The Definitive, One-Volume So
Mythic Females

About the Author

Patricia Monaghan, Ph.D., is one of the pioneers of the women's spirituality movement. In addition to *The New Book of Goddesses and Heroines*, she has also written *Magical Gardens: Myth, Mulch and Marigolds; O Mother Sun: A New View of the Cosmic Feminine;* and *Seasons of the Witch*. She is a member of the Resident Faculty of the School for New Learning at DePaul University in Chicago.

To Write to the Author

If you wish to contact the author or would like more information about this book, please write to the author in care of Llewellyn Worldwide, and we will forward your request. Both the author and publisher appreciate hearing from you and welcome your comments. Llewellyn Worldwide cannot guarantee a reply to all letters, but all will be forwarded. Please write to:

Patricia Monaghan
c/o Llewellyn Worldwide
P.O. Box 64383, Dept. K465-0
St. Paul, MN 55164-0383, U.S.A.
If outside the U.S.A., enclose international postal reply coupon.
Please enclose a self-addressed, stamped envelope for reply,
or $1.00 to cover costs.

THE NEW BOOK OF

Goddesses & HEROINES

Patricia Monaghan

All photographs courtesy of The Field Museum of Natural History,
Chicago, Illinois

1997
Llewellyn Publications
St. Paul, Minnesota 55164-0383

THIRD EDITION
First Printing, 1997
SECOND EDITION, 1989 (Previously titled *The Book of Goddesses and Heroines*)
Published by Llewellyn Publications
FIRST EDITION, 1981
Published by E. P. Dutton Publishing Co., Inc.

Cover Art and Design: Anne Marie Garrison
Photographs: The Field Museum of Natural History, Chicago
Cover Photograph: Douglas Deutscher
Statues on Cover: Oberon Zell and Morning Glory Zell, used courtesy of Mythic Images, P.O. Box 1775, Laytonville, CA 95454. (707) 984-0024
Photographic Research Assistance: Nina Cummings, Director of Photography, The Field Museum of Natural History
Editing and Proofreading: Jan Feeney
Design and Layout: Designed to Sell
Project Management: Kimberly Nightingale

Library of Congress Cataloging-in-Publication Data
Monaghan, Patricia.
      The new book of goddesses & heroines / Patricia Monaghan. --3rd ed.
          p. cm.
      Rev. ed. of The book of goddesses & heroines.
      Includes bibliographical references and index.
      ISBN 1-56718-465-0
      1. Goddesses. 2. Mythology. I. Monaghan, Patricia. Book of
goddesses & heroines. II. Title.
      BL473.5.M66 1997
      291.2'114--dc21
                                          97-17471
                                           CIP

Publisher's note:
Llewellyn Worldwide does not participate in, endorse, or have any authority or responsibility concerning private business transactions between our authors and the public. All mail addressed to the author is forwarded but the publisher cannot, unless specifically instructed by the author, give out an address or phone number.

Llewellyn Publications
A Division of Llewellyn Worldwide, Ltd.
P.O. Box 64383, Dept. K465-0
St. Paul, Minnesota 55164-0383, U.S.A.

Dedication

To my mother

and

to Our Mother

Other Books by Patricia Monaghan

Magical Gardens: Myth, Mulch, and Marigolds (Llewellyn, 1997)
Oh Mother Sun! A New View of the Cosmic Feminine (The Crossing Press, 1994)
Working Wisdom (Harper SanFrancisco, 1994)
Seasons of the Witch (Delphi Press, 1992)
Winterburning (Fireweed Press, 1991)

Forthcoming

Goddesses and Heroines: A Daily Meditation Book

Contents

Photographs

All photographs that appear in *The New Book of Goddesses and Heroines* were provided by The Field Museum of Natural History, Chicago, Illinois. The listing below gives the descriptions of the photographs, the goddesses and cultures associated with them, corresponding negative numbers, and page numbers where they can be found.

Preface to the Third Edition

When I was seven, I made a vow of perpetual virginity. I made it in a dim church, kneeling before an altar, my head bowed over a lit candle—the whole megilla.

Not that I had any idea what "perpetual" meant, much less "virginity." But I'd noticed, in my St. Joseph's Daily Missal, that only a few of my sex got ratings high enough to be assigned their own feast days. There was the Mother of God, a position already filled by a suitable candidate. There were a couple of queens—I especially remember Margaret and Elizabeth, because my grandmothers had those names.

Beyond that, I found only virgins. Lots and lots of virgins.

Not a very extensive list of role models for a girl aspiring to sainthood. Not only that, but queenship was out of the question, once my Irish grandfather informed me that, saints or no saints, royalty deserved hatred. (He seemed to imply that choice, not blood, was what kept us from being royalty ourselves.)

That left virginity.

Oh, yes—there was also martyrdom. Unlike virginity, I was pretty clear on the details of this one. Frankly, death seemed easier than the prelude—being flayed alive, boiled in oil, beheaded, burned, dismembered. Faced with lurid descriptions of these pathways to heaven, I became both squeamish and flat-out cowardly. But I evaded acknowledging these craven feelings by

telling myself that martyrdom was getting harder and harder to arrange. This was, after all, the 50s.

Now virginity—whatever it was, it didn't sound painful. And it definitely got you into the calendar of saints. It was this line of reasoning that led to candles on a Saturday morning, the padded kneeler in front of the altar, and a whispered vow—

I remember that moment whenever someone asks me why I believe in goddesses.

Believe? I'm not sure that's the right word for my abiding sense of the universe's sacredness. It's like asking whether I believe in air. In food. In the earth beneath my feet. I feel like Mark Twain, when he was asked if he believed in baptism. "Believe?" he answered. "Lady, I've *seen* it done!"

That is how I feel about divinity. I do not so much believe in it as know, in my bones, in my elusive soul, that it is there, that it surrounds us, sustains us, recognizes us.

Yet I do not always think of divinity as feminine. Rather, I often conjure a non-gendered image: "the light within," for instance. The universal force of creation and destruction, the quantum potential of electron and quark, the implicate order behind all matter: surely this power cannot be a person. And thus it cannot have gender. Surely, its awesome otherness transcends the limitations of "masculine" and "feminine."

But if I imagine divinity, in its totality, as beyond personification, why do I spend my vacations searching for lost goddesses in off-the-track museums, on windy hillsides, within the yellowing pages of old books? Because of the same inner compulsion that led me to take that vow, one Saturday morning in the 1950s, in Corpus Christi Church. Because our gods are more than an expression of our ideas about divine totality. They also express our own human capacity for god-ness.

At seven, ignorant of goddesses, I'd turned to the lives of the saints to find out how divinity looks when it wears a body like mine. (Of course I had been told that saints were not gods, but they seemed the nearest I could personally get.) These stories had offered various plots for my life. I'd examined them and settled on the most likely part for me to play. If queenship was impossible and martyrdom unendurable, I'd take the only other role available.

Shortly after I'd made that solemn vow, however, I found that there were other possibilities. I discovered stories of hunters and warriors, leaders and dreamers, artists and inventors, saviors of their people, creators of the universe. All of them girls or women—people like me.

I discovered mythology.

Like many girls, I first discovered modern re-tellings—dazzling, vivid, heart-stopping. I read through every book on mythology (almost all about the Greeks) in the children's and young adult section of the library. That only whetted my appetite. I learned from the encyclopedia that there were goddess stories from other lands as well. How I wanted to learn them!

This led to my first conscious attempt at law-breaking: I got busted trying to sneak *Bulfinch's Mythology* out of the library. It was classified an "adult" book, and youngsters like me were forbidden to read it within the library, much less remove it to corrupt our minds at home. I stuck it into a pile of duly checked-out young-adult novels and walked casually towards the door. At the final check—this was before electronic scanning, when librarians tediously hand-checked every book—my theft was discovered. I tearfully

begged the librarian to let me have just that one book, just that once. Imperiously, she denied me and removed my stolen treasure—thus strengthening my resolve to have the information it contained.

I talked an older friend into checking out the book. It's not an easy read, but I savored every page. The fierce Icelandic tale of Ragnaroc, when the beautiful hard-working sun goddess is devoured by the evil Fen-ris Wolf—but not before she gives birth to her shining daughter. The powerful Welsh tale of Arianrhod, who mates with the king of the sea. The mysterious women of Arthurian legends: Viviane, Guinevere, the Lady of Shalott. Unlike the civilized versions I'd read from the children's section, Bulfinch introduced me to myth in its primal power—and to the goddess in hers.

Decades have passed, but I am still thrilled when I discover a new goddess story. I love the one about Amaterasu, the Japanese sun goddess who grows angry at her importunate brother and hides herself in a dark rock cave, from which only dancing and joke-telling can lure her. I love the Inuit tale of the little girl who is so noisy that she's sent up to the sky, where she becomes the thunder. I love the beautiful Irish story of Fionnuala and her brothers, the Children of Lir turned into singing swans. I love the classic Greek myth of earth-mother Demeter and her lost daughter Perse-phone, who returns like spring at story's end.

These stories nurture me. There is boldness in them, and courage, and lust, and joy. There is also pain and disappointment and the enormity of grief. I find in these stories images of all the ways a woman can be. I find wild freedom there, embodied in the virginal huntress Artemis, who roves with her hounds and maidens in the moon-swept forests. I find the home-loving comfort of Hestia, whose emblem is the hearth fire that warms and joins the family. I can see myself as an artist like the Hindu Sarasvati, a gardener like Rome's Pomona, a weaver like Athena of the Greeks.

Our lives are lived in story. When the stories offered us are limited, our lives are limited as well. Few have the courage, drive and imagination to invent life-narratives drastically different from those they've been told are possible. And unfortunately, some self-invented narratives are really just reversals of the limiting stereotype; thus a sensual woman, where only virginity is honored, can believe herself marred or even evil. Heroic myths, by comparison, offer positive life narratives, inspirations for living in power and strength.

But it is not just as patterns for action that myths are important—otherwise, good novels and excellent movie roles would serve just as well. Myths are not about human life; they are about the divine within. Thus when only the masculine is dignified as god, human women suffer. If we cannot imagine ourselves as god—as men so easily can—we can never become fully human either. Our gods express us. If we cannot find ourselves in god, we find it hard to find god in ourselves.

The most important fact about goddesses, it seems to me, is that they are invariably connected to polytheism. Put another way: there is no monotheistic religion based on a goddess. Not a single goddess appears without friends, companions, lovers, children. The presence of the goddess demands the presence of other goddesses, and gods as well. This is comforting to me, for in my vision of the world redeemed, the world made whole, I yearn for connection, not for separation. Throughout human history, gods have banished the goddess, demanding that we hold no other gods before them. But the goddess did not respond in kind. In the religions that honor her, she had welcomed—even embraced—the other. By welcoming her back, we do not banish the god but only make space for the connection so many of his followers have, for millennia, denied.

So, in a sense, I do believe in goddesses—for I believe that women touch the divine as men do, in as many ways. We are children and parents and lovers and creators and warriors and artists and dancers and healers—

We are also, sometimes, queens and virgins and martyrs. But we're so much more besides. In the mythology of the goddess, we find stories that testify to the vast variety of women's ways of bearing witness to the divine. It is these stories that I remain forever grateful I found as a girl.

As for the results of my vow of perpetual virginity—well, let's just say that that's another story.

$\mathcal{I}$ntroduction to the Third Edition

Twenty years ago, research for the first edition of this book meant using a card catalog or printed bibliography to find an appropriate reference, then copying notes by hand onto three-by-five cards, which were filed in little plastic boxes or manilla folders. The first edition was written on a correcting electric type-writer—which seemed marvelously high-tech, because it didn't involve using a dreaded white fluid to correct typographical errors. Each entry was typed on a separate sheet of paper, so that the entire dictionary could be alphabetized upon completion. The final manuscript was, as a result, over two feet tall.

Ten years ago, the second edition added scores of entries and an index. Information for the additional entries was located through computerized searches on site at several major libraries, but once again, these new entries had to be prepared on individual sheets, for the new word processor could not readily handle complex reshufflings. Similarly, the index was created by hand-writing lists of goddesses into the appropriate categories, then alphabetizing and typing them. Proof-reading, not surprisingly, was arduous and slow, both at manuscript and galley stage. Art, when included, had to be isolated from text, as the typesetting programs did not have a text-wrap feature.

For this third edition, online searches through multiple library holdings, from a single terminal, has meant the addition of many goddesses. The text was prepared on a personal computer, which not only permitted easy storage of notes but also quickly alphabetized and spell-checked the entries. Similarly, word-finder programs permitted extraordinarily fast location of relevant materials to expand the indexes. Finally, page layout software allowed for insertion of art easily within the text.

Plus ça change—However, as the saying goes, the more some things change, the more others remain the same. While technology has advanced with almost incredible speed since the 1970s, there are depressing similarities between this time and that. New "comprehensive" encyclopedias of mythology still concentrate on male divinities, dismissing female ones with the briefest of mentions. Sexual stereotypes still exist, with male/god being equated to power, the sky, and intellect while female/goddess is still assumed to be identical to passivity, the earth, and the body; thus "earth mothers" get more press than sky goddesses, "love goddesses" more time than world creators.

Significantly, the names of goddesses are still infrequently mentioned; a hero, his name carefully recorded, still serves "the earth goddess" or "his mother." A god, his name carefully recorded, still mates with someone called "a goddess of the land" or "a princess." This latter interaction then makes the goddess into "the wife" of the god—even when the intercourse occurred once and included force, a circumstance that contemporary courts would likely call rape. An aged goddess is described as "ugly," a self-possessed one is labeled "overbearing," while a maiden is "beautiful" and a sexually active one "fertile." The language of mythological reference books remains permeated with the attitudes of patriarchal scholarship.

After twenty years, then, this book is as useful—alas—as it was when first published. It remains difficult to find information about the vast panorama of female possibilities which has been recorded in the world's myths. It is difficult to find material that represents a diversity of cultures and world views. It is difficult to find texts in which the goddess, in her infinite variety, is at center stage. While it has been a delight to work again on a text close to my heart, it would be even more delightful to see it become unnecessary, to see the female aspect of divinity accorded its due place in all texts on the subject.

This third edition adds many new entries to the original text—hundreds of goddesses, information on whom is available only in rare or limited editions, in periodicals with small circulation, or in otherwise obscure sources. As with the older entries, there is no attempt to define all the variations of academic interpretation; rather, this book's purpose remains to tell goddess myths and to describe goddess symbols. As before, the focus is on the goddess as seen by her original worshipers; thus there is little reference to psychological or archetypal theories. Older entries remain predominantly unchanged, except where additional information about the myth, ritual or symbol of the goddess has been unearthed in recent years. And as before, the book includes "heroines," mythic or legendary women who might not have been named "goddesses" by the people who honored them, but whose stories express the essence of the feminine divine.

Finally, much additional material has been added to this edition to make it useful to the non-specialist reader. Primary among these additions is the new section on "Cultures of the Goddess," which provides information on the location, time and general features of the major religious systems detailed in the goddess myths. A comprehensive listing, titled "Names of the Goddess," provides all available names for each goddess, along with many variant spellings. Where a goddess is obscure or minor, her cultural identity and significant features are recorded along with her name, and can be found only in that listing. In cases where a myth or ritual has been recorded, the name of the goddess appears in boldfaced type. This indicates that you will find her story listed in the "Myths of the Goddess" section.

This book can be used in many ways. Firstly, it provides information about goddesses, which the reader may discover through other references; a novel set in Wales might yield the name Branwen, or a lecture might send one off looking for information on Medusa. Secondly, it is useful for those engaged in goddess study who wish to locate goddesses with specific features. Those seeking goddesses of a particular heritage or ethnic identity will find it easiest to locate them through the "Cultures of the Goddess" listing, where the major cultural groups of each continent and their goddess myths can be found. Those who seek goddesses whose domain includes an area of concern—health, for instance—or those composing art or ritual based in goddess culture will find the "Symbols of the Goddess" listing useful, both as a source of information and inspiration.

Contemporary women and men have many reasons for interest in the goddess. While a single book cannot meet all needs, this encyclopedia is designed to be useful both to those who perceive the goddess as immanent, as a part of the human psyche, and those who see her as a transcendent or cosmic force outside humanity. (Some, of course, see her in both manifestations.) Those who see the goddess as immanent will find this book useful in self-searching. Images from dreams and art, for instance, can be interpreted with its help, or matron goddesses located that represent aspects of the self. For those who recognize the goddess as transcendent, this book provides evidence of the great diversity of her power. For all those who honor her in ritual, *The New Book of Goddesses and Heroines* offers images, myths, calendar feasts, and traditional rites.

Even the creation of this book has been, in part, a ritual, for as Erich Neumann has said, "In naming all of these, we are practicing an age-old rite. Such lists…are a form of ritual worship." To have practiced such a ritual for more than twenty years has been a great joy, and it is with joy that this third edition is offered to readers.

Cultures of the Goddess

The myths and legends in this book are gathered from many civilizations, many lands, and many eras. The following section looks at the major cultural groups of each continent and the ways they define the importance of feminine divinity. A list of the major goddess myths from each culture is provided. All names in these listings can be found in the Myths of the Goddess section. Many additional goddesses from each culture can be found in the list of Names of the Goddess in the back of the book. Dates are given as B.C.E. (before common era) and C.E. (common era).

Entries in this section have been provided by Priscilla Buffalohead, Cecilia Corcoran, Miriam Robbins Dexter, Normandi Ellis, Susan Gitlin-Emmer, Deborah Holton, Edain McCoy, Janet McCrickard, and Luisa Teish, as well as the author. Contributors' names follow their entries; contributors' biographies appear at the end of this section.

Africa

African

Comprised of over fifty countries, each with its own language, laws and culture, Africa is the world's second largest continent—so large that not only would the United States fit comfortably within it, but Europe, China, India, New Zealand, and Argentina as well. At least 800 different languages are spoken in Africa, and it is home to over 700 million people. Currently, there are over 3,000 diverse ethnic groups in Africa, including Asante (Ashanti), Yoruba, Ibo, Fulani, Mandingo, Hausa, Dogon, Akan, Tuareg, Maasai, Zulu, Xosa, and Shona.

Geographically, Africa is one of the oldest continents on earth, comprised of deserts (the Sahara, Kalahari, and Namib), vast rain forests, numerous lakes and major rivers (including the Niger and Zambezi), tall mountains, and savannahs. The world's largest river, the Nile, runs from Lake Victoria in Uganda at its southern end, through Sudan, into Egypt and north to the Mediterranean sea.

Scientists agree that Africa is the land of the first humans. Discovered in East Africa, artifacts indicate the earliest evidence of complex social structures. Some have wrongly believed that Africa is a land of primitive people, and although highly prized and regarded by Western art historians, its art still holds this inaccurate and negative connotation. However, like its art, music, dance, and oral traditions, Africa is both complex and diverse. And it can rightfully boast spiritual and religious achievements that rival any in the world.

Common to most African people, regardless of country of origin, language or religious faith, is belief in a creator divinity. For Africans, the creator is present everywhere, in all things, at all times, in both sacred spaces and secular realms. This overarching belief in a supreme deity informs regional and individual practices of Islam, Christianity (Coptic, Catholic, and Protestant), and indigenous traditional forms of worship. Often seen as bisexual or beyond gender, the creator sometimes divides into two primary divinities, a mother goddess connected to the earth and human fertility, and a father god associated with celestial phenomena. This mother goddess further becomes an ancestor, the primal mother who gives birth to the first humans.

Another belief that informs daily life, particularly among those who follow traditional practices, is that the ancestors—those deceased elders who lived morally exemplary lives and were revered by their clan—still offer advice and protection to the living. Ancestors are worshiped not only because of their past wisdom, but also because in death they are empowered by their proximity to the creator. In regions where the forces of nature are directly linked to the survival and sustainment of its inhabitants, paying homage to those forces through animal sacrifice and consultation with priests and healers is not uncommon. Although other institutionalized religions may prevail, the daughters and sons of Africa retain their strong connection to the creative life force exemplified in their beliefs in one creator, ancestor veneration, and devoted spiritual practice.

Throughout African history, trade was of special importance, for the continent is rich in gold, diamonds, silver, iron, and other minerals. But part of Africa's unfortunate legacy was created by the trade of human beings, which laid the foundation for colonial rule. The Arab slave trade had been widely practiced in northern Africa above and below the Sahara. It was significantly different and incomparable in magnitude to the European slave trade, however, which spanned 400 years. The Portuguese were the first, and the last, to establish trading posts in Africa. They were followed and accompanied by the Spanish, English, North Americans, Dutch, French, Swedish and Danish, who crossed the Atlantic to Africa to acquire captives for slavery. After crossing the Atlantic, following an infamous route called the Middle Passage, they deposited their human cargo in the Caribbean, and the Americas—North, South, and Central—where plantations prospered from slave laborers. In exchange, slavers brought back indigo, cotton, sugar cane, and rum from those regions, and took other African captives to Europe where factories produced beads and guns to eventually exchange, along with the rum, for more people.

Thus an invidious triangle of trade was established and maintained, and remains the major source for the African diaspora, the dispersal of people of African descent in the world. It is estimated that as many as twenty million people—men, women, and children—were sent across the Middle Passage as chattel. When the slave trade officially ended in 1853, colonial occupation of Africa by European nations was just beginning. In 1957, almost one hundred years later, an African country would be the first to gain independence from colonial rule: Ghana, thus marking a long and arduous struggle to break from European domination and control.

Africans across ethnic divides highly value and are widely celebrated for their sophisticated and complex music, dance, art forms, and oral traditions. One outcome of the European slave trade is the shared valuing of these cultural expressions by African descendants throughout the African diaspora. Similarly, African people across the continent and throughout the diaspora share elemental spiritual beliefs while practicing various religions. —*Deborah Holton*

African Goddess Myths: Abuk, Agwe, Akonadi, Ala, Andriam-Vabi-Rano, Annalia Tu-Bari, Asase Yaa, Ashiakle, Atete, Chichinguane, Fatouma, Gleti, Gonzuole, Ilankaka, Inaruchaba, Isong, Itoerambola-totsy, Kahindo, Kaikara, Kimpa Vita, Ko, Lueji, Mahalbiya, Malika Habashiya, Mamlambo, Maruwa, Mawu, Mbaba Mwana Waresa, Mbombe, Mella, Monje, Motsesa, Muhongo, Mujaji, Mulindwa, Muso

Koroni, Mut, Muzita, Nambi, Nambubi, Nana Buluku, Nawangwulan, Nchienge, Nenakatu, Ngolimento, Ngwa Ndundu, Notambu, Nsomeka, Nsomeka, Nsongo, Nyadeang, Nyamitondo, Nyamwanda, Nyapilnu, Nyavirezi, Nyi Pohaci, Nyina Mweru Oeno, Ochumare, Oddudua, Oshun, Oya, Ra-mitoviaman-dreniny, Ranoro, Sabulana, Sela, Selekana, Sukulung, Tangalimbibo, Titichane, Ymoja.

Arabic

Although the primary religion of Arabic peoples today is Islam, that form of patriarchal monotheism was not inaugurated until the tenth century. Prior to that—as in Europe prior to Christianization—Arabs and their cultural cousins the Nabataeans worshiped many goddesses as well as gods.

These ancient people lived in Arabia Felix ("Happy Arabia"), which extended across the fertile south of the Arabian peninsula. There, small kingdoms and states rose and fell throughout the millennia before the common era; little is known about these states, most of which were subjugated by Romans propelled by their interest in the incense and perfume trades. Similarly, little is known about their religion. Their divinities were honored with sacrifices; in addition to animal and fruit, Arabic peoples also offered incense and perfumes. Other ancient practices included pilgrimage, public confessionals, and religious banquets.

On the great desert in northern and central Arabia, nomadic shepherds and camel breeders roamed among oases populated by merchants and artisans. They worshiped three goddesses who took the form of sacred stones—including the one honored today in the Ka'aba in Mecca. These stones substituted for temples, for the tradition of the area was to worship under the open air rather than in an enclosed space.

A final Arabic culture, the Nabataean, was affected by nearby Semitic culture. A vital and prosperous people, the Nabataeans established a profitable trading capital at Petra, on the border of Palestine and Syria. Unlike their Arab neighbors, the Nabataeans built sumptuous temples, many built into rock sanctuaries. However, sacred stones remained important to them as well, as did sacrifice and divination. —*Patricia Monaghan*

Arabic Goddess Myths: Al-Lat, Al-Uzza, Candace, Dhat-Badan, Fatima, Kalisha, Menat.

Egyptian

There were two Egypts, historically as well as geographically: Lower Egypt, the fertile, dark soil of the northern delta or the Black Land; and Upper Egypt, which was predominantly southern desert, or the Red Land. One Egypt existed during the Predynastic era (10,000–3,000 B.C.E.) and the other sparked the three major dynasties: Old Kingdom (3000–2175 B.C.E.), Middle Kingdom (1971–1797 B.C.E.), and New Kingdom (1570–525 B.C.E.) What we have come to know as Egypt is primarily the arable land of the Nile River Valley and the Delta; the rest includes a vast desert on the west and high mountain desert on the east.

Prehistoric Egypt arose from a melting pot of cultures. Perhaps as early as 10,000 B.C.E., nomadic European tribes following game crossed a land bridge between Italy and Libya, entering the African savannah. When the climate changed, the land bridge vanished and the savannah turned to desert, trapping them. To survive, they moved toward the Nile Delta, their nearest food source, thus forging an agricultural society as early as 5000 B.C.E. These people may account for the red-haired, blonde and blue-eyed images of people sometimes found in Old Kingdom statuary. Simultaneously, groups of Mesopotamian settlers followed the Mediterranean coastline, crossed Sinai and entered the Delta, bringing with them cattle and wild emmer, previously unknown on the African continent. From this mix arose three great Lower Egyptian cultures, the Merimda (oasis), Omari, and Maadi (delta), known for their basketry and weaving.

The horned goddess—whom the Pyramid Texts called The Great She, and who later was called Hathor or Isis—is the oldest divine being in ancient Egypt. Her image appears on the rock face of a now nearly inaccessible plateau in the Sahara Desert, but when the image was created around 7000 B.C.E., that desert was a blooming savannah. Around 5000 B.C.E.—two thousand years before the male-dominated bull cults—she reappears carved on a rock face in the Fayuum oasis. Wearing long plaits of hair and a woven dress, she blesses the cattle brought by her naked, dancing people.

At the same time, central African tribes followed the northward-flowing Nile tributaries from Sudan and Ethiopia. The harsh desert landscape of Southern Egypt—where arable land appears only in narrow strips along the river bank—caused these traveling tribes to retain some of their hunter-gatherer ways. What agriculture they practiced was scattering seeds in fertile places, then returning to harvest them. The goddess of these early peoples was a divine sky queen, a dancing bird woman, later called Het-her, or Hathor. The earliest cultures in Southern Egypt were the Badarian, Amratian and Gerzean cultures, known for their exquisite pottery.

Apparently around 3500 B.C.E., a third culture entered Egypt near Naqada and Abydos, through a gap in the mountains, coming from the east in large sea-going boats. This group became the catalyst for creating a high culture of architecture, pyramid-building, writing and temple worship that lasted from the Old Kingdom era through the New Kingdom. They emerged as the protodynastic kings, the first of whom was a Southern Egyptian man named Narmer who married Queen Neithhotep of Northern Egypt, thus merging the Red and Black Lands. During this integration period, many of the goddesses merged. The Great She in her various guises was both natural and spiritual, representing earth and sky, fecundity and salvation. She exhibited a fiery side as well, often appearing in the Middle and New Kingdoms under the veil of the warrior goddess.

During the Fifth Dynasty of the Old Kingdom the creative power of the feminine was slowly usurped by the patriarchal priests promoting such gods of light as Ra, and later Amen and Aten. The gods acquired the means of creation by duplicating the fecund qualities of the goddess; they created humankind through masturbation, or magical words, or the sculpting of humankind from clay.

As pharaonic Egypt acquired its wealth and the means of trade and travel, the goddess of other cultures, including Babylon, made their way into the Egyptian pantheon, and the goddess culture of Egypt spread throughout the Mediterranean world, appearing in various guises as Minoan and other Greek goddesses.

More so than in any other ancient Mediterranean culture, women were treated as equal partners in ancient Egypt. It was a fact that bewildered and irritated later Greek historians who began to visit Egypt around 600 B.C.E. The early historian Herodotus described Egypt as a place where women worked the fields and men stayed home weaving—not entirely accurate, but certainly a farming woman and a weaving man would have surprised the Greek traveler. During the Ptolemaic era following the conquest of Egypt by Alexander the Great (332–30 B.C.E.). Egyptian-born Greek women like Cleopatra and her sisters still enjoyed the advantages of an equitable Egyptian society.   —*Normandi Ellis*

Egyptian Goddess Myths: Ahemait, Ama, Ament, Anuket, Bast, Hathor, Hekt, Isis, Maat, Mafdet, Mehurt, Mertseger, Meskhoni, Mut, Neith, Nekhebet, Nephthys, Nut, Qebhsnuf, Renenet, Renpet, Saosis, Sati, Sekhmet, Selkhet, Shait, Sheshat, Tauret, Tefnut, Uadgit.

North African/Carthaginian/Phoenician

The queen city of Northern Africa was Carthage, and her queen was Tanit, the cosmic goddess who ruled the heavens and the earth. Tanit was a perfect symbol for Carthage, for she was an indigenous goddess of the nomadic Berber people of the area, whose image and power were assimilated to that of Astarte, goddess of Phoenician settlers. These Phoenicians were sea-faring traders from what is now Lebanon, whose famous cities included Arvad, Bylbos, Berythus (today's Beirut), Sidon, and Tyre. Despite their common heritage, the Phoenician city-states developed independently, never forming a unified nation. Each city had its own Ba'alat (lady or mistress), who ruled with a Ba'al or consort; each had its own currency, its own rulers, its own rituals. This complexity has meant that Phoenician religion is less readily studied than many others of the ancient Mediterranean; the remaining inscriptions and monuments, in their diverse languages, have not permitted a complete picture of Phoenician religion to be assembled.

These ethnic groups joined to develop Carthaginian culture, keeping their own folkways relatively intact. The religion of Tanit held sway for many centuries, while other goddesses were worshiped on the outskirts of Carthage's cosmopolitan culture. The coming of Islam in the tenth to eleventh century, however, meant the loss of ancient religions in this region as in many others. The old religion of Carthage did not fare any better; although it had lasted from the ninth century B.C.E. through the period of Roman conquest, Islamic conversion ended Tanit's almost 2,000-year reign.   —*Patricia Monaghan*

Phoenician Goddess Myths: Ba'alat, Bau, Beruth, Mylitta, Ri.

Carthaginian Goddess Myths: Dido, Tanit.

Other North African Goddess Myths: 'Aisha Qandisha, Lemkechen.

The Americas

African Diaspora

Ymoja and Asase Yaa, Oshun and Oya: These are the names of black goddesses, queens and spirit women of the African diaspora. They represent the forces of nature, the wisdom of the ancestors and the dynamics of culture. In precolonial Africa, the powers of nature were personified as anthropomorphic figures in the folklore of the people. They were joyfully worshiped; beautiful songs were sung to polyrhythmic orchestras as undulating dances recounted the stories of their adventures. They changed themselves in fantastic ways: from pure energy into water, earth and animals. They whispered their desires into the ears of human women, then spoke through their mouths and walked the land with their feet. The black woman goddess roamed the continent, birthing everywhere she stopped.

Most of her children nestled in the deep green of the rainforest, some settled on the savannah while others roamed the desert to bathe in the Nile. A mysterious few strayed far away from home, into the northern regions of the globe. There they forgot where they came from and that she was their mother.

Millennia passed before the pale ones returned. They came by ship seeking ivory and gold, and rattling chains of iron.

The trans-Atlantic slave trade extended deep into the womb of Mother Africa. It reached from Gambia to Angola, and deep into the Kongo, gathering her children from their many different tribes and cultures. The Yorubas, the Kongolese, and many unnamed others were herded into slave ships and pushed out to sea.

It is estimated that as many as twenty million Africans were exported to the Americas. They were sent to Brazil and Haiti, to Cuba and Jamaica, to New Orleans and New York. When they landed on the shores of this "new found land," they were confronted with two spiritual phenomena. Christian baptism was imposed on them so that they might be proper slaves; and their own spiritual traditions were made illegal and punishable by death. At the same time they found the traditions of the indigenous people to be very much like their own. Like African traditions, these were rooted in the environment, celebrated through prayer and music and offerings, and integral to daily life. European pagans who had come as indentured servants also practiced traditions based in a reverence for nature.

But the Catholic church, which supported the slave trade, insisted that its icons and saints be worshiped by the people who had become its property. So the Africans identified their goddesses with those of indigenous people and European pagans, and with the saints of the Catholic Church. In this way they maintained vestiges of their mother culture and generated other spiritual traditions, such as Candomble, Santeria and Voudoun.

This syncretism changed the name and the face of the goddesses. Ymoja, goddess of the Ogun River in Nigeria, became Yemaya (in Cuba) and Yemanja (in Brazil), the goddess of the ocean. Her domain was changed by those Africans who survived the Middle Passage, the arduous journey across the Atlantic. Her image was further changed by identification with

Catholic saints, which tended to lighten her skin, repress her sexuality, and limit her power.

In the New World, Christian patriarchy almost eliminated the secret societies (such as Awan Iyaami) and public ceremonies (Gelede) that honored female power in Africa. Nevertheless, the memory of great rulers such as Nzinga of Ndongo (Angola) was preserved in the carnivals of Brazil. Even today, a woman who is chosen to represent her parades through the streets wearing a crown.

The spirit women who spoke the will of the ancestors in trance; the medicine women who healed the sick with herbs and cool water; and the market women who created and distributed the magnificent arts and crafts derived from the forest have survived in the western hemisphere. They are known as Mothers of the Spirit in Brazil, as Mambos in Haiti, as Tante in the Caribbean, and as the two-headed woman, Mam'zelle Marie LaVeau, in the southern United States.

African spiritual practices identify humans as having personalities befitting the forces of nature. Humans who have exhibited noteworthy behavior during their lives on earth can be deified as ancestors and are believed to speak to their descendants through mediums. Thus the goddesses are present in nature and active in the lives of everyday women.

In this book you will find the goddesses of Africa dressed in western clothes and speaking pidgin languages. Here also are images of powerful women driven by a passion for freedom, sustained by the courage of their ancestors. As you meet them, remember who they are and where they have been. Then open your eyes wide and engage your imagination, so that you can see them crossing the ocean and waiting at the bus stop down the street. —*Louisa Teish*

African Diaspora Goddess Myths: Ochumare, Oddudua, Oshun, Oya, Ymoja.

Central American/Mexican

In the immense sprawl of Mexico City is found the most visited of sacred sites, the hill of Tepeyac, where the Virgin of Guadalupe is honored. This Catholic shrine attracts millions of people each year, not only because it honors Mary, the mother of Jesus, but also because La Morenita ("the dear, dark one") represents the mestiza people who make up the population of most of Latin America as well as parts of the United States. But before Hernado Cortez marched on the Aztec Empire, a goddess named Tonantzin (Our Mother) was worshiped at Tepeyac. This, then, is a significant site, for it serves as the link that connected ancient religious belief to the contemporary Catholic faith.

Mesoamerica is made up of five regions that share distinctive characteristics: pyramidal temples, the ritual ball game, advanced astronomy and mathematics, precise calculation of a calendar, use of steam baths for ritual cleansing and health, use of cotton cloth for clothes, and a diet based mainly on corn, squash and beans. This area, crossed by three mountain ranges, extends south in Mexico from the Central Plateau Region (Mexico City) to the Gulf of Mexico, over to the Pacific Coast, and through the Mayan lands of southern Mexico, Belize, Guatemala and parts of Honduras and El Salvador.

Most of what is known about this area comes through the eyes of the Spanish conquerors who arrived in 1519 C.E. There was no historic contact between Europe and Mesoamerica before that time, which means that right up until the sixteenth century the indigenous goddess and goddesses reigned in Mesoamerica. Ancient civilizations replaced one another through three millennia, leaving traces that indicate developments of early beliefs in the sacredness of nature. The earliest signs of magical or religious consciousness have been found in rock art, cave paintings and petroglyphs dating to 10,000 B.C.E. As small villages evolved that could be supported through the cultivation of crops, and hunting and fishing close to the settlements, fertility figures called "pretty women" signify a further development in human relationship to the divine power.

The "mother" culture of Mesoamerica is thought to be the Olmec civilization that flourished in the Gulf Coast Region near Vera Cruz, in 1200 B.C.E. The Olmecs rapidly developed a high culture, and their influence has been found extensively in the other regions. Studies of ancient remnants indicate that for the Olmecs the deity was fluid, being endowed with characteristics that continually changed, to be re-assembled in new configurations. This idea of god as a "shape-shifter" is very much part of the other high cultures spawned by Olmec prodigality.

While the Olmecs were developing a Classic culture, most developments before the Common Era in Mesoamerica have what archaeologists call Formative and Preclassic qualities. It was only in the period between 200–700 C.E. that high cultures, known for sophisticated urban centers, began to develop. Here religious celebration and sacrifice was the unifying force that supported a stratified society. Priests direct-ed cultic practices and, indeed, represented the gods and goddesses.

For example, Teotihuacan in Mexico and Tikal in Guatemala, two distinct and basically unrelated cultures, developed societies that accomplished feats of architecture, mathematical calculation, and complex calendars. Both cities were sacred spaces created for the deities, laid out in alignment with the stars and planets rather than with the natural geography. This indicates the importance of cosmology in understanding the peoples of Mesoamerica.

Though the names are different in the different cultures of Mesoamerica, the basic creation story has some common elements. The chief divinity was androgynous or paired. The Lord and Lady of Duality, or Our Mother/Father God or Heart of Earth/Heart of Sky began the world by creating divine doubles: four gods to reign over the four directions; others to prevail in the 13 heavens and the 9 underworlds. From earliest times it was believed that humans emerged from the mouth or cave of the divine creator. From the Olmec civilization on through the Toltec culture in central Mexico, images of this event—showing people emerging from the mouth of a monster-like figures—have been found.

The Aztecs were latecomers into the Valley of Mexico, arriving towards the end of the thirteenth century. They claimed the Toltecs, distinguished for their arts and wisdom, as their ancestors and established an empire under the tutelage of the warrior sun god. Though the ancient fertility gods and goddesses, and the belief in the inspirited power of nature, were still incorporated into Aztec religious beliefs, the Aztecs introduced a concept of "Flowery Wars" to satisfy the thirst of their principal god for blood sacrifice. Thus wars were fought to take captives for sacrifice. To die such a death was to be ensured an honored place in the heavens. At the same time the need for ritual victims justified the continual wars that expanded the Aztec Empire. Such was the situation when Cortez landed in Mexico. Many people in the outlying areas were tired of the years of war and were restive as subjects of Mexico/Tenochtlican. It was not difficult for the Spaniard to enlist the support of native tribes to join him in attacking Montezuma, the Aztec ruler.

In territories inhabited by the Mayas, warring among ethnic groups facilitated the conquests of that region. It was simply a matter of time for Pedro Alvardo, who found ways of manipulating the intrigue and betrayal to further the cause of the Spanish crown.

With the Spaniards came the friars whose first task was to serve the Spaniards; after it became clear that Spain was claiming the land for the crown, they began the task of evangelizing the so-called pagan Indians. Unfortunately, in the process of conquest and conversion, the great native cultures were devastated. War, plagues and mistreatment decimated the people, who believed their gods had abandoned them. Signs interpreted by the sages confirmed this. Yet as the pilgrimages to La Morenita show, ancient figures and beliefs continued, albeit in mutated form, to this very day.

—*Cecilia Corcoran*

Aztec Goddess Myths: Chalchiuhtlicue, Chicomecoatl, Coatlicue, Coyolxauhqui, Huixtocihuatl, Mictecacibu-atl, Omecihuatl, Tlazolteotl, Toci, Tonan, Xochiquetzal.

Mayan Goddess Myths: Alaghom Naom Tzentel, Ix Chel.

Nahuatl Goddess Myths: Cipactli, Mayahuel.

North American

What came to be known as the Americas is the homeland of hundreds of Indian nations. At the time of the

Columbus encounter, some 500 years ago, the nations of North America thrived as distinct cultures adapted to the widely varying landscape of this vast country. The salmon-filled rivers of the Pacific Northwest provided an ample livelihood for the Tlingit, Bella Coola and Klamath nations. An abundance of oak trees in the interior valleys of California provided the Pomo, Miwok and Maidu with acorns as a staple food.

Precious sources of water in the desert Southwest allowed the desert to bloom with green crops of maize, beans and squash planted by the Navajo, Hopi, Rio Grande Pueblos and Pima nations. Vast herds of buffalo on the Great Plains became a major food source for the Lakota, Cheyenne, Omaha and Comanche. Deer, elk and moose, hundreds of varieties of fish, and agricultural crops formed the diet of the Indian nations of the Eastern woodlands. The homelands of the Ojibwa, the six nations of the Iroquois Confederacy, the Cherokee, Creek and Eastern Algonkians encompassed most of this spacious woodland country.

In the centuries that followed the arrival of Christopher Columbus, the Native land base gradually shrank into small enclaves known today as Indian reserves or reservations. While assimilation into the cultural practices of the invaders, primarily Euro-Americans, has taken place at a rapid pace over the last 200 years, traditional beliefs and practices survive. Indian nations of the past as well as today exhibit great cultural diversity. Within this diversity, however, are common values and themes with regard to spirituality.

The spiritual beliefs of America's Native people differed from those found in most parts of Europe and Asia. Indian nations were primarily, although not exclusively, egalitarian societies. The spirit world mirrors the human world, and because most Indian nations were not hierarchical, the notion of gods and goddesses ruling over their people constituted an alien concept. Instead, the Native people of North America spoke of a spiritual presence pervading the natural world. This spiritual presence was referred to as "wakan" among the plains-dwelling Lakota, and "manidou" among the neighboring Ojibwa people. This spiritual presence was everywhere but could be found concentrated in sacred spaces and places.

"Wakan" or "manidou" is literally translated as "great mystery" and is not necessarily associated with gender. However, the female principle can be found in the beliefs of many Native people. This principle is especially present among Indian nations whose traditions include plant agriculture. Most of the plant oriented nations practice descent through the female line. Children belong to the family and clan group of their mothers. The female principle as mother exhibits a strong presence in the spirit world of these plant cultivators.

The homelands of the Navajo nation are bound by four sacred female mountains jutting out of mother earth from flat-topped mesas and red sand deserts. For the Navajo of the American southwest, cornfields and sheep herds are sources of life, and they are called "sacred mothers." In human affairs, it is the Navajo clan mother who makes decisions regarding this female space of fields and herds.

Far to the east in the fertile woodland country of Eastern North America, many other Indian nations also cultivated corn, beans and squash for their livelihood. These nations—the Iroquois, Cherokee, Creek and Algonkian-speaking people—also traced descent through the female line. In addition to their central place in family life, the women produced the crops and exercised a strong measure of control over the affairs of men.

Women nominated the civil chiefs to office among the Iroquois, and they could recall those chiefs who did not properly voice the concerns of the women. Clan mothers could veto any decisions made by the great civil chiefs, if the women felt such decisions were not in their best interests. A female officeholder, the Mother of Nations, maintained a sanctuary lodge for anyone, including enemies, escaping from harm. The power of women is well expressed in the original story of the Iroquois first mother, Ataensic, who created the earth and everything that exists upon it.

The female principle can also be found among Native nations whose economies emphasized the primacy of the male-oriented hunt. Millions of buffalo once moved like rivers over the vast grasslands of the North American plains, homeland to the Lakota nation. Men were the buffalo hunters, and as warriors, they held honored positions as their nation's protectors. Despite the prominence of Lakota men, the female principle can be found in one of their most sacred objects, the Sacred Pipe given to humanity by White Buffalo Calf Woman.

The neighboring Ojibwa of the Great Lakes region told a similar story regarding how they acquired the Big Drum. The Drum holds as much sacred meaning as the Pipe, and according to traditional teachings, a Lakota woman gave the first Drum to the Ojibwa. Her gift symbolized her strong desire for peace between these neighboring nations. The common theme in both stories is the idea that women are the life-givers. They are the source of all that is alive and all that is sacred. Women have power, and according to Ojibwa scholar Basil Johnston, "It is men who must constantly struggle to seek power in their being."—*Priscilla Buffalohead*

Northeast/Northcentral Goddess Myths: Ataensic, Atira, Djigonasee, Gawaunduk, Gendenwitha, Genetaska, Geezhigo-Quae, Godasiyo, Kiwakweskwa, Leelinau, Maya Owichapaha, Muzzu-Kummik-Quae, Nokomis, Nunnehi, Omamama, Oniata, Winonah.

Northwest/Aleut Goddess Myths: Agischanak, Asintmah, Chuginadak, Dzalarhons, Gyhldeptis, Loo-Wit, Mem Loimis, Nahkeeta, Pahto, Qamaits, Queskapenek, Rhpisunt, Sneneik, Somagalags, Tacoma, Tlitcaplitana, Tsagigla'lal, Wah-Kah-Nee.

Plains Goddess Myths: Hanwi, Pawosee, Pohaha, Rukko, White Buffalo Woman.

Southeast Goddess Myths: Ailsie, Ohoyo Osh Chishba, Selu, SpearFinger, Tahci, Unelanuhi.

Southwest Goddess Myths: Atse Estsan, Awitelin Tsita, Changing Woman, Estsanatlehi, Glispa, Kachina, Kuwanlelenta, Shiwanokia, Spider Woman, Tse che nako, Uti Hiata, Utset/Nowutset, Yolkai Estsan.

California Goddess Myths: Amayicoyondi, Hekoolas, Hulluk Miyumko, Norwan.

Circumpolar Goddess Myths: Aakuluujjusi, Akycha, Apasinasee, Irdlirvirisissong, Kadlu, Nuliayoq, Pukimna, Sedna, Uinigumasuittuq.

South American/Caribbean

The arrival of humans in South America dates back as far as 30,000 years ago. When Europeans arrived in the fifteenth century C.E., the entire continent was populated, supporting tens of millions of residents. The lush Amazon basin, the snowy peaks of the Andes, the high plateau of the Altiplano, the tropical islands stretching out into the Caribbean Sea—these diverse geographical features separated the peoples of South America and the Caribbean, encouraging the development of civilizations, with their attendant mythologies, which varied widely. The coming of European conquistadors placed a Christian veneer over some native religions, a process that was especially easy given the lack of an indigenous script for recording the ancient material; in addition, the arrival of enslaved Africans created the opportunity for a new, cross-cultural spirituality (see African diaspora).

Native South Americans, like their island neighbors, included both hunter/gatherers and agriculturalists; the first practiced a shamanic religion, while the latter developed pantheons related to nature and the weather. There were, however, some areas that included both shamanic elements and agricultural sacrifices, as among the llama-raising agriculturalists of the south Andes. In addition, several important advanced societies—including the Inca as well as the unknown peoples who built the mysterious Nazca lines of Peru and colonized the city of Tiahuanaco by Lake Titicaca—further complicate the religious picture of this varied continent.

The feminine divinity was clearly important to these cultures, most of which—the patriarchal Inca being an exception—had a central earth goddess. Often she was an ancestral mother to the people; sometimes she was seen as the first being to create food, which nurtures her descendants. Several myths suggest an ancient cultural primacy of women; these myths tell of the stripping of power by men, who sometimes were said to kill all the women who had already learned enough language to speak, keeping only girl infants to reproduce the tribe. Despite this, concern for the earth as a maternal being who, in turn, relies on the care of her children, is widespread in native South America and nearby islands. —*Patricia Monaghan*

South American Goddess Myths: Akewa, Auchimalgen, Bachue, Cavillaca, Ceiuci, Cocomama, Evaki, Huitaca, Hun-Ahpu-Mtye, India Rosa, Inga Woman, Ituana, Korobona, Mama Allpa, Mama Cocha, Mama Ocllo, Mama Quilla, Mamapacha, Sibilaneuman, Sicasica, Zaramama, Zipaltonal.

Central American Goddess Myths: Cihuacoatl, Cihuateteo, Dabaiba, Masaya, Mu Olokukurtilisop.

Caribbean Goddess Myths: Anuanaitu, Atabei, Guabancex, Itiba Tahuvava.

Asia

Chinese/Mongolian/Korean

The history of what we now call China reaches back into deep antiquity; the first dynasty, the Shang, ruled between 1500–1000 B.C.E., with the Chou ruling for the next 800 years. The dynasty that gave its name to the land mass today, the Ch'in, ruled only briefly, between 221–206 B.C.E., with later dynasties (Han, Three Kingdoms, Western Chin, Sui, and Tang) following in the early common era.

The earliest civilizations of China were not the highly centralized bureaucracies of later Chinese life, nor were their mythologies the highly structured regimes of later centuries. Rather, eastern continental Asia was home to tribal people whose mythologies were never entirely lost, but were absorbed into the developing religions. Among these ethnic groups, female shamans (*wu* in China, *mu* in Korea) mediated between this world and worlds beyond; these female religious leaders did not survive into later historical times in China. However, they remain a vital cultural

and spiritual force even today in Korea, where as many as 100,000 dancing *mudang* still evoke the ancient mysteries.

It is from the earliest period that most of the great myths of China derive. Many were recorded in the illustrated Shanhai Jing (Book of Mountains and Seas), a compilation of myths transcribed during several B.C.E. periods. The dancing woman ruler/shaman finds her reflection in strong and active goddess figures, many of whom conflict with later philosophy that saw the feminine as an essentially passive force.

This aboriginal Chinese religion forms the basis for Taoism, which called for the balance of the feminine (yin) and masculine (yang) aspects of life. Yet Taoism grew well beyond its roots. Taoism's traditional founder is the sage Lao-Tzu of the sixth century B.C.E., author of the important Tao-te Ching (Book of the First Principles). Originally a man of the fifth century B.C.E., Lao-Tzu was transmogrified into a demon-fighting elemental force who never died but disappeared instead, riding a green ox towards the west. As Taoism became the religion of choice for the new imperial China, its pantheon began to reflect the social organization of earthly life, resembling nothing so much as a bureaucratic hierarchy complete with monthly reports to superior gods and annual performance reviews.

Later, the ideas of Confucius (the sage K'ung Ch'iu of the fifth century B.C.E.) became the basis for an ethically sophisticated, philosophically oriented way of life. The abstractness of the Confucian way gave rise to few myths, although it provided rituals that celebrated the passing seasons and the ancestral powers. Rather, Confucian ideas and ideals were appended to extant myths, producing in some cases a disjuncture between mythic action and its interpretation. Or ancient myth was recast as history, producing some intriguingly supernatural "historical" characters including impressively powerful queens.

In the third century C.E., Buddhism immigrated from India, by way of Tibet and Afghanistan, bringing with it many vivid myths and mythic figures. Few of these were feminine, but the most powerful female figure in China for more than a millennium—the kindly bodhisattva or Buddha-to-be, Kuan-Yin—derives from this mythic tradition. Like other Buddhist figures, Kuan-Yin was adapted from the original; often these figures were renamed, sometimes their genders were altered, and often new myths arose to explain them.

Despite the imperial strength of China, evident in such major public works as the Great Wall, the court did not dictate all religious ways to the people of the great land. Messages alternative to the mainstream religion were found in two places: in the residue of the indigenous religions, as in the folktales and folkways of ethnic groups like the Miao; and in the religious myths of neighboring peoples, the Turks and Manchus as well as those frequent invaders of the middle kingdom, the Mongols. Thus, even while the court may have held a limited patriarchal world view, alternatives that were more open to feminine energies were kept alive in villages and outlying areas.   —*Patricia Monaghan*

Chinese Goddess Myths: Chang-O, Chih Nu, Feng Pho-Pho, Fu-Pao, Gaomei, Gum Lin, Ho Hsien-Ku, Hsi-Ling Shih, Hsi Wang Mu, Hsi-Ho, Hsian Fu-Jen, Hu-Tu, Jiandi, Jiangyuan, Kuan-yin, Lan Ts'ai-Ho, Li Chi, Meng-Jiang Jyu, Meng-Po Niang-Niang, Moye, Nuxiu, Nu Kua, Pi-Hsia Yuan-Chin, Sao-Ts'ing Niang, Tai Yuan, Tien-Hou, Tien-Mu, Tou-Mou, Tsi-Ku, Wa, Yaoji.

Korean Goddess Myths: Grand-Aunt Tiger, Hae-Sun, Mama, Mulhalmoni, Pali-Kongju, Ryuhwa, Samsin Halmoni, Sungmo, Yondung Halmoni.

Mongolian Goddess Myths: Aigiarm, Alan Qo'a, Altan-Telgey, Etugen, Vatiaz.

Indian

From about 4500 B.C.E. to about 2800 B.C.E., semi-nomadic Proto-Indo-European warrior folk migrated in several waves from the grassy and forested steppe area north of the Caucasus Mountains and the Black Sea to many areas of Europe and Asia. The Proto-Indo-Europeans, whose social structure was patriarchal, patrilineal, patrilocal, and hierarchical, particularly honored the priest and warrior castes. After centuries of slow migrations, the Proto-Indo-

Europeans reached the geographical regions where they would finally settle, and in many cases they assimilated with the relatively peaceful, sedentary, agricultural, beauty-loving indigenous peoples of Neolithic and Bronze Age Europe and Asia.

By the second millennium B.C.E., some Proto-Indo-Europeans had reached the Iranian Plateau. Those who remained in this area became the Iranians (ancient Persians). Others continued migrating, reaching what became historic India and Pakistan around 1500 B.C.E. The Indic and Iranian languages show a very close relationship, suggesting that their speakers were once united as an Indo-European subgroup before further separating linguistically and culturally.

In what became Pakistan, the Proto-Indo-Europeans assimilated with the indigenous peoples of the Indus River Valley civilization, the peoples of Harappa and Mohenjo-Daro, cities that flourished from about 2500–1500 B.C.E. Fortified citadels encircled by walls about three miles long, these cities had streets—complete with drains—laid out in a grid plan.

The structures of Mohenjo Daro were made of undecorated red bricks. Originally, the ornamentation may have been confined to the woodwork, which would have perished with time. Sculptures from Mohenjo Daro include a small bronze figurine of a dancing woman and a figurine of a bearded man. Sculptures from Harappa include two very finely worked figurines, both of which have socket holes in the neck and shoulders that would allow a head and arms to be attached. The Harappan artists produced lifelike figurines as good as those which the classical Greeks produced over a millennium later. They also produced earthenware vessels turned on the wheel, often decorated with designs. The Indus Valley peoples also spun and wove cloth. They had several kinds of weapons—bow and arrow, spear, axe, dagger, and mace—but had not yet developed the sword. It would appear that their weapons and fortifications did not serve them on the advent of the Indo-Europeans, because around 1500 B.C.E. the Indus people were massacred in their streets and in their dwellings. For example, one excavated room revealed the skeletons of thirteen adults and one child. Two of the adult skulls showed signs of violence.

The Indus Valley peoples have left us sealstones inscribed with a form of pictographic script, which has not been deciphered. But after the advent of the Indo-Europeans, there was a Dark Age that lasted several centuries. There is no evidence of writing again for several centuries, when the earliest writings of the Indic peoples appear.

The oldest Indic writings are the Rigveda, sacred hymns to the Indic deities composed in approximately 1200 B.C.E. Although most of the Rigvedic hymns are addressed to male deities, several are in praise of goddesses. The most cited goddess in the Rigveda is Ushas, a goddess carried by the Proto-Indo-European peoples from their steppe homeland. Another Proto-Indo-European goddess found in the Rigveda and later writings is the sun-maiden Surya, daughter of the (male) sun, Surya. This sun-maiden was wooed by two sets of lovers, the twin Asvins, the divine horsemen; and by Soma, god of the moon (and of the sacred soma plant). The myth is a Proto-Indo-European one, found also in Latvian mythological songs and Greek epic. A third Proto-Indo-European Goddess found in the Rigveda is Danu, mother of the watery monster Vitra. Danu and her son withhold the celestial waters, and the young male warrior deity, Indra, kills them both. This is a recurring theme throughout Indo-European and Near Eastern mythology, wherein a young warrior hero kills a female snaky monster who is usually but not always connected with water. This murder of an indigenous snaky goddess probably recalls the destruction/subjugation of the indigenous peoples and their deities by the Proto-Indo-Europeans.

Another goddess invoked frequently in the Rigveda is Sarasvati, goddess of wisdom, music, and the river. Sarasvati "causes milk, melted butter, [and] sweet water to pour forth" and she "bestows beautiful things." A goddess of bounty, she places the fetus in the womb, but she also "dashes to the ground those who hate the gods."

Other Vedic writings were composed somewhat later, for example the Atharvaveda, which includes, again, laudatory hymns to gods and goddesses, but also includes charms: magical charms for love, for prosperity, for children, to banish troubles, to banish jealousy. Puranas were tales of ancient times, celebrating the powers of deities (for example, the Devimahatmyam, from the Markaeya-Purana, celebrated the birth and potency of the Goddess Devi). Classical Sanskrit literature dates from the early centuries C.E. through the Middle Ages. One intriguing trait of Classical Sanskrit literature is that two languages are used to indicate gender differentiation. Gods and male heroes use the Sanskrit language, while female heroes use forms of the Prakrit language, further differentiated according to social rank. The Indo-European Indic society was exceptionally hierarchical.

In the first millennium of this era, vestiges of the pre-Indo-European great goddess—perhaps the tutelary deity of the Indus River Valley—began to re-emerge in Indic religion: the goddess Devi first appeared in the great Indic epic, the Mahabharata, but her honor and status grew in the later Puranas and Tantric ("rule, ritual") texts. Devi eventually subsumed many of the other Indic female figures, becoming known under many names. In some of her forms, she carried the snake and she rode "in a chariot yoked with swans." Thus she bore the icons of the prehistoric bird and snake goddess of Neolithic and Bronze Age Europe. This re-emergence of Devi is most probably a re-emergence of the religion of the indigenous peoples of India and Pakistan, who also left their mark on the Sanskrit language; Sanskrit has an entire extra set of consonants ("linguals") that the other Indo-European languages do not share.

Thus the Indic language and religion are a result of the interweaving of pre-Indo-European substrate and Indo-European superstrate peoples. In India, this influence is still strong, because Devi is a living goddess.
—*Miriam Robbins Dexter*

Indian Goddess Myths: Abhramu, Aditi, Alakhani, Amba, Anapurna, Banka-Mundi, Bardaichila, Bentakumari, Bhavani, Bisal-Mariamna, Bomong, Budhi Pallien, Candi, Churalin, Dakini, Devi, Diti, Draupadi, Durga, Ganga, Gauri, Ghar-Jenti, Hada Bai, Hariti,

Hathay, Holika, Huligamma, Ila, Janguli, Kadru, Kali, Kamadhenu, Karaikkal-Asmmaiyar, Kottavi, Kunti, Kusumamodini, Lopamudra, Lakshmi, Lolita, Maitreya, Manasa, Maya, Minachiamman, Mindhal, Naina Devi, Nidra, Nirriti, Parooa, Parvati, Pidari, Prajnaparamita, Prakriti, Prithivi, Radha, Rakshasi, Rambha, Ranaghant, Rangda, Ranu Bai, Rati, Rohini, Samjuna, Sarasvati, Sati, Savitri, Shakti, Sita, Sitala, Surabhi, Tari Pennu, Uma, Urvasi, Ushas, Uyu-sum, Vajravaraki.

Japanese/Ainu

The archipelago of Japan was the home of the Ainu people when new settlers arrived, in approximately 1500 B.C.E., from Korea. These newcomers drove the Ainu to the far northern islands, where their descendants still live; other early tribal people such as those on the southern island of Kyushu were assimilated into the culture of the newcomers, their beliefs appearing in vestigial form in later Japanese legends.

The newcomers practiced what came to be known as Shinto, a religion with its roots in a shamanism practiced by women—including the empress, who sought counsel among her spirits to make political decisions. Although Japanese rulers are no longer women, the connection of the imperial throne to the spirits continues to this day, for the current emperor was "reborn" on his inauguration as the child of the sun goddess, ancient central divinity of Shinto.

Shinto means "way of the *kami*"—the *kami* being powers that, although clothed in human form in the myths and legends, were recognized to be universal forces. Within the natural world around us, Shinto sees these forces, which can appear in their positive, gentle form (*nigi-mi-tama*) or their sterner, more violent one (*ara-mi-tama*). There is no real sense of evil in Shinto, merely of things being out of place or at the wrong time. Shinto, still practiced by many Japanese today, is the only living religion centered on a goddess—the sun *kami*, Amaterasu.

With the coming of Buddhism to Japan in 522, the early myths and legends of the kami were almost lost to history. But in 681, Heido-no-Are, a court woman

of phenomenal memory, was assigned to memorize all the tales. Thirty years later, the empress Gemmyo assigned a scribe to take down the material. Called the Kojiki, these myths form the basis of Shinto beliefs. A few years later Gemmyo had additional material compiled from other sources; this, the Nihon shoki or Nihongi, is another primary source of information on Japanese mythology.

The court was, by this time, controlled by the Yamato clan, which still holds the imperial throne today. Their divinities, including the clan mother Amaterasu, were elevated above those of other tribes and became the primary divinities of Shinto. But the other divinities remained alive among their clan followers. Thus several divinities may "rule" a certain aspect of nature, the "lesser" kami being those of less powerful clans.

As the court became more Buddhist, some figures from that religion, and attendant myths, were brought into Japanese culture. As most of the buddhas and bodhisattvas were male, this change diminished the mythic role of women in Japan. Yet Shinto continued, even influencing Buddhism enough that a nature-oriented Buddhism called Zen emerged from the contact between the two religions. Both are actively practiced in Japan today.   —*Patricia Monaghan*

Japanese Goddess Myths: Akoya, Amaterasu, Aryong-Jong, Benten, Fuji, Hiedo-no-Ame, Himiko, Ikuta-mayorihime, Inari, Ishikore-Dome, Izanami, Jingo, Kishimogin, Kongsim, Kono-Hana-Sakuya-Hime, Naru-Kami, Ningyo, No-Il Jae-Dae, Ootonobe-no-Kami, O-Ryu, Oto-Hime, Rafu-Sen, Sayo-Hime, Seya-datarahime, Suhijini-no-Kami, Tamayorihime, Tatsuta-Hime, Toyota-Mahime, Toy-Uke, Tsuru, Uke-Mochi, Uzume, Wakahirume, Yama no Kami, Yamato-Hime-no-Miko, Yaya-Zakura, Yuki-Onne.

Ainu Goddess Myths: Chu-Kamui, Kamui Fuchi, Turesh.

Siberian

Across the vast tundra and sheltering taiga (arctic forest) of Siberia live five distinct nations. To the west are the Finno-Ugric people (see separate entry), represented in Siberia by the Ugrian Xants and the Samoyeds (Nencs, Encs, Nganasans and Selkups). The

Altaic tribes include the Buryats, who originated in Mongolia but now live around Lake Baikal in southwestern Siberia; the Turks, who include the far-ranging Yakut of central Siberia as well as several smaller groups (Yakut, Tuva, Tofalar and Xakas); and the Tungus-Manchu, composed of the Tungus (also called Evenk), Lamut (Even), Gold (Nanaj or Nanai), Ulc, Udege, Orok and Orochon peoples. Almost a million of these people still reside in their ancestral lands in central and northern Siberia. Of the remaining groups—the Paleo-Arctic peoples (Chukchee, Koryak, Kamchadais, Yukaghir and Gilyak), the Ket and the Eskimo—perhaps only 30,000 still reside in the far western areas of Siberia.

Despite the vastness of their lands and the dramatic difference in their languages, Siberians are joined by several important religious conceptions: a vision of a tripartate world; the initiatory process whereby shamans are made; and the importance of the clan or ancestral mother. The universe is seen as divided into three parts. There is the middle world, in which humans live. From this familiar world, a river descends to the lower world, where immortal female shamans are found. Reaching upwards from the middle world is a vast tree, whose branches reach the upper world. In this tree's branches, the souls of the dead perch; when their time has come for rebirth, they drop through smoke holes into tents, enter the hearth fire, and from there reenter a womb.

It was the role of shamans to navigate these three worlds, rising into the upper world to reclaim lost souls; traveling on the middle world to see distant events and to locate game animals; and descending to the lower world to reaffirm the order of creation. Shamans were called to their duties by an initiatory illness, sometimes called "arctic hysteria." In this visionary state, they were dismembered and then reassembled; the reborn shaman was thus an utterly new being, no longer completely human, empowered to fly above our earth and descend beneath it.

In those descents, the shaman would encounter powerful female figures. The presence of such divine foremothers in the nether world has led Soviet theorists to hypothesize an ancient Siberian matriarchy, supplanted by a later more patriarchal society. Western researchers remain unconvinced of these Soviet theories, but they do not contest the importance of female divinities among the Siberians. One of the greatest was the fire goddess who lived in the hearth of each home and guarded the family who lived there; she was especially honored by women of the home, who cared for her and made sure she was never extinguished. Ancestral mothers, too, were important figures who provided food for their descendants; animal mothers may have been the non-human form of the ancestral mothers, or divinities in their own right. Whether these are vestigial forms of ancient matriarchs or not, their importance in Siberian religion is without dispute. —*Patricia Monaghan*

Siberian Goddess Myths: Ajysyt, Bugady Enintyn, Bugady Musun, Dunne Enin, Ja-Neba, Kasum-Naj-Ekva, Kou-Njami, Mou-Njami, Poza-Mama, Tu-Njami, Umaj, Vut-Imi, Zonget.

Southeast Asian

The peninsulas, archipelagoes and islands of Southeast Asia are home to some of the richest and most complex mythologies on the planet. Located between India and China, the lands of Southeast Asia had their own aboriginal religion (called Austroasiatic, Austric or Austronesian) long before the influences of Hinduism, Buddhism and Taoism arrived. These immigrant religions, with their divinities, were integrated and adapted into the cultures of Southeast Asia—in lands we now call Singapore, Thailand, Vietnam, Bali, Laos, Indonesia, Java, Cambodia, Malaysia, and the Philippines. The syncretic (melded) religions of Southeast Asia today vary from area to area, including in various proportions the mythologies and rituals of both indigenous and imported cultures.

The aboriginal cultures had no written languages. People lived in small settlements on the lush river deltas, in the forested mountains, along the fertile plains, adapting their lives to the necessities of the land. Rice growing was important, but so was fishing and sea trading, weaving and pottery making. In approximately the beginning of the common era, influences from India brought writing and art to these lands; China's influence began substantially later, around 1000 C.E. Great kingdoms began to emerge, with attendant cities and monuments like the majestic Angkor Wat. Yet in the shadows of these centralized kingdoms, such indigenous cultures as the Hmong in Vietnam continued to exist and even to flourish. Thus the recorded mythology of this region offers a wide variety of goddess figures from the various cultural strata. *—Patricia Monaghan*

Southeast Asian Goddess Myths: Agusan Devi, Au-Co, Biman Chan, Dayang Racca, Dayang Sumbi, Dewi Nayang Shasi, Dewi Shri, Emboq Sri, Giri Devi, Giriputri, Ibu Pertiwi, Kannagi, Ka Nam, Kiri Amma, Kling, Kn Sgni, Lieu Hahn, Mera, Min Mahagiri, Pattini, Po Ino Nogar, Rangada, Ratu Kidul, Royot, Si Boru Deak Parujar, Silewe Nazarata, Tisnawati, Trung-Trac.

Tibetan

The towering Himalayan mountains might not seem like a natural crossroads, but such it has been for religious culture. It was there, in the countries now called Tibet and Nepal, that the religions of India (Hinduism and Buddhism) encountered those of China (Taoism and Confucianism) as well as the indigenous religions of the mountain dwellers. What resulted was a rich and complex religion, sometimes called Lamaism, which was flavored by all of these ingredients.

Texts rediscovered at the beginning of the twentieth century show that Tibetan myths and rituals existed until the eighth or ninth century C.E. untainted by Buddhism, which was resisted on its arrival by the native clergy. Even after its arrival, Buddhism—which is essentially a non-narrative religion, relying less on the exploits of divinities than any other major faith—did not seriously impede the conveyance of ancient myths. However, Tibetan myths were not codified and organized in the way that, for instance, Greek mythology was. Therefore we find a diverse and sometimes self-contradicting variety of figures and stories in what is called the Bon-po or vestigial ancient religion.

Among these stories are many that involve goddesses of great power. Despite Buddhism's lack of narrative emphasis, the figures of the Buddha and the Bodhisattvas are predominantly male; thus most of the main Tibetan goddess figures are from the Bon-po, with a few others being Hindu imports. The feminine divinity of these Bon-po myths is never simplistically portrayed; she is both vengeful and kind, destructive and creative. Tibetan art is replete with images of these fierce and powerful beings who, despite many centuries of official demotion, remain a vital part of Tibetan culture. *—Patricia Monaghan*

Tibetan Goddess Myths: Brag-srin-mo, Dakini, Khon-Ma, Klu-mo, Lla-Mo, Maitreya, Marici, Tara, Srid-Icam 'phrul-mo-che, Vajravaraki.

The Pacific

Australian Aboriginal

The Dreamtime, that conception of another space/time continuum wherein creation is continuous and divinity still walks the earth, is one of the great contributions of Australian aboriginal religion to world culture. This Dreamtime (also called "The Dreaming") is not, as the term might suggest, something false or unreal. Rather, it is more true, more real, than the visible, tangible world. Nor is it separate from the waking world; it exists simultaneously, yet is unreachable in ordinary consciousness.

In this Dreamtime, the great myths are still unfolding. The great mother goddesses still walk the land, naming its features. The rainbow serpent still lures young women into danger. Animal totems continuously create races to honor them. It would be wrong to say that these myths are happening in a linear fashion; imagine, instead, that they are happening all at once, not as a progressive narrative. Into this fertile, powerful Dreamtime all humans can venture, in mystic states or through ritual as well as when unconscious. Religious leaders are especially adept at making the transition from Dreamtime to ordinary time, and like shamanic practitioners in other cultures, use this talent to assist in healing and otherwise serving their communities.

The land itself—this earth on which humans live—actively participates in Dreamtime. It is a sacred place wherein creative acts occur continuously. It is the duty of humanity to be aware of this sacredness and to mark those creative acts. Thus "walkabout," the tradition of walking the land and marking its "songlines" with ritual words and prayers, is an important action to traditional Australian peoples. Through these actions, Dreaming is strengthened, and humanity is strengthened as a result.

The role of women is vitally important in this endeavor. When European researchers began to write about Australian aboriginal religion earlier in this century, cultural biases became immediately evident. Because traditional Australian society was divided into male and female spheres, male researchers were unable to gather information about women's role in religion. They simply assumed, therefore, that there was none. Woman was declared "profane"—to use the term popular at the time—while men were "sacred." It was only when women researchers, working alone, began to together information from the aboriginal communities, that existence of women's rituals and their importance to the continuity of society were realized.

Although much of the blame for this decades-long derogation of the value of women to Australian traditional society must rest with biased researchers, the secrecy in which rituals are conducted was also a factor. Rituals were conducted with scrupulous secrecy, so that men in a community might actually be unaware of the ritual workings of the women within it. Sacred equals secret in Australian religion. The conveyance of spiritual and religious information took place in carefully structured settings, at specific locations and times. Nothing was written down; the myths and their meanings were conveyed orally, often in songs.

Given the size of the island continent, it is to be expected that there are substantial regional and cultural differences to be found; the features mentioned above, however, are generally shared. The major geographical distinctions are: Arnhem Land, the central northern part of the island with its relatively lush vegetation; the great central plains, centered on majestic Ayers Rock; and the rich coastal areas, where most European colonization occurred. Additionally, there were doubtless important cultural features of the island of Tanzania, to the south of Australia, but the indigenous residents were slaughtered and their culture lost to written history.   *—Patricia Monaghan*

Australian Goddess Myths: Bila, Djanggawul Sisters, Eingana, Erathipa, Gnowee, Julunggul, Junkgowa, Kalwadi, Kunapipi, Lia,Numma Moiyuk, Nyapilnu, Walo, Waramurungundji, Wawalag Sisters, Wuriupranili, Yhi.

Oceanic/Polynesian

Scattered across the vast Pacific Ocean are thousands and thousands of islands and atolls, some tiny and others large, most separated from the next island by days, sometimes weeks, of sailing. Despite these distances, the lush islands were a beacon for early migrants. Beginning an estimated 22,000 years ago, hunter/gatherers began to populate New Guinea and parts of Melanesia, as well as Australia. Much later—perhaps 17,000 years later—other settlers came, bringing with them a farming culture that also relied on animal husbandry. Migration within the region continued to at least 1000 C.E. In double outrigger canoes and other seafaring vessels, the Pacific peoples spread themselves over tens of thousands of ocean miles.

As might be expected under such geographical conditions, there is no centralized or hierarchical framework to Oceanic mythology as a whole. Many regional divinities—sometimes goddesses who rule only a single small atoll—are to be found; some seem derived from, or associated with, similar figures on other islands, yet each has distinctive features as well. Despite this complexity, there are a number of similarities among Oceanic myths, including the importance of an ancestral mother figure, whose cosmological role includes creating the islands on which people live, as well as the people themselves. This goddess figure appears as a shapeshifter, able to move between the realms of earth, underworld and heaven, as well as to change from bird or animal—even vegetable or mineral—form to human shape at will.

Among the many islands of Oceania, there are several of significant size and with significant populations; in addition, there are a number of archipelagos and other island systems with shared cultures. The religious traditions of such areas, as might be expected, are better known than are those of the smaller, more isolated islands. These cultures include that of the Maori, the native people of New Zealand; the multiple cultures of Papau-New Guinea, which include the Sepik, Kuma, and Arapesh; and the peoples of Hawaii, the New Hebrides, Samoa, Tahiti and Fiji. Yet the appeal of Oceania's rich cultures on its beautiful islands has drawn the attention of researchers as well to less populous areas. Thus the number of known mythic figures from this area is large, the myths fascinating and complex. —*Patricia Monaghan*

Oceanic Goddess Myths: Aponibolinayen, Arrang Dibatu, Atanea, Biliku, Ciau, Darago, Goga, Hainuwele, Haumea, Hikuleo, Hina, Hine-ahu-one, Hine-titama, Hit, Indara, Jata, Jugumishanta, Ka Ahu Pahau, Koevasi, La'ila'i, Laka, Le-Hev-Hev, Ligoapup, Lorop, Lumin-Ut, Mahuilki, Mele, Miru, Niniganni, Noika, Pani, Papa, Pare, Parewhenua-Mea, Pele, Rabie, Rona, Satine, Taranga, Toririhnan, Tuli, Wahini-Hai, Walutahanga, Wari-Ma-Te-Takere, Whaitiri, Wigan.

Eastern Mediterranean

Anatolian

The land mass we call Turkey used to be called Asia Minor, because of a fancy that it imitated, in miniature, the shape of the entire Asian continent. From earliest times this peninsula and the lands surrounding it have been a cultural crossroads on the route between Europe and Asia, and its mythologies and religions show the influences of both.

In approximately 6000 B.C.E., Anatolia was home to a culture whose massive cities like Catal Huyuk have been recently excavated. Although we do not know her name, the fleshy, birth-giving goddess worshiped there may have survived in later figures like the powerful mountain mother Cybele. Thousands of years later, the historical record of the area begins with the arrival of the Hittites. Until early this century, known only from a single treaty with Egypt and a Biblical mention, the Hittites were believed to be only a minor tribe. But discovery of the imperial records in Boghazkoy, their former capital, revealed the extent of their influence and power. These Hittites built upon the civilizations of earlier people, the Hurrians and Hattites. Ruled by a queen who was considered the embodiment of the primary goddess, these ancient people established an empire that stretched far beyond the plains of Anatolia.

The empire collapsed after several hundred years, leaving only isolated city-states—some of which, like Troy and Ephesus, became significant and powerful in their own right. Later, in approximately 1200 B.C.E., the Phrygian culture arose in the central part of the peninsula, the Phrygians themselves having apparently migrated from Europe. In what is now Iran, the culture called the Sythian or Sarmatian emerged, terrorizing the ancient world with its military prowess. During classical times, Greek and Roman colonies on the coasts of Anatolia brought together the richness of those cultures with the indigenous ones. Figures such as those of Medea and Medusa probably represent the conjunction of native with imported religious material.

In late classical times, the religion of Zoroaster—with its extreme dualism and belief in a war between light and dark—was born and flourished in Anatolia and Persia, spread especially by the prophet Zarathustra. It became the first Anatolian religion to spread outside its homeland, influencing western culture especially through Manicheanism. This extremely dualistic philosophy, founded by the Anatolian sage Mani, so strongly influenced Christian church father Augustine that its effects are still felt today. Similarly, the light-worshiping religion of Mithras spread through the Roman legions, who carried it to the farthest reaches of the empire. In these dualist world views, the feminine was invariably connected with the dark, with evil, with mortality. The coming of Islam was joined to these native roots in the form of the Shiite heresy, which believed that the first Arabian caliphs illegally deprived Mohammed's son-in-law of succession to rulership; from this source several semidivine figures, including Mohammed's daughter Fatima, derive.

Thus a land that in prehistory portrayed the divine as a birth-giving mother has been, for most of the historical period, the center of patriarchal world views that derogate the feminine. Despite this, powerful feminine figures continue to exist in folklore and in unorthodox religion in the area.—*Patricia Monaghan*

Anatolian Goddess Myths (includes Hittite, Sythian, Phrygian, Persian): Aka, Ala Nur, Al-Karisi, Anahita, Ararat, Armaiti, Cybele, Eni Mahanahi, Ephesia, Firanak, Halmasuit, Hannahanna, Hebat, Inaras, Jaki, Jeh, Kamrusepas, Kara-Kura, Kubaba, Lilwani, Mitra, Myrrha, Rudabeh, Semiramis, Shauskha, Tabiti, Wurusemu.

Mesopotamian

In our time, it is a strife-torn area. The current names this land bears—Iraq, Syria, Palestine, Israel, Jordan, Lebanon—come into our consciousness daily, almost invariably connected with slaughter and war. In ancient times, this fertile area was the cradle of civilization, a paradise on earth. But even then, it was also a land of conflict and dispute, where civilizations rose and fell over more than three thousand years. Called Mesopotamia or the Near East, this contested land is the source of some of the greatest mythic figures known to religious history.

The Tigris and the Euphrates, the two great rivers that flow through Iran, embrace between them the land of the ancient Sumerians, whose famous cities included Eridu, Nippur, Lagash, Erech and Ur; these people originated, it is believed, in Asia or Siberia, and had established themselves in southern Mesopotamia by 3400 B.C.E. Their neighbors were the Semitic Akkadians, whose cities included Babylon, Kish and Sippar. Thus the religion that emerged in this area includes some elements of both original cultures.

The rich land supported both herding and farming; it also supported great cities, each with its own religious pantheon as well as its own currency and rulers. As centuries passed and lands were conquered, the

pantheons merged, with deities from one being identified with those in another. Some divinities disappeared completely, leaving only their names as a title of the conquering god or goddess. Among these competing city-states were the Sumerian civilizations of Babylon, Assyria, Chaldea, and Ugarit and the Semitic cultures of the Amorites and Akkadians.

Two great myths of the region concern the goddess who descends into the realm of death but re-emerges safely, and the goddess whose consort dies and must be mourned. These goddesses were worshiped in citywide festivals as well as in lavishly endowed temples. It was in the latter that such vital skills as mathematics and cuneiform writing were invented, presumably by priestesses who served the goddess.   —*Patricia Monaghan*

Assyrian/Syrian Goddess Myths: An-Zu, Atargatis, Eye Goddess.

Babylonian Goddess Myths: Aja, Anunitu, Astarte, Bau, Belit-Ilani, Belit-Seri, Gatamdug, Gestinanna, Gula, Irnini, Ishtar, Kadi, Kilili, Mami, Myrrha, Nana, Sarbanda, Siduri, Tiamat, Zarpandit.

Chaldean Goddess Myths: A, Adamu, Eshara, Ki, Lamamu, Mamitu, Orore.

Sumerian Goddess Myths: Ashnan, Damkina, Eriskegal, Inanna, Lamasthu, Mami, Nammu, Ningal, Ninhursag, Ninlil, Nisaba.

Ugaritic Goddess Myths: Anat, Kathirat, Shapash.

Semitic/Hebrew

Their scriptures still are viewed by many as historical fact, but much in the Hebrew bible is colored by the politics of patriarchy; it is a partisan tract rather than an objective record of fact. For it was among these roving bands in Palestine, in the millennium before the common era, that the idea of monotheism based on a single male god arose—an idea that took root and, in the form of Judaism and Christianity, still flourishes today. However, the Semitic tribes originally had a polytheistic religion that included recognition of the goddess.

In historical terms, the Semites are the people who lived in the Near East beginning in approximately 3000

B.C.E. Their name comes from Noah's son Shem, one of those who repopulated the earth after the mythical Great Flood. But Semitic language is more relevant than the blood of Shem, for scholars suggest that the connection among Semitic people is linguistic rather than biological. Eastern Semitic—called Akkadian, or later Assyro-Babylonian—was used by the people of ancient Babylon. More complicated is the family of western Semitic languages, which includes Phoenician and Aramaic, as well as Arabic and Hebrew.

Among these western Semitic people, only the Hebrews and—two thousand years later—the Arabs adopted male-oriented monotheism. Most Canaanite people, relatives of the Hebrews like the Phoenicians, worshiped the goddess into historical times. The Hebrews of the two kingdoms of Israel and Judea were not themselves instantly converted. Their scriptures tell of continual revival, and continual repression, of goddess culture among them. Even when the official religion had soundly routed the goddess, she remained in folk culture and in some rituals, a living if somewhat ghostly presence.

When the official elimination of the goddess was completed, the ancient symbol of a woman and a fruit-bearing tree—for generations an emblem of the connection between human fertility and that of the land—had become a warning sign. No longer did the great mother point to the joys of this earth; rather, she lured us into sin and destruction. The serpent, similarly, was transformed from a symbol of rebirth to one of death.

Yet as in other areas where the goddess was suppressed, she lived on despite lack of official acknowledgment. She was the Sabbath queen, welcomed in the rituals of the home and the Matronit, mother of the esoteric Kabbala. She may have been described as metaphor or as a mere linguistic curiosity, but many centuries after her apparent death, the Hebrew goddess still inspired and comforted her people.   —*Patricia Monaghan*

Canaanite Goddess Myths: Adath, Asherah, Astarte, Husbishag, Ishara, Naamah.

Semitic/Hebrew Goddess Myths: Abigail, Adah, Agasaya, Agrat Bat Mahalat, Ardat Lili, Athaliah, Beruryah, Bilhah, Broxa, Cherubim, Daughters of Zelophehad, Deborah, Dinah, Esther, Eve, Hagar, Hannah, Hokkma, Iahu Anat, Igirit, Istehar, Jezebel, Jocebed, Judith, Leah, Leviathan, Lilith, Mahalat, Miriam, Rachel, Rebecca, Sarah, Sheilah, Shekinah, Tamar, Torah, Vashti. Zipporah, Zuleika.

Kabbalistic Goddess Myths: The Matronit.

Europe

Baltic

About 2500 B.C.E., the Indo-European ancestors of the Lithuanians and Latvians arrived in the fertile lowlands east of the Baltic Sea, probably from an original homeland in the Eurasian steppes. They brought with them a tribal, patriarchal form of culture that resembled that of the Celts, in that warrior-chieftains ruled but women held high status, and in which possible traces of a remote matriarchate may be perceived.

These Baltic peoples had no written language— their existence is first recorded in the works of Classical writers such as Tacitus, who in the *Germania* of 98 C.E. describes them as patient cultivators of grain and collectors of fine Baltic amber. Archaeology confirms their farming skills in traces of wheat, rye, millet, barley, oat, flax, hemp, apples and livestock, especially horses, cattle and pigs. Later writers concur in the view of the Balts as peaceable farmers and traders, but formidable in combat.

The amber trade linked Baltic culture with central and southern Europe from at least the Bronze Age, bringing it into contact with Celts, Slavs and Scythians in particular. In the ancient world, Baltic amber was more precious than gold. It has been found in the shaft-graves of Mycenae (c. 1580 B.C.E.) and as far south as Egypt and Syria. Intensive trade with Roman provinces from the second to sixth centuries C.E. led to a golden age of material prosperity for the Balts in general, reflected in the splendid use of precious metals. Bronze, brass, gold and silver were prized, and appear as lavish jewelry in female burials and weapons in male interments.

The Baltic group of languages, which includes Lithuanian, Latvian and Old Prussian (the latter extinct) is the most ancient of the Indo-European family, bearing a close relationship to Sanskrit. Moreover the Balts preserved, in a vast oral tradition of verse, a proto-Indo-European mythology in which cultic primacy was given to a sun goddess, reflecting the elevated position of women. Despite influences from Scandinavian, Germanic, Slavic and Finno-Ugrian neighbors, the Balts maintained a remarkably conservative religious heritage, in which the most archaic types of deity can be traced via living traditions into modern times. The pantheon emphasized sky-deities—sun, moon, stars, rain and thunder—while spirits of rivers, springs, trees and earth took an important though lesser place. The deities' characters and myths were passed on in the form of sacred songs called dainas. There are more than a million collected versions in the national libraries. Chiefly composed by women, they exalt and invoke much-loved deities in contexts of everyday life: the concerns of farmstead, field and marriage, or the sorrows of the Balts during their troubled history, when they were oppressed by German and Slav overlords. Overwhelmingly the dainas exalt the sun goddess, her beauty and beneficence, in thousands of songs for the summer solstice feast and the harvest-home. The song-tradition sustained the Balts though hundreds of years of suffering, and today is still a flourishing, living tradition, an essential part of Baltic identity.

Although richly described in song, the Baltic deities were seldom depicted in art. From prehistoric through historic times, sacred art is aniconic, with a wealth of astral symbols, predominantly solar, decorating jewelry, weapons, burial urns, textiles and household objects. From early times married women wore diadems profusely ornamented with sun symbols. Similar crowns, adorned with red and white streamers representing sunrays, are part of women's folk costume to the present day. Baltic women's ancient reputation as skilled weavers and embroiderers is still displayed in these charming and dignified robes, worn now for festive and choral occasions. Solar emblems beautify hems, crowns and plaids, and the use of tartans and massive brooches gives a somewhat Celtic appearance. The Baltic woman in her traditional finery is still said to be dressed as the sun herself is dressed, and women in folk costume are called "daughters of the sun."

Lithuania and Latvia were the last strongholds of paganism in Europe. The priests who first attempted to Christianize the Balts grudgingly admired their altruism, while lamenting their "stubborn heathenism." When threatened, the Balts were ruthless in self-defense and protection of their holy places. Missionaries who dared, for example, to fell sacred trees met a violent end. In retaliation the German "Knights of the Sword" undertook a crusade, with papal blessing, to exterminate Baltic heathenism. Thus in 1201 began the long and bitter persecution of the Baltic religion and peoples, in brutal atrocities and forced baptisms. The Lithuanians in particular resisted conversion. No real headway was made until the seventeenth century, and even then Christianity remained a veneer. In some remote forest regions and on farmsteads isolated by swamplands, the old religion persisted even into the nineteenth century, with Christian priests still finding it necessary to cut down sacred trees and preach against the old gods. By then Lithuania was officially Roman Catholic (though with many saints and symbols borrowed from pagan forerunners), while Latvia had become Lutheran.   —*Janet McCrickard*

Baltic Goddess Myths: Amberella, Aspelenie, Austrine, Breksta, Dugnai, Egle, Laume, Laima, Juras Mate, Jurate, Maria, Milda, Perkuna Tete, Rugiu Boba, Saule, Saules Meita, Vakyrine, Zemyna.

Celtic

The precise origins of the war-loving Celts are clouded in the haze of prehistory. The consensus among today's scholars is that the Celts swept out of the Caucasus and into southeastern Europe as early as 3000 B.C.E., bringing with them their goddesses of land and war. The supreme Celtic divinity was embodied within in the land itself, personified as a goddess of sovereignty from whom all bounty flowed. From southern Gaul to western Ireland, male rulers—chosen for their unblemished bodies and their ability as warriors—underwent sacred ceremonies in which they were wedded to this goddess of the land before they could assume leadership. Statuary and icons of these goddesses can be found throughout modern France, England, and Ireland. Often they are depicted cradling fruits of the harvest, children, or warriors' weapons.

Celtic civilization and social structure was built around warfare, an activity that assumed spiritual dimensions modern people can barely grasp. The blessings of the Druids, a male-dominated priesthood, and of the priestesses was essential. Offerings were made to war goddesses on the eve of battle, and divinations were undertaken in lavish ceremonies to attempt either to foresee the outcome of the battle or to discover the best battle strategy.

Because one of the primary objectives of war was the acquisition of new land or of cattle (animals sacred to the goddesses of the land), it is not surprising that war deities were mostly feminine. Probably the most famous Celtic war goddess was the triple deity known as the Morrigan. This fearsome figure appeared as a raven screeching over the battlefield calling up the spirits of slain warriors to continue the fight in the Otherworld. War "trophies," or the severed heads of the enemy, were sacred to her and were referred to as "the Morrigan's acorn crop."

Celtic tribes covered much of central and western Europe during the late Bronze and early Iron Ages, and iconographic evidence of their occupation can be found throughout modern-day Switzerland, Denmark, Spain, Germany, Italy, and Romania. Sometime between 1200 and 500 B.C.E. they settled in what are today thought of as the "Celtic lands": northwestern France (Brittany), Ireland, Scotland, Wales, and large sections of England, particularly the Duchy of Cornwall. When the Celts reached these areas they came into contact with races of people who also worshiped the earth's sanctity, and who had built stone monu-

ments to their deities and to the cycles of the seasons. The Celts vanquished these peoples through war and then adopted their sacred sites and many of their deities as their own.

Once settled in their new lands, the Celtic languages divided themselves into two categories: the Brythonic group (called the P Celts, for their softening of the hard k/c/q sound) which includes Welsh, Breiz (spoken in Brittany), and Cornish; and the Goidelic group (called the Q Celts) which is comprised of Irish, Manx, and Scots Gaelic.

Of all the Celtic myths, those of Ireland are the oldest and best preserved, and through them echo the themes of women as warriors and as sovereigns. Many of the myths were blended with actual historical events so that it is often difficult to decide where the mythic aspects of women warriors/queens such as Queen Maeve of Connacht or Boudicca of the Iceni stop and their factual aspects begin. The oldest collection of Irish myths were written in a seventh-century manuscript known as *The Book of the Dun Cow*, though only parts of it still exist. Another important Irish manuscript is the twelfth-century work, *The Irish Book of Invasions*, containing the myth of the heroine Cessair, the first human to set foot in Ireland.

The Welsh myths were committed to paper much later—between the twelfth and sixteenth centuries—and because of this many of the original Celtic meanings have been given a veneer of Christian morality and ideology. Two of the most influential Welsh manuscripts are the *The Black Book of Caermarthen* (twelfth century), and *The Red Book of Hergest* (thirteenth century). The latter contains part of the famous quartet of myths known as the Mabinogion (eleventh to thirteenth centuries), including what many believe are references to the Arthurian legends. The other portion of the Mabinogion can be found in the *White Book of Rhydderch* (twelfth century). This collection also contains the myths surrounding the popular goddess Rhiannon and offers glimpses into the Celtic beliefs about the nature of the underworld.

By the fourth century C.E. Gaul was long in the hands of the Romans, and the newly Christian Normans were making inroads into Brittany. Christianity was also gaining a grip on Britain and Ireland, and many goddesses of the old religion were given rebirth as saints of the new. Ireland's once supreme sovereign goddess, Brigid, became Catholicism's St. Bridget, retaining many of her original mythic attributes. Even her old festival day, February 2, was kept as the feast day of the saint.

Today many Catholics use the term "The Celtic Church" when referring to their Irish co-religionists. Ireland's Christianity has adopted many pagan practices into its festival year and considers many pagan sacred sites among its holy places. Pilgrimages to petition saints at sacred wells—openings once thought to represent the birth canal of the sovereign Goddess of the land—are still popular features of the Celtic Church. *—Edain McCoy*

Irish Goddess Myths: Achall, Achtan, Achtland, Aeval, Aibheaog, Aiofe, Aige, Ailinn, Ain, Aine, Airmed, Anu, Badb, Banba, Ban Naomha, Banshee, Bebhionn, Becuma, Biddy, Biddy Mannion, Bo Find, Boann, Brigid, Bronach, Buan, Caer, Cailleach, Cally Berry, Canola, Caolainn, Carman, Carravogue, Ceibhfhionn, Cessair, Cethlion, Clidna, Cred, Danu, Dechtere, Deirdre, Devorgilla, Dia Griene, Ebhlinne, Echtghe, Edain, Emer, Epona, Eri, Eriu, Ess Euchen, Etain, Ethne, Fand, Feithline, Finchoem, Findabar, Fiongalla, Fionnuala, Fithir, Flidais, Inghean Bhuidhe, Latiaran, Lavercam, Leanan Sidhe, Liban, Luaths Lurgann, Macha, Maeve, Mal, Mala Liath, Moriath, Morrigan, Moruadh, Muireartach, Munanna, Nar, Nemain, Nessa, Niamh, Odras, Oona, Saba, Sheila na Gig, Sin, Sinann, Taillte, Turrean, Varia.

Welsh Goddess Myths: Arianrhod, Blathnat, Blodewedd, Branwen, Cerridwen, Don, Goleuddydd, Guinevere, Gwendydd, Gwyar, Gwyllion, Iseult, Mabb, Morgan Le Fay, Olwen, Rhiannon, Viviane.

Scottish Goddess Myths: Bean Nighe, Carlin, Ceasg, Fideal, Scathach, Scota, Triduana.

British Goddess Myths: Albina, Andraste, Black Annis, Brigantia, Cartimandua, Coventina, Elen, Gentle Annie, Gillian, Godiva, Habetrot, Henwen, Marcia

Proba, Nemetona, Nimue, Rosmerta, Sequana, Silkie, Sirona, Sulis, Sele, Silly Witches.

Continental Celtic Goddess Myths: Adsagsona, Ardwina, Artio, Aveta, Brunissen, Dames Vertes, Dea Nutrix, Deae Matres, Dahut, Epona, Habondia, Korrigan, Marcassa, Melusine, Minerva Medica, Natosuelta, Nehalennia, Rosmerta, Veleda.

Christian

While it often makes orthodox worshipers uncomfortable to acknowledge it, much of Christian religion incorporates the symbols, myths and rituals of earlier cultures—including those in which the feminine is given much more spiritual authority than in Christianity. The primal narrative of Christianity, that of the birth of the savior from a virgin mother and his later sacrifice, echoes the typical dying-god myths of the ancient Near East where Christianity was born. Similarly, indigenous divinities were often subsumed into the Christian story, sometimes becoming "saints" along the way. Since the middle of the twentieth century, there has been a purging of some especially suspicious saints by the Roman Catholic church ("saint" Priapus, whose name and symbols were embarrassingly close to those of the ancient Roman god of male erections, is no more). But others remain too important to eliminate. Most vital of these is Mary, the mother of Christ, a figure that absorbed most of the attributes of the major goddesses with whom she came into contact. *—Patricia Monaghan*

Christian Goddess Myths: The Black Madonna, Brigid, Falvara, Guadalupe, Mary, Mary Magdalene, Ursula.

Finno-Ugric

The Finno-Ugric peoples are spread across a vast, mostly circumpolar, area stretching through Siberia and Scandinavia. A few related ethnic groups, like the Hungarians, are found in central Europe. The diverse peoples that make up the Finno-Ugrians were once—perhaps as far back as 2000 B.C.E.—a single culture, with the Ugrian branch (today's Hungarians, as well as the Voguls and Ostyaks, also called Mansi and Hanti, of Russia) departing the original Asiatic homeland to move east. This was followed by a second migration, of the Zyrian (Komi) and Votyak (Udmurt) peoples, who also moved east. A third migration, by the Cheremis (Mari) and Mordwin, brought them to eastern Russia. The Saami or Lapps moved north, into Scandinavia, and finally the Balto-Finnish people, who include the Finns and the Estonians, migrated to the shores of the northern seas.

The connections among these groups are more linguistic than cultural. Hungarians share more, in terms of folkways and lifestyle, with their central European neighbors than with their distant linguistic cousins among the reindeer-herding Saami. Similarly, the myths and rituals of nearby cultures have left their mark, so that Estonian religion has as much in common with the nearby Lithuanian as with more distant Ugrian myths. This corruption or conflation makes it difficult for scholars to sort out what is indigenously Finno-Ugric from what has been absorbed over the centuries.

Two religious traditions, however, seem to have been shared among the ancient Finno-Ugric people. These are the famous bear ritual, in which that fierce beast is hunted in sacrificial fashion and shared among the people; and a shamanism that is very similar to that found among Siberian people. The role of the goddess among these people is as difficult to sort out as any other aspect of their religions, although without question the earth goddess had an important ritual and religious role. Among Soviet researchers, it has been popular to assume an ancient matriarchal society that underlies the later-developing patriarchy; the fact that a creator goddess is found in many Finno-Ugrian cultures offers some support for such an interpretation which, however, is unpopular among Western researchers.

Finnish Goddess Myths: Haltia, Louhi, Luonnotar, Mere-Ama, Metsannetsyt, Mielikki, Ovda, Paivatar, Rauni, Suonetar, Tuonetar, Veden Emo, Vellamo.

Hungarian Goddess Myths: Tundr Ilona, Xatel-Ekwa, Xoli-Kaltes.

Saami/Lapp Goddess Myths: Avfruvva, Barbmo-Akka, Beiwe, uks-Akka, Luot-Hozjit, Madder-Akka, Mere-Ama, Paive, Pohjan-Akka, Poshjo-Akka, Radien-Akka, Radien-Kiedde, Rana Neida, Sar-Akka, uks-Akka, Yabme-Akka.

Other Ugrian Goddess Myths: Azer-Ava, Cuvto-Ava, Idem-Huva, Jumala, Keca Aba, Mardeq Avalon, Port-Kuva, Sundi-Mumi, Ved-Ava, Vitsa-Kuva.

Germanic/Scandinavian/Old Norse

The Germanic peoples, who originally occupied the Baltic islands and North German plain between the Rhine and Vistula Rivers, were composed of three separate ethnic groups who spoke differing dialects of a lost proto-Germanic language. The East Germans or Goths, who came from the area near the Vistula River, moved towards the Baltic Sea c. 200 B.C.E. The West Germans—ancestors of the modern German people and of the Anglo-Saxons who eventually settled the British Isles—moved outward towards the Rhine in the West and the Danube in the South. The Old Norse moved north, into the countries of Scandinavia.

Our understanding of early Scandinavian beliefs has been greatly expanded by archaeological evidence. In the late Neolithic there is evidence of ceremonial rituals, linked with the cycles of the agricultural year, performed at tombs that held the cleansed bones of ancestors. The primary deity appears to have been a goddess responsible for the fertility of earth and crops. She brought increase and health to the animals and to humans, and she was also the welcoming tomb of death and rebirth. Pots from the funnel-necked Beaker culture of neolithic Denmark are incised with the features of the ancient bird goddess in her owl/death form, with eyes that are also suns. The huge round eyes of the goddess can be seen again in small bronze figurines of a female deity that date from the Bronze Age. Bare-breasted, she wears a necklace or torc and a short skirt. One of these figures, found in Jutland, kneels with one hand on her breast and the other apparently holding the reins of a wagon. Found with her was a bronze snake.

The Bronze Age came late to Scandinavia and lasted from 1600–450 B.C.E. The mythology of the Bronze Age seems to center on a wagon of the sun crossing the heavens. A small bronze wagon bearing a gilded sun disc, made in approximately 1000 B.C.E., was found at Trundholm, Denmark. Wagons and ships, which carried the sun to where it disappears below the western sea, can be found in Scandinavian rock art. Along with the wagon, a tree, water birds and reindeer or elk also appear. Male fertility figures appear to carry axes or staffs and may represent twin year gods.

Such is the archaeological evidence. Our first written information about the Germanic people and their beliefs comes from their contact with the Romans who, in the first century B.C.E., invaded German lands. The Roman historian Tacitus, in *Germania*, described the Germanic peoples as having a patriarchal society composed of male warriors and farmers. Still, among the rituals he describes is one familiar from the earlier pre-Indo-European evidence of the area. The celebrations of the earth goddess Nerthus were most likely an ancient form of ritual renewal of the goddess and her energy.

The earliest writing in Scandinavia appears in runic inscriptions on stone, wood, metal or bone. These inscriptions remain difficult to understand clearly, because the runes were primarily a symbolic magical alphabet. The earliest form of the runes was the Elder Futhark, an alphabet of twenty-four letters. The Meldorf brooch, found in Jutland and dating from c. 50 C.E., is the oldest object yet discovered with runic writing. There is evidence of runic writing in this form in Denmark, southern Sweden and southeastern Norway, prior to 200 C.E. Only one standing stone, in Kylver, Gotland, contains the entire alphabet. Runic writing continued until about 1000 C.E., but the oldest form faded out about 800 C.E. Its origins are uncertain, but it was probably developed from a northern Italian (Etruscan) alphabet. There is a remarkable similarity between the runes of the Elder Futhark and the markings associated with the goddess on older archaeological finds. It is likely that they represent a remnant of ancient script from Old Europe that symbolically represents the mysteries of the ancient goddess of life, death and rebirth. The runes are often interpreted in the light of rune poems from the Viking era, and it is evident that they were considered of magical use and

importance through the early Christian times. The runes contain many of the same symbols as earlier rock art: sun, wagon, tree, water birds, and reindeer, and retain a concern for fertility of crops and humans, prosperity and peace.

In the fourth century C.E., the Goths were converted to Christianity. The earliest written records to speak of the Goths make no mention of their beliefs before conversion, and the first Gothic records consist of a translation of the Christian Gospels. Very little of the beliefs of the West German people have survived, except as comments in Christian works intended to point out the error of pagan ways. Most of what we know of German beliefs and mythology comes to us from Scandinavia, which remained pagan until around the tenth century C.E. From that century comes a collection of poems, written by different poets, known as the Elder (or Poetic) Edda. The poems, which reflect earlier oral traditions, recount epic stories and legends about gods and goddesses of the Germanic pantheon. The second source of ancient German literature available to us is the Prose Edda, written by an Icelander, Snorri Sturluson, dated approximately 1200 C.E. Sturluson's work retells many myths in different versions and refers to others that are lost to us. It tells the sagas or histories of the first kings of Norway and Sweden and stories of the early days of Iceland, which had been settled in the ninth century C.E., primarily by Norwegians. While this amazing work is one of our primary sources, we must not forget that Sturluson himself was a Christian writing more than 200 years after the acceptance of Christianity by the Icelandic council. Aside from the Eddas, there is a many-volumed work in Latin by a Danish church historian, written in the twelfth century C.E., that gives us Danish versions of the myths and religious practices and the histories of the Danish kings.

The Eddas describe a pantheon of gods and goddesses composed of two groups, the Vanir and the Aesir. The Vanir—reminiscent of the description Tacitus gave of Nerthus—are primarily concerned with fertility and prosperity, while the Aesir are warrior gods. In the Eddas the two groups fight and eventually merge. Snorri tells us that the goddesses of the Eddas are no less sacred or powerful than the gods. The world of the Eddas is, however, mainly a male-centered world. Far fewer myths of the goddesses survived than those of war and battles. Of the goddesses who remain, a few, such as Freya and Hel, still hold vestiges of the powers of Nerthus and her predecessors. There are still others described in the Eddas as giantesses, such as Skadi or Gerd, who may reflect an older pre-Indo-European form of female deity absorbed into the Scandinavian pantheon.

Despite the male-centered, warrior nature of the Germanic world, there is evidence both from the Eddas and from Tacitus that German women held domain in the area of prophetic magic, which was highly valued. It was believed that seers and priestesses were able to foretell, and even control, the future and the fate of men, through the use of trance, the casting of spells and the reading of lots or wooden runestaves. This form of magic was known as seidhr. The god Odin knew its ways and could practice it, but had learned it from the goddess Freya. The counsel of such wise women was highly regarded, even in the area of battle. The belief that women controlled the processes of fate, of life, death and rebirth seems to have survived well into the Viking era.

It seems likely that an Old European-style form of the goddess existed in Scandinavia as late as the Bronze Age. Her descendants in historic times were the goddesses and gods of the Vanir, who were absorbed into the Indo-European pantheon of warrior Gods. We see in many of these historic goddesses the characteristics and attributes of the goddess as bringer of life, death, and regeneration.—*Susan Gitlin-Emmer*

Germanic Goddess Myths: Alfhild, Angerboda, Audbumbla, Bestla, Bil, Brynhild, Buschfrauen, Dekla, Dis, Edda, Eir, Elle, Embla, Fangge, Fengi, Fjorgyn, Frau Holle, Freya, Frigg, Fulla, Fylgja, Gefion, Gerd, Gna, Gollveig, Gondul, Gonlod, Groa, Hedrun, Heith, Hel, Hertha, Hervor, Hild, Hlin, Hlodyn, Hnossa, Huldra, Hyrrokin, Idunn, Ingebord, Jord, Kara, La Reine Pedaque, Lorelei, Lofn, Ma-Emma, Mari-Ama, Matergabiae, Modgud, Menglod, Misere, Ostara, Nana,

Nerthus, Nixies, Norns, Nott, Oddibiord, Perchta, Ran, Rind, Rapunzel, Rheda, Saga, Sibilja, Sif, Sigurdrifta, Sjofn, Skadi, Skogsnufvar, Skuld, Sunna, Swan Maidens, Sweigsdunka, Syn, Syrith, Thorgerd, Valkyries, Var, Voluspa, Waldmichen, Wanne Thekla, Wave Maidens, Weisse Frauen, Wilden Wip, Zisa.

Greek/Cretan

The Greeks, and their pantheon of goddesses and gods, were an amalgam of Indo-European with Neolithic and Bronze Age European peoples. Between about 4500 B.C.E. and 2800 B.C.E., the semi-nomadic, pastoral, horse-riding, patriarchal, warrior-honoring Proto-Indo-Europeans, or Kurgan people, migrated from their homeland (probably north of the Black Sea and the Caucasus Mountains, in the grassy and forested Russian Steppes) to many parts of Europe. The Proto-Indo-Europeans had developed various types of weapons, and they had domesticated the horse; this gave them a military advantage, and therefore they were able to impose their language and their hierarchical social structure on the indigenous peoples with whom they came into contact.

The first Indo-Europeans reached what became Greece around 3000 B.C.E., assimilating with the indigenous peoples, the peoples of the Balkan peninsula and surrounding islands. The Proto-Indo-Europeans found a flourishing culture in this part of southeastern Europe. The indigenous peoples were sedentary agriculturalists, probably with a goddess-centered culture. The Neolithic and Bronze Age Europeans, called by archaeologist Marija Gimbutas "Old Europeans," created beautiful polychromatic pottery and may have developed an early script. There are few remains of weapons from this area, indicating that the culture was probably not a martial one. If we take the excavated proportions of female figurines and male figurines into account, their pantheon was female-centered. These figurines often depict bird goddesses and snake goddesses, and hybrids of the two.

Although many scholars dismiss the idea of an Old European matriarchy, the social structure of these Old

Europeans may well have been egalitarian, with regard to gender, and non-hierarchical. The first Proto-Indo-Europeans who arrived in this area went to both the mainland and the island of Crete. These were known as the Mycenaean Greeks, and they flourished from about 1600 B.C.E. to about 1200 B.C.E. Instead of destroying the advanced culture of Minoan Crete, the Mycenaeans adopted the culture and writing system of the Minoans, adapting the Minoan linear script (known as Linear A) to their own language and writing inscriptions in the early Greek script known as Linear B or Mycenaean Greek. Linear B inscriptions tell us much about the earliest Greek pantheon of goddesses and gods: Hera, Artemis, and Athena are among the goddesses mentioned in these inscriptions. Unfortunately, only inscriptions exist in Linear B; there are no fully formed written myths or folktales that date to this period.

These Mycenaeans were the protagonists in Homer's epics of the Trojan War, *The Iliad* and *The Odyssey*, which supposedly took place around 1450 B.C.E. Tales of the Trojan war very likely were composed at this time, and they were then orally transmitted for several centuries, until they were developed by Homer (or plural Homers) into coherent epics, around 800 B.C.E. Although the Mycenaeans were warlike, they were not as patriarchal and misogynistic as the Greeks of the Classical era. The fierce patriarchy manifested by the Classical Greeks was brought by yet another group of Indo-Europeans.

In the twelfth century B.C.E., Greece was invaded by this other group of Indo-Europeans, who became known as the Dorians. The Dorians were so martial that their invasions unleashed a Dark Age in Greece that lasted from about 1200 B.C.E. to about 800 B.C.E. The Linear B script fell out of use, and there was no writing system in Greece for several hundred years. Literature did not appear again until the time of Homer, about 800 B.C.E. In the writings of Homer, and the poet Hesiod about one hundred years later, there appeared a fully developed pantheon of goddesses and gods. Although most of the Greek literature was written by males, there is one female poet who was lauded

throughout the Classical world: the lyric poet Sappho (b. 612 B.C.E.), who established a school for young women on the Aegean island of Lesbos and wrote exquisite poems, often in honor of the love goddess Aphrodite. Her work was collected in seven books, but only about 160 fragments remain, some only a few words long. These fragments were preserved in the works of later Greek writers, including those of the Classical era (the fifth century B.C.E.), and in Egyptian papyri, but not in medieval manuscripts. Thus, almost all of her work was lost.

The Greek pantheon is a composite of Proto-Indo-European and Old European. The Proto-Indo-European pantheon—which incorporated a sky god, a warrior god, various other male deities and a very few female deities (a sun maiden, a dawn goddess, a water goddess, and an earth goddess)—assimilated with the pantheon of the Old Europeans, in particular adopting several forms of the prehistoric goddess or goddesses. As a result, multi-functional goddesses such as Artemis, Hera, and Athena became important figures in the Greek Olympian pantheon. It is important to stress that these latter multi-functional goddesses were not of Proto-Indo-European origin. They were products of earlier, goddess-worshiping cultures.

Although powerful "great" goddesses with multiple functions may have been worshiped in prehistoric Europe, the divine feminine became fragmented in Indo-European Greece. Even the most powerful Greek goddess, Athena, was subservient to Zeus, the ruler of the pantheon. Further, although Athena was multi-functional, holding sway over the realms of wisdom, victory in war, and handicrafts, her sexuality was taken away. Whereas her Near Eastern avatars, such as the Syrian Anat and the Sumerian Inanna, represented both war and love, and were sexually autonomous, Athena was a virgin, touched by no man. Among the Classical Greeks, there was little sexual autonomy, among either the mortal women or the divine females. Among the Classical Athenian Greeks only the love goddess Aphrodite (who was probably borrowed from the Near East) was sexually autonomous.

Hera was associated with Zeus early on, although not exclusively: a Linear B inscription reads, "For Zeus, one gold bowl and one male attendant; for Hera, one gold bowl and one female attendant," but other Linear B inscriptions associate Zeus and Dione. Further, the inscription does not indicate a dominant-subordinate relationship between Hera and Zeus; in fact, Hera's power was substantial in some Greek cities. For example, in Elis, there was a statue of Hera and Zeus; Hera was enthroned while Zeus stood beside her: just as in the Linear B inscription, Hera is not subordinated here. Nonetheless, in the writings of Classical (male) authors, Hera was not very powerful, and she certainly was not sexually autonomous. She slept only with Zeus. Thus the cultural requirements for mortal women were superimposed on the divine idealizations: the goddesses.

The Greek authors presented a unified picture of the Greek goddesses and gods, but this picture is misleading. Cult inscriptions allow us to formulate a clearer picture of the deities, who were worshiped in many local manifestations. Further, it appears that although the goddesses are often subordinated in the literature, they retained many of their pre-Indo-European powers in actual ritual and cult practice. Thus, despite the Classical fragmentation and diminution of powers, there are intriguing hints of the significant power of the Greek goddesses. —*Miriam Robbins Dexter*

Greek/Cretan Goddess Myths: Acantha, Achlys, Adamanthea, Aedon, Aega, Aella, Agave, Agdos, Aithuia, Alcippe, Alecto, Alectrona, Althaea, Amalthea, Amazons, Amphitrite, Ananke, Anaxarete, Andromeda, Anieros, Antianara, Antigone, Antiope, Aphrodite, Arachne, Arete, Ariadne, Artemis, Artemisia, Asteria, Astraea, Atalanta, Ate, Athana Lindia, Athena, Augralids, Aura, Baubo, Bia, Biblys, Britomartis, Brizo, Caenis, Caligo, Callisto, Calypso, Campe, Carya, Cassandra, Cassiopeia, Castalia, Ker, Cerberus, Ceto, Charila, Charybdis, Caryatids, Chthonia, Chelone, Chimera, Chloe, Circe, Cleone, Cloelia, Clymene, Clytemnestra, Clytie, Cydippe, Cynosura, Cyone, Cyrene, Da, Dactyls, Damia, Danae, Danaids, Daphne, Dejanira, Demeter, Despoina, Dike, Dione, Doris, Dryads, Dryope, Echenais, Echidna, Echo, Eileithyia, Eireisone, Electra, Eos, Ececheira, Eleos, Eris, Erigone, Erinyes, Eumenides, Europa, Eurydice, Eurynome, Fat Lady, Gaia, Galatea, Ganymeda, Gorgons, Graces, Graeae, Halcyone, Harmonia, Harpies, Hebe, Hecate, Hegemone, Helen, Heliades, Helle, Hera, Hero, Hesperides, Hestia, Hiera, Hippia, Hippo, Hippodamia, Hippolyta, Horae, Hydra, Hypermnestra, Ia, Iambe, Ida, Idothea, Ino, Io, Iphigenia, Invidia, Iphis, Irene, Iris, Ismene, Jocasta, Kakia, Kore, Lada, Lamia, Larissa, Lethe, Lampetia, Latona, Leda, Lemna, Leto, Leucippe, Limnades, Lotis, Lysippe, Lyssa, Macaria, Macris, Maenads, Maia, Manto, Marpesia, Marpessa, Medea, Medusa, Megaera, Meliae, Melissa, Melanie, Menalippe, Mentha, Meroe, Merope, Meta, Meter, Metis, Mnasa, Mnemosyne, Moirae, Muses, Myrine, Myrmex, Nomia, Naiads, Nausicaa, Nemesis, Nephele, Nereids, Nike, Niobe, Nyx, Oceanids, Omphale, Oreads, Oreithyia, Orthia, Otiona, Otrere, Pallas, Pamphile, Pandia, Pandora, Pantariste, Paphos, Pasiphae, Penelope, Penthesilea, Pero, Perse, Persephone, Phaedra, Pherenice, Philemon, Philomena, Phyllis, Pitys, Pitho, Pleiades, Polycaste, Polydamna, Praxidike, Procris, Protagenia, Psyche, Pyrrha, Pythia, Python, Rhea, Rhode, Rumor, Salmacis, Scylla, Selene, Semele, Sibyl, Sirens, Smilax, Spako, Sphinx, Styx, Syrinx, Telesilla, Telphassa, Telphusa, Tethys, Thalassa, Thalestris, Thea, Themis, Thetis, Tomyris.

Roman/Etruscan

Before there was a Rome, there were dozens of ethnic groups living in that boot-shaped peninsula we call Italy; some of the best known called themselves Latini, Sabini, Etrusci, Veneti and Calabri. Their distinct languages and cultures can be divided into three groups: the Indo-European-speaking Italics; the Etruscans, whose non-Indo-European language remains untranslated today; and the Greek colonists of southern Italy and Sicily. In addition, northern Italy saw regular incursions of Celtic peoples from the sixth century B.C.E. onwards.

All these groups left their traces on what became classical Roman religion, which arose after the founding of the city in 753 B.C.E. Unfortunately, it is extremely hard to unweave the tapestry of Roman mythology to determine which strands are connected to which previous culture. The Etruscan divinity Menrva, for instance, very likely gave rise to the classical figure of Minerva—but with evidence of Etruscan belief found only in visual arts, the connection must remain conjectural.

Unknotting Roman mythology is made even more difficult by the unusual circumstance that Rome, after conquering the Greek city-states, absorbed their divinities so thoroughly that some of the distinguishing features of the Italian originals were lost. Many of the Roman originals were far less complex than the arriving pantheons. Where divinities seemed similar, they were simply joined; thus Artemis was melded to Italic Diana, Aphrodite to Venus, and so forth. But other divinities had no Greek correlative. These included the almost innumerable special-function divinities listed in the Indigitamenta, the catalog of divinities. There one could find goddesses assigned the oversight of various aspects of daily life: Rumina for the moment flowers turn to seed, Cinxia for the untying of the bridal belt, Pietas for filial affection.

To compound the confusion of divinities, the Roman Empire threw its mantle over many diverse regions and as many diverse religions. Into Rome, the imperial capital, flooded initiates of religions from all around the ancient Mediterranean. Thus the religion of Cybele, the great mountain mother of Asia Minor, was at home in Rome together with the rites of Egyptian Isis and of Celtic Epona. Rome was a cross-cultural cauldron for centuries. Its own native goddesses were touched and transformed by the effervescence of rites and myths from lands both near and unimaginably distant.   —*Patricia Monaghan*

Etruscan Goddess Myths: Lara, Lasa, Menrva, Nortia, Turan, Turresh, Tuchulcha, Uni, Vacuna, Vanths.

Roman/Italic Goddess Myths: Acca Larentia, Aetna, Angerona, Angitia, Anima Mundi, Anna Perenna, Aricia, Aurora, Averna, Barbata, Befana, Bona Dea, Camenae, Camilla, Cura, Calva, Cardea, Carmenta, Carna, Ceres, Claudia Quinta, Concordia, Copia, Diana, Diuturna, Egeria, Empanda, Fama, Felicitas, Feronia, Fides, Flora, Fortuna, Furrina, Galiana, Hybla, Intercidona, Juno, Juventas, Levana, Libertas, Libitina, Lupa, Lua, Lignaco-Dex, Lucina, Maia, Mania, Mater Matuta, Mens, Minerva, Ocrisia, Ops, Orbona, Pietas, Pomona, Postvorta, Proserpina, Pudicitia, Ques, Rhea Silvia, Salacia, Rumina, Spes, Tanaquil, Telete, Tellus Mater, Vegoia, Venus, Vesta, Voluptia.

Roman/Non-Italic Goddess Myths: Bellona, Dea Dia, Giane, Ggigantia.

Slavic/Thracian/Georgian

The relation between the Slavic peoples and the ancient culture of Thrace is unclear. However, much of the area later occupied by the Slavs was assigned by Greek and Roman commentators to Thrace. Known for its astonishingly beautiful goldwork, Thrace occupied the lands we now call northern Greece, Bulgaria, and parts of the Balkan peninsula and Turkey. Although the area came under the rule of Greece with Philip of Macedon in 342 B.C.E., and the Romans later conquered it as well, the inhabitants held on to their ancient ways under these new regimes. Some of their mythic figures became incorporated into the conquering mythologies (the wine god Dionysus, the singer Orpheus, the goddesses of arts called the Muses) while others remained unassimilated (the sex goddess Cotys).

After the fall of Rome, the area entered a dark age, where the movements of people are hidden from history. By the time the Slavs enter the historical record, they had already been in close contact with Celts and Germanic people—as well as having endured some Christian and Islamic influences—so it is difficult to sort out their original beliefs. Some written documents, some archaeological finds, and many folkloric remnants provide what we know of Slavic (sometimes called Slavonic) religion.

It is thought that the culture began in the rugged Carpathian mountains, where the Slavs spoke an Indo-European language. From there, beginning in the first century C.E., migrants traveled outward to become the Southern, Western and Eastern Slavs, living in areas that today we call Russia, Czechoslovakia, Croatia, Bulgaria, Serbia, Slovinia and Poland. Mostly agriculturalists, these ancient people were fundamentally peace-loving. Scholars have noted the lack of military organization among Slavs at this time; where it occurs, it is found to have been imported from a neighboring culture. Rather, the Slavs turned their attention to the encouragement of the land's fertility, to providing for human comfort, and to the encouragement of family/clan bonding. Religion, similarly, revolved primarily around honoring the forces of nature and the deified ancestors of the tribe.

The worship of nature was very important to the Slavs, whose rituals included honoring of specific natural places such as mountains, rivers and boulders. Trees were especially important, whether in the form of significant isolated oaks, elders and walnuts, or as sacred forests to which entry was forbidden. These sacred places were associated with the concept of the earth as a feminine force, personified as the goddess Mokosh. Her connection with agriculture is obvious from the fact that she not only ruled the soil, but also rain and running water.

Finally, in the area of the Russian Caucasus Mountains known as Georgia, there is a unique culture that is apparently not connected with that of the neighboring Slavs. Although strongly patriarchal and hierarchical, as recorded, the culture features several vivid female divinities that suggest that the feminine contribution to nature and society was once highly valued. Incestuous brother/sister divinities are a special feature of this culture, a pairing that elsewhere indicates a primeval creation myth in which the goddess is equal in importance to the god.   —*Patricia Monaghan*

Thracian Goddess Myths: Bendis, Cotys, Hecate, Muses, Philomena, Phyllis.

Slavic Goddess Myths: Baba Yaga, Beregyni, Cinderella, Colleda, Doda, Dolya, Dziewona, Dziwozony, Elena, Erce, Falvara, Jezenky, Jumala, Kikimora, Kostrubonko, Kupalo, Marzana, Mati, Mokosh, Mora, Mother Friday, Navky, Papalluga, Poldunica, Rusalky, Selci Syt Emysyt, Siva, Sreca, Sroya, Stepova-Baba, Sudice, Solntse, Snegurochka, Veshtitze, Vesna, Vila, Vodni Panny, Wlasca,Vasilisa, Zima, Zywie, Rozanicy, Zorya, Zvezda Dennitsa.

Georgian Goddess Myths: Dali, Tamar, Samdzimari.

Contributors

Priscilla Buffalohead teaches women's studies classes at Augsburg College in Minneapolis, Minnesota.

Miriam Robbins Dexter, who teaches at the University of California in Los Angeles, is author of *Whence the Goddesses: A Sourcebook.*

Artist and ritualist **Susan Gitlin-Emmer** is author of *Lady of the Northern Light: A Feminist Guide to the Runes.*

Cecilia Corcoran, O.P., directs the GATE program to introduce North Americans to Central American culture; her doctoral work centers on the importance of the feminine divine in Mexican culture.

Luisa Teish is a faculty member at the Institute for Creation Spirituality and is author of *Jambalaya.*

Janet McCrickard, a British writer and artist, is author of *Eclipse of the Sun.*

Edain McCoy has written a number of books on Celtic religion, including *Celtic Women.*

Deborah Wood Holton, associate professor at DePaul University School for New Learning, is a daughter of Africa and a writer of urban folktales who draws from the mythic to inform her creative writing.

Normandi Ellis is the author of *Dreams of Isis* and *Awakening Osiris.* She leads tours to Egypt and teaches workshops in Egyptian myth, metaphysics, and hieroglyphics.

A A Chaldean moon goddess, her emblem is a disk with eight rays, a number that—like the octagon—is associated with the goddess of light in many cultures.

Aakuluujjusi The great creator mother among the Inuit people, Aakuluujjusi made the animals that feed humankind. First she created the caribou, simply by taking off her trousers and setting them on the earth—for anyone knows that caribou look a great deal like a walking pair of women's trousers. With a wave of her hand, she gave the new animal sharp long tusks. Then she took off her jacket and threw it on the ground. There it turned into a walrus—which anyone knows looks just like a lumpy woman's jacket. On its head she placed a nice rack of antlers. But her Inuit children were far from happy with these gifts, because the new animals kept attacking the people who tried to hunt them. So Aakuluujjusi made some minor revisions to her creation. She swapped the horns and tusks. The walrus were now perfect, but the caribou were too quick for the hunters. So she turned their belly-hair around, so that the hairs caught on the wind and slowed the creatures down. And then she knew her creation was finished.

Abhramu The "cloud-knitter" was the original female elephant who—like her offspring for many generations—was a supernatural winged being who could change shape at will, like the clouds that resemble her children. But according to Indian legend, Abhramu's tribe lost its wings and its magic by mischance.

One day a flock of elephants was flying slowly through the sky, changing into various shapes. Tiring, they spied a huge tree and alighted upon it. Alas, the combined weight of the elephant flock broke the tree's branches.

And alas for the winged elephants, for an ascetic was sitting in yogic posture beneath the tree, teaching his pupils. He was unharmed, but the falling branches and elephant bodies crushed all his students. The sage, furious at having his school destroyed, cursed the elephants and their wings dropped off. Abhramu's progeny have been earthbound ever since, trapped in the enormous cloud shapes they were wearing during the unfortunate encounter with the sage.

Abigail This woman of Hebrew legend is similar in many respects to the ancient goddesses of the eastern Mediterranean in being both the sister and the spouse of a king, David of Israel. Married first to the "churlish and evil" non-Hebrew Nabal, a shepherd who grazed his flocks under David's protection along Judea's border, Abigail intervened when Nabal insulted David, who threatened to send 400 soldiers to punish the shepherd. Hearing that his wife had saved him, the shepherd fell over dead, leaving Abigail available for remarriage to David—who, in other texts, is described as her brother by the same mother. Such tales of brother-sister incest often indicate a connection to ancient myths of creation.

Abrya   Nymph of a freshwater spring, she fell in love with the shepherd Selemnus. Taking a human form, she climbed from her spring and seduced him. But then—nymphs will do this—she lost interest and resumed her watery form. But Selemnus could not forget so easily. He pined away until Aphrodite, taking pity on him, turned him into a river so that he could share Abrya's waterly element. This still did not suffice, so Aphrodite gave his waters the power to remove the sting of failed love.

Abuk   The first woman, say the Dinka people of the African Sudan, was created very tiny but fully formed, then put like a bean in a big pot, where she swelled up overnight. The creator god stingily gave Abuk and her mate Garang only one grain of corn to eat each day. The human race would have starved had Abuk not simply taken what people needed and ground it into meal. As patron goddess of women and gardens, Abuk has for her emblem a little snake.

Acantha   According to the Greeks, the resident spirit of the acanthus was once a nymph loved by the sun god. At her death, she was transformed into a sun-loving herb whose deeply cut leaves are frequently seen as an architectural motif.

Acca Larentia   "Lady Mother," an important Etruscan goddess, passed into the mythology of the conquering Romans as a semidivine prostitute. Benefactress of the lower class, Acca Larentia was

In northeastern Liberia, among the Mano and Geh people, woman-shaped wooden spoons like this were used for eating rice on ceremonial occasions. Goddesses of food are very important to African people; see Abuk, Asase Yaa, Maruwa and Nchienge.

said to have risen from poverty by worshiping an entire night in the temple of Heracles. As she departed, she met a rich man with whom she lived for some time. He died, leaving her a fortune; when she died, she willed her vast wealth to the Roman people, who celebrated the gift each year on December 23 in a raucous festival called the Larentalia. In other legends, Acca Larentia is named as the foster mother of Rome's founders, Romulus and Remus, and even as the she-wolf who suckled them. Her connection to the city's ancestral past is clear from the connection of her name to that of the Lares, who connected the Romans to their past, and by the sacred day she shared with them.

Achall In Irish legend, Achall was a loving sister who died of sorrow when her brother was killed in battle. Her love was memorialized at the Hill of Achall near Tara, the island's mystic center.

Achlys To the Greeks, this was the name of eternal night, the only being that preceded Chaos in the universe's history. Pale and thin, with long fingernails and bloody cheeks, she wept constantly, her teeth chattering loudly. Despite the lack of appeal of her image, she must be seen as a primordial creative being, for from her came the entire world.

Achtan The Irish heroine Achtan slept with, and conceived a child by, the land's high king the night before the battle in which he was killed. Accidentally separated from Achtan, the child was suckled by a wolf. He grew up wild but healthy, and was ultimately returned to Achtan by a hunter. The reunited mother and son set out to climb the wild Irish mountains, protected by animals as they traveled. When they reached the seat of Irish sovereignty, the Hill of Tara, Cormac took his father's place as king, while his mother settled down nearby with the hunter who had found her child.

Achtland In ancient Celtic legend, this mortal queen could not be satisfied with human men so instead took a giant as her spouse. Her greatest pleasure came from combing his yards of long hair.

Aclla This was the name given to the sacred sun virgins among the Incas of Peru. Chosen for their grace and beauty from among all the young women of the land, the maidens lived together in convents where they spent their time weaving vicuna and alpaca into fabric sacrificed to the gods. They also fermented corn to make chicha, a sacred drink used in ceremonies. In case of dire emergency such as the earthquakes that still ravage the land, such maidens would sacrifice their lives to appease the angry gods and save their people.

Adah Her name means "ornament," and Hebrew legend names her as one of the great matriarchs of the neighboring tribe called the Edomites.

Adamanthea Zeus could never have became the preeminent Greek god without the help of this woman, for his father Cronos intended to swallow the infant god, as he had swallowed the older siblings. To spare her offspring, earth mother Rhea hid the infant in Crete, in the care of the nymph (or princess) Adamanthea. Cronos had dominion over the earth, the heavens, and the sea; he could see anything that existed in his realm. But the infant's new nurse was clever. Adamanthea hung a cradle from a tree and there—suspended between earth, sea, and sky—Zeus was invisible to his destructive father. In other versions of the story, the nurse of Zeus is named Ida, Adrastea, Neda, Helice, Aega or Cynosura.

Adamu In Chaldea, this was the name of the female principle of matter. Her name means "red," and she represented the blood of the womb and of menstruation.

Adath This Canaanite word, the counterpart of Adonis ("lord"), means "lady" and was applied to both goddesses and distinguished mortal women.

Aditi Some have tried to call her mother earth, but this Hindu goddess properly is called mother space, a feminine embodiment of whatever transcends measurement: infinity, the cosmos, the continuing creation, divinity itself. Although unquestionably feminine, she was sufficiently androgynous to be called "father and son" by the Vedic scriptures.

The preexistent first goddess had no mother and no birth; she existed from all time. She was, however, the genetrix of other divinities: some say of the powerful Vishnu, others of Indra, others, Mithra. Almost all sources agree that in her aspect of sky goddess she produced the multiple divinities who bear her name, the Adityas.

Although Aditi was more often invoked or prayed to than described in myth, there are tales that explain how the goddess produced children. Some say she bore twelve Adityas, one for each month, and that Aditi thus marked limits on previously boundless time. It was also said that she had seven normal sons, then birthed a huge egg that rose into the sky to become the sun. Yet another version of the story says she had only one son, but one so splendid that his mere presence hurt Aditi's eyes; she divided the single son into twelve, setting them to rule the order of nature.

Adsagsona Celtic goddess of the underworld and of magic, invoked as "weaver of spells" and "she who seeks out"—the latter apparently a flattering title used in cursing, to assure that the accursed would receive the full effect of her power.

Aedon The queen of ancient Thebes plotted to murder the eldest son of her rival Niobe but accidentally killed her own child. Stricken by remorse and grief, Aedon attempted suicide and was transformed into the first nightingale, a bird that still haunts the night with its mournful cry.

Aega Like her sisters Circe and Pasiphae, this daughter of the sun was hypnotically beautiful. She was so beautiful that when the earthborn Titans attacked the gods of Olympus, the earth mother Gaia placed Aega in a cave to hide her shimmering loveliness. It is probable that behind these Greek legends lies a myth in which the three sisters were a triple goddess of the sun, for Pasiphae means "she who shines for all" while Circe means "circle." Sun goddesses in other cultures, like Japanese Amaterasu and Finnish Paivatar, are hidden in caves as part of their myths.

Aella The Greeks set sail for the shores of the Black Sea, intending to make war on the Amazons and to despoil their queen of her famous golden belt. But the women resisted. Aella flew first at the invaders like a "whirlwind" (the meaning of her name). But this heroic defender of Queen Hippolyta, this valiant wielder of the double axe, was cut down by the Greek hero Heracles.

Aetna The Roman mountain goddess after whom the Italian volcano Mount Etna is named. In many cultures, fire is female; in most, mountains are considered to be so; thus people living near volcanoes often perceive the fiery mountains as particularly powerful goddesses. Some legends say that Aetna was the wife of the smith god Vulcan. Under her mountain, his hidden thunderbolts could be heard, making a constant dull roar.

Aeval A fairy queen of Munster, the southwestern quarter of Ireland, Aeval judged a debate on whether the men in her district were satisfying the women's sexual needs. It took all night to give evidence at Aeval's "midnight court," but when the queen had heard both sides, she determined that the men were guilty. Their sentence: they were ordered to overcome their prudishness and accede to the women's wishes.

Agasaya "Shrieker," Semitic war goddess who merged into Ishtar in her identity as fearless warrior of the sky.

Agave The daughter of Harmonia, Agave had a son, King Pentheus of Thebes. Her sister Semele had a son, too—the god Dionysus, inventor of viniculture and leader of secret rites. Agave and another sister, Autonoe, quickly recognized the divinity of their nephew and joined the new religion as Maenads.

Only women were allowed to participate in—even to witness— the all-night festivals of the new religion; thus the Maenads sought the privacy of forested mountains for their rituals of dancing and drinking, during which they felt themselves to be part of the divinity of life. Prudish King Pentheus, however, saw no good in such religious intoxication and deplored the attendance by his aunt and, worse yet, his mother.

Despite warnings, King Pentheus decided to spy on them. Climbing a tall pine near the ritual site, he thought to go unnoticed while he penetrated the women's privacy. But the Maenads spotted him, and not even a mother could ask forgiveness for such sacrilege. They dragged Pentheus from the tree and tore him to shreds as if he were a wild animal. Then the women bore his bloody remains back to Thebes—his mother bearing the head aloft—as a warning to anyone considering a similar infringement of the women's ceremonials.

Agdos A name for the great rock of Asia Minor (Cybele in disguise) that Zeus tried to rape. The name survived in the hermaphrodite offspring of the union, Agdistis.

Agischanak Among the Tlingits in southeastern Alaska, this kindly goddess lived on top of Mount Edgecumbe, near the town of Sitka, where you can still see the depression near the peak where she disappeared into the earth. She is a powerful being, strong enough to support the pillar on which the earth rests. Were it not for her, the pillar would have collapsed and the whole earth would have disappeared into the cosmic ocean. But she stands there strongly, upholding the world because people please her by lighting warm fires. Once a year, her brother flies up to the mountain to visit her and bring news of this world; he speaks with thunder, and his eyes dart lightning.

Another frequent visitor is the trickster Raven, who tries to trick Agischanak into abandoning her post. She never does, and sometimes he pushes her in annoyance—which causes earthquakes.

Agrat Bat Mahalat In Jewish legend, she is the commander of 180,000 demons and drives her chariot around the world on Wednesday and Friday evenings, hunting down anything that moves. On other days, the Talmud tells us, the "spirit of uncleanness" is contained by the power of the

A splendid golden image from Midaanao, in the Philippines, shows a goddess locally called Agusan Devi. She probably represents a syncretism between a local goddess and Devi, the Hindu cosmic goddess.

rabbis. But as Jewish couples were traditionally expected to have intercourse on Friday evenings, it is possible that Agrat represents unbridled sexuality, which the rabbis attempt to "bind" but which they admit will never be banished completely until the end of time.

Agusan Devi   A goddess found in the Philippines, where indigenous divinities melded with imported Hindu gods to form a new pantheon.

Agwe   In Benin, this goddess is the mother of the sea; she is affectionate and nurturing to humans who honor her.

Ahemait   An Egyptian underworld goddess ("devourer"), part hippopotamus, part lion, part crocodile, who eats the souls of the unworthy dead.

Aibheaeg   Ancient fire goddess of County Donegal in Ireland, she was worshiped at a well whose waters were held to be an effective remedy against toothache, so long as the petitioner left a little white stone beside the well as a substitute for the sore tooth.

Aida Wedo   The snake *loa* (spirit) in Benin and Haiti, she is the companion of the most popular god, Damballah-Wedo, also a serpent. She rules fire, water, wind and the rainbow. When she appears in voudoun ritual, she slithers across the ground wearing a jeweled headdress that—like the treasure at the end of the rainbow—is elusive but enriches anyone who can grasp it. She is a New World form of the African goddess Oya.

Aige   A woman of Irish legend, she was turned by elfin spite into a fawn. In this form, Aige wandered across the island until she died by plunging into a bay, which today bears her name.

Aigiarm   Marco Polo said of this Mongolian princess, "She could meet no man able to conquer her." Whenever one came to woo her, Aigiarm wagered her virginity against the suitor's horses and challenged him to wrestle her to the ground.

There is no record of her marrying, but it is recorded that Aigiarm won 10,000 horses.

Ailinn   The heroine of one of Ireland's great romantic legends was born a princess of Leinster, the southeastern part of the island. She was passionately attached to Baile, a prince of northern Ireland, and they agreed to meet for a night of love midway between their realms.

But an evil sprite met Baile at the trysting place and told him that Ailinn was dead; the shock killed the prince instantly. The wicked sprite then traveled to Ailinn, this time telling the truth. Hearing that her lover was dead, the princess died of grief.

Their people, recognizing the depth of their affection, buried Ailinn and Baile in adjoining graves, from which grew two magical trees: an apple from Ailinn's grave, a yew from Baile's. As they grew, the trees twined themselves around each other. Centuries later, poets cut down the famous trees and made wands, on which all the tragic love songs of the Irish were recorded in runes and carried to the Hill of Tara.

Ailsie   A Cherokee heroine, she was a tall woman beloved of both the crane and the hummingbird. Her father wished for her to marry the powerful crane, but she preferred the swift-flying hummingbird. She set her suitors a challenge: the one who could fly fastest would win her.

She trusted in the hummingbird's speed, but after five circuits around the racecourse the hummingbird had tired, and the crane won handily. Furious at the loss, Ailsie vowed never to marry rather than wed an ugly bird like the crane. But her father, happy at the race's outcome, pledged to kill her unless she married. Ailsie asked for a reprieve of seven days alone. During that time she wept so much that she turned into a deep pool in the Etowah River.

Ain   The sister of Iaine and probably her double, she was the mythical reason for women's high status in ancient Ireland. When the two sisters married their two brothers, the men invented war so that each could claim as large a share of the island as possible. As a result of the conflict, the rights of women, single or married, were spelled out carefully in the ancient Brehon Laws, which among other things guaranteed that no child be called illegitimate except those engendered by satirists who changed sides with each dispute. These laws were singularly comprehensive in assuring women's property rights and freedom, but later occupation by the Normans meant the end of the Brehon system.

Aine One of the great goddesses of ancient Ireland survives in modern times as the queen of the fairies of south Munster, the southwest corner of the island, who is said to haunt Knockainy Hill there. Originally Aine was a sun goddess who assumed the form of Lair Derg ("red mare"), the horse that none could outrun. Her special feast was Midsummer Night, when farmers carried torches of straw in procession around Knockainy and waved them over the cattle and the fields for protection and fruitfulness.

Two stories are told of Aine. In one, she was the daughter of an early Irish god and was infatuated with the semidivine hero Fionn. She had taken a *geasa* (magical vow) that she would never sleep with a man with gray hair, but Fionn was young with no silver streaking his bushy hair. One of Aine's sisters, Miluchrach, was also interested in Fionn: she enchanted a lake and tempted Fionn to take a dip. When the hero emerged from the magic waters, his body was still youthful and strong, but his hair was stained gray. True to her *geasa*, Aine thereafter scorned the hero.

In another story, Gerald, the human Earl of Desmond, captured Aine while she was combing her hair on the banks of her sacred lake. Aine bore the first Earl Fitzgerald to the man, but made Gerald promise never to express surprise at the powers his son might develop. All went well for many years until one day when Gerald saw his son jump into and out of a bottle. He could not

contain an exclamation of shock and the boy disappeared, flying away in the shape of a wild goose. Disappointed in her human mate, Aine disappeared into Knockainy, where she is said still to live in a splendid castle.

Airmed She was a goddess of the Tuatha de Danaan, the most ancient deities of Ireland; like all of them, she had great magical powers. She was the particular goddess of witchcraft and herb lore, for she knew the uses of every plant, knowledge gained at the death of her beloved brother Miach. She buried him with great mourning, and innumerable plants sprang from his grave. These were all the world's herbs, which instructed her in their use as she tended Miach's grave.

'Aisha Qandisha Arabic people along the coast of Northern Morocco sometimes saw this *jinniya* (female spirit), recognized by her beautiful face, pendulous breasts and goat legs. She was wanton and free, seducing young men, despite having a *jinn* consort named Hammu Qaiyu.

Her name strongly suggests a connection to the Qadesha, the sexually free temple women who served Astarte. Like 'Aisha, Astarte was a water goddess; a possible translation of her name may be "loving to be watered," apparently with semen. Another connection hides in the name of Astarte's consort Haman, seemingly the original of Hammu. The route of transmission was likely through Carthage, where Astarte had a temple. Carthage had colonies in Morocco; the bedouins of the Beni Ahsen, living on the site of the ancient Carthaginian colonies, were most prone to visitations by 'Aisha.

Aithuia "Diver bird" was the Greek goddess Athena in the shape of a seabird, or a separate goddess later assimilated into the powerful Athenian goddess. As the symbol of the seabird also signified a ship, this image represented Athena in one of her major cultural roles, as the goddess who taught the arts of shipbuilding and navigation to humanity.

Aja "The bride," the Babylonian dawn goddess, was consort of the sun god. Like other dawn goddesses, Aja was associated with the eastern mountains, which boost the sun into the sky. Independent at first, she later was merged with Ishtar.

Aje Yoruba goddess of wealth in all its forms, she sometimes takes on the form of money. But at other times, she appears as a five-toed chicken, as she did at time's beginning, when she scratched on the earth's hard surface until it became rich soil for farmers.

Ajysyt Among the Yakuts of Siberia, this birth goddess had two functions: to help laboring women bear safely, and to breathe a soul into the child once born. She was also the divinity of domestic animals, especially cattle. Perhaps her rulership of birth made this a natural evolution of her duties, for the safe birthing of cattle was necessary in economically marginal societies.

The ceremonies glorifying Ajysyt after birth were held secret by the Yakut women; a man's presence would have been sacrilege. Parts of a sacrificed animal (usually the inner organs) were served to the goddess on a special dinner table in the birth chamber. As the birth proceeded, the midwife offered butter to the goddess by placing it on the heart, praying, "We thank you, Ajysyt, for what you have given and ask for it even in future." For three days the birthing woman had to remain sequestered; her friends visited and ate butter with her. After three days, the midwife took the straw on which the new mother had lain and tied it into the top of a tall tree; after this, the goddess left the house until the next birth.

Aka The mother goddess in ancient Turkey; her name remains in some dialects as the common noun for *mother*.

Akewa The sun goddess of the Toba of Argentina was said to be the sister of all earthly women. Once they, like her, were shining residents of the heavens, while hairy male savages inhabited the earth. Curious about their downstairs neighbors, the women one day climbed down a vine rope to explore the earth. But one of the brutish men bit the heavenly ladder in two and stranded the angelic women on this planet forever, leaving only Akewa to remind them of what they had been.

Akonadi In the Accra region of Ghana, Akonadi is an oracle goddess who brought justice at whatever the cost. When her oracles captured a thief, recovered property was donated to the village poor, for Akaonadi was also the protector of women and children in need.

Akoya Once, in ancient Japan, there was a young woman who was a gifted player of the stringed instrument called the koto. One day, as she was practicing, she heard a sweet sound outside her door. It was a young man, dressed all in green, who had been accompanying her harmoniously. His name was Natori Taro, he told her, and he lived at the foot of Mount Citose. Each day he came to accompany her and, predictably, they fell in love. But their love was ill-fated, for one day he arrived in despair, to tell her he could never come again, for he was soon to die. Then he disappeared, leaving her distraught. She raced to the mountain where he said he lived, only to find nothing but a construction camp. A bridge was being built, and a huge pine had been cut down to make way. But it had only fallen halfway, and the crew could not dislodge it. Only when Akoya touched it with tender hands did the tree finally fall. She never left the site, living there until she died. A new tree grew up in place of the old one, and then another, and another. And the Pine of Akoya still stands today, in the suburbs of Yamagata-Shi, at the foot of Mount Chitose.

Akycha The people of Greenland, Canada and Alaska say that the sun and the moon, before they lived above us, were residents of the earth. The sun was the young woman Akycha, the moon was her brother, and they lived in a small village where the people gathered each night to dance in the dance hut.

One night, while everyone else was dancing, Akycha was surprised by a man breaking into her home. He raped her, and in the dark, she could not recognize her assailant. After that she never knew when the man would come, but he frequently repeated the crime.

One night, Akycha determined to discover the identity of the man. She rubbed her fingers across her oil lamp, covering them with soot; after the attacker had finished with her, Akycha rubbed his face with her smeary fingers. He left, but she trailed him to the dance hut. There, to her horror, Akycha saw her own brother with a smeared face. She grabbed a knife and cut off her left breast, flinging it to him with the words, "Since you desire me so much, eat this."

Then Akycha grabbed a burning brand of wood and ran from the village. Her brother followed her, his desire inflamed by the sight of her blood. He too grabbed a lighting branch, but he tripped and dampened its flame in the snow. On and on they ran until they were transported to the sky, where they continue their endless pursuit.

Ala   The most popular divinity of the Igbo (Ibo) tribe in Nigeria is the earth mother Ala, creator of the living and queen of the dead, provider of communal loyalty and lawgiver of society; her worship survives today. She is the guardian of morality, the one on whom oaths are sworn and in whose name courts of law are held. The village shrine of Ala is the central one in any Igbo village; it is at her sacred tree shrine that the people offer sacrifices at planting, at first fruits, and at the harvest.

Alaghom Naom Tzentel   "Mother of mind" was the ancient Mayan goddess of thought and intellect.

Alakhani   Under the bamboo groves in a mushroom-shaped plant called *alakhanibah* ("cell of Alakhani") lived this puckish imp known to the Assamese of North India. Anyone who passed was suddenly possessed by her, though never harmed.

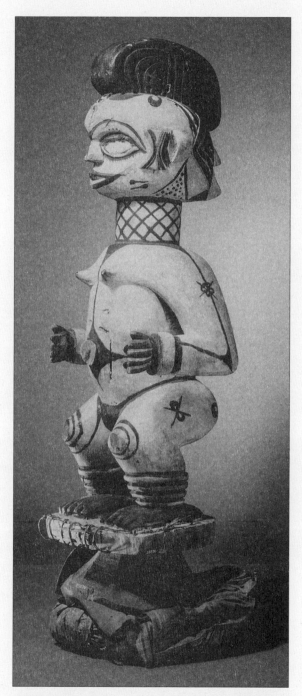

This standing shell-eyed carved figure from the Kongo area of Africa is typical of those used by people of this area as symbols of feminine spirit-power. An important divinity to the Igbo people is Ala, still worshiped with offerings at her tree-shrines throughout Nigeria.

This tall female figure, carved of red wood, was created in Gabon, along the Ogoue River. Wood is not only plentiful in western Africa but is connected with such goddesses as Ala, who is worshiped in the form of a tree.

A form of vegetation spirit, she was essentially benign, though mischievous.

Alan Qo'a The ancestress of the Mongol hero Ghenghis Khan was visited nightly by a shiny yellow man who descended through the smoke-hole in the woman's yurt, rubbed his stomach, emitted a yellow light, then turned into a yellow dog.

Ala Nur "Red Light" was a heroic ancestral mother of western Turkey. Coming face to face with a lion, she fainted from fear; shortly afterwards she found herself miraculously pregnant and gave birth to a folk hero.

Albina The ancient Roman writer Pliny identifies this goddess with the island of Britain, a land sometimes called Albion. Her name suggests she was a white goddess, perhaps the goddess of the chalky British soil. The most famous goddess image from prehistoric Britain may represent her, or an ancestor of her. It is a tiny rotund figure carved from chalk. Miraculously found underfoot in a chalk mine, Grimes' Grave Goddess has a broadly smiling expression that recalls that other mysterious figure of the island, the Sheila na Gig.

Alcippe According to the Greeks, the rape of this daughter of Aglauros occasioned the first murder trial. The young goddess was criminally assaulted by a son of Poseidon, whereupon her father Ares killed the offender. Called to trial by the gods to account for his actions, Ares presented the brutal facts and was swiftly acquitted.

Alecto One of the Erinyes; sometimes a separate Greek goddess of war and death.

Alectrona An early Greek goddess, she was the daughter of the sun. No beast of burden could enter her sanctuary in Rhodes. Anyone riding an ass, horse, or mule to her shrine had to undergo ritual purification.

Alfhild A maiden goddess of Scandinavia who, according to the ancient Historica Danica, dressed as a warrior to avoid being taken in marriage by King Alf. Only when they had fought to the death, and he had proven himself as strong as she, did she agree to mate with him.

Al-Karisi In Moslem Turkey, "The Red Woman" or "The Red Mother" is the name given to a wild and fearsome female figure. Like the Slavic Mora, Al-Karisi rides horses all night, so that they're found covered with frothy perspiration in the morning. Like Indian Sitala and similar goddesses, she brings disease: in this case, puerperal fever to women in childbirth. Such "demons" are often goddesses of earlier cultures who are said to destroy what they previously protected; thus Al-Karisi may have originally been an Artemis-like figure who protected both animals and human women.

Al-Lat In Arabic, Allah means "god." Similarly, Al-Lat means simply "goddess," the supreme reality in female form. Al-Lat is a mythic figure of great antiquity, one of the trinity of desert goddesses named in the Koran, Al-Uzza and Menat being the others. Like the Greek Demeter, Al-Lat represented the earth and its fruits; it follows that she also ruled human generation.

Al-Lat was worshiped at Ta'if near Mecca in the form of a great uncut block of white granite, which her worshipers addressed as "My Lady" or Rusa ("good fortune"). Women were required to appear before her naked and circle the sacred rock; if these conditions were met, the goddess would grant all requests. Solid as the earth she represented, Al-Lat was considered unshakable and immovable. Thus her people swore their most solemn oaths by her, with the following words: "By the salt, by the fire, and by Al-Lat who is the greatest of all."

Altan-Telgey The earth goddess bore this name, which means "golden surface," among the Mongol people.

Althaea This Greek woman had two sons: one was a hero in campaigns against tribal enemies, the other a priest of the secret rites. When the hero Meleager killed his brother, the priest, Althaea cried out to the underworld to take the murderer away.

Al-Uzza Before declaring himself a prophet of male divinity, Mohammed worshiped this desert goddess of the morning star, whose name means "the mighty" or "the strongest." He turned on her, however, destroying her sanctuary of acacia trees south of Mecca, where Al-Uzza's worshipers had gathered for generations to revere the sacred stone representing her. Belief in her power long survived the destruction of her holy place, not dying out until almost 1,000 years had passed. With Al-Lat and Menat, this goddess composed the great religious trinity of the ancient Arabians.

Ama "Muse" and "mother" in Semitic and Indo-European tongues. In Egypt, there was a goddess of this name whose consort was the sun god; in Dravidian southern India, a similar-named goddess, Amba, is "Mother Earth."

Amalthea Whatever the name of Zeus' Cretan nurse (see Adamanthea), she fed the infant god on the milk of this magical nanny goat. When he grew up, Zeus broke off one of Amalthea's horns and gave it to his nurse; it then turned into the magical "cornucopia." Just as the magic goat could produce milk rich and copious enough for a god, so part of her could provide sufficient nourishment for the children of earth. After thus providing for humankind, the one-horned nanny disappeared into heaven, where she was transformed into the constellation of Capricorn.

Amaterasu Of all the religions currently practiced by significant numbers of people, the only one whose chief divinity is female is Japanese Shinto, based on the worship of the sun goddess Amaterasu ("great shining heaven"). In her simple shrines—notable for their architectural purity and unpretentiousness and for the central mirror that represents the goddess—Amaterasu is honored as the ruler of all deities, as the guardian of Japan's people, and as the symbol of Japanese

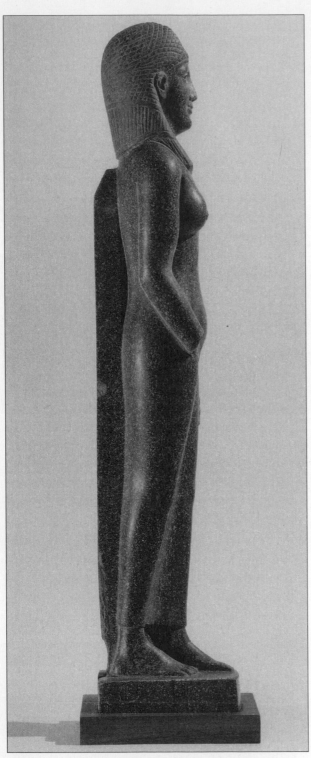

This diorite statue from the Ptolemaic period in the late B.C.E. centuries is typical of the Egyptian sculptural style of the time. "The Great She," Egyptians called the goddess, who also bore many individual names including Ama, Isis, Maat, Mut, Neith, Nut, and Tefnut.

cultural unity. Her emblem, the rising sun, still flies on Japan's flag. Even the inroads of patriarchal Buddhism have not destroyed the worship of the bejeweled ancestor of all humanity.

There is one central myth of Amaterasu. She quarreled with the storm god Susanoo and brought winter to the world. Two reasons are given for her annoyance with him: one, because of his murder of Amaterasu's sister, the food-giving goddess Uke-Mochi; the other, because of his deliberately provocative acts against Amaterasu herself.

The latter version has it that Amaterasu did not trust her brother Susanoo because of his excesses and his constant shouting. One day he came to heaven to see her, claiming that he meant no harm. She was wary, but he promised that he would undergo a ritual test to prove his goodwill. He said he would give birth, and that if his intentions were peaceful, the children would all be boys.

Amaterasu grabbed Susanoo's sword and broke it with her teeth, spitting out three pieces which, striking the ground, became goddesses. Susanoo asked Amaterasu for some of her jewels. She gave him five; he cracked them open and made them into gods. But then Susanoo grew wild with excitement at his creative feat and tore through the world destroying everything in his path: he even piled feces under Amaterasu's throne. As though that were not enough, he stole into her quarters and threw a flayed horse's corpse through the roof of her weaving room, so startling one of Amaterasu's companions that she pricked herself and died.

This was too much for the sun goddess. She left this mad world and shut herself up in a comfortable cave. Without the sun, the entire world was blanketed with unending blackness. The eight million gods and goddesses, desperate for their queen's light, gathered to call out pleas that she return. But in her cave the goddess stayed.

The shaman Uzume, goddess of merriment, finally took matters into her hands. She turned over a washtub, climbed on top, and began dancing and singing and screaming bawdy remarks.

Soon the dance became a striptease. When she had shed all her clothes, Uzume began dancing so wildly and obscenely that the eight million gods and goddesses started to shout with delight.

Inside her cave, Amaterasu heard the noise. As it grew to a commotion, she called to ask what was going on. Someone paused to answer that they had found a better goddess than the sun. Provoked—and curious—Amaterasu opened the door of her cave just a crack.

The gods and goddesses had, with great foresight, installed a mirror directly outside of the cave. Amaterasu, who had never seen her own beauty before, was dazzled. While she stood there dazed, the other divinities grabbed the door and pulled it open. Thus the sun returned to warm the earth. Mounted again on her heavenly throne, Amaterasu punished Susanoo by having his fingernails and toenails pulled out and by throwing him out of her heaven.

Amayicoyondi The sky mother of the Pericu of California had three children by a bodiless god. One of them was killed by people from the south, but he was incorruptible, so his blood still flows on the desert.

Amazons A land populated entirely by these women—the Greeks believed in it, believed it existed on their very borders, a country on the River Thermodon. Once or twice a year, on the borders of their country, the Amazons had intercourse with men from surrounding tribes, keeping their daughters and returning the sons to the tribe of origin— or possibly killing or crippling the boys.

Two queens, one for defense and one for domestic affairs, shared sovereign rule. Under their military queen, the Amazons were a mighty army of mounted warriors bearing ivy-shaped shields and double-bladed battleaxes. At home, the Amazons lived peacefully, supplying all their own economic needs and producing artistic treasures coveted far outside their borders. For some 400 years (1000–600 B.C.E.), they held sway over the part of

Asia Minor along the shores of the Black Sea. Or so the Greeks believed for hundreds of years after the legendary warriors last engaged them in battle. Later Greeks attempted to dismiss the earlier tales as untrue. The historicity of Amazonia still provokes scholarly skirmishes. Did the Amazons exist? There are many theories, some dating all the way back to the days of classical Greece.

Some attempts to disprove the nation's existence are simply ludicrous, like the suggestion that, because Greek men wore beards, they thought anyone without a beard was a woman; a beardless army would have been perceived as composed of women. Other theorists speculate that, because some northern tribeswomen fought alongside their men, their existence was extrapolated into an entire northern kingdom of women warriors. Finally, there are those who contend that the Amazons were a mere projection of the (male) Greek mind and never existed outside of psychopathology.

But if they never existed, they could never have invaded Athens as Plutarch (among others) assures us they did. Of course, one could argue that the Greeks also believed that monsters like the Sphinx and Gorgons also fought with historical kings. While the issue of historicity remains far from settled, the stories of the Amazons continue to inspire the generations.

There is a persistent belief that the word *Amazon* means "breastless," although no convincing etymology has been established. Allegedly Amazons tore off their right breasts, the better to draw the bow and throw the javelin. This is a smear campaign, for there is not a single bit of evidence in Greek art that they considered their neighbors to be self-mutilated women. On the contrary, Amazons are invariably shown with one breast bare, and both quite visibly intact.

Once, so their legend says, the strong man Heracles murdered his three children. For this crime, he was sentenced to perform twelve virtually impossible tasks. One of these was to travel to Amazonia and to bring back the women's most famous treasure, their golden belt of queenship. With a large force of men, Heracles debarked at the land of women. Bands of Amazons guarded him and his comrades as they approached the queen's residence.

But Queen Hippolyta liked the looks of the hefty Heracles and offered him the belt in peace, and her bed with it. Unfortunately, rumor flew among the gathered Amazons that their queen Hippolyta was under attack, and they counterattacked instantly, driving the Greeks right back to their boats. Many warriors fell on both sides before the battle could be halted. It ended poorly for the Amazons. The valiant women were no match for the superhuman strength of Heracles. They were forced to surrender their leaders Melanippe and Antiope, and beautiful Hippolyta herself lay dead. Antiope was carried back to Athens as a spoil of war and given to King Theseus; this was too much of an outrage for the Amazons, who mounted an attack on Greece.

The queenless warriors fought their way the length of the Greek territories, finally entering Athens and penetrating right to the sacred hill, the Acropolis. There the battle reached an awful pitch, with Antiope dying still a captive and many other Amazons losing their lives in the heroic but futile effort. They retreated north to Amazonia, so many of the wounded dying en route that the trail home was lined with their shield-shaped gravestones.

Amba   Possibly pre-Indo-European, this Indian goddess (her name means "mother") was assimilated to other Hindu divinities, among them Durga, Parvati, and Uma. Near Jaipur into modern times she was honored with dawn sacrifices of black goats. Her name is similar to the old Semitic and Indo-European word for "mother"—*ama*.

Amberella   In Baltic folklore, Amberella was a golden-haired woman with eyes the color of the sea in which she liked to swim. One day, grasping at a piece of floating amber, she was pulled to the bottom of the water by the Prince of the Seas, who had fallen in love with her.

Distraught, her parents walked daily by the ocean, looking for their child and calling her name. A goldfish came to the surface and offered them precious amber in exchange for the girl, but the mother refused. The goldfish, taking pity on the woman, vowed to find her daughter.

The fish swam until she found the prince's bejeweled castle, where green amber lined the hallways and foaming amber wreathed the clear amber columns. In a hall of the palace on a sunbright throne, Amberella sat. The goldfish spoke her sad message, and while it softened the girl's heart, it made the prince furious. As he stormed, so did the sea. Mounting his raging white horses, he bore Amberella back to the shore.

Her parents stood amazed at the vision of their daughter glowing like a goddess. She began to throw large chunks of amber to them as gifts. Then, as suddenly as they had come, Amberella and her lover vanished. The people of the Baltic say that when the sea rages it is Amberella coming home, and as proof they show the shores full of amber that are left when the storm subsides.

Ambika   After the great Hindu warrior goddess Durga had destroyed the buffalo-demon who was threatening the world, there were still some devils lurking about the world, which needed to be disposed of. And so Parvati sent forth her feminine power, which appeared as Ambika, "Little Mother," a surpassingly beautiful woman who lured the demons to their deaths. Her approach was a clever one: first she told them she'd made a vow that she would not sleep with anyone who had not bested her in battle. Then, when the demons—smirking to themselves about how easy this weak creature would be to defeat—approached, she killed their servants with a supersonic hum. Then she transformed herself into the terrible goddess Kali. Armed with sword and noose, covered with the skulls of those she'd defeated, she set to work adding to her record.

Ament The "westerner," Ament was an Egyptian goddess who lived in a tree on the edge of the desert. She watched the gates to the afterworld and welcomed the newly deceased with bread and water. Those who took her offerings became "friends of the dead" and could never return to the land of the living. Originally from Libya, this goddess appears in hieroglyphs wearing an ostrich feather on her head; not only was this a common ornament among Libyans but it was the ideogram for her name. In time, the "West," which at first meant Libya to the Egyptians, began to mean the land of death as well.

Ammavaru North of Madras in India it is said that this ancient goddess existed before the beginning of time. Over eons she laid three eggs in the cosmic milk-sea, one at a time. The first egg spoiled. The second filled up with air, but the third hatched into the divine trinity of Brahma, Vishnu and Shiva. The egg's lower half became the earth, its upper half the sky. Ammavaru may well have been a very ancient, pre-Indo-European creator goddess.

Amphitrite A great Greek sea goddess with a non-Greek name who, the poet Homer tells us, was the female manifestation of the ocean itself. She may have been the pre-Hellenic sea goddess of the Aegean, whom the invading Greeks "married" to their image of oceanic strength, the god Poseidon, demoting her to Nereid or sea sprite. However, Amphitrite retained her individuality and her ownership of the caves under the sea, where she stored her precious jewels and from which she emerged to tend her cattle, the fish and mammals of the deep.

Anahita "Immaculate one," also called Ardvi Sura Anahita ("humid, strong, immaculate one"), she was one of the ruling deities of the Persian Empire. Anahita embodied the physical and metaphoric qualities of water, the fertilizing force that flowed from her supernatural fountain in the stars. By extension she ruled semen—which flows forth and fertilizes—and thus human generation as well as all other forms of earthly propagation.

She originated in Babylonia, whence she traveled to Egypt to appear as an armed and mounted goddess. Her worship spread east as well; she became the most popular Persian deity, worshiped, it is said, even by the great god Ahura Mazda himself. Nevertheless, Zoroaster did his best to ignore Anahita, although later writings reveal that the sage was specifically commanded by his male god to honor her.

In this tall and powerful maiden, her people saw the image of both the mother and the warrior; she was a protective mother to her people, generously nurturing them while fiercely defending them from enemies. In statuary, Anahita was the "golden mother," arrayed in golden kerchief, square gold earrings, and a jeweled diadem, wrapped in a gold-embroidered cloak adorned with thirty otter skins. She was also described as driving through our world in a chariot drawn by four white horses that signify wind, rain, clouds, and hail.

"Great Lady Anahita, glory and life-giver of our nation, mother of sobriety and benefactor of mankind," the Armenians called out to their beloved goddess. They honored her with offerings of green branches and white heifers brought to her sanctuaries. They may have offered themselves as well; the traveler Strabo said that sacramental promiscuity was part of the honor due this ruler of reproduction who "purifies the seed of males and the womb and milk of females." Healer, mother, and protector of her people, she was worshiped throughout the Persian Empire for many centuries. To the west she was said to be identical to Anat; the Greeks contended she was Aphrodite, when they did not claim she was Athena.

Ananke Plato called her the mother of the Moirae or Fates, but she seems less an actual goddess than the Greek personification of the abstraction necessity, or that force of destiny perceived in most cultures as female.

Anat The great goddess of the Ugaritic pantheon had four separate aspects: warrior, mother, virgin, and wanton. "Mother of nations," she remained "Virgin" in spite of being "Mistress of All Gods"; she never lost her hymen despite her promiscuity. Creator of her people, she could also be a bloodthirsty killer who went berserk and destroyed every living thing within reach.

The energy she personified was immense—no less than life itself in all its ecstatic and terrifying aspects. The goddess of desire, Anat was the favored sex partner of her brother Baal, for whose embraces she prepared herself with a bath of dew and a shower of ambergris. Their appetite for each other was prodigious: in one case Anat, overcome by lust, sought Baal while he was hunting, whereupon they copulated seventy-seven times in the wilderness. For this occasion, she took the form of a cow, and the progeny she bore afterward were oxen and buffalo.

Her rage for blood was equally noteworthy. Once, when her brother had waged a victorious battle, Anat ordered a huge celebratory feast prepared on the heavenly mountain, to which she invited the defeated. Retiring, Anat painted herself with rouge and henna. Then she entered the hall and closed the doors. She slew everyone in sight, wading maniacally in knee-deep blood and strapping dismembered bodies to her waist. In this, Anat embodied the fearful indifference of sexuality, which endlessly reproduces mortality: sex producing life, which ends in death.

Anat was later fused with Asherah, a less noticeably contradictory goddess. But her worship had already traveled from Canaan to Egypt, and there she was honored as the warrior Anath even by the Jews.

Anatu   Ruler of the earth and queen of the sky, a great goddess of Mesopotamia who was merged with Ishtar. Originally, however, it appears she was not only a separate figure but Ishtar's mother.

Anaxarete   Iphis, a commoner, loved this stony-hearted Greek princess. But she ridiculed him and his affection until, in a fit of depression, he hanged himself at her door. She laughed even then, and for this, Aphrodite, the goddess of sexuality who commanded all to mate, turned Anaxarete to stone.

Andraste   The "invincible one" was invoked by Celtic Britons before they entered battle. The warrior goddess was the particular favorite of the famous queen Boudicca of the Iceni, who offered Andraste sacrifice in a sacred grove before launching an anti-Roman campaign. Boudicca was almost successful, but overpowered at last by the Roman legions, she committed suicide rather than submit to slavery and probable rape.

Andriam-Vabi-Rano   On the island of Madagascar off the coast of east Africa, the "Princess of the Water" originally lived in the sky. But, curious about humanity, she turned herself into a leaf and dropped into a lake on the top of Mount Angavo. There, she was found by a prince who—apparently detecting something unusual about the floating leaf—captured it and locked it in prison until Andriam reappeared as a goddess. The children of their marriage became heroes and heroines.

Andromeda   The Greeks said that Joppa's queen Cassiopeia bragged once too often of her beauty; in punishment, Poseidon—proud of the beauty of his own daughters, the Nereids—sent a monster to ravage her land. Cassiopeia's daughter Andromeda was then exposed on a barren rock as an offering to the monster, who threatened but did not devour her. Eventually the Greek hero Perseus saw the endangered maiden and rescued her, and they lived together afterward. At her death Andromeda was placed by Athena among the stars as the constellation that bears her name.

Her original story may be older, and different, from this familiar version, however. Her name may be interpreted as "ruler of men" as well as "human sacrifice." Some consider her to be a personification of the moon, constantly under siege by the demon of darkness. Rather than being a victimized maiden, Andromeda may have originally been a pre-Hellenic moon goddess whose legend was incorporated into that of a Greek hero.

Angerboda The "one who warns of (bodes) danger" was given a cameo role in the Scandinavian eddas, where she was called a giant and the mate of the trickster god Loki. Her attributes were not described, but she was given credit—or blame—for bringing into the world three strange offspring. One of these was Jormungander or Midgard Serpent, who grew so large that he surrounded the earth. The second was the Fenris Wolf, an impressively vicious beast that will bring about the end of the world when let loose at Ragnarok, the end of this time cycle. Third was Angerboda's daughter Hel, the death queen. It seems that Angerboda was a form of the goddess of mortality, for her children circled the world of men (Jormungander) so that they could not escape their fate (Hel) or the inevitable end (Fenris) of the entire creation.

Angerona The Roman goddess of the winter solstice was shown with a bandaged mouth and with a finger to her lips enjoining silence. At her feast on December 21—called the Divalia or Angeronalia—the sun passed its weakest moment in the year and the sunlight began to increase. At the very moment of the solstice, however, before the balance tipped toward light, the goddess' image reminded her worshipers of the need to remember the fragility of the natural balance; for this reason she was sometimes called a death goddess.

Angitia An early Italian goddess of the Oscan tribe, she ruled the powers of healing and witchcraft and was known as a great expert in verbal and herbal charms. She especially knew how to remedy snakebite, as her name, which refers to killing snakes through enchantment, attests. She has been identified with Medea, who allegedly fled to Italy after driving off from Greece in her dragon-chariot; but the Romans said she was the same as Bona Dea, the "good goddess." Angitia was partic-

ularly honored in Italy's Marsian district, still famous today for its witches.

Anieros During Roman times, in the northeastern provinces of Phrygia and the island of Samothrace, this name was given to a Demeter-like earth

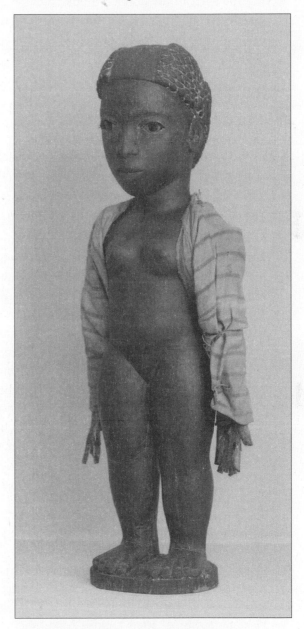

This delightful small wooden sculpture from South Bara, Madagascar, was created around the turn of the twentieth century. Heavenly goddesses called Andriams descended to earth to help create human society, according to Malagasey legend. See Andriam-Vabi-Rano.

goddess who had a Persephone-like daughter named Axiocersa. They were doubles of each other: the young earth of springtime and the mature earth of autumn; the young woman of promise and the fulfilled matron. Their religion was the ancient one of Asia Minor, based on the divinity of the female body, which was seen as a microcosm of the forces of life, growth, death, and rebirth.

Anima Mundi To the Gnostic philosophers of the Roman Empire, the "soul of the world" was female, a concept that corresponds to our mother nature.

Ankt A spear-carrying war goddess of the Egyptians who was depicted wearing a curved and feathered crown.

Annalia Tu-Bari In ancient Wa-Ghana, the legendary city of gold in west Africa, this princess became queen of her region when her father died, leaving her his only heir. But the land was divided among eighty disputatious kinglings, each of whom waged continual war on the others. Annalia offered herself to whomever could bring the warring princes under control. The king of Ghana, Samba ("strong one") did so, and his marriage to Annalia joined two vast and wealthy realms. But shortly after their wedding, a drought devastated the area, which was found to be caused by a dragon drinking up the Niger River water upstream of Ghana. It took eighty years for the king to kill the dragon, and he used 800 spears in the fight, but finally the dragon was killed and the Niger flowed again.

Anna Perenna The origin and original legend of this Roman goddess is a subject of conjecture, for she seems to be so ancient that even in early historical times her beginnings were unclear. One legend tells us that she was the sister of Dido of Carthage. Fleeing to Rome after Dido's death, she was received by Aeneas, Dido's unfaithful lover, by then married. The new wife grew jealous of the mistress' sister, and Anna Perenna ran away, changing herself into a river.

Another story says that Anna was an old woman of the town of Bovillae; when the plebeian revolutionaries were besieged on Mons Sacer, she found a secret way to convey food to them, enabling them to endure the siege. For this, Anna Perenna was deified after her death.

Current scholarship suggests that she was originally an Etruscan goddess who ruled human and vegetative reproduction. Each year at her March 15 festival, rowdiness, merrymaking, and promiscuity were expected of all pious Romans. The spring date of the festival and its nature indicate that Anna Perenna was the goddess of the fruitful earth, who would be pleased by the reproductive activities of human beings and respond by bringing forth an abundance of edibles for them.

Anapurna "Food-giver" was the name of this ancient Indian goddess whom some scholars connect with Rome's Anna Perenna. A common household deity, often depicted enthroned and feeding a child from a full ladle, Anapurna was especially significant to the city of Benares, where harvest festivals honored her. The Hindus, finding it necessary to systematize their complex pantheon, called her a form of Durga or of Devi, but she retained her rulership over food production and distribution.

Antaboga Near Java, this Indonesian underworld serpent goddess produced rice—which provides the main nutritional staple there—by weeping eggs that hatched into the rice divinities.

Antevorta Roman goddess of prophecy, she was especially invoked by expectant mothers, who prayed to her to know the outcome of their pregnancies. She is seen as a companion of the spring goddess Carmenta, or is sometimes said to be an aspect of her.

Antianara This Amazon queen, when asked why her male slaves were all crippled, replied, "The lame best perform the acts of love." This comment, recorded by the Byzantine scholar Eustathius, runs counter to the common image of Amazons as disinterested in, or repelled by, heterosexual relations.

Antigone   The loyal daughter of Oedipus of Thebes, she followed her blinded father into exile at Colonus; some say that she attended his death and dug his grave. Then she returned to Thebes and found two of her brothers had been killed in a revolt against their uncle Creon, ruler of the city. Creon forbade anyone to bury the rebels, but Antigone knew that unless her brother Polynices' body was returned to the earth's womb, he could never be reborn. She risked death to spread dust over the corpse so that the earth mother would recognize Polynices' desire for reincarnation. Caught, Antigone was buried alive; some stories say, however, that her lover-cousin Haemon secretly carried her away.

Antiope   One of the most beautiful women of her age, this Amazon queen was kidnapped by Heracles (some say Theseus) from her homeland north of Greece, brought to Athens, and presented to King Theseus. Some sources say he made her his legal wife, others claim he merely kept her as a captive concubine. She bore him a son, naming the child Hippolytus after her sister Hippolyta. But Theseus eventually tired of Antiope, as he had previously tired of the helpful Ariadne, and moved on to his next affair with Phaedra. (In some versions of the tale, the Amazon queen who lived with Theseus is Hippolyta herself.) Antiope died in the Amazon attack on Athens, either as a traitor fighting beside Theseus against her own kin or as a captive of the Greeks and a casualty of the war.

Anu   One of the ancestor goddesses of Ireland, some say she is the same goddess as Aine. Others say she is identical to Danu. In any case, she was known as a force of prosperity and abundance; two breast-shaped mountains in western Ireland are called, in her name, "the paps of Anu."

Anuanaitu   In the days just after creation, said the Caribbean peoples, men were usually ugly and women were magnificently beautiful. But there was one handsome man, Maconaura, who lived with his mother in the peaceful jungle of primordial time, when there was no evil and no fear.

One day Maconaura found that someone had been raiding his fishnet—the world's first crime. To make matters worse, the thief had ripped the nets. Maconaura set a woodpecker to guard the nets and soon heard the bird's cry. Running back to the pond, the young man saw a water monster and swiftly shot it. Then he discovered on the shore a young girl, not yet pubescent, whom he took home and whom his mother raised.

When she grew, Anuanaitu was Maconaura's first choice for a wife. She demurred at first, for she could not marry without her parents' consent and she refused to reveal their identity. Eventually, she gave way to her affection and desire and married Maconaura. The pair decided it would still be best to travel to the woman's village and seek the blessing of her parents. Anuanaitu's mother quickly agreed to the match, but her father subjected Maconaura to near-impossible tests of skill and courage. The young man performed well and remained with Anuanaitu as her husband.

One day Maconaura decided to visit his own family; on his return to Anuanaitu's village, her father shot him dead with an arrow. War broke out between the two families, with Anuanaitu's kin being destroyed in the magical battles. She remained alive and became entranced with the spirits of the dead. Traveling in rattlesnake form to her husband's village, she determined to take her revenge. The human woman who had raised her appealed to her gentler instincts, and for a moment Anuanaitu hesitated. But then she struck her poisonous blow, revealing that the water monster slain by Maconaura had been her own brother, for she was from a race of such creatures.

Her heart had been moved, although duty had silenced love. Anuanaitu ran through the world—which turned dark and fearsome as she crossed it—until she reached the ocean. There she threw herself into the water and drowned in a place where today a dangerous whirlpool sucks; there she was reunited with her lover, and there she reigns as the Soul of the Ocean.

Anuket   At Aswan in Egypt, and particularly on the sacred island of Seheil, this water goddess was adored. Her name means the "embracer" and may refer to the embrace of the Nile waters by the river's banks. Her sacred animal was the gazelle, whose speed matched that of her waters. In hieroglyphs she wore a feather headdress; late in her history, she was merged with Nephthys.

Anunitu   Originally goddess of the city of Akkad in northern Babylonia, she was later called Ishtar of Akkad and finally was submerged in the powerful figure of Ishtar. While independent, Anunitu ruled either the moon or the evening star and, like other light goddesses, was symbolized by a disk with eight rays. "Mistress of battle, bearer of bow and quiver," she was called, but despite her martial nature she was kindly disposed toward humankind and interceded for them with the moon god Sin, her father or brother.

An.Zu   Assyrian goddess of chaos, pictured as sickle moon with seven-pointed star and sacred tree; her emblems also include a fish and a lozenge/vulva. Like Tiamat, she was killed in order to form the universe.

Aoife   A legendary Celtic queen, whose name is pronounced "eefa," she lived in Scotland near her rival, the Amazonian queen Scathach, with whom she was constantly at war. They were well-matched foes; Scathach had magical powers, whereas Aoife was invulnerable to them, as she was to everything but fast horses and pretty horsewomen. Eventually, Aoife was defeated by the Irish hero Cuchulain and accepted as part of the truce his demands that she bear his son; she did; he returned to Ireland and, years later, killed his son without recognizing him.

Another—or possibly the same—Aoife was the consort of the sea god Mananaan. She stole the secret alphabet of knowledge from the gods to give to humanity and was transformed into a crane in punishment. However, in a bag made from her own skin, Aoife delivered the magic letters to the people.

Apasinasee   Once, the Inuit of Hudson Bay say, there was a haughty young woman who refused all the men in her village; she did not wish to marry but stayed instead in her parents' home. One day, her father angrily suggested that, considering her behavior, the family dog was the proper mate for her.

The next day the dog disappeared, and a beautiful young man dressed in dogskin clothing arrived at the hut, ate sitting next to the girl, and then slept with her. They stayed together until the young woman gave birth to a litter of puppies. Her children were so noisy that Apasinasee's father put the whole lot, with the dog and his wife, into a boat and carried them across the river to live.

Apasinasee's father continued to provide for them, however; he sent meat to the family every day, tying it around the dog's neck. Eventually tiring of this, he tied rocks around the dog's neck instead, so it drowned. Apasinasee instructed her children to eat her father, and they did.

Then Apasinasee was utterly without support. So she mournfully sent her children away to forage for themselves. One group traveled far inland, where they became giants; another, living on the coast, became walrus-eating dwarves. A few she put into a magical ship, and they disappeared entirely. And a very few stayed beside their mother—and they became the Inuit.

Aphrodite   One of the most familiar of Greek goddesses, Aphrodite was not originally Greek at all. She was the ancient mother goddess of the eastern Mediterranean who established herself first on the islands off Greece before entering the country itself. There, her journey with the sea traders who brought her across the waters was expressed in a symbolic tale.

In the ancient days, it was said, the old heaven god Uranus was castrated by his children, the Titans; his penis fell into the ocean and ejaculated a final divine squirt. The sea reddened where it fell, and then the foam gathered itself into a figure: the long-haired Aphrodite riding on a mussel shell (whence the epithet Anadyomene, "she who rises from the waves"). She shook the seawater from her locks and watched drops fall, instantly turning to pearls, at her feet. She floated to the islands off Greece, for which she is sometimes named Cytherea or Cypris. She landed at Cyprus and was greeted by the lovely Horae, who provided attire worthy of her beauty and who became her constant companions.

The story of her birth is an obvious description of the journey of this Near Eastern goddess to her new home in Greece. It is also allegorical: the sky god impregnates the great sea womb with dynamic life, a story that the Greeks reiterated in the alternate version of Aphrodite's birth by the sea sprite Dione and the sky god Zeus.

Once she arrived, the Greeks provided Aphrodite with a husband: Hephaestus, the crippled god of smithcraft. Aphrodite could not be contained in a single relationship, though, and spread her favors liberally among divine and mortal males. She bore children by half a dozen mates, none her husband. In many of these unions, the allegory is glaringly obvious, as when Aphrodite (sexuality) mates with Dionysus (wine) to produce Priapus (permanent erection).

The most famous—or perhaps notorious—of Aphrodite's affairs were those with Ares and with the beautiful young Adonis. She carried on scandalously and publicly with the god of war; their union was a fascinating symbol of the relationship of female carnality and male competitiveness. All heaven knew of their assignations, the Greeks said, before someone finally tattled to the husband. Furious at Aphrodite's unfaithfulness (although in her homeland such behavior would have been expected), the cuckolded Hephaestus fashioned a mesh of gold in which he caught the lovers. Ares and Aphrodite were the laughing-stock of heaven then, naked and damp, their limbs entangled in each other's and in the golden web that held them.

As for Adonis, it was said that Aphrodite fell in love with his youthful beauty and hid him in a chest that she gave to Persephone for safekeeping. The queen of the underworld, however, peeked inside to see what treasure she was guarding and, smitten, refused to give Adonis back to Aphrodite. Zeus was called in to arbitrate, and he ruled that Adonis could live one-third of each year by himself, one-third with Persephone, and the remaining one-third with Aphrodite. Each year thereafter Adonis was killed while hunting a wild boar, and his spilled blood turned the Lebanese river named for him red.

The energy that Aphrodite represented, however humanly true, was almost incompatible with Greek culture. The great goddess of impersonal, indiscriminate lust meshed poorly with the emerging Greek intellectualism. Thus the tale of the goddess' love for the ever-dying god ceased to be central to her legend and became that of just another casual attraction to a pretty face. The rather smutty little tale is a far cry from those masterpieces of theological understanding, the stories of Ishtar, Inanna, and Cybele, with their symbolic description of the hopeless love of the earth herself for the life she continually produces and inevitably consumes.

In their attempt to assimilate the alien goddess, the Greeks converted Aphrodite into a personification of physical beauty. But she remained so problematic that Plato distinguished her by two titles: Urania, who ruled spiritualized (platonic, if you will) love; and Aphrodite Pandemos, the Aphrodite of the commoners, who retained her original character in debased form. In this form she was called Porne, the "titillator." It was this latter Aphrodite who was worshiped at Corinth, where the Near Eastern practice of sacramental promiscuity deteriorated into a costly prostitution about which the Greeks warned travelers, "The voyage to Corinth is not for everyone." However degraded the practice became in a patriarchal context, the "hospitable women" (Pindar) who engaged in it were highly valued, serving as priestesses in public festivals, and of such rank and importance that at state occasions as many hetaerae as possible were required to attend.

Aponibolinayen   In the islands now called the Philippines, it was said that this divine sky woman supported the heavens by a vine wrapped around her waist. Possibly she was a moon goddess, for she was said to live during the day in the sun's home; Aponibolinayen produced children by him, giving birth from her little finger.

Arachne   The daughter of a dyer, this proud young mortal was an exquisite weaver who challenged the goddess Athena to a weaving contest—a presumptuous act, as Athena was the very spirit of the craft itself. In an attempt to embarrass the goddess into making a mistake, Arachne wove a gorgeous tapestry revealing the whole Greek pantheon in indelicate poses. Athena shredded the woman's cloth in anger, and Arachne hanged herself in shame. Her spirit scurried away from the loom in the body of the first spider, and spiders (arachnids) still bear Arachne's name today.

Ararat   The ancient Anatolian world-creator goddess was embodied in this famous mountain in modern Armenia, where Noah's ark was said to have landed after the biblical great flood.

Ardat Lili   In Semitic lore, this storm demon caused nocturnal emissions, mounting sleeping men and capturing their ejaculations to form her demon children.

Ardwinna   The Continental Celtic goddess of the wildwood, she demanded a "fine" of money for every animal killed in her wood; in addition, her people were expected to bring her sacrificial animals on feast days. Her favorite haunt was the forest of Ardennes, which Ardwinna was said to oversee mounted on a wild boar.

Arete   The Greek goddess of justice, teacher of the hero Heracles, was a personified abstraction with no real legendary background.

Ariadne   The myth and character of this Cretan goddess come to us in confused form. Political and cultural changes in ancient Greece were mirrored in religious shifts, and Ariadne's worshipers—the losing side in one such shift—found their native religion suppressed. In her original Minoan form, Ariadne ("very holy") was apparently a goddess worshiped exclusively by women, a goddess of the underworld and of germination, a vegetation goddess much like the Greek Persephone. When the Greeks arrived, they "converted" Ariadne's worshipers and demoted the former goddess to the heroine of the following tale.

The daughter of Queen Pasiphae and King Minos of Crete, Ariadne gave the Athenian hero Theseus a spool of thread for his escape from the Minoan labyrinth. Together they fled, but Theseus abandoned Ariadne on the island of Naxos (or Dia). There she was discovered by the newly mature god of wine, Semele's son, Dionysus, and they joined forces. She became the leader of the Dionysian women, the Maenads, and bore many children to the god before dying in childbed. (Another version says that Artemis killed her; as that goddess ruled childbirth, the tale remains essentially the same.) Then Ariadne was raised to heaven and given the new name of Aridella, "the very visible one."

Arianrhod   The goddess of the "silver wheel" was a Welsh sorceress who, surrounded by women attendants, lived on the isolated coastal island of Caer Arianrhod. Beautiful and pale of complexion, Arianrhod was the most powerful of the mythic children of the mother goddess Don.

It was said that she lived a wanton life, mating with mermen on the beach near her castle and casting her magic inside its walls. She tried to pretend virginity, but a trial by the magician Math revealed that she had conceived two children whom she had not carried to term: in leaping over a wizard's staff, Arianrhod magically gave birth to the twins Dylan-son-of-Wave and the fetus of Llew Llaw Gyffes. Dylan slithered away and disappeared. Arianrhod's brother, the poet Gwydion, recognized the fetus as his own child, born of his unexpressed love for his sister.

Gwydion took the fetus and hid it in a magical chest until it was ready to breathe. Arianrhod, furious at this invasion of her privacy, denied the child a name or the right to bear arms—two prerogatives of a Welsh mother—but Gwydion tricked Arianrhod into granting them. Eventually the goddess overreached herself, creating more magic than she could contain; her island split apart, and she and her maidservants drowned.

Some scholars read the legend as the record of a change from mother right to father rule, claiming that the heavenly Arianrhod was a matriarchal moon goddess whose particular place in heaven was in the constellation called Corona Borealis. The argument has much in its favor, particularly the archetypal relation of Arianrhod to her sister moon goddesses on the continent, who like Artemis lived in orgiastic maidenhood surrounded entirely by women. Other scholars, unconvinced that the Celts were matriarchal at any time, see Arianrhod simply as an epic heroine.

Aricia The name of the most famous shrine of Diana was also the name of a minor Roman goddess who ruled the prophetic visions sometimes experienced in wild places far from human habitation.

Armaiti An aspect of the androgynous divinity of Zoroastrianism, Armaiti ("devotion") is the righteous virgin who also ruled reproduction, fructification, and destiny. Sometimes she is called Spendta Armatai, "holy devotion," or in shortened form, Spendarmat. Of the seven aspects of Ahura Mazda, three were feminine: Armaiti and the sis-

ter divinities Haurvatat ("integrity") and Ameretat ("immortality"), who ruled the physical as well as the spiritual manifestations of these qualities. In some myths, Armatai created the first humans, suggesting a derivation from an early creator goddess.

Arrang Dibatu A rock-born creator goddess of the Toraja of the south Celebes in Indonesia, she invented the idea of using bellows to superheat fire for forging metals. From this invention, the stars, animals and even humanity were created.

Arria A heroic Roman matron, she was the wife of Caecina Paetus, who was ordered by the emperor to end his life in 42 B.C.E. He shrank from obeying

This delightful small red marble sculpture from Italy represents the goddess of the wilderness, Artemis, in an especially girlish fashion. More frequently she was shown hunting, running, or striding strongly.

the command, so his wife stabbed herself first, then handed the dagger to her husband with the words, "It does not hurt."

Artemis   As we see her in Western art, Artemis is the virginal moon goddess roaming the forest with her band of nymphs, bearing the bow and quiver, avoiding men and killing any male who looks on her. But this familiar form was only one of the identities assumed by this complex Greek goddess, for she was also the many-breasted Artemis of Ephesus, a semi-human symbol of fecundity, and the warlike Artemis said to have been the special goddess of the Amazons. It is problematic whether she was originally an all-encompassing goddess later divided into separate identities, or if Artemis became so complex by assuming the attributes of lesser goddesses as her worshipers took control of Greece. But, like Isis or Ishtar, Artemis came to represent the variable energies of the feminine. She was therefore contradictory: she was the virgin who promoted promiscuity; she was the huntress who protected animals; she was a tree, a bear, the moon. Artemis was the image of a woman moving through her life and assuming different roles at different times; she was a veritable encyclopedia of feminine possibility.

In one form she was a nymph and ruler of all nymphs, an elemental force whose domain was the greenwood. There an order exists so unlike human order that it seems to us formless and free, but this freedom is that of complete obedience to instinct, which animals still follow while humans do not. Artemis in this form was the Lady of the Beasts, the force who assured their individual deaths and the survival of the species. As mistress of the animals, she was the invisible game warden of the Greeks, killing with sharp arrows anyone who hunted pregnant beasts or their young. Again as instinct, she ruled reproduction, both sex and birth. She ruled the childbed; even in late legend, when her dominance was undercut by male gods, Artemis was said to have been the elder twin of the sun (not originally her brother) and midwife

at Apollo's birth. It was to Artemis, the force of creation, that Greek mothers called when the pangs of birth began, and they found comfort in their belief that she nursed them through labor just as she did any of her other animals.

As the nymph of the greenwood, then, she is not really different from her other most famous form: Mother Artemis, whose vast rich temple at Amazonian Ephesus was one of the wonders of the ancient world. There her massive statue stood, rising from a legless base into a huge torso ringed with breasts, then up to a head surmounted by the turret crown of her city. This Artemis was merely a different visualization of the same energy represented by the woodland nymph: the instinct to live, to produce and reproduce constantly, to devour, and to die. There is power in the image of Ephesia—as Artemis in this form was sometimes called—a power that could be seen as terrifying, so vast and inhuman is it.

The most beloved goddess of Greece, Artemis was honored in rituals that were wildly popular although as varied as the forms of the goddess herself. At Ephesus, in her well-endowed temple, Artemis was served by chaste priestesses called Mellisai, or "bees," and by eunuch priests. In Sparta she was Korythalia, worshiped in orgiastic dancing. The Amazons honored the war mother Astateia, the mother as protector of her children, in a circle dance amid the clashing of shields and swords and the stomping of battle-clad feet. But apparently the most popular festivals of Artemis were those celebrated on nights of the full moon, when worshipers would gather in the goddess' wood and give themselves over to her power in revels and anonymous matings. The beloved goddess of Greece was the personification of natural law, so different from the laws of society, so much more ancient, so everlasting.

Artemisia   A famous naval strategist of Caria in Asia Minor, she fought her way to fame in the wars between Persia and the Greek city-states.

Artio All across Celtic Gaul and Britain, this great goddess of wildlife was worshiped. She appeared to her people in the form of a bear, as did Artemis, a Greek goddess with a similar name.

Aryong-Jong Korea's "Lady of Dragon Palace," the first queen of the land, was a goddess who controlled rainfall. In times of drought, shamans poured water through a sieve on the parched soil, and Aryong-Jong opened the clouds.

Asase Yaa "Old Woman Earth" is a rough translation of the name of this great divinity of the Ashanti people of Ghana in western Africa. She gave birth to humanity and today still reclaims her children at death. Each person who has worked a field and who, on dying, returns to Asase Yaa becomes a co-power of fertility. At planting, therefore, the Ashanti farmer prays to his ancestors and to Asase Yaa, who lent the rights of cultivation to the living.

Thursday is the sacred day of the earth goddess; farmers then allow her a day of rest from their plows and other sharp tools. When Christianity came to western Africa with its Sunday festival, the issue of which day was the more truly sacred posed a great problem to those seeking converts. Another difficulty was that this supreme divinity does not live in houses or temples but in every plowed field; the Ashanti do not have to retreat to special places to acknowledge her power and presence. Although Christianity has nominally won the battle, vestiges of the worship of the "Old Woman" remain, and some Akan people still pray, "Earth, when I am about to die, I lean on you. Earth, while I am alive, I depend on you."

Asherah From a root meaning "straight," this Canaanite goddess derived a name that implied not only the moral rectitude she demanded of her followers but also the upright posts or living trees in which they perceived her essence. In her temples, Asherah's image was non-human, merely an unshaped piece of wood called by her name. But in private devotions she was represented by a simple woman-shaped clay figurine with, instead of

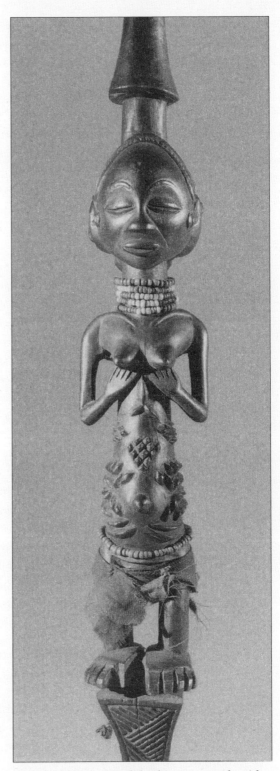

Ceremonial spears such as this one—made with iron, wood, cloth and beads—represented the female power in Africa. See Ala and Asase Yaa for important African goddesses of womanly power.

55

legs, a base for insertion in the soft earthen floor of the home. She also appeared as a naked, curly-haired goddess riding a sacred lion and holding lilies and serpents in upraised hands.

"Wet nurse of the gods" and "she who gives birth" to seventy of them, Asherah was one of the Ugaritic mother goddesses. Not only did she physically nurture the gods—and human rulers too—she offered spiritual sustenance through her oracular wizards. She was the force of life, experienced as benevolent and enduring, found in flocks of cattle and groves of trees, evoked in childbirth and at planting time.

The character of "Lady Asherah of the Sea" (her full name) is vague and unclear, coming down as it does to us predominantly through the writings of her sworn enemies, the patriarchal Hebrews who often, perhaps deliberately, confused her with Astarte (which they spelled Ashtoreth). But this official view often did not coincide with popular opinion. In the Old Testament we can read the catalog of a centuries-long campaign against the joyfully orgiastic rites of this benevolent goddess. Asherah would apparently be rooted out of the people's hearts, only to reemerge, giving rise to another wave of reforms. Queen Maacah, mother of Asa and Jezebel, publicly worshiped her; Hebrew zealots, however, took the life of Jezebel on the charge of "harlotry" during festivals of the goddess. But so popular did the worship of Asherah remain that there is substantial evidence that she was worshiped, with all attendant public pleasures, within the Jerusalem temple itself.

Ashiakle In the Accra region of Ghana, she is the goddess of wealth and the sea. Eldest daughter of the chief god, she was born in the ocean and travels along the coast in her canoe. Her colors are red and white, and her name includes the word *shika* (money).

Ashnan The Sumerian goddess of grain and her friend Lahar were charged with the provision of food and drink for the gods. Alas, they got drunk and failed in their duties, with the result that humankind was created to take up the slack.

Asintmah Among the Athabascans of western Canada, she was the first woman, midwife to the earth mother. Born at the foot of Mount Atika near the Athabaskan River, Asintmah found a land of ice and snow and clear water. But it was empty of animal life. And so Asintmah carefully built a loom of saplings and wove a blanket of fireweed blossoms. Carefully, she spread this across the land, anchoring it at the sacred mountains at the world's corners. Then she began to sing, a beautiful song of life and movement. Inspired by the woman's song, the earth began to give birth under her blanket of flowers. First mouse was born, then rabbit, then cougar. Caribou and moose were next, each born to the song of the first woman, who lifted them carefully from beneath earth's blanket. Thus was the earth populated, by woman's art and by her song.

Aspelenie This Lithuanian goddess ruled the corner of the house behind the stove. She could sometimes be spotted in her animal form as the *zaltys*, the little ringed snake that was not only harmless but useful as a rodenticide. Sometimes Aspelenie was so friendly with the family that her snake was an actual house pet.

Astarte It is often difficult to distinguish the like-named goddesses of the ancient Near East, partially because the persecuting Hebrews blurred the distinctions between them and partly because over the ages tribes identified their native goddesses with those of conquering or neighboring peoples. Such is the case with Astarte, often confused or merged with Anat, Asherah, even Atargatis. Whether she was originally an independent deity whose identity grew indistinct, or whether her name was at first a title of Asherah or another goddess, may never be known. But Astarte was probably the West Semitic (especially Phoenician) version of that goddess named, in other languages, Ishtar and Aphrodite.

Astarte ("womb" or "she of the womb") was the goddess who appears in the Old Testament as Ashtoreth, a non-name formed by misreading the goddess' name with different vowels so that the word becomes "shameful thing." What seems to have been shameful to the patriarchal Hebrews was the untrammeled sexuality of the goddess, one of those who "conceived but did not bear" offspring for her partners. In this, her identity as the Canaanite version of Ishtar becomes clear, for in the ancient eastern Mediterranean the spirit of sexuality was the goddess who ruled the planet Venus. As the morning star Astarte was, like Anat, a war goddess robed in flames and armed with a sword and two quivers full of death-dealing arrows, flying into battle like a swallow. But as the evening star, a goddess of desire, Astarte descended to the underworld to reclaim a lost lover, thereby causing all human and animal copulation to cease until she returned.

Her colors were red and white; in her honor the acacia tree produced flowers in these colors, so she called it her emblem. She also loved the cypresses of her country and the stallions that she rode, the first fruits of the harvest, the firstborn of the womb, and all bloodless sacrifices. In some pictures, Astarte stands small-breasted and naked on the back of a lioness, with a lotus and a mirror in one hand and two snakes in the other. At other times, to show her fierce and hungry nature, she was shown with the head of a lioness.

Asteria Assaulted by the Greek god Zeus, this nymph changed herself into a quail to avoid rape. Stories like this one may allegorically record the invasion of the patriarchal Greeks and their religious persecution of the pre-Hellenic goddess worshipers native to the peninsula. In this case, the story of Asteria would contain the name and symbol of one of the many local goddesses lost in the pre-Hellenic mists.

Astraea Daughter of Themis, she lived on earth in the golden age when all lived in peace together. But as humankind grew more and more violent, the gods abandoned this world and retreated to the heavens. Patient and hopeful, Astraea was the last of the immortals to leave, but finally even she was forced to abandon the earth.

Asynjr Generic term for female Scandinavian divinities and giantesses.

Atabei The primary being of the pre-Hispanic people of the Antilles bore five names other than Atabei: Attabeira, Momona, Guacarapita, Iella, and Guimazoa. She was served by a messenger, Guatauva, and by the hurricane goddess Coatrischie. Little is known of her rites, although she was recognized as a form of the earth goddess by the Antillean people, whose culture was such that invading Spaniards called the women "Amazons" and said that they lived alone and engaged in war. In some areas, the women even spoke a different language from the men of the same group.

Ataensic Once, said the Iroquois and their neighbors, there was no land, just a vast blue lake upon which water birds floated with otters, turtles, and other seadwelling creatures. High above in a heavenly land was the celestial society into which Ataensic was born.

Her father died before her birth—the first death in the universe. He was placed on a burial scaffold where the girl used to go to converse with his spirit. He instructed her, when she was grown, to travel a long distance through heaven to Earth-Holding Chief, her intended mate.

Through tempests and danger she traveled; the chief tested her with torture, but she endured and returned to her own village, pregnant by him. Her daughter, Gusts-of-Wind, was born, but her people threw Ataensic down to the earth-lake. (Or was it an accident?—the myths differ.) She fell and fell through the blue air, her daughter returning to Ataensic's womb.

Below, a loon looking into the water saw a figure rising from the depths. He mentioned this curiosity to the bittern. The puzzled birds slowly realized that Ataensic was falling, not rising from the lake. They had never known that their lake had a bottom, which thus had formed a mirror. The knowledge came just in time, for to save the falling woman, the birds and animals had to build land from the lake mud. Otter and turtle tried, and muskrat, and finally Ketq Skwayne ("Grandmother Toad") dove deep and returned exhausted, spitting up some of the magical earth just before she died.

The earth landed on the turtle's back and instantly began to grow. By the time Ataensic reached the water—her fall broken by the water birds' wings—there was enough land for her to rest on as Gusts-of-Wind was reborn. (Some stories say that she fell onto what is now a mountain near Oswego River Falls in New York.)

Gusts-of-Wind became pregnant and died giving birth to twins; from her body Ataensic fashioned the sun and the moon, and that is the way the earth and its luminaries came into being.

Atalanta The "impassable one," a pre-Hellenic divinity of mountainous Arcadia in northern Greece, was probably originally the death goddess whom no one can outrun. The conquering Greeks told her legend this way: Atalanta's father, disappointed at the birth of a daughter, took the infant to Parthenia ("virgin hill") and left her there to die. But she survived by being suckled and raised by a mother bear. She grew wild and strong in the wilderness, grew into a centaur-killing heroine, the match of any man in Greece, a woman of vigorous beauty who took her lovers from the men at whose side she fought.

Her father eventually decided to claim fatherhood of the famous warrior, and with it he claimed such paternal rights as the choice of Atalanta's husband. But the heroine refused to marry any man whom she could outrun and demanded the right to kill any who lost to her. So compelling

was her beauty that many risked, and lost, their lives racing for her hand. One competitor, given golden apples by Aphrodite, flung them down before the fleet woman who, stopping to scoop them out of the dust, lost the advantage. Won by guile, Atalanta nevertheless wed happily. But she and her lover, engrossed in their passion, neglected to make proper marital sacrifices and were punished by being transformed into the lions who drew Cybele's chariot.

Atanea The dawn goddess of the Marquesas Islands was the daughter of the high divinity Atea. (Some scholars claim that Atea, cited in most sources as a male deity, was in fact originally female, an overarching sky mother.) Atanea created the sea accidentally when she miscarried and filled the hollows of the earth with amniotic fluid.

Atargatis No one is certain of the original name of this Syrian or Aramaic goddess. The names we now use are Greek transliterations, similar to Isis for Au Set. But philologists suggest that her original name ("divine Ata") was related to Ishtar and Astarte.

The spirit of fertilizing moisture, Atargatis descended from heaven in the form of an egg, from which the mermaid goddess emerged. Beautiful and wise, she roused the jealousy of a rival who cursed her with consuming love for a beautiful youth. She became pregnant by the boy and bore the goddess Semiramis, then assured the boy's eternal fidelity by causing him to disappear. After placing her daughter in the wilderness with doves to attend and feed her, Atargatis threw herself into a lake and became the omnipotent fish mother. In honor of her and her daughter, the Syrians refused to eat fish or doves.

Although this was the basic form of her legend, Atargatis appeared in other guises as well: as a vegetation goddess who protected the cities that her produce enriched; as a sky goddess in a cloudlike veil with eagles around her head; as a dolphin-crowned sea goddess. Her sanctuaries, such as the one at Delos, were centered on quiet fish-filled ponds, and doves roosted in the sacred trees around them.

During the Roman era, Atargatis was worshiped in ecstatic dances by eunuch priests who devoted their lives to dervishlike whirlings and self-inflicted pain. Her worship was ancient by that time, for in the pre-Christian centuries her believers had come under Hebrew attack when Judas Maccabaeus lured them into her temple with assurances of safety and then ruthlessly slaughtered them. Atargatis is a figure comparable to Ishtar and Cybele.

Ate Daughter of Eris, she was a minor Greek goddess of folly, moral blindness and infatuation who was banished from Olympus for her mischief-making. She now lives among humans, who cannot escape her cruel games. Her plaything, the golden apple of discord, began the far-from-minor discord called the Trojan War.

Atete This name is thought to have been the original one of the Ethiopian goddess who became subsumed under the guise of Saint Mary, who in historical times was celebrated in all-female rituals involving processions to riverbanks and the singing of ritual songs.

Athaliah The daughter of Jezebel, she was, with her mother, one of the pair of women who bore the singular distinction of ruling the early Hebrews. Athaliah was a zealous worshiper of the ancient life-and-death goddess Asherah and, like her mother, was martyred for her faith.

Athana Lindia This goddess of the city of Lindos was one of the early Mediterranean symbols of the united power of fruitful fields and a peaceful community. Like the Roman Ceres, she embodied the reproductive energies of the harvest, as well as the prosperity and culture that a stable food supply could sustain. In statuary, Athana Lindia's torso and limbs were represented simply by an uncut plank, from which rose a sculpted head crowned

with the walls of her city, while across her unshaped breast were strung necklace garlands.

Athena She was not always accepted as patron of the famous city that bears her name. Greek legend says that the sea god Poseidon disputed with the goddess for rulership of the city. It came to a vote of the people of the town in question. The citizens, men and women alike, gathered to cast their ballots. Naturally, the men voted for the god, the women for the goddess. As it happened, there was one more voter on the women's side, and so

Dressed in a fiber skirt, this tattooed woman from Oceania wears armbands and shell rings. She may represent a creator goddess such as Atanea.

Athena won the day. (An alternative version says that the Olympian deities judged the contest. They ruled that because Athena had planted the first olive tree, whereas all Poseidon could offer was the changeful sea, the goddess would be a better city ruler than the god.)

The men of Athens bitterly agreed to accept the goddess as their patron. But being poor losers, they levied three heavy requirements on the women: that they should forgo being called citizens, that they should no longer vote, and that their children should be called by their fathers' rather than their mothers' names.

They then prepared a new identity for the city's goddess. They claimed that she was a virginal goddess without sexuality, a motherless goddess who sprang full-grown from the head of Zeus, who had swallowed her mother Metis. This Athena was "all for the father" (as Aeschylus had her say), who voted on the side of the new patriarchal order against the earlier system of mother right. But hidden in the legend of the Athenian vote are clues to Athena's original identity. If children did not bear their mothers' names, if women were not full citizens, if women did not vote, why bother to legislate against it?

There was yet another version of the birth of Athena, one that is far less flattering to male divinity. This story says that she was the daughter of Pallas, a winged giant. He tried to rape his virginal daughter, so she killed him. She tanned his skin to make a shield and cut off his wings to fasten to her feet. Another myth in which Athena's virginity is threatened says that Hephaestus, the smith god, attempted to rape her, but only managed to ejaculate on her leg. The goddess wiped it off in disgust. But the semen touched all-fertile Gaia, whereupon a half-serpent boy named Erichthonius was born. Athena accepted the boy as her offspring and gave him to the Augralids to guard.

A curious part of this relatively obscure story is the snaky nature of the boy. As Hephaestus had no known reptile ancestors, it must be that Athena provided the serpent blood. Her intimate connection with Medusa, whose snake-haired visage Athena wears on her goat-skin cloak called the aegis, is also relevant. Similarly, the massive snake that reared beside her statue in the Parthenon, her major temple on the Athenian Acropolis, suggests that the snake was one of the primary symbols of the virgin goddess.

It is now well established that Athena—her name is so ancient that it has never been translated—was originally a Minoan or Mycenaean household goddess—possibly related to the barebreasted Cretan figures seen embracing snakes or holding them overhead. This original Athena was the essence of the family bond, symbolized by the home and its hearth—and by the mild serpent who, like a household cat, lived in the storehouse and protected the family's food supplies against destructive rodents. As household goddess, Athena ruled the implements of domestic crafts: the spindle, the pot, and the loom. By extrapolation, she was the guardian of the ruler's home, the goddess of the palace; by further extrapolation, she was the symbol of the community itself, the larger social unit based on countless homes.

Although Minoan civilization declined, Athena was not lost. A maiden goddess, apparently called Pallas, arrived with the Greeks; she was a warrior, a kind of Valkyrie, a protector of the tribe. This figure was bonded to that of the indigenous tribal symbol to form Pallas Athena, and her legend was re-created to suit the new social order. But Athena's ritual recalled her origins. Each year at midsummer her splendid image was taken from her temple on the Acropolis and borne ceremoniously down to the sea. There Athena was carefully washed and, renewed in strength and purity, was decked in a newly made robe woven by the city's best craftswomen. It was the same ritual that honored Hera and showed Athena as a woman's deity—the mistress of household industry and family unity.

Atira   To the Pawnee, the omniscient earth was the mother of life and death; she both fed the living and embraced the dead. Uniting with the god of heaven, Atira brought forth life in the form of a daughter, Uti Hiata ("mother corn").

So sacred was Atira that the heroic Smohalla, upholding traditional Pawnee values under pressure from white invaders, asked rhetorically: "You ask me to dig for stone—shall I dig under her skin for her bones? Then when I die I cannot enter her body to be born again. You ask me to cut grass and make hay and sell it—but how dare I cut off my mother's hair? It is a bad law, and my people cannot obey it."

Atse Estsan   The first woman of Navaho religion was born in the darkness of the First World and gradually rose to the surface of our Fifth World. To do so, she passed with the first man and the trickster god Coyote through the Second World, where a man assaulted her. Coyote called together the other dwellers in the Second World, and all determined to climb farther, to the Third World.

There, in a lake-filled mountain territory, Atse Estsan and the others met a water monster named Tieholtsodi, whose children Coyote stole. The monster, unable to find his offspring but suspecting that they were in the mountains, began to raise the level of his lake. The people piled all the world's four mountains atop each other, so that they almost reached the sky. Still the waters rose until they reached the feet of the animals and people who, climbing up a water weed that punctured the sky, gained the Fourth World.

There a great argument arose between men and women. The women claimed social precedence because they were the fire makers, the childbearers, and the planters. The men contended that because they hunted and danced, they were the more important sex. The alienated sexes went their separate ways. But within four years, weary of their isolation, they agreed to reunite.

During this time the water monster's lake had been slowly seeping into their land. Finally, Tieholtsodi's waters turned the soil to mud, and the lake again rose about them. A long reed was again lifted to pierce the sky, and everyone climbed through to the Fifth World. And what did they find but the bottom of a lake! The Locust volunteered to find a way out, and passing through the ordeals set for him by the many-colored swans who lived on the lake, he brought forth the people. Behind them was the monster Tieholtsodi, in hot pursuit of his children.

Until then the people did not know that in Coyote's pack were the water monster's children. Discovering his theft, the people forced Coyote to toss back the monster babies, and the underworld waters retreated. Then Atse Estsan and her people built the earth as we know it, with its changing seasons, its moving luminaries, and the death of its inhabitants.

But the humans from the Third World grew haughty and selfish in the Fifth World. Atse Estsan began to create monsters to plague them: the giant Yeitso, the man-eating antelope Delgeth, and others. After a time, the goddess felt her people had been punished enough and she brought them a reward: the goddess Estsanatlehi, the Navaho savior, the wife of the sun. Leaving her on the Fifth World to combat the dangers facing her people, Atse Estsan retreated to the eastern sky where she still lives.

Auchimalgen   This kindly moon goddess was the divinity of the Araucanians of Chile, who believed that she protected them from her not-so-kindly subject-spirits. Auchimalgen was a seer, foretelling great events by changing the color of her face.

Au-Co   In Vietnam, Lady Au-Co was an immortal queen who lived in the mountains while her consort, the dragon king, lived in the ocean. Au-Co created humanity in a unique way: she gave birth to a sticky pouch from which, after a week, a hundred eggs emerged. The parents divided the hatched offspring between them; thus some Vietnamese people live in the highlands, others by the sea.

Audbumbla Before this world, the Scandinavians said, there was a land of frost in the north, a land of constant fire in the south, and between them a gulf of elemental chaos. The interaction of heat and cold, expansion and contraction, eventually formed two creatures: Audbumbla, the cow rich in milk, and an evil man named Ymir, who sweated forth offspring from his armpits and feet while nursing at the teats of the divine cow. Audbumbla herself needed nothing but the salty ice of chaos, which she converted into four great rivers of milk on which Ymir fed.

Eons passed as the great cow browsed the ice fields for her food. One day, under her thirsty tongue, a hard spot appeared in the ice. It was the head of a man born of the ice just as Audbumbla had been. She licked the ice, freeing first one part, then another, of the man who after three days was free. This was Bur, grandfather of the great god Odin, and with his icy birth the world we know began.

Augralids Long before Athena came to rule the city that bore her name, there were other native goddesses in Attica. Pre-Hellenic residents worshiped a trinity of goddesses, the Augralids: Agraulos, the mother or oldest sister, and the "dewy sisters," Herse and Pandrosos. Apparently they were goddesses of the earth and its produce, signifying the social organization of the people who lived on the land. As the centuries brought social and political change to the area, the religion also changed until the ancient goddesses were bonded to the new city ruler by a complex myth.

The Augralids, it was then said, were entrusted by the goddess Athena with a box that they were told to guard but not to open. The goddesses performed their task as instructed—for a while. Eventually curiosity overtook them, and they peeked into the box, discovering the terrible snake son of Athena, Erichthonius ("earthborn one"). (This, clearly, happened while Athena was still a fertile earth mother, before her transformation into a motherless virgin.) The myth then loses its way in theological complexities, for all of the following are said to have happened: Agraulos and Herse threw themselves in terror off the Acropolis; Agraulos was turned into a stone; and Agraulos was appointed Athena's first priestess. However distorted their legend became, the remnants of the Augralids' worship lasted into the days of Athens' glory.

Aura A maiden who followed Artemis through the wildwood, Aura caught the fancy of the wine god Dionysus. But she spurned him, true to her vow of chastity, until he turned to Aphrodite. No one can resist the love goddess. And so Aura became a Maenad, bearing twin sons to the god.

Artemis had not forgotten her, however, nor had she forgotten Aura's vow of chastity. In punishment, Artemis caused her to go mad. And so, in the intoxication of the Dionysian rituals, Aura killed and ate one of her newborn children. Then, despairing, she drowned herself.

There are several similar tales told of the impassioned Maenads, and several interpretations offered. Some see infanticide as a symptom of the negative feminine, usually controlled but unleashed in the Dionysian religion; others, as a clue to the tremendous oppression that was apt to explode into violence, under which Greek women lived; still others, as a spiritual convulsion in which women, perhaps sacrilegiously, impersonated the great goddess of death and rebirth.

Aurora The Roman dawn goddess of whom the same tales are told as of the Greek Eos, her name means "light."

Austrine "Lady of the morning star," the daughter of the Baltic goddess Saule who was raped by the moon man Menesis, she formed a trinity with Breksta and Zleja.

Averna The Queen of the Dead, according to the Romans, bore this name, which derives from the underworld river Avernus. She may have originally been a separate goddess from Persephone, called Proserpina in Italy.

Aveta   The ancient Celts saw water as an aspect of the sacred feminine. Such water goddesses took two major forms: they were healers, or they were ancestral mothers whose river forms represented the territory of their children. One such goddess was honored at the famous healing spring of Trier in Germany; the fact that she was depicted as a nursing mother suggests that she had the role of a tribal ancestress.

Avfruvva   This mermaid goddess of the Finnish Saami performed a very important task for them: at appropriate times, she gathered schools of fish and herded them into the mouths of rivers, then led them upstream to their spawning ground.

Awitelin Tsita   A "fourfold vessel," the earth was a mother to the Zuni of the American Southwest as to most people in the world. She was thought to lie in constant intercourse with her lover the sky, until she filled her four wombs with his seed. Then she withdrew to carry and birth her children—the human race.

But men and women, confused by the new world around them, needed more than life from their mother. So she gave them directions to find their way around her surface; mountains, so that the land's divisions would be clear; clouds filled with rain, so that the earth's surface might bloom. Challenged by her generosity, the sky father waved beneficial lights over the earth dwellers. Thereafter the Zuni lived in a happy world, well provided for by their immortal parents.

Azer-Ava   The Mordvins were a Finno-Ugric people who settled in eastern Russia with their pantheon of nature divinities. Azer-Ava, the rain-bringing sky goddess, was one of the most important. Her name, meaning "mistress," appeared in many other goddesses' names, suggesting that her people saw her as one goddess in a number of different guises.

The Mordvins invoked a goddess for each place they occupied and had a name as well for each natural phenomenon. Around the settled areas there were Jurt-Azer-Ava, the goddess of the home, and Ban-Ava, the ruler of the outhouse. Farther afield we find Norov-Ava, the corn mistress, and Nar-Azer-Ava, the meadow spirit. On an even larger scale were Mor-Ava, the sea mother; Varma-Ava, the wind woman; and Tol-Ava, the spirit of fire.

A few of the goddess' most important forms were Mastor-Ava, the earth mother herself; the women's goddess, Niski-Ava; and the very ancient Otsuved-Azer-Ava. Mastor-Ava was the goddess in her most honorable form, the ruler of the earth and all its dwellers; sacrifices were offered to her by the entire community at agricultural holidays. Niski-Ava, now generally confounded with the Virgin Mary, was a form of the goddess worshiped by women in the privacy of their homes. Otsuved-Azer-Ava (or simply Ved Ava) was the spirit of moisture who made the earth ready to bear fruit; she resided in a different form in each different body of water, just as Niski-Ava took a different form for each woman's body she occupied.

One of the most delightful forms that Azer-Ava took was Vir-Ava or Vir-Azer-Ava, the forest mother. She assumed a different shape for each forest, often looking very much like a tree. A friendly goddess, she welcomed berry pickers and mushroom hunters, directing them to the best foraging areas if gifts were left for her. Hunters, too, prayed to her for luck in the hunt and protection against accidental injury and death. The energy of the forest hostess stretched out to the fields nearby; if the right kind of attention was paid her, she would increase the crop yield for her worshipers. It was rumored that communal festivals, at certain trees that enjoyed gifts of money and food, had good results.

Ba'Alat Her name means "Lady" or "Our Lady" and is equivalent to that of the god Baal ("Lord"). The chief deity of the Phoenicians, she was sculpted as a heavily built naked woman whose hands supported her mature breasts, a sign of her generosity toward the children of earth. When dressed, she was a stylish matron in a shoulder-strapped tight robe and an elaborate Egyptian hairstyle. The Sumerians called her the "wise old lady" of the trees; this connection of goddess and tree was common in the ancient Near East.

Baba Yaga The "old woman" of autumn was called Baba by the Slavic inhabitants of eastern Europe, Boba by the Lithuanians. This seasonal divinity lived in the last sheaf of grain harvested annually, and the woman who bound it would bear a child that year. Baba passed into Russian folk legend as the awesome Baba Yaga, a witchlike woman who rowed through the air in a mortar, using a pestle for her oar, sweeping the traces of her flight from the air with a broom. A prototype of the fairytale witch, Baba Yaga lived deep in the forest and scared passersby to death just by appearing to them. She then devoured her victims, which is why her picket fence was topped with skulls. Behind this fierce legend looms the figure of the ancient birth-and-

death goddess, one whose autumn death in the cornfield led to a new birth in spring.

Bachue The great ancestor goddess of the Chibcha, who lived in what is now Colombia, was Bachue or Turachoque. At first she lived beneath the waters of a huge lake, but one day she decided to live on land and rose from the waves, hand in hand with her young son. Raising him to manhood beside the lake, Bachue then had intercourse with him to produce the human race. Teaching her offspring civilized manners and religious rites suitable to her divinity, Bachue finally satisfied herself that her human children could live without her. Transforming herself and her son-husband into dragons, Bachue returned with him to their original home.

Badb One of the forms of the Morrigan, the great Irish war goddess, Badb (pronounced "beeve") usually took the form of a hooded crow, although she sometimes haunted battlefields disguised as a wolf, a bear, or a heifer. When she took human form, she was a gigantic woman who straddled a river. One foot on each bank, Badb washed the clothing and armor of the men she had doomed to die in battle. When she lowered her hands to the water, it ran red with blood; when she raised them, the water disappeared entirely, leaving a fordable crossing.

Ban Naomha Kilna-Greina in Ireland's County Cork was the ancient well of the sun, a place of prophecy and wisdom. In it swam Ban Naomha, a magical trout invisible to all save the second-sighted. You could force the fish goddess to show herself—thus permitting you to ask any question and be answered truthfully—by taking three drinks from the well three times, crawling around the well three times between drinks, and laying a stone the size of a dove's egg on the altar with each circle. At the end of the ritual, and ready with your question, stare into the well to catch your glimpse of the wisdom trout.

Banba "Land unplowed for a year" is the meaning of this Irish earth goddess' name. With Eriu and Folta she formed the triad of ancient rulers of the island. A talented sorceress, she met the Mile-sians—a mythic race of invaders—at the Slieve Mish Mountains in Kerry, the farthest southwest county in modern Ireland; there she unsuccessfully tried to prevent their occupation of the country.

Banka-Mundi Among the Khond in India, she was a hunting goddess; merely uttering her name made one fearless against jungle beasts.

Banshee Her gray cloak covering a green dress, with streaming hair and eyes, the Banshee or spirit woman is still said to appear to Irish families to foretell the coming death of one of its members. Sometimes she chooses not to be seen, instead conveying her message of bereavement by pro-ducing an unearthly keening sound outside the window. When more than one Banshee is heard or seen, a great person faces death.

Barbata "The Bearded" may seem a strange name for a goddess, but bearded goddesses are far from unknown. This name was applied to late classical Mediterranean statues showing a divinity who wore female attire but had obvious facial hair. Often, she was called Venus, after the Roman god-dess of love and infatuation. The statues may rep-resent either festivals in which cross-dressing was required or an androgynous deity.

Barbmo-Akka This goddess of the Saami controlled the migratory paths of birds, whose arrival and departure marked the coming of spring and fall, respectively, in the subarctic of western Lappland.

Bardaichila This storm goddess of the North Indi-an Assamese created gales when she traveled from her airy homeland to earth for the festival of Bohag Bihu; thus it was traditional to speak of the two storms, one just before, one immediately after, the annual event.

Bast She originated in the Nile delta, but by 930 B.C.E., the power of Bast was acknowledged by all Egyptians, even those a thousand miles south of her original home. At first she was a lion goddess of sunset, symbolizing the fertilizing force of the sun's rays. Later her image grew tamer: she became a cat carrying the sun, or a cat-headed woman who bore on her breastplate the lion of her former self.

Bast ruled pleasure and dancing, music and joy. At the city of Bubastis ("house of Bast"), the center of her worship, great celebrations were held. Boatloads of worshipers—hundreds of thousands of them, Herodotus said—were greet-ed by pleasant flute melodies as they debarked for a worship service combined with a vast trade fair. Bast's followers believed that in return for this reverent celebration Bast bestowed both mental and physical health.

As part of Bast's worship, Egyptians honored live cats. Domesticated (if cats can ever truly be said to be domesticated) during the early period of agriculture, cats were useful to keep down the rodent population and therefore to assure a stable diet for humans. Egyptians cherished their cats, often decking them with golden earrings or other jewelry. When they died, the cats were mummified and buried in the vast cat cemetery at Bubastis.

Bau She emerged into history as a sky goddess (praised as "eldest of heaven"), bearing a name that means "space." In early times, Bau was the mother goddess of Babylonia and Phoenicia, a life-giving figure who appeared in each morning's light. But she merged with Gatamdug, then with Gula, and the separate identities of these goddesses became lost, with only Gula surviving the process.

Baubo Her name means "belly," and Baubo was the Greek goddess of belly laughter, the kind that indecent gestures and suggestive jokes provoke. Baubo was sculpted as a headless and limbless body, with her genitals forming a bearded mouth and her breasts staring like eyes. She was the sister or double of Iambe, the goddess of indecent speech, and a similar story is told of both: the weeping Demeter, searching the earth for her lost Persephone, reached the coastal town of Eleusis and there, convulsed with sorrow, sat down by a deep well. Baubo came to draw water and, touched by the goddess' sorrow, tried to console her. But Demeter refused her sympathy. So Baubo lifted her skirts and exposed her vulva. Demeter's sorrow was broken by a smile; the sterile earth stirred; soon Persephone returned. (Almost the same tale is told in Japan of Uzume and the sun goddess Amaterasu.) That such a minor character should have such power over the great goddess seems unlikely to some, who contend that Baubo is really a form of Hecate, the night-riding goddess of mystery and power who also plays other significant parts in Demeter's legend.

Bean Nighe A woman who dies in childbirth, say the Irish and the Highland Scots, better not leave laundry unfinished; otherwise, she will be forced to remain on earth as a ghost, washing linens until the day she would have died of old age. These Washers at the Ford are a form of the Banshee, foretelling imminent death when they appear to human eyes. The Bean Nighe is described as a

Sacred to the goddess Bast, the cat was depicted in innumerable Egyptian sculptures such as this bronze from the twenty-sixth dynasty. A crystal scarab on the cat's head and a magical eye on its chest make this an especially beautiful artifact, displayed in the Bast shrine in The Field Museum.

small woman dressed in green, with red webbed feet, one nostril, and one tooth. Her breasts are very long and, if you can grab and suck one of them, you will be granted any wish. Like other water spirits, the Bean Nighe are prophets; if you meet one, you can ask her three questions, which she will answer. However, she will ask you three questions in return, and if you lie in answering her, things will go badly for you thereafter.

Bebhionn As huge as she was beautiful, this supernatural woman was from Maiden's Land, the Isle of Women, far off the Irish west coast. Some legends say she was originally an underworld goddess and a patron of pleasure, that she traveled surrounded by magical birds, and that she knew all the powers of healing. Another legend says that she came from her magical island to live with the king of the Isle of Man. But he soon proved brutal and she, rather than endure his beatings, headed home. The king pursued and killed Bebhionn.

Becuma In Irish legend, this goddess of the magic boat was one of the earliest divinities of the island, one of the Tuatha de Danaan, the people of the goddess Danu. She lived in the heart of the country on the magic Hill of Tara, where by sleeping with her a king could gain sovereignty over the countryside. The Tuatha de Danaan ostracized the beautiful goddess for this behavior, but they could not change the tide of history, for the kings remained and the Tuatha were banished from their green homeland.

Befana A figure of Italian folk legend, she is the "lady of twelfth night" in Rome, where custom still calls for an image of an old woman made of rags to be hung outside the home on January 5, probably to witness the passing of winter's deepest darkness.

Beiwe This Saami goddess of Lappland traveled with her daughter Beiwe-Neida through the sky in an enclosure of reindeer antlers. In the Arctic spring, she brought back greenness to the land, making new plants grow so that reindeer could prosper and reproduce. At each solstice her worshipers sacrificed white female animals, the meat of which was threaded on a stick, then bent into rings and tied with bright ribbons. When she was invoked, a special prayer was always said for the insane; Rafael Karsten explains that madness was thought to be caused by Beiwe's winter absence.

On the day when light first appeared in the Arctic, the Saami smeared their doors with butter so Beiwe could eat the rich food with her hot beams and begin her yearly recovery. On summer solstice, "sun rings"—twists of leafy branches—were hung about and butter "sun porridge" was sacramentally eaten. Prayers were offered that the sun virgin would "pour her merciful rays over the reindeer, and everything else."

Belit-Ilani A Babylonian title meaning "mistress of the gods," Belit-Ilani was the name of the evening star of desire. Some consider it a title of Astarte, some of Ninlil, some of Nintud. In any case, Belit-Ilani is inscribed on portraits of the goddess as a woman who bears on her left arm a babe that she suckles, blessing the child with her right hand.

Belit-Seri In Babylonian theology, she was the scribe of the afterlife who kept records of all human activities. The lady of the underworld wilderness, she squatted in front of the queen of the dead to call out judgments on the lives of the newly deceased.

Bellona Often described as a feminine shadow of the god Mars, Bellona was actually much more, for her domain included the entire arena of conflict, diplomatic as well as military. Even her name shows her importance, for the Latin word for war, *bellum*, derives from her name.

In the temple of this serpent-haired goddess who bore a bloody lash, the Romans began and ended their military campaigns. Before Bellona's temple, her priest began a war by raising a ceremonial spear and hurling it into a section of ground that symbolized enemy territory. When the war was finished, it was in Bellona's temple that the Senate determined the best reward for the victorious generals. And during wars as well as in peacetime, the Senate used Bellona's temple to receive the ambassadors of countries in conflict with Rome.

When Roman divinities began to be identified with those of the countries Rome conquered, Bellona found herself assimilating the Cappadocian goddess Mah, a late form of the Sumerian Mami. Both symbolized territorial sovereignty and both represented the armed conflict necessary to defend claims to rulership. The Roman goddess was called Mah-Bellona in the later days of the Roman Empire. She was associated as well with the Erinys (Furies) and with Discordia.

Bendis A Thracian goddess whose worship traveled south to Greece, Bendis was depicted holding a twig, which was said to grant passage to the underworld. Her name meant "to bind" and is said to indicate her supervision of marriage. Yet her orgiastic rituals seem quite contrary to the usual idea of marriage. Later, her religion was somewhat tamed, with torch races and processions substituting for other more amorous rites.

Bentakomari A water goddess of the North Indian Assamese, she was owed the first fish caught each season.

Benten Among the seven Japanese divinities of good luck, only one was a goddess: Benten, who brought inspiration and talent, wealth and romance to those who honored her. Benten was also queen of the sea, a dragon woman who swam in state through her domain with a retinue of white snakes. In her dragon body she protected her devotees from earthquakes by mating with the monstrous snakes who thrashed under the Japanese islands. But she could also wear the form of a lovely human woman, and in this form she was usually portrayed, mounted on a dragon who was both her steed and her paramour.

Berecynthia This goddess appears in several ancient texts, but her identity is not clear, although she is clearly connected with the mountain in Anatolia called by her name. The word is used as a title of Cybele, the mountain goddess of that area whose worship spread as far as Rome in classical times.

Beregyni Slavic spirits of female vampires, they hide on lakeshores and in rocky crags, where they capture human victims. They are connected to, or may be a form of, the Rusalky.

Beruryah A Jewish heroine of the 2nd century A.D., she was a judge known for her wise sayings, her wisdom, and her kindness.

Beruth Her name still lives in her city—Beirut—recalling the days when she was high goddess of the Phoenicians, their image of the earth who mothered the human race. It is not known whether her name means "earth," "mother," or "covenant"—an instructive set of possibilities.

Bestla The first woman-shaped female of Scandinavian mythology (the earlier creation goddess was a cow), Bestla received scant notice in the written eddas, except for the mention of her status as the Norse Eve and mother of the great god Odin.

Bhavani One of the common names of the mother goddess of India, Bhavani means "bestower of existence" and is thought to have been the goddess' name in Dravidian languages spoken by non-Indo-European people of the subcontinent. But unlike Durga, Parvati or Kali, the goddess of this name developed no distinguishing legends or attributes, save that she was evoked by women in labor, who burned perfume to honor her.

Bia A warrior maiden of Greek mythology, her name means "force." It was Bia who bound the Titan Prometheus to a rocky crag when he was condemned to perpetual torment for stealing heavenly fire for humanity.

Biblys One of a pair of Greek twins, she fell in love with her brother. But he refused her love and Biblys, tormented and ashamed, was transformed into a constantly weeping fountain.

Biddy A shortened version of the name Bridget, used in Ireland on February 1 when a girl impersonating the goddess-turned-saint (or a group carrying her effigy) went begging from house to house. In Kerry, on the far southwest coast, she sang, "Something for poor Biddy! Her clothes are torn. Her shoes are worn. Something for poor Biddy!" When the group was only young men, who dressed in women's attire, they were called "Biddy boys." Giving food and money to the Biddy callers was thought to bring a good harvest in the following season.

Biddy Mannion   A midwife of Inishshark, a tiny island off the Irish coast, she was stolen from earthly life by the king and queen of the fairies. They had a sickly child, and Biddy's reputation for healing had spread to fairyland. Biddy did indeed bring the child back to life. Returning to her home, Biddy found a fairy double in her place; not even her family had suspected the switch.

Bil   Once she was a human girl, but Bil did not stay long on earth. One morning, she was sent to fetch water with her brother Hjuki. The moonman, still in the sky, saw them, descended to earth, and stole them to be his servants. Thus did Norse mythology record the story, which some scholars say is the same one told in the familiar children's chant "Jack and Jill."

Bila   Among the Australian aboriginals of the Flinders Range, the cannibalistic sun goddess provided light for the world by cooking her victims, dragged into camp by her dogs, over a huge open fire. When the lizardman Kudnu wounded her with his boomerang, she blew up into a ball of fire and disappeared, plunging the world into darkness. When he realized what he had done, Kudnu was frightened and sent his boomerang off into the north to try to recover the sun—but to no avail. Then to the west, and the south—but still no light came forth. The lizardman threw his boomerang to the east, and it carried the sun goddess high above the horizon, then down again in the west, as she does to this day. Because the lizardman saved the world from extinction, the Flinders Range aboriginals never killed a goanna or a gecko.

Bilhah   One of the great matriarchs of Jewish tradition, she was the mother of the tribes of Dan and Naphtali. She was the "handmaiden" of Rachel and her double, sharing her house and her husband. Little is told of her in Hebrew legend; her character presumably was merged with Rachel's.

Biliku   The chief divinity of the Andamanese Islands in the Pacific, Biliku was a complex goddess, both kindly and fearsome. The creator of the earth, sometimes embodied in a spider's form, she was the first to own fire. But the kingfisher stole this magic substance from her and, furious at the sacrilege, Biliku abandoned the earth forever.

Biman Chan   Her name means "sojourn in the moon," and that describes her story as well. This Cambodian heroine was taken up into the sky by the moon, who had fallen in love with her. But he had other wives, who grew jealous of her. Fearful that they might do her ill, Biman Chan begged the moon to take her higher into the sky—but alas, the wind blows strongly there, so strongly that it blew her to pieces. Her head fell to earth, into the pond of a monastery, and there she was brought back to human life.

Bisal-Mariamna   This Shakti of sunlight in Mysore, India, is symbolized by a brass pot full of water called the Kunna-Kannadi or "eye mirror." Pepper leaves and coconut flowers are put into this pot; a small metal mirror leans against it. One of seven sister goddesses, Bisal-Mariamna is worshiped in an unroofed shrine into which sunlight pours.

Black Annis   A blue-faced cannibal with long white teeth who snatched people from their firesides to devour them, this British form of the Cailleach was said to live in a cave in Argyll. There she crouched among the branches of an old pollard oak, the last remnant of her huge forest, which grew out of a cleft in the rock at the mouth of her cave—an opening she dug out with her fingernails.

In Leicester, according to Lewis Spence, Black Annis lived in a round cave in the Dane Hills. Children who dared play there "were warned that Black Agnes, or Annis, lay in wait to snatch them away to her cave, where she would scratch them to death." Annually, it was an early spring custom to drag a dead cat in front of a pack of hounds near Black Annis' bower—originally a ceremonial cat hunt, resulting in the ceremonial killing of the hag of winter.

It is axiomatic that conquered deities survive as devils and monsters, and Black Annis is an example. Although it is probable her origins are pre-Celtic, she may have melded with Danu as Cat Ana, another name for Anu.

The Black Madonna This form of the Christian Virgin Mary may have roots in healing goddesses of Europe from the era preceding Christianization. Usually now found in churches, the images of these sacred mothers are sometimes said to have been altered by fire, as was Germany's Our Lady of Altotting, the Black Mother of God. Other times, however, no explanation is given for the dark visage. As black is often connected with the soil, especially in Slavic countries where these images abound, the darkness of these madonnas reveals their ancient heritage as emblems of fertility. Other famous black goddesses appear at Montserrat in Spain, Einsiedeln in Switzerland, Chartres and Le Puy in France, and Tindari and Enna in Sicily.

One of the most famous Black Madonnas is the Virgin of Jasna Gorna, also called Czestochawa, the Black Virgin of Poland. According to legend, the icon that bears her name was painted by Luke the apostle, who captured Mary on a cedar wood table where Mary dined. St. Helen, mother of the first Christian emperor Constantine, then brought the painting from Jerusalem to Constantinople, from whence it was carried by angels to Poland. A lovely tale, but in fact, the image dates to the thirteenth to fourteenth century C.E., and it is probably a local production, presumably painted by a non-apostle. More legends surround the scar on the cheek of the Madonna: alternatively, it was caused by a Swedish, German or Turkish invader, who slashed the portrait, which bled real human blood. The image inspires a famous pilgrimage each year.

Blathnat "Little flower" was the daughter of Midir, high king of the Irish fairies. She traveled across the island with three cows hitched to her magic caldron, demanding that heroes serve her with feats of superhuman strength. She was apparently a late survival of an early goddess of sex and death, another version living on in Wales as the deceitful queen Blodewedd.

Blodewedd Arianhod, unwilling mother of the Welsh hero Llew Llaw Gyffes, laid a curse on him that he would never have a human wife. So two magicians made Blodewedd from nine kinds of wildflowers, among them meadowsweet, oak, broom, primrose, and cockle. The magicians piled blossom upon blossom to create "Flowerface."

The beautiful Blodewedd was also treacherous. She lived with Llew Llaw for a time. One day, though, she saw a band of hunters pass outside her window and, falling in love with one of them, plotted the death of her husband. Llew Llaw had a magical safeguard. He could be killed only under curious circumstances: in a bath by the side of a river, under a thatched roof over a caldron, while standing with one foot on a deer. Blodewedd set up those circumstances, daring Llew Llaw to stand in his only dangerous position. He took the dare and her hidden lover killed the king.

Blodewedd eventually was found out, captured by the magicians who created her, and turned into an owl. This strange legend, which parallels the Irish story of Blathmat and the Semitic Delilah, seems to record an ancient legend of the goddess, the clues to which are now lost. Some, like Robert Graves, see Blodewedd as a type of May Queen, wedded ritually to the king who would eventually be sacrificed to her. Others see her as a flowery rebel, an image of women's opposition to patriarchal bondage. But it is also possible that the flower goddess of betrayal was simply the goddess of life and death, a form of the earth goddess who, like Ishtar or Cybele, both loved and devoured the living.

Boann Among the Celtic people, rivers were the residences—indeed, the tangible forms—of powerful goddesses of inspiration and fertility. Such was the case in Celtic Ireland, where the goddess of the mighty River Boyne was Boann ("she of the white cows"). It was said that Boann was a curious woman who heard of the magical Well of Segais at the source of the Boyne. There, nine magical hazel trees grew and bore nuts of knowledge. The nuts dropped into the well, where they were eaten by a little salmon—the wisest creature in the world.

Even goddesses were forbidden to approach the grove, but Boann, undeterred, traveled to the Well of Segais. Furious and defensive of its treasure, the well rose from its depths and poured out in a mighty flood, drowning the approaching Boann. But it could never return to its original place deep in the earth, and henceforth had to carry its waters, which brought spiritual and mental food to humans, down across the Irish hills.

Bo Find Before Ireland became renowned as a green isle, when it was still barren and unpopulated, this magical white cow appeared from the western sea, together with the red cow Bo Ruadh and the black cow Bo Dhu. Each headed in a different direction: the black cow to the south, the red cow to the north, and Bo Find to the center of the country. (She may have been a form of Boann, central Ireland's white cow goddess of fertility, called Bouvinda in early Ireland.)

Bo Find stopped twice along her journey to drink: at Loughna-Bo, cow's lake; and at Tober-Bo-Finn, well of the white cow. When she reached the island's center, she gave birth to magical twin calves, one male and one female; from them descended all the cattle the Irish owned for centuries. Then Bo Find, having provided for the island's people, disappeared into the west again, to sink down entranced in a dark cave where she still rests.

Some legends say that Bo Find originally had a human woman's form, but that she could not regain it unless she slept for centuries on the summits of Erin's three highest mountains; even if that magical duty were fulfilled, only an Irish high king would be able to wake her. The ancient divinity of fertility thus survives in Irish folklore,

enchanted beneath the earth, awaiting the signal to return.

Bomong In addition to the Hindu and Buddhist pantheons of India, there are thousands of smaller goddess groups belonging to various ethnic groups. One of these is the Minyong, whose cosmic goddesses were two sisters, Bong and Bomong. Daughters of the earth and sky, they glowed from the moment they were born. Brighter and brighter they grew under the care of their treasured nurse, but when she suddenly died, they died too.

In the prolonged darkness that followed, the earth's creatures grew afraid. Thinking that the nurse had somehow stolen the light, they dug up her body. But it had rotted away—except for the eyes, which held mirror images of Bong and Bomong. The people, thinking they had the goddesses back, took the eyes to a stream and washed them for five days and five nights. Then a carpenter carefully cut the images from the reflecting eyes, and the two girls jumped back to life.

The people did all they could to keep the goddesses with them. But Bomong, dressing herself in her finest jewelry, ran away into the sky. Bong followed her, shining brightly. Together, their intense brilliance made the earth crack and bubble.

People were fainting from the heat, so they sent a frog hunter to kill Bong. He shot her twice, and she fell dead. Her body lay for a long time until a rat dragged it to Bomong who, seeing her sister dead, covered herself with a huge rock in sorrow.

In the darkness that followed, all living beings grew frightened. A rat, a bird and a cock went to find Bomong, who said that she would never return until her sister was revived. In animating the goddess, a carpenter made her smaller so that she could become a moon. Bomong, joyous at her sister's rebirth, rose into the sky in all her splendor, and all the beasts and birds sang out in welcome.

Bona Dea The "good goddess" was originally a descriptive term—some say a mistranslation of the name Damia—but Bona Dea later became the most popular name by which the goddess Fauna or Fatua was known in Rome. She was worshiped only by women, and only in utter secrecy at rites in early December. No men could attend these, and even portraits of men were covered over in the halls of celebration. Conducted by the Vestal priestesses, these events were held at the home of a high-ranking Roman matron and may have been rather bawdy affairs; it is known that the room was decorated with vine branches and that wine flowed freely in honor of the goddess of abundance and of prophecy. The wine was, however, referred to as "milk," for there was a story that Bona Dea had been beaten once for appearing in public intoxicated.

In 62 B.C.E., when the women's festival was in progress at the home of Caesar himself, a certain Publius Clodius disguised himself in women's clothing and invaded the rites; discovered, he was duly prosecuted. The crime caused considerable political upheaval. Unfortunately for curious moderns, the invader kept secret the rites he had illegally witnessed, as did Bona Dea's rightful worshipers.

Brag-srin-mo The ancestral goddess of the Tibetan people once encountered a monkey in yogic meditation. Becoming sexually aroused by seeing the little fellow in this unlikely position, she encouraged him to mate with her. But he claimed a vow of chastity kept him from doing so, until the goddess Tara intervened and explained that his cooperation was necessary for people to be born. Thereafter, Brag-srin-mo ("ogress of the cliffs") bore six little monkeys which, when she fed them special food, lost their tails and fur and became human.

Branwen The "White-Bosomed One" was the Welsh love goddess, sometimes called "the Venus of the northern sea." In The Mabinogion, the Welsh epic, Branwen was said to have been married by her brothers to an Irish chieftain, who, once he got Branwen back to his land, treated her terribly. From the miserable kitchen where she was

enslaved, the goddess sent a trained crow—possibly her spirit or familiar, for sometimes her name is translated "white crow"—across the waters to alert her brothers to her predicament. They launched a massive campaign to get her back, paying dearly in lives to reclaim Branwen.

Breksta In Lithuania, three goddesses ruled the passing hours: Austrine, the dawn; Zleja, high day; and Breksta, the darkness. They may all be forms of the great sun mother Saule.

Brigantia In Celtic Ireland, Brigid was one of the greatest of goddesses, and the Celtic Britons worshiped the same goddess as Brigantia. Ancestral goddess of the people that bore her name, the Brigantes, she was especially worshiped in Yorkshire; her presence is memorialized in the names of the rivers Briant in Anglesey and Brent in Middlesex. It is possible that she was never envisioned in human form, worshiped instead—as are other Celtic water goddesses—as the power of the rushing rivers and thrusting hills of her countryside.

Brigid Probably the clearest example of the survival of an early goddess into Christian times is Brigid (pronounced "breed"), the great triple goddess of the Celtic Irish who appeared as Brigantia in England, Bride in Scotland, and Brigandu in Celtic France. So entrenched was the devotion of the Irish to their goddess that the Christians "converted" her along with her people, calling her Bridget, the human daughter of a Druid, and claiming she was baptized by the great patriarch St. Patrick himself. Bridget took religious vows, the story went on, and was canonized after her death by her adoptive church, which then allowed the saint a curious list of attributes, coincidentally identical to those of the earlier goddess.

The Christian Bridget, for instance, was said to have had the power to appoint the bishops of her area, a strange role for an abbess, made stranger by her requirement that her bishops also be practicing goldsmiths. The ancient Brigid, however, was in one of her three forms the goddess of smithcraft. Brigid also ruled poetry and inspiration, carrying for this purpose a famous caldron; her third identity was as a goddess of healing and medicine. Not surprisingly, the Christian Bridget was invoked both as a muse and as a healer, continuing the traditions of the goddess.

There were three Brigids, who were probably never construed as separate goddesses but as aspects of one divinity; unlike other triple goddesses, they were identical, not aging through the typical maiden-mother-crone sequence. The Brigids were unified in the symbol of fire, for her name means "bright arrow," or simply the "bright one." Almost into modern times, the ancient worship of the fire goddess Brigid continued at her sacred shrine in Kildare, where nineteen virgins tended the undying fire and where, on the twentieth day of each cycle, the fire was miraculously tended by Brigid herself. There, into the eighteenth century, the ancient song was sung to her: "Brigid, excellent woman, sudden flame, may the bright fiery sun take us to the lasting kingdom." But for more than ten centuries, the Bridget invoked was a saint rather than a goddess; her attendants, nuns rather than priestesses.

The Irish said that the goddess Brigid brought to humanity a number of useful things, including whistling, which she invented one night when she wanted to call her friends. And when her beloved son was killed, Brigid invented keening, the mournful song of the bereaved Irishwoman. This story draws her close to the great mother goddesses of the eastern Mediterranean, and like them, Brigid was identified with the earth herself and with the soil's fertility.

Ritual, that most conservative of forces, preserved Brigid's name and symbols for more than 1,000 years after she ceased to be acknowledged as a goddess. But little is left of the legends told of one of the greatest of all Celtic goddesses, a deity so high that her brass shoe was the most sacred object that could be imagined, a divinity so intensely related to the feminine force that no man was allowed to pass beyond the hedge surrounding her sanctuary.

Some rituals and legends suggest that Brigid's history may date back even beyond the era of the Celts—that she may have taken on some of the aspects of an even more ancient seasonal goddess of the pre-Celtic inhabitants of Ireland and Scotland. In the latter, a series of stories relate how the Cailleach kept a maiden named Bride imprisoned in the high mountains of Ben Nevis. But her own son fell in love with the girl and, at winter's end, he eloped with her. The hag chased them across the landscape, causing fierce storms as she went, but finally she turned to stone as Bride was freed. In such stories, which may date back as far as 2,000 to 3,000 years, Brigid becomes a surrogate for a spring/summer goddess whose rule over the land alternated with that of a fall/winter hag. Similarly, the fact that the massive sandstones called sarsens, used in the building of such ancient pre-Celtic monuments as Stonehenge and Avebury, are called Bridestones, suggests that Brigid's identity as a primary goddess caused her name to be used of Neolithic (late Stone Age) divinities of the area.

Britomartis Early Crete boasted an elaborate and wealthy culture based on the worship of the female principle of nature, embodied in such goddesses as Rhea and Ariadne. But when the patriarchal Greeks overran the island, the theology of the early settlers was passed through the distorting prism of the invaders' sensibility. Cretan goddesses were demoted to heroines, and their legends were grafted onto those of Greek heroes. The complex symbolism and imagery that expressed Minoan theological insights were, in the main, reinterpreted or misunderstood.

In some cases, a goddess' picture and name are still known, but scanty legendary material survives to explain her original symbolic and psychological significance. Such a figure is Britomartis ("sweet girl"), whom some scholars suspect was the greatest goddess of Minoan Crete. We know little of her except how she was traditionally depicted: a young, lithe, and strong hunter, often carrying arrows.

This image was given as a spoil of war to the invading goddess Artemis, and it remained for 2,000 years the traditional depiction of that Greek deity. But Britomartis also had as her companions a suckling babe and a snake, two powerful symbols of the generative force that were never identified with the moon goddess to whom the Cretan divinity was assimilated.

What little we know of Britomartis' myth is sketchy but suggestive. Minos of Crete, it was said, intended to rape the virginal goddess. He chased her for nine months through the forested island, but she finally eluded capture by flinging herself off a high cliff into the ocean. There she was miraculously saved, caught in the fishnets that she herself had invented as a gift to humanity.

After this, the goddess was called Dictynna ("netted one"), some sources say; others claim the great Cretan goddess was Britomartis in the eastern end of the island, Dictynna in the west. But the story that joins them, with its pursuit that lasted the length of a human pregnancy and its rebirth from the sea, suggests that this goddess, in Crete's labyrinthine theology, symbolized the integrity of the feminine soul and the promise of salvation or rebirth.

Brizo This goddess, worshiped on the Greek isle of Delos, was a prophet who specialized in revealing the meaning of dreams. She was also a goddess of the sea, invoked to protect ships and their crews, and honored with images of boats.

Bronach This goddess is a form of the Cailleach known in the west of Ireland, especially in the rocky northern Burren near the famous Cliffs of Moher. One of the highest of these cliffs is Hag's Head, or Ceann Cailighe. Bronach's title, Cailleach Cinn Boirne, means "the hag of Black Head," another of the Moher Cliffs.

Broxa In Jewish folklore, a name for the nightstalker Lilith as a nightjar, a bird believed to suck the milk of goats while the family sleeps.

Brunissen "The Brown One" was the fairy queen of Provence in France, hailed in song and story. She was a young orphan who could not stop weeping over her lost family. Seven years she wept, constantly, exhaustingly: four times each day, three times every night. Only bird-song could ease her sorrow, which suggests that she was derived from a continental Celtic bird goddess like Rhiannon in Wales. Finally, the birds eased her grief completely, and she lived thereafter in peace in her palace Monbrun, "dark mountain."

Brynhild She was a shieldmaiden, a woman warrior, when she first encountered the hero Sigurd Fafnirsbane, who desperately desired her. But this Norse heroine, aware that the Norns (Fates) opposed their love, refused to sleep with Sigurd. His constant pleas, however, finally wore down her resolve, and the result of their union was a daughter named Aslaung.

Sigurd would not stay with Brynhild, however; he wandered south of the Rhine where he met with the powerful sorceress Grimhild. Knowing how great a hero he would become, Grimhild wanted him as spouse for her daughter Gudrun. Sigurd protested that he was promised to Brynhild, but the sorceress drugged him so that he forgot his promise. Soon Grimhild had her way: Sigurd and Gudrun were wed.

Grimhild next decided that she wanted Brynhild for her son Gunnar, whom she sent off to gain the warrior maiden. Impossible: she was lying in a trance surrounded by a ring of fire. (In some versions, she was on a glass mountain; other stories confound her with the Valkyrie named Sigurdrifta.) Gunnar could not get his horse to cross the barrier; he tried mounting Sigurd's magic horse but still could not cross through the flames. So Sigurd magically exchanged identities with his brother-in-law and passed safely through the fire.

There he slept for three nights—albeit without having intercourse—with Brynhild, marrying her while still in Gunnar's body.

Sigurd then resumed his usual appearance, but the interlude had restored his memory and he was thereafter miserable with Gudrun. Gudrun, for her part, hastened the end of this unhappy story by teasing Brynhild with the information that she'd actually married Sigurd in Gunnar's body; Brynhild's heart was embittered toward her former lover because of the trick. When, urged on by Gudrun, Gunnar killed Sigurd, Brynhild laughed with hysterical joy. Then, remembering the fated link between them and the depth of her love for Sigurd, she committed suicide quietly by piercing her chest with a dagger. The lovers were burned on the same pyre.

Buan   This Irish heroine had the psychic power of understanding her husband, Mes Gegra, after his death. When his severed head was brought home to her, she asked it questions about how he was killed, translating the faint reddening and whitening of the flesh to gain her answer. Understanding that he had died by treachery, she cried herself to death. The magical hazel tree Coll Buana grew from her grave as testimony to the steadfastness of her love.

Budhi Pallien   A forest goddess of the Assamese in North India, she appears in the shape of a tiger roving through the jungle.

Bugady Enintyn   Her name includes the word which, to her worshipers among the Evenki of Siberia, meant sky, universe, and homeland—for familiar land and the sky above it constituted the whole universe for these people. The mythic mother of the clan, Bugady Enintyn lived beneath sacred rocks or in the roots of sacred trees. There, she swallowed the soul of the shaman at initiation, providing the route for rebirth in animal form and eventual return to serve as healer.

Bugady Musun   Among the Evenki of Siberia, this mother of animals was imagined as a very old, very strong woman. In her animal form, she was a huge female elk or a wild reindeer. She ruled all life, from the plants of the taiga to the food supplies of her villagers. Because of her connection with food, it was proper to offer bits of meat and especially fat to her by throwing them into the fire with the prayer, "Eat to satiety, do not be angry with us, protect us." She was sometimes worshiped outside the hearth at sacred rocks that looked like petrified elk or reindeer.

Buschfrauen   The "bush women" of central Europe were a little taller than dwarfs, golden-haired and shaggy-skinned, with pendant breasts and hollow backs. They lived in companies in old hollow trees, where they guarded the forests and the kindly people who followed their three rules: never use caraway in baking bread (it makes it impossible for spirits to eat the food), never peel off tree bark (it hurts the tree), and never tell your dreams. They also preferred that you never count dumplings while they're still cooking.

The Buschfrauen had a queen named the Buschgrossmutter, the Grandmother of the Bushes, an ancient white-haired elf with mossy feet. She was constantly pursued by an evil spirit, a wild hunter who would only leave her alone if she sat on a fallen tree marked with three crosses; those walking through the forest who wished her aid blazed the sign of safety on trees they passed. When the Buschfrauen and their queen were pleased, they revealed the secrets of herbs and healing, danced in the fields to make the plants grow, and gave endless magical balls of yarn to knitters. Although it is not known if the Buschfrauen still exist in Europe, the fact that they were said to live only in virgin forests suggests that, if not extinct, they are hard to find.

Caenis   A woman of Thessaly in ancient Greece, Caenis was brutally raped by the sea god Poseidon. Furious and humiliated, she appealed to the gods of Olympus for revenge: transform her, she begged, into an invulnerable man so that she might maim and murder the sex that had injured her. Her wish having been granted, she became a great hero named Caeneus, unstoppable on the battlefield, fierce and destructive. When she died a heroic death, she resumed her female body and original name, and enjoyed a hero's welcome in the afterlife.

Caer   "Yew berry" was an Irish swan maiden who lived on the Lake of Dragon's Mouths, swimming about decked in a golden necklace hung with 130 chains set with golden balls. There Aengus, god of poetry, loved her. Caer lured him into the lake where he, too, became a swan. In that form the pair flew off to Brugh na Boinne—the megalithic monument north of Tara—singing so sweetly that everyone on the island slept for three days and three nights.

Cailleach   Her name, pronounced correctly, sounds like someone clearing her throat, but "coyluck" is a near approximation. One of the world's Great Goddesses, she went by many names: Cailleach Bheur or Carlin in Scotland; Cally Berry in northern Ireland; Cailleach ny Groamch on the Isle of Man; Black Annis in Britain; the Hag of Beare or Digne in Ireland. She was vastly ancient; the Irish Triads say: "The three great ages: the age of the yew tree, the age of the eagle, the age of the Hag of Beare." She could endlessly renew her youth. All the men she loved—and they were countless—died of old age as she went on, returning to the prime of life, finding another pretty young one with whom to share youth.

She had one eye in the middle of a blue-black face, an eye of preternatural keenness. She had red teeth and matted hair "white as an apron covered with hoarfrost." Over it she wore a kerchief and over her gray clothing, a faded plaid shawl. She owned a farm and hired workers for six months with the stipulation that none would be paid who could not outwork her. Looking at the hunched old thing, many a man fell for the trick and paid with his life, dying of overwork while trying to keep the pace she set. So strong was she that she carried boulders in her apron; the ones she dropped became mountain ranges.

She controlled the seasons and the weather; she was the cosmic goddess of earth and sky, moon and sun. Because she does not appear in the written myths of Ireland and Scotland, but only in ancient tales and place names, it is presumed that she was the goddess of the pre-Celtic settlers of the islands off Europe. She was so powerful and beloved that even when newcomers imported their own divinities, the Cailleach was remembered.

Caligo This was the name the Greeks applied to the "vaporous" condition, perceived as feminine, that preceded even primordial chaos. She was Chaos' mother, and by him she became mother of Nyx (night).

Callirrhoe This was the name given to the priestesses of Hera who served her at the Heraion, the great temple of the goddess near the city of Argos.

Callisto In the mountains of provincial Arcadia, this pre-Hellenic goddess personified the force of instinct: in human form, as a lithe young athlete and hunter, racing barefoot through the woods she owned; in animal form, as the powerful and protective mother bear. But the invading Greek tribes had their own image for this energy, and they called her Artemis. A forced merger of the two similar goddesses resulted in the legend that Callisto was a mere nymph, treasured by Artemis but accidentally killed by her. The saddened Greek goddess took on the "Nymph's" name and all her symbols, calling herself Artemis Calliste ("Artemis the fairest").

Cally Berry This was the northern Irish name for the "old gloomy woman," called the winter hag, Cailleach Bheur in Scotland and Caileach Bhera in southern Ireland. She was a spirit of the lakes and protected them from being drained; she also controlled the weather, appearing as a crane with sticks in her beak to forecast storms in Scotland. In Ireland, she was a builder of mountains, wearing an apron full of stones until the ties broke and the rocks fell in gigantic heaps.

Some scholars think that the Highland Cailleach Bheur ("hag of winter") was the same goddess who is called Black Annis in Britain; British researcher Katherine Briggs sees her as a primitive Artemis-type figure who guarded the animals from predators and hunters. She may have had an alternative form as the goddess of spring, for a young maiden appears in a number of stories related to this supernatural crone.

Calva "The Bald" was a title for Venus at Rome, apparently given her in memory of the selfless action of Roman women during a siege against the Gauls. When the soldiers began to fail, the city matrons cut their hair off and wove it into bowstrings for their protectors. In honor of this action, women cut a lock of their hair on their wedding day and sacrificed it to Calva.

Calypso One of the daughters of the ocean, this Oceanid lived on the island of Ogygia. The wandering Greek king Odysseus was shipwrecked there; Calypso was attracted to him and offered Odysseus immortality if he would stay and sleep with her. Odysseus took advantage of Calypso's offer to stay as long as he desired her. Then, after seven years, Odysseus abandoned the disconsolate Calypso on her wave-ringed isle, which some identify as the island of Gozo, off Malta.

Camenae In ancient Italy, these goddesses dwelt in freshwater springs and rivers, their most notable haunt being the sacred spring at the Porta Capena, just outside Rome. Their name means "foretellers," for, like many other feminine water spirits, they were prophetic forces. As Roman divinities were assimilated to those of Greece, the Camenae were seen as a local variation of the Muses. Their festival, the Fontinalia, was celebrated on October 13 by the tossing of good-luck wreaths into wells. Some of the names they bear as individual goddesses are Antevorta, Postvorta, Prorsa, Proversa and Carmenta.

Camilla A legendary Volscian queen of ancient Italy, she appears in Virgil's Aeneid as a warrior dedicated to the service of the virgin goddess Diana. Camilla led their armies against Aeneas and his invading Trojans. On foot and with breasts bare, she fought at the head of the army, but was killed by a spear of the Trojan leader. Some scholars see in her the remnant of a very early territorial goddess with a name meaning "fiery one."

Campe This huge female dragon was set to guard the monster children of the Greek earth mother, Gaia, in their prison beneath her surface, deep in her stony womb.

Candace For at least 800 years, Candace was the name or title of the hereditary queens of the desert empire of Meroe. During the early Roman Empire, Strabo recorded that the reigning Candace was "a masculine sort of woman, blind in one eye." She may have been the same Candace who led an army of 10,000 rebels against the Roman occupation of Egypt. In some traditions, this was the name of the Queen of Sheba who visited Solomon of the Hebrews.

Candi In ancient India, the moon was a male divinity named Chandra. The fierce goddess Durga had a similar name: Candi ("furious"). Over the centuries, the nominal similarity gave rise to the idea that the moon was a goddess. Because this clearly contradicted earlier legend, yet another arose: that the moon was a god one month, a goddess the next.

Canola The inventor of the Irish harp was Canola, one of the most ancient of Eire's deities. She had a disagreement one day with a lover, and so she left his bed to wander the night. Hearing beautiful music, she stopped and sat down; soon she fell asleep in the open air. Wakening to daylight, Canola discovered the music had been made by the wind, blowing through the rotted sinews clinging to the skeleton of a whale. Inspired by the sight and remembering its magical sound, she built the first harp.

Caolainn A form of the Cailleach, she was the ruler of a healing well in County Roscommon of Ireland. A man, it was said, happened to admire this maiden's beautiful eyes, whereupon she gouged them out, throwing them at him. She then groped her way to a sacred spot, where she pulled rushes from the ground. Where the plants were uprooted, water gushed forth; when Caolainn wiped her bloody sockets with the rushes, her eyes grew back. The same story is told of three nearby wells, all devoted to Brigid, who in her "saint" form was said to have gouged out her eyes to avoid marriage.

Cardea Roman religion included many minor goddesses who personified the spiritual value of certain acts, certain times of life, or certain household objects. Cardea was one of these, signifying the hinges of the front door, and therefore the comings and goings essential to family life. She was particularly invoked to protect sleeping children against night-spirits who might harm or kill them.

Carlin "Old woman" was the name of this Scottish spirit of the eve of Samhain—the Celtic festival we call Halloween—the night the year turned to winter, and the ghosts of the dead roamed the world of the living. Into modern times, her effigy—a figure built from the last sheaf of harvested corn—was exhibited to protect farming families from unearthly visitations.

Carman A powerfully destructive witch of Irish legend, she was goddess of malevolent magic and could destroy anything by chanting her spells. She had three destructive sons, with appropriately violent names: Dub ("darkness"), Dother ("evil"), and Dian ("violence"). Not magicians like their mother, they wreaked havoc with their bare hands.

Carman spitefully came to Ireland to lay waste its fields and to blight its corn. But the Tuatha de Danaan, the deities ruled by the goddess Danu, fought against Carman with their most powerful weapons. First, they sent a poet to stop Carman; he failed. Second, a satirist, but he too failed. Third, the sorceress Bechuille, who was able to undo Carman's curses. The sons of the goddess were destroyed and Carman put in chains, where she died of grief. Thereafter, an annual festival was held at her death place to ensure the continued growth of food plants; this suggests that Carman was perceived as a goddess of sterility who needed to be magically propitiated.

Carmenta   Originally there seems to have been one Carmenta, a Roman goddess of prophecy and midwifery; she also brought the art of writing to her land. She was worshiped in magical ceremonies each January 11 and 15, celebrated by the flamines who were her priests. Later there were said to be many Carmentes; they appeared to assist a woman in labor and to tell the future of the newborn.

Carna   Every June 1, at the feast of Calendae Fabrariae, the Romans celebrated this goddess by offering her a soup of beans and bacon, thanking her for helping them maintain good health. Sometimes simply explained as a goddess of food assimilation, Carna was more than that—she was, in fact, the carnal reality of human existence, a personification of the physical processes of survival.

Carravogue   In eastern Ireland in County Meath, a myth was told until early this century of a woman by this name who, because she ate berries on the way to church, became a monstrous snake. St. Patrick was called upon to throw holy water at her, and she dissolved into lakes from which she will someday rise again. The story, says Maire Mac-Neill, can be interpreted in several ways—perhaps it epitomizes Christianity's disdain for the island's original faith and its attempt to destroy it; or perhaps St. Patrick merely stands in for an earlier hero who, at the goddess' urging, banishes the Hag of Winter to bring spring to the earth.

Cartimandua   A legendary British warrior queen who waged war against the Roman Empire, she was the leader of the Brigantes, descendants of the goddess Brigantia.

Carya   Like Callisto, this goddess lost her independent identity as the religion of the great Artemis swept over the Greek provinces. In southern Laconia, of which Sparta was the capital in classical times, the pre-Hellenic settlers perceived the force of nature in trees, where their goddesses (Helen being one) were embodied. But the invading Greeks assimilated these tree divinities into their own Artemis, spirit of the wildwood. The memory of the era's social upheaval was preserved in the legend that Carya ("walnut") died and was transformed into a walnut tree. Artemis then carried the news north that the Laconian "woman" was dead. For this simple task, she was awarded the title of Caryatis ("she of the walnut tree") in a transparent tale of the assimilation of an indigenous goddess' cult.

Caryatids   We are familiar with the name from architecture, for until the nineteenth century builders used columns in the shape of standing women to support roofs. The word comes from the town of Caryae in Greece, where a famous festival of the goddess was held every year. Their dances included statuesque poses that were reputed to have inspired the architectural motif.

Cassandra   The most beautiful of the twelve daughters of Queen Hecuba of Troy, Cassandra was a priestess of the sun who caught the eye of her god. The lust-stricken Apollo promised the maiden that he would grant any wish if she would sleep with him. Cassandra demanded the power of prophecy; Apollo quickly granted the wish. But once she had what she wanted, Cassandra coquettishly refused the god's advances. So Apollo wet Cassandra's lips tenderly with his tongue and disappeared.

After that kiss, Cassandra was cursed. Everything she prophesied was true, but was received as falsehood. Her people, the Trojans, thought her crazy. They ignored her when she warned her brother Paris not to go to Greece; they didn't believe that there were armed soldiers in the wooden horse; they ridiculed Cassandra for saying Troy would lose the war.

When Troy did lose, Cassandra was taken captive to Mycenae as a concubine of the Greek king Agamemnon and was murdered with him. Like many dishonored prophets, however, she was respected after death; in Laconia she was worshiped as the goddess Alexandra ("helper of men").

Cassiopeia   The boastful mother of Andromeda was, like her daughter, turned into a constellation. Of the thirteen stars that bear her name, five support the queen's seated figure and are familiarly known by the name of Cassiopeia's Chair.

Castalia   The power that resided in a spring on Mt. Parnassus, this goddess was apparently a force of artistic inspiration, for the Muses (called "Castalides" in her honor) made her fountain their sacred place.

Cavillaca   The natives of Huarochiri in Peru said that the moon god rolled his sperm into a fruit that this beautiful virgin goddess ate. It impregnated her; she bore a son. On her son's first birthday, Cavillaca gathered all the gods together and demanded to know the boy's father. None would admit to it, so she set the child down on the ground and he crawled to the moon god Coniraya. Feeling ashamed—for the moon was a poor and slovenly god—Cavillaca ran from the gathering with her child. She fled to the coast of Peru, where she turned herself and her child into rocks. The pursuing Coniraya traveled long and far seeking them, but found them too late to prevent the goddess' transformation.

Ceasg   The mermaid of the Highland Scots was said to be half girl, half salmon, and to enjoy affairs with human males, from which sea captains were often born.

Ceibhfhionn   Her name, which looks unpronounceable, sounds rather like Yvonne. In Irish legend, she was a goddess of inspiration, who stood next to the Well of Knowledge, constantly filling a vessel with its water and pouring it out without letting wisdom-seeking humans taste it.

Ceiuci   Along the Amazon River in South America, the story is told that Ceiuci ("famished old woman"), one of the Pleiades come to earth, was having bad luck fishing one day. A shadow fell across her pond; it was a young man. Ceiuci told him to dive into the pool. The young man refused, laughing, and the goddess set a swarm of stinging red ants on him. Quickly, he obeyed her.

Once she had him in the water, Ceiuci snagged the man with her fishing line and put him in her creel. At home, while the goddess was gathering wood to cook her catch, Ceiuci's daughter hid him. When Ceiuci demanded her prey, the girl and the boy ran away, dropping palm branches behind them as they went. These were transformed into animals, the first in this world, which Ceiuci ate, barely stopping her pursuit to taste. Even when all the species had been created, Ceiuci still pursued the runaways. Finally, the girl stopped her flight, but the young man continued through many adventures until he found himself, old and white-haired, at the home of his own mother, who offered the final protection from Ceiuci.

Cerberus   A hybrid of lioness, lynx, and sow, Cerberus was one of the great Greek monsters. Standing at the entry to Hades, she is a typical "guardian at the gates," who in myth and dream challenges anyone passing between two states of consciousness. Before being incorporated into the Greek map of the underworld, Cerberus was one of the calendar beasts of the great pre-Hellenic earth goddess.

Ceres   "Propitiate the mothers of cultivation, Tellus and Ceres," Ovid told his Roman audience, "with their own spelt and the entrails of a pregnant cow. Ceres and Tellus guarantee the same function: one provides the tillages with their origin, the other with their place." The two great earth goddesses of Rome were thus distinguished by the great Roman poet: Tellus was the earth herself, the dark rich soil that lies waiting for the seed; Ceres, however, was the force of vegetable growth personified.

Before Ceres was adopted as the Italian version of the great Greek goddess Demeter, she doubtless had her own identity and legend. But what remains of her today is a Hellenized goddess, of whom Demeter's story is told. To determine her original meaning, we can examine her name, which comes from the same root as our word *create*. And we can study her ritual. She was celebrated each April 19 in the Cerealia, when foxes with burning sticks tied to their tails were set loose in the Roman Circus to dash desperately about while the public cheered them on. This exotic rite has given rise to much speculation, some scholars contending that the ritual was to protect the growing crops from disease, others that it was to assure bountiful harvests by increasing sunshine. In either case, the connection of Ceres and the success of the crop is evident.

But the goddess of growth also took responsibility for its inevitable end. Thus Ceres, a goddess of crop-rich August, when women celebrated secret rituals in her honor, was also a funeral divinity, to whom sacrifice was made to purify homes after death had occurred therein. The force of creation, Ceres was also goddess of the death of plants that makes them edible—and the death of human beings that returns them to Tellus Mater, the earth.

Cerridwen The people of Wales—who call themselves the Cymri or "friends," for the term "Welsh" means "foreigner" in the language of their British neighbors—worshiped this goddess. Cerridwen lived on an island in the middle of Lake Tegid with her two children—the beautiful Creidwy and the ugliest boy in the world, Afagdu. To compensate her son for bestowing such a body on him, the goddess brewed a magical formula that would make her son the most brilliant and inspired of men. For a year and a day, she kept

From Jalisco, in Mexico, came this clay figure of a kneeling woman. Mexican religion today incorporates ancient cultural figures who have been absorbed into Christianity. Some early Mexican goddesses are Chalchiuhtlicue, Chicomecoatl, Coatlicue, Tlazolteotl, Toci, Tonan, and Xochiquetzal.

herbs simmering in her caldron, which she left under the care of a little boy named Gwion.

One day, while the goddess was out collecting more herbs for her brew, a few drops of the bubbling liquid splattered onto Gwion's finger. Scowling in pain, he stuck his hand instantly into his mouth. Miraculously, he was able to hear everything in the world and to understand the secrets of both the past and the future.

His enchanted foresight showed him how angry Cerridwen would be when she found a mere mortal had acquired the inspiration intended for her son. So he ran away; the all-knowing Cerridwen realized what had happened and pursued him.

Gwion changed himself into a hare; Cerridwen pursued him as a greyhound. So they ran: he as a fish, she as an otter; he as a bird, she as a hawk; he as a grain of wheat, she as a hen.

It was in the final form that she caught and devoured him, bearing him nine months later as a child. She threw the baby into the water where he was caught by a prince and grew into the poet Taliesin, the greatest poet in his language. Thus the Welsh expressed their understanding that death and rebirth were necessary for true inspiration to be brought into this world, showing the Muse, the goddess of inspiration, in a somewhat more terrible form than she appears in other cultures.

Cessair After the colonizing Christians arrived in Ireland, the island's ancient legends were altered to incorporate elements from the new tradition. Thus we find some rather strange amalgams of native and imported myth, like the one in which Cessair appears.

She was apparently an early Irish earth goddess, later called a historical woman, who was a granddaughter of Noah and married to a man of the blood of Seth. With this heritage, it was no small feat to get her to Ireland; the annalists simply defied Judeo-Christian tradition by allowing Cessair to survive the flood, along with three men and fifty women, who in three ships plied the deluge waters from Palestine to Eire.

Ireland, of course, was spared the flood—one of the many miracles in the land's mythic history. Cessair and crew arrived, after forty days and the loss of two ships, at Corca Guiny in Ireland. There the last ship was wrecked, and Cessair drowned. So did her daughters Birrin and Blama, along with almost everyone from the ship. Cessair leveled mighty curses at Jehovah as she went down.

Cethlion "Crooked teeth" was a goddess of ancient Ireland who, as queen of the sea people called the Fomorians, prophesied their doom at the hands of the invading Tuatha de Danaan, the children of the goddess Danu.

Ceto This vague figure in Greek mythology was probably the Syrian fish mother Derceto incorporated into Hellenic legend, where little was said of her except that she was a sea goddess. Nonetheless, she was said to have produced some of the most fabulous daughters in Greek legend: the Graeae, with one eye and one tooth between them; the snake-haired Gorgons; the serpent Echidna; and the seductive wind demons, the Sirens.

Chalchiuhtlicue According to the Aztecs, our world is the fifth in a series; the fourth was destroyed by a great flood sent by Chalchiuhtlicue to punish humanity for its wickedness. Before she did so, the goddess built a multicolored bridge into the Fifth World for the righteous—a bridge that reappears

This magnificent stone figure of Chalchihuitlicue, the Aztec water goddess, was found in Mexico City in the early years of the twentieth century.

today, sometimes, as a rainbow. Other versions of the myth say that she turned the elect into fish, so they could swim out the flood. A symbol of metamorphosis, the "jade-skirted goddess" ruled all waters: earth's flowing streams, rain from the heavens, and the nourishing waters used for drinking and baptisms. When painted or sculpted, the goddess was shown decked out in a jade necklace, turquoise earrings, a crown of iridescent blue feathers, and a skirt trimmed with water lilies.

Changing Woman The Apache called the earth goddess by this name, for she never grew old. When her age began to show, she simply walked toward the east until she saw her form coming toward herself. She kept walking until her young self merged with her aging self and then, renewed, returned to her home. Among the Chiricahua Apache, the name of this eternal goddess was Painted Woman.

Chang-O In ancient China it was said that this moon goddess originally lived on earth, where her husband was a famous archer. To honor the man's prowess, the gods gave him the drink of immortality, but Chang-O beat him to the bottle and drank it down. Then she fled to the moon, where she asked the hare who lived there for protection from her (probably righteously) furious husband.

There, some say, Chang-O gained immortality—as a toad. Other legends say that Chang-O's residence was one of the twelve moons, each a different shape, that cross the sky.

Charila Once upon a time, the Greek town of Delphi was parching under a terrible drought. The people starved as the crops burned up in the field, and the king grew concerned for his realm. At the height of the disaster, a little girl came to the king to beg for food. Annoyed, the king struck Charila in the face; she hanged herself in shame. Later, an oracle told the king that he should have been more kind to the supplicant, and that Delphi must thereafter offer propitiatory sacrifices to Charila's spirit every nine years.

Charybdis This monster daughter of the sea and the earth originally lived on land. But the Greek god Zeus threw her into the ocean, which she afterward constantly swallowed and vomited. Charybdis was the personification of the terrifying whirlpools of the sea, later individualized as the dangerous maelstrom off the Italian coast, opposite the ship-eating rock Scylla.

Chelone This nymph, the Greeks said, ridiculed the marriage of Zeus and Hera and was metamorphosed into a speechless turtle (*chelonia*) in pun-

From the T'ang Dynasty (618–906 C.E.) in China comes this dancing woman figurine in clay, used in burial rituals. Important Chinese goddess include Chang-O, Chih Nu, Feng Pho-Pho and Hsi Wang Mu.

ishment. Another way the story is told is that Chelone stayed home from the wedding, and was therefore punished by having to take her home with her everywhere. The marriage of Hera to Zeus, scholars argue, was a forced joining of indigenous pre-Hellenic goddess religions with the male-centered theology of the Indo-European tribes. This story, then, may have been a slightly veiled threat to anyone objecting to the enforced religious change; it may also memorialize priestesses who were "silenced" during that era of social upheaval.

Cherubim   Hebrew scholar Raphael Patai, examining the legends of the Cherubim, concluded that there were two such beings: one male, one female. A statue of the pair, engrossed in unending intercourse, was the secret held by the sacred Holy of Holies in the Jewish temple. Patai argues that the mating Cherubim originally symbolized a unifying and transfiguring spiritual force, but that later Hebrews failed to understand the intent of the symbol. Unable to integrate the Cherubim into their developing theology, they suppressed descriptions of the temple's sacred precinct.

Chichinguane   A folktale heroine of Mozambique, Chichinguane was the oldest daughter of the chief's favorite wife. But the other wives were envious of the love her parents bore her, so they urged their own offspring to persecute her. Every day they tormented her, but the climax came when they abandoned her at the lakeshore. All the village girls had been sent to draw up clay for pottery, and the others forced Chichinguane into the pit, from which she handed out baskets filled with clay. When they had filled their own baskets, the girls ran away, leaving Chichinguane unable to climb out of the pit.

But there was one side of the pit through which the girl could walk. Unfortunately, that led into the waters of the lake. As night began to near, the desperate girl took that route—only to find her escape hatch leading her directly into the jaws of a

great fish. The fish did not swallow her, but carried her to a beautiful land beneath the lake, where all the people were kind to her.

There Chichinguane lived for many months. But one day, as she was swimming near the shore, she saw the girls tormenting her little sister as they once had harassed her. The girl was trying to draw water, but was too small to carry the water jug properly on her head. She sat by the lakeside, weeping helplessly. But she looked up in surprise and delight when her older sister suddenly appeared from the lake. Chichinguane walked the little girl back to the village, carrying her water jug, then made her promise to say nothing about the visit.

Thereafter, Chichinguane appeared every day to help her sister. But finally their mother became suspicious and extracted the truth from the little girl. The next time Chichinguane assumed human form, she was greeted by her mother, who begged her to return to human life. She declined, explaining that she was a fish now and was well treated by her people. Yet when she returned under the waves, Chichinguane could not shake her homesickness. Finally, the fish who had brought her to the lake world took pity on her, gave her a magic wand, and delivered her back to her village. There, he told her, she should wave the wand over her scaly body. And when she did so, the scales fell off, transforming themselves into silver coins—and she was able to live in wealth and comfort ever after.

Chicomecoatl   This maize goddess of the Aztecs had many forms, as many as did the growing corn: she was a maiden decked with water flowers, a young woman whose embrace brought death, a mother carrying the sun as a shield. One of the most popular divinities of ancient Mexico, she was depicted wearing a four-sided headdress and carrying a magic corncob labeled "forgiving strength." It is possible that Chicomecoatl was originally worshiped by the residents of central Mexico who preceded the Aztecs, and that her rites in their era were less bloody than the Aztec sacrifices of young girls in Chicomecoatl's name.

Chien-Ti This Chinese ancestral mother accidentally swallowed an egg while she was swimming in a river. It was a beautiful swallow's egg, colored in five different hues—so it's hard to imagine how this could have been an accident. The egg impregnated her, and she gave birth to the ancestors of the Shang dynasty.

Chih Nu One of the most beloved goddesses of China was the "weaving woman" of heaven, whose task it was to weave the iridescent seamless robes of the divinities. Once, Chih Nu fell in love with the cow-herd god; she spent so much time in his bed that the silk robes of the heavenly ones began to tatter, and there were no new ones in the works. The chief god removed Chih Nu to one side of the heavens, her lover to the other, allowing them one night together annually. On that evening, magpies flew across the sky carrying branches to build a footbridge for the pair's reunion. When it rained, however, the magpies were stranded on earth, and the lovers had to forgo their yearly lovemaking.

Chimera Part goat, part lion, part dragon, this Greek monster was said to have endangered the land of Lycia. Probably she was originally a volcano goddess like Pele or Fuji or Chuginadak, for there was a volcano of her name in the very country she allegedly terrorized.

Chthonia A title rather than a name, this word means "goddess of the earth" and is applied to such underworld deities as Hecate and Nyx, as well as to Demeter in her role as protector of fields. From the title, we get our word *chthonic*, meaning "of the earth."

Chuginadak One of the world's greatest volcano goddesses of the world appears in the myths of the Aleuts, who occupy the islands on the far north edge of the volcanic Pacific Ocean rim. They say the mountain now called Mt. Cleveland was once a proud woman who refused to marry any man in her village. She had a mate in mind: a man she once knew who shot rosy finches. Because of her disdain

for the men there, she became unwelcome in her village and set out to find her chosen mate.

Making magic as she went, Chuginadak walked across impossible waters from island to island on the windy Aleutian Chain. Eventually she came to a village where a dance festival was in progress, and there she saw the man she wanted. She called to

Carved from pink sandstone, this Aztec figure shows the corn goddess Chicomecoatl holding ears of corn in each hand.

him and he came to her. They embraced and fell to the ground in a fever of love.

When Chuginadak arose, the man lay dead beneath her. Disappointed, she retreated to a cave with several birds to mourn her loss. It was not long, however, before the man's father—the village chief—found the body of his son. Angry, he was able to divine, with the help of several old women, who had killed his son, and then he sent armies of warriors and magical spirits against Chuginadak.

None could conquer her, however. A fox spirit finally convinced her to travel to the village and explain her deed. When Chuginadak did so, the chief realized that she had truly loved and desired his son. He sent everyone away. Then, alone in his home, he danced and sang until the body of his son rose up and again embraced his lover. Then the old chief passed on his leadership of the people to his son, and Chuginadak became his wife.

Chup-Kamui Among the aboriginal Ainu of Japan, the sun was worshiped as the highest divinity. Each morning the Ainu greeted Chup-Kamui as though she were a living woman; they were also careful not to step into sunbeams flooding from the window towards the stove, for that was the sun's greeting to the hearth goddess Kamui Fuchi. Originally Chup-Kamui was the moon, but after one night overhead watching illicit trysts on earth, the modest girl asked the male moon to trade places with her. Henceforth, she rose each morning from the mouth of a devil who had spent the night trying to eat her. A magical helper shoved crows and foxes into the devil's mouth while Chup-Kamui escaped; hence, these animals were sacred to the Ainu.

During an eclipse, the Ainu called out *chup rat*, meaning the sun was dying, or *chup chikai anu*, meaning she was fainting. Then they dipped willow branches in water and cast droplets upwards while calling out *kamuiatemka*, or "Oh goddess, we revive you!" As soon as the eclipse passed, they drank themselves into a maudlin state with sake, telling

A pottery figurine from Mexico shows the ancient Aztec vision of femininity. Aztec goddesses in this volume include Chalchiuhtlicue, Chicomecoatl, Coatlicue, Coyolxauhqui, Huixtocihuatl, Mictecacibuatl, Omecihuatl, Tlazolteotl, Toci, Tonan, and Xochiquetzal.

tales of their escape from a world without the luminous sun goddess.

Churalin The Hindus say that a woman who dies in childbirth loses her soul, which melts into the powerful repository of frustrated maternity called Churalin, a monster that roams the countryside looking for pretty infants to kill.

Ciau In the Pacific's Loyalty Islands, the people of Oceania tell the story of this heroine, daughter of a chief. She and her attendants regularly went to a white-sand beach, where Ciau bleached her hair with the salty sea waters. One day, as she was performing her ablutions, two fish appeared and, each swimming under one of her armpits, quickly swam away. They carried her to a tiny island, where the sun sets each evening.

There she was introduced to the mother of the sun, who was delighted to have such charming company. However, she warned, Ciau must hide as the sun arrived, for otherwise his rays would scorch and burn her. The girl did hide, but after dinner the sun suspected her presence and searched the house until he found her. Falling in love with her instantly, he made her his wife.

To the couple, a son was born. But he was not a quiet child, and his noise frequently upset his father. One evening, furious at the constant interruptions to his peace, the sun insulted his wife, calling her a foreigner. Immediately, she took her child and dived into the ocean, where the magical fish appeared and took her back to her original home.

There her people welcomed her with joy and set about to celebrate her return. But the sun, angry at having his child taken from him, arrived and began to burn up everything in the land. All the people hid underground, but still the heat nearly killed them. Finally, they decided that all humankind would be wiped out if they did not return the sun's son. Tearfully, Ciau allowed them to set her son on fire; immediately he turned into smoke and returned to his heavenly parent. And just as quickly, the sun resumed his regular course, and the earth survived.

Cihuacoatl The Mexican goddess of life's trials, Cihuacoatl invented productive labor. She also prophesied doom, wandering through the world decked out in jewels and face paint, moaning in despair over coming disasters.

Cihuateteo To the ancient Mexicans, these were the roving spirits of women who died in childbirth.

Cinderella That familiar childhood story of the orphaned girl ("elf of the cinders") enslaved by her evil stepmother and stepsisters, and whose fairy godmother gives her the power to attract the attention of a local princeling, is a mere shadow of the earlier figure. Children's tales often capture something of the legend, if not the power, of ancient divinities, for despite conversion to new (and often invading) religions, mothers still spin the old yarns for their children. Among the Slavs of central Europe and Germans who lived near them, Cinderella was originally goddess of fire, whose name signified the sparks cast off by forgers and blacksmiths. In some versions of the story, she lived naked in a cave or at the bottom of a well; or she wore a coat of cat's skins or golden chimes; or she wears shoes of the sun. Her domain may, therefore, have included the sun as well as earthly fire.

Cipactli Before there was an earth, said the Nahua of ancient Mexico, the goddess Cipactli existed, a monstrous alligator swimming through the waters of primordial chaos. All potential life was contained within her, but it could not be freed until—like Tiamat across the oceans in the eastern Mediterranean—Cipactli offered her very body.

Two serpent gods tore the goddess apart. Her lower body fell through chaos to form the earth, while her upper body rose to form the heavens. Her scaly coat became the mountains; her eyes and mouth turned into caves. Sometimes, the Nahua said, she could still be heard sobbing at night, wishing life to die back into her—a symbolic rendering of death's significance that the Aztecs later took literally, tearing living bodies apart to feed the goddess.

Another legend, in which the goddess was called Tlaltecuhtli, says that this primordial goddess was the most magnificent creature in the universe, a beautiful woman with eyes and teeth at every joint so that she could look everywhere and protect herself. But she could not avoid the two gods who tore her in half, whereupon her hair grew into trees, flowers, and grass, her eyes into rivers, her shoulders into mountains.

Circe A daughter of the sun and sister of the famous Cretan queen Pasiphae, this illustrious witch was said to have gained the rulership of Colchis near the Black Sea by marrying its prince. Then she killed him so that she could rule alone. When

Circe's subjects discovered her crime, they rose against her. The enchantress fled, escaping on her father's rays to the island of Aeaea.

There Circe lived in a little stone house set in a clearing, surrounded by lions and wolves. She entertained herself by blending magic potions of herbs that she tried on human subjects ship-wrecked in her vicinity. She was most famous for turning Odysseus' men into swine; the wandering Greek king himself managed to escape her spells, but he could not escape her charms and fathered two sons by the witch, who, Hesiod said, became Etruscan princes.

Claudia Quinta   The legendary matriarch of the Claudian family of Rome, she was accused of promiscuity in 204 B.C.E. At that time, the goddess Cybele was traveling to Rome, and her boat stuck fast in the Tiber River. Claudia, proclaiming herself ready for a test of her continence, took hold of the ropes tied to Cybele's boat. Invoking the goddess, she pulled, and singlehandedly pulled Cybele into Rome, thus acquitting herself of the false charge.

Cleone   A pre-Hellenic water goddess who was the divine ancestor of the Cleonae, a tribe who lived between Argos and Corinth.

Clidna   The beautiful bird goddess of the Irish after-life survives today as a fairy queen of southwest Ireland, ruler of the sacred hill in Cork called Car-rig Cliodna. In ancient legend, Clidna was one of the Tuatha de Danaan, the magical divinities sub-ject to the goddess Danu; she was said to rule the Land of Promise, where there is no death, vio-lence, or decay.

Legend says that she ruled the ninth wave of every series, which was thought to be larger than the preceding eight; huge swells were therefore called "Clidna's waves." These waves were one of the goddess' forms; she also appeared as a swoop-ing seabird. When she took human form, she was the most beautiful woman ever seen, hence her name, "shapely one."

Like many ancient goddesses, Clidna took mortal lovers. John Fitzjames, for instance, she stole from Eire's mainland. But he already had a human lover, a witty and argumentative Irish woman named Caitileen Og. This Caitileen was the only woman ever to berate Clidna for her careless ways with human affection. She trailed the goddess all the way to the afterlife, demanding her lover's return. Indeed, she almost prevailed against Clidna's lust. Almost persuaded by the woman's clever speech, Clidna finally decided to keep Fitzjames for herself.

Cloelia   In Roman legend, this woman was given as a hostage to Lars Porsena, an Etruscan king, but she escaped by throwing herself into the Tiber River and swimming strongly back to her people. The Etruscans demanded their hostage's return, and so she found herself back among them. But the king so admired her bravery and strength that he released her again.

Clymene   A common name among Greek heroines. We find at least a dozen in that mythology, includ-ing the mothers of Atalanta and Mnemosyne.

Clytemnestra   The Greek woman Leda was raped by—or, some say, willingly mated with—a huge swan, the disguised Zeus. Shortly afterward, she had intercourse with her husband, the king of Sparta. Nine months later Leda laid two eggs. One broke open to reveal the immortal Helen (later "of Troy") and her brother Pollux; the other produced two mortal children, Clytemnestra and her brother Castor.

As she grew, Clytemnestra was overshadowed by her immortally beautiful half-sister. It was Helen who attained the crown of the city, raising her consort Menelaus to the throne. Clytemnestra, on the other hand, became part of a foreign fami-ly by marrying Helen's brother-in-law, Agamem-non of Mycenae. They had three children: two daughters, Iphigenia and Electra, and a son, Orestes.

Then Agamemnon was called to Troy to regain Helen—and with her, the crown of Sparta—for his brother. At the town of Aulis on the Aegean coast, the luckless Greek navy was stalled by ill winds. To further their campaign, the brothers decided they needed a human sacrifice. They sent back to Mycenae for Iphigenia, pretending to her mother that the girl was intended as the hero Achilles' bride. But they put Iphigenia to death. The bloody sacrifice pleased the wind deities; the Greeks gained the advantageous winds they needed to sail to Troy.

Back home in Mycenae, Clytemnestra was stricken with furious grief at her loss. For a decade she planned vengeance. She took as consort Agamemnon's cousin, Aegisthus—also his bitter enemy because of crimes committed in their families' past. The queen and her lover plotted revenge suitable for a man who valued his brother's crown over his own child's life.

When Agamemnon returned, he brought with him Cassandra. The doomed Trojan prophet foresaw the results of maternal anger, but the king ignored her warnings. King and captive were quickly murdered by Clytemnestra and Aegisthus. But the queen herself met a violent death, for her own children avenged their father's murder.

This complicated cycle of killings and revenge murders expressed, some interpreters claim, the social upheaval in the Greek city-states when the era of mother right ended and the patriarchal family was established as the base of society. Under a matriarchal system, Clytemnestra acted intelligibly, if brutally, meting out death to her child's killer. Under the new patriarchal system, Clytemnestra's children acted correctly by destroying their father's murderer. Those who favor this interpretation of the myth cite the end of Aeschylus' Oresteia: Clytemnestra's son, pursued by the matriarchal Erinyes, is absolved of his mother's murder by the supporters of the patriarchy.

Clytie   The spirit of the sunflower or the heliotrope, Clytie was once a Greek nymph who slept with the sun. Transformed into a flower, she still worshipfully follows his movement across the sky.

Coatlicue   The earth was a fivefold "serpent-skirted goddess" to the ancient Mexicans, who counted four directions and a central point, up and down, on their compasses. The fivefold earth goddess therefore sometimes appeared to them as a woman with four sisters; they gathered, it was said, on Coatepec ("Snake Hill") to meditate. There Coatlicue gathered white feathers to adorn her breasts. Becoming pregnant while remaining a virgin (she was impregnated by emeralds or jade stones), she gave birth to the savior god Quetzalcoatl.

Sometimes the fivefold goddess was called a moon divinity, wife of the sun god. She was also called the creator: she was preeminent and preexistent, floating for eons in a misty world. Even the sun and his magicians did not realize her magnificence. Once they did, however, they brought her love charms, and she suddenly flowered forth as the great mother of all living.

But Coatlicue was the death mother as well. Her most famous images show her as the ruler of life and its end, garlanded with hearts and hands, wearing a skirt of swinging serpents, hung with skulls, vested in a flayed human skin. Coatlicue, honored with spring's earliest flowers, was also rightly attired in claws and snakes, for to the ancient Mexicans the goddess was both Tlaltecuhtli, the ugly earth toad, and Tonantzin, the mother redeemer.

Cocomama   The resident divinity of the coca plant was, to the people of the Andes, a goddess who granted healing and happiness to her worshipers. Originally, it was told, she was a promiscuous woman cut in half by jealous lovers; her body grew into the first coca bush, whose leaves men were not to chew until they had satisfied a woman's sexual needs.

Colleda   Serbian goddess of winter solstice, she was the recipient of the ceremonial Yule log that was burned as the year's light drained away. When daylight was reborn, her devotees served sweet cakes to the children, who went from house to house begging favors for the "sweet maiden goddess" who promised the revival of light and growth. In northern Russia, the same goddess appears as Koliada, a woman who re-creates the world each winter solstice by embroidering a new one.

Concordia   The Roman goddess of peace, her name survives in English as *concord*. In Roman art, she was shown as a heavyset matron, holding a cornucopia in one hand and an olive branch in the other. Her worship goes back to the era before the Roman empire, for a temple was dedicated to her as personification of community harmony in the fourth century B.C.E. Another was built in the first century C.E. by the emperor Tiberius, who pleaded with her to end the murderous feuds that were tearing the imperial family apart. Concordia's special feast was April 30, at which time Pax and Salus—peace and health—were also honored.

Copia   A Roman goddess of plenty, her name survives in the cornucopia, which she was often depicted holding, and in *copious*, our word for "abundance."

Cotys   In Thrace, far in the north of Greece, this goddess of sexuality was revered. There her servants, the *baptai* ("baptized ones"), celebrated secret festivals in her honor, releasing the forces of life through erotic celebration. The secrecy of the rituals was so treasured that anyone who described them to non-initiates was put to death by other devotees. When the Greeks invaded this goddess' homeland, they saw no religious content to the life-evoking rituals, dubbing the Thracian goddess the "patron of debauchery."

Coventina   Among the Celts, both insular and Continental, goddesses were often perceived in the form of flowing water; the "earth goddess" of a territory was seen, not in the landscape, but in the river that drained it. Best described as "goddesses of the watershed," these divinities included Boann of the Boyne, Belisama of the Mersey, Sinann of the Shannon, and Coventina of the Carrawburgh in England.

At Coventina's sacred well in Northumberland, relics were recovered, including portraits of the elegant-looking goddess. In one sculpture, the goddess was shown lying on water weeds, pouring the river from an urn that she carried. In others, she stood holding branches of water plants, while thoughtlessly tipping her bucket.

Many of these goddesses, like Sulis at Bath, were considered to be healing divinities, and offerings for good health were dedicated to them at their sacred sites, as to Mary of Lourdes today. In addition, the Celtic water goddesses were also spirits of inspiration and prophecy, rather like the Greek Muses or the Roman Carmenta.

Coyolxauhqui   "Golden bells" was the name of this Aztec moon goddess, daughter of Coatlicue. Some legends say that when the fearful stars tried to kill their mother rather than let her bear rivals to them, Coyolxauhqui was among them. But the traitorous siblings then turned on her, decapitating her and throwing her head into the sky. (Other versions say that she tried to warn Coatlicue of the conspiracy against her, so that the sun god killed Coyolxauhqui to keep her from speaking; her mother, grieving, placed Coyolxanhqui's shining head in the night sky.)

One of the great monuments to Coyolxauhqui was unearthed during construction work in Mexico City in 1978: a ten-ton circle of stone showing her dismemberment, as important a piece of Aztec art as the Calendar Stone found in 1790. The archaeologists were so moved by the stone's discovery that they sang a hymn to the goddess who was buried for more than 500 years but emerged intact. Later excavations have revealed one of the greatest religious centers of Aztec Mexico surrounding the stone.

Cred   This Irish fairy queen of the famous goddess-mountains, "the paps of Anu," promised never to sleep with a man until she found one who could create a magnificent poem for her. Not only did it have to be perfectly constructed, but it had to describe in vivid detail her home and its splendid furnishings. As her palace was heavily guarded and no man had ever entered, it seemed likely she would die a virgin. But the poet-seer Coll came to her and sang a poem so accurate and so beautiful that she instantly wed him. "Wounded men spouting heavy blood would sleep to the music of fairy birds singing above the bright leaves of her bower," were the words that convinced her to become his Leanan Sidhe, or otherworld lover.

Creiddylad   We know this ancient Welsh goddess as Cordelia, daughter of Lear in Shakespeare's play; she was originally a sea queen, daughter of the sea god Lyr. Geoffrey of Monmouth claimed that Cordelia, the human form of the goddess, ruled the land after her father died. Shakespeare, of course, killed her off along with Lear. By then, the real legend of Creiddylad and Lyr was probably lost.

Crobh Dearg   "Red claw" was an ancient Irish goddess who was sometimes said to be the sister of Latiaran; possibly she was a form of Badb.

Cunina   "Cunae" in Latin meant "cradle," and this goddess was honored as the protector of infants asleep in their cradles, together with her sister goddess Rumina, whose name derives from the word for "mother's milk."

Cura   According to Roman myth, Cura was the goddess who first fashioned humans from clay. She possesses us, giving us *cures* (a word derived from her name) for whatever ails us, until we die.

Cuvto-Ava   The "tree mother" of the Mordvins was addressed in many charms—probably because she was a haughty deity, always on the lookout for injuries done to her or her tree daughters. If you were to break off branches thoughtlessly or otherwise offend her, Cuvto-Ava would punish you with withering diseases.

Cybele   Of all the great mothers of the ancient world, the one whose myth and cult came down to us most clearly was Cybele, for her worship survived in Rome centuries into the Christian era. A mountain-dwelling goddess of holy madness, Cybele's worship originated in Phrygia, in northern Anatolia (modern Turkey); it traveled through the northern Mediterranean, together with her image as a full-breasted mature woman, crowned and carrying corn and keys, arrayed in a robe containing all the flower colors of the earth she ruled.

Here is the story told of her: one day, disguised as the rock Agdos, Cybele was sleeping. Zeus, a far younger divinity, came upon her and attempted to rape her. Unable to penetrate her, he was so excited by the contest that he ejaculated onto the ground. But the ground, too, was Cybele the earth mother, and so she conceived.

The child of this unresolved conflict was the hermaphrodite Agdistis, as unpleasant and violent a child as his conception could warrant. The wine god Dionysus drugged him with alcohol and, to make his life easier, tied his male members to a tree so that, on awakening, he would pull them off. Unfortunately, Agdistis died of the wound, and from his blood sprang up a beautiful almond—some say pomegranate—tree.

From this tree, the nymph Nana picked a lovely fruit and placed it next to her skin; it impregnated her with a lovely child whom she named Attis. When he grew into the perfection of young manhood, Attis roused the passion of Cybele. She took him as her lover, bearing him through the world in her lion-drawn chariot, engaging him in ecstatic embraces. This wasn't enough for Attis, though, and he foolishly turned his attentions to another woman. Because his grandmother-lover was the earth itself, there was nowhere that Attis could accomplish his infidelity without Cybele's knowing. He nonetheless tried; Cybele naturally surprised him at it, and in punishment she drove him mad. In an anguish of contrition, Attis tore from himself the cause of all the trouble and, castrated, bled to death beneath a pine tree.

Most interpreters find in this tale a representation of the flowering passage of the short growing season over the face of the constant earth. Indeed, the Cybeline ceremonies focused on springtime. In Rome, they began with the triumphal entry of the young Attis, symbolized by a pine tree, into the city; then followed a day of mourning and fasting for his death; finally, an Easterlike "Festival of Joy" celebrated the arrival of the new growing season. This joyful conclusion is noteworthy in that the myth does not mention Attis' rebirth, although similar stories (Ishtar, Isis) do show the young lover reborn or restored to Mother Earth's embraces.

Called the "Mountain Mother" in her homeland, Cybele's religion entered Rome in 204 B.C.E. At that time, the city was threatened by Hannibal, and consultation of the books of the Sibyl showed that the Carthaginian would be conquered only if the black stone of Cybele was brought in ceremony to the capital. This stone, apparently a meteorite that had fallen to earth before astonished witnesses, was honored in Asia Minor as the very stone that Zeus had tried to rape. Five distinguished Romans duly sought out the irregularly shaped piece of betyl and brought it ceremoniously into the temple of Victoria. Thirteen years later Cybele is said to have caused the defeat of the Carthaginians.

However, the ritual, which arrived with the sacred stone, was controversial from the start and was sporadically banned. At issue was the self-castration of Cybele's priests, performed as an act of identification with the goddess' beloved, and even today the focus of emotional academic dispute. Amid wild music and throbbing cymbals, the initiate allowed himself to be overcome by mystic abandon and used whatever was near at hand—a blunt knife, a stone would do—to accomplish the act.

Ovid described it thus: "His [Attis'] unmanly ministers cut their offending members while they toss their hair." After becoming eunuchs, the initiates danced in elaborate costumes and served the goddess in music and dance. All this horrified the masculinity-conscious Romans, who are recorded to have killed slaves in punishment for self-castration, as though death were a fitting retribution for sacrilege of this sort.

But citizens could partake of the goddess' mysteries without such total devotion. Once in a lifetime—or, if one were rich, every twenty years—a worshiper of Cybele could be reborn. In the Taurobolium, one stood in an earth pit under an ox. The beast was slaughtered and drenched the worshiper with its blood. Then, bloody as a babe and spiritually refreshed, the baptized would emerge from the earthwomb, confirmed in his devotion to the mountain mother Cybele.

Cydippe An Argive priestess of Hera, she had two sons to whom she was devoted. She prayed to her goddess to grant them what was best for mortals; that night they died in their sleep.

Cynosura The Cretan goddess Cynosura leaves us her name in *cynosure*, a word that means "center of attraction" and recalls the navigational uses of her constellation, Ursa Minor or the Little Dipper. Some legends call her the nurse of the Greek god Zeus.

Cyone This woman of Syracuse in ancient Greece was raped by her own father. She promptly marched him into a temple and sacrificed him on its altar.

Cyrene A powerful princess of early Greece, Cyrene entertained herself by wrestling with lions. She was also, Pindar said, excellent with the javelin and sword and hated merely to "pace to and fro before the loom."

Da This may have been the original name of the ancient Greek earth mother, who later was Ge or Gaia. Da's name survives in that of the god Poseidon, whose name means "husband of Da," for the woman-centered culture that preceded the Hellenes saw the ocean as the fertilizing husband of the land.

Dabaiba "Mother of creation," the great goddess of early Panama.

Dactyls Ten little women born with no father to the Greek woman Anchiale, they were fabulously inventive and brought to us all we know of metalwork and smithcraft. The Dactyls represent the ten fingers of the human hands; their legend suggests that women were the discoverers of metal and its working.

Dahut This pagan princess lived in Brittany, the far-western Celtic wilderness of France, during the period when Christian monks were destroying the remnants of the old European religion—the worship of maternal nature. These flesh-despising monks ruined the princess' pleasures until Dahut begged her father, King Gradlon, to build her a retreat from the cruelties of the new way.

Gradlon seemed to ignore her, but all the while he was secretly building a magnificent city for her.

Located on the rocky Pointe du Raz and called Ys, it was to be hers to do with as she wished. When he presented it to Dahut, the sensual princess was wild with joy at the splendid homes arranged to catch the setting sun's rays.

Dahut's people were rich and happy, but it soon became clear that Ys had been built too close to the sea. Storms endangered the small fishing craft by which the people of Ys earned their wealth. Dahut asked Gradlon to build them a safe harbor, but the king, threatened with damnation by the monks, built instead a fine new church to the Christian god right in the center of Ys.

Furious, Dahut rowed that night through dangerous coastal waters to a secret island where women—possibly immortals—continued to celebrate the ancient rites. There she asked them to command the sea spirits, the Korrigans, to help her; she offered eternal fidelity to the old ways in return.

But then Dahut's ambition poisoned her. Granted the aid Ys needed, Dahut asked for yet another miracle: that magical powers would raise her palace high above the new Christian church. She was granted that, too, but her selfish desire took its toll. For many years Dahut and her people lived in splendor and pleasure. But the princess' sickness grew. Eventually she began to take one-night lovers, having them destroyed immediately after they left her. The powers of passion and ambition that Dahut had stirred grew so strong that finally the king of the waters himself came to claim the princess—and he drowned the entire city of Ys when he did.

Although the above story is told as a local historical legend, it is probable that Dahut was originally a Breton goddess—possibly Celtic, for her image recalls that of the Welsh Arianhod, who similarly mated with the ocean king. But Brittany was also a center for pre-Celtic civilizations of note, including that of the megalith builders whose alignments to the winter solstice surround the hamlet of Carnac. Dahut's heritage could thus, like that of Celtic Brigid, include ancient material transformed as times changed.

Dakini   In Indian Hinduism, these powerful female beings are attendants on the death goddess Kali. Like her, they are of a terrifying aspect, sometimes fish-bodied, sometimes huge as an ogre, often eating raw flesh or drinking blood (from which they are called Asrapas, "blood sippers"). In the esoteric tradition in Tibet, however, they have another aspect, for beneath their horrific guise they carry the power of "the mothers," as Tibetan yogis call them, and grant supernormal powers and insights to the sincere practitioner of yoga, particularly Kundalini yoga.

Dali   In Russian Georgia, this huntress goddess rules all wild horned animals: mountain sheep, deer, chamois. Like any wildwood goddess, she lives in the inaccessible regions, fancying most to establish her camp in a cave within a glacier's face. Hunters are captivated by her, for she is beautiful, with solid gold hair worn in long braids. Sometimes she allows herself to be seduced by strong men, because she knows such matings result in especially talented hunters.

One such mate was careless about her affections, and he met a bad end indeed. One cannot hide infidelity from an all-seeing goddess, yet he believed he could sleep with whom he chose. The very next night, he saw an incredibly large white deer, which led him into the highest peaks of the mountains. He was a great hunter, so he often came near—but never quite near enough to shoot his prey. At last he found himself high above an abyss, balanced on a rock outcropping. And all at once, the rock crumbled beneath him. Headfirst he fell into the chasm—but, at the last moment, his foot caught on a little branch. There he hung, day after day, thirsty, hungry, in agonizing pain. Nothing could be done, for no rope could reach him. Every time someone tried to rescue him, the mountain grew taller and the abyss grew deeper. Finally, realizing he had wronged the goddess and had to pay the price, the hunter let himself drop into the abyss and died.

Dames Vertes   The "Green Ladies" of Celtic French folklore were seductive but cruel, luring travelers from the forest paths and holding them upside down over waterfalls, laughing all the while. As wind spirits, they traveled speedily over their chosen countryside, invigorating all the plant life they touched. When visible in human form, the Dames Vertes were said to be tall and seductive, dressed in long green robes, passing so lightly over the grass that it seemed only winds had disturbed it.

Damia   An alternative form of the corn goddess Demeter, she was paired with a Persephonelike daughter named Auxesia in ancient Greece. In a famous story, a famine struck the Epidaurians that, it was prophesied, would not end until statues of the goddesses were carved of Athenian olive wood. The Athenians gave their neighbors the wood, but afterward demanded heavy tribute. During a rebellion, the Epidaurians stopped payment of the tribute; the Athenians invaded, intent on carrying home the goddesses' statues. But they would not move, and a fierce battle followed. A messenger carrying tidings to Athens of the sacrilege to Damia and Auxesia was murdered by angry Athenian women; the men of Athens used this attack to strip the women of their few remaining rights.

Damkina In the Akkadian language, this name means "lady of earth," and she was to the Sumerians the earth mother familiar to us in Greece as Demeter and in Rome as Tellus Mater.

Danae, the Danaids There is a Greek story about a woman of Argos who, confined to a tower so that she could not conceive, was raped by the god Zeus, who fell in through the window disguised as a shower of gold. Danae then bore the hero Perseus. And there is another Greek story about forty-nine Danaid sisters who, forced into marriage, killed their husbands on their wedding night; the thirtieth sister, Hypermnestra, spared her mate and conceived by him the ruling dynasty of Argos.

The names of the Argive heroine and of the husband-slaying sisters are nearly identical, although legends never connect them. In addition, the Argives bore the tribal name of Danai. In Greek times, the excuse was given that the name came from the father of the Danaids, Danaos. Clearly an attempt to disguise the matrilineality of the pre-Hellenic settlers of the Peloponnese, this reveals its bias by assuming that the daughter bears the father's name and her children bear the daughter's.

There is evidence that the Danaids were originally water goddesses of the region around Argos; Hypermnestra gave her name to a fountain, an odd honor for a mortal woman of that time. If the Danaids were indeed connected with Danae, then she (whose name fittingly means "dawn") would be the ancestor goddess of the Argive tribe.

Danu The greatest of the goddesses of ancient Ireland, Danu was the ruler of a tribe of divinities called Tuatha de Danaan, the people of Danu, who were demoted to fairies called Daoine Sidhe in later times. Her name derives from the Old Celtic *dan*, meaning "knowledge," and she was probably the same goddess as the Welsh Don. Some scholars see her as the same goddess as Anu, while others contend that she is an aspect of

Brigid. There are no legends of her left to elucidate the search for her meaning, but her preeminence among ancient Irish deities remains clear.

Daphne A priestess of Gaea, this nymph led secret women's rituals in celebration of the earth's femininity. But the mortal Leucippus tried to penetrate their rituals in female disguise. The all-seeing sun, who had ulterior motives for his action, suggested to the women that they conduct their rituals nude, to be certain that there were no male intruders.

So the mortal was found and destroyed for his sacrilege. Then the sun god's motives became clear. He accosted the beautiful priestess and demanded that she sleep with him. She refused. Apollo grew violent. Chasing her, intent on rape,

In Tibet, indigenous goddesses combined with those imported from Buddhism to form bon-po figures like this one, a Dakini with four arms holding a bow and arrow and clad in tiger's skin.

he overpowered Daphne. But she cried out to the goddess she served, Mother Earth, and instantly was transformed into a laurel tree. The repentant Apollo thereafter wore laurel wreaths in his hair and honored the tree as the symbol of inspiration.

Darago   The volcano goddess of the Philippines was said to be a warrior woman who lived in fiery mountains and demanded human sacrifices once a year to keep her from angry eruptions.

Daughters of Zelophehad   The individual names of these Jewish heroines are no longer recorded, an ironic aspect of this story of an ancient fight for women's equal rights. When the Hebrews conquered Canaan, they began to divide the country among the males of the tribe. But the Daughters—convinced of their own rights as members of the same tribe and as survivors of the desert exile—waited until a day when Moses was preaching. His subject was the laws of "levirate marriage," the forced marriage of barren widows to the brothers of their dead husbands. Pointing out that their own father was dead and that they, apparently, did not count as offspring, they claimed Moses should demand strict adherence to the Hebrew marriage law by forcing their aged mother into marriage. Shamed, Moses agreed that the Daughters had found a legal inconsistency and thereafter granted them equal land rights with the men.

Dayang Raca   On the island of Bornea, among the Iban people, this woman was the only human being to survive a monstrous flood. How, then, could humanity be reborn, if there was only one woman and no man left alive? Dayang Raca managed: she lit a fire, then mated with its flame to become pregnant and begin the repopulation of the planet.

Dayang Sumbi   A heroine of western Javanese legend, she once grew disturbed at her young son's incessant noise and hit him with a spoon. To her horror, this outburst left the child's face scarred. Not only that, but the boy was scarred

emotionally as well, and soon ran away (toddled away, rather) from home and could not be found. Many years later, a handsome young stranger came to town and fell in love with the still-lovely Dayang Sumbi. But she recognized the scar and so set impossible tasks for him to perform before she would grant him her hand: he must transform her lands into a lake in one night, then build a boat

The many cultures of southeast Asia offer numerous visions of the feminine divine, many of which result from the combination of indigenous and imported (often Hindu) religious ideas. This Javanese sculpture, a stone woman with one hand resting on the head of a child, may represent Dayang Sumbi, one of the area's mother goddesses.

before dawn so that she could witness the sunrise on the water. But the young man, with massive help from spirit forces, dammed a river and creates a lake. He was hard at work building the boat and might have made his deadline, but Dayang Sumbi had magic up her sleeve as well: she unfurled a fabric which caused a rain of leaves to fall, thwarting the shipbuilding by covering the materials densely. Day broke, and the wedding was called off. The young man left disappointed—but saved from an incestuous marriage.

Deae Matres Their names—bestowed by scholars—may be Latin, but the Deae Matres were Celtic, the primary divine image of the continental tribes. No legends survive of this trinity of earth goddesses, although hundreds of inscriptions and sculptures attest to the strength of their worship.

Their religion was apparently destroyed early in the Roman occupation, but their names and images survived into the days of the empire. They were then called sorceresses of the early days, thus holding the attention and reverence of their people in ancient Gaul and Germany.

The "mother goddesses"—for this is what their Latin name means—were always shown as three robed women bearing baskets of fruit and flowers; sometimes they also carried babies. Seated under an archway, they were depicted wearing round halolike headdresses; the central goddess was distinguished from the others by standing while they sat or by sitting while they stood. They were probably ancestral goddesses, rulers of the fruitfulness of humanity as well as that of the earth.

Dea Nutrix "Nurturing Mother" was the Romanized name given to a Celtic goddess, perhaps a form of Deae Matres, whose images were found in central France and southern Germany. The figures, discovered in sacred springs like Vichy and in graves, showed a young woman seated in a wicker chair and nursing an infant.

Dea Syria The Romans usually used this name, "the Syrian Goddess," to describe Atargatis. Sometimes, however, they lumped together other goddesses of the eastern Mediterranean—Ishtar, Cybele, Anahita—under this broad term.

Deborah A Hebrew prophet, Deborah was married to a man named Barak, called "the ignoramus." She was a high-handed woman who took no commands from her husband, instead ordering him around. A great poet and a judge, she sat in the open air dispensing judgments and composing poems rather than hiding her talents indoors.

Dechtere The mother of the superhuman Irish hero Cuchulain was herself a magical creature, able to transform herself and her fifty maidservants into birds so that they could travel more quickly through the green hills of the island. Wherever they stopped, they ate voraciously, especially the enormous queen who headed them, for Dechtere was of more than normal height.

Drinking wine one day, she accidentally swallowed a mayfly floating in the cup, whereby she conceived Cuchulain. That, however, is but one of the three versions of the conception: another says that she flew away as a bird with the god Lugh; yet another says that Dechtere was miraculously impregnated by Lugh with his own soul. She gave birth to the reborn god by vomiting him into daylight, thus retaining her virginity.

Deirdre The most tragic heroine in all of Irish legend, Deirdre was the most beautiful woman in the world, and one who bore the curse that only sorrow would come from her beauty. The warriors of the Irish north, on hearing the prophecy at Deirdre's birth, demanded her death. But the Ulster king Conchobar, pitying her, sent her into exile in the distant reaches of Ireland.

As she grew into the lovely woman prophecy had foreseen, Deirdre lived happily enough in her exile. One day, though, she saw blood on the snowy ground and a raven nearby. Instantly she remembered an insistent dream of a young man with the same coloring: black hair, white skin, and red lips. She sank into depression until her nurse Lavercam told her of Naoise, who lived with his brothers, Ardan and Ainle, nearby. Lavercam arranged a secret meeting, and Deirdre, literally seeing the man of her dreams, demanded that he free her from her woodland exile.

They fled to Scotland, where they took refuge with noble people. But Deirdre attracted the attention of the king, who laid plans to steal her from her lover. To avoid this, Deirdre and Naoise, together with his brothers, fled to the windy coast. There they lived a rugged but happy life, until rumor reached them that Conchobar would welcome them back in Ireland. But the rumor had been deliberately planted; the king, angry at having his captive sprung from his grasp, wanted her back only for evil purposes.

Deirdre knew by intuition that if they returned to Ireland, tragedy would follow. But Naoise was a proud man, loyal to his king, and he overruled his lover. The party of four sailed across to Ireland while Deirdre continued to see gloomy portents, including a blood-red cloud. Naoise and his brothers, however, continued to ignore her warnings.

Alas for them all, Deirdre's premonitions proved correct. Through treachery, Naoise and his brothers were murdered by the warriors of Conchobar; Deirdre herself was taken captive. Submitting to her captors, Deirdre saw that she had one way out. So, as she was being transported to the king in a speedy chariot, she suddenly stood up and let her head smash against a tree, splattering her blood and brains across the Irish soil.

Dejanira   The Greek hero Heracles had a bad record in relationships. He had countless affairs before, during, and after his first marriage, which ended with his killing his wife Megaera. Despite his reputation, a woman warrior, Dejanira, fell in love with Heracles, and he with her. They were married, and she bore him several children. But Hera-

cles soon returned to his usual behavior, even bringing a mistress into Dejanira's home.

Desperate to regain Heracles' love, Dejanira wove a splendid garment for her husband and soaked it in what she hoped was an infallible charm: blood and semen from a dying centaur, killed by Heracles. But the centaur had revenge in his heart when he confided the secret potion to Dejanira. His blood burned so terribly on Heracles' flesh that—finding he could not tear the garment off—the hero pleaded to the gods for death. The remorseful Dejanira followed him to the afterlife, dying by her own hand.

Dekla   This sympathetic Latvian fate goddess watched over infants. When she was forced to witness the birth of a child for whom a tragic life was destined, she wept bitterly. She may be a localized form of the Baltic Laima.

Demeter   Once the flowerlike Persephone, the lovely daughter of earth, disappeared; her mother, Demeter, could find her nowhere. The weeping Demeter searched and searched through the fields, crying out for the daughter who was so close as to seem her very self, her childhood, her gentle youth. Demeter fretfully clutched her blue-green cloak, then thoughtlessly shredded it into tiny pieces, scattering them as cornflowers in the grasses. But flowers and grasses soon faded, for Demeter was the source of all growth; as she mourned, the goddess withdrew her energy from the plants, which began to wilt and shrivel. So, it was said, Chloe ("green one"), the happy earth, changed for the first time into the yellow-gold, autumnal Demeter.

The goddess wandered through the dying earth until she came to a town near Athens. There she took a job as nursemaid to the queen of Eleusis, Metanira, whose son Triptolemos she wanted to make immortal by smoking him like a log in the fireplace (see Isis). The frantic queen found her, and the disguised goddess was revealed. Demeter stayed on in Eleusis, however, often sitting sadly by a well as she wept for the loss of her beloved daughter.

One day the queen's daughter Baubo (or Iambe) saw the sad goddess at the well and tried to comfort her. Demeter refused all her consoling words and so, to make the goddess smile, Baubo exposed her vulva salaciously. Surprised, Demeter chuckled, the first laughter the starving earth had heard from its goddess in many months. Shortly afterward, Persephone was restored to her mother, and spring bloomed again on the earth. In gratitude for the hospitality of the Eleusinians, Demeter taught the arts of agriculture to Prince Triptolemos and thereafter based her mysterious rites at that city.

This Greek story of the great goddess is clearly a seasonal metaphor; it contains as well a beautifully tender archetype of the bond between mothers and daughters. A variant of the common Mediterranean myth that explains how the earth loves and consumes its own green growth, this legend is singular in epitomizing this love, not in a sexual relationship between the ever-dying son and his mother, but in a familial bond between the maternal Demeter and her adored daughter Persephone.

This daughter, the springtime earth, was really another form of Demeter herself. In Sicily, the identity of Demeter and Persephone was canonical; they were dubbed Damatres ("mothers") and were portrayed as indistinguishable. But the most common form of the great goddess was a trinity, rather than a pair of deities, and many scholars have sifted through the famous Demeter myths, hoping to find the third part of the feminine triad, the winter earth, the aged crone, the hibernating seed. Speculation has generally settled on Hecate, who certainly seems to be the most cronelike of the possible divine figures in the story. In addition, she appears at important junctures; she was, for instance, the only one to witness Persephone's disappearance. Because the omniscient earth, Demeter, could hardly have been oblivious to happenings on her surface, Hecate therefore

seems to be an aspect of Demeter as "earth mother."

But "earth mother" is only one of the possible meanings of Demeter's name. The second part of the word unarguably means "mother." The first part, however, translates as easily into "cereal" as "earth," making her the goddess not of the earth's surface but only of cultivated, food-providing plants, parallel to the Roman Ceres. If Demeter derives from the words for "earth mother," the goddess would be another form of Gaia. As such,

A goddess or her priestess holding a mirror decorates this small plate found in Italy and dated to the fourth century B.C.E. Mirrors were associated with several goddesses, such as Demeter and Aphrodite, and have a solar significance.

she appears in some legends mated to Poseidon, "the husband of Da."

Whether she symbolized all the earth or just its edible plants, Demeter was worshiped in fireless sacrifices, demanding all offerings in their natural state. Honeycombs, unspun wool, unpressed grapes, and uncooked grain were laid on her altars. Not for her the offerings of wine, mead, cakes, and cloth, for Demeter was the principle of natural, rather than artificial, production.

Her greatest festival, shared with Persephone, was at Eleusis, where the Greeks annually celebrated mysteries that brought the initiate into a gracious and grateful relationship to the Mother. At the three-day festival, the *mystai* imitated the searching Demeter and rejoiced as, once again, she was reunited with her daughter. In their mimicry, they were at first Demeter Erynes ("angry"), furious and sad at the loss of Persephone; then they acted the happy role of Demeter Louisa ("kindly one"), the mother transformed by reunion. In other places and at other times, Demeter bore other names: Kidaria ("mask"), Chamaine ("soil"), and the powerful Thesmophoros ("lawgiver"), orderer of the seasons of the earth and of human life as well.

Derceto A Greek translation of Atargatis. This word may have originated in *dagitu*, the feminine form of the word for "fish," a symbol of Atargatis.

Despoina "Mistress," a name for the Kore worshiped with Demeter at the Greek city of Thelpousa. There, it was said, Hippia ("horsefaced" Demeter) took Poseidon as a lover and afterward bore this wild girl, sometimes called Artemis.

Devi Hinduism is polytheistic in that it grants many names and forms to the divine force, but it is ultimately monotheistic as well in that all forms of divinity can be reduced to one: Devi ("the goddess"). True, there are preeminent gods, some of whom have more power than the goddess. But without her, they would have no power at all, or even a form. For it is Devi, the Hindus say, who gives birth to all force and form, who creates separation out of unity, who is the energy without which all would still be chaos.

All goddesses are Devi, the one goddess; all the myths told of black Kali, of golden Parvati or Gauri, of the fierce Durga, are myths of Devi. Many of these legends are recounted in the Puranas, Indian religious works created after the indigenous goddess culture was assimilated into the religion of the Indo-European invaders of the Vedas. What these legends were in pre-Vedic India we have no record. The civilization of the Indus Valley in the second millennium B.C.E. is known to have been centered on a religion of the goddess. But generations of invasions and warfare almost obliterated the early worship. Still, followers of the goddess retained their beliefs and rituals, which erupted in later Indian history in the Shaktic and Tantric movements, heterodox at first but later incorporated into orthodox Hinduism. Almost 3,000 years passed between the heyday of Devi's worship and the Indian Middle Ages, but when she reemerged it was not only as the people's deity, the popular recipient of their devotions, but as the philosophic basis of the perceived universe.

Devorgilla There was a woman of this name in Irish history who, by running off with her lover, Diarmuid, brought ruin to the island by allowing the entrance of Norman warriors. That woman was the namesake of an earlier Devorgilla, an ancient Irish sorceress. Given to the hero Cuchulain by her father, the king of Ireland, Devorgilla was spurned and passed on to another man. Hurt by the slight, she instantly changed herself and her handmaiden into birds; together they flew away. But out hunting one day, Cuchulain brought Devorgilla to earth with a rock; she instantly resumed her human form, to the hero's dismay. The pebble, big enough to stun a bird, was buried deep in Devorgilla's flesh; Cuchulain got on his knees and sucked it out, thereby saving the woman's life. But he swallowed some of her blood in his rescue effort, thereby becoming Devorgilla's blood kin; thereafter there was no possibility of them sharing a bed.

Dewi Nawang Sasih Among the Sundanese, who live near Java in the Pacific Ocean, this celestial nymph taught people how to cook rice. The recipe, in that ancient time, was very easy: place one grain in a pot, and wait until it divides and subdivides into an entire meal. People lived in comfort for many generations, because the men always obeyed Dewi Nawang's one commandment: never to touch a woman's cooking implement. But there came a king who believed himself above all laws, and he deliberately broke the goddess' one rule. Dewi Nawang Sasih, disgusted, departed forever from this earth. And since that time, it takes a whole bunch of rice to fill a pot, because although the grains swell up, they no longer divide and reproduce.

Dewi Shri The rice goddess of Bali has a name like Sri, the Hindu goddess of prosperity. But Dewi Shri is a more primeval force than her Indian namesake. Goddess of both the underworld and the moon, she has thus both earthly and celestial powers. Although she rules life, through her control of the foodstuffs of the earth, she also controls death, which returns us to her bosom.

Dhat-Badan The primary goddess of the Himyaritic Arabs of Yemen, her names mean "she of the wild goats" and "she of the sanctuary." This suggests that she was a goddess of the natural forces of the wilderness, worshiped especially in tree-circled oases.

Dia Her ancient name shows that she was one of Italy's original goddesses, but little survived into historical times of Dea Dia. More historically prominent than the goddess' name is that of her servants, the twelve Arval Brothers (Fratres Arvales), a renowned college of priests charged with tending Dea Dia's sacred grove on the Tiber River. So sacred was this laurel and oak grove that whenever a rotten limb fell in a storm or an old tree was blown to the ground, the Fratres had to offer lambs and sows in reparation.

Dia Griene The daughter of the sun in ancient Scotland was called "the sun's tear" for reasons that remain mysterious. She appears in a folktale in which, held captive in the Land of the Big Women, she is freed by the Cailleach, disguised as a fox, and a helpful young bumbler named Brian.

Diana Today we confuse Diana with the Greek Artemis, seeing both in the familiar picture of the lightly clad, bow-bearing goddess who rides the moon or strides through the forest with her nymphs. And in later Roman times, Diana was indeed so pictured, but only after the original Italian goddess was assimilated into the powerful figure of Artemis, the goddess of the conquered Greeks.

Diana was originally queen of the open sky, worshiped only outdoors, where her domain stretched overhead. Possibly she was ruler of the sun as well as the moon, for the early Italians had no sun god and had to adopt Apollo for that role. Diana's name comes from the word for "light"; probably she was the original Italian ruler of the sun.

She ruled on earth as well, as bestower of sovereignty and granter of conception; thus she was sometimes called the threefold Diana Trivia. With two other deities she made up another trinity: Egeria the water nymph, her servant and assistant midwife; and Virbius, the mysterious woodland god. The three lived together in the famous Wood of Nemi near Aricia, where runaway slaves competed for the mistletoe—the Golden Bough that would give them a fighting chance for the position of Diana's priest. Not a job a modern man would covet, the priesthood meant continual vigilance against the next contender for the post, and ultimate death at a successful rival's hands.

This fatal kingship was one of the few roles men could play in the worship of Diana. Otherwise, the sky queen was entirely a woman's goddess. On her feast day, August 15—today the Catholic feast day of Mary's assumption into heaven—processions of women would journey to Aricia to offer thanks in Diana's grove for her help that year and to implore her continuing aid. The hunting dogs who accompanied them were crowned but kept leashed so as not to disturb the wild creatures who lived under Diana's sky. Eventually Diana's worship moved closer to the population center, to the Aventine Hill in Rome itself, where women continued to flock to her shrine for ritual hairwashing and invocations for aid in childbed.

Dido   To most people steeped in European culture, this name evokes the Carthaginian queen who, seduced and abandoned by the wandering Trojan Aeneas, killed herself rather than face public dishonor as a ruler whose wishes could be flouted. But behind this legendary figure is another, for Dido was also the name of the founder of Carthage. It is possible to assume that Dido lived for many centuries and committed suicide twice; this would be necessary to incorporate all the events of "Dido's" life into one story. It seems more probable that the name of a deified ancestor and city founder was adopted, in turn, by each of the Carthaginian queens and that Dido—like Candace and Helen—was the title that went with the crown. Dido of the Aeneid, then, would have been one of a line of so-named Punic rulers.

The first Dido probably took her name from *dida* ("to wander") and was originally Elissa or Alitta ("the goddess") of Tyre or Cyprus. When she discovered that her brother had treacherously murdered her husband, she fled her homeland with a retinue of eighty women. Dido traveled to North Africa and purchased "a hide's worth" of land, then cleverly cut the hide into strips and claimed all the land they could surround. Her city, Cartha-Elissa ("city of the goddess"), flourished under the more familiar name of Carthage, but its first queen killed herself when a neighboring king threatened war unless she would sleep with him. The sacred grove of Elissa, the divine queen, remained in the middle of Carthage until the Punic city was obliterated by the Romans.

Dike   Personification of justice to the Greeks, she was less a goddess than an abstract ideal. She was said to protect those who administered justice; she encouraged rewarding the good as well as punishing the evil. Her assistant was Poena, the goddess of retaliation and retribution.

Dinah   Mother of the last matriarchal Hebrew tribe, she was the daughter of Leah and was changed from male to female in her mother's womb—an inversion of the usual biological development—when her mother, pitying her childless sister Rachel, prayed that her child be a worthless female rather than her seventh son.

Hebrew legend tells us that Dinah was kept in a chest by her father Jacob whenever possible suitors were in sight, so concerned was he that she would marry an uncircumcised man. Nonetheless, Dinah went walking one night and stumbled into a joyous group of dancers—one of whom, a prince named Shechem, asked her to come home with him, and slept with her.

Shechem planned to make Dinah his lawful wife, but the Hebrews objected to Dinah's marriage to a man from an uncircumcised tribe. So Shechem's people agreed to forfeit their foreskins and did so. Then, on the third day after the ritual, when all the men were bedridden with post-operative inflammations, the Hebrews fell upon the tribe and massacred them, taking Dinah away, pregnant with a daughter. It is likely this tale holds a political allegory concerning the attempt of the Dinah tribe to ally itself with other, non-Hebrew people of the Near East and an eventual realignment according to blood. Dinah herself was provided with a proper Hebrew mate, suggesting that the matriarchal vestiges were purged from the tribes of Israel.

Dione   She was a very ancient goddess of the territory that became Greece, and what we know of her is confusing and sometimes contradictory. In late Greek legend, Dione is an Oceanid, daughter of the ocean, mother of Aphrodite. But this is geographically impossible, as the alleged daughter was imported from the eastern Mediterranean long after Dione's worship had faded.

In the invented genealogy of Aphrodite, Dione was said to have been impregnated by Zeus. Zeus appears in another relation to Dione: he was the second ruler of her oracle at Dodona. At that very ancient spot, the rustling of a tree answered questions on personal, never state or religious, matters; only aged women were allowed to interpret the tree's words. Even after Zeus took over Dione's oracle, men were barred from presiding at the rituals.

It is likely, these clues suggest, that Dione was originally an important goddess of inspiration and sexuality of pre-Hellenic Greece. Her name is a cognate of Juno and Diana, the Roman sky goddesses; this hints at an early theological preeminence. But the truth about Dione's significance has been virtually obliterated, with rustlings as faint as the Dodona beeches left for us to interpret.

Dis, Disir (pl.)   Originally the deified woman ancestor of a family, this word came to mean any Scandinavian goddess. But the Disir also remained an undistinguished blur of fate goddesses, worshiped in services called *disablot*. With much drinking and storytelling, a family celebrated "winter nights," the festival that honored these goddesses of heredity, who controlled an individual's talents and defects.

Diti   If the Indian goddess Aditi is "boundless," her counterpart, Diti, is "the bounded one." Many interpreters see Aditi as the endless sky, Diti as the earth. Both apparently come from a non-Aryan source of Hindu mythology, for their children, though recognized as supernatural, were never part of the official pantheon.

Diti's children were *asuras*, non-gods. They were powerful beings, especially the warrior Maruts, who might have conquered the gods. Diti, whose earlier children Indra had killed, practiced magic when pregnant again. So threatened was Indra that he watched her constantly. When Diti fell into a doze, Indra entered her vagina, traveled to her womb, and dismembered the fetus. Even cut to pieces, the fetus was so powerful that it reformed into forty-nine separate warriors.

Djanggawul Sisters   Daughters of the sun, these Australian goddesses unceasingly brought forth living creatures from their endlessly pregnant bodies. Plants and animals, sacred articles, and even rituals fell from them as they wandered the world. Their long vulvas broke off piece by piece with these births, producing the world's first sacred artifacts.

But, Australian myth says, the women's power was stolen by their brother. One day as the women were fishing, their brother and a companion sneaked into the camp and stole the women's power objects. Instantly, the women were alerted by psychic alarms, but they returned too late to save their possessions. Bereft of their magic, the women departed to follow the sun's path, continuing to produce new creatures as they traveled.

Djigonasee   A heroine of the Ontario Hurons, Djigonasee was the mother of the peacebringer Deganiwada, founder of the Six Nations: Seneca, Cayuga, Onondaga, Oneida, Mohawk, and Tuscarora. Like many mothers of heroes, Djigonasee was a virgin when her son was born. A herald from beyond this world announced the birth.

When her son was grown, Djigonasee served the cause of peace by conveying messages and treaties among the nations. In this role, she upheld her woodland people's traditions, for their chiefs were chosen by wise women, who also removed from power chiefs who acted selfishly or foolishly.

Dolya   In Russia, the goddess of fate was said to live behind the stove. When she was in a fine mood, she was called Dolya, the little old lady who brought good luck; when annoyed, she was Nedolya, the shabbily dressed old hag of bad fortune. Occasionally she appeared as a young woman rather than the usual gray-haired granny; in either shape she presided over birth, for it was at that moment that her prophetic powers were most invoked.

Don   The ancient ancestral goddess of the Welsh, Don had no real place in their legends except as the mother of all divinities. Most scholars agree that she was the same goddess as the Irish Danu—for the Celts of the two islands were related—but there is considerable dispute whether she was related to Danae of the Greeks. Irish legend claims that the people of Danu, driven from their Peloponnesian homeland by the Syrians, traveled through Denmark to arrive in the Atlantic islands in 1472 B.C.E. If this Irish tradition is accepted, then one must see Don as a pre-Hellenic goddess suppressed in Greece who reemerged centuries later in Wales.

Doris   An ancient, probably pre-Hellenic goddess of the waters, she may have been the ancestor goddess of the Dorians. She was the mother of the Nereids and, possibly, Thetis.

Draupadi   One of the main heroines of the Mahabharata, the Indian epic, Draupadi was a polyandrous woman who slept in turn with each of her five husbands, who were all brothers; she had a favorite, however, named Arjuna.

Dryads   The Greeks believed every tree had an individual soul, an elemental force incarnated in a barky body. They were, as in most cultures, female; they were mortal, dying with the tree. Sometimes, it was believed, a Dryad would punish a mortal for thoughtlessly injuring her by breaking branches.

Dryope   There were a number of Greek heroines by this name. One was a water nymph who, infatuated with a mortal man, lured him into her embrace, and drowned him. Another was a nymph from wild Arcadia who gave birth to that late addition to the Greek pantheon, the lascivious Pan. Finally, there was an unfortunate nymph of this name, raped by the sun god and turned into a poplar tree. As such a tale often indicates an indigenous goddess suppressed by invading Indo-Europeans, it is possible that Dryope was originally much more than a doomed "nymph," possibly a tree goddess.

Dugnai   This Lithuanian goddess ruled the kneading of dough. Her name, "that which is at the bottom," suggests that she also controlled the lees or dregs of fermenting liquor.

Dunne Enin   An important goddess of the Tungus of Siberia, she rules the territory of the clan. It is to her that an offering (a piece of old cloth, a bit of ribbon, a broken bowl) must be left as an offering whenever camp is broken. It is from her that women must ask permission whenever a new camp is established, a new tent erected, a new fire lit. It is she who sets the rules of community behavior—and she enforces them by withholding game if taboos are broken. Should that occur, an individual must offer a black ribbon and a white ribbon on trees or bushes near the tent, which reflect Dunne Enin's control of the underworld and the sky. But if she is not content with this offering, then the shaman must travel to her, begging that she look kindly on her children again. At first she will always resist, but finally her heart will be softened and she will release the food animals—provided her sister goddess, Bugady Enintyn, agrees.

Durga   All goddesses in Hindu belief are ultimately the same goddess, often called simply "the Goddess" or Devi. But she appears in different forms with different names. One of the fiercest of Devi's forms is Durga. She was also the eldest: during the primordial war between gods and antigods, Durga was the first manifestation of goddess energy.

The war was a standoff; neither side was winning, and the battles dragged on without victory. Almost hopeless, the gods gathered and concentrated their energies. Flames sprang from their mouths and formed Durga, the first female divinity in the universe. Although produced by the gods, the goddess was stronger than any of them, or all of them together, and she was fiercely eager to fight.

Recognizing her power, the gods handed their weapons to Durga. She mounted a lion to ride toward the antigods' chief, the demon Mahisa. That magical being, terrified of this new apparition, used his powers to assume one fearsome form after another. Still the goddess advanced, until finally, as the demon assumed the form of a buffalo, Durga slaughtered him. The demon nonetheless tried to escape through the dying beast's mouth, but Durga caught him by the hair and butchered him, thereby freeing the earth for the gods to inhabit.

The goddess in this form not only symbolizes the fierce power of the combat against evil but also the rule of the intellectual sphere, for Durga ("unapproachable") represents the end of all things; to seek to understand her is to engage in the most powerful intellectual exploration possible.

Dzalarhons The volcano woman of the Haida of the northwest Pacific coast was a powerful spirit who ruled the creatures of the earth and punished people who abused them. Once, it was said, Dzalarhons was a mortal woman who migrated into Haida country with her uncle, Gitrhawn the Salmon-Eater. There she fell in love with a Haida man and, according to the matriarchal customs of the indigenous people, had her uncle arrange a marriage.

Bedecked with sea-otter furs and dentalia-trimmed leather, Dzalarhons was escorted across the bays of the Queen Charlotte Islands to the village of her chosen mate. There, splendid ceremonies marked the wedding but, when the couple retired to bed, Dzalarhons found she had mistaken the character of her new husband. He demanded that she spend the night, not beside him, but holding a lighted torch above his head. As the torch shrank through the night, the woman protected her arms with her garments, which were singed, then burned.

The next morning the Haida, shocked at the young man's behavior, warned him about bringing Gitrhawn's vengeance on the people. The bridegroom did not care, however, and continued to demand that Dzalarhons hold his torch until all her garments were burned and she was forced to go naked.

Hearing of Dzalarhons's shame, the Salmon-Eater people came to her rescue. They burned the Haida village but found no maiden, only a stone statue from between whose legs a stream flowed. The stream formed a lake; at the lake's head, the stone woman stood, holding a burning staff topped by a copper frog. Thereafter the metamorphosed maiden was a powerful and feared divinity.

Along the Nass River, it was said that Dzalarhons almost destroyed a village because its residents were careless of life. At first, the people lived in comfort, for the land provided them with berries, salmon, and other wild things to harvest. But growing accustomed to the wealth, they began to forget the land's strictures; they killed animals needlessly and left the carcasses for carrion eaters. They even invented a terrible game: they caught spawning salmon, slit their backs and inserted pitch-soaked branches, then lit the candlefish and set them back in the water. Bleeding and suffering, the shoals of salmon lit up the rivers spectacularly.

This horrible sight roused the fury of the volcano woman. Soon the people of the Wolf Clan heard terrible rumblings, like ghostly drums. Fright ran through the guilty village, but it was too late for repentance. Dzalarhons, goddess of the earth's treasures and owner of its metals, poured forth a fiery wrath on the Haida. Few escaped the holocaust, for even the rivers ran hot with the goddess' fury.

Dziewona Polish goddess of the hunt, she rode through the forests mounted on a speedy horse and accompanied by a pack of hunting dogs.

Dzivaguru In Zimbabwe, among the Korekore, she was an earth goddess whose palace stood on the shores of an ancient lake. Dressed in goatskin, she walked through her rich meadows and forests, drinking from her cornucopia, her magic horn which gave forth anything she requested of it. But the son of the sky god grew envious of Dzivaguru's wealth, and descended to earth to capture it from her. Dzivaguru wrapped her land in fog to hide it, but the god tied a ribbon around his head which allowed his sight to penetrate the fog. When the god entered Dzivaguru's palace, he found that she had fled, taking the sunlight with her. In the darkness, the god set a trap for her, and caught the goddess as she reappeared. Angry at his demands, she announced that she would leave him the lands, but she would take her lake with her. Thus the people of that country are forever crying out to Dzivaguru to send rain, for although she has vanished from the earth, she still controls the waters that nourish it.

Dziwozony This was the Polish name for the wild women of the woods, whom the Bulgarians called Divi-Te-Zeni and the Bohemians, Divozenky. They lived in the forest in underground burrows, seeking to understand the secrets of nature, especially those of herbal medicine. The Dziwozony were said to have large square heads, long fingers, and very ruddy bodies.

Ebhlinne This Irish goddess was worshiped in the southern county of Tipperary; her home was in the Twelve Mountains of Ebhlinne, the highest of which was called Mathair-Sliabh, the Mother-Mountain. In the *dindshenchas*, the geographical poetry of Ireland, Ebhlinne was said to be the daughter of Guaire from the Brugh na Boine—a fabulous pre-Celtic series of shrines that were called fairy-mounds in Christian times, and whose occupants were often disguised as ancient divinities. Married to a king of Cashel, Ebhlinne ran away with his handsome son. Until the first part of this century, the ancient goddess behind this legendary fairy-woman was honored by midsummer celebrations in her mountains.

Ececheira The Greek personification of armistice or truce, this goddess appears at the shrine of Zeus in Olympia, for during the Olympic games, all hostilities are forbidden.

Echenais This Greek nymph fell in love with a mortal, Daphnis, and made him promise sexual fidelity to her. But he got drunk with a priestess and made love to her. Echenais discovered the infidelity and, to assure that Daphnis would never again be tempted by mortal beauty, blinded her lover.

Echidna This monstrous serpent woman, daughter of the earth, mated with her own brother to produce some of the strangest creatures inhabiting Greek myth: the raging Nemean lion, the dangerous Scylla, the many-headed Hydra, the ferocious Chimera, and possibly even the Sphinx.

Echtghe Believed to be an ancient form or title of the pre-Celtic goddess Ana or Danu, the Mother of the Gods. Until recently, her name was used for a range of mountains in the west of Ireland, Sliabh na Echtghe (Slieve Aughty). Daughter of the god Nuada Silver-Arm, Echtghe was given the hills by her lover. Feakle Parish, the area surrounding the hills, was the haunt in the early part of this century of Biddy Early, the White Witch of Clare. She was an outrageous free-living woman with renowned healing powers which, she claimed, she derived from a magical blue bottle. Just before she died, Biddy threw the bottle into nearby lake Lough Rea, where it still rests, its magical power waiting to be reclaimed.

Echo An elemental of the mountains, one of the Oreads, Echo became an attendant of the sky goddess Hera. But Zeus, ruler of Olympus and Hera's mate, liked to confide in the nymph; he filled

Echo's ears with tales of his philandering. Hera, to prevent her strained marriage from becoming the laughingstock of heaven, struck Echo mute; Zeus counterattacked by giving her power to repeat anything she heard. Another version of the story says that Echo used to engage the goddess in gossip whenever Zeus wished to dally with one of her sister-nymphs, and this unsisterly deceit was what drew Hera's wrath.

The beautiful, silent woman was the lover of the wilderness god Pan, by whom she had two daughters, Iambe and Iynx. But she left the god to fall in love with a pretty mortal named Narcissus. The vain young man, however, would not sleep with her. In retribution, Narcissus was condemned to fall in love with his image in a forest pool. He pined away by the pool, eventually becoming a flower. And Echo, still trying to catch his attention, became a rock by the poolside. She still had the power of speech, but could only repeat what was spoken. This pretty story is almost without question a literary invention or fairy tale rather than a real myth, for there were no religious rituals which attended it.

Edain   Born in the southwest of Ireland, the legendary heroine Edain married the king of Munster who, a gambler with poor luck, lost her in a chess match to the fairy king Midir. Fairies in Ireland enjoyed affairs with humans, whom they held captive in underground palaces; so it was with Edain, who was imprisoned in Midir's crystal mansion.

The human king followed his wife, storming the fairy fort with his armies. But that, as anyone versed in fairy strength would know, was foolish as well as useless. The king then persuaded the old gods, the Tuatha de Danaan, to cast magical imprecations against Midir; that too was of no avail.

Finally, the king gathered another army and, joining forces with several powerful Druids, marched to Midir's fort. The fairy king was frightened by this show of human force. Unwilling, however, to let his captive go, he sent forth a group of fairies, all magically identical to Edain, who was forced to accompany them.

The fairies stood before the king, who could not distinguish the human woman among them. Despite this lapse in her husband—for true love should have allowed him to see through the fairies' glamour-spell—Edain remained staunch in her love for him and, straining against the enchantment that held her, broke the fairy king's power and returned to her mate. Thus, Irish legend says, did a woman destroy the magical power of the fairies, who thereafter could not capture humans at will.

Edda   Her name means "great grandmother," a word also used to describe the great compilations of Scandinavian mythology called the eddas ("tales of great-grandmother"). In the Norse creation story, the dwarfish Edda was the first woman to produce offspring; with her husband Ai, or possibly with the fire god Heimdal, she gave birth to the race of Thralls, the ones "enthralled" to service as food producers. The next great mother was Amma ("grandmother"), who gave birth to the race of Churls, who thenceforth (not always churlishly) conducted businesses and learned trades. The final mother figure of the story was Mothir herself, who produced the Jarls or leaders, the ones who hunted, fought, and attended school.

Egeria   An early Italian goddess of wisdom and foresight, her name is still used for women advisers. She may have been a form of Diana, with whom she shared a sacred shrine in the forest of Nemi. Or she may have been connected or identified with Vesta, for from a spring at her shrine, Vesta's virgins drew water for their rituals. Egeria appeared in Roman legend as a semi-divine water nymph enamored of the Roman king Numa Pompilius. She took him as her husband and thereafter served as his supernatural adviser. Egeria was the one who taught the correct rites for earth worship; she was the one who pronounced the first laws of the city. Later Egeria became a full-fledged divinity, worshiped by pregnant women desirous of easy delivery and (like many midwife goddesses) responsible for foretelling the future of the newborn.

Egle In Lithuania, this folklore heroine, whose name means "fir," had a dozen brothers, but only two sisters. One hot summer evening, the sisters went to a nearby lake to cool themselves. After a pleasant nude swim, a revived Egle waded to shore to dress. But there she saw a snake—a poisonous adder—coiled in the sleeve of her blouse. The oldest sister grabbed a stick and tried to poke the snake away, but it would not move.

Then, suddenly, the adder spoke in the voice of a man. "Be my wife, Egle," he said, "and I will not harm any of you." Realizing that she had little choice, Egle agreed. She and her sisters returned home, weeping with fright. Their fright did not diminsh when hundreds of adders swarmed over the house that night, singing merrily. Egle, resigned to her fate, went with them back to the lakeshore.

But to her amazement and delight, she found a handsome youth awaiting her there. He was king of the snakes, he explained, and he'd often admired her while she swam. He intended to make her very, very happy, he said. And then he waved, and a boat appeared, on which the couple traveled to an island paradise where a three-week wedding banquet was celebrated. From then on, Egle was supremely happy. She loved her husband, and he loved and cared for her. Before ten years had passed, she had three lovely children: her sons Oak, Ash and Birch, and her sweet daughter Trembling-Aspen.

As they grew, her children expressed curiosity about their human grandparents and cousins. So Egle planned an expedition home—although she was not herself homesick and had never been. Her husband explained that such a sojourn was possible, but first a hank of silk had to be spun. Egle spun and spun, but the silk never seemed to diminish. Consulting a sorcerer, Egle discovered that the silk was bewitched; she threw it into the fire and it instantly spun itself. Her husband then

gave her slippers that had to be broken in; she took them to the blacksmith and cooked them in the forge-fire. Then her husband wanted her to cook a rabbit pie, but she found all the pots had been removed; she made herself a pan from dough and cooked the pie. And so, sighing, her husband agreed to let her leave the kingdom of snakes to return to her people.

But he warned her that, should she see red foam on water, she would know he was dead. Shrugging off his ominous words, she packed for her journey. But once she had returned, Egle's brothers plotted to kill her husband, whom they wrongly believed was evil. And so, when the young woman returned to the lake to travel back to her happy home, she found red foam, which showed they had succeeded. Instantly, she and her children were all turned into the trees that bear their names.

Eileithyia A birth goddess who spun the thread of life, Eileithyia was worshiped in pre-Hellenic Greece; later she was assimilated to the goddess Artemis. Though superseded, Eileithyia did not disappear; her name was used even into Roman times. Immeasurably ancient, she was said to have midwived the gods and goddesses of classical Greece. Some legends even call her the mother of Eros—not the frivolous later godling, but the primordial force of creation hatched from the world egg.

Eileithyia could curse a birthing mother by crossing her knees and clasping her hands; until she unfolded her body, the woman's child would not enter the world of light. Dogs and horses were her symbols; the sacrifice of a dog assured that Eileithyia would sit with uncrossed knees during birth. Later peoples used this ancient goddess' name as a title of their own birth goddess, and so Eileithyia came to be used of Juno Lucina and even Hecate.

Eingana The people of the oldest continuing culture on the earth's face, the Australian natives, tell us that Mother Eingana was the world-creator, maker of all water, land, animals, and kangaroos. This huge snake goddess still lives, they say, in the Dreamtime, rising up occasionally to create yet more life.

At first, Eingana vomited living beings from her mouth. Then, dissatisfied with this method of birth, she swallowed them again. The primordial snake had no vagina; as her offspring grew inside her, the goddess swelled up. Eventually, tortured with the pregnancy, Eingana began to roll around and around. The god Barraiya saw her agony and speared her near the anus so that birth could take place as all creatures now give birth. From Eingana poured her reborn creatures, which were chased by a dingo and took on their earthly forms as they flew, ran, or hopped away.

The birth mother, to these aboriginal people, is also the death mother. They say Eingana holds a sinew of life attached to each of her creatures; when she lets it go, that life stops. If she herself should die, they say everything would cease to exist.

Eir   The Scandinavian goddess of mercy was the "best physician" or the "caring one," the youthful goddess Eir who sat upon her hill Lyfjaberg ("healing"), granting health to any woman who could climb up to her.

Eireisone   The female personification of a Greek ritual object: a branch of olive wood, twined with wool and hung with fruits, which was carried in festivals by children with two living parents. Goddesses are created in many ways: sometimes as personifications of natural forces, sometimes as rulers of specific passage-points in a woman's life, sometimes as the spiritual essence of a season or of a significant geographical point. Occasionally, as in the case of Eireisone, an object of ritual becomes imbued with feminine force and identity, but there is often no myth attatched to the name.

Elat   This word, meaning "goddess," was applied to towns in the eastern Mediterranean where goddess worship was strong in pre-Christian days.

Electra   There were many Greek heroines of this name; most were notable only for being the mother of someone or the sister of someone else. Most famous was the daughter of Queen Clytemnestra, an Electra who plotted her mother's murder in revenge for Clytemnestra's murder of her father Agamemnon—which in turn was inspired by Agamemnon's murder of his child, Electra's sister Iphegenia. This character was, most scholars agree, a purely literary contrivance with no basis in the original myth. As such, she served as a mouthpiece for authors who wished to support the diminishment of women's power; the goddess Athena was used in similar fashion in the same myth cycle, when she was shown to find Electra's brother Orestes innocent of Clythemnestra's murder on the odd grounds that a mother is genetically unrelated to her offspring, serving only as a sort of biological holding-tank for sperm-created babies. Electra's name is used by psychologists today who refer to an "Electra complex" among young women inappropriately dependent on their fathers.

Elen   In the Mabinogian, the Welsh mythic epic, this heroine appears as the world's first highway engineer. When her land was threatened, she magically built highways across the country so that her soldiers could gather and defend it. Because her invention provided a way for her armies to gather, she is sometimes called Elen of the Hosts.

Elena   The famous Russian folktale of the firebird parallels that of Dia Grene the Scottish sun-maiden. It begins when a young man ordered to find the magical firebird. With the help of a friendly wolf, he did so, but the bird's owner awakened as he was stealing it, and demanded that he get a magnificent horse in return for the bird. The young man found the horse, but the owner awakened and demanded Elena in return for the animal. But when the hero met Elena, he fell in love with her. Luckily for him, the wolf was a shapeshifter who turned into a false woman and a false horse, allowing the youth to come home with Elena, mounted on the magnificent horse and carrying the firebird. But his own brothers set upon him and killed him, stealing Elena and the other treasures. The wolf, however, magically revived him—just in time for him to prevent Elena's marriage to one of the murderous brothers.

Eleos To the Greeks, she was the goddess of mercy. She had one altar, in the center of Athens, and there anyone who wished to gain the assistance of the city-state had to worship before requesting an alliance.

Elle This mythic woman, who represented Age, once wrestled with the thunder god Thor. Even though she looked like a frail old woman when they gripped each other's arms, her strength proved greater than his—for no one can beat old age.

Embla The first woman on earth was, according to the Scandinavians, an ash tree. (Some say she was an elder, and that the ash tree formed the first man.) "Empty of force and empty of fate," Embla lay alive but soulless on the new earth. Into the wooden female form, the god Odin breathed an enlivening spirit, as he did into her mate.

Emer This most desirable of Irish heroines was endowed with everything a woman could possess: wisdom, talent, and wit. Besides all that, she was lovely to look upon, and she pridefully acknowledged her own excellence. "I am," she told one suitor, "a Tara among women, the whitest of maidens, one who is gazed at but gazes not back; I am the untrodden way." That suitor was the hero Cuchulain, of whom she demanded heroic exploits before she would sleep with him, reasoning that her superior endowments warranted them.

Empanda This Roman goddess personified the idea of openness and generosity. Her temple was always open, and food was always available there,

as was asylum for escaping slaves and criminals. Sometimes the word appears as a title of Juno.

Eni Mahanahi In ancient Anatolia, this was the name given to a goddess known as Leto to the Greeks, mother of Artemis. As Artemis was also a goddess of human and animal birth, her "divine mother" Eni Mahanahi would presumably have had more cosmic duties. She may thus be described either as goddess of the land and its produce, or as ruler of the universal force of life.

Eos The Greek goddess of dawn, Eos was the daughter of two early light deities, Hyperion and Thea. The lovely winged creature drove a chariot hitched to four swift steeds, dragging light across the sky; she changed at midday into another goddess, Hemera ("light of day"), and later into sunset goddess Hesperide.

Eos had a strong sexual appetite—almost as strong as that of the love goddess Aphrodite herself. She had many lovers, often kidnapping handsome men to serve her needs. One was the gigantic Orion, a rather brutal human who, because of his constant mistreatment of his wife Merope, was blinded by Merope's father and by the wine god Dionysus. In order to restore his sight, Orion was told to bathe his face in Eos' rays. She saw him standing on a hilltop and not only restored Orion's sight but stole him away for her lover. Orion never did remedy his violent ways, however, and was eventually removed to the stars for an offense against Artemis.

Another mortal lover was Tithonus, for whom Eos conceived so lasting an affection that she begged immortality for him. Alas for him, Eos forgot to add a request for eternal youth. Slowly Tithonus wizened, and Eos' love faded. She fled his bed, but took enough pity on her former lover to turn Tithonus into a cricket and install him in a little cage near her door, whence he could chirp good-bye to her as she left on her day's journey.

Ephesia The goddess of Ephesus in Anatolia is often called simply Artemis, or their names are joined as Artemis Ephesia. Originally, however, she was distinct from the Greek goddess of the wild places. Her statue still stands in the sanctuary that bears her name, a place considered one of the Seven Wonders of the ancient world. It is a familiar image: a tall woman whose chest is covered with globes. Breasts? Honeycombs? The genitals of cattle? Those of castrated men? All these have been offered as possibilities, and any (or all) could be correct. The protuberances look like breasts and appear on the torso; her priestesses were called Melissae, "bees"; and she was served by castrated priests. Whatever the sculptor meant, it cannot be argued that the image is one of abundance. And Ephesia was a goddess who, like other mother goddesses, offered abundant life and protection to her children.

Epona Epona was the name given to the horse goddess among the Celts. Her worship, widely popular in territories occupied by Rome, was eventually adopted by the Roman armies as well, who honored her as the goddess who protected their stabled horses, while a similar goddess named Bubona was allotted the protection of oxen and other cattle. Although she was honored among the insular Celts in Britain and Ireland, the greater number of inscriptions and statues of Epona come from the continent. She was depicted in three poses: astride a horse, standing beside a horse or (least frequently) lying naked on a horse. When these sculptures and bas-reliefs show her holding an emblem, it varies also: sometimes Epona carries a cornucopia, sometimes a goblet, but most often a round bowl or plate.

Said to be the offspring of a mare and a man, Epona could take the tangible forms of both parents. Sometimes, too, she appeared as a rushing river, which suggests that Epona was a fertility goddess, often seen in Celtic culture as a water spirit. Similarly, the connection among Celtic peoples of the horse and the sun suggests a solar nature to

Epona, supported as well by the *patera* or round sunlike plate that she carries in many sculptures.

The sacred mare Epona appeared as the bestower of sovereignty in the ancient Celtic rituals of kingship, which may have included a rite of marriage with the mare goddess. Among Indo-European peoples in India, a rite of mare-marriage, which solidified a man's claim on the rulership of a geographical area, is attested and has been connected by scholars to the figure of Epona.

Recent excavations of the magnificent British monument, the White Horse of Uffington, strongly suggest that the 360-foot-long horse represents Epona. Using a new technique, archaeologists have been studying the rate at which the hillside, upon which the White Horse is carved into the chalky soil, has descended towards the deep valley (the Vale of the White Horse) beneath. The White Horse has puzzled researchers for many years, some maintaining that it was a late medieval creation, others that it derived from the post-Celtic era. Even before the recent attempt to date the monument itself, it had been noted that the horse's design echoed that of coins issued by the Celtic warrior queen Boudicca. The identification of the White Horse with the Celts is now virtually certain—and as the Celts had only one horse-divinity, the likelihood is that the horse on the hill was Epona. Vestiges of her are also found in the figure of Lady Godiva and the mysterious white-horse-riding woman of Banbury Cross.

Erathipa In central Australia, there is a huge boulder in the shape of a pregnant woman that bears this name. Down the side of the stone runs a long opening, and through that opening the souls of children are imprisoned. They hide there, watching until a woman of suitable age walks by, and then they slip out into her womb to be reborn. Women of childbearing age, who do not wish to become pregnant at that time, stoop as they walk past Erathipa's rock. Pretending to use a cane to walk, they mutter, "I am an old woman, I cannot carry children."

Erce   In Slavic tradition, the earth mother Erce was honored by greeting the newly turned soil each spring and pouring milk, flour, and water into the furrows.

Eri   A goddess of the Tuatha de Danaan, the magical divinities of early Ireland, Eri "of the golden hair" found a lover in an unusual way. She was a virgin until the day a silver boat traveling in the path of the sun arrived. It contained a man, shining like his boat, with whom Eri made love almost immediately. But the visitor stayed on shore only long enough to impregnate Eri with the beautiful god Bres, then left to return to his own people, leaving only a golden ring with the goddess as a token of his stay.

Erigone   The usual story of the Greek queen Clytemnestra says that she lost one daughter, Iphegenia, to her husband's callous plotting, while the other, Electra, turned against her mother and plotted her murder. But other versions of the story exist in which Clytemnestra had another daughter, this one with her lover Aegisthus. Named Erigone, she remained faithful to the queen, her mother. In this less commonly known version of the famous story, it was Erigone who brought her half-brother Orestes to trial for Clytemnestra's murder. When he was acquitted, Erigone hanged herself, rather than live in a world that forgave matricide.

Erinyes   Long before the Olympians ruled the territory we now call Greece, the people there recognized three immortal black maidens with serpent hair and poisonous blood that dripped from their eyes. Clad in gray, bearing brass-studded whips, baying and barking like bitches, they roamed the pre-Hellenic world in pursuit of those who dared offend the primordial laws of kinship. They were the force that held a matriarchal world together, for these half-human women waited as punishment for anyone who dared commit the sacrilege of spilling kindred blood. The dreaded Erinyes hounded to death, like a tortured conscience, anyone who spilled such blood, painfully created by his maternal relatives, for kinship was traced through the mother.

There were three Erinyes, or there was one Erinys with three forms: Alecto ("unresting one"), Megaera ("envious anger"), and Tisiphone ("avenger"). They were born from the blood of the castrated sky god Uranus where it touched the earth mother Gaia. Standing by the throne of the sun or in the dark world of Tartarus, these implacable goddesses could be stayed by neither sacrifice nor tears once their righteous anger was aroused. Nonetheless, those hoping to avert their gaze from minor misdeeds would lay by their sanctuaries black sheep and honeyed water, white doves and narcissus flowers.

The trinity of goddesses bore many names. As the Semnae, they were worshiped as "kindly ones," although they were invariably just rather than gentle; when guilty conspirators sought their forgiveness by attaching themselves by a thread to the goddesses' statue, the Erinyes miraculously broke free, showing the Athenians that criminals deserved punishment. As the Dirae, they were "curses" personified. As Maniae or Furiae, they were the mad ones—the Furies. Most often they were called Erinyes, "the strong ones," a force so instinctive and primeval that the Greeks assured each other, "Even dogs have their Erinyes."

It was the poet Aeschylus who identified them with the helpful Eumenides, a theologically radical position, for the trinities of goddesses were originally distinct. In the famous climax to Aeschylus' Oresteia, the laws of mother right—of which the Erinyes were the fiercest symbol—are shown giving way to the newer form of social organization imported into Greece by the patriarchal Indo-Europeans. Orestes, son of Clytemnestra, killed his mother in a vengeful fury; the Erinyes hounded him until they reached the temple of Apollo, where he took sanctuary. The first trial by jury was then held, with Athena presiding; the vote was tied.

Athena cast the deciding vote, against punishment of the matricide. The Erinyes were convulsed with anger at the decision, at having a morsel stolen from their plates. "Gods of the younger generation," they screamed, "you have ridden down the laws of elder times, torn them out of my hand." They threatened to ravage the land in retaliation, but Athena consoled them with promises of sacrifices and honor. Finally, they grew reconciled to the new order and were renamed Eumenides, taking on the name and identity of a triplet of goddesses who originally had little but number in common with the Erinyes. Allowed to keep their original function, the goddesses were thereafter to exercise their calling only at the behest of the Olympian divinities.

Eris Like the Roman goddess Discordia, she was to the Greeks the embodiment of folly, moral blindness, infatuation and mischief. Her famous toy the Apple of Discord (sometimes said to be that of her daughter Ate), was the cause of the Trojan War. Her familial heritage is unclear, as perhaps is suitable for such a disordered goddess. Usually, Eris is said to be the daughter of the ancient Nyx, goddess of night. But occasionally she is said to be the sister of the war god Ares, which would make her a descendent of the sky father Zeus; yet other writers make her the mate of Ares, mother by him of a gaggle of woes named Pontus (sorrow), Lethe (forgetfulness), Limus (hunger), Algaea (pain), Ate (error) and Harucs (the oath).

Eriskegal In Sumerian theology, a vast black-haired woman slept naked in a palace of lapis lazuli in the afterlife, drawing the naked dead into herself. This goddess, Eriskegal, was another form of the earth mother known by so many names in the eastern Mediterranean: Ishtar, Mami, Inanna, and others.

Originally Eriskegal alone ruled the wilderness at the world's end, surrounded by rainbow gardens. But then the violent god Nergal invaded her territory. Eriskegal wanted peace. So she had intercourse with Nergal, thus imparting some of her wisdom to him and bringing him closer to equality with her—close enough, at least, that she henceforth shared her throne with him. They ruled together over Kigalla ("dead land"), living in the "House of Dust."

In art Eriskegal appeared as a lion-headed woman suckling lion cubs. She was also shown in a boat, kneeling on the horse of death and traversing the boundary river between her world and ours, gazing toward the offerings that the living place on its shores.

Eriu In Gaelic, Ireland is called Erin, a word that means the "land of Eriu," the green isle's ancient earth goddess. In old Ireland, there were two related goddesses, Banba and Folta, and the following story is told of the trinity.

Many tribes had invaded the island, conquered it, and assimilated its indigenous people. Last in prehistory to arrive on Ireland's shores were the sons of Milesius. First, they met Banba ("land unplowed for a year"), the sorceress queen. They promised the goddess that if allowed to pass, they would name the country after her. Banba stepped aside.

Second, they met Folta. They promised her, too, that the island would bear her name; again, the goddess let them pass. Third, the Milesians faced Eriu. As you looked at her, the goddess sometimes appeared as a huge beautiful woman, sometimes as a long-beaked gray crow. A masterful magician, she lived on a hill in Ireland's center; as the goddess aged, her hill grew in size. Eriu could pick up clods from her mountain and fling them at invading armies; the earth turned into warriors and Eriu invariably won the ensuing battle.

But the Milesians, though stunned by the goddess' size and obvious power, were also magicians. They negotiated a truce with Eriu—offering, of course, to name the island after her. This time they were too frightened of her power to break their promise, and Erin remains today the land of Eriu.

Ergane "The Worker" is an important title of the Greek goddess Athena as patron of arts. Descended from a Cretan goddess of household industry, Athena remained a goddess closely identified with the women's craft of weaving after her transportation to the mainland of Greece. In this guise, this otherwise virgin goddess was sometimes said to be the mother of Plutus, "wealth," which results from hard work.

Eshara The Chaldean goddess of the productive fields, she was also a war goddess who symbolized the armed defense of property that accompanies private ownership of land.

Ess Euchen When the Irish warrior Cuchulain killed Ess Euchen's three sons, this fierce mother turned herself into an aged crone and ambushed the murderer on a narrow mountain path. She asked for right of passage and Cuchulain, deferring to her sex and age, stepped off the path, clinging to the road with his toes as he hung over the cliff. Ess Euchen immediately stomped hard on his toes, hoping to send him tumbling to his death. However, Cuchulain had been trained by the warrior goddess Scathach; using one of Scathach's magical jumps, he leaped up and killed the woman.

Esther It is now well established that this Old Testament heroine was the goddess Ishtar in thin disguise. Start from the clues in her name: in Aramaic, Esther is the word for Ishtar; in Persian, it means "star," and Ishtar was the goddess of the morning and evening star. Even the woman's Hebrew name, Hadassah, means "myrtle," a tree with star-shaped flowers.

In addition, the Book of Esther—recorded in the third or second century B.C.E.—is the only one in which Jehovah's name does not appear. Instead, the book relates the unlikely story that a Persian queen, Vashti (the name of an Elamite goddess), and a prime minister, Haman (an Elamite god), were replaced by a pair of Hebrew cousins, Esther and Mordecai. By this time, it should be no surprise that Mordecai too had a namesake: none other than the Babylonian hero Marduk (Hebrew, Morodach), the cousin of Ishtar. Marduk fought dragons; Mordecai dreamt of them.

In essence, the Book of Esther records the overthrow of the Elamite pantheon and its replacement by that of the Babylonians. Small wonder, then, that for many centuries the book was considered to be of questionable orthodoxy. Doubts somehow were set to rest, however, and the book is now part of authorized Judeo-Christian belief.

Estsanatlehi "Turquoise woman" was the Navaho sky goddess, wife of the sun. She lived in a turquoise palace at the western horizon, where each night she received her luminous husband. Sister (or twin or double) of Yolkai Estsan, the moon's wife, Estsanatlehi was able to make herself young each time she began to age, thus her name, which means the "self-renewing one."

Here is her story: the ancestral goddess Atse Estsan, discovering Estsanatlehi on the ground beneath a mountain, reared her to be the savior of earth's people. When she was grown, Estsanatlehi met a young man; each day they went to the woods to make love. When her parents looked on the ground and saw only one set of footprints, they knew their daughter had taken the sun as a lover.

Delighted at the honor granted their family, they were delighted again when Estsanatlehi gave birth to twins, who grew so miraculously that eight days after birth they were men, ready to seek their father. But when they found his house, the twins found another woman there. Angry at the intrusion, she threatened them with their father's anger as well.

Undeterred, the twins remained and won from their father magic weapons, which they needed to clear the earth of monsters. This they did. After dancing with their mother in celebration, the twins built Estsanatlehi a magnificent home at the sky's end, so that the sun could visit her again.

But the twins' wars with the monsters had depopulated the earth. Estsanatlehi brushed the dust from her breasts. From the white flour that fell from her right breast and the yellow meal from her left, she made paste and molded a man and a woman. Placing them beneath a magical blanket, Estsanatlehi left them. The next morning they were alive and breathing, and Estsanatlehi blessed the creation. For the next four days, the pair reproduced constantly, forming the four great Navaho clans. But the creative urge of Estsanatlehi was not fulfilled. She made four more groups of people, this time from the dust of her nipples—and the women of these clans were thereafter famous for their nipples.

Feeling her creation to be complete, Estsanatlehi retired to her turquoise palace from which she continued to bestow blessings on her people: seasons, plants and food, and the tender sprouts of spring. Only four monsters survived her sons' wars on evil: age, winter, poverty, and famine, which she allowed to live on so that her people would treasure her gifts the more.

Etain   The "swift one" was one of the early sun goddesses of ancient Ireland and—like other Celtic solar divinities—was also a horse goddess, a divine mare no mortal steed could outrun. Her worshipers said Etain lived in the sacred hill of Eochaid Airem, or at the entrance to the underworld, Bri Leith, in a *griannon* or house open to the sun.

The most famous story of Etain told how she, though a powerful goddess of the de Danaan tribe, nonetheless fell under the power of the fairy queen Fuamnach, who transformed her into a purple fly. For seven years Etain buzzed bewitched through the world. Then she fell into a cup, was swallowed by a woman, and was reborn in human form. The reborn Etain wed the king of Ireland, then took his brother as a lover. The fairy king Midir, to bring Etain back to the supernatural world, disguised himself as her husband, surprised her with her lover, and demanded that she return home with him. Then, resuming his original form, King Midir flew her off to Bri Leith at the sun's rising point, where they are said to still live happily today.

Another Etain, called Etain of the Fair Hair, was a fairy woman of the hill Ben Edar; married to a mortal, she died of grief when he was killed. Yet another Etain—although possibly all are forms of the original goddess—was the ruler of Beare Island, a well-known ritual spot in Bantry Bay, off the west coast of Ireland.

Ethne   Originally, Ethne was a primitive Irish goddess who lived on nothing but the milk of a sacred cow from India and was guarded by a demon who staved off any approaching men. She came into later legend as a princess of the Fomorians, the early Irish sea deities; her people offered Ethne to the later gods, the Tuatha de Danaan, in an attempt to unite the peoples. Ethne ("sweet nutmeat") wedded Diancecht of the Tuatha and gave birth to the god Lugh.

Another story says that Ethne was locked in a high tower where no man could reach her because of a prophecy that her sons would kill her father. But a hero, MacKineely, disguised himself as a woman to gain entrance to the tower; he slept with Ethne, but was killed by her father for his rashness. In this variation of the tale, Ethne's sons met a tragic fate, all dying in infancy.

Etugen   An ancient Mongol earth goddess, her name was derived from Otuken, the holy mountain of the Tujue people. She was honored by eating clay-filled earth, which was obtained from sacred sites called "earths of strength." Although there is little recorded about this goddess, she seems to have been a virginal mother, for it was said that earthquakes were caused by Etugen shaking herself to get rid of impurities.

Eumenides   The "kindly ones" were early Greek goddesses of the underworld, who pushed edible plants through the ground as gifts to humanity. By extension, the Eumenides ruled human reproduction and the establishment of families. Originally distinct from the Erinyes, they were later assimilated into that triad of goddesses, and the names became interchangeable. Their sacred cave on the

Athenian Acropolis became the preserve of the Erinyes as well. There, in the sanctuary of kindness, a court met in darkness to discuss matters of state. In darkness, too, the rituals of these goddesses were held at low-lying altars, celebrated by worshipers wearing purple robes and bearing torches.

Europa The "wide-eyed one," the moon goddess after whom the subcontinent of Europe is named, was originally the mother goddess of Crete. Europa owned a magic spear that never missed its target and a monstrous brass warrior that protected her island while she rode the night on her servant, the lunar bull. But Europa's guard failed to repulse the invading Greeks, who brought their own gods to Crete and rewrote Europa's legend substantially. As they told it, she was a mere Phoenician princess, and the lunar bull was the sky god Zeus, who spied the lovely woman bathing and carried her to Crete to rape her. Abandoned there, she married well and bore three famous kings of Crete: Minos, Sarpedon, and Rhadamanthus. That the Greek tale has Europa born in Phoenicia suggests to many scholars a Near Eastern origin for Cretan culture and religion.

Eurydice There were many Greek heroines of this name, which means "wide-judging," but the most famous was the spouse of the singer Orpheus. When she died, he was so stricken with grief that he followed her to the kingdom of Persephone. To reclaim her, he charmed the queen of the dead with a song begging for Eurydice's release. Granted that, Orpheus was instructed not to look behind as he led his lover to the light. But he could not restrain his curiosity and, looking back, saw only the shade of Eurydice disappearing forever. Some scholars, notably Robert Graves, remind us that one Eurydice was an underworld serpent goddess to whom human males were sacrificed; whether this goddess and Orpheus' beloved were once the same is unclear, though the singer was killed by women shortly after his return to the earth's surface.

Eurynome The most ancient of Greek goddesses, she rose naked from primordial chaos and instantly began to dance: a dance that separated light from darkness and sea from sky. Whirling in a passion of movement, Eurynome created behind herself a wind that grew lustful toward her. Turning to face it, she grasped the wind in her hands, rolled it like clay into a serpent, and named it Ophion.

Then Eurynome had intercourse with the wind serpent and, transforming herself into a dove, laid the universal egg from which creation hatched. Installing herself high above the new earth on Mt. Olympus, Eurynome looked down on it complacently. But Ophion, her own creation, bragged that he had been responsible for all that was tangible. Forthwith Eurynome kicked out his teeth and threw him into an underworld dungeon.

There was another goddess of this name—or perhaps the later Eurynome was an elaboration of the creator goddess. Said by the Greeks to rule the sea, she may have been the same goddess as—or part of a trinity with—the great sea rulers Tethys and Thetis. The "wide ruling one," Eurynome had a temple in wild Arcadia, difficult to reach and open only once a year. If pilgrims penetrated the sanctuary, they found the image of the goddess as a woman with a snake's tail, tied with golden chains. In this form, Eurynome of the sea was said to have been the mother of all pleasure, embodied in the beautiful triplets, the Graces.

Evaki Along the Amazon, people said that this goddess of darkness had a pot with a lid; when she closed the lid of the heavens, the sun was left outside. When she took the lid off the pot again, the sky filled with daylight.

Eve The "mother of all living," also called Ishah or, in Hebrew, Hawwah. Familiar to us from Hebrew mythology, Eve is called in the Book of Genesis the first man's *ezer*, usually translated "helper" or "helpmeet." But the masculine word is read, in other biblical contexts, as "instructor."

Immediately we can guess that there is more to Eve than the disobedient temptress wife of the Bible. And indeed, in Hebrew folklore and Jewish legend, we find another figure, a more complex Eve clearly related to the ancestor goddesses of the ancient eastern Mediterranean.

Many writers have pointed out that the biblical creation myth actually contains two contradictory stories. In one, Jehovah created Adam and Eve (or possibly Lilith) simultaneously. But a second story follows, in which Eve was drawn from Adam's rib—currently the more familiar version.

Slavic folklore—probably merging Eve with a similar goddess from pre-Christian mythology—offers some interesting variants on the conventional tale. In Bulgaria, it was said that Adam and Eve were created, naked and blind, at the same instant; a billy goat told Eve to climb an apple tree and take a bite of the fruit, whereupon her blindness disappeared. In another Balkan story, Eve was created by the devil, who borrowed a quill Jehovah had used to breathe life into Adam and invigorated his female creation; although Satan's breath could not enliven Eve, the remnant of divine breath did so. Similarly, a Turkish and Mongol legend says that Edji (Eve) was naked and hairy but that when she touched the fruit, all her apelike hair fell away.

Turning back to the Hebrew mythology from which Eve sprang, we find again that folklore sheds an interesting light on her character. Jewish folklore says that Adam, certain that Eve was his inferior, did not trust her with the truth about Jehovah's prohibition; instead, overcautious, he told his companion that Jehovah had forbidden them, on pain of death, even to touch the Tree of Life. The serpent—said to have stood upright and to look just like a man—shoved Eve against the tree.

She brushed against one of the dropping fruits. Satan then argued, convincingly enough, that Jehovah had lied, that the tree was perfectly safe. Seduced by reason, Eve ate the famous fruit. Then she gave it not only to Adam but to all the animals

of Paradise, bringing death to all except the phoenix, the magical bird who refused to taste.

This Eve has much in common with the great birth-and-death goddesses of every culture—Ishtar, Kali, Tlazoltéotl—and seems, like them, to symbolize the knowledge that woman, by bearing life, brings death into our world as well. But in Jewish legend, Eve brings us rebirth as well. The last part of the tale—rarely included in current tellings—shows Eve traveling from earth to Jehovah's throne while Adam lies near death. She pleads for his life, offering to take half of Adam's pain on herself. She eventually draws Jehovah's pity. Although for their sin the first human couple (and their descendants) were still sentenced to die, Jehovah promised Eve that they would be reborn. Thus Eve, like other mother goddesses of her area, traveled beyond this world to beg the boon of rebirth—and won it.

After Adam died, Eve (like Demeter or Ishtar) wept incessantly for days and nights and more days. Finally she rose from her grief to teach her children the first grave rites. A prophet, she foresaw the afterlife clearly and was able to design appropriate passage rituals.

About Eve's children, some Jewish legends say that Cain and Abel were conceived by Eve in intercourse with the serpent, whom she believed to be an angel—an echo of the myths of mother goddesses impregnated by numinous animals common in Greek mythology. Eve, foreseeing that Cain would kill Abel, named her younger son "born only to die."

And so, behind the shriveled and guilt-laden figure familiar from Judeo-Christian mythology, we find the powerful great goddesses of the earth, progenitors of the race and prime divinities of the tribes of the ancient Near East. Like Eve, they were confidantes of the snakes of rebirth; like her, they were the mothers of humanity. Like her, too, they bore responsibility for the downfall of their lovers. And like Eve, they were the saviors of humankind, seeking and winning the prize of resurrection.

Eye Goddess   The name her people used for her is lost in the mists of time, but her images remain: startling, staring eyes that appear on megalithic temples in Malta and across the eastern Mediterranean. These eyes sometimes appear clearly, complete with eyelashes, as at the temple in Tel Brak in eastern Syria, where the goddess watches not only from the temple walls but also from the altar itself. At other times, the eyes dissolve into a design of spirals, as they do on the carvings of the temples of Malta. Scholars, often following E.O.G. Crawford, suggest that the eye goddess ruled both birth and death. Her image may survive in variations of the "eye of god" found in Mediterranean cultures.

Ezili-Freda-Dahomey   The *loa* (spirit) of sensuality in Haitian voudoun, Ezili is generous to the point of extravagance with her worshipers, and expects the same in return. She is a form of the African goddess Oshun, who accompanied her people to the New World.

Falvara In the Caucasus mountains of Russia, the Osset people honored this "saint" whose name combines the names of Flora and Laura—patrons, respectively, of vegetation and of sheep—thus creating a figure of prosperity who was loved for her kindness and patience. As the Ossets were distant descendants of the Sythians, Falvara may encompass their ancient fertility goddess. Her feast day was in August, when a sheep was offered to her by each family; during the rest of the year she was content with a paste of flour, butter and milk.

Fama The Roman goddess of fame, she lived in a bronze palace with a thousand windows that were always left open, so that she could hear anything said about anyone, anywhere on earth. She kept company with other similar divinities: Credulitas (error), Laetitia (unfounded joy), Timores (terror), Susuri (rumor). Her Greek name was Ossa.

Fand The greatest of the fairy queens of Ireland, Fand was the daughter of the sea and ruler of the beautiful Land-over-Wave, from which she flew as a seabird to our world, usually to entrap human lovers.

Fangge The wood wife of the Tyrol was said to live within trees, rather like the Dryads of the Greeks; to kill her, you twisted a tree's branches or sliced off the bark of the trunk. Fangge could be very bloodthirsty, however, if she survived the attempted murder; an assailant would not be safe in the woodlands after such an act. Fangge liked fresh-baked bread and would steal it when possible; of course, loaves could always be protected from her by being baked with caraway seeds, which the forest folk detested.

Fatima The daughter of Mohammed is not a goddess in Islam, any more than the virgin Mary is a goddess in Christianity. However, each of these "human" women occupies a unique position in their patriarchal religions—as surrogate goddesses, figures to whom the power granted to goddesses in polytheistic cultures accrues. Fatima was married to Ali, and when her father died, he expected to succeed to the Prophet's position as leader of the people. But the first three caliphs kept Ali from assuming that position—which caused the first Islamic schism, resulting in the establishment of Shiite Islam in the area that is now Iran. There, a quasi-mythic status was given to Fatima, who was said to be mistress of waters (thus the Koranic verse, "Water is the source of all life," is held to refer to her) as well as mistress of salt.

When she died, Fatima left orders that upon her breast should be placed a tiny box holding a contract, written in green ink, that gives directions for the salvation of all Shiites. Thus green, the color of the garden paradise to which Fatima ascended, is the emblematic color of Shiite Islam.

Fat Lady This name is applied to several goddess figures from cultures so ancient that they left no written language that would tell us the divinity's original name. One such figure is the Fat Lady of Saliagos, from the Cycladic culture that inhabited the Greek islands in prehistory. Carved in approximately 5000 B.C.E., she is a plump woman whose form seems as monumental as a mountain—despite the fact that the sculpture is only two and one-fourth inches long. Another is the Fat Lady of Malta, a name applied to several rotund figures from that sacred island. Cut from the golden limestone of the island, these show a rather flat-chested woman with enormous calves and thighs. Although these Fat Ladies are usually headless, holes near the neck suggest that the head was separate and mounted in such a way as to allow the head to nod, perhaps in answer to questions from her worshipers.

Fatouma In Mali, this heroine was born near the shores of a lake inhabited by a virgin-devouring dragon who annually claimed tribute in return for the water drawn for the lakeside villages. After many sacrifices, a year came when Fatouma was the only eligible virgin. As she stood there, awaiting her doom, a hero named Hammadi arrived, attacked the dragon, and freed her. As in similar stories around the world, they married happily and grew old together.

Feithline This seer lived at the hill in western Ireland called the Gateway to Hell, or Cruachen. She appeared to Maeve, attired in a golden crown with seven burnt-gold braids hanging down her shoulders, to foretell the queen's death.

Felicitas "Good fortune" was a Roman goddess distinct from Fortuna, another divinity of fate. Shown on Roman coins in the form of a heavyset matron, Felicitas was goddess of personal happiness, while Fortuna ruled the fates of cities and nations.

Feng Pho-Pho Riding herd on the winds of China, Feng Pho-Pho had a tiger for a steed and clouds for her roadway. On calm days, it was thought that the old woman had rounded up the winds and stuffed them into the bag she carried over her shoulder.

Fengi When a child in ancient Scandinavia asked "Why is the sea so salty?" her parents had a ready answer. Once, they would say, in the days of the heroic king Frodi, there were two magical female giants who worked a mill called Grotti. Fengi and Mengi were the only beings strong enough to turn the giant millstone that magically produced peace and plenty for Frodi's land.

The king, anxious for endless prosperity, kept them working constantly, letting them rest only as long as it took them to sing a song. One night, angry and exhausted, they sang a magical charm that caused Frodi's death at the hand of the sea king, Mysing. But Mysing set the giants to work again, this time grinding salt—of which they ground so much that the entire kingdom of the sea was filled with it.

Feronia Far from the growing cities of Italy, this solitary goddess made her simple home in woodlands like those at Campania or at the foot of mountains like Soracte. She may date to the era before Rome; some believe she is a vestigal Etruscan goddess, powerful enough to maintain her own identity after Roman conquest, for her major sanctuaries were in the central Italian areas where the Etruscans once lived. Orchards and fields, volcanoes and thermal springs were her abode, for she was a fire goddess ruling the heat of reproductive life as well as the fires beneath the earth's crust. At her festivals on the Ides of November, great fairs were held and first fruits offered; freedom was bestowed on slaves; men walked barefoot across coals to the cheering of crowds.

The energy of Feronia could not be contained within cities, and her sanctuaries were therefore in the open country. So unsociable was she that when her Campanian forest shrine once burned and her worshipers planned to remove her temple to the safety of a town, the goddess instantly restored the charred trees to leafy greenness.

Fideal　The water demon of the Highland Scots, Fideal was one of those seductive maidens who, after luring their lovers into the water, dragged them under to drown.

Fides　Often dismissed by modern writers as a personified abstraction, "good faith," this goddess was in fact one of the most ancient divinities of Rome and, like the Greek Themis, personified the very basis of human community. Without her influence, no two people could trust each other long enough to cooperate; Fides was the guardian of integrity and honesty in all dealings between individuals and groups.

She was depicted as an old woman wearing an olive wreath and carrying a basket of fruit; thus her iconography shows her to be connected to peace and prosperity. Once each year, on October 1, Rome's three major priests gathered at her sanctuary to offer sacrifice, their right hands wrapped in white cloth. The solemn ritual was carefully guarded from ill omen, for there was no feast more sacred than that which sanctified the bonds of trust among the worshipers of Fides.

Finchoem　Irish goddesses often had unusual ways of conceiving, and Finchoem was no exception: she swallowed a worm from a magic well, hoping it would impregnate her with a hero. Indeed it did; his name was Conall, and he figures significantly in Irish heroic legend.

Findabar　Her name derives from the same word as Guinevere in English; this Irish heroine was the daughter of the fiery queen Maeve and her consort, the king Aillil. Aillil opposed Findabar's choice of a husband, but Findabar simply overruled him and married the beautiful mortal named Froach.

Fiongalla　The "fair-cheeked one" lived in the far southwestern corner of Ireland, where legend says that she was held in enchantment by the powerful Druid Amerach from Ulster, who grew no older as years passed. She made Fiongalla vow never to sleep with a man until one brought magical yew berries, holly boughs, and marigolds from the earthly seat of power. Amerach lost power over Fiongalla when a hero named Feargal actually managed to perform the almost impossible task.

Fionnuala　The story of Fionnuala, one of the most famous of Irish myths, began when the woman Aebh married the Irish king Lir. She died in childbirth, after bearing Fionnuala and three brothers. Lir married again: the sorceress Aiofe, who, jealous of her stepchildren's claim on Lir's affections, decided to kill them. Aiofe feigned illness in order to hatch her plot, then sent the children on the long trek to Connaught, their mother's wilderness home. While they were traveling, Aiofe cast her spell on them. The children, shedding their human forms, rose into the air as swans.

Aiofe's magic was so strong that there was no one in Ireland who could free the children of Lir for 900 years. But King Bobh, Aebh's father and Fionnuala's grandfather, discerned what had happened and vowed to punish Aiofe. He trapped her and asked what shape she hated most. "That," Aife responded, "of the demon of the air." Instantly she was changed to one, and in that form—or, it is said, as a crane—she still haunts the Irish countryside.

Meanwhile Fionnuala and her brothers, who sang so sweetly that people fell enchanted to the ground as they flew overhead, remained trapped. Once, separated from her brothers by a fierce storm on the Sea of Moyle, Fionnuala thought she had lost the enchanted boys. Her lament—written in English in Thomas Moore's "Silent, O Moyle"— was one of the saddest and most lovely laments in

Ireland. But it proved happily unnecessary, for the siblings were reunited on the northern Irish coast.

Fionnuala ("fair-shouldered one") nurtured her brothers during almost a millennium of banishment from human form. Finally, during the reign of Queen Decca, they were freed from enchantment and, crumpling into impossibly aged people, died almost immediately. As old Irish tradition demanded—though the countryside had been Christianized during their enchantment—Fionnuala and her brothers were buried standing upright, together in the grave, as they had been in the sky.

Firanak This Persian heroine was the mother of the hero Feridun, whom she saved from a threatened massacre by hiding him in a garden where a miraculous cow named Prumajeh suckled him, and later by trekking with the baby to the Himalayas, where she found safe fosterage for him.

Fithir The younger daughter of an Irish king, Fithir drew the attention of the king of Leinster, in southeastern Ireland. But her older sister Darine was still unmarried, and their father refused to let the younger girl wed before her. The king of Leinster then kidnapped Darine and trapped her, together with nine handmaidens, in a tower in the woods. He returned to the palace at Tara, claiming Darine was dead. Fithir was then, although mourning for her sister, free to wed.

Years later, while she was wandering in the woods, Fithir happened upon her beloved, sorely missed Darine. The shock killed Fithir; Darine, seeing her sister dead, killed herself with weeping.

Fjorgyn The mother of the Norse thunderer Thor, she appears in few myths, but she may have originally had a more significant identity, as her name appears frequently as a title of other goddesses, including Frigg, Hertha and Jord—a practice that is frequently found where an ancient divinity is deposed and replaced with the deities of later immigrants to a region.

Flidais Almost every old European culture had a goddess who roamed the woodlands, owned all animals, and embodied the fruitfulness and freedom of the wilderness. Among the Irish, she was called Flidais, the stag-mistress who roamed the earth in a chariot drawn by supernatural deer. She possessed a cow whose milk supplied thirty people in one night; she also called the wild creatures of the countryside her cattle. Flidais had one daughter, Fland, a lake maiden who sat beneath her waters and lured mortals to herself—and death.

Flora Apparently forgetting that flowers are the sex organs of plants, most mythographers express shock and puzzlement that the blooming Flora was the patron of prostitutes, worshiped in public orgies from April 28 to May 3. But this very ancient Roman goddess was the embodiment of the flowering of all nature, including human nature. Thus it was presumed that the best way to honor Flora was to pass obscene medallions around, scatter beans and lupines, and make love to passersby.

The female body was especially honored at the Floralia, the festival of nude women celebrated until the third century C.E., when Roman authorities grew prudish and demanded garments on the revelers. This Floralia was not frivolous partying, for Flora was the queen of all plants, including edible ones—for flowers lead to fruit as intercourse to conception, a basic truth that the Romans recognized by calling Flora the secret patron of Rome, without whose help the city would die.

Fortuna In early Italy, this was the name of the goddess who controlled the destiny of every human being. She was shown as a blind woman holding a rudder (for steering a course for each of us) and a cornucopia (for the wealth that she could bring). No mere "Lady Luck," she was the energy that drove men and women to reproduce themselves, a truly irresistible Fors (her later Latin name). Fortuna was originally "she who brings," the goddess who permitted the fertilization of humans, animals, and plants; thus was she worshiped by women desiring pregnancy and gardeners seeking bumper crops. Even when she grew into the monumental figure of Tyche, the destiny of the human community, she still retained her earlier reproductive function as Fortuna Virilis, the goddess who made women irresistible to men, who was worshiped by a regular invasion of the men's public baths by luck-seeking Roman women. Under that name, she was invoked by newly married women, who dedicated their virgin garments to her.

Frau Holle Throughout German, Austrian and Swiss folktales we find this former goddess demoted, together with her twin Perchta, to a witch. Frau Holle was the more pleasant of the two: sunshine streamed from her hair when she combed it, snow covered the earth when she shook a feather comforter, and rain fell when she threw away laundry water. She was a splendid white lady who appeared each noon to bathe in the fountain, from which children were said to be born. She lived in a cave in the mountain or in a well, and people could visit her by diving into it.

She rode on the wind in a wagon. Once she had to have a broken lynchpin repaired, and the man who helped her later found that shavings of wood from the project had fumed to gold. In addition to gold, she rewarded good people with useful gifts, such as the invention of flax and spinning.

Her feast day was celebrated on winter solstice, when she checked the quality of each spinner's work. A good spinner would wake to find Frau Holle had left her a single golden thread, but sloppy ones found their work tangled, their spinning wheels shattered or burnt.

The period between December 25 and January 6—the "twelve days of Christmas"—were sacred to Frau Holle during that time she traveled the world in her wagon. No rotary actions were allowed; sleighs were used instead of wagons, and all meal-grinding had to cease. Her twin Perchta was, if not welcomed, at least acknowledged at the same season.

Freya Far from the ancient Near East, home of the lustful warrior Anat, we find a goddess who is virtually her double: a Scandinavian mistress of all the gods who was also the ruler of death. Leader of the Valkyries, war's corpse-maidens, this goddess was also the one to whom love prayers were most effectively addressed. The goddess who gave her name to the sixth day of our week, Freya was one form of the "large-wombed earth," another version of which her people called Frigg the heavenly matron. Here was how Freya appeared to her worshipers: the most beautiful of all goddesses, she wore a feathered cloak over her magical amber necklace as she rode through the sky in a chariot drawn by cats, or sometimes on a huge golden-bristled boar who may have been her own brother, the fertility god Frey.

When Freya was in Asgard, the home of the deities, she lived on Folkvangr ("people's plain") in a vast palace called Sessrumnir ("rich in seats"). She needed such a huge palace to hold the spirit hordes she claimed on the battlefields, for the first choice of the dead was hers, with leftovers falling to Odin. Like Persephone, the Greek death queen, Freya was also the spirit of the earth's fertility; like Persephone too, Freya was absent from earth during autumn and winter, a departure that caused the leaves to fall and the earth to wear a mourning cloak of snow. And like Hecate, an alternate form of Persephone, Freya was the goddess of magic, the one who first brought the power of sorcery to the people of the north.

Despite her connection with death, Freya was never a terrifying goddess, for the Scandinavians knew she was the essence of sexuality. Utterly promiscuous, she took all the gods as her lovers—including the wicked Loki, who mated with her in the form of a flea—but her special favorite was her brother Frey, recalling Anat's selection of her brother Baal as playmate. But Freya had a husband, too, an aspect of Odin named Odr; he was the father of her daughter Hnossa ("jewel"). When Odr left home to wander the earth, Freya shed tears of amber. But she soon followed Odr, assuming various names as she sought him: here she was Mardol, the beauty of light on water, there Horn, the linen woman; sometimes she was Syr, the sow, other times Gefn, the generous one. But always she was "mistress," for that is the meaning of her own name, and a particularly appropriate double entendre it proves in her case.

Frigg Scholars and mythographers still argue whether Frigg was the same as, or different from, the goddess Freya (the same argument would probably not rage over the god Jehovah and his son). Whatever the understanding of the people who worshiped them—whether the Scandinavians distinguished the two goddesses from each other or saw them as aspects of the same female energy—Frigg unquestionably embodied a different aspect of womanhood from Freya. They were as alike, and as different, as mother and daughter; if they were identical, it was in the way that Frigg was identical to her mother, the great earth herself, Fyorgyn.

And who, really, could confuse the White Lady of Midsummer, the flaxen-haired matron Frigg ("bearer") with the promiscuous battle maiden Freya? The goddesses were distinct in their symbols and in the images of womanhood they reflected. Freya may have been the favorite goddess of lovers, but the overall rulership of Asgard, the home of the gods, was granted to the motherly Frigg, named as the primary goddess in the famous compilation of Scandinavian mythology called the eddas. "Frigg," claimed the compiler, Snorri Sturluson, "comes before any." He described her as a quiet but knowing goddess, dressed in the plumage of hawks and falcons, who spent her days in her home Fensalir ("seahall"), surrounded by the goddesses who were actually forms of herself: the physician Eir, the wise Saga, the virginal Gefion, the secretive Fulla, and others.

The story told of Frigg is strikingly like that of Ishtar, Cybele and other Near Eastern earth goddesses whose son, the vegetation god, dies through his mother's will. In the Scandinavian story, Balder was not the lover of his mother, Frigg, as Attis was to Cybele; rather, he was said to be married to Nana, a goddess with no identity of her own whose name resembles that of Attis' mother. (Some scholars believe that the entire story migrated north from its original home in the Mediterranean, so similar is the Scandinavian tale to the southern version.) Frigg, the story goes, loved her son Balder so much that she extracted a promise from all earth's creatures that they would never harm him. The most loved god became the source of great sport at Asgard; the divinities used to gather and throw darts and rocks and arrows at Balder and were entertained by the way the weapons glanced off without harming the beautiful god.

But wicked Loki was disgusted with the sport. His envy of Balder made him sick with fury. So he disguised himself as an old woman and approached the spot where the gods were throwing darts at Balder. Spotting Frigg, who sat calmly watching, he asked if she was not concerned for his safety. Frigg answered, of course, that she'd seen to it: nothing on earth would hurt her son. Nothing? Loki inquired carefully. Well, the goddess admitted, there was that little sprig of mistletoe. It had been just a baby when she'd been extracting promises, too small to hurt anything…Loki was off like a shot, gathering the mistletoe and forming it into a sharp arrow. This he placed in the hand of the blind god Hoder, convincing him to take part in the sport. The arrow found its way to its mark, and Balder dropped dead. He went off to the realm of Hel, accompanied by Nana, who died of heartbreak at her husband's death. Frigg organized a rescue effort, which meant convincing every creature on earth to weep for Balder's return. And all did, save a strange female giant who turned out to be Loki in disguise. And thus Frigg lost Balder to Hel's captivity, not to be freed until a son of Rind had been born and had matured into a hero.

Fuji   On all continents, people have seen volcanoes as female forces, hailed them as goddesses: Aetna in Italy, Pele in Hawaii, and Chuginadak in the Aleutians are among the many female divinities of earthly fire. The aboriginal Japanese Ainus, too, saw volcanic fire as female, naming their chief divinity Fuji, goddess of the famous mountain that bears her name.

Now the highest mountain in Japan, Fuji was once almost the same height as nearby Mt. Hakusan, wherein a god lived. A dispute arose about which was, in fact, the higher mountain, and the Amida Buddha invented an ingenious way to measure: he connected the two peaks with a long pipe and poured water in one end. Alas for the proud goddess, the water fell on her head. Her humiliation didn't last long, however. Fuji forthwith struck Mt. Hakusan eight blows, creating the eight peaks of today's mountain.

Fulla   From her name we get our word for abundance, and this Scandinavian goddess embodied the fullness of the fruitful earth. She was a servant of Frigg (and probably another version of that great goddess), the one who carried the coffer in which Frigg kept her riches. She was pictured as a young woman with long, full hair bound at the temple with a golden band.

Fu-Pao   It is customary in most countries to ascribe a miraculous conception to culture heroes, and the Yellow Emperor of China was no exception. His mother, a well-traveled intellectual, sat outdoors one spring night watching an unearthly light play across the sky. Soon Fu-Pao found herself pregnant. Her child Huang-Ti gestated for two years—another common phenomenon among heroes, who often spend more time than usual in their mother's wombs.

Furrina   The prominence of this ancient Italian goddess is obvious from the fact that—although by Cicero's time no one knew what Furrina represented—one of the twelve Roman priesthoods was dedicated to her. She had a feast, the Furrinalia, on July 25; some conjecture she was one of the Furies, goddesses of vengeance.

Fylgja, Fylgakona (pl.)   A family's guardian spirit was called by this name in Iceland and other parts of Scandinavia; sometimes the spirit was called Haminga. Though in some senses the Fylgakona resembled the goddesses called Disir, the former were never actually worshiped. The Fylgakona rarely appeared to human sight; when they did, it betokened misfortune; some scholars contend that they were external souls, visible only when death was nigh. But some legends consider them to be protective as well as ominous spirits of the future in either good or unfortunate form.

Gaia   In the beginning, the Greeks said, there was only formless chaos: light and dark, sea and land, blended in a shapeless pudding. Then chaos settled into form, and that form was the huge Gaia, the deep-breasted one, the earth. She existed before time began, for Time was one of her children. In the timeless spans before creation, she existed, to herself and of herself alone.

But finally Gaia desired love, and for this purpose she made herself a son: Uranus, the heaven, who arched over his mother and satisfied her desire. Their mating released Gaia's creative force, and she began to produce innumerable creatures, both marvelous and monstrous. Uranus hated and envied Gaia's other children, so the primeval mother kept them hidden from his destructiveness.

Eventually, however, her dark and crowded womb grew too heavy to endure. So Gaia created a new element: gray adamant. And from it she fashioned a new tool, never known before in her creation: a jagged-toothed sickle. With this Gaia armed her son Cronos (Time), who took the weapon from his mother's hand and hid himself.

Soon Uranus came, drawing a dark-sky blanket over himself as he approached to mount his mother-lover. Then his brother-son Cronos sprang into action, grasping Uranus' genitals and

sawing them off with the rough blade. Blood fell in a heavenly rain on Mother Gaia. So fertile was she that even the blood of the mutilated sky impregnated her. The Erinyes sprang up; so did the Giants; and so did the ash-tree nymphs, the Meliae, humanity's ancestors.

This was the familiar creation story that the ancient Greeks told their children. Even after the earth mother had been supplanted as the primary divinity by invading Olympians, the Greeks worshiped Gaia's power with barley and honey cakes placed at sacred openings in her surface. At such fissures, too, gifted people would read the will of the Great Mother, for she was through all ages the "primeval prophet" who inspired the oracles at Delphi, Dodona, and elsewhere. And it was to Gaia—even in the days when Zeus ruled the pantheon—that the Greeks swore their most sacred oaths, thus recognizing her ancient theological sovereignty.

Galatea   There are two figures by this name in Greek mythology, one of whom was a minor sea goddess whose legend revolves around the two men who desired her. The more familiar Galatea appeared in the story of Pygmalion, a man afraid of the desires of mortal women but devoted to the static beauty of statuary. He especially lusted after the pale marble form of a statue of Aphrodite herself and carved an ivory replica of the goddess, with which he used to sleep. Such unnatural love was distasteful to Aphrodite, who encouraged the free and generous sharing of physical love among living beings.

Aphrodite cursed Pygmalion by constantly increasing his desire for the ivory statue. It could not, of course, return his affection, neither could his love find satisfaction against its hard thighs. Driven to despair, Pygmalion finally threw himself upon Aphrodite's mercy. Touched, the goddess breathed life into the statue, which came alive as Galatea. The lovers quickly produced a child, a daughter whom they named Paphos in honor of the "promiscuous" Aphrodite, who bore this name and shared it with her most active worshipers.

Galiana This Etruscan heroine saved her city—today called Viterbo—from a Roman invasion by the simple expedient of appearing naked on the battlements. Her appearance had a magical effect on the Roman legions, which fell back in disarray at this vision of female courage.

Ganga The Hindu mother of rivers once lived in heaven with her sister, the virginal Uma. When sea-dwelling demons harassed the earth, the sage Agastya swallowed the ocean where they hid. Agastya got rid of the demons, but the earth was left parched and dry; such was the heat in the sage's stomach that the waters evaporated immediately.

Because of the prayers of her people, the heavenly water goddess Ganga threw herself down to earth. Unbroken, Ganga's power could have washed away the world; but the god Shiva received her torrent on his head and saved the earth. Henceforth the goddess, embodied in the sacred river Ganges, flowed through India.

Some said that Ganga remained in heaven as well, as the celestial river we call the Milky Way; another part of the Ganges flowed under the earth. The intersection of the three Ganges at Benares was considered to be Ganga's most sacred spot. There people daily washed themselves in the purifying waters. Once a year pilgrims traveled—still travel—to avail themselves of Ganga's promise to wash away ten sins from each of a bather's last ten lives. And many a devout Hindu seeks to die immersed in Ganga—for the goddess, who has no human form, actually lives in her river—and the goddess then ensures instant freedom from both punishment and reincarnation.

One of the greatest of Hindu goddesses, Ganga appears often in groupings with other powerful divinities: as a pair with Uma; as a trinity with the other river goddesses, Sarasaoti and Yauni; as a fivefold group with Sarasvati, Laksmi, Durga, Savitri, all as aspects of Devi ("the Goddess") or Prakriti ("earth"). Her role in any of these groupings is as bestower of health, happiness, fertility, and material wealth.

Ganymeda Originally the goddess who served ambrosia and nectar at Olympian feasts, she was later split in two. Her name and her position as bearer of immortal food and liquid were granted to an invented figure, Ganymede, a mortal boy elevated to heaven to replace her. But her other attributes remained in Greek mythology under the guise of Hebe.

Gaomei Originally an ancient Chinese goddess whose name—which means "first mother" or "great mother"—suggests a creator divinity, she was later transformed into a male divinity.

Gatamdug The mother goddess of the Tigris area, counselor to kings and interpreter of dreams, was eventually assimilated into Gula.

Gauri Because Hindu philosophy recognizes that divinity is ultimately indivisible, all goddesses are called aspects of Devi, or simply "the Goddess." Despite this philosophy, however, Indian culture provides innumerable goddess names that seem remarkably like separate divinities. To explain away this apparent contradiction, Gauri ("golden one") is said to be a form of the mighty Durga;

before she made her reputation as a warrior, Durga was Gauri, the golden sky virgin. But sometimes Gauri is called Parvati, Shiva's dark lover, after she underwent magical skin-lightening beauty treatments. Yet again, some say Gauri is another name for Varuni, goddess of golden liquor.

In any case, Gauri is the name used for the goddess worshiped in August festivals; this is said to be the best time to arrange marriages and to name babies. Gauri's particular day is August's new moon, when bedtime sweets are eaten to bring Gauri's honeyed grace into the soul for the year.

Gauri-Sankar An Indian mountain goddess embodied in the world's highest peak, the one we call Mt. Everest.

Gawaunduk "The Guardianess," heroine of an Ojibwa legend, was a young woman given in marriage to a distinguished elder of the tribe, many years older than her. She went obediently but without joy, feeling that her life would be less satisfying than if she had found a love-mate her own age. Yet, as the years passed and she bore children to the old man, her heart softened towards him. When in his eighty-fifth year he grew sick, Gawaunduk was frantic for his survival. He recovered and lived another fifteen years. Then, a full century old, he died quietly in his sleep. She mourned so wildly at his grave that she finally died of grief and they were buried together. Mists that rise from spruce forests are her tears as she mourns for her beloved.

Geezhigo-Quae To the Ojibwa, she was the sky mother, a manitou or great spirit who dwelt in the heavens and watched over her people from there. The creator of humanity, she also created the bountiful earth, for it was Geezhigo-Quae who descended into the primal soup to find land under the waves. She brought it forth and fashioned it into hills and valleys and mountain ranges.

Gefjon It is difficult to determine whether or not the Scandinavian giant Gefjon and the virgin goddess of the same name were identical. The former Gefjon was a trickster-creator; a vagrant, she was promised as much land as four oxen could plow in a day. So she conceived four ox-shaped sons by a resident of Giantland; when her sons had grown, Gefjon brought them back to Sweden, plowed off a part of that country and dragged it south, where it became Seeland. The other Gefjon, a goddess, sold her hymen for a jewel but miraculously retained her virginity. She was an attendant upon Frigg and possibly a form of that earth goddess as the "generous giver." All women who die maidens were said to pass into Gefjon's possession.

Gendenwitha The Iroquois called the morning star by this name, which translates as "she who brings the day." Their religion recalled the time when the great hunter Sosondowah ("great night") was stalking a supernatural elk. The hunt brought him to the heavens where the jealous goddess Dawn snared Sosondowah as her doorkeeper.

But the new slave could not remain faithful to his duties. Down on earth he saw Gendenwitha, then a mortal woman, and daily left his duties to court her. While Dawn was busy coloring the sky, the hunter was singing to his beloved: in spring as a bluebird; in summer, a blackbird; in autumn, a hawk. And it was as a hawk that he tried to carry Gendenwitha to heaven with him. But Dawn, angry at his disappearance from her doorstep, turned the woman into a star and set Gendenwitha just above Dawn's door, where she shines today, just out of reach of her dark hunter-lover.

Genetaska "Maiden peace queen" of the Iroquois was a human woman so wise that lawsuits were brought to her for settlement. Genetaska was, for a long time, impartial, but finally fell in love with a defendant; when she married him, her office was abolished.

Gentle Annie The pleasant aspect of Black Annis was said to bring good weather to the English countryside, as well as to the nearby waters. Sometimes the weather goddess thought by some to be descended from Anu—turned on those she had recently favored, ravaging their boats and crops with high winds. In many cultures, weather goddesses were similarly pictured: beautiful but dangerous maidens, alternatively seductive and treacherous.

Gerd   A Scandinavian deity of light, Gerd was said to live in a house ringed by fire and to shoot flames from her hands. She was the most beautiful of creatures, the daughter of a female giant and a mortal man. The fertility god Frey became infatuated with Gerd and sent his servant to bring her to him. Gerd refused, but Frey kept sending gifts and, finally, threats. A spell in runes finally won Gerd, and she traveled to Asgard, the home of the gods, to live with Frey. Some interpreters, tracing Gerd's name to a word for "field," see the legend as an allegory of the springtime earth ready to produce fruit under the god of fertility's influence, but still living in the grip of winter, symbolized by the Frost Giants.

Gestinanna   Around the figure of the dying god Dumuzi we find one of the great trinities of eastern Mediterranean religion: the lover Inanna, the mother Ninsun, and the sister Gestinanna ("lady of desolation"). Tortured by nightmares, Dumuzi brought the dreams to his sister for interpretation. Skilled in such matters, Gestinanna immediately realized her brother was under attack by demons. Warned, Dumuzi fled, swearing Gestinanna to secrecy. The demons arrived as predicted, attacking Gestinanna to force her to reveal her brother's whereabouts. But she remained steadfastly silent. Nevertheless, the demons found Dumuzi, hiding in the form of a gazelle in his sister's sheepfold. He was carried to the underworld; Gestinanna set off in pursuit, and the siblings were eventually reunited. The goddess then persuaded the underworld divinities to grant Dumuzi half her own life; henceforth, each was allowed to live on earth six months of each year.

Ggigantia   The massively fat goddess of the tiny island of Gozo, just north of Malta, she is seen as both mother and daughter, into whose wombs

their worshipers walked when they entered the goddess-shaped temples.

Ghar-Jenti   "Light of the house" was what this name meant to the North Indian Assamese; she was the spirit of good fortune within the home who manifested herself by making ticking noises at night—only the sounds of nails pulling out of wood, so we're told. When she walked around the darkened house, residents felt her passing like cats' paws in their dreams.

Giane   In Sardinia, this was the name of the woodland spinning spirit, an average-sized woman with steel fingernails and long disheveled hair. Giane also had long, pendant breasts that, as she was working her magic loom, she threw over her shoulders. As she wove, Giane sang plaintive love songs. If a human man should respond, Giane would have intercourse with him. The man, overcome with the spirit's force, would die, and his child, a half-breed brute, would be born only three days later.

Gillian   In Britain, this name is associated with mazes formed of turf, through which springtime ritual races are run. Often a woman is "imprisoned" in the middle of the maze, called a Gillian Bower or Troy Town, and "freed" by a young man. Behind this folkloric ritual rests an ancient spring goddess who needed to be released from the grip of winter by heroic human effort.

Giri Devi   In rituals associated with the great goddess Pattini of Sri Lanka, this legendary woman is invoked in dances and songs. She was the sister of the evil demon Dala Kumara ("Tusk Prince") who indulged himself in illicit desires for her. This grew to be an obsession, until at Giri Devi's wedding, Dala Kumara went crazy, ate all the food, then kidnapped her. Taking her to the forest, he raped her there and kept her prisoner. After enduring this for some time, Giri Devi committed suicide by hanging herself from a tree. The demon never recovered from his loss, but the efforts of Pattini kept him from devastating the world by instituting rituals to hold him at bay.

Giriputri On the island of Bali, there is a sacred mountain called Gunung Agaung, ruled by the benevolent goddess Giriputri. There, each year, sacred water is drawn which is used to bless the harvest. Rituals in honor of the goddess are still a vital part of Balinese society.

Gleti Moon goddess of Benin, the country formerly called Dahomey, Gleti is the mother of all the stars, who are called Gletivi, the moon's children. An eclipse is caused by the shadow of the moon's husband crossing her face.

Glispa This great Navaho heroine who brought the healing beauty chant to her people may have been a form of the great goddess Estsanatlehi, for she was a turquoise woman, while her sister (like Estsanatlehi's sister, Yolkai Estsan) was associated with white shells. The two girls were lured away from their village by young men; when dawn came, however, the men were withered and old. Her sister was too terrified to escape, but Glispa fought her way through venomous snakes to freedom.

At the center of the world, the place of emergence from the lower worlds, Glispa stopped to drink. Snake people appeared and lifted the magical lake so that Glispa could travel beneath it. There she met her lover, again firm and handsome. He was, he explained, a shaman of the snake people. To keep her with him, he taught Glispa the healing chant called Hozoni and its rituals. Quick to learn, Glispa instantly memorized the information.

After many years, Glispa grew homesick for the surface world, and the snake god allowed her to return. Once on earth, she tried to teach the song of beauty to her brother, but he was slow-witted and could not remember the elaborately beautiful song. With magic and maize she taught him then so that when she returned to the lower world the Navaho were left with the gift of healing, per-

formed in four-day ceremonies in honor of Glispa.

Gna Riding her horse, Hoof-Tosser, this goddess was the messenger of heaven and of heaven's queen, Frigg; a wind deity, Gna's name was used as a synonym for "woman" in Scandinavian poetry.

Gnowee The sun goddess of the Wotjabaluk, aboriginal people of southeast Australia, Gnowee once lived on the earth at a time when the sky was always dark and people walked around carrying torches in order to see. One day while Gnowee was out gathering yams, her child wandered away from camp. She set off to search for him, bearing a huge torch, but never found him. She still climbs the sky daily, trying to find her son.

Godasiyo A tale of human folly is told among the North American people called the Tuscarora. At the beginning of time, all the people spoke the same language. The heroine Godasiyo was the chief of the biggest village—one so big that it filled both banks of a wide river. A strong bridge connected the two halves of the town. One day, Godasiyo's favorite dog gave birth to seven puppies, the last-born of which was the cutest puppy the world has ever seen. It was completely white with little dark markings over each eye, and it played so cleverly that the people just wanted to watch and pet it. This magical puppy was so cute that Godasiyo's people on the other side of the river grew envious. They began to fight violently for possession of the dog, and in terror, Godasiyo burned the bridge. But still the people raged and threatened. So Godasiyo invented canoes and ordered her people into them. She wanted them to travel to a new place, where they could establish a new village and live in peace with the adorable puppy.

But arguments began about which canoe the chief and her puppy should ride in. Godasiyo invented an outrigger made of saplings, so she could ride between several canoes. But even this was not good enough. The migrating people reached a place where the river divided and began to argue furiously about which way to go. During the argument, the chief and her dog were thrown into the water and drowned. But immediately they were reborn, she as a huge sturgeon, the puppy as a little whitefish. And when the people tried to comment on this miracle, they found they could no longer understand each other. Because of the conflict over possession of a puppy, the many human languages were born.

Godiva   Her story is one of the best-known British folktales. Once the earl of Mercia, Leonfric, put such onerous taxes on his people that they were starving in order to keep up their payments. His wife, Lady Godiva, pleaded for mercy. Leonfric's reply was cruel and casual: if Godiva would ride naked through the town of Coventry, he would release the people from the taxes.

Godiva took up the challenge. She ordered that all windows should be covered at noon on a certain day, and that all residents should remain indoors without looking out. On that day she rode proudly through the town, her long hair as her only garment. Shamed, Leonfric lifted the taxes, and the people celebrated their heroine.

One part of the story is less well known: that a single resident defied the ban on looking at the passing horsewoman. He was Peeping Tom, and he was struck blind the instant he gazed upon Godiva's nakedness.

The power to blind is not one most Mercian ladies of the time had, and this incident reveals the true nature of "Lady" Godiva: that she is a folkloric remembrance of a powerful goddess, probably the horse goddess Epona. Similar figures appear in other towns near Coventry, an area occupied by the ancient Celtic tribe of the Brigantes. One of the most famous such horsewomen was found at Banbury Cross, where as the rhyme says, one could "see a fine lady upon a white horse (with) rings on her fingers and bells on her toes." At Southam, a Godiva festival took place until the eighteenth century, which required two semi-nude women, one wearing white lace, the other black lace, who rode on horseback through the town. The purpose of these festivals was to encourage agricultural abundance—which appears in the "historical" Godiva legend as well, because the people of Coventry after her famous ride were able to keep more of their land's produce for themselves.

Goga   In Melanesia—Papua New Guinea and nearby islands—the primal being was an agelessly old woman. In her body, Goga nurtured fire, which a human boy stole from her. She pursued the boy; he dropped the burning branch he was carrying onto a tree, which caught fire; inside the tree was a snake, whose tail caught fire. Though Goga deluged the world with rain, hoping to quench the stolen fire, the snake's tail continued to smolder, and humans used it to light the first earthly blaze.

The Kiwai of Papua said that the primal woman was the first to kill an earthly creature. Hunting down a wallaby, she left it to rot; human beings emerged from it like maggots, and the old woman taught them the necessary rituals and regulations of earthly life.

Goleuddydd   "Bright Day" was a Welsh princess who married a prince but, remaining barren, caused consternation among the people, who prayed ceaselessly for an heir to the thrown. But when she finally became pregnant, Goleuddydd went mad and refused to live indoors. She went into the forest and hid, avoiding all inhabited places. When her time came to give birth, however, her mind returned to her and she found herself in a swineherd's yard. There she gave birth, and because of these circumstances her son was named Culhwch or "pig." This folktale heroine probably disguises an ancient sow goddess of fertility.

Gollveig   The story of "Gold-Might" is a mysterious part of Scandinavian mythology. Many interpretations have been offered to explain why this mighty witch entered the halls of divine Asgard demanding vengeance for an injury, why she was killed three times but still lived, and why she possessed the power of the Vanir, a group of divinities distinct from the Aesir of Asgard.

Some see her simply as a symbol of the corruption of wealth, interpreting her name as "drunkenness of gold." Others say that the Vanir were an invading people's gods and that Gollveig (also called Heid, the Volva, or sibyl) embodies a historical combat. Among the latter scholars are some who see Gollveig as a disguise for the mightiest of the Vanir, Freya, who possessed a golden necklace and the power of prophecy.

Gondul   One of the most famous Valkyries, Gondul was sent to earth to bring back the spirits of famous kings who fell in battle. She figured prominently in the legend of Hild, for she was the creator of the everlasting battle involving that woman's lover; for this reason, some legends say Gondul was Freya, the queen of the Valkyries, in disguise.

Gonlod   The mother of poetry, she was a giant in Scandinavian mythology who owned the caldron of inspiration that the god Odin took by trickery; she was also said to be the mother of Bragi, god of poets.

Gonzuole   Among Gangwi of Liberia, she was the first woman, a farmer who provided her own living from the land. Without needing a mate, she gave birth to many beautiful daughters who, like her, were industrious and strong. Soon they lived together in a wealthy village of women. Nearby were some men, who were attracted as much to the women's wealth as to their beauty. They consulted a diviner, who told them that the women had a very difficult time resisting the taste and odor of mushrooms. So the men fixed traps with mushrooms and, when the women arrived, captured them, even mother Gonzuole. She, fearing for her daughters, agreed to give them in marriage to the men, who had to pledge never to harm them. But the women could never forgive being stolen from their mother, and so resorted to spells and witchcraft to punish their captors.

Gorgons   Their faces and figures were beautiful, and above their shoulders arched golden wings. But they were as terrifying as they were lovely, for these three sisters were covered with lizardlike scaly skin and had hair of hissing serpents. The Gorgons had huge boarlike tusks and brass fingers, and their gaze was so powerful that a single glance could petrify the onlooker.

The three sisters lived together beyond the sea, almost at the end of night, and their triplet sisters, the Graeae, guarded the way to their preserve. Of the three, two Gorgons were immortal; they were Sthenno ("strength") and Euryale ("wide sea"). But they were less prominent in Greek legend than their mortal sister Medusa ("ruler").

Poet Robert Graves saw the Gorgons as priestesses of the triple moon goddess, mask-wearing women who guarded the secrets of the women's mysteries. Graves pointed out that the moon's face was called "Gorgon's head" by the Orphics and that Greek bakers mounted Gorgon's heads on their ovens to warn the inquisitive not to pry and ruin the bread. A different interpretation is offered by Helen Diner, who argued that Gorgon was the name of a tribe of Libyan Amazons, who, conquered by the Greeks, were thereafter described by their murderers as monsters.

Graces   The most common English name for these three goddesses comes from the Latin Graciae; in Greek these divinities were called Charites. Both words mean the same thing: the grace of movement, for they were dancing goddesses; the grace of manners, for they were always gentle and polite; and the greatest grace, the gift of love itself, which these goddesses ruled with Aphrodite.

The goddesses themselves were called Thaleia ("abundant, overflowing, flowering one"), Aglaia ("radiance" or "splendor," the glow of youth and love), and Euphrosyne ("joy and merriment and delight"). In the early days in Athens, there were two, Auxo ("waning one") and Hegemone ("mastery"); they were probably moon goddesses, like the Laconian Graces named Cleta ("invoked") and Phaenna ("brilliant"), goddesses said always to dance by moonlight. But the ancient triple goddess could appear as easily as a single or a double goddess; thus we find Charis (Roman Gratia), the single Grace, called the double of Aphrodite and, like that goddess, said to be the mate of the smith god Hephaestus.

Single, double, or triple, Grace or the Graces represented the delight in living that produces art, dance, music, and love. Agelessly young, they nonetheless were older than Aphrodite, whom they met as she rose from the sea; they provided fitting garments for the love goddess and thereafter always accompanied her, dressing her, arranging her hair, massaging her with sweet oils. They were always pleasant and charming, bringing to human encounters a wistful longing. The Greeks described the difference between the Graces and other goddesses in the proverb that the first cup of wine at a banquet was theirs; the second belonged to the lustful Aphrodite, while the third was ruled by the argumentative Ate.

Graeae The three sisters of the Gorgons were swan maidens who lived at the world's edge, guarding the path to their sisters' sanctuary. The Graeae were beautiful although gray-haired from birth; some tales say they were also deformed, having only one eye and one tooth among them.

Their names were Pemphredo ("wasp"), the beautifully clothed one; Enyo ("warrior"), who always dressed in yellow; and Deino ("terrible"). Their shared name means "the gray ones" or "the crones," and they may have given their name to the Greeks themselves, if Graeci is translated "worshipers of the crone."

Grainne Her name means "hateful goddess," suggesting that she was originally divine. However, Grainne comes into Irish mythology as the heroine of its most famous romance in which the strong-willed beauty chose her own lover and traveled the entire island with him, sleeping out of

doors and sanctifying the countryside (like a goddess) with their love.

A princess of Ulster, Grainne was promised by her father to the hero Fionn MacCumhaill. But at their wedding feast, a sudden breeze lifted the long bangs of the handsome Diarmuid (in English, Dermot). On the man's forehead was a magical love spot that, if any woman saw it, left her helplessly in love with him. And so it was with Grainne.

Some versions of the legend claim that Grainne offered herself to first one, then the next, of the assembled heroes, and that only Diarmuid was foolish enough to accept her advances. Another version says that Diarmuid refused Grainne, unless she came to him neither clothed nor unclothed, on horse or afoot, in daylight or at night. Grainne went to a wise fairy woman to borrow a cloak of mountain mist, then came to Diarmuid just at sunset mounted on a goat. Thus avoiding his prohibitions, Grainne won Diarmuid.

But the most familiar tale was that of Fionn's wedding feast and the magical love spot that enraptured her. She quickly slipped soporific drugs into the drinks of the company, and when everyone else was sleeping, demanded that Diarmuid escape with her. At first, afraid of Fionn MacCumhaill's anger, he demurred, but Grainne prevailed. She knew that Diarmuid had once pledged never to refuse aid to a woman, so Grainne cleverly enforced the *geasa* (magical vow) and, to maintain his honor, Diarmuid had to do as she demanded. They fled together to the Shannon River, to the Wood of the Two Tents—so called because for their first few nights together Diarmuid refused to sleep with Grainne. Again, however, Grainne prevailed. This time a gigantic monster accosted her and Diarmuid rescued her; Grainne sarcastically remarked that at least something was interested in touching her, and Diarmuid, humiliated, moved into her tent.

The new lovers were found by the pursuing Fionn and his band, the Fianna, but Diarmuid gave Grainne a cape of invisibility in which to escape while with superhuman strength he leaped from the pursuers' grasp. A god then appeared to the pair, saying they could never again sleep in a cave with one entrance, land on an island with one approach, eat a cooked supper, or sleep two nights in one place.

And so the lovers began their travels, sleeping in rocky alcoves called even today "the beds of Diarmuid and Grainne." Eventually, tired of constant travel, they took refuge under a magical rowan tree guarded by a giant named Sharvan the Surly. He let Diarmuid and Grainne hide in the tree, provided they did not eat the berries. Grainne, again, had other ideas, and on her urging Diarmuid killed the giant and they feasted on the magical food.

The screams of the dying giant gave the couple's location away to Fionn, who had continued to pursue them. Grainne and Diarmuid quickly climbed the tree; Fionn, suspecting that they were hiding there, sat down to a game of chess with the poet Oisin and challenged him to guess the winning move. Three times Diarmuid—proud of his chess-playing skill—tossed berries from the tree to signal the correct move to Oisin. Fionn, sure that Diarmuid was nearby, called his name and Diarmuid, like a good Irish hero, had to answer.

Grainne wrapped herself in the cloak of invisibility and fled, while Diarmuid took a mighty leap and landed beyond the reach of the Fianna. And so the pursuit began again, until the poets' god, Aengus, appeared to Fionn to plead the rovers' cause. Fionn's heart was touched, and Grainne and her beloved were allowed to return to the company. And thus did the "hateful goddess" have her will.

Grainne ni Malley The legendary Irish pirate queen from County Galway was a contemporary of England's Elizabeth I. Trying to convince Grainne to stop harassing the British fleet, Elizabeth invited her to the English court and presented the Irishwoman with a lapdog and embroidered gifts. Grainne scoffed at the useless trinkets and left the court without making Elizabeth the desired promises. Grainne returned to Ireland and promptly kidnapped the Englishman who lived in Dublin's Howth Castle, holding him hostage until her point was made: that she acknowledged only her own sovereignty.

Grainne was as strong-willed about men as she was about rival queens. Each year she took a new lover and, on the first day of the second year, maintained the right to evict him by standing in the castle yard and loudly announcing that she wanted him out. If the man refused to leave, she would kill him. At last, however, Grainne found a man who satisfied her—an Irish nobleman with whom, when the first day of the second year arrived, she could not bear to part.

Grand-Aunt Tiger The image of a primeval tigress goddess is prominent in China, Taiwan, Korea and southern Japan, leading many researchers to propose an ancient pan-Asian myth in which a tiger mother is the ancestral divinity, possibly even the creator-mother of the universe. In Korea, where she stalks and threatens the sun maiden Hai-Soon, early historians recorded that the primary divinity was the tiger spirit, while throughout southeast Asia, the tiger mother initiates all shamans. Throughout Asia, the tiger-mother appears in similar folktales that are vestiges of otherwise-forgotten archaic mythologies.

Grian Her name means "sun," which this early Irish goddess ruled. As her daughters, Irish women lived in open homes called *griannon* ("sun houses,") after their goddess. There are no surviving legends of Grian, just her name, but some researchers think that she was the twin of Aine, another Irish solar deity. One goddess might, in that case, represent the weak winter sun, the other the more powerful sun of summer.

Groa In the Scandinavian mythological books, the eddas, this wise woman combined the attributes of sorcery, healing, spellcasting and housekeeping.

Guabancex   The Caribbean people of the Antilles use this name for the goddess of storms, wind and water; she was served by the messenger goddess Guantuava.

Guadalupe   On December 9, 1531, a Mexican man named Juan Diego was climbing the hill of Tepeyac, sacred to the Aztec goddess Tonan. There he met a beautiful dark-skinned woman who was a stranger to him. In his own language, Nahuatl, she commanded him to build a church there, where once a shrine to Tonan stood. Juan Diego went immediately to the Spanish bishop of the area, who refused to honor the lady's command. Juan returned to the spot, and the woman told him to gather roses—which do not normally bloom in December, even in Mexico—and take them to the bishop. Not only was the bishop convinced by the roses, but the image of the lady herself appeared miraculously on Juan Diego's cloak.

The bishop said she was the virgin Mary, mother of the Christian god Jesus. But her name did not matter. Whether she was Tonan, returned to help her people through the Spanish subjugation, or Mary the mother, Guadalupe was recognized as a female power who would intercede for the needs of the Mexican people. Her image is still the national symbol of Mexico, and pilgrimages to Tepeyac hill still honor her image—although, ironically, women are not allowed to approach the sacred relic, displayed behind the altar in the cathedral of Guadalupe.

Guinevere   The ancient Welsh triple goddess came almost undisguised into Arthurian legend. In some tales, King Arthur was said to have married three women, all named Guinevere; this recalls the ancient tradition that the king must "marry" the earth's triple goddess to be fully invested with kingship. In another recollection of the ancient tradition, Guinevere betrayed Arthur by sleeping with a younger man; this was a common part of stories of such goddesses who, like Blodewedd or Maeve, both made and unmade kings and heroes.

Gula   During the slow process whereby similar goddesses were assimilated into one grand figure, this Near Eastern goddess took over the attributes of Bau and Gatamdug, emerging as one of the primary divinities of the Akkadian and Babylonian peoples. She was the mother goddess as the "great physician," with the power both to inflict and to cure disease; she was shown with the eight-rayed orb of vital heat, the heat of the body that sustains life and, as fever, can destroy it. Sometimes in recognition both of the goddess she assimilated and of her own duality, she was called Gula-Bau.

Gula lived in a garden at the center of the world, where she watered the tree that forms its axis. The moon man, her mate, stood in the sky over the tree, from which Gula plucked fruit to offer her worshipers. In art, Gula was shown accompanied by a dog, for she defended the boundaries of her people's fields as a hound might. At other times, Gula was depicted with both hands raised in the air, showing humans the proper position to assume when entreating her aid.

Gum Lin   A Chinese folklore heroine, she was a poor peasant girl whose task it was to weave mats of bamboo and sell them in the market. But a drought struck her village, and it grew harder and harder to find enough bamboo to sustain her family.

One day, wandering far from her village, she arrived at the shores of Ye Tiyoh lake, high in the mountains, where she drank deeply of its sweet waters and then gathered some of the plentiful bamboo from its shores.

That night, after returning home to her dusty and thirsty village, Gum Lin had an inspiration. The next day she went forth with shovel and pick, planning to open a canal between the distant lake and her village. But when she got to the lake, she discovered one already cut—but the flow of water was stopped with a huge stone gate, kept closed by a big iron lock. Wild birds told her to seek help from Loy Yi Lung, the daughter of the dragon who lived in the lake.

And so Gum Lin stood in the shallows of the lake and began to sing sweetly. And within seconds, Loy Yi Lung was standing next to her, joining in the song. But the spirit had bad news for Gum Lin: the key to the lake was in the possession of her dragon father. Together, however, the girls came up with a plan. Loy Yi Lung sang beautifully, distracting her father while Gum Lin swam into his cave and stole his key. She opened the floodgates and the waters rushed down the mountain to her village, saving her people from slow death from starvation. The new river went right by Gum Lin's house, and her friend Loy Yi Lung came to visit her often there.

Gwendydd Also known as Gwendolyn and Gandieda, this Welsh woman was the sister of the renowned magician Merlin—perhaps his twin, perhaps his lover as well. It was to her that Merlin passed on his magical powers and his knowledge, once Vivienne had trapped him in her magical forest.

Gwyar The story of this ancient Welsh goddess, the wife of the god of heaven, is virtually lost. All that is left is the meaning of her name ("gore"); the fact of her relationship to King Arthur, said to have been her brother; and the information that she had two sons, one good, the other bad.

Gwyllion Wandering alone in the Welsh mountains, you might come face to face with this fierce spirit of wilderness, an old woman who spitefully told you the wrong road, whereupon you would lose your way in the hills and die. Carrying an object of iron protected against her enchantment.

Gyhldeptis "Lady hanging hair" was a kindly forest spirit of the Tlingit and Haida in southeastern Alaska; they saw her in the long, hanging mossy branches of the great cedars of the rain forest. A protector of Indians and other humans, Gyhldeptis was disturbed by the activities of Kaegyihl Depgeesk ("upside-down place"), a tremendous whirlpool that devoured entire ships of travelers. To break this power, Gyhldeptis staged a huge feast and invited all the coastal powers: the ice, the forest fire, the wind, and others. Magically feeding them in her underwater Festival House, Gyhldeptis convinced the forces that human beings needed more protection from Kaegyihl Depgeesk. Thereupon, all the well-fed natural powers set to work rearranging the coast so that the whirlpool was smoothed into a gentle river.

Habetrot   One of the most famous English sprites was the spinning goddess Habetrot, who was also goddess of healing; the wearer of her handmade garments would never suffer from ailments.

Habondia   This goddess of abundance was celebrated, particularly in medieval European times, as the special divinity of witches. Apparently she was, or was descended from, an ancient Germanic or Celtic earth goddess.

Hada Bai   A goddess of wealth to the Assamese of North India, she was also invoked when one wished to financially ruin an enemy.

Hae-Soon   In the yennai yaegi—Korea's "old tales"—this is the name of the sun goddess. Originally a girl on earth, she lived with her mother and two sisters in an isolated valley. One morning the mother went to market, warning the girls not to open the door until she got home, for the land was full of tigers. And sure enough, the woman was eaten by a tigress (who appears as Grand-Aunt Tiger in many other Asian tales), who then tried to pass herself off to the children as their mother.

The girls were too smart, however: they ran out the back door and climbed a tree. The tigress followed them out but couldn't didn't see their hiding place. As the tigress stood there looking around in bewilderment, the girls began to giggle. "Get down," the tigress ordered. But they refused. "Then I'm coming to get you," the tigress said. But however she tried, she could not climb the tree.

When she demanded to know how the girls had gotten to the treetop, they told her to pour oil on the trunk. The tigress did and slid down to the ground to the children's laughter. Then, furious, she got an axe and began to carve steps into the tree. Terrified, the children called to heaven for help. They grabbed the magical golden chain that swung down to them just as the tigress reached the treetop. She too called for help, but a rotten straw rope was all that descended. She grabbed hold anyway, only to be smashed to death when the rope broke. Meanwhile, in heaven the girls were given duties: Hae-Soon, to ride the sun, Dae-Soon, the moon, and Byul-Soon, a star.

Hagar   In the Old Testament, Hagar was Abraham's slave and mother of his son Ishmael. But originally she was a desert mountain goddess; her son's name means the "goddess' favorite," and the Ishmaelite people were goddess worshipers. The Christian Paul distinctly linked her with Mt. Sinai in Arabia, an interesting connection in view of

Yahweh's decision to bestow the Hebrew commandments there. Some traditions say that Hagar had, in all, six sons for whom she built a city and to whom she taught magic.

Hainuwele   West of Papua New Guinea, on the island of Ceram, this supernatural woman was the source of food plants. It was said that a man named Ameta ("night"), hunting with his dog, pursued a wild pig into a deep pool. The animal drowned, and Ameta tried to pull out the body for meat. What emerged from the water was a coconut, stabbed with a boar's tusk.

Ameta planted the coconut, which grew miraculously and flowered within a week. From one of its leaves, fertilized by a bit of Ameta's blood, a nine-day gestation led to the birth of Hainuwele. Like the tree from which she sprang, Hainuwele grew swiftly. Less than a week after her birth, she led her father's people in the world's first ritual dance. Around and around the people spiraled, with Hainuwele at the procession's head until she began to sink into the ground. Around and around the people danced, over her head, until Hainuwele was completely buried. And from her place of descent grew wonderful food plants, never before seen on earth.

Halcyone   The faithful human lover of the Greek fisherman Ceyx, Halcyone was warned by a dream of his death at sea. She stood watch thereafter by the seashore and caught Ceyx's body as it washed to shore. Transported by grief and unquenchable longing, Halcyone burst out of human form into the shape of the first kingfisher, and her dead mate magically revived and joined her in the same shape. So kindly did the Greek divinities look on this loyal love that they blessed the couple. Now, when the kingfisher is ready to lay its eggs, a calm descends on the sea until they hatch, called by the ancient name of the loving mortal—the halcyon days.

Halmasuit   A Hittite throne goddess, she represented divine legitimation of earthly rulership. Her name is Hattian, suggesting that she descended from a goddess of that pre-Hittite culture. She is addressed in prayers as "the friend behind the mountains," which has suggested to some that she was a primary Hattian divinity adopted by the invading Hittites who wished to keep their new subjects at a safe distance.

Haltia   This was the name among the Baltic Finns for the house goddess, called Holdja in Estonia. She was said to live in each room's roof beam, bringing good luck and health to the residents if they greeted her on entering. Haltia was so attached to her domicile that she would call down mournful curses on a family who destroyed her home to move to a new one; the only way to assure her continued goodwill was to bring a log from the old house to the new (Haltia moved in as soon as three logs were crossed) or to bring a bit of ash from the old hearth to the new one.

Hannah   The name of a Jewish prophet, she was the mother of Mary, and according to apocryphal legend was married three times and produced three daughters of the same name.

Hannahanna   Once, Hittite legend says, the fertility god Telipinu disappeared, and with him disappeared all happiness and fruitfulness from the earth. Water ceased to flow; animals ceased to bear; even the milk of human mothers dried up within the breast. Everywhere gods and humans searched for the missing divinity, and everywhere they found him absent. Food became scarce. Even the wind god, blowing through the universe, could not find Telipinu.

But the queen of heaven, the mother of all people, knew what to do. While other gods mocked, she instructed a tiny bee to fly out in search of Telipinu. When she found him, the bee was to sting the god awake, for it was clear that he must be sound asleep indeed to have missed the commotion of the search parties.

Fly the little bee did, until almost exhausted. And in a village so tiny that previous searchers had overlooked it, the bee found Telipinu fast asleep. She stung him mightily, and mighty was his fury as he awoke.

Telipinu flew into a destructive rage, destroying everything animate or inanimate within reach. But Hannahanna was ready for this. Quickly she sent a huge eagle to fetch the god. Then, with the help of lovely maidens bearing sesame and nectar and accompanied by the enchantments of the magician Kamrusepas, Hannahanna cleansed all fury from the god. Thus was fertility restored to the earth, all happiness, all celebration, and all growth.

Hanwi The moon goddess of the Oglala originally lived with Wi the sun god, but another woman tricked Hanwi into giving up her seat next to Wi. Coming late to a banquet, Hanwi saw Ite in her place and hid her head with shame. As a judgment on the sun god for allowing another woman to take the moon's place, Hanwi was allowed to leave Wi's residence and go her own way; to compensate for her humiliation, she was given rulership over dawn and twilight, but henceforth always hid her face when near the sun.

Hariti This great ogress had 500 children, whom she loved passionately. She converted to Buddhism when the Buddha took away one of her children and refused to release the kidnapped child until Hariti had accepted his faith. Both the devourer and bestower of children, she enjoyed great popularity in India, across Southeast Asia, and into China. This popularity, as well as the areas wherein she was honored, hint at a possible great goddess hiding in demonic form.

Harmonia The "uniter" was the daughter of love (Aphrodite) and war (Ares), and from her the legendary Amazons claimed descent. Harmonia was also said to have founded the dynasty of Thebes and to have borne the famous Dionysian women Semele, Agave, and Autonoe, as well as their sister Ino. At Harmonia's marriage ceremony, all the Olympians bore magical gifts, including a famous necklace bestowed by Aphrodite that gave irresistible sexuality to its wearer.

Harpies Originally they were aspects of the death goddess, who came to snatch away the living. Death appeared to the people of the ancient Aegean as a seabird, so they left food offerings for her. Later Greek legend shows the goddess transformed into the Harpies ("snatchers"), three fair-haired winged maidens, swifter than birds or winds, daughters of the earth mother Gaia. They had the pale faces of beautiful starving women, the bodies of vultures, sharp claws, and bear's ears. Many names were given them, but the most common were Aello ("howler"), Celaeno ("screamer"), and Ocypete ("swift").

Hathay In South India, this goddess ("grandmother") was originally a girl who refused to marry the man her father selected for her. She went to the pool in the center of the village and drowned herself there. When she appeared in dreams to people, announcing that she had been an incarnation of Parvati, her worship was assured.

Hathor One of the world's greatest goddesses, Hathor was worshiped for more than a millennium longer than the life, to date, of Christianity. For more than 3,000 years her joyful religion held sway over Egypt. Small wonder, then, that a profusion of legends surrounded her, or that she was depicted in so many different guises: at once mother and daughter of the sun, both a lioness and a cow, sometimes a woman, and sometimes a tree. Goddess of the underworld, she was also ruler of the sky. Patron of foreigners, she was mother of the Egyptians. Like Ishtar to the east, she was a complex embodiment of feminine possibilities.

One of Hathor's most familiar forms was the winged cow of creation who gave birth to the universe. Because she bore them, she owned the bodies of the dead; thus she was queen of the underworld. Again, she appeared as the seven (or nine) Hathors who materialized at a child's birth and foretold its inescapable destiny. Then too, she was the special guardian spirit of all women and all female animals.

"Habitation of the hawk and birdcage of the soul," Hathor was essentially the body in which the soul resides. As such, she was patron of bodily pleasures: the pleasures of sound, in music and song; the joys of the eye, in art, cosmetics, the weaving of garlands; the delight of motion in dance and in love; and all the pleasures of touch. In her temples, priestesses danced and played their tinkling tambourines, probably enjoying other sensual pleasures with the worshipers as well. (Not without cause did the Greeks compare her to Aphrodite.) Her festivals were carnivals of intoxication, especially that held at Dendera on New Year's Day, when Hathor's image was brought forth from her temple to catch the rays of the newborn sun, whereupon revels broke out and throbbed through the streets. (In this capacity she was called Tanetu.) She was a most beloved goddess to her people, and they held fast to her pleasurable rites long into historical times.

Haumea   Originally, Hawaiian myth tells us, human women could not give birth. They swelled with pregnancy and, when it was time for delivery, they were cut open—a dangerous procedure. But the goddess Haumea came to their rescue, teaching women how to push the child out between their legs.

Haumea was not so much ageless as ever-renewing. Frequently she grew old, but as often she transformed herself into a young woman. Generations went by and still she lived among humans, sleeping with the handsome young men even when they were her grandchildren and distant descendants. One of her favored mates was named Wakea. Once, it was said, the people intended to sacrifice him. Taking him to the forest, which was her domain, Haumea ran directly through the tree trunks, leaving shreds of her skirts blooming as morning glory vines, and carried her lover to safety.

Because she owned all the wild plants, Haumea could withdraw her energy, leaving people to

starve. This she did when angry, but most often Haumea was a kindly goddess. Some say she is part of a trinity whose other aspects are the creator Hina and the fiery Pele.

Hebat   Originally the presiding goddess of the Hurrian pantheon, she merged with Wurusemu, the Hittite sun goddess; this, as well as her title of queen of heaven, suggests that she was a solar figure. She was depicted as a distinguished, well-dressed matron, wearing a crown, jewelry, and fancy shoes, standing on a lion.

Hebe   Her ancient name was Ganymeda and under that name she was the Olympian cupbearer, refreshing the divinities with the ambrosia and nectar of immortal youth. The "downy one" who represented spring's young herbage, Hebe was reverenced with ivy cuttings at her sanctuary in Phlius. The incarnation of all that is young and fresh, she could renew youth magically.

The young spring goddess was the younger, maiden self of the great heavenly matron Hera, the primary deity of pre-Hellenic Greece. But just as Hera's preeminence gave way to that of Zeus, so did Hebe lose her position to a male divinity: Ganymede, a homosexual youth kidnapped from earth by Zeus to bear the Olympian cup of immortality. Greek legend recorded an excuse for replacing the goddess with a deified mortal: Hebe, it was said, had been clumsy enough to fall while serving, embarrassing the divine assembly by exposing her genitals as she fell. From the maiden form of the great goddess, she was demoted to the daughter of Hera and was eventually just a shadowy pale goddess with little legend and no cult practices.

Hecate   At night, particularly at the dark of the moon, this goddess walked the roads of ancient Greece, accompanied by sacred dogs and bearing a blazing torch. Occasionally she stopped to gather offerings left by her devotees where three roads crossed, for this threefold goddess was best honored where one could look three ways at once.

Sometimes, it was even said that Hecate could look three ways because she had three heads: a serpent, a horse, and a dog.

While Hecate walked outdoors, her worshipers gathered inside to eat Hecate suppers in her honor, gatherings at which magical knowledge was shared, the secrets of sorcery whispered, and dogs, honey, and black female lambs sacrificed. The bitch goddess and the snake goddess ruled these powers, and she bestowed them on those who worshiped her honorably. When supper was over, the leftovers were placed outdoors as offerings to Hecate and her hounds. And if the poor of Greece gathered at the doorsteps of wealthier households to snatch the offerings, what matter?

Some scholars say that Hecate was not originally Greek, her worship having traveled south from her original Thracian homeland. Others contend that she was a form of the earth mother Demeter, yet another of whose forms was the maiden Persephone. Legends, they claim, of Persephone's abduction and later residence in Hades give clear prominence to Hecate, who therefore must represent the old wise woman, the crone, the final stage of woman's growth—the aged Demeter herself, just as Demeter is the mature Persephone.

In either case, the antiquity of Hecate's worship was recognized by the Greeks, who called her a Titan, one of those pre-Olympian divinities whom Zeus and his cohort had ousted. The newcomers also bowed to her antiquity by granting to Hecate alone a power shared with Zeus, that of granting or withholding from humanity anything she wished. Hecate's worship continued into classical times, both in the private form of Hecate suppers and in public sacrifices, celebrated by "great ones" or Caberioi, of honey, black female lambs, and dogs, and sometimes black human slaves.

As queen of the night, Hecate was sometimes said to be the moon goddess in her dark form, as Artemis was the waxing moon and Selene the full

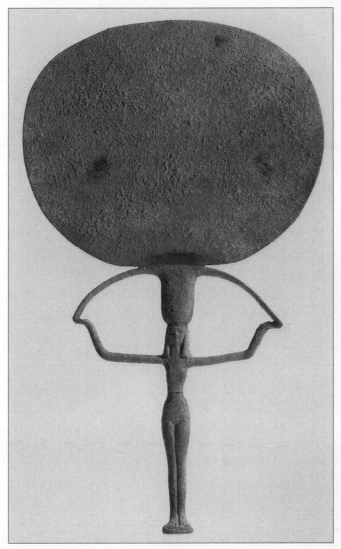

Hathor, Egyptian goddess of light and the sun, was often depicted in the form of a woman holding a mirror above her head, as in this bronze wherein the mirror is shaped like a papyrus blossom. Such mirrors served both as ritual reminders of the goddess' energy and as household ornaments.

moon. But she may as readily have been the earth goddess, for she ruled the spirits of the dead, humans who had been returned to the earth. As queen of death she ruled the magical powers of regeneration; in addition, she could hold back her spectral hordes from the living if she chose. And so Greek women evoked Hecate for protection from her hosts whenever they left the house, and they erected her threefold images at their doors, as if to tell wandering spirits that therein lived friends of their queen, who must not be bothered with night noises and spooky apparitions.

Hedrun In the Scandinavian Valhalla, the hall of heroes where the Valkyries brought those slain in battle but not selected for Freya's retinue, a magical nanny goat lived. Every day Hedrun stood on her hind legs nibbling needles from a magical pine tree, possibly the very tree that held up the world. She converted this nourishment not into goat's milk but into intoxicating mead, which she produced so copiously that all the heroes spent every day getting roaring drunk, and would do so until the world's end.

Hegemone An ancient goddess of the soil whose name survives in a word for sovereignty, Hegemone appeared so early in Greek history that we have no real record of her independent worship. As wave after wave of invaders reached the Aegean, they assimilated this early goddess to various deities of their own: to Artemis, to the horse goddess Despoina, and to the Graces as a double goddess. In this last identity, she was honored at Athens with her sister Auxo, their names signifying "increase" and "mastery." The power of her original identity, as the force that allows humankind to produce foodstuffs from her land, is indicated only by the power her name still evokes, for no legend survives of her.

Heith In the Voluspa, the Scandinavian lay of the shaman-woman, this name is given to a wise woman whose witchcraft includes casting spells upon the minds of those she wished to enchant.

Hekoolas The body of this California Miwok sun goddess was completely covered with shining abalone shells so that she glowed in the sky. But she did not always live in this world, which was once dark and cold, with only the faint glow in the east from her reflection. Coyote sent two men to bring the sun to our side of the earth, but she refused. Then Coyote sent enough men to tie her

up with ropes and drag her back across the world. Once here, she made her home above us and provided the sunlight our world needed.

Another tale from the Miwok, in which the sun woman is named Heima, tells how she had to be convinced to light this world. The story begins when the sun shut herself up in her stone house and refused to come out. The sky was dark, and Hawk Chief was very far away. He went to his grandfather and demanded daylight. Coyote, his grandfather, said he'd see what he could do and went to visit the doves. He told them his grandson didn't like the dark, and they said they'd fix the problem.

The doves had been to the sun's house and knew where it was, so they set off. When they got there, they sat down and waited, hoping she'd come out of her own accord. They waited and waited, but nothing happened. Finally they decided to shoot stones at her house to make her rise. Trouble was, they couldn't agree on who should do the shooting. The older wanted to try, but the younger claimed to be stronger. And so the young dove took up a slingshot and whirled it around. The stone, flying from the slingshot, hit the sun's house and went right through the wall. The sun was frightened and rose from her smokehole to check on the damage. But she found that there was only a little house, so she went back in.

The older dove then took up the slingshot and whirled it round, and round and round. When he let the stone fly, it sailed through the air so fast that it smashed right into the sun's house, right in the center. The sun, frightened out of her wits, rose straight up into the air and stood overhead. And so Coyote and his grandson were very, very happy.

Hekt The frog-headed goddess, the "great magician" of Egypt, Hekt represented the embryonic grain that apparently dies, rots, and then sends forth roots and sprouts. One of the most ancient of Egyptian divinities, Hekt was midwife at the birth of the sun and continued each day to help it into the sky. It was she who gave the Egyptians—indeed, all people—life, for at the original creation she touched the lifeless humans with the ankh, causing them to breathe and move. Like other birth goddesses, she was a prophetess, perhaps because the croaking of frogs was held to predict rain, and thus the rising of the Nile.

Hel The goddess who gave her name to the Christian place of eternal punishment was the Scandinavian ruler of the misty world under the earth. Her name means the "one who covers up" or the "one who hides," and the ones Hel hid in her nine-circled realm were those who died of disease or old age. Those who died heroically, in battle or by other violence, were carried off by the Valkyries to the heavenly halls of Freya or Odin.

Hel was the daughter of the giant woman Angerboda and was thought to be an ugly pinto woman, half black and half white, who rode to earth to enfold the dying in her horrible arms and to rest her drooping head against theirs. Down in her nine-ringed realm, where the inhabitants kept up a constant wail, Hel lived in a miserable palace called Sleet-Cold, where the walls were built of worms and human bones. She ate with a knife and fork called Famine from a plate named Hunger. Her slave, Senility, served her, as did her maidservant, Dotage. When she slept, it was on her cot, Bedridden, covered by curtains named Woefully Pale.

The entry to her queendom was guarded by the hell-hound, Garm; before you reached the threshold you had to travel Helveg ("Troublesome Road") to Hel, past the strange guardian maiden, Modgud. Some scholars say the conception of Hel is more ancient than the heroic myth of Valhalla, the hall of dead heroes.

Helen Before the Dorian Greeks invaded her territory in the Peloponnese, Helen was a full-fledged goddess whose second name was Dendritus ("she of the trees"). A vegetation deity, she was depicted with two mates, the Dioscuri, later said to be her "brothers" Castor and Pollux. All were born of an egg laid by the mother goddess Leda, possibly a

recollection of a tradition that connected the tree-dwelling goddess with birds.

Helen is such a complex figure that her myths sometimes seem self-contradictory. Even the meaning of her name is disputed. Some translate it as meaning "fair" or "bright one," seeing her as a form of the moon goddess—although she could as easily be a sun divinity, given the similarity of her myths with other Indo-European dawn maidens. Others connect her name with roots that mean "spring" or that refer to baskets carried in Demetrian festivals—both appropriate for a vegetation goddess.

There was a folk tradition that, in her human form, Helen was so perfect that when the potters of Greece learned their art, they molded the first bowls upon her breasts. Her beauty connects her to Aphrodite—so much so that Paul Friederich calls her an "Aphroditoid." Some myths call Aphrodite her mother—although yet others say she was born of Nemesis, goddess of vengeance, who was at the time a goddess of fertility but who became deformed with anger after Zeus raped her. Perhaps it is this ancient lineage that is recalled by the curiously ambivalent name given to Helen: Rhigedanes, the one who stiffens, apparently in rigor mortis as well as erotic erection.

As a goddess, Helen had several famous sanctuaries. In Rhamnus she was worshiped as the daughter of Nemesis; at Argos, in the temple of the goddess of childbirth, Eileithyia. And in Sparta, home of the heroine who bore her name, Helen was honored in a shrine of trees; figurines of her were hung in orchards as votive offerings for a good harvest.

The goddess of the land's fertility gave her name to the queens of that land. Thus the most familiar Helen, the queen of Sparta who figured so prominently in the epic struggle of Greeks against Trojans. Raped by the Athenian king Theseus when she was but a girl, Helen grew into a strong-minded ruler who took Menelaus as her spouse, thereby granting him the right to her city's throne. But soon Helen left Menelaus for the beautiful Trojan prince, Paris. To regain his throne, Menelaus had to regain the queen. He chased Helen to Troy and fought for years to win her back. But there is a persistent tradition that—because the queen was so necessary to the seasonal cycle of her land, Lacedaemon—Helen could not be removed from it. Only a ghost, therefore, accompanied Paris to Troy, and the famous war was fought over a specter.

Heliades   The daughters of the sun, these sisters were poplar-tree goddesses who cried amber tears at the death of their beloved brother Phaethon. Some of their names were Aegilae, Aegle, Lamethusa, Lampetia, and Phatusa.

Helle   Once, it was said, King Athamas of Boeotia, north of Greece, and the cloud queen Nephele had two children, Phrixus and Helle. But the king turned his attentions to another woman, Ino, who conspired against Nephele's children by urging the Boeotian women to parch the seed corn, inducing a famine when the burned seeds did not germinate and grow.

According to custom, someone had to be sacrificed to restore the earth's fertility, and Ino bribed an oracle to claim that the earth spirits demanded Nephele's children. But a golden, winged ram magically appeared and took Helle and her brother northeast to the land of Colchis. Helle grew dizzy and fell into the narrow strait that separates Europe and Asia, even today called Hellespont in her honor. Her brother arrived safely in Colchis and sacrificed the ram, whose golden fleece figured in the later legend of the sorceress Medea.

Poet Robert Graves saw in this myth the residue of an earlier one in which Helle was the moon goddess who ruled the sea and its tides. He identified Helle with Helen and Selene and called her the ancestral goddess of the preIonian residents of Boeotia, who persuaded the invading patriarchal tribes to adopt the "bright" goddess Helle. The invaders made her a male ancestor, Hellenus of the "Hellenes," and scrambled the goddess' legend together with their own religious tales to produce the hybrid and complex stories about Helle and Helen known today.

Henwen   In British mythology, this magical sow goddess came forth early in creation to give life to the world. As she roamed the hilly countryside, she gave birth to litter after litter. But instead of piglets, Henwen produced a grain of wheat and a bee; a grain of barley and a bee; a wolf cub, an eaglet, and a kitten, each strange litter in a different part of the country.

Hera   Many generations before Zeus was known in Greece, the people there worshiped as their chief divinity the cow-eyed sky queen whom we call Hera, although that title means only "Our Lady" and may not have been the goddess' actual name. Magnificent of form and feature, ruler of the earth and its dwellers, Hera was particularly the goddess of women and their sexuality. Like the women who worshiped her, she was the daughter of flesh and time, Rhea and Cronos. Also like human women, she passed through three life stages: youth, prime, and age.

First, she was the maiden Hebe or Parthenia, called virginal not because she avoided intercourse but because, having no children, she was free of responsibility. In this stage, she was also called Antheia ("flowering one"), symbol of both the flower of human youth and the budding earth. Second, she was revealed as the mature woman, Nymphenomene ("seeking a mate") or Teleia ("perfect one"); she was then the earth in summer, the mother in the prime of life. Third, she grew into Theira ("crone"), the woman who has passed through and beyond maternity and lives again to herself.

In honor of the three phases of Hera, the ancient residents of Greece celebrated the Heraea, a competitive festival that dates to earlier times than the Olympics. Every four years, or perhaps annually, women came to a field near Hera's town of Argos for the 160-yard races. They ran barebreasted and with hair unbound in three age groups to honor the goddess' three stages. There were three winners, each receiving identical olive crowns and a share in the cow sacrificed at the festival. Each winner—young, mature, and old—had the right to leave a statuette of herself in Hera's shrine.

Another part of her religion was Hera's annual revival. Her worshipers bathed her image, renewing her youth and preparing her again for the seasonal cycle of maturation and death. Carrying the goddess' statue to the water to cleanse the winter away from her marked how they, too, like the earth, would forever be reborn. As goddess of birth and death, of the tender spring and the weary autumn, Hera held the emblems, respectively, of a cuckoo and a pomegranate.

Originally Hera had no consort, but when the patriarchal tribes of the north descended on Greece, they brought with them their sky god Zeus. Because Hera's religion was too strong to destroy, a marriage of convenience was forged between the two predominant divinities. From this melding of the pre-Hellenic goddess of women and the newly arrived thunderbolt wielder, the Hera of classical times emerged.

This new Hera was not a very attractive figure, a jealous and petulant wife who hounded her unfaithful husband and his lovers. Of course, legend says, she never wanted the marriage to begin with. Zeus so desired the statuesque goddess that he transformed himself into a cuckoo—the bird for which Hera had a special fondness—and flew bedraggled into her lap. Taking pity on the bird and soothing it, Hera found herself being raped by Zeus. Shamed by the violation, the goddess agreed to restore her dignity by joining in marriage with Zeus. But it wasn't long, the stories say, that she wearied of his ceaseless pursuit of other women and goddesses—probably a mythic recollection of the destruction of indigenous goddess cults by Zeus' worshipers—and Hera organized a heavenly revolt against the tyrannical Zeus. She and other Olympians tied him to his bed and gathered to mock him. Freed by one of the deities, Zeus took his revenge on the instigator of the palace revolt by stringing Hera from the sky, her wrists tied to golden bracelets and her ankles weighted by anvils. When freed, Hera resumed her persecution of Io, Semele, and other paramours of Zeus, siding against him in the Trojan War and otherwise making a mythic nuisance of herself to the father symbol of the patriarchy. Eventually, little remained of the ancient threefold goddess of dignified womanhood except the insistence of Greek mythology on the periodic retreat of Hera into solitude, a remembrance of the days in which that was her

The seated goddess receiving gifts was a common artistic motif in Mediterranean cultures. Here a goddess, probably Hera or her Italian counterpart Juno, is shown on a black amphora with designs in pinkish glaze.

honored third phase, the prophetic crone, the distinguished wise one, the woman alone.

Hero A priestess of Aphrodite at Sestos, she took a young man named Leander as a lover. Each night he swam across the waters that separated them, made love with her, and swam back at dawn. One night, however, Leander dove into stormy waters, so great was his passion for Hero. He drowned, and the priestess joined him in death.

Hertha   No legends survive of the Germanic goddess from whom we get our word for earth. It is known, however, that she was worshiped into historic times, when plows were carried in Christian Shrovetide processions in honor of the earth's fertility. Hertha was also frequently invoked by medieval witches as their special patron.

Hervor   One of the few Scandinavian heroines to whom a saga—the Hervarar Saga—is devoted, Hervor was a warrior maiden. Needing a magical sword for her campaigns, Hervor dared to enter the rocky grave of her father and uncles. There, battling their violent spirits, she claimed her prize.

Hesperides   Far to the west of the world, at the edge of night, lived the evening stars, the sweet-singing daughters of Nyx, the night goddess. The Greeks said that they and a majestic serpent guarded the golden-fruited apple tree that the earth goddess Gaia gave to the sky queen, Hera. Sometimes legend said there were three Hesperides, sometimes four. Sometimes they were said to be like Harpies, at other times like Sirens. But consistent in their legend was their stewardship of magical objects. Thus they might have been embodiments of the guardians of secret rites held at nightfall to soft music, conducted by goddess worshipers long after the conversion of Greece to patriarchal worship.

Hestia   There were never statues of this most ancient Greek goddess, for she took no human form. Hestia was seen only in the fire of the hearth, living in the center of every home, an honored guest and helpful to her hosts. As the hearth goddess, Hestia symbolized family unity; by extension, as goddess of the public hearth, she embodied the social contract. At this ever-burning public hearth, the *prytaneion*, she bore the name of Prytantis; there first fruits, water, oil, wine and year-old cows were sacrified to her.

According to Greek legend, Hestia was the first-born of the Olympian goddesses. Her antiquity is attested by the Greek proverb "Start with Hestia," meaning "Begin things at the beginning." In the beginning of her worship, matrilineal succession seems to have been the rule, and traces of it survived in the custom of classical Greece whereby a new home was not considered established until a woman brought fire from her mother's hearth to light her own. In the same way, Greek colonists brought fire from the mother city's public hearth to assure the cohesion of their new communities.

Hiedo-no-Ame   A court woman of phenomenal memory, she was assigned by the empress Gemmyo to memorize all the tales of Japan's primordial goddesses and gods, for the invasion of Buddhism had threatened the survival of Shinto. For thirty-two years Heido kept the ancient tales in mind until a scribe was finally assigned to take dictation from her. The written compilation of her tales, called the Kojiki, has served as the Japanese scripture for more than a thousand years.

Hiera   A famous woman warrior, general of the Mysians, she fought in the Trojan War but was edited from Homer's account because, Philostratus says, "this greatest and finest of women would have outshone his heroine Helen."

Hikuleo   The underworld goddess of the Tongans of Polynesia owned a land called Pulotu, to which several men traveled to seek food for their people. Drinking, diving, and surfing contests were held; the men performed admirably. But the gods did not really want to share the precious food. So Hikuleo chased the humans out of her realm, not realizing that they had hidden the seeds of yam and taro in their clothing.

Hild   Scandinavian legend said that when this heroine's father refused to make peace with her lover—declaring war on him instead—Hild used magic nightly to raise the dead warriors. Then the battle could never end with capitulation to her father. Hild's fight, legend said, would go on forever, to the doom of this world called Ragnarok.

Himiko   "The great child of the sun," this Japanese empress never left her palace, governing by means of messages received while in a trance. It is possible the name was a title held by all shaman queens of early Japan.

Hina   The greatest Polynesian goddess was a complex figure of whom many myths were told. Like other major divinities, she was associated with many aspects of life and had many symbols: she was the tapa-beating woman who lived in the moon; she was Great Hina, the death mother; she was a warrior queen of the Island of Women. An all-inclusive divine archetype, Hina appeared in many Polynesian legends, some of which—not surprisingly, for such a complex and long-lived goddess—contradicted others.

In some legends, Hina was said to have been created of red clay by the first man. But others—in Tahiti, for instance—knew Hina as the preeminent goddess, for whose sexual pleasure the first man was created. This goddess had two faces, one in the front as humans do, one at the back of her head. She was the first female being on earth, from whose fertile womb fell innumerable others, many bearing her name.

One of these was the dawn goddess Hine-titama, who was seduced by her own father, while unaware of his identity. Furious and ashamed on discovering this trickery, Hina ran away to Po, the Polynesian underworld; this was the first death in creation. Her fury was so unquenchable that she announced her intention of henceforth killing any children begotten by her father, thereby assuring that death would remain a force on earth.

How the goddess Hina reached the moon— she who had originally lived on earth and populated it—was a matter of numerous myths. In Tahiti, Hina was a canoeist who enjoyed the sport so much that she sailed to the moon, which proved to be such a good boat that she stayed

there, guarding earthly sojourners. Others told of Hina being sent to the moon by violence. Her brother, hung over from indulgence in kava, became infuriated at the noise Hina made while beating tape cloth. When she would not cease her labors for her brother's convenience, he hit her, sending her sailing into the sky. Because tapa-beating was thought to be like the process by which the human body is slowly beaten down into death, this Hina of the moon, the tapa-maker of the sky, was closely related to the Great Hina of the underworld. Finally, a Hawaiian variant of these legends said that Hina, a married woman, grew tired of constantly picking up after her family and she simply left the earth to pursue a career as the moon's clothmaker.

One guise Hina wore was as a warrior of the Island of Women, a place where no men were allowed, where trees alone impregnated the residents. A man was washed up on the shore and slept with Hina, the ageless and beautiful leader. He stayed for some time. But every time she began to show her years, Hina went surfing and came back renewed and restored. At the same time, her human lover gradually bowed under the years. Hina returned the man to his people on a whale, which the humans impudently and imprudently killed. The whale was Hina's brother, and she sent terrible sufferings on the people as a result.

Among all the many stories of Hina, however, probably the most commonly known one was that of the goddess and her lover, the eel. Living on earth as a mortal woman, Hina bathed in a quiet pool where, one day, she had intercourse with an eel. Her people, afraid of the power of the serpent, killed him, only to find that Hina had been mating with a god. Furious and despairing at having her affair so terminated, Hina took the eel's head and buried it. Five nights later the first coconut grew there, a staple product thereafter to Hina's folk.

Hine-ahu-one   Among the Maori of New Zealand, this goddess—a version of the Polynesian great goddess Hina—was the primary female principle, formed when the goddess Papa died, leaving her seventy male descendants with no way to reproduce themselves. Papa's last instructions were that the heroic Tane should find red clay at the beach of Kuruwaka—the earth mother's vagina—and sculpt a woman from it. He followed Papa's instructions, and this ancestral woman came to life.

Hine-titama   The Maori dawn goddess was the first real human woman born on this earth, and was the first child of Hine-ahu-one, the primary female principle. All unknowing, she married her own father, thus becoming the mother of humanity. But when she discovered the truth about her husband, she left this world, transforming herself into Hine-nui-te-Po, "Great Lady of the Night," goddess of the underworld who cares for spirits after death.

An important myth of Hine-titama explains why we must all die. The hero Maui bet that he could crawl into the goddess' vagina, through her body, right to her heart. He would then, he boasted, eat her heart and conquer death. And so Maui turned himself into a lizard and prepared to enter the goddess' birth canal. But his bird companion burst into laughter at the sight of this hero, shrunken into a lizard, crawling into Hine-titama's pubic hair. The laughter woke up the goddess, who crushed Maui between her sturdy legs. And thus the hero lost, and so we must all die and rejoin the goddess in her underworld realm.

Hippia   The "horseheaded" Demeter was worshiped in rural Arcadia, where the story was told that the Greek Earth mother was once pursued by the sea god Poseidon. She changed her shape several times, but he changed shape as well. Finally she became a mare, and he a stallion, in which form he was able to mount her and engender the marvelous horse Arion and, possibly, the young goddess Despoina.

Hippo   Her name means "horse," a word found in many Amazon names. She was a general who, with Marpesia and Lampado, inaugurated the worship of the Amazonian Artemis at Ephesus; that city became one of the goddess' most famous shrines. After conquering Asia Minor and Syria, the warrior women set up a wooden image of Artemis near a beech tree at Ephesus. There they performed a shield dance. Then they circled in a second dance, one in which they stamped the ground rhythmically and shook their arrow-filled quivers as pipes played a wild, warlike melody.

Hippodamia   She was originally a goddess of pre-Hellenic Olympia honored annually in secret rites of women, but she passed into Greek legend merely as the ancestral queen of the tragic house of king Atreus.

Hippolyta   The "stamping mare" was one of the greatest queens of the Amazons. One of the most beautiful and strongest women of her time, she wore the golden belt of Amazonian queenship, a gift from her father, the war god Ares. The fabulous treasure was coveted by the Greeks to the south, who sent a raiding party to despoil the women warriors. The burly Heracles ("glory of Hera") led the raid.

A fight ensued, the legends about which are confused and sometimes contradictory. Apparently Hippolyta found Heracles attractive but, as was customary, wished to wrestle with him before she would sleep with him; thus she tested the strength of her potential lovers so there was no chance that she might bear a weak child. Her loyal retainers, however, thought that the Greek champion was attacking their queen and sprang to arms. Alas, the women were defeated.

Here the legend becomes almost hopelessly confused, with Hippolyta merging with her sister Antiope and with Queen Oreithyia. Sometimes the tales say Hippolyta died in the first battle over the golden belt. Then again, it was said she was carried off as hostage and granted to the Athenian king Theseus as a concubine. Some versions even have Theseus leading the raid on Amazonia. Finally, there were stories that Queen Antiope was carried off to Athens and that her sister Hippolyta led the women warriors to regain her. Defeated by Theseus, Hippolyta led her decimated legions north again, dying of grief en route. Her mourning comrades, these stories say, buried her in Megara under a tombstone shaped like an Amazon's shield.

Hit In the Caroline Islands of Micronesia, this name was given to an octopus goddess. Hit's daughter was sleeping with one of the gods, who already had a wife in heaven. The sky woman followed her husband, trying to drag him away from his mistress, but Hit began dancing lewdly. So erotic was her performance that the sky woman fainted from excitement and had to be carried back to heaven. Each time she tried to stop her husband's intercourse with the octopus' daughter, Hit began dancing again, thus allowing for the conception of the hero Olifat.

Hlin Either a minor Scandinavian goddess or an aspect of the great goddess Frigg, Hlin's name means "protector," and her role was to defend Frigg's favorite humans. Sometimes she was invoked as "mildness" or "warmth," possibly a reference to the Scandinavian summertime as a "servant" to the earth.

Hlodyn "Protectress of the hearth" may have been a title of the Germanic earth mother Hertha or a distinct goddess whose special province was the human home.

Hnossa The youthful goddess of infatuation in Scandinavia, she was the daughter of the goddess of sensuality, Freya. Her name means "jewel" and was used of precious stones by her worshipers.

Ho Hsien-Ku In Chinese mythology, there were, in addition to divinities, a number of "immortal beings" or apotheosized humans. One of these Eight Immortals was Ho Hsien-Ku, who dreamed at puberty that, by eating mother of pearl, she could gain eternal life. She did so, and soon her body began to fade away; she could pass through solid objects and travel at impossible speeds. While she still dwelled on earth, Ho Hsien-Ku spent all night wandering the hills gathering flowers and herbs. Eventually she simply faded away, but was seen a half-century later floating on a cloud, whereupon it was recognized that she was living with the goddess Hsi Wang Mu in the heavens.

Hokkma The Hebrew god Jehovah had Hokkma ("wisdom") from the first, and almost from the first this quality isolated itself in female form and became a demi goddess. Some contend that Hokkma was merely allegorical, but she speaks from the Bible in terms that make such a reading difficult to support. In two books—Proverbs and Ecclesiasticus—she makes particularly strong claims to a separate identity.

The earliest creation of Jehovah, Hokkma was also his favorite. "At the first, before the beginning of earth," she brags in Proverbs, "when he established the heavens, I was there, when he drew out a circle on the face of the deep" (8:23, 28). Having established her temporal seniority, she further claims, "I was daily his delight" (8:30). It was Hokkma who cast her shadow on the primeval waters, stilling them so that creation could continue. It was Hokkma who gave consciousness to humankind, for humans crawled like worms until she endowed them with spirit. Hokkma goes so far as to call herself the playmate, even the wife, of Jehovah. Allegorical or not, this figure and others (Shekinah, Sabbath) undercut and softened the patriarchal religion of the Jews with their semidivine femininity.

Horae Also called the "hours" or the "seasons," they were a group of Greek goddesses and, like other groups, appeared in various numbers. Sometimes there were two of them: Thallo ("spring") and Carpo ("autumn"). Sometimes there were three: Eunomia ("lawful order"), Dike ("justice"), and Irene ("peace"). They were the goddesses of the natural order, of the yearly cycle, of plant growth;

they ruled the varied weather of the seasons. By extrapolation they became the goddesses who ruled the order of human society.

Few legends were told of them, although they made cameo appearances in Olympian celebrations and myths of other goddesses—clothing the newly born Aphrodite, for example, dancing with the Graces, or opening the gates of heaven for Hera's escapes to solitude. Only Dike had an actual myth to her name. The younger self of her mother Themis—as Hebe was of Hera and Persephone of Demeter—she grew so weary of the constant wars of humankind that she withdrew to the mountains, to await a more peaceful order. Ages passed, and conditions grew worse instead of better. Finally Dike, losing hope in humanity, ascended to heaven to become the constellation Virgo.

Hsi-Ho Mother of the ten suns, this ancient Chinese heroine created the calendar by selecting the order in which she would bathe her children—thus establishing which day came before which. After bathing the child in the sweet waters of the Kan Yuan Gulf, she hung the day's sun in a mulberry tree and raised it into the sky.

Hsi-Ling Shih This ancient and legendary Chinese empress was said to have invented silk and the culture of silkworms and to have taught it to her people.

Hsi Wang Mu The highest goddess of ancient China was the Queen of the West, who lived in a golden palace in the Kunlun Mountains, where once every 3,000 years, she threw a birthday party for herself. It was a special day for all the gods, for on that occasion the peach tree, *p'ant'ao*, ripened, providing the fruit of immortality. Also on the menu for the party were such delicacies as dragon livers and monkey lips.

Like the Roman Juno, Wang Mu was the goddess of female energy, the essence of yin and the ruler of individual female beings. In her most ancient form, she was a monster-mother, a wild-haired human-faced female with tiger's teeth and

a cat's tail—perhaps a form of the great Grand-Aunt Tiger. She lived, in those days, not in a palace but in a cave, where magical three-footed birds fed her and from which she sent forth disease and death. Later Wang Mu took a gentler form as a beautiful ageless woman dispensing peaches that,

From the Ming period (1368–1643 C.E.) in China comes this stone statue painted green, red and black. The worshiping maiden formed part of a bodyguard of figures placed in a grave; the dead were considered to have returned to the Queen of the West, Hsi Wang Mu.

mixed with the ashes of mulberry trees, cured rather than caused disease. Clearly, these forms were two sides of the same archetype.

Huaxi This Chinese heroine was one of many legendary women who became pregnant under unusual circumstances. In Huaxi's case, she found a giant footprint in a marsh; there lived the dragon-shaped thunder god, whose essence passed into her through the footprint; Huaxi gave birth to a serpent-bodied god.

Huitaca The moon goddess of intoxication and joy to the Chibcha, residents of what is now Colombia, Huitaca was the rival of the industrious male preacher Bochica. In the Chibcha legends, Bochica wandered through the countryside teaching not only useful crafts but a puritanical attitude toward life. Following him, and undoing his efforts, was the owl woman Huitaca, whose reckless delight in life was contagious.

Sometimes this goddess was called Chia and was said to be the wife of Bochica. The story of their conflict remained the same in this version, except that the "woman" became so angry at Bochica's influence that she raised a great flood by magic, drowning Bochica's followers; her husband then threw Chia into the sky, where she became the moon.

Huixtocihuatl The sister of the Aztec rain gods quarreled with them one day and left home to live by herself in the ocean, where she became the goddess of salt. Her June festival celebrated Huixtocihuatl's invention of salt extraction by exposing ocean water in pans; she was thus considered to be the patron goddess of salt-makers.

Huldra Huldra ("hill lady") was the queen of the Germanic hill fairies, and her people were thus the Huldrafolk. Elegant mountain dwellers, they were addicted to dancing and music making. Unfortunately for humans, the mournful melodies of Huldra's people were hypnotic, none more so than the harping of Huldra herself. She was a tall being who

seemed from the front like a beautiful human woman; her back, however, was hollow like other fairies' backs, and she had a long tail.

Hulluk Miyumko The star chiefs of the California Miwok were beautiful women who lived beneath a whistling elderberry tree, which kept them awake so they could work all the time. They included the Morning Star and the Pleiades.

Hun-Ahpu-Mtye The Guatamalan goddess of the moon appeared as a human woman with the face of a tapir, an animal sacred to her people.

Husbishag The ancient Semitic goddess who kept the secret book in which the hour of death was written for every living thing, she was possibly an aspect of the underworld queen Eriskegal.

Hu-Tu As did all other recorded cultures except the Egyptian, the Chinese saw the earth as a female divinity ("Empress Earth"), patron of fertility, worshiped until this century on a square marble altar in the Forbidden City, whereon the ruler offered sacrifices each summer solstice.

Hybla The name of the greatest goddess of ancient Sicily still appears in Italian place names; she was an earth goddess and ancestor of humanity.

Hydra The beast of Hera, daughter of the serpent-goddess Echidna, guarded the entrance to the underworld at Lerna. There, her many heads hissed at any mortal who tried to enter death's kingdom; if a head were chopped off, another—or two, or seven, more—took its place. The dangerous swamp of Lerna was also a sanctuary where murderers could purify themselves of spilled blood, giving rise to the Greek saying, "a Lerna of evils."

The blood of the Hydra was so poisonous that, touched by it, the immortal centaur Chiron begged to die to escape its torture. And in some Greek tales, it was Hydra blood that destroyed Heracles—a bit of mythological irony, for the strong man had previously killed the serpent.

Hydra's blood, these tales say, was the poison imbued in the robe that Dejanira wove for Heracles, the robe that burned him to death.

Poet Robert Graves saw in the Hydra myth a memory of the patriarchal Greek tribes'extermination of the worship of the pre-Hellenic divinities. Meeting in secret groves, these religious groups grew through persecution: for every goddess-honoring group destroyed or converted, another sprang forth in its place. Even the ancients, finding the Hydra a puzzling figure, offered their own explanations. One early scholar, for instance, thought that the Hydra was an underground river whose waters, if stopped up in one place, would burst forth in another.

Hypermnestra   Oldest of the Danaid sisters, she was worshiped in Greek Argos as the founder of its royal dynasty. It is theorized that she was originally not a Danaid but a water goddess. She did not join her husband-murdering sisters but spared her mate in order to give divine sanction to the Argive monarchy.

Hyrrokin   After the Scandinavian goddess Frigg's son Balder was killed, the earth mourned so much that his death ship could not travel to the underworld. But this giant, strongest of a strong race, was brought to heaven to throw her weight against the ship. She arrived riding a wolf, using snakes for a bridle, and performed the near-impossible task of launching Balder into Hel's world.

Ia In one version of the story of the goddess Cybele, the hermaphrodite Agdistis did not die from the trauma of castration, but survived as a woman. The discarded penis and testicles bled into the earth, which engendered a tree whose fruit impregnated Nana, who in turn gave birth to the lovely youth Attis. Attis, meeting the womanly Agdistis, fell instantly in love, as did the former hermaphrodite with the handsome boy. But King Midas, opposed to the union, arranged a marriage between Attis and his own daughter Ia. At the wedding supper, the jilted Agdistis burst upon the scene in fury. She drove all the guests mad, most notably Attis, who castrated himself on the spot, throwing his genitals aside and condemning them as "the cause of all evil." Then he died, and the newly widowed bride, Ia, killed herself.

Iahu Anat According to some scholars, this was the most ancient name of the Hebrew divinity—a goddess who, over the ages, was changed into the god Yahweh, later called Jehovah.

Iambe "Abuse" or "indecent speech" this Greek princess was called, for her talk was bawdy and full of raillery. By telling salacious jokes, she brought the first smile to great mother Demeter's face after the loss of her precious Persephone. When Demeter smiled at these obscenities, Iambe offered her a cup of wine. The goddess refused, asking instead for water mixed with barley meal and pennyroyal. Some say Iambe was the same as Baubo; in any case they both signified the crude humor that invariably accompanied the solemn Eleusinian mysteries of the earth mother.

Ibu Pertiwi In Bali, where the goddess is celebrated today in lavish song and festival, this is the name given to the ruler of the earth's fertility. Sometimes she is considered an aspect, or title, of Dewi Shri, the rice goddess.

Ida The name for Rhea as goddess of Mt. Ida also given to Rhea's son, suggesting that an embodiment of the goddess' own nurturing energy protected the newborn god.

Idem-Huva This harvest goddess of the Cheremis, a Finno-Ugric people of northern Europe, was said to haunt the threshing area in early morning to ensure all was in order; she was shy, however, and fled if approached.

Idothea A minor Greek sea goddess, she was daughter of the multi-formed Proteus; a favorite of sailors, she was so disrespectful of her father that she revealed Proteus' weather tricks to humans.

Idunn In the Scandinavian eddas, this goddess performed the same function as Hebe did for the Greeks: she fed the gods magical food that kept them young and hale. The Norse gods and goddesses were not immortal; they relied on Idunn's magical apples to survive. But once the evil Loki let Idunn and her apples fall into the hands of the enemies of the gods, the giants who lived in the fortress of Jotunheim. The divinities immediately began to age and weaken. Charged with reclaiming the goddess of youth and strength, Loki flew to Jotunheim in the form of a falcon, turned Idunn into a walnut, and carried her safely home.

Ikutamayorihime From the Kojiki—Japanese myths and folktales compiled in the sixth century by the noblewoman Hiedo-no-Ame—comes the story of this woman who conceived a child from a mysterious unknown lover. To discover the man's identity, Ikutamayorihime's parents told her to sew a thin, long hemp thread to him to follow it after his departure. Next morning, oddly, the thread was not found to go under the door but through the keyhole. Then it led straight to the snake god's shrine on Mt. Miwa. The child in the girl's womb became the ancestor of the shrine's priestly family. In this tale Carmen Blacker, noted scholar of shamanism, detects a link with a matrilineal tradition of an ancestral human mother and an unearthly father.

Ila Apparently a very ancient name for the Indian earth goddess, Ila appears in ancient scripture in several contradictory stories that attest to her antiquity while disguising her original form. (In some stories, indeed, she is said to be male, or to have changed sex several times, not an uncommon circumstance among goddesses whose people were overcome by patriarchal Indo-Europeans.) In the oldest Indian scripture, the Rig Veda, Ila was said to be the goddess progenitrix of humanity, the earth as producer of living intelligence; in addition, she

invented all the food and milk to feed her children. She also invented speech—which streams forth like food—and the first religious rituals.

Ilankaka The sun goddess of the Nkundo of central Zaire was trapped by a man who was hunting during the night. She begged to be released and promised him much wealth for doing so, but the only wealth he wanted was her, and so she agreed to marry him. Soon pregnant, she refused to eat anything but forest rats. Because it was known that a man had to provide for any whim of a pregnant woman, the man was kept very busy trapping for her. One night, however, she awakened to realize she was no longer pregnant. Shocked, she discovered the baby had slipped out of the womb and was already eating meat. He grew up to be the hero Itonde, who captured the heart of the Elephant Girl Mbombe.

Inanna The Sumerians knew how civilization had come to the ancient Near East, and here is how they told the tale. Across the immeasurable distances of the sweetwater abyss lived Enki, god of wisdom, and with him were the Tablets of Destiny and other magic civilizing implements. These were his treasures, and he kept them from humankind. But his daughter, the crafty queen of heaven, took pity on the miserable primitives of earth and fitted her boat to travel to her father's hall. There she was grandly welcomed with a banquet of food and wine. Wise he may have been, but Enki loved his daughter beyond wisdom, so much that he took cup after cup from her at table and then, drunk, promised her anything she desired. Instantly Inanna asked for the Tablets of Destiny and 100 other objects of culture. What could a fond father do but grant the request?

Inanna immediately loaded the objects onto the boat of heaven and set sail for her city, Erech. Awakening the next day from his stupor, Enki remembered what he had done—and regretted it. But he was incapacitated by a hangover as massive as the previous evening's pleasure, and he could not pursue his daughter until he recovered. By then, of course, Inanna had gained the safety of her kingdom, and even the seven tricks Enki played on her did not regain him his treasures.

And the Sumerians knew how the various seasons came to the desert in which they lived. It started long ago, when the lovely queen of heaven had two suitors, the farmer Enkidu and the shepherd Dumuzi. Both brought her gifts; both wooed her with flattery. Her brother urged the farmer's suit, but the soft woolens that Dumuzi brought tipped the scales of Inanna's heart. And so Dumuzi became the goddess' favorite, in a tale like Cain and Abel's that must have recorded a common dispute in the days when the new agricultural science was gaining ground from the nomadic culture of the cattle and sheep herders.

It was not long before Dumuzi grew arrogant in his favored position. But that leaps ahead in the story, for first Inanna—compelled, some say, by curiosity, while others accuse the goddess of ambition—made plans to descend from her sky throne and visit the underworld. She arranged with her prime minister, Ninshuba, that if she did not return within three days and three nights, he would stage mourning ceremonies and would appeal to the highest deities to rescue her. And then Inanna began her descent.

At the first of the seven gates of the underworld, the goddess was stopped by the gatekeeper, Neti, who demanded part of her attire. So it was at each gate. Piece by piece, Inanna gave up her jewelry and clothing until she stood splendid and naked before Eriskegal, the naked black-haired goddess of death, who turned her eyes of stone on the goddess from the upper world.

At that Inanna lost all life and hung for three days and three nights a corpse in the realm of death. When Inanna failed to return to her sky kingdom, Ninshuba did as instructed. Enki, the goddess' father, came to her aid. Fashioning two strange creatures, Kurgurra and Kalaturra, from the dirt beneath his fingernails, he sent them into the wilderness of the afterlife with food and water to revive the lifeless Inanna.

But no one can leave the underworld unless a substitute is found to hang forever naked in the land of doom. And so demons followed the goddess as she ascended to her kingdom. One after another, the demons grabbed the gods they met. Each in turn Inanna freed, remembering good deeds they had performed for her. But when Inanna reached her holy city, Erech, she found that her paramour Dumuzi had set himself up as ruler in her stead. Angered at his presumption, the goddess commanded that he be taken as her substitute to Eriskegal's kingdom. Luckily for Dumuzi, his loving sister Gestinanna followed him to the underworld and won from Eriskegal her brother's life for half each year—the half of the year when the desert plants flower, for Dumuzi was the god of vegetation.

In some versions of the tale it was Inanna herself, not Gestinanna, who freed Dumuzi. But Gestinanna's name incorporates that of the other goddess, and Inanna herself was sometimes said to be Dumuzi's mother, while Ninsun claimed that role in other versions. All these apparent contradictions cease to be problematic, however, if one extends the "three persons in one god" concept to this trinity of Sumerian divinities. Then we see that the mother, the lover, and the sister were all aspects of a single grand figure: the queen of heaven, who may have been the life-giving sun itself, as able to parch the earth into a desert as to reclaim vegetation seasonally from beneath the earth's surface.

Inaras In the Anatolian embodiment of the heavenly queen Inanna, Inaras went to the rescue of the earth's people when they were threatened by the great dragon Illuyuksa. The goddess filled vessel after vessel with liquor, inviting a man to set them as bait for the dragon. That night Inaras rewarded the human's industry by sleeping with him. The next morning the pair found the dragon and her children unconscious from intoxication, easy to slay.

As a reward for service in battle and bed, Inaras installed the man in a splendid house on a high cliff, and there they lived in pleasure until the goddess was called on a journey. Inaras instructed her paramour not to gaze out the window while she was away, but after twenty days he disobeyed. Seeing his human wife and children in the sands outside, the man grew suddenly homesick for mortal company. His complaints angered Inaras when she returned, and she dispatched him to the underworld for his disobedience.

The story of the destruction of the dragon of darkness was celebrated each new year by Inaras' worshipers. A man enacting the part of the goddess' human helper seems to have met his death after spending the night with the goddess, who for the occasion took the form of a priestess. He could not continue to live, for should he ever have intercourse with a mortal woman after sleeping with the goddess, he might transfer some of Inaras' magical power to her and thereby weaken the goddess.

Inari The Japanese rice goddess liked to wrap herself in a fox's body. Sometimes, too, she took the shape of a human woman in order to sleep with men, who had excellent crops as a result. One of these men, it was said, realized he was sleeping with the goddess when he saw a long, furry red tail sticking out from beneath the blankets. He said nothing of it, and she rewarded his discretion by causing all his rice to grow upside down, thus bearing a full harvest that was exempt from the rice tax.

The legendary woman Tamamono-Maye, possibly an incarnation of Inari, lived at court and could change at will into a flying fox. An enemy, however, ended her power of transformation (and her life, some say) by confronting her with a mirror, which was powerful medicine against her magic.

Inaruchaba Among the Burundi of Africa, Inaruachaba was the daughter of the first man, the black-and-white Kihanga, whose skin was striped like that of a zebra. One day, she got lost in the forest and was forced to live entirely on wild strawberries until she found her way to a swamp where a herd of cows were cooling themselves. Noticing a calf suckling, Inaruachaba joined it at the udder and sucked forth the sweet milk. Having made this bond with the animals, she was able to bring them back to her people, who thereafter relied on them for sustenance.

Indara Her name means "maiden"; she was the creator goddess of the people of central Celebes in the Pacific, forming human beings from stone and awakening them to life with her winds.

India Rosa A form of Kuma, great goddess of the Yaruros of Venezuela, India Rosa was the inventor of women's culture, teaching pottery skills and basket weaving. She also gave birth to the sun and the moon, the snake and the jaguar. In some myths, she is the ancestor of all humanity as well.

Inga Woman In Brazil, Columbia and eastern Venezuela, the story is told that the selfishly lustful moon visited his sister Inga Woman's hammock nightly, when it was too dark for the woman to see who had seduced her. One night she painted his face with black dye, which he saw the next morning in the mirror. Try as he might, he could not scrub it off. Horrified at what she had discovered, and pregnant with their incestuous child, Inga Woman wandered from their camps and was dismembered by jaguars. Such sun sister/moon brother incest is often connected with an ancient myth of creation, with the woman's body being torn apart to form this world.

Ingebord A magical maiden of Scandinavian mythology, Ingebord took a mortal for her lover. After spending three nights with him, she blinded him so that he would never love another woman.

Inghean Bhuidhe The Yellow-Haired Girl, sister of Latiaran, was honored in ancient Ireland on May 6, which was considered the first day of summer. Until recent times that day was celebrated in her honor with rituals around a sacred well.

Ino The daughter of Harmonia, "she who makes sinewy" was originally a goddess of orgiastic agricultural rites in pre-Hellenic Greece, to whom human victims apparently were sacrificed in a magical attempt to make rain fall as freely as blood on the soil. When later tribes brought their own pantheon into Ino's realm, the religious conflict that ensued was recorded in the legend that Ino was a rival of the king's wife Nephele. Ino brought on a famine and in punishment was pursued into the sea bearing her son Melicertes. Both were then "transformed" into sea deities by Greek legend.

Intercidona After birth of a Roman child, this goddess was invoked as the "axe" or "cleaver" that separated the newborn from evil and danger.

Invidia The Greek personification of envy, she was the daughter of the goddess of forgetfulness, Styx; from her name we derive our word *invidious*.

Io The first king of Argos, the Greeks said, was a river god who voted against Poseidon and for Hera when the two divinities contested ownership of the city. To punish the Argives for refusing him, Poseidon cursed the area around Argos with dry summer streams, for the sea god could withdraw nourishing water from the land at will.

But the Argives were not concerned. They worshiped the moon as the heifer Io, or the "cow-eyed" Hera, and the moon was the maker of rain. The king's daughter Io, named for the moon, led them in rainmaking dances, in which priestesses mimicked the desperate actions of cattle driven mad by gadflies in the scorching heat.

Then came the invasions by Zeus-sworshiping tribes. The indigenous cow goddess of the moon found her legend grafted onto that of the patriarchal sky god. And so it was told that Hera, jealous of the love of Zeus for Io—who was originally her servant or an aspect of herself—accused her husband of infidelity. He transformed Io into a heifer and denied the accusation, but Hera was too smart to be taken in by the ruse. She asked for the cow, and Zeus could hardly refuse. Hera tied Io to a tree in her own sanctuary, setting the 100-eyed Argos to guard her. Hermes, on order of Zeus, freed the heifer; Hera then sent a gadfly to torment her. Io ceaselessly wandered the world, a vestige in later legend of the original portrait of the moon-cow wandering restlessly across the sky.

Iphigenia The daughter of Clytemnestra, she was sacrificed by her father to bring favorable winds for the Greek voyage to Troy. Some legends say that she was miraculously saved from sacrifice by Artemis, who replaced Iphigenia with a stag and wafted the girl off to live in Asia Minor as her priestess. There, after his trial for matricide, Iphigenia's brother, Orestes, came to steal the statue of Artemis, which an oracle said would relieve his tortured conscience. Iphigenia was supposed to sacrifice all noble strangers to the goddess, but when she discovered her brother's identity, she spared him and assisted him in moving the statue from its sanctuary. Other legends say that Iphegenia was transformed into a goddess in Taurus, and called there Orthia or Brauronia—both titles of the wildwood mother Artemis. Yet other sources claim she was transformed by Artemis into Hecate. Such confusions often indicate that a "legendary" character bore the name or title, and some of the mythic resonance, of an ancient goddess.

Iphis A Cretan woman, she was reared as a boy because her father planned to kill any daughters he begot. Iphis grew into a beautiful youth with whom the woman Ianthe became infatuated. Iphis too fell in love; she begged Isis to be changed into a man. The goddess answered her prayer and the lovers were wed. "The boy pays what the girl vowed," she wrote on her wedding offering to Isis.

Irdlirvirisissong The crazy cousin of the Yupik and Inupiat sun goddess Akycha, this clownish dancer lived in the sky with the sun's brother, the moon. Sometimes she danced through the sky to make people laugh; she was probably the ruler of the northern lights.

Irene The Greek goddess of peace, she was worshiped with bloodless sacrifices at Athens. Some legends named her as one of the Horae.

Iris The rainbow goddess Iris was Hera's messenger, a winged maiden who—when not delivering messages for her mistress—slept under Hera's bed. It was Iris who, when her mistress slept with Zeus, prepared their bed with sanctified hands. She was one of the few Olympians who could journey at will to the underworld, where she fetched water for solemn oaths; for this reason, she was sometimes called a form of the witch goddess Hecate.

Irnini The patron goddess of the cedar mountains of Lebanon, she was originally distinct from Ishtar but later merged with her.

Iseult In the cycle of British myths that came into literature as the "Matter of Britain"—the stories of the fabled realm of Camelot—this heroine is the center of a tale of fated love. A single strand of her gorgeously golden hair attracted the attention of Mark of Cornwall, who sent his knight Tristan to find and fetch her. On the boat back to Mark, the couple mistakenly drank a potion intended to make the newlywed couple fall hopelessly in love—and thus Iseult found herself irrevocably in love with Tristan. They attempted to fulfill their assigned roles, Iseult as Mark's wife and Tristan as his vassal, but they were doomed to love each other, and their love eventually led to Tristan's banishment and Iseult's death. Afterwards, Tristan married another woman, Iseult of the White Hands. As Arthurian legend frequently hides ancient Celtic and even pre-Celtic mythology, we can here detect an ancient goddess of sovereignty, who must mate with the king to solidify his claim to the land. In a struggle between contenders to the goddess' hand (or bed), the younger and more vigorous finally wins—although the late legend disguises this fact by offering a second Iseult to the victorious Tristan.

Ishara Semitic goddess of promiscuity, originally distinct from Ishtar but later merged with her.

Ishikore-Dome Stone-Coagulating Old Woman was the smith goddess of ancient Japan who created the first mirror from copper-bearing stones of the Isuzu River. Three times she tried, working in the darkness that befell the world when the sun goddess Amaterasu hid herself in heaven's Sky-Rock-Cave; twice she failed to create a perfect reflection of the sun's beauty, but when at last she succeeded, her mirror became the most sacred relic of Japanese Shinto. It is kept to this day in the Imperial Shrine at Ise, south of Nagoya. So sacred is this mirror that every twenty years the shrine buildings are rebuilt according to elaborate 1,500-year-old plans. When the new shrine is completed, a complex ceremony is held to apologize to the mirror for the inconvenience and possible harm that accompanies moving.

No one can see the mirror, for it is hidden in brocade coverings and carved boxes, but tradition has it that Ishikore's creation is eight-sided or shaped like an eight-petaled flower. Each of the more than 90,000 Shinto shrines across Japan has as its most sacred object a similar mirror.

Ishtar As the process of assimilation of similar goddesses took place in the ancient Near East, the mighty Ishtar slowly emerged from a throng of lesser divinities (Anatu, Anunit, Gumshea, Irnini, Ishara) to become a complex image of the multiple possibilities of womanhood. She was the mother holding her massive breasts, symbols of her benevolence. She was the ever-virgin warrior, never giving her essence to anyone, warring with any who tried to take it. She was the wanton, constantly plotting to find a new lover—divine, human, bestial, it did not matter. And she was judge and counselor, the old wise one whom women emulated in the courts and the homes of her lands.

The Babylonian Ishtar was a later, more complex form of the Sumerian Inanna, and their myths were similar in many respects. Both loved a vegetation god who died constantly and was constantly reborn; both were responsible for the death as well as the rebirth of the beloved. Like Inanna, Ishtar descended to the underworld in search of Tammuz, the lover whose death she had caused. But unlike the timid Inanna, the bold Ishtar demanded entry at the gate of death, threatening to smash it open and set the dead loose on the earth's surface if her request were denied.

But even a divine visitor to the hell queen, Eriskegal, must go naked, so Ishtar was forced to give up her jewels and clothes as she descended. As the moon darkens, so Ishtar too was stripped: her crown taken from her at the first gate, then her earrings, her necklace, her diadem, her belt, her bracelets, and finally—at the seventh gate—her very garment. All these were courting presents

Ishtar was one of the great goddesses of the ancient eastern Mediterranean. Innumerable small statuettes of her, often in this welcoming pose, have been found throughout Iraq and nearby areas.

from Tammuz, and Ishtar was loath to part with them. But to gain her desire—the resurrection of the vegetation god Tammuz for whom earth's women were wailing—Ishtar allowed herself to be stripped and stood naked before Eriskegal. Her wish granted, Ishtar reemerged slowly through the gates of darkness, regaining her attire as the moon regains its white light, until it glows full in the sky as Sharrat Shame ("queen of heaven").

Not only did she rule the moon, but Ishtar owned the morning and evening stars, invariably the symbol to the people of the Tigris and Euphrates of the alternately warlike and lustful energies of the feminine. As the morning star, Dilbah, the goddess arrayed herself in armor and hitched her chariot to seven lions before setting off in the dawn to hunt animals or humans. As Zib, the evening star, she was served by promiscuous temple women who adored the "glad-eyed Ishtar of desire, the goddess of sighing," the one "who turns the male to the female, and the female to the male," the goddess "whose song is sweeter than honey and wine, sweeter than sprouts and herbs, superior even to pure cream."

Sometimes these two energies were combined into a figure of threatening sexuality. Thus the hero Gilgamesh spurned the goddess, claiming that her lovers came to naught (for all who live, who love, will die), then fell into a terrible sickness, his body's self-punishment. The hero's comrade Eabani similarly rejected the honor due the goddess and died miserably, his final agony lasting twelve days. For Ishtar was life itself, which leads to death and (so her devotees would say) to a new birth. And who denies sex denies life, who denies death denies life, and such a one will find neither life joyful, nor death easy.

Isis Isis of the winged arms, first daughter of Nut, the overarching sky, and the little earth god Geb, was born in the Nile swamps on the first day between the first years of creation. From the beginning, Isis turned a kind eye on the people of earth, teaching women to grind corn, spin flax, weave cloth, and tame men sufficiently to live with them. The goddess herself lived with her brother, Osiris, god of Nile waters and the vegetation that springs up when the river floods.

Alas for Isis, her beloved was killed by their evil brother, Set. The mourning goddess cut off her hair and tore her robes to shreds, wailing in grief. Then she set forth to locate her brother's body. Eventually Isis arrived in Phoenicia, where Queen Astarte, pitying but not recognizing the pathetic goddess, hired her as nursemaid to the infant prince. Isis took good care of the child, placing him like a log in the palace fire, where the terrified mother found him smoldering. She grabbed the child from the fire, thus undoing the magic of immortality that Isis had been working on the child. (A similar story was told of the mourning Demeter.)

Isis was called on to explain her action, and thus the goddess' identity was revealed and her search explained. And then Astarte had her own revelation: that the fragrant tamarisk tree in the palace contained the body of the lost Osiris. Isis carried the tree-sheltered corpse back to Egypt for burial. But the evil Set was not to be thwarted; he found the body, stole it, and dismembered it.

Isis' search began anew. And this time her goal was not a single corpse, but a dozen pieces to be found and reassembled. The goddess did find the arms and legs and head and torso of her beloved, but she could not find his penis and substituted a piece of shaped gold. Then Isis invented the rites of embalming for which the Egyptians are famous, and she applied them with magical words to the body of Osiris. The god rose, as alive as the corn after spring floods in Egypt. Isis magically conceived a child through the golden phallus of the revived Osiris, and that child was the sun god Horus.

There was another tale told of the magician Isis. Determined to have power over all the gods, she fashioned a snake and sent it to bite Ra, highest of gods. Sick and growing weaker, he called for Isis to apply her renowned curative powers to the wound. But the goddess claimed to be powerless to purge the poison unless she knew the god's secret name, his name of power, his very essence. Ra demurred and hesitated, growing ever weaker. Finally, in desperation, he was forced to whisper the word to her. Isis cured him, but Ra had paid the price of giving her eternal power over him. (A similar tale was told of Lilith and Jehovah.)

When she was born in Egypt, the goddess' name was Au Set (Auzit, Eset), which means "exceeding queen" or simply "spirit." But the colonizing Greeks altered the pronunciation to yield the now-familiar Isis, a name used through the generations as the goddess' worship spread from the delta of the Nile to the banks of the Rhine. Like Ishtar (of whom a similar tale of loss and restoration was told), Isis took on the identities of lesser goddesses until she was revered as the universal goddess, the total femininity of whom other goddesses represented only isolated aspects.

She became the Lady of Ten Thousand Names, whose true name was Isis. She grew into Isis Panthea ("Isis the All Goddess"). She was the moon and the mother of the sun; she was mourning wife and tender sister; she was the culture-bringer and health-giver. She was the "throne" and the "Goddess Fifteen." She was a form of Hathor (or that goddess a form of her). She was also Meri, goddess of the sea, and Sochit, the "cornfield."

But she was everlastingly, to her fervent devotees, the blessed goddess who was herself all things and who promised: "You shall live in blessing, you shall live glorious in my protection; and when you have fulfilled your allotted span of life and descend to the underworld, there too you shall see me, as you see me now, shining. And if you show yourself obedient to my divinity…you will know that I alone have permitted you to extend your life beyond the time allocated you by your destiny." Isis, who overcame death to bring her lover back to life, could as readily hold off death for her faithful followers, for the all-powerful Isis alone could boast, "I will overcome Fate."

Ismene A daughter of King Oedipus and Queen Jocasta, she was the sister of the noble Antigone, the Greek heroine who gave her life for her brother's eternal happiness. In today's society, such dedication would be eccentric at best, but in matrilineal societies—such as early Greece seems to have been—a woman's closest male relation was her brother, the man who had shared her mother's womb; thus Antigone's devotion was a social duty. Ismene felt this tie of blood as strongly as her sister, but Antigone denied Ismene's claim of equal guilt and went to her death alone.

Isong The tortoise-shell goddess of the earth's fertility, she was one of the primary divinities of the Ibibio and Ekoi peoples of West Africa.

Istehar A maiden with a name suspiciously like Ishtar's, she appeared in Jewish legend as the prey of the angel Shemhazai, who planned to rape her. Instead, Istehar agreed to sleep with him if the angel would reveal the secret name of Jehovah. He did so, and she, breaking the bargain, used it as a magical charm to ascend to heaven, where she became one of the stars we call the Pleiades.

Itiba Tahuvava Among the Taino, a pre-Hispanic people of Cuba and other Caribbean islands, this woman was the great ancestor, who gave birth to four sons by Caesarean section; these boys accidentally created the sea while playing.

I-toeram-bola-totsy "She whose nature is silver" was a folkloric heroine of Madagascar. After her beloved husband had been fatally wounded by a rival, she learned that only a magic potion owned by a terrifying ogre would bring him back to life. So loving was she that she located the monster, confronted it and won the right to use the potion—and was reunited with her loving mate.

Ituana "Mother Scorpion," the great goddess of the Amazon River people, was said to live at the end of the Milky Way. There she ruled an afterworld, where she reincarnated each soul to new life, nursing earth's innumerable children from her innumerable breasts.

Isis was one of the greatest of Egyptian goddesses. In this bronze Greco-Roman figure, Isis wears the sun disc and the magical serpent called the uraeus, as she nurses her son Horus.

167

Jaki   The Persian menstruation spirit, she was perceived as a *drujs*, a kind of demon, who urged men to evil deeds. It was because she was kissed by Ahriman, the great demon, that women began to bleed. The British poet John Milton used her as the model for his image of guilt. But this literally "demonized" creature may well hide an ancient women's goddess whose power was acknowledged but vilified by those who wished to diminish her.

Ja-Neba   The Samoyeds of Siberia invoked mother earth under this name; she was mother of animals and ancestor of humanity. Among the nearby Udegeis, the same goddess was Sangia-Mama; among the Nasnai, Sengi-Mama. Statues of these goddesses were covered with blood of animals killed in the hunt in order to encourage her to bring more game. Usually the heart and head were sacrificed as well if the prey were reindeer; if elk, the tongue and nostrils were the gift to the goddess.

Janguli   Three-mouthed, six-handed golden Tantric snake goddess of Bengal, she is shown holding a sword, a thunderbolt and an arrow with her right hands, while her left held a noose, a blue lotus and a bow. Invoked as "remover of poison, born of a lotus," for as a snake goddess she could remove venom, she may be the same goddess as Manasa.

Jata   In Borneo, among the people who call themselves the Ngaju, the complete name of this snake goddess is Bawin Jata Balawang Bulan, and she is the feminine first principle, half of the original divine couple. A double goddess of earth and sky, Jata has two homes: one in the bottom of the ocean, from which she rules the land of the dead; the other at the top of a golden mountain, from which she rules the moon.

Jeh   The Indo-Iranian first woman, called the "queen of all whores" because she arrived at the creation with the devil already in tow and had intercourse with him immediately.

Jezebel   This famous queen was one of only two women who ruled the Hebrew tribe; the other was Athaliah. Jezebel, famous today as a "harlot," was in reality a devoted follower of the goddesses of her region, some of whose religious rites sanctified sexuality. Even the Hebrews who murdered her could not help but admire their victim, whom they remembered as having "a capacity for sympathy with others in joy and sorrow."

Jezenky In Czechoslovakia, these spirit women were said to travel the night looking for human children to kidnap and cage as pets, feeding them with morsels through the bars. They could also be even more violent, putting out human eyes as they traveled the night.

Jiandi Chinese ancestral mothers find interesting ways to get themselves pregnant, and Jiandi—ancestor-mother of the Yin clan—is no exception. Walking through a land rich in mulberry trees with her companions, she felt a need to take a bath. She and the other maidens found a nice pool and, descending into it, refreshed themselves with its water. While bathing, Jiandi saw a black bird lay an egg, which she claimed and swallowed whole. Shortly afterwards, she found herself pregnant, and the child she bore was the heroic ancestor of the Yins.

Jiangyuan Like other Chinese ancestral mothers, Jiangyuan was a virgin mother, one who was able to get pregnant simply by stepping into a giant footprint. She bore a child who was the ancestor of the Zhou clan.

Jingo There is no evidence that this Japanese warrior queen's name formed the base of the current term *jingoism*, but it is known that she was a magical being who remained pregnant for three years, rather than stop her war on Korea to give birth to her son. Jingo utterly devastated the three Korean kingdoms, which pledged undying loyalty to her sovereignty; some credit not her battle prowess but her supernatural control of the tides for the victory.

Jocasta Thanks to Sigmund Freud, the story of Oedipus of Thebes is undoubtedly the most familiar Greek legend in the twentieth century West. But the myth on which the Austrian psychoanalyst based his theories was unfortunately not so universal as he believed; rather, it was a late and literary record of a historical event in Greek religious history.

Scholar Robert Graves has suggested this reconstruction of the original tale: Oedipus successfully besieged Thebes, but he had no real claim to the throne until he married the local priestess, Jocasta, whose earlier consort, Laius, was first dragged to death in a ritual slaughter. Then Jocasta ceremoniously "gave birth" to the new king, who immediately announced his intention to overthrow Theban traditions and replace them with those of Corinth. Jocasta committed suicide in protest; the land rose up against him; and Oedipus was forced from the throne. The dead priestess' nearest male relative, her brother Creon, took over the Theban throne as regent. But the tide of which Oedipus had been the first wave—the patrilineage already practiced in Corinth—was rising, and the sons of Oedipus again put the town under siege, demanding the throne that was rightfully theirs under the new social order.

Jocebed The mother of Miriam, her name means "divine splendor" and was thought to refer to the unearthly light that surrounded her body. She seems to be a vestige of the ancient mother goddess who appeared in the legends of the patriarchal Hebrews.

Jord The goddess of the primeval earth—the world before the creation of humankind—had this name among the Scandinavians. The daughter of Nott ("night"), she was worshiped on high mountains where she was thought to have mated with the sky.

Judith The great Jewish war heroine is held by many to be a fictional creation of the fourth century B.C.E., a sort of "Miss Liberty," useful as a symbolic figurehead of rebellion. But other scholars claim that there actually was a historical woman who lived in that era and who braved the battle lines to butcher the oppressive general Holofernes. Yet others claim that Judith was originally a barley goddess, for her husband died during the harvest, like a ritual king of vegetation.

Jugumishanta Ancestral mother of the people of Papua New Guinea, Jugumishanta liked a great deal of privacy. And so, although she was married, she built herself a little hut, away from the main part of her village, and she told everyone to leave her alone when she went there. Around her place she planted wild ginger, and within the wild ginger she hid a little handmade flute, wherein she placed one of her own pubic hairs, so that it would cry out if anyone else touched it.

Often Jugumishanta would take her flute out, and play plaintive melodies to herself, there in the forest. One day her husband heard the sad sound, and sneaked up to discover what caused it. Watching Jugumishanta, he saw not only how she made the fluting sounds, but also where she hid the instrument. The next day he sneaked back, planning to make the melodies himself. But the flute raised the alert, and Jugumishanta came back angrily, demanding its return. In the ensuing fight, the flute fell onto the ground—and a huge forest of bamboo suddenly sprang up, where ever after Jugumishanta's people could gather material for flutes. These instruments are placed back into the forest at rituals, so that food animals might increase—a part of this story that implies that Jugumishanta's power was similar to that of other great goddesses, in that she provides the food that sustains her children.

Juks-Akka The daughter of Madder-Akka. Among the Saami, the "old lady of the bow" was also called the "gunwoman" (obviously a later name) and was a symbol of fierce motherhood who guarded children from harm.

Julunggul The rainbow snake goddess of Australia was able to be male, to be neuter, or to be androgynous. She was said to be embodied in the ocean and waterfalls, in pearls and crystals, and in the deep pools in which she lived. A goddess of initiations, Julunggul was approached in Arnhem Land by boys who, symbolically swallowed and regurgitated by the mother snake, were vomited out again as men.

Jumala The sun goddess of the Russian Ugrians, she was worshiped until very recently—and may be still, in remote and rural parts of the land. In 1549, a German nobleman visited a Ugrian shrine where he found a golden goddess rather like the familiar Matrioshka dolls-within-dolls, with three figures enclosing each other. These statues were said to speak, in clanging tones like a bell. Offerings of gold were hung in the sacred trees by worshipers; when enough was accumulated, a new outer figure was forged. As late as 1967, in the village of Tiumen, treasure-hunters were informed that Jumala was still honored, but her precious image was hidden to protect her from gold-seekers.

Junkgowa The great ancestor goddess of the Yulengor of Australia's Arnhem Land lived during Dreamtime in the spirit-land of Buraklor. It was she—in multiple form, as female ancestors—who created the food producing zones of the earth, as well as forming the waterholes that link humankind with the spirit world. The Junkgowa Sisters made the sea so that they could build the seagoing canoe. Setting off, they sang the world's first songs to accompany their rowing. As they passed over the sea, they created fish and ocean mammals. Finally, when they realized how slowly they progressed, they created wind to blow them along. But a long black rock, far out in the ocean, overturned their boat and forced them back to land. There they established sacred zones and constructed necessary crafts so that their descendants would have a spiritual life: they invented the dilly bag, amulets, yam sticks and feather belts; they designated tribal totems and bore their first children; they invented fire to keep their babies warm.

The Junkgowa Sisters invented and managed all ceremonial life. But some of their sons, jealous of their power and magical skills, decided to steal the sacred totems. And so they did. The Junkgowa Sisters then vanished into the sea, never to return to the Yulengor.

Juno   A vestige remains of her worship in today's culture: brides still choose to marry in the month of June, thus assuring themselves of the beneficence of the goddess after whom the month is named. Indeed, under her different names Juno ruled not only marriage but the entire reproductive life of each woman: she was called Pronuba, arranger of appropriate matches; Cioxia, ruler of the first undressing by the husband; Populonia, goddess of conception; Ossipago, who strengthens fetal bones; Sospita, the labor goddess; Lucina, who leads the child to light, the birth goddess; and Viriplaca, who settles arguments between spouses.

Juno ruled these uniquely feminine occasions because she was herself the ruler of femininity, its very essence. To the Romans, each man had a *genius*, the spirit that made him alive and sexually active; in the same way, each woman had her *juno*, not so much a guardian spirit as an enlivening inner force of femaleness. She had many feast-days: one for each woman's birthday, when Natalis, her own special Juno, was celebrated.

A very ancient Italian goddess, Juno was originally quite different from the Greek Hera; both, however, were essentially goddesses of women. When the Greek sky queen came to Rome during the days of cultural assimilation, she merged with the Roman goddess and her legends were told of Juno. Juno's separate mythology was lost, except for the tale that, impregnated by a flower, Juno bore the god Mars—a story never told of Hera.

Not only was she ancient but she was long recognized as one of the predominant Roman divinities. Juno, with Minerva and Jupiter, made up the Capitoline triad, the trinity that ruled Rome. As such she was Regina ("the queen"). One of her most famous names was Moneta, "warner," which was earned many times over: once when her sacred geese once set up such a squawking that the city was warned of invading Gauls, another time when an earthquake threatened and Juno's voice from heaven alerted the city, and finally when the underfunded Roman generals came to Juno's temple for advice and were told that any war fought ethically would find popular (and financial) support. This last effort made her matron of the Roman mint, which was located in her temple, and turned her title into a word for "money."

Most important, Juno was the goddess of time. Daughter of Saturn, she was a symbol of the menstrual cycle as time's indicator; goddess of the new moon, she was worshiped by Roman women on the Calends, or first, of each lunar month. In addition to these monthly celebrations, Juno was honored in two festivals: the unrestrained Nonae Caprotinae on July 7, when serving girls staged mock fights under a wild fig tree; and the more sedate Matronalia on March 1, when married women demanded money from their husbands to offer to the goddess of womanhood.

Juras Mate   The Latvian sea mother may be the same goddess as the Lithuanian mermaid Jurate.

Jurate   Mermaid goddess of the Baltic, she lived in a magnificent castle at the bottom of that sea. Its walls were of white amber, its threshold of golden amber, its floors of bronze amber. Diamonds formed the windowpanes, and the palace was roofed in seashells, fish scales, and pearls. Spurning the love of the thunder god Perkunas, she selected her own mate from among the fisherman who worked her shores. But the thunderer chained Jurate's lover to a rock in the bottom of the sea, then killed the goddess. All the precious amber that washes up on the Baltic shores is said to be her palace, slowly crumbling away.

Juturna   This Roman spring goddess was celebrated in a healing festival on January 11. A fountain rose near her temple in the Forum, and bathing in it was said to renew health.

Juventas   The Roman goddess of youth was honored together with the healing goddess Minerva on the Capitoline Hill, but she was not a goddess of rejuvenation, for only those who were young in years—not just in attitude or in health—fell under her rulership.

K

Ka Ahu Pahau In Hawaiian mythology, she is the queen of the ocean waters, who appears in the form of an enormous shark.

Kachina This word combines *ka* (spirit) and *china* (respect), and to the Hopi of the American southwest, the figures that bear this name are indeed spirits worthy of our respect. Appearing in dances, embodied in their human followers, or in carved representations, the Kachinas are the most powerful spirits of nature—plants and planets, animals and ancestors, even stars whose light we cannot yet see. There are between 220 and 335 Kachinas, among whom are many important female figures. There is the old Warrior Mother Hehewuti, who appears in ritual half-dressed and with messy hair, in memory of the time she helped defend her people against a dawn attack without even pausing to dress fully. There is Whipper Mother Angwushahai'i, mother of those who whip boys and girls in initiation ceremonies, and the Butterfly Maidens who represent spring's fertile energy. And there is the beautiful Crow Mother Angwusnasomtaqa, who dresses in bridal attire and a magnificent crow headdress, in honor of the time when she left her own wedding to aid her Hopi children.

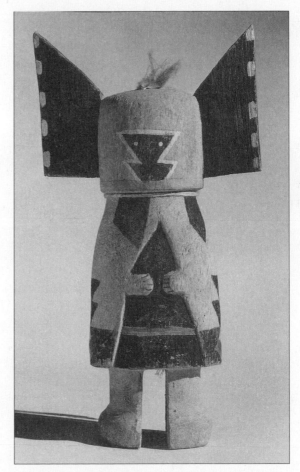

From Shipavlovi, Arizona, at the turn of the twentieth century came this kachina doll representing the Crow Mother of the Hopi people.

175

Kadi The Babylonian-Assyrian goddess of justice, she symbolized the earth, upon which solemn oaths were sworn because she was witness to all that happened on her surface. Kadi was shown as a snake with human head and shoulders.

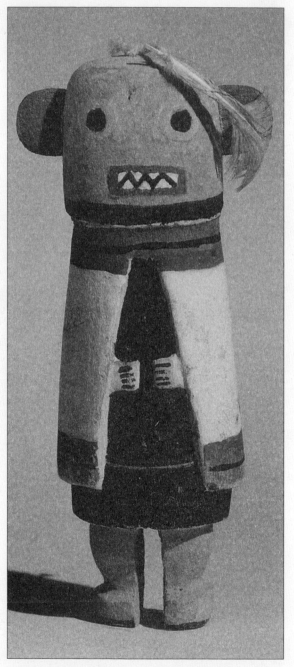

Kachina dolls such as this Ogre Woman were used by the Hopi people to teach mythic truth and to acknowledge the power of the feminine divine.

Kadlu The Eskimo thunder goddess was originally a little girl who played so noisily that her parents told her and her sisters to go outside to play. So they did, inventing a game in which Kadlu jumped on hollow ice, causing a thunderous sound; Kweetoo rubbed flint stones together to create lightning; and an unnamed sister urinated so profusely that she created rain.

Transported to the sky, the goddesses lived in a whalebone house far in the west, away from the sea, where the sisters wore no clothing but blackened their faces with soot. For food, they went hunting for caribou, striking them down with lightning.

Some legends said that Kadlu made thunder by rubbing dry sealskins together or by singing. In some areas, women were said to be able to avert thunderstorms, or to create them, by leaving offerings for the trinity of weather goddesses: needles, bits of ivory, old pieces of sealskin.

Kadru Sometimes called Aditi, she was an Indian one-eyed goddess who also went by the name Sarpamatar or "Mother of Serpents." She wagered with her sister Vinata as to who could see farthest. But then she attempted to cheat and, as a result, had to forfeit one of her eyes. Kadru prayed to become the mother of a thousand snakes, while her sister prayed for two children more powerful than all her sister's. And sure enough, Kadru laid a thousand eggs, Vinata two. For 500 years they rested together in a jar of water. Then Kadru's eggs hatched into a thousand splendid snakes. Anxious, Vinata broke open one of her own eggs to see if anything was alive within. She found a son, but the lower half of his body was malformed from hatching too early. He cursed his mother to serve her sister for another 500 years, at the end of which time the second egg hatched into the giant snake-eating bird Garuda, which avenged his mother by eating Kadru's offspring.

Kahindo Daughter of the fire god among the Nyanga of Zaire, she saved the culture hero Mwindo

This Hopi kachina came from Carleys Post, Arizona, in the middle of the twentieth century. It shows the White Corn Maiden (Ang-chin Mana) whose whorled hair represents her unmarried status.

from her father by telling him how to survive the god's tricky assaults.

Kaikara Ugandan goddess of harvest who spoke through a woman medium; millet was offered to her to ensure a good crop.

Kakia The Greek "goddess" of vice was merely a personified abstraction, invented as a foil to Arete, goddess of virtue. In legend, the two fought over the champion Heracles, whose teacher was Arete and whom Kakia attempted to seduce with promises of love, ease, and riches.

Kali In Hindu India, all goddesses are ultimately one: Devi, whose name simply means "the goddess." But she takes different forms—perhaps a way of allowing limited human minds to fix on first one, then another, of her multiple possibilities. One of the most powerful, most common, and—to Western eyes—most terrifying of these forms is Kali ("Black Mother Time"), the goddess who perpetually transforms life into a fascinating dance of death.

This Butterfly Maiden is a kachina doll used to honor spirit entities among the Hopi of Arizona.

Her tongue juts out of her black face; her hands hold weapons; her necklace and earrings are strung with dismembered bodies. She seems at best a stern mistress, this Shakti ("animating power") of the creator-destroyer Shiva, the dancing god. As Durga, Devi is personified as a just warrior, purging the world of evil; as Parvati, the same energy exemplifies passionate attachment to sexuality. But as Kali, the goddess is uncompromisingly alone, the mother of death that swims in her womb like a babe; she is the force of time leading ever onward to destruction. And then, when she has destroyed everything, Kali will be the timeless sleep from which new ages will awaken.

Kali first manifested herself when the demon Daruka appropriated divine power and threatened the gods. The powerful goddess Parvati knitted her brows in fury, and from her sprang three-eyed Kali, already armed with her trident. This emanation of Parvati quickly dispatched the demon and made the heavens safe again. Once born, this goddess remained in existence, beyond the control of even Parvati (of whom, it must be remembered, she is an aspect).

Several famous myths tell just how uncontrollable Kali's energy is. Once, it was said, she dared to dance with Shiva, the Lord of the Dance. They grew wilder and wilder, more competitive in their dancing, until it seemed the world would shake itself to pieces—and so it will, for beneath all appearances that dance continues. Another time, it is said, Kali fought and killed two demons and celebrated her victory by draining their bodies of blood. Then, drunk with slaughter, she began to dance. Thrilling to the feel of lifeless flesh beneath her naked feet, Kali danced more and more wildly—until she realized that Shiva himself was underneath her and that she was dancing him to death. The god's tactic slowed Kali's wildness, but only for the moment, and eventually she will resume the dance that ends the world.

Kali is still one of India's most popular goddesses: her picture hangs in many homes, her name is familiar in Calcutta (Anglicized from Kali-Ghatt, or "steps of Kali," her temple city). Served at one time by murderers called *thuggee* (from which derives the English word *thug*), the goddess of cemeteries was thought to thrive on blood; most often, however, goat rather than human blood was sacrificed to her, and it is still poured out in some parts of India today.

So terrifying do these bloody rites seem that few understand Kali's spiritual significance. As a symbol of the worst we can imagine, as the most extreme picture of our fears, she offers us a chance to face down our own terror of annihilation. Ramakrishna and other great Indian poets sang rapturously of Kali, for they understood that she is a blissful goddess. Once faced and understood, these mystics say, Kali frees her worshipers of all fear and becomes the greatest of mothers, the most comforting of all goddesses.

Kalisha "Purity," an ancient Arabian goddess worshiped, as most other female deities of that culture, in the shape of a stone.

Kalwadi An old woman with the human name of Mujingga, this Australian goddess worked as a babysitter. Unfortunately, she had a powerful craving for infant flesh, and occasionally one of her charges would mysteriously disappear. People—even her children, for she had watched her own grandchildren—were understandably upset by the babies' disappearance. Then Kalwadi too disappeared. They tracked the goddess to an underwater lair and—regretfully, for they loved her dearly—killed Kalwadi and released the children, who were still alive within her. The children were not in Kalwadi's stomach, but in her womb, awaiting rebirth. Australian aborigines celebrated this second birth in their initiation rituals. Some scholars feel that Kalwadi was known elsewhere in Australia as Kunapipi.

Kamadhenu This name is the most common one used of the sacred cow, which symbolizes prosperity in India; she especially represents the wealth of the brahman class, and as such provides the ghee (clarified butter) that provides fuel for sacrificial fires. In Sanskrit, the words *cow* and *earth* are synonyms, indicating the deep connection between this figure and the earth goddess.

Kamrusepas The Hittite goddess of magic who assisted the heavenly queen Hannahanna in restoring the earth's fertility by purging the god Telipinu of wrath. She ruled chanting, healing, and ritual purification.

Kamui Fuchi Ainu goddess of the hearth, visited each morning by the sun goddess Chup-Kamai as she rose. It was extremely impolite to walk through sunbeams as they streamed across the floor each morning, for this was the sun's greeting to the hearth goddess.

Ka Nam Among the Khasi, an ethnic group in India, Ka Nam was born so beautiful that her mother, fearing she would be kidnapped, kept the child imprisoned in a secluded part of the village. The girl's father, however, finally convinced her that the child should lead a more normal life. This was to be her undoing.

One day, as Ka Nam was drawing water from a well, a huge tiger dragged her off to its lair. The tiger, U Khla, was very hungry. When he realized what a tiny morsel the girl was, he decided to fatten her up. He brought her little candies and made her feel at home. Ka Nam forgot to be afraid and grew into a young woman with perfect trust in tigers.

Her host, however, had not lost sight of the ultimate objective in rearing the girl. When she had reached full growth, he invited all his tiger friends for a feast. A little mouse, however, warned Ka Nam. She ran away and, as the mouse had told her, went right to the cave of the magician toad U Hynroh. He said he would protect her, but in fact he only intended to make her a slave. Telling her he was going to make sure she would be safe from the tiger, he turned her into a truly hideous toad.

The tiger, returning to his den, found his captive had escaped. He grew furiously angry and

This six-armed Tibetan brass image shows Mahakala, the local variant of the death goddess known in India as Kali.

called down curses on whoever had stolen his prey. The other tigers, when they realized they wouldn't get anything to eat, turned on U Khla and tore him to death.

Meanwhile, back at U Hynroh's, the little mouse had witnessed Ka Nam's transformation. Taking pity on the girl, she led Ka Nam to a magical tree that led to the sky. The maiden climbed into the tree and spoke the mouse's magic words: "Grow tall, dear tree, the sky is near, expand and grow." The tree grew and grew until it reached the sky, and there the maiden entered the Blue Realm.

Ka Nam, looking like a toad, went from palace to palace begging for help, but the heavenly folk were so repulsed by her ugliness that they threw her out. Finally she approached the palace of Ka Sgni, the sun mother, who gave her an outhouse to live in.

There she sat one day, with her toadskin off, combing her hair. And there the son of Ka Sgni saw her and fell in love with her. He ran to his mother and asked her to move the maiden indoors so he could be near her. Ka Sgni, a wise mother, waited to see if the infatuation would pass. She also went out to spy on the toad in the outhouse and, sure enough, saw the maiden without her toad disguise shining with loveliness.

Realizing that the maiden had been bewitched, Ka Sgni knew she would have to find the maiden asleep, and then burn the toadskin. She did so, releasing the maiden but incurring the fury of the magician toad. For days he tried to devour Ka Sgni, causing the world's first eclipse. Below on earth, the people stood in fear, watching the goddess fighting for her life. They screamed and they cried, they beat on drums and cymbals. When he heard the commotion, U Hynroh thought an army was about to advance on him. He released the sun goddess, but continues to attack her periodically, hoping humans will be too busy to help. For this reason, the Khasi say, it is important always to make a lot of noise during an eclipse.

Kanene Ski Amai Yehi The Cherokee Grandmother Spider brought the sun to our world, the only creature able to succeed after Possum had burned off his tail, and Buzzard, his clawfeathers, attempting to do so. She wove herself a little basket and then, spinning out a web to carry her, she traveled to the other side of the world. Then she reached out one of her many arms and grabbed the sun out of the sky. Popping it into her basket, she fled back across the waiting web to light our sky.

Kannagi Among the forty million Tamils in southern India, Sri Lanka and Malaysia, this is the name of the great mother goddess. She is the ancestral mother of all Tamils, who now rules the faithfulness of wives. This emphasis on faithfulness in an ancestral mother is unusual, for such divinities often produce their children through parthenogenesis or through multiple matings, so it is possible that Kannagi's myth once depicted her as engaging in less-than-chaste behavior which was later dis-

couraged. The great epic of Sri Lanka, the Lay of the Ankle Bracelet or the Silapathikaram, tells the story, which is identical to that told of the goddess Pattini.

Kantarupi In the Indian city of Mysore, there is a famous tale told of the goddess Bisal-Mariamna and her six sisters. Once, it is said, they stole the husband of a young woman, Kantarupi, for their sexual pleasure. They held him captive, but one night decided to let him return to his wife. Mischievously, they hypnotized Kantarupi, so that she was ignorant of what occurred. A few months later Kantarupi realized she was pregnant, but knew not why. Her father cast her out into the woods, certain that she'd been unfaithful with a secret lover. There she was adopted by a prostitute who exposed the baby boy in a snake temple, where his own grandfather found him and raised him.

Years later, the now-grown man passed through the prostitute's quarters and, seeing Kantarupi, fell in love and arranged a meeting—en route to which he stumbled over a calf whose mother soothed him by saying, "What can you expect of someone about to sleep with his own mother?" The young man was baffled at that. Imagine, then, his surprise when, approaching Kantarupi, all the mother's milk she had never given him to drink exploded from her breasts at him. All ended happily, however, when Bisal-Mariamna released the stolen husband, and the little family was united at last.

Kanuga Among the Tlingits, residents of Alaska's coastal rainforests, this human woman was turned to stone and now controls the winds.

Kara A Valkyrie, one of the Germanic war maidens, she accompanied her lover Helgi to battle, swooping above him in her swan plumage and singing such a sweet song that his enemies laid down their arms to listen admiringly. But one day Helgi raised his sword too high, too abruptly, and stabbed his loving protector. He lived in misery and guilt until he joined her in death.

Karaikkal-Asmmaiyar This Hindu saint and poet of the Vaishnava (honoring the warrior Vishnu) tradition was a renowned ascetic honored by those who wished to conquer bodily appetites.

Kara-Kura It is almost axiomatic that, when a natural energy is thwarted, it will appear threatening and dangerous. It follows that rigidly patriarchal societies frequently are plagued by female demons like this tiny goat-woman who, according to Turkish folklore, suffocates men while they sleep.

Kasum-Naj-Ekva The ancestral goddess of the Siberian Mansi, who lived on the Kasym River, she was called Kasum-Naj-Ekva (Great Woman) or Teterka (Greybird). Daughter of the highest god, she wore bird-pendants, which jingled as she walked, in her hair. Massively powerful, she was known to kill six opponents at one blow; she was also a magician known for the strength of her curses.

Two suitors wooed her. She lived with one for a time, then abandoned him and their daughter, whom she turned into a mountain. Then she lived with the other, but discovering that they were siblings, she left him as well and settled on the Kasym River to become ancestor of all the people there. She was honored as a bird goddess by them; they embroidered her image on baby pillows as a plea that she protect the newborn.

Kathirat The "wise goddess" of the Ugaritic religion, she set the bride-price for every woman, including the mighty Ishtar. As she who decides the proper order in which all things must be done, she corresponds to the Greek Graces.

Keca Aba Mother Sun, to the Cheremis of Russia, was worshiped by bowing in the direction of the east each morning as she rose. She was also called Os Keca Aba ("White Sun Mother"). Huge festivals were held annually in a sacred grove in which horses and other animals were sacrificed if they wished to be, signified by their shuddering at a certain moment in the ritual.

Ker The Greek goddess of violent death, she was a daughter of Nyx ("night") and sister of the Moirae ("fates"), and is sometimes personified as a black carrion bird hovering over the corpse. This name was also used of the malevolent ghost of any dead person. In the plural form, as Keres, she symbolizes the many forms that death can take.

Khon-Ma The "ancient mother" of Tibet, a ghostly queen rode on a ram through the night, dressed in golden robes and carrying a golden noose; she sought unguarded doors to enter, bringing her earth demons with her to attack the household. She was easily thwarted, however: one merely placed a ram's skull and food outside the door, along with pictures of the inhabitants; should Khon-Ma pass, she would mistake the pictures for reality and eat them.

Ki The Chaldean primeval earth goddess was the original female principle of matter.

Kikimora In Russia, this little woman lived behind the oven in every home. She was thought to be tangible to the family she haunted—usually in the form of mysterious night sounds—but only if danger threatened; otherwise, she was an invisible pest who particularly sought to torment women while they were spinning.

Kilili Ishtar the promiscuous, the bringer of tremendous anxiety to the men who desired her. She was symbolized by windows and birds.

Kimpa Vita A seventeenth-century prophetess of the Bakongo people of Africa, she was baptized a Christian under the name of Donna Beatrice. But by the time she was twenty, she was offending the church hierarchy by teaching heretical doctrines: that Christ was born black, that the ancient African kingdoms would be restored, that her child was conceived of the Holy Ghost. Such ideas were not popular, and she was burned as a witch, together with her baby son, in 1706.

Kinnari In Thailand, these bird women like to descend to earth to dance and sing on the edges of lakes and in forest clearings. There they sometimes meet and mate with human men, but such affairs are usually short-lived.

Kiri Amma Her name has several meanings—milk mother, wet nurse, and grandmother—all of which indicate her nurturing interest in the Sri Lankan people who worship her. Although she is honored throughout the island, Kiri Amma is the major goddess of central villages, seen as both a group of seven divinities but also in singular form. When a child falls ill, seven women impersonate this goddess, arriving at the house with rice and cakes. The blessing of lactating women is especially effective in healing childhood diseases, for in such women the strength of this protective goddess is strongest.

Kishimogin In Japan, this spirit once ate children, but she was converted by a saint and now works as a kind of infants' guardian angel.

Kiwakweskwa Among the Sokoki, woodland Indians of the American northeast, this forest-dwelling monster had enormous strength and loved to feast on human flesh. Such cannibals are frequent in Native American mythology, and may represent the danger that faced hunting people who spent much time away from their villages in the wilderness.

Kla In West Africa, there are two types of souls, a male Kla and a female. The male Kla, the Ashanti say, is full of evil, but the female Kla is the force of goodness in this world.

Kling In Indonesia, this falcon goddess was the mother of many sons, who had the curious habit of waging war using kites, to which they tied themselves. Flying beneath their drifting kites, they attacked and conquered their enemies.

Klu-mo The full name of this Tibetan demon queen was Klu-rgyal-mo srid-pa gtan-la phab-pa, the Klu Queen Who Set in Order the Visible World. She is part of the tradition of Bon-po, the ancient religion that preceded Buddhism in the Himalayan lands, and her full name indicates that she once had more power than simply terrifying human beings. She was the first being ever to emerge from the void of creation, and from her all the universe we know was born. From the top of her head, the sky erupted. Then the moon flashed forth from her right eye, the sun from her left, and the stars from her teeth. Her voice created thunder and her tongue lightning; her breath forms the clouds, her tears the rain. Her very flesh forms the earth, and the rivers that run across it are her veins. When her eyes are open, it is day; when she closes them to sleep, night descends. Described as she is in this way, her identity with the cosmic goddess of earth and sky seems clear.

Kn Sgni Her name means sun, and she had two sisters—Ka Um (water) and Ka Ding (fire)—and a brother U Bynai, the moon. In the beginning, say the Indian people called the Khasi, the moon was as bright as the sun. But he was a spoiled and self-centered young man. He wandered around aimlessly, consorting with bad companions. He spent many nights away from home, without telling anyone where he was going. He drank, he gambled, he pursued whatever pleasure caught his fancy.

Then be began to desire his sister. When she realized what he was planning, she grew furious. Scorching his face with hot ashes, she said, "How dare you think such thoughts of me, your elder sister, who has taken care of you and held you in her arms, carried you on her back like a mother does?" U Bynai was so ashamed of himself that he left home to wander through the heavens. His sisters, however, stayed home with their mother until she died. Then they formed the earth from her body.

Ko Among the bushmen of South Africa, Ko is the patron goddess of hunting, a shining white figure who dances with hunters and shares with them secrets of where game is hiding. Anyone who is touched by her during the pre-hunt dance has a sharp eye and perfect coordination during the hunt. Her appearance at the dance is not guaranteed, and sometimes she descends for only an instant, disappearing behind a mob of attendant spirits.

Koevasi Although she was suffering from a bad cold, the creator goddess of Melanesia walked through the world creating humanity. Because her speech was so difficult to understand through her stuffed-up nose, all the different islanders did their best to approximate it—which is why they all speak in different dialects.

Kongsim In a variant of the Korean legend of Pali Kongju, this heroine became insane—perhaps suffering from *shin byong* or "spirit sickness" that precedes shamanic initiation—and was thrown out of her palace. She wandered through Seoul towards the magical South Mountain, but the king banished her further to distant Mt. Diamond in Kangwon province. There she dreamed that a blue-winged crane flew into her mouth and caused her to conceive. Her twin sons each became the fathers of four daughters, all of whom became healers. Through their efforts, the princess became an honored ancestor.

In another myth attached to this name, Kongsim was a desperately ill princess confined to a dark-curtained room. Through her own prayers, and those of the maid she'd inspired to pray, Kongsim cured herself and was honored as the originator of the *mudang* or spirit religion.

Kono-Hana-Sakuya-Hime The Japanese cherry-tree goddess had a name that means the "lady who makes the trees bloom." Daughter of the mountain god, she was sister to the rock goddess Iha-Naga. Both desired the man Ninigi, who chose the younger flower goddess; for that, Iha-Naga cursed their children with lives only as long as a blossom, while hers would have lived as long as the rocks.

All did not go well with the couple, however, for Kono-Hana gave birth nine months to the day after their marriage. As she swelled with pregnancy, her new husband began to suspect she had conceived before they met. Angered at his doubt, Kono-Hana built a magic house that, when labor began, she set afire, saying any children born who were not Ninigi's would die in the blaze. Triplets were born, all safe, disproving the man's doubts. As the same story was told of Sengen Sama, goddess of Mt. Fuji, it is probable that Kono-Hana may be the same goddess under a different name or title.

Kore The most familiar "maiden" goddess (for that is the meaning of her name) to bear this title in Greece was Persephone, but the term was also used of such nubile deities as Despoina, Athene, and Artemis. Kore was the youngest form of the threefold goddess, the others being matron and crone. As such, she represented the youthful earth, the fresh season of buds and flowers, and the fragrant breezes of springtime.

Korobona With her sister Korobonako, this Warrau divinity from South America's tropical forests was said to live beside a sweetwater lake that the girls were forbidden to enter. However, the rebellious Korobona went swimming in the lake one day. Colliding with a stick in the middle of the pond, she released a captive divinity who dragged her down into the water and had intercourse with her.

Korobona soon gave birth to a wholly human child. She decided to visit the water deity again; this time she returned pregnant with a half-serpent baby that, though she tried to hide it, was killed by her brothers. Korobona offered the dead babe her breasts, and it revived. Discovered again by Korobona's brothers, the baby was this time not only killed but dismembered. The grieving mother gathered the pieces, planted them deep in the earth, and kept watch until, fully armed, the first Carib warrior sprang forth and drove the brothers, the Warrau, away. Scholars believe that Korobona was

The maiden goddess was a familiar figure to her worshipers in ancient Greece and Rome, honored under names like Kore, Persephone and Proserpina. This small stone sculpture shows the typical straight posture of the maiden goddess.

a local name for Kururumany, the creator goddess of the Antillean people called the Arawak.

Korrigan   In France, especially in Brittany, this was the name of the goddess of underground springs near dolmens and other ancient monuments; some legends said that Korrigan was the granddaughter of a great female Druid of ancient Gaul. A beautiful, translucent, and tiny spirit, she seemed to be a young maiden at night, when her power was at its height; during the day, she looked like a wrinkled crone.

Like other ancient goddesses who survived in the form of fairies, Korrigan was said to be dangerous. Women were not at all endangered, even if they should stumble upon Korrigan bathing or performing ancient rituals; men who saw her, however, were either killed or forced to marry Korrigan and never return to human society. The most dangerous time was the spring festival, when the Korrigans all met to pass the crystal goblet of inspiration and wisdom; a man who happened on the rite would instantly die.

Kostrubonko   This Russian goddess was impersonated each spring by a young woman who would lie on the earth as though dead. People of her village would form a ring around her, singing mournfully that "Kostrubonko is dead, our loved one is dead." Then the girl enacted the resurrection of the spring goddess, accompanied by the joyful songs of her friends and family.

Kottavi   This popular aboriginal South Indian mother goddess was later assimilated into Durga. She was shown nude, with mussed hair, sometimes with the upper part of her body covered with armor. Her name is found in many places in the south and west of the continent, suggesting that her worship was widespread.

Kou-Njami   The sun goddess of the Tvagi Samoyeds of Siberia was sent away into her winter absence each year with a sacrifice of white reindeer hung on a south-facing tree. Among the related Nenets, she was the eye of the heavens; because of her, no arrows or guns were ever shot into the air, lest the goddess be blinded.

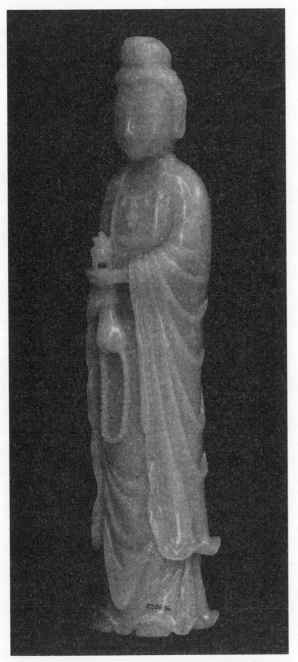

Kuan-Yin is one of the most beloved of Chinese divinities. This representation of the goddess of mercy was sculpted by Chien Lung in the mid-eighteenth century. She holds a rosary in one hand, indicating her constant prayerfulness.

Kuan-Yin   Just as Catholic Christianity has provided an antidote to pure theological patriarchy by encouraging the reverence of the Virgin Mary, so Chinese Buddhism evolved a feminine bodhisattva, or Buddha-to-be, named Kuan-Yin. And just as Mary captured the hearts of Catholic worshipers, so Kuan-Yin far outstripped the male bodhisattvas in popularity. Both in Japan (as Kwannon, who is often pictured as male) and in pre-revolutionary China, this semi-divine being was honored in virtually every home; she was the

This attendant upon the goddess Kuan-Yin is called a "guardian at the gate" by archetypal theorists, who find such fierce creatures often protecting secrets from the unworthy or frivolous inquirer.

most powerful being in the entire Chinese pantheon.

It was said that Kuan-Yin was so concerned for humanity that, upon receiving enlightenment, she chose to retain human form rather than transcend it as pure energy. And so she would stay until every single living creature attained enlightenment. Her name translates "she who hears the weeping world"; Kuan-Yin sat on her paradise island P'u T'o Shan answering every prayer addressed to her. The mere utterance of her name in prayer was said to assure salvation from physical and spiritual harm. Even better was the observance of Kuan-Yin's own testimony of peace and mercy; her most devout worshipers ate no flesh and lived entirely without doing violence to other beings.

Sometimes it was said that Kuan-Yin originally lived on earth as Miao Shan, a young woman of unearthly virtue. Although her father wished her to marry, Miao Shan decided to visit a monastery, which, contrary to her expectations, was a hotbed of vice. Her father, hearing of her presence in the convent and suspecting the worst, burned it to the ground. A rainbow carried her to heaven, where her innocent death earned her transmutation into the divine world.

On the other hand, it was sometimes said that the bodhisattva emerged directly from the light of Amitabha Buddha's eye. As this story is also told of the male Indian bodhisattva Avalokita, some scholars believe that Kuan-Yin represents a merger of that compassionate figure with the Tibetan star goddess Tara.

In either case, the feminine Kuan-Yin has for centuries been the chief symbol of human compassion in the Orient. Her statues show her dressed in flowing garments and often hung with golden necklaces, attended by the dragon-girl Lung Nu and the male child Shan Ts'ai. Often she holds willows or jewels; she makes symbolic gestures of generosity and the banishment of fear and hardship. Usually a virgin goddess, she is in China occasionally connected with physical love, which can indeed be an expression of love and compassion such as Kuan-Yin encourages. She also appears as a temple guardian, with a thousand arms or a thousand eyes, always alert and on guard. Such statues were designed as guides to meditation, but the most effective meditation was the constant repetition of Kuan-Yin's name. That continual inner reminder of Kuan-Yin's peace and generosity brought such qualities into every aspect of her worshiper's life.

Kubaba   A very ancient Hattian goddess, the "mountain mother," from whom the better-known Cybele derives her name. Later writings call her Queen of Kargamis, a Hittite metropolis; there she was called Khipa or Khebe, then Kubabas, and finally Kubaba. Mounted on or between two lions, Kubaba is a link between the mother goddess of the vast Anatolian city of Catal Huyuk, whose name is unknown, and the later image of Cybele.

Kuma   Among the Yaruros of Venezuela, the creator goddess was mother of the sun and of all people on earth. She always appeared dressed as a shaman, but with beautiful gold jewelry.

She was the first living being to appear on earth; afterwards came the gods. Desiring to become pregnant, she asked the god Puana to have intercourse with her thumb. Convincing her that she would become too productive that way, he impregnated her womb instead. She gave birth, then sent her children, the gods, scurrying about the earth looking for people. After a lengthy search, they found them in a hole in the ground. Kuma gave the gods a rope and hook, with which they pulled forth human life from under the earth.

Kunapipi   Eternally pregnant, the great mother goddess of northern Australia is the creator of every living being. Sometimes represented (like Julunggul) as a rainbow snake, Kunapipi is the overseer of initiations and puberty rituals. She came, it was said, in Dreamtime from a sinking land to establish herself and her worship in Arnhem Land.

Along the Roper River, people say that Kunapipi had several daughters whom she used as bait for her favorite meal: human men. Kunapipi ate so many men that it attracted the attention of a hero who, catching her in the act, destroyed her. But the moans she made while dying struck into all the trees in the world, and still can be heard if the wood is carved into bullroarers, which cry out "Mumuna," Kunapipi's ritual name.

Kunti   An ancient Indian mother goddess was Kunti ("woman"), the ever-virginal lover of the gods who, like the earth, could take innumerable men into herself without changing her essence. Although replaced in Hindu worship by later goddesses, Kunti figured in the epic, the Mahabharata, as well as giving her name to a north Indian people and their territory.

Kupalo The Slavic goddess of midsummer, Kupalo takes her name from a word that means "to bathe," and her worshipers bathed both in rivers and in the dew gathered on June mornings. Slavic people greatly venerated water, which was held to have healing as well as purifactory powers; to gain relief from an illness, for instance, it was suggested that one toss bread into a stream, then beg the water's pardon and ask for healing.

Kupalo was embodied as well in the purifying fire, which also figures into her rituals. These were part of an annual fire ritual in Russia: young men and women leaped over a huge bonfire, dragging a straw maiden with them. The next day, everyone joined in ritually bathing the figure, which was then released into the water to drift away. The goddess magically removed all evil from the village as she floated downstream.

Such images were also constructed in Serbia and other Slavic countries. Dressed in the finest gown, hung with floral garlands, the Kupalo image was hung from a tree (a ritual that recalls the Greek tree goddess Helen Dendritis) which had been ceremoniously cut and carried from its forest home. All but the upper branches were trimmed, so that the tree itself seemed to form the image of a green-haired woman; sometimes the tree itself was sufficient for the ritual, and no straw maiden was constructed. These rituals, to be effective, had to be performed by women only; men could not even touch the tree or the hanging figure.

As a healing goddess, Kupalo ruled the herbs of the field. Purple loosestrife—the same plant found so readily on North American roadsides—was one of her favorites; its roots had the power to banish demons and bad dreams, but it had to be gathered at dawn on solstice morning. The flowering fern would also grant its possessor great power—the power to understand the language of trees, which on the night before solstice are no longer rooted but can wander through the world—but gathering it meant slipping by fearful guardian demons.

Kuwanlelenta "To Make Beautiful Surroundings" is the meaning of this Hopi spirit's name. She was the guardian of the sunflower plant, and thus ancestral mother to the sunflower clan. In Owaqlt, a women's ceremony, Kuwanlelenta appears in double form, represented by two girls whose faces are painted with the ground petals of sunflowers.

Lada   There are several goddesses with this name. One, the Slavic spring goddess, was honored with tinsel-decked clay images of larks, smeared with honey, which were carried in song-filled processions. This Lada ruled love and marital happiness.

The other Lada was a goddess of Lycia, in southwestern Anatolia, whose myth has been lost although the meaning of her name—indicating both "woman" and "goddess"—remains. She made her way into Greek mythology as Leda, mother of Helen, and possibly as Leto, mother of Artemis.

Lady of the Beasts   This phrase is used to describe a number of goddesses of various cultures, all of which share a similar identification with wild places and the animals that live therein. A form of the great mother goddess who births and cares for humanity, this Lady usually is found in cultures where game animals provide a signficant part of the diet. Not surprisingly, she is often a goddess of birth as well, invoked for aid by human mothers, but also invoked to encourage animal reproduction. Where a culture has begun to move into agriculture, the Lady often adds rulership of vegetation to her original identity as mother of animals.

La'ila'i   Among the Hawaiians, this was the name of the first goddess born after chaos settled into form; mating with the sky, she produced humanity.

Laima   The Baltic goddess of fate sometimes appears as three or seven goddesses to symbolize the many fates possible. Laima, like the Norns and Fates, measures the length and happiness of a person's life. Sometimes called Laima-Dalia, "happy fate," she was invoked in prayers: "Oh, Laima, thou art healthy; give me thy health." Often mentioned in the same prayer was the sun goddess Saule, for Laima measured the length of the sun's day as well as a woman's life. Laima was her name in Latvia; she was Laime in Lithuania; in both countries she was sometimes pictured as a swan maiden or as a multiple goddess.

Laka   Patron of hula dancers, this Hawaiian goddess was said to rule the islands' uncultivated areas; her dancers also represented the untamed element of human nature. Originally, hula troupers were satirists and puppeteers as well as performers of the now-familiar dances; they worshiped Laka in the shape of a piece of wood covered with yellow cloth and decked with wildflowers.

Lakshmi   Ancient India did not erect temples to this goddess, for why try to contain the one who embodies herself in all forms of wealth? Lakshmi is everywhere: in jewels, in coins, in rare shells, in every child born to welcoming parents, and particularly in cows.

The well-known reverence for cows in Hindu India is based on the worship of this goddess, called the Shakti of life-preserving Vishnu. Hindu philosophy defined male godhead as passive and abstract, distant and powerless, unless activated by the goddess. In Vishnu's case, his power to maintain and enrich life only functions when Lakshmi inspires it. Therefore it is thought good policy to bestow reverence on those embodiments of wealth—the cows who in some parts of India are simply called *lakshmi* after their owner.

Some myths say that Lakshmi existed from all time, floating before creation on a lotus; for this she is called Padma ("lotus goddess"), whose symbol became the sign for spiritual enlightenment throughout Asia. Some stories say that Lakshmi sprang up from the ocean when it was churned by the gods, emerging like a jewel in all her beauty and power, covered with necklaces and pearls, crowned and braceleted, her body fat and golden. Many interpreters see the variant legends as recording Lakshmi's preeminence in pre-Aryan India, where she was goddess of the earth and its fructifying moisture, and her later incorporation into Vedic theology when her worshipers would not abandon their devotion to the lotus goddess. Once established in the religious amalgam called Hinduism, Lakshmi grew to symbolize not only the wealth of the earth but of the soul as well, becoming a magnificent symbol of the delights of spiritual prosperity.

Lamamu   The daughter of Tiamat the sea goddess, she derived her name from the Chaldean word for "primeval sediments" and apparently symbolized the first bits of created matter. This primal matter was invoked at the completion of human creations, especially buildings.

Lamasthu   Almost every culture produced a figure like her: the lion-headed "daughter of heaven," desperately covetous of human beings and their offspring. She was Lamia to the Greeks, Lilith or Gilou to the Hebrews, Kishimogin to the Japanese, Baba Yaga to the Russians. The Sumerians named her Lamasthu, a plague-bearing woman who carried double-headed serpents and suckled dogs and pigs. She infected children with disease whenever possible, but she would attack adults as well, drinking their blood and consuming their flesh.

It was possible to avoid this demon of destruction, however. One merely hung on all the doors of the household plaques or amulets bearing Lamasthu's name. (Women hung them on their breasts.) The demon, thinking them greetings or signs of reverence, reacted in her usual perverse way: she went elsewhere, somewhere she was not wanted.

Lamia   To the Greeks, she was a nursery bogey, useful for scaring children, as Lilith was to the Semitic tribes. "Be good, now," Greek mothers would say, describing how the beautiful features of Lamia's face grew twisted, how her eyes detached themselves from their sockets. Lamia was, they said, originally a mortal woman who lived in a cave; she bore Zeus several children. The jealous Hera destroyed all her offspring but Scylla, and Lamia went crazy with grief. That is why (this was most effective in silencing toddlers) the "greedy one" started stealing other women's children and sucking out their blood.

Some scholars contend that Lamia was a case of one people's goddess becoming the next culture's demon. They find in this half-snake figure the vestige of a Cretan snake goddess, in turn an image of the death mother, the earth who ultimately devours all who walk on her. This Lamia seems to have been honored at mystic rituals similar to those of Demeter at Eleusis. But the children of classical Greece were no scholars, and they doubtless grew silent with fright at Lamia's name.

Lampetia   The English word *lamp* comes from this Greek goddess' name. The sun's daughter, she was his chief herdswoman as well, guarding his fabulous cattle. *The Odyssey* tells how the Greeks arrived on the island of Trinacria (modern Sicily), where this goddess and her sister Phathusa lived. King Odysseus warned his men not to touch the sacred cattle, but a few disobeyed.

The immortal cattle suffered greatly: the hides walked around by themselves; the spitted flesh groaned over the fires. Lampetia reported the sacrilege to her father, who sent a punishing storm to destroy the Greek boats. Only Odysseus was saved from the sun god's anger; he was washed ashore on the island of Calypso.

Lan Tstai-Ho   Among the Eight Immortals of ancient China was this androgynous being who dressed as a woman but had a male voice. She was the singing Immortal, originally an earthly street musician who wandered about bringing joy until she was lifted to heaven on a stork's wings. Afterward, she brought delight to the heavenly gatherings, always carrying her flute and a basket of fruit to any party.

Lara   Roman sources mention this goddess passingly as "mother of the dead," an underworld goddess who may have been the same one who granted Rome prosperity as Acca Larentia. She was sometimes called Tacita or Muta ("deadly silent one"); she was invoked by that name in magical attempts to stop the mouths of detractors, in which women would tie the mouths of dead fish so that gossips would suffer the same fate.

La Reine Pedaque   "The flat-footed queen," a jeering name for the Germanic spinning goddess Perchta because one of her feet had become oversized from vigorously pushing the pedal on the spinning wheel.

Larissa   This Greek woman faced an incestuous assault from her father in a quick-witted and effective way: she pushed him into a wine barrel, wherein he drowned.

Lasa   An Etruscan goddess who supplied comfort to her worshipers when they invoked her in times of need. Her name may be a title, meaning "Lady" or "Goddess," for it appears as part of several goddess-names in this early Italian culture.

Latiaran   An Irish goddess who had two sisters: the eldest Lasair ("flame") and the middle sister Inghean Bhuidhe ("yellow-haired girl"). They survived into the Christian era disguised as saints, Lasair ruling the first spring; Inghean Bhuidhe, the beginning of summer; and Latiaran, the beginning of harvest time. Originally, it can be assumed, they were seasonal goddesses.

The story that survives of Latiaran is that each morning she carried a "seed of fire" from her nun's cell to a nearby forge. One morning the smith complimented her on her beautiful feet, and she, vainly, looked down. As she did, her apron caught fire, but though her clothes burned she remained unharmed. Then she sank into the ground under a heart-shaped stone and was never seen again.

Laume   A Lithuanian fairy queen, she appeared at night on footbridges or in thickets, a large-breasted woman with long blond hair accompanied by a cat. Or you might see her in her alternative guise, looking like an animal with human breasts and hen's feet. But best not to laugh at her, for those who did could find themselves changed into animals themselves. She visited homes to judge the industry she found therein; where people worked hard, she would reward them with gifts, often of linen, but where she found laziness she punished it by eating the culprits, especially if they were children. But she loved hard-working children, whom she often captured and took off for a spirit-vacation, dressing them in lovely clothes. Generous but easily angered, she might do all the farm work and then, at a wrong word, destroy her handiwork and disappear. Sometimes she appears as a multiple goddess, or she was said to have many daughters who would change into animals at the snap of her fingers. In Latvia, she was known as Lauma.

Lavercam This Irish poet made an appearance in the famous tale of Deirdre of the Sorrows, but she was more than the tragic heroine's nurse and companion. Born a slave, she was so brilliantly witty—though uncommonly ugly—that she rose in society, right to the court of Irish nobility. She was exceedingly strong and so fleet that she would run Ireland's entire length in a single day, gathering news. Lavercam would return to the court of King Conchobar by dinnertime to relate the tidings of his realm.

Once assigned to care for the doomed Deirdre, she transferred her loyalty from the king to the woman. When, after escaping with her lover, Deirdre was foolish enough to return to Ireland, Lavercam warned her and prophesied death if she should stay; Naoise, Deirdre's beloved, would not heed the poet's words. So Lavercam went to the king and lied about Deirdre's appearance, saying her beauty had been ruined by hardship; the deceit might have worked, had Conchobar not chanced to see the tragic heroine again.

Leah The sister of Rachel; both were part of Jacob's harem. Like her sister, Leah gave birth to founders of the great Hebrew tribes; her sons were Reuben, Simeon, Levi, Judah, Issachar, and Zebulon.

Leanan Sidhe The sister and opposite of the dreaded Banshee, this Irish goddess was the spirit of life and muse of singers. She appeared as the poet Eodain who wooed her human lovers with beautiful compositions. One of these, a king of Munster, so attracted Eodain that she granted him victory in war and wealth in peace. Ungrateful as he was, the king took his riches to Spain and spent nine years squandering them. He finally returned to a kingdom in ruins. Eodain, however, was loyal to her love. She restored him to the throne and, henceforth, was the power behind it, making sure the king did not slip into dissolute behavior again.

Leanan Sidhe ("fairy sweetheart") was sometimes thought destructive to her chosen mate; a man, once witnessing her unearthly beauty, would find mortal life dull and meaningless. Through no fault of the beautiful spirit, he would pine away whenever she was not with him, eventually dying of depression.

Leda Originally she was probably Lada ("woman"); her name may also be related to that of the goddess Leto. In her most familiar Greek legend, she was raped by Zeus, who took the form of a swan for the occasion; Leda slept with her husband the same night and laid an egg. Out hatched two sets of twins, male and female, mortal and immortal. The mortal children were Clytemnestra and Pollux; the immortal ones, Helen and Castor. Leda was then raised to heaven, the legends say, as the goddess Nemesis.

Other variants say that Zeus raped the avenging goddess Nemesis herself. She fled from him, changing shape as she ran, but finally overpowered in the body of a bird, Nemesis laid an egg that the woman Leda found and cared for. Another tale says Zeus tricked Nemesis as he had Hera: disguising himself as a swan, he hid in the goddess' bosom and then turned on her in violence. The egg that resulted was laid between Leda's legs so that she was the foster mother of the four children. The complexities of these variations indicate that, hidden in the dim pre-Hellenic past, Leda was important in her own right, not merely as a mortal victim of Zeus. But it is currently impossible to assign her a character and myth unbiased by Greek influences.

Leelinau Among the Ojibwa of the northern forests, this girl used to meditate near a lakeshore spirit grove inhabited by turtle spirits. Whenever people needed to pass through the grove or to seek shelter under its trees, they would leave offerings of sacred tobacco for these protective deities. When Leelinau grew to marriageable age, her parents told her they had found a fine young man to be her husband. Unaccountably, the girl burst into tears and ran from their home. She ran through the village, all the way to her meditation spot. There she sat, sobbing in dispair, although she did not know why she felt such grief. Then a voice spoke kindly to her. She turned, and saw a young man step forward from a young pine tree. He offered her his love, and she accepted it. Then she returned to her village. On her wedding day, dressed in her wedding finery, she disappeared again. The last that was seen of Leelinau, she was walking into the grove, whose trees embraced her and made her one of them.

Le-Hev-Hev Before a departing soul could pass to the afterlife, the Melanesians said, it had to confront this goddess, who tried to trick the soul with games. Drawing on the sand in front of her, she challenged the soul to complete her diagram. Should the dead one be unable to do so—or did so incorrectly—Le-Hev-Hev had the soul for dinner.

The Malekulans who honored Le-Hev-Hev considered her a goddess, not a monster, offering her boars so she would not eat human corpses. Her earthly forms were the spider, the crab, and the rat; she was also embodied in female genitalia. Her name has been roughly translated as "she who smiles so that we draw near and she can eat us."

Lemkechen Among the Berbers of North Africa, the polestar was a black woman who held the reins of a camel (Ursa Minor) while its mother (Ursa Major) was milked. Fearful of her life, for she believed the other stars wished to kill her, she stood motionless in the sky in fright.

Lemna The little island of Lemnos is in the far north of the Aegean Sea—near the land of Amazonia, if that country existed where the ancient Greeks believed it did. The people of Lemnos had other connections to those women warriors, for they claimed descent from Myrine, one of the greatest Amazon queens. And the tiny isle was the setting for one of the most amazonian of Greek myths.

The women of Lemnos—worshipers, probably, of an earth goddess named Lemna—were so

This beautiful carved female figure is from Tonga, in Polynesia. For some Pacific goddesses, see Le-Hev-Hev, Hananuele, Lorop, Papa, Satine and Taranga.

confident of their renowned beauty that they began to neglect proper sacrifices to the goddess of desire, Aphrodite. In punishment she put a curse on them, a curse appropriate to their neglect. They were stricken with a terrible odor, some legends say; other stories say they became sexually repulsive. In either case, the men began consorting with slave women, conceiving children upon their concubines. In revenge, the proud Lemnian women killed the men. They also killed the slave women and the children born of the illicit unions.

Only their queen, Hypsipyle, broke the women's covenant by hiding her father from death. Later, the Greek hero Jason and his Argonaut companions stopped at the island. To repopulate their land, the women had intercourse with the strangers, Hypsipyle choosing Jason himself. It was said that the women—realizing that their murders had changed their society utterly—thereafter called the children begotten by the Argonauts by their fathers' names, rather than by their own.

Lethe   The Greek goddess of oblivion was the daughter of the matron of disorder, Eris. The underworld river through which the dead pass, and which causes them to forget their lives on this earth, is named for her. Some myths call Lethe the mother of Dionysus—the god of wine, whose heritage would explain the reason for drunken forgetfulness.

Leto   The Greeks said that she was a paramour of Zeus who bore the sun and moon, Apollo and Artemis, despite the persecutions of Hera. But Apollo was an immigrant god said to have traveled from the north, the realm of the Hyperboreans ("people beyond the north wind"). And Artemis existed in Greece before her twin, a circumstance recorded in the legend that says she was the first child born, with no labor pains, to Leto. She then sprang up and aided her mother in delivery of the later god, a long and difficult birth.

Who, then, was the "mother" of these unrelated deities? Her name means "darkness" and she

was invoked as the "nocturnal one," suggesting a parallel to the Greek Nyx, the primordial night that also gave birth to light. In matriarchal symbolism, many scholars point out, night is said to precede day and winter precedes summer, while in patriarchal societies the opposite is usually the case. Leto may therefore have been part of the substratum of Greek religion shared with Hera and other pre-Hellenic women's goddesses. She may also have been an imported goddess, for some researchers argue that she was the same as Lat, or Al-Lat, the Near Eastern goddess.

Leucippe   The daughter of a Greek king, she jeered at the women who participated in the rituals of Dionysus. In punishment she was stricken mad and, while entranced, ripped her sons to pieces in an action worthy of the most frenzied Maenad.

Levana   The Romans, who had a divinity to every hour and every tree, had a special goddess for the moment when a father, to ritually indicate his intention to rear his child, picked up a newborn infant from the ground. Her name comes from *levare*, to lift up.

Leviathan   The snake-shaped monster of the Old Testament, she was said to have been a daughter of Adam's first wife, Lilith. Thus she was probably an ancient dragon goddess in disguise; Jehovah's victory over her may have symbolized the successful Hebrew campaign against their region's indigenous goddesses.

Lia   Among the aboriginal people of Gippsland in Australia, this heroine led a revolt of the women of her village against the men, when the latter were found to have been greedily keeping water to themselves. Each day the men left the village, saying that they would search for water; each night they returned bearing only the smallest amounts. Though the women were dusty and thirsty, the men seemed content.

One day, Lia decided to break the rules that the men had set up, which required the women to stay in camp and, especially, not to climb the nearby mountains. She left in early morning and climbed and climbed, but her thirst had made her weak, and she passed out in a cave on the mountain. There the little people, the Tukonee, visited her in her Dreaming, pointing out a place to dig with her digging-stick.

The next day, she brought the women to the spot she had learned of, and began to dig as instructed. A huge wall of water rose, and when it had settled down into a steady flow, it had formed the river Mumumbidgee. Across its banks, the women saw the men of their village, but they could not cross and had to find other, less selfish mates on their own side.

Liban This early Irish goddess was the daughter of the god Eochaid who, because he eloped with his stepmother and neglected the sacred rites, angered the other divinities. A punishing flood was sent on his household, and everyone save Liban was drowned; the only other living survivor was the goddess' lapdog.

For the next 300 years Liban and her dog lived beneath the lake formed by the flood. Eventually they changed into sea creatures, Liban into a salmon, her lapdog into an otter. But Liban finally grew curious about happenings on earth and allowed herself to be caught in a net. Hauled to land, the goddess looked like a *berooch*, or mermaid, clinging to an otter.

The two were exhibited as curiosities until a cruel man killed the otter without reason. The goddess, deprived of her lifelong companion, turned herself back to human form and died. Liban still haunts the sea, however, in the form of a seabird.

Libera With Ceres and the god Liber, this goddess composed a triad of Roman agricultural divinities worshiped at the Liberalia on March 17. At that time, to celebrate the return of vegetation to the earth's surface, old women would serve as Libera's priestesses, sitting at little portable street stands

The Tibetan goddess Lla-Mo rides on a mule over a sea of blood, bones, limbs and entrails, in this beaten-copper sculpture from Tibet, from the late nineteenth century.

selling fried honey pancakes. Romans bought the lucky cakes from the ivy-decked old ones, offering a bit to the goddess and devouring the rest. When Greek influence modulated the Roman pantheon, Libera was assimilated to Persephone, and the same stories were told of both.

Libertas This goddess of liberty, depicted as a matron wearing a laurel wreath, was worshiped in three temples in Rome. In one of them, criminal records were kept, hostages held, and censors did their censorious deeds; later it was used as a public archive.

Libitina Her temple was the center for Roman burials, for it was there that the bereaved could buy or rent everything necessary for a funeral. The goddess of

195

death and its attendant rituals, she gave her name to the morticians, *libitinarii*, who served her.

Li Chi This Chinese heroine is celebrated in many ballads, which tell of how she was set out as a morsel for a great serpent to eat. Many others had been sacrificed, and they had all died in terror. But Li Chi fought back and killed the serpent. Although she mourned the girls who had preceded her as sacrifices, she claimed that gentleness and timidity had been their downfall. Girls who followed her lead, however, would find they could protect themselves.

Lieu Hahn This Vietnamese goddess, the most important of the Holy Mothers, was sent into exile on earth because she broke a jade wine cup in the home of her father, the Jade Emperor. She lived an unremarkable life on earth, marrying and bearing a son, then dying when her exile was over. But after she returned to heaven, she was haunted by memories of her life on earth. So she returned, clothing herself for her second incarnation in the form of a beautiful flute-player. She ran a teahouse in the capital, which miraculously disappeared whenever she left it, then reappeared at her return. But Lieu Hahn was often seen in other places in the country, especially secluded sites of natural beauty. Meanwhile, the husband of her first incarnation died and reincarnated as a great scholar, whom she married and with whom she lived another happy lifetime.

When she died, she ascended yet again to heaven, but still wished to return to earth, and so in her third and final incarnation she became the goddess of a village. There she happily remained, caring for her people, until the seventeenth century, when an emperor destroyed her shrine and ruled that she was a demon. Infuriated, she afflicted both men and animals for many miles around with a fatal illness, until the emperor was forced to admit his error and rebuild her shrine.

Lignaco-Dex The early Italians knew that the forest had laws of its own, and Lignaco-Dex was their name for the goddess who pointed out which trees were acceptable for human use. Before chopping down a tree for fuel, the Italians invoked this "inmost-forest-revealing" goddess, who threatened appropriate punishment if her orders were ignored.

Ligoapup In Micronesia, the creator goddess made all land in the form of islands. Some legends said that she drank water from a hollow tree, swallowing invisible animals who fertilized her. She bore a girl as humans do, but also produced three other children from unusual organs: a son from her arm, another from one eye, and a second daughter from the other eye. These four beings were the ancestors of the human race we know.

Lilith "Male and female he created them," proclaims Genesis in its first version of humanity's creation. But the Bible later changes its mind, explaining the creation of woman as Jehovah's afterthought. Jewish tradition outside the Bible understood the disparity: there was a female created simultaneously with Adam, and her name was Lilith. (There were variants: she was created before him; or after him, from the slime of the earth; or much later, as the twin of the evil Samael.) When the first man suggested intercourse to the primal female, she enthusiastically agreed. Adam then instructed Lilith to lie down beneath him. Insulted, she refused, pointing out that they had been created equally and should mate so.

Lilith then went to Jehovah and tricked him into revealing his secret name, his name of power. (See Isis for a similar tale.) Once she had power over him, Lilith demanded that Jehovah give her wings; she then flew from Eden to the western deserts. There she happily had orgies with elemental spirits and sand demons, producing demon children by the score. (Here, too, there were variants of the story: perhaps Lilith was banished from Paradise; perhaps she was born with wings; maybe she flew off to the Land of Nod. Again, some say that Jehovah cursed her with sterility.)

Adam was provided with a new mate, but he and Eve fell from Jehovah's favor. As penance for his sin, Adam vowed to avoid the pleasures of marriage for a century. Then Lilith had her revenge. Each night she came to Adam and had intercourse with him (in her preferred positions, one assumes), capturing his emissions to form little demon babies. One of these, some say, was Samael the evil prince, whom Lilith then took as her playmate and companion.

You would think her beautiful, Lilith of the luxurious hair and the arching wings—until you saw the talons she had instead of feet. Her unearthly beauty was dangerous to young men, who lusted after her and pined away, never aroused by mortal women. Lilith threatened children as well, for she had power over all infants in their first week, all babies on the first of the month and on Sabbath evenings, and all children born of unmarried people. Mothers could protect their young, however, by hanging an amulet marked "Sen Sam San"—for the protective angels Sensenoi, Samangalaph, and Sanoi—around the child's neck.

When Lilith came to steal a child, it was usually at night, when the babe was tucked in crib or cradle. Because she liked her victims smiling, she tickled the infant's feet. It giggled; thereupon Lilith strangled it. Mothers hearing their children laughing in dreams, or noticing them smiling as they slept, hit the baby's nose three times, crying out, "Away, Lilith, you have no place here." Mothers were also wary of kites, pelicans, owls, jackals, wildcats, and wolves, all disguises favored by Lilith, who went as well by forty other names.

Lilwani The Hittite earth goddess, at whose shrine near Babylon the festival of Inaras was celebrated.

Limnades These Greek nature spirits never attained immortal status but, like English fairies or Celtic Banshees, were part of the daily lives of unlettered folk. The Limnades haunted lakes, marshes, and swamps; they sang soft songs to passing strangers, luring them to a watery death, or called out desperately as though they were drowning women, luring passersby into mire and mud. The Limoniades were more gentle folk, nymphs who lived in open meadows and entertained themselves by dancing with the flowers.

Litae Innumerable sweet-natured goddesses, they represented penitential prayers, which—light as the frail bodies of the Litae—wafted to Olympus

From the highlands of Sumatra comes this figure of an ancestral mother, for whom offerings were regularly made so that she might ensure the health and safety of her descendants. Such goddesses include Ligoapup, Lorop, Hina and Papa.

to be answered by the Greek gods and goddesses. We derive our word *litigate*—to plead one's case—from their name.

Lla-Mo One of the great goddesses of Tibetan Llamaism, her rule encompasses life, death and regeneration. She is depicted as enveloped in flame, riding across a lake of blood, riding a mule whose saddle is made of the skin of her own son. Her companions are goddesses of the seasons, the jewel goddesses and the goddesses of long life. Guardian divinity to the Dalai Lama, she is reputed to have appeared to the Tibetan spiritual leader to pledge her unwavering protection.

Loddis-Edne This goddess of the western Saami controlled the nesting instincts of birds, which brought them back annually to the arctic, where they both served as a reminder of the earth's springtime rebirth and provided sustenance for the people.

Lofn This Scandinavian love goddess had a special purpose: she was charged with smoothing over love's difficulties. Lofn ("mild") received the prayers of those separated from their lovers and was empowered to bring together those she favored.

Lolita The divine essence of the universe is sometimes said by the Hindus to take the form of this adolescent woman, delighting both in girlish play and in womanly intercourse. Lolita is a symbol of the carelessness of the divine energy; to her, creation is merely another pleasant toy.

Loo-Wit The goddess of the volcanic Mt. St. Helens. Loo-Wit was said by the Multnomah and Klickitat to be an old woman who, because of her generosity, was granted one boon by the sky spirit. She wished for eternal youth and beauty.

Granted, said the sky father. He told Loo-Wit to build a fire on the magical bridge that separated the Multnomah and the Klickitat. These selfish and greedy people had been stricken with killing weather; all their fires had gone out. So when the now-magnificent woman appeared on the magic bridge, bringing them fire, they made peace between the tribes.

But trouble soon started. Loo-Wit was courted by both Chief Wyeast of the south and Klickitat of the north; she could not choose between them.

The men started a war over Loo-Wit, breaking the magical bridge in the battle.

Finally, the sky father intervened, turning Wyeast and Klickitat into the fiery peaks of Mt. Hood and Mt. Adams (the latter sometimes said to be a goddess) and Loo-Wit into Mt. St. Helens. Long after they were raised into mountains, the chiefs continued to make war, shooting fire at each other and spilling rocks—the Columbia Cascades—into the space where the magical bridge once stood.

Lopamudra A marvelous heroine of the Indian Mahabarata, she was created from the parts of many creatures by the sage Agastya, who arranged to have her born to a queen who yearned for a daughter. As Lopamudra grew, she became all that the sage had intended, beautiful and graceful beyond compare. When she was still very young, he married her, to assure himself that no one else would have access to her glorious body. He waited, not patiently, until his child-bride bled her first blood, then had her brought to his bed. Who knows what he expected? Probably not that the young girl would teach him a lesson. Reasoning with him that the conception of children should take place in beauty and joy, she instructed him in the proper ways to make love to her, demanding that he approach her in fine clothes and garlands of flowers, that he lie with her in a magnificent bed, and that he grant her as much pleasure as he wished to receive.

Lorelei Daughter of the river god of the Rhine, she was a beautiful maiden who sat on the rock that bore her name, near the town of St. Goar. There she sang a sweet and plaintive song that lured more than one mariner to his death on the sharp treacherous rocks.

Lorop The creator goddess of the Micronesian islanders of Yap, Lorop was the daughter of an earlier creator named Liomarar, who tossed sand into the ocean to form the first islands, then squatted on one to bear her daughter. Lorop herself had three sons whom she fed with miraculous food.

They did not know where Lorop got the plentiful rations, and two did not care. But the third, the youngest, stayed home one day, curious to see where his mother gathered dinner. Seeing Lorop dive into the sea, chanting a spell, he followed her to the underworld. There he saw her filling baskets with food—a discovery that meant she must remain below the earth. But Lorop continued to provide for her offspring, sending them many fish each day, and occasionally even a new island on which to live. A similar goddess was called Nomoi or Mortlock in other parts of Micronesia.

Lotis   In Greek legend, this nymph was pursued by Priapus, intent on rape. She called out to her mother the earth and her father the sea; they transformed her into the first lotus tree.

Louhi   The fierce and magical queen of the Arctic in the Finnish epic, Kalevala, Louhi was the great antagonist to the hero Vainamoinen. He tried to steal her treasured sampo, a charm that brought prosperity to her country. Louhi raised a huge ocean storm to prevent the thief from escaping; she called down her son, Winter, to freeze the sea to restrain Vainamoinen's flight. But all she managed to do was shatter the sampo. Vainamoinen escaped with the fragments, which were still powerful enough to bring abundance and wealth to his country.

Lua   Little information remains about this early Italian divinity, to whom arms of defeated enemies were sacrificed and in whose name plagues were called down.

Luaths Lurgann   "Speedy foot," the fastest runner in Ireland, was the aunt of the hero Fionn. At birth, Fionn was threatened by those fearful of his eventual power, but Luaths Lurgann, who had been his midwife, swiftly carried the child away. Deep in the woodlands, she raised the boy, teaching him all the physical arts. But Fionn accidentally killed his aunt. An enemy was pursuing them; Fionn picked up the aging athlete and ran as fast as he could—so fast that the wind he created tore the woman's body apart, leaving only her thighbones. The mourning Fionn planted these in the earth, where they formed Ireland's Loch Lurgann.

Lucina   The little red ladybug was the emblem of this Roman goddess, later merged with Juno and Diana, and even later converted to Christianity as St. Lucy. The early Italic Lucina was a goddess of light and therefore—because birth is the first time we see her—of labor and childbed as well. She was variously honored in September and in December— still the times for festivals of Lucina as the candlebearing saint; her holidays were enforced by the superstition that any work done on those days would be undone by the morrow.

Lueji   Among the Lunda and Bemba, Bantu-speaking peoples of Africa, this moon goddess is embodied in the black stork whose white underbelly looks like the moon when it flies during the night. She also represents a ritual object, the torch of life, which is lit at dawn after a night when young people have been initiated.

Luminu-Ut   The ancestor of humanity, among the people of the Minahassa peninsula in the South Pacific, was Luminu-Ut, a goddess born of rock sweat. She constructed the earth from a handful of soil foraged from primeval chaos; then she opened her legs to the wind and conceived a son. The boy, when grown, was sent off by his mother and instructed that his wife should be shorter than Luminu-Ut's staff. The son circled the world but did not find a mate. When he returned to his starting point, Luminu-Ut had so shrunk with age that she fit her own description. The son did not recognize Luminu-Ut and had intercourse with her, and she gave birth to all the gods.

Luonnotar   The "daughter of nature," Finnish myth recalls, floated in the sky for serene ages, content and virginal. Eventually, however, Luonnotar grew lonely and threw herself into the ocean. For seven centuries, she floated there.

One day, as Luonnotar rested near the turbulent surface of the water, another creature appeared—a duck, seeking a place to nest. Luonnotar's knee was breaking through the water; the duck, seeing this, built a nest on it and laid her eggs. But Luonnotar could not remain still long enough for the eggs to hatch. After three days, she felt a cramp in her legs and suddenly twisted involuntarily so that the eggs fell into the primeval slime.

There the eggs were transformed into the universe: the lower part into the earth, the upper part into the overarching sky, the yolk into the sun, the white into the moon. Luonnotar afterward took a hand in the emerging creation, forming islands and peninsulas, building the earth.

Luot-Hozjit The reindeer virgin of the Russian Saami was a friend to humanity who watched the roaming cattle in the summer forests. Although a wild spirit, she cooperated with human hunters in locating untamed reindeer herds. Luot-Hozjit was said to look just like a human girl, except that she was covered with reindeer fur.

Lupa This is the name given to the wolf who nursed Romulus and Remus, the legendary founders of Rome. Other myths name Acca Larentia as the nursing wolf. As she was a deified courtesan, and Lupa's name was applied as slang to prostitutes, they may have originally been the same goddess.

Lysippe In a Greek legend of Amazonia, this queen had a lovely young son, Tanais, who found no woman so beautiful as his mother. Some say he drowned himself in despair at his hopeless love, while others say that death was accidental. In either case, Lysippe lost her sorrow in work consolidating her queendom, building the city of Themiscyra and raising temples to Artemis with the spoils of her many victories. "She who looses the horses" led a force of women (for by law her men lived at home and kept house, contrary to tales that all Amazons lived without men); those ancient warriors were the first to use cavalry in battle. Dressed in wild animal skins and bearing brass bows, Lysippe's warriors expanded her empire throughout Asia Minor. Even after Lysippe was slain in battle, her Amazons advanced under the leadership of Marpesia and other renowned generals.

Lyssa "Canine madness" was the name of this Greek underworld goddess, who drove her dogs through the world, spurring the divine intoxication of the Maenads to destructive fury.

Maat The Egyptian goddess of truth, she took the form of an ostrich feather on the underworld balancing scales, opposite a recently dead person's heart. If the dishes balanced—if the heart of the deceased was light with justice—the judge, Osiris, said, "Let the deceased depart victorious. Let her go wherever she wishes to mingle freely with the gods and spirits of the dead." Alas for the soul if the dishes did not balance, for the heart heavy with evil was instantly eaten by the monstrous goddess Ahemait. Sometimes divided into two identical goddesses, Maat had no temples but was worshiped in the rhythm of truth, wherever it was perceived.

Mabb A close relative in Celtic Wales of the Irish warrior Maeve, Mabb descended into English fairy lore as a nightmare-bringing little sprite described by Shakespeare at length in *Romeo and Juliet* as Queen Mab, "the fairies' midwife."

Macaria The "blessed one" was the only daughter of the champion Heracles and the warrior woman, Dejanira. During a siege of Athens, an oracle announced that the city would be overrun unless a child of Heracles should die; to save her home, Macaria committed suicide. The city saved, a spring was named in Macaria's honor.

Macha Like many other Celtic goddesses, the Irish Macha was threefold: athlete, queen, and warrior, called "Macha, wife of Nemed; Macha, wife of Cruchchu; and Macha the Red" to distinguish the legendary exploits of the goddess' different aspects.

The most famous Macha, "the sun of women," was a magnificently beautiful queen of northern Ireland. She lived with a Nemed, a mortal king, and became pregnant with his twins. When he proudly boasted that the goddess could outrun any horse, Macha warned him against such arrogance. Ignoring her, he entered Macha in a horse race, winning his point when the hugely pregnant goddess handily won. But at the finish line Macha gave birth to twins, then died—for Irish goddesses were not immune to death. As she did so, she cursed her husband's people.

This "curse of Macha" figured importantly in Irish legend. Because of her humiliation, the goddess caused all Ulster men to be stricken in time of danger with labor pains lasting five days and four nights. Only one man, the hero Cuchulain, was immune to the curse.

Some legends said that Macha was a form of the Morrigan or of Badb, both war goddesses. Like Badb, Macha took the form of a hooded crow; conversely, her three aspects were similar to the threefold Morrigan. As an independent figure, Macha especially ruled the *mesred machae*, the pillars on which, following Celtic tradition, the severed heads of those who died in battle were displayed.

Macris   The daughter of Autonoe, she helped raise the infant wine god Dionysus in a cave where she spoonfed him with honey.

Madder-Akka   The Saami birth goddess had three daughters: Sar-Akka, Juks-Akka and Uks-Akka, a trinity of fate goddesses who lived with their mother beneath the earth's surface. While Madder-Akka had general control of fertility, her daughters were more directly involved with human reproduction. Sar-Akka opened the womb; as magical assistance for her, wood was chopped outside the birthing tent so that the woman's flesh would divide as neatly as cleft wood. The new mother also drank brandy in Sar-Akka's honor before giving birth; afterward, her first meal was of Sar-Akka porridge, in which three magical sticks had been cooked. Whether you found the white one (good luck), the black one (death), or the cleft one (success) was important in determining how Sar-Akka saw the child's future.

Juks-Akka ("old lady of the bow") was also honored in the porridge ceremony; if the newborn were a boy, she assured him successful hunting, provided a tiny bow was placed in the porridge and fished out by one of the diners. The third sister, Uks-Akka ("old lady of the door"), was charged with receiving the newborn into the world of light. She, however, was said to live away from daylight, just beneath the tent's entry. There she blessed and protected anyone leaving home, just as she protected those crossing out of the womb into daylight.

Ma-Emma   The Estonian earth mother was one of the great deities of that Baltic people, reverenced wherever an old tree stood alone in a meadow or where a pile of stones marked the foundation of a long since burnt-down house. Because Ma-Emma controlled all the earth's creatures, human beings depended on her for food; in thanksgiving for what she offered, they returned to her the first fruits of milk, butter and wool.

One of her favorite feast days was midsummer, when fires were lit in celebration of her fruitfulness. Animals were herded around these fires so the sacrificial smoke could bless them for the year. Flowers and grasses, carried through the smoke by children, were fed to the cattle. The evening ended when the village's most distinguished woman led three processions around the fire, then placed food on the earth, thanking Ma-Emma with these words: "Mother, you gave to me, now I give to you. Accept from me what I have accepted from you."

Maenads   The ecstatic worship that overtook the women of Greece, descending from wild Thrace in the eighth century B.C.E., is still the subject of scholarly conjecture. What was this mania, this religion of madwomen? Was it transcendent or pathological? The women in question followed the wine god Dionysus. A latecomer to the Olympian pantheon, he was born of Zeus and Semele. Hidden from other gods, Dionysus grew to young manhood nursed only by women, then began his triumphal procession across Greece. With him came the intoxication of unity with the divine, as well as throngs of women, entranced and transformed by communion with the spirit he represented.

They gathered, these Maenads, dressed in wild animal skins, bearing ivy-wreathed staffs of fennel, erecting altars in the wilderness to their god. And they flung themselves into their religion with such fury that it often seemed terrifying to men—who were forbidden to witness, much less to join, their secret rites. The Maenads ran through forests and mountains, heads flung back and hair unbound, in a strange wild dance accompanied by flutes, drums, and tambourines. Sometimes they hunted, killing with bare hands and devouring raw flesh in a primal communion, drinking warm blood to sustain themselves in their sleepless rituals.

An intruder on these secret festivals was subject to terrible punishment, for it was sacrilege to spy on women transformed by "the rage" or mania of their ecstasy. Many are the stories of men who, like Agave's son, Pentheus of Thebes, ignored these strictures and met death; there are stories as well of women who mocked the sacred religion of "the women's Zeus," as Dionysus was called, and who were driven mad in punishment. Attempts to jeer at or persecute the religion out of existence failed, and the ritual procession marched triumphantly through Greece, with Dionysus recognized as a full-fledged god by the seventh century B.C.E.

The maenads were members of a women's religious cult of ancient Greece. They were frequently depicted on red-figured kraters such as this one, found in Southern Italy and dated to the fourth century B.C.E.

At the head of his women he paraded, this intoxicated god, clad in women's robes, beautiful to see. Perhaps Dionysus was once "the shoot" (the meaning of one of his names), a god of vegetation destined to be destroyed as a human symbol of growth and death. According to this interpretation, the Maenads embodied the goddess of life and death, the nurse of life and then its devourer.

Not all women participated in the all-night wilderness revels, but it was said that all Greek women honored the rights of their sisters who chose this magical, dangerous form of worship. Once, it was said, the Maenads descended to their village from the mountains where they'd spent the night running beneath the moon. They collapsed beside the central fountain, unable to drag themselves to their homes. When they awoke, they saw ringed about them, silently holding hands, all the town's matrons, solemnly guarding their sisters from assault.

Scholars of religion offer various and conflicting interpretations of the motivations that drove the Maenads wild. Some agree with the nineteenth-century theorist Bachofen that the women were possessed, insane, or criminal. Others suggest that the oppression under which Greek women lived was such that their anger erupted in occasional furious orgies; Philip Slater suggests that the killing of boy children was a direct attack on the children's fathers. Still others believe the Dionysian religion to have been an essentially female form of spirituality, a chance for women to enact the divine and horrible roles of goddesses.

Eventually the Dionysian religion suffered the same fate as the other woman-centered religions of the ancient Aegean: it was reinterpreted by men and taken from the hands of the original priestesses. The singer Orpheus, urging men to refuse women's lusts and find contentment with other men, created a substitute religion for Greece. Though the singer himself was torn to death by Maenads seeking to preserve their religious independence, there was no stopping the singing of Orpheus' head or the progress of the Orphic religion.

Maeve   Of the great female figures of Ireland, Maeve was probably the most splendid. Originally a goddess of the land's sovereignty and of its mystic center at Tara, she was demoted in myth, as the centuries went on and Irish culture changed under Christian influence, to a mere mortal queen.

But no mortal queen could have been like this one, this "intoxication" or "drunken woman" (variant meanings of her name), who ran faster than horses, slept with innumerable kings whom she then discarded, and wore live birds and animals across her shoulders and arms. If there ever was a woman named Maeve who reigned as queen of Ireland, it is probable that she was the namesake of the goddess; the goddess' legends may have attached themselves to a mortal bearer of her name.

Maeve is the central figure of the most important old Irish epic, the Tain Bo Cuillaigne, or Cattle Raid of Cooley. The story begins with Maeve, ruler of the Connaught wilderness in the Irish west, lying abed with her current consort, King Aillil. They compare possessions, Aillil attempting to prove he owns more than she does. Point for point, Maeve matches him. Finally, Aillil mentions a magical bull—and wins the argument, for Maeve has no such animal.

But she knows of one, the magic bull of Cooley in northern Eire. And so Maeve gathers her armies to steal it. She rides into battle in an open car, with four chariots surrounding her, for she is glamorously attired and does not wish to muddy her robes. She is a fierce opponent, laying waste the armies of the land, for no man could look on Maeve without falling down in a paroxysm of desire.

The armies of Ulster, stricken with the curse of the goddess Macha, fall down in labor pains upon the arrival of Queen Maeve's army in their land. Only the hero Cuchulain resists, killing Locha, Maeve's handmaiden, as well as many male heroes of Connaught. Maeve tries to buy victory with her "willing thighs," stops the battle whenever she is menstruating, and otherwise shows herself to be an unusual warrior. After much bloodshed, she does indeed win her bull—but it and Aillil's bull fling themselves upon each other, tear each other to bits, and die in the bloodiest anticlimax in world literature.

Mafdet   The Lady of the Castle of Life was an early (First Dynasty) Egyptian goddess whose totemic animals were the cat (or its fiercer cousin, the lion) and the mongoose; she was invoked against snakebite.

Mahalat   In Jewish legend, Queen Mahalat commanded 478 bands of dancing demons. On the day of judgment, she will march them into the desert to meet her rival Lilith in fierce combat. Mahalat, a compulsive dancer, will whirl and gyrate in an attempt to terrify her enemy. Legend does not predict the outcome of the conflict.

Mahalbiya   The Hausa people of West Africa use this name for the spirit who causes tropical ulcers and skin diseases. When she possesses a dancer during ritual, that person can thereafter effect cures for her diseases.

Mahui-Iki   The underworld, the Polynesians said, was a fiery realm whose queen was Mahui-Iki. Her grandson was the trickster hero Maui, who one day decided to extinguish her power despite the warnings of his mother Taranga.

Maui traveled to Mahui-Iki's domain, where he found her stirring a cooking pot. Begging for help, Maui said he needed fire to cook some food. Mahui-Iki pulled out a fingernail and gave it to him; he secretly quenched the half-moon's fire. Then Maui asked for another, then another, until Mahui-Iki had given all her fingernails and nine of her toenails. Just as Maui was asking for her last toenail, Mahui-Iki's fury exploded and, pulling out the nail, she flung it on the earth, causing a massive fire. Maui called down rain from the heavens to extinguish the blaze, but what landed in the trees remained there, so that humans could thereafter kindle fire from wood.

Maia We derive the name of our most beautiful springtime month from this ancient goddess who appeared in both Greek and Roman legend. In Greece, she was "grandmother," "midwife," or "wise one" (variant meanings of her name). Originally the goddess of the night sky, later the oldest of the Pleiades, Maia survives in name only, for all of her myth is lost except for the mention of her as mother of the phallic god Hermes. The Romans identified the Greek Maia with their fire goddess of the same name who, with Flora and Feronia, ruled the forces of growth and warmth, including sexual heat. Maia's festival was held on the first day of her month, a rite that still survives in the Christian dedication of May to Mary, queen of flowers.

Maitreya This divinity of Indian and Tibetan Buddhism appears sometimes as male, sometimes as female. Sex changes in divinities may indicate that a force is seen as essentially non-sexual; the changing sexual identity alerts the viewer not to limit the divine essence to its human form. This seems to be the case with Maitreya. In other cases, however, as with Amaterasu in Japan and the Dactyls in Greece, sex change comes with political or social change; a powerful goddess transmuted into a god can indicate that the power represented by that divinity has been transferred from human women to men.

Ma-Ku Chinese maiden goddess of springtime.

Mal The crone goddess of Hag's Head, the most famous of the Cliffs of Moher in Ireland's far west, she was an overeager lover who died pursuing a much younger man along the Irish coast. The village of Miltown Malbay was named for her.

Mala Liath "Gray eyebrows" was the name given to the Cailleach in Ross and Cromarty in Scotland. She was said to tend a herd of pigs, which included the wild boar of Glen Glass.

Malika Habashiya The great mythic queen of Ethiopia who bore this name dreamed that she was holding a baby goat; when she awoke, she discovered she was pregnant. A daughter was born—a

The Chinese goddess Ma Ku, the spirit of springtime, appears here in a bronze figurine from the Ming period (1368–1643 C.E.).

perfect child, except for her one goat's foot. There were no other children, so when Malika Habashiya died, the goat-foot princess inherited the throne. This daughter traveled to the court of the wise Solomon, hoping to be healed of her deformity; indeed she was, and was revealed as such a beauty that Solomon himself desired her. A night of love left her pregnant, but she returned to her own domain. Many years later, her son David traveled to Solomon's court to claim his inheritance. Solomon gave him all of Africa, and since then the Ethiopian kings have been called "Lions of Judah."

Mama   The great smallpox goddess of Korea leaves spirit footprints, which appear as little pimples, on the bodies of those she visits. If children talk while in the grip of fever, it is believed to be her voice. The ritual to send away Mama begins five days after infection, when the poxes appear; clean drinking water ritually welcomes the spirit of Mama. Conducted by a woman shaman, the ceremony is called *Skimun* ("gate of sickness") This preventive rite continues through the twelfth day, when the patient is no longer in danger; then Mama is sent away on a mugwort mount. Called *Sangma*, it is made of three pieces of mugwort formed into a horse and saddled with baskets of steamed rice, cakes and money.

Mama Cocha   The eldest divinity of ancient Peru was the ocean ("Mother Sea"), worshiped not only by the Inca but by all the tribes of South America's Pacific Coast. Mountain dwellers would regularly descend to her, carrying their infants, for Mama Cocha was the source of health. Indeed, as the fish provider, the whale goddess, Mama Cocha was also the source of all food.

Mama Ocllo   When the Spanish invaded South America, they found a variety of names given to the foremothers of their race by the Incas. There were four—or six—of them, and they bore the names of Mama Ocllo or Mama Ocllo Huaca, Mama Huaco, Mama Coya, and Mama Rahua; or Topa Huaco, Mama Coya, Cori Ocllo, and Ipa

Huaco. Coming, with their brothers, into time at the creation, these women populated the world.

Of Mama Ocllo, it was said that she was the most intelligent sister and that she found inhabitable land for the group by scouting until she came to where the city of Cuzco rose. She killed a passing Poque Indian, cut his chest open, and removed his lungs. Carrying the bloody organs in her mouth, Mama Ocllo entered the area's impoverished towns. The residents, terrified at this murderous apparition, instantly fled, leaving the region to the people of Mama Ocllo.

Mama Quilla   In ancient Peru, this was the name of the moon goddess, imagined as a silver disk with a woman's face. "Mother Moon" was honored at regular calendar-fixed rituals, especially held during eclipses, when a supernatural jaguar attempted to devour her.

Maman Brigitte   A *loa* (spirit) of death in Haitian voudoun, she owns all cemeteries, particularly those in which the first body interred was a woman. Her children are the spirits who outline, dig, and mark graves.

Mamapacha   Among the Inca of South America, the earth was seen as a dragon goddess who lived beneath the mountains; occasionally she quivered, sending earthquakes through the world. Mamapacha was also the deity of agriculture; rituals in her honor had to be performed daily to assure a sufficient food supply. During planting and harvest, women would travel to the fields to talk softly to Mamapacha, sometimes pouring a thank-offering of cornmeal on her surface.

Mami   Just as the Hebrew creation legend described humankind's creation from the earth's clay, so did other myths of the ancient eastern Mediterranean. The Sumerians, for instance, had a myth that sounds like that in Genesis—except that they believed the creator was not a god but the almighty All-Mother Mami, the lapis-crowned ruler of earth.

A potter, the goddess mixed clay over the cosmic abyss to form fourteen images of herself, placing them in two rows, seven on her right hand and seven on her left. Between the rows, Mami set a baked brick. She uttered life-giving incantations over the clay images, and they sprang to life: those on her right hand as men, those on her left as women, both in the goddess' image, hence her titles Nindum ("lady of procreation") and, in Sumerian, Ninmah ("lady mother").

Delighted with her creations, Mami called together the other gods for a celebration. It was not long before the goddess, now drunk, began playing with the remnant clay of creation. In her intoxication, she created barren women, eunuchs, and four other unrecorded human types. This excited Enki, the god of wisdom, who decided to display his creativity. He was too drunk: up from the ground wobbled a crippled, retarded man. Horrified at the creature, Enki begged Mami to correct it, but the creator goddess had no power to change what already existed.

Mami's symbolic brick was a pillow to Sumerian women as in labor they partook of the All-Mother's power. They also called her name during childbirth; she was especially kind to those birthing second children. Any woman's work was an image of the mother's creativity; when men served her, they did so as eunuchs who danced in wild ecstasy to trumpet and tambourine, wounding themselves in Mami's honor.

As Mami's worship traveled across the Mediterranean, she became less and less a gentle earth mother, more and more a warrior goddess of private property, protector of rich fields. As owner of the earth, she demanded that a corner of every tilled field be left wild in her honor; if this were done, she would protect the entire holding against bad crops and covetous neighbors. In these later times, Mami was portrayed standing or riding on fierce lions, bejeweled with the riches of her people. By the time she reached Rome, she was the image of that people's warrior, Bellona, and so the gentle earth mother of the East passed into Western history as Mah-Bellona.

Mamitu The Chaldean divine ancestor responsible for all that happens to her descendants, this destiny goddess is a sort of deified chromosome.

Maneca In Colombia and eastern Venezuela, this mother goddess had a miraculous single teat that gave as much milk as a mortal mother's pair.

Mania We use the name of this Roman goddess to describe an obsession, possibly a reminder of the days when her children, the Manes, came back after death to drive the living mad. Mania was the mother of ghosts, who were penned in Rome's center, in a deep well capped with a stone that was removed several times annually. Those nights as the dead roamed the streets in search of victims, woolen effigies were hung on doorposts, one for every free person in the house, a different style of doll for every slave—all in the hope that Mania's hosts would leave the house in peace.

Manto We still call prophetic words *mantic speech* after the name of this Greek heroine, daughter of the seer Tiresias and herself a gifted prophet. A Theban woman, she was captured by the people of Argos who, impressed with her gifts, carried her off to become oracle at Delphi.

Marcassa The legend of this princess of Brittany is filled with mythic overtones, suggesting that she is a diminished goddess figure, possibly a sun goddess like Dia Griene, whose myth is similar. The story starts when a king was found to be ill with a sickness that could only be cured by a magical bird. But the bird was in a cage in an inaccessible castle, behind a courtyard of giants, which was behind a courtyard of tigers, which in turn was behind a courtyard of poisonous snakes. The hero survived and found not only the bird but Marcassa, a princess beautiful as dawn, asleep on a purple bed. Escaping with both the princess and the magical bird, he returned to his king—only to discover that it was Marcassa's power, not the bird's, which was necessary to effect the cure.

Marcia Proba   A legendary Celtic queen of Britain, she ruled in the third century B.C.E. Her people's law, notably fair in its treatment of women, was inscribed into the Marcian Statutes; the same law in Ireland became the Brehon Laws, which provided legal equity for ancient Irish women. Many provisions of the Marcian Statutes became part of the later Magna Charta, although the legal equality of the sexes was virtually ignored.

Mardeq Avalon   The wind goddess of the Cheremis of Russia was worshiped in sacred groves that included both oak and birch. Eighth in order of precedence among divinities, she was honored even more than the earth goddess.

Maria   In Lithuania and Latvia, this Christian name was used to disguise goddess imagery. It is thought that the goddess who most frequently hid behind this title was Perkuna Tete, mother of thunder and lightning.

Mari-Ama   This Scandinavian goddess was invoked as "Mother Death" by her people, who depicted her with four hands holding in turn a trident, a skull, a rope, and a drum.

Marici   This Tantric Buddhist goddess, connected with the sun, was masculinized in China and Japan.

Marinette   A powerful *loa* (spirit), Marinette "of the dry arms" is a screech-owl sorceress who, when she possesses Haitian voudoun worshipers, causes them to move their arms like wings and hook their fingers into claws. Like Hecate among the Greeks, Marinette is a night goddess who searches the woodlands for offerings left for her. Special services in her honor are held far out in the country, under a tent beside a huge fire fueled with salt and oil, where chickens, pigs, and goats are sacrificed.

Marpesia   One of the great Amazon military queens, she began her victorious campaign at the Black Sea, the Greeks tell us, and soon conquered Thrace and Syria. Then, with Queen Hippo, she marched through Ephesus and Cyrene, finally reaching the Aegean Sea. Marpesia settled back to rule her empire. But she was called back to the battlefield to defend it, losing her life putting down an uprising of her subjects.

Marpessa   Homer called this Greek heroine, the lover of the mortal Idas, the "fair-ankled daughter." When the immortal Apollo tried to rape her, Marpessa appealed to Zeus for aid. He gave her a choice of mates: the god or the man. Not surprisingly, she chose Idas rather than her assailant.

Maruwa   Among the Wachanga and Chaga of Kenya, this ancient story is told: Maruwa and her little sister were set to guard the family bean garden. Thirsty, Maruwa walked to a nearby pond for a drink, leaving her sister to watch the beans. While Maruwa was gone, a baboon troop descended and devoured the entire crop in front of the frightened little girl.

Maruwa, ashamed of losing her family's food supply, threw herself into the pond. Sinking to the bottom, she found a village where she was welcomed and given hospitality. Wise in the ways of spirit people, Maruwa refused to eat their food, claiming that people above the waters lived on bitter foods, unlike the tasty meals served beneath.

The old woman whom Maruwa was staying with gave her daily instructions, which she disobeyed every day. This drew a little girl to her; she told Maruwa to ask to go home, and then to obey the old woman's orders. The old woman told Maruwa to jump into a pile of manure. She did, and instantly she found herself at home, covered with silver chains and expensive beads.

Another village girl, envious of Maruwa's new wealth, imitated her actions. When she arrived beneath the waters, she followed the old woman's orders to the letter—including leaving all the housework to Maruwa's helper, the little under-water girl. This child told the visitor to ask to go home, but reversed the advice she'd given Maruwa. The girl returned home, indeed, but full of poisonous fire that drove her to drown herself in waters that remain bitter to this day.

Mary There is a time-honored tradition among goddesses: people never truly give up the ones they love and worship. So, when the early Europeans were slowly Christianized as Roman imperial power grew, they faced conversion—often forcible—to a faith that denied a major portion of their traditional beliefs.

What Christianity denied was the possibility of divine femininity, that force worshiped in ancient Europe as Epona, Freya, Hertha, Mokosh, and under countless other names. More than just a nominal change was entailed when the utterly non-feminine Christian theology was introduced to these goddesses' devotees. Christianity provided no image of the mother goddess to substitute for the ones they revered so highly.

It was not long, however, before the people located within Christian mythology a female figure that could serve quite adequately. The Virgin Mary, daughter of the grandmotherly Anna, lost and regained her divine son. Once elevated to queen of heaven, she had all the necessary qualifications. Try as the church might, it could not stop the spread of Mariolatry, an extreme reverence toward the power of the Mother of God.

Many scholars have traced the spread of the Marian devotions; some contend that from the first, Christianity contained female-oriented rituals which, like the all-women feasts of the Roman Bona Dea, honored the mother above the son. Whether or not that was so, the excesses of Mary's devoted followers brought warning after warning from church officials that she was not a goddess—despite bearing all the titles and attributes of one. Even today, long after other goddesses have been forgotten, Mary remains a threat to patriarchal Christianity; the greater proportion of churches

This fabulous copper sculpture shows the Tibetan goddess Marici with three heads (one of them a pig's), riding in a chariot drawn by nine tiny pigs.

are dedicated to her, not her son, and she is the one to whom many Catholics prefer to address their prayers.

Mary Magdalene There are several Marys in the Christian scripture, several of which have been combined to form the quasi-mythic character called Mary Magdalene. A woman of that name does appear in the stories of Jesus Christ, but she is not identified as a prostitute. Yet the need to balance the motherly but sexless female imagery that Christianity offered seems to have led to the evolution of this figure who is the Virgin Mary's opposite: a woman with sexual experience but no children.

Apocryphal legends abound regarding this woman, supposedly a prostitute who reformed under the influence of Jesus. But according to some of the more extreme forms of the legend, her reform did not take the form of celibacy. Rather, she became Jesus' wife or his mistress; she bore his child, either before or after his crucifixion. One sequence of myths brings her to France, where she raised Jesus' son to become the ancestor of the French royalty; sometimes Jesus accompanied her on this emigration. In other versions of the Magdalene story, the converted woman lived out her life on the desert as an anchorite or hermit.

Marzana This was the Polish name for the goddess of winter and death, called Marena in Russia. Each spring an effigy of "Old Woman Winter" was carried through the village and thrown, amid rejoicing, out of town.

Masaya The ancient Nicaraguan goddess of volcanoes and earthquakes was the source of oracles; she was described as having black skin, thinning hair, and long, sagging breasts.

Matergabiae "Womanfire" was the Lithuanian household goddess. To her the house mistress offered the first loaf from each bread-baking; ornamental markings were molded into the dough with the fingers to designate the loaf as belonging to the goddess, a custom still used by some Lithuanian women. The last loaf was offered to the baker herself, as a representative of the goddess; she ate it at her pleasure as a communion with her productive energies.

Mater Matuta To the Romans, Dawn was not the reckless, lustful goddess that many other people saw. Instead, she was a matron, the mother bringing day to her frightened children. They worshiped her in a touching ceremony on July 11, when women held their sisters' children in their arms and begged Dawn's blessings for them. At the same rite, the Matralia, the women drove from the temple a slavewoman who symbolized night, thereby incarnating their divinity's own activity in human form.

Mati It was a grave sin in the Slavic culture to strike the earth with iron implements before March 25. Mati ("Mother Earth") was pregnant until that time, and one does not strike a pregnant woman. Mati's full name was Mati Syra Zemlja ("moist Mother Earth"), and she was the great source of power and strength to her people. When they swore oaths, they did so by eating soil or placing lumps of dirt on their head; when they married, each party swallowed a bit of earth.

Among the Russians, who also honored Mati as supreme, her prophetic powers were acknowledged; to know how the harvest would turn out, you only had to dig a hole in the ground and place your ear to it. The sound of a full sleigh meant a good harvest; the tinkling of an empty one meant trouble ahead. The Russians also cared for their Mother's honor by demanding that anyone who spit on her apologize immediately.

Matronit In the Kabbala's esoteric Judaism, we find two demi-goddesses formed by analyzing the mystic name of god, YHWH. Each letter was given a human character: thus, the *Y* of Yahweh became the Father and the first *H* the Mother, who proceeded from the Father. These two produced *W*, the Son, the King, and finally a second *H*, the blameless Daughter, the essence of kingship, Makhut or the Matronit.

However abstract the analysis that produced her, the Matronit soon became a livelier personage than uplifting allegory should permit. The lowest of the ten mystic emanations of the male godhead, she was the one that human senses could perceive. Jacob, for instance, perceived her, as did Moses. She not only took the latter's soul to heaven when he died, but she apparently took human form in order to sleep with him. But her usual lover was her brother, the king, with whom she regularly cohabited in the temple on Friday nights. (Jewish couples were encouraged to have intercourse then, in emulation of the sacred couple.)

Whenever the children of Israel fell into sin, however, the Matronit and her king were separated; the king mated instead with Lilith while the demon king Samael was allowed to have intercourse with the pristine Matronit. All this—even read as allegory—is rather seamy and melodramatic material; it seems that Judaism, in denying the possibility of female divinity, left itself open to this kind of overblown and seductive quasi-mythology.

Mawu The creator goddess of Benin in northwest Africa, Mawu not only made the earth but created human beings as well. At first she used clay mixed with water, but running short of materials, Mawu began to enliven the bodies of dead people, which explains why people sometimes look like their forebearers.

But her experiment was not entirely successful, for humanity began to grow arrogant. Annoyed with her earthly creation, Mawu retreated to her home in the sky. Things did not go well on earth after her departure, so Mawu sent her son Lisa to teach useful arts to humanity, then instructed him to watch the people each day to ensure obedience to her rules. Because Lisa was sometimes identified with the sun and because of the proverb "When Lisa punishes, Mawu forgives," the goddess was sometimes assumed to be a moon spirit.

Maya Like Shakti ("energy") and Prakriti ("nature"), Maya is less a goddess than one of the great philosophic concepts of Indian Hinduism embodied in female form. In Hindu thought, the male energy is essentially passive, while the female is the force of action. Maya is one of those active powers: the constant movement of the universe, pervasive to the atomic level. There is no life—no existence, even—without Maya, but she is so powerful that we cannot see the essence of things, and mistake her movements for reality. For this reason, Maya is often called "the veil of illusion," the dance of multiplicity that distracts us so that we cannot see all matter as essentially identical. Illusion, however—as the sages have stressed—is not the same as falsehood. Maya is not a negative force, but can be a mesh through which we perceive the ultimate reality of existence—if we are not distracted by her magnificent creativity and complexity.

Mayahuel There were two major myths told by the ancient Mexicans of the goddess whose name means the "strangling one," ruler of the earth and the night sky as well as of hallucinations and drunkenness. The 400-breasted goddess was said to nurse the stars, who were fish in the oceanic heaven; in art Mayahuel was shown sitting naked on a throne of tortoises and snakes, offering a dish of intoxicating pulque to her worshipers.

The Nahua, who lived in central Mexico before and after the Aztec, said that Mayahuel originally lived in the heavens, where she slept continuously, guarded by the stern goddess Tzitzimitl. But the god of winds blew across her, caressing and arousing her until she awoke. To consummate their desire, they descended to earth where, as soon as their feet touched the ground, they melted together into a beautiful tree with two branches—one of which, the goddess, instantly flowered.

But the chaperone Tzitzimitl, who had been dozing, awoke to find the maiden goddess gone. Furious, she gathered an army of gods and started in pursuit. Finding the heavenly tree rooted in the earth's soil, she cursed the divinities it held. The tree cracked in two and Tzitzimitl fed the flowering branch to the young gods, who ate their former friend.

When the gods had departed, the wind god resumed his own shape and gathered the few bits and bones of his lover, burying them with care in the earth. There they sprouted into the maguey plant, which gives forth a winy sap that can be fermented into pulque, then distilled into mescal or tequila.

The other version of the story says that Mayahuel lived on earth as a peasant woman. One day she passed a merry mouse who not only refused to shy at her approach but actually danced and scurried about under her gaze. Mayahuel noticed that the rodent had been nibbling the maguey plant; she put a pot under the broken stem and caught some of the sap. This she took home with her, discovering the basis of intoxication, which she introduced to the gods. The gift was so popular that they welcomed her as one of them and her earthly husband as the god of gambling and of flowers.

Maya Owichapaha "She Who Pushes Them Over the Bank" is a Lakota goddess who lives in the southern part of the Milky Way. There she judges the souls of the dead; those who lived good lives she assists in their travel across the sky, but those who did evil, she pushes off the star-path into oblivion.

Mbaba Mwana Waresa The Zulu rain goddess fell in love with a mortal youth and wished to bring him to heaven. He seemed devoted to her, but she wished to test that devotion before giving herself to him fully. And so she dressed her maidservant as a bride, with beaded belts and copper bracelets; she braided the maid's hair with jewels and painted copper dye on her cheeks and lips. Then Mbaba shaved her own head, smeared her face with ashes, and donned a tattered zebra hide. On branched lightning, the two traveled to earth, where they found the goddess' intended worshiping at her shrine. Immediately he recognized Mbaba and, having won her trust, he was carried back to heaven to enjoy life with her

Mbombe Several goddesses in Zaire bear this name. One was the mother of all humans and animals; her eldest daughter, Nsongo, was the first human female born. The name is also given to a folklore heroine, the Elephant Girl, daughter of the thunder god. The hero Itonde fell desperately in love with Mbombe, but she refused to marry him unless he could best her in wrestling. After a fierce fight, she admitted his strength and agreed to be his wife. Her thunder father gave as dowry a magical catskin on which Mbombe flew through the air, together with her eighty servants, to the wedding.

Medea Without the aid of the "cunning one," the Greek hero Jason would have been unable to obtain the golden fleece from the kingdom of Colchis. The princess Medea, adept in magic, first led the Greek through dangers surrounding the well-guarded treasure; then she sailed off with him on his ship the *Argo*, bringing her brother with her so that, when pursued and in danger of

capture, she could kill him and cast him piecemeal overboard. The people of Colchis, stopping to catch for burial the pieces of their prince, let the Greeks escape.

When they reached Greece, however, all that she had done was forgotten. Medea found that nothing could hold the wandering attentions of Jason. Though Medea had borne him several children—fourteen, some sources say—he married again, a well-endowed princess. He seemed, however, to have forgotten the temperament of his first spouse, who promptly killed his children and new wife, mounted her serpent chariot, and flew away.

An ancient version of the tale says that Medea, far from slaying her offspring, placed them under the protection of Hera and left Jason's city. But a plague broke out, and the Corinthians killed the children as a sacrifice; thereafter they offered 14 children each year as servants to the goddess. In this version, Medea is not only connected with the goddess of womanhood, Hera, but is herself considered divine.

Jason ended poorly, wandering homeless through Greece until he wretchedly slumped beneath his old ship, the Argo, pitying himself and his aimless life. A piece of the rotting hulk suddenly detached itself and brained him.

Medea did better. Flying to Athens, she married King Aegeus. But she grew jealous of the attention he lavished on his son Theseus, whom he favored over Medea's son Medus. So she mounted her chariot again and flew home to the north, to Colchis, where she continued her magical practices until deciding to leave earth. So great a sorceress did not need to pass through death's portals; she went straight to the Elysian Fields, where she became a goddess, worshiped in Italy as the snake divinity Angitia.

Medusa Once she was a beautiful woman who took the sea god as a lover. Often Medusa would lie with Poseidon in the spring grass, the heavy fragrance of blossoming trees around them. But once, the Greeks said, the pair made their bed within a chapel of Athena. The offended goddess turned Medusa into a Gorgon, later engineering Medusa's murder.

As she died at the hand of Athena's servant, Medusa gave birth. From her neck sprang the magnificent winged Pegasus and the hero Chrysaor as well. Drops fell on the desert, and there engendered snakes. The Gorgon's remaining blood was caught in vials; it had such power that a single droplet from the left side could raise the dead, and the same tiny amount from the right could instantly kill. A lock of her hair was given to the champion Heracles, who hid it in an urn; while it did not have the power of her blood or her head, Heracles did find it useful for causing entire armies to be seized with inexplicable panic.

Behind this eerie figure seems to be an early goddess, possibly similar to the corn mother Demeter, also said to have mated in the form of a mare with Poseidon, a name that merely means "husband of earth." Medusa is also believed to derive from an Anatolian sun goddess. The fierce snake-haired head of late legend probably was originally the mask worn by priestesses when they impersonated the goddess; later peoples, not remembering the old rites, explained the image as a decapitated woman.

Her connection with Athena also bears consideration, for once her head had left her winged shoulders, Medusa was henceforth always seen mounted on the virgin goddess' aegis, her goatskin robe. The two goddesses become inseparable. Athena has other suspicious connections with the monster goddess: the snake that appears on Medusa's head accompanies Athena as well. A massive snake rose next to Athena's image in the Parthenon, and there is that illegitimate serpent son, embarrassing for a virgin goddess. And the connection may be even stronger, for a pithos from 700 B.C.E. shows a winged, enthroned goddess sitting calmly while another winged figure—helmeted and armed with spear—leaps from her

head. Medusa and Athena, far from being opposites, seem deeply intertwined.

Megaera This Greek word named the cleft in the earth into which sacrificial pigs were driven during the festival of Thesmophoria; the bodies of the sacred animals restored the fertility of the earth mother. Megaera ("anger") was also the name of one of the Erinyes and of the first wife of Heracles, whom he murdered and for whose death he was sentenced to perform twelve near-impossible tasks.

Mehurt The Egyptian goddess Neith as the sacred cow of creation, the mystic animal mother of the world. She was shown as a pregnant woman with

The head of Medusa was a favorite motif in art and architecture throughout Greece and Italy. A terra-cotta plaque from Capua, in Etruscan Italy, has been dated to 400–300 B.C.E. and shows the typical jutting tongue and flattened nose of the early Medusa. Later Roman art showed the goddess with eyes closed and snake hair writhing.

huge breasts, or as a cow-headed woman holding the lotus of the world.

Melanie Variants of this name, "dark one," have been given to several goddesses. Melaenis was a title of Aphrodite, given to her because she urged love-making when dusk arrived. Demeter was called

Melaina or Melantho in honor of the blackness of rich fertile soil. After Christianization of Europe, the name Melanie was given to girls in honor of the Black Madonna.

Melanippe The "black mare" was an illustrious Amazon warrior, one of three queens of the Thermodon empire. When the Greek hero Heracles sacked the Amazons' capital, he took Melanippe captive, but later released her when he acquired the women's most priceless treasure, their golden belt of sovereignty. In some legends, Melanippe accompanied the Amazon forces in their raids on Athens.

Mele On the Wallis Islands in the Pacific, a tale of survival and friendship is told about the heroine Mele. She was the daughter of a cannibal woman, Lona, who left the girl alone at home while she raged through the islands, swallowing people whole. Mele was lonely, but did not know any other way of life until she found another little girl, Pikipikilauifi, hiding in a tree. Still terrified by what she had witnessed, Pikipikilauifi told Mele that her entire family had been killed by a cannibal woman. Mele took Pikipikilauifi home and made her comfortable. But Lona, when she arrived, picked up and swallowed the girl. Mele, outraged at losing her first friend, forced her mother to vomit her up. Pikipikilauifi was thus saved, and the action killed Lona—thus saving the other islanders as well.

Meliae The Greek creation stories say that when Mother Gaia arranged the castration of her oppressive son-lover Uranus, drops of his blood fell on her fertile body. In those spots, Gaia conceived. Among her daughters by that strange and brutal mating were the ash-tree spirits called Meliae. The world's original women, they were mothers of humankind, for people rose from the earth at their roots.

Melissa This name, meaning "bee," was applied to the priestesses of the earth goddess Demeter and of Artemis of Ephesus. It was also said that one Melissa was a Cretan princess who learned to collect honey as food for the infant Zeus, who, when he grew into a supreme god, turned his nurse into a bee.

Mella Among the Buhera Ba Rowzi people of Zimbabwe, this heroine saved her father from a fatal illness with the help of the moon goddess Bomu Rambi, who told the despairing girl that, to gain a remedy, she had to travel to the home of the Python Healer. Despite the terror this creature evoked in human hearts—even Mella's own brothers had been frightened by it—the girl traveled many days to reach the cave where the snake lived. There she was challenged even more frighteningly, for the snake slithered forward and coiled itself around her body. She permitted it, and the snake asked to be taken to the sick man. Once there, the magical snake instantly cured Mella's father, then asked to be carried back to its cave. Mella did so and was instructed to enter. Inside, the girl found piles of jewels and treasure. The snake urged Mella to take a token, but she asked him to select something for her. His choice was appropriate: a necklace that depicted Bomu Rambi. When she returned wearing her magnificent trophy, Mella attracted her greedy brothers' attention. They determined to kill the snake and take its treasure. But Mella, grateful for the snake's healing power, warned it. The boys were banished for their greed, and Mella became the chief of the village.

Melusine In Celtic France they tell of a water spirit, Pressina, who married a mortal king but made him promise never to visit her when she was in childbed. But when their first children—the triplets Melusine, Meliot, and Palatina—were born, the king forgot himself and rushed in excitement into the queen's chambers. Angrily reminding her husband of his promise, Pressina gathered the children and disappeared to a miragelike coastal island.

There Pressina brought up her children. The oldest girl, Melusine, was infected by her mother's disappointment at the marriage's outcome. She organized her sisters for a magical raid on their father and encased him in a mountain, together with his castle and servants. Returning, they found their mother angry, for this revenge had gone too far. Pressina, unable to contain her vengefulness, cursed Melusine to become part serpent each Sunday.

Melusine wandered across the continent, hoping to find a man who would agree to a marriage contract with a "never on Sunday" clause. Finally she fell in love with Raymond of Poitou. They lived passionately together until Raymond grew curious about Melusine's prohibition and spied on his wife. She discovered the oath-breaking and fled from him, becoming a Bansheelike creature who afterward haunted his family.

Mem Loimis Among the Wintuns of the Pacific Coast, this underworld goddess controlled the earth's water supply.

Menalippe Because she could so accurately predict the future, the Greek gods hated this daughter of centaurs. So they sent the wind god Aeolus to rape her, then transformed her into a horse, the mare Ocyrrhoe.

Menat With Al-Lat and Al-Uzza, this goddess of fate and time was the third member of the ancient Arabian religious trinity. The three goddesses seem a single woman, passing through the three parts of her life: in youth, the virgin warrior Al-Uzza; in the prime of life, the fertile, benevolent Al-Lat; and as an aged woman, Menat, a force of fate and an embodiment of death.

The religion of Menat stretched across most of ancient Arabia. Her principal sanctuary was located on the road between Mecca and Medina, at the shrine of Kodail. There she was worshiped in the form of a black uncut stone, destroyed by Mohammed as he struggled to establish his own male-centered religion. Despite the destruction of her shrine, this goddess' worship long continued. But her people, impressed by the success of the masculine religions around them, changed Menat slightly: from a goddess into a god.

Meng-Jiang Jyu The Chinese folktale heroine of this name was born in a miraculous way. Two neighboring families, both of them childless, found a watermelon exactly halfway between their homes. Within it was this magical girl, whom the families decided to raise jointly. Meng-Jiang was a good girl who made both sets of parents happy. When she came to marry, she was lucky enough to find a young man in the village who cherished her. All went well until one summer day the emperor's soldiers came and, without giving him a choice, conscripted Meng-Jiang's husband to build the Great Wall.

Months passed and, worried that her husband would be cold without his winter clothes, Meng-Jiang set off to find him. She walked and walked, asking everyone for her lover, but each village sent her further. She almost drowned crossing the Yellow River, but the river god became sympathetic to her cause and saved her. Finally, she reached her destination, only to find that her beloved husband had died; his bones had been interred somewhere in the Wall. She cried out to heaven, and the Wall collapsed—revealing thousands of bones. How could she find her husband's? Recalling their vow to be blood of each other's blood, she bit herself and, bleeding, walked among the bones. Those of her husband's recognized and absorbed her blood, so she was able to give them a proper burial.

Menglod In Scandinavian mythic literature, this "sun-bright maiden" appears surrounded by a wall of flame from which a hero must rescue her. This peculiar entrapment was a frequent hazard to ancient Norse heroines, suggesting an emblematic meaning that has been lost, but may well connect women with fire and the sun.

Meng-Po Niang-Niang "Lady Meng" was said by the Chinese to live just inside the exit door of hell.

There she brewed a secret broth that, forcibly administered to those departing for a new incarnation, caused them to forget not only where they lived between lives but also their previous lives—and even the words of their last human language.

Mens "Menstruation" does not, as some women fear, include the English word for the other sex within it. Instead, it derives from the name of the Roman goddess of the "right moment."

Mentha The spirit of the mint plant was said to be the beloved of the Greek underworld ruler; she may have been an aspect of Hades' other "wife," the spring goddess Persephone.

Mera In southeast Asia, this celestial dancer or Apsara seduced a celibate ascetic; their descendants founded the land of Cambodia.

Mere-Ama The "sea mother" of the Finns and Saami was also called Vete-Ema or Mier-Iema, according to the language of her worshipers. But she was conceived identically by all of them: as the spirit of water. Her most powerful manifestation was the ocean, but she resided as well in streams and brooks.

At ceremonies in honor of this goddess of silky, silver-streaked hair, her people were sprinkled with water, an embodiment of Mere-Ama. When a bride moved into a new home to start a family, one of the first things she did was to make the acquaintance of the water mother of the area, walking to the stream nearest the new house and offering bread and cheese, or cloth and thread, to the goddess. The bride would then wash her face and hands, or at least sprinkle herself with water. Those married in winter, when Mere-Ama was distant beneath the ice, would gather after the ice broke up for a ceremony of friendliness; all who participated were blessed with healthy children, for the water mother controlled human, as well as animal and vegetative, reproduction.

Mere-Ama also ruled sea creatures, especially the fish her people depended on for food. To woo her good nature, humans only had to pour liquor into the sea; then many fish would bite when fishing began, for Mere-Ama loved brandy.

Meroe This Greek witch could lower the sky, extinguish the stars, raise the dead, and send the gods to hell. When angry, she could turn people into beavers, snakes, or rams; she also teleported them hundreds of miles from home. Whenever Meroe needed human blood, she simply selected someone, stole his heart, and substituted a sponge; the man died as the sponge drank his blood. Like other witches of Thessaly in the north of Greece, she was renowned for her magical craft.

Merope Of the seven starry sisters called the Pleiades, one of them—the shy sister or Lost Pleiad—is virtually invisible to stargazers. In Greek times, she was sometimes called Electra, crying for the loss of Troy. At other times, she was Merope, wife of the criminal king Sisyphus who stewed his children and was sentenced to eternal punishment; in embarrassment and shame, his star wife faded from human sight. The name Merope was also used of a victim of rape; Orion, her assailant, was blinded by Merope's father in retaliation.

Mertseger "Friend of silence," she lived on the pyramidal peak of the burial ground at Egyptian Thebes. Benevolent and punishing by turns, she was sometimes shown as a snake with three heads—one its own, one human, one that of a vulture—and sometimes as a snake with a human head.

Meskhoni Like the Sumerian Mami, this Egyptian birth goddess was symbolized by a brick, but a human-headed one in her case. On such a goddess image an Egyptian woman crouched during labor. Meskhoni appeared—usually in company with Ermutu—at the precise moment when contractions began and remained through the delivery to predict the future of the newborn. In

Egyptian bas-reliefs, Meskhoni appeared as a woman wearing palm shoots on her head.

Meta In Greek legend, she was the daughter of the mortal Erysichthon, whom Demeter afflicted with insatiable hunger. The sea god Poseidon, who desired Meta, offered her the power of metamorphosis in return for sexual favors. She concurred, and her father—discovering her new talent for shapeshifting—afterward regularly sold her in animal form at market, spent the money for food, then sold her again when she returned.

Meter The oldest of Greek goddesses, her name means simply "mother" and survives in that of Demeter ("corn mother" or "earth mother"). Statues of Meter were half-carved: the top a stately maternal figure, the lower half uncut rock.

Metis "Prudent counsel" was a Titan, daughter of the ocean queen of early Greece. When the new pantheon headed by Zeus arrived in her territory, Metis' priority was noted by the invaders, who named her as their sky god's first wife. They said that Metis told Zeus what emetic would make his father, Cronos, disgorge the other gods; ironically, Zeus later swallowed Metis. Afraid—as his own father, Cronos, had been—of being surpassed by his offspring, Zeus devoured his pregnant spouse and gave birth to her daughter Athena through his head. This legend is a pastiche of elements from different tribal myths and eras, consistent only in its attempt to disguise the early mother-oriented religion, of which both Metis and Athena seem to have been part—a legend that is less a true myth than what Jane Ellen Harrison called a "theological expedient," for art showing Athena being born from a goddess' head exist to dispute the father-birth story.

Metsannetsyt Among the people of western Finland, this forest woman was said to live in the woods where she exposed herself to passing men, hoping to seduce them. However, if they were to take her in their arms, they would find themselves embracing a tree stump.

Mictecacihuatl In pre-Columbian Mexico, this goddess ruled the nine rivers of the afterlife to which evil souls were condemned. There, however, they did not suffer torments or pain; instead, they led afterlives of boredom and monotony, while better souls enjoyed the colorful existence of heaven.

Mielikki The Finnish Kalevala, the epic poem of that northern land, names Mielikki as the goddess of forests, protector of animals, and goddess of the hunt. Her favorite animal was the bear-cub; when she found orphaned cubs, she nurtured them herself into adulthood. She is associated with the tradition of placing a bear skull in the forest as an offering.

Milda The Lithuanian goddess of love especially favored those who sang silly love songs to her, bringing them very good luck with matters of the heart.

Minachiamman Local goddess of Madura in India, she incarnated as a little girl to revenge herself on a king who dared to close her temples. She appeared miraculously in the palace, wearing a tiny bracelet that duplicated a favorite diadem of the queen's. Astrologers warned the king not to adopt the babe, so he cast Minachiamman into the river from which a merchant plucked her. He raised her to be a fine young woman, who attracted the eye of Shiva, incarnated as a poor man in a village on the River Kaveri. They were so poor that Shiva took the bracelet from his wife's arm and attempted to sell it. But, alas, he was accused of stealing the queen's jewel and was put to death. The goddess, taking her demon form, under which she was called Thurgai, immediately killed the king in retaliation.

Mindhal In India's Himachal Pradesh, this was the name given to a goddess who emerged from the ground in the form of a huge black stone. The woman from whose yard Mindhal issued tried to push the stone back into the earth by pounding on it, but to no avail. Converted to awareness of the goddess' power, the woman tried to convert her friends. When they laughed, she transformed herself and her seven sons into standing stones around Mindhal's image.

Minerva   Familiar though her name is, the origin and descent of this Roman goddess are vague. Some scholars claim the figure of Minerva fused Etruscan and Italian deities of handicrafts and war, respectively; some claim she was always the artisans' patron and that the imposition of the Greek figure Athena on her meant the addition of war to her domain. (The Latins already had a proper war goddess, Bellona.)

It is clear that the goddess' name derives from the ancient root for "mind," and her domain was—even more than Athena's—intellectual. She was wisdom incarnate in female form, the goddess therefore of the application of intellect to everyday work, thus of commerce and crafts. She was also said to be the inventor of music, that most mathematical of arts, as well as the instruments on which it is played.

The Romans celebrated her worship from March 19 to 23 during the Quinquatrus, the artisans' holiday which was also a festival of purification. The "goddess of a thousand works," as Ovid called her, was pleased to see scholars and schoolmasters join in spring vacation with those who labored with their hands.

Minerva Medica   If her name seems Roman, it is only because of the imperial legions' policy of *interpretatio Romano* whereby Celtic goddesses were assimilated to those from their homeland. Many local and tribal goddesses lost their identities this way; many became Minervas, perhaps because they were originally connected with household industry, war, or healing—all of which fell under the dominion of the Italian original. At least one "Minerva"—Sul of Bath in England—

was strong enough to resist renaming; she became Sulis Minerva.

Min Mahagiri   This feminine spirit or nat in Burma lived outdoors, high in the mountains; when lured indoors to become a protective spirit, she sought similar places and made her headquarters on the highest point of an interior post.

Miriam   The greatest woman prophet of Jewish tradition, she began to foretell the future at the age of five, at which time she also began working with her mother, Jocebed, as a midwife. She foresaw the birth of her brother Moses, and it was Miriam who knew the babe could be saved from death if placed in a reedy basket and hidden in a river. Her prophetic gift was matched by her genius for poetry; it was Miriam's song that celebrated the Hebrew escape from Egypt's pharaoh.

Like many prophetic females, Miriam was associated with water. Her name seems to be derived from *marah*, the "bitter water," and she sang her most famous poem after crossing the Red Sea. Most important, she gave her name to the miraculous spring that burst forth from the desert rock struck by Moses; Jewish legend says that it was an ancient spring, brought into existence at twilight of creation's sixth day and rediscovered by Miriam.

But even a great woman prophet and poet can overreach herself in a patriarchal society. Miriam did so by siding with her sister-in-law Zipporah when the latter complained that Moses' divine revelations had led to his abandoning conjugal duties. (Miriam herself continued to cohabit frequently with her husband, leaving her inspirational work outside the bedroom.) Jehovah, furious at Miriam's condemnation of Moses, spit in her face, and the poet grew leprous. But the father god then cured her, demanding only a seven-day infection as punishment; during that time the Hebrew people would not leave the spot of Miriam's confinement.

Miru Throughout Polynesia the queen of the last three circles of the underworld was a goddess, with Miru being one of her common names. The soul, departing earthly life, was supposed to take a great leap, landing safely in the arms of ancestors. But standing nearby with a net, hoping to catch weaklings and evildoers, was Miru; she threw captured souls into her oven. There they did not suffer, but were instantly consumed, while better souls lived calmly in a world identical to earth but eternal.

Misere She was the thirteenth fairy, the one who in Germanic folktales was left out of the guest-list for the christening of the girl who would become Briar Rose. Her name means "misery," and that is what she brought to the girl, whom she cursed to sleep for a hundred years behind a hedge of roses.

Mitra The great Greek historian and geographer Herodotus mentions a sky goddess with this name, which seems to be a feminine form of Mithras, the name of a more familiar Persian divinity. In that language, *mihr* meant sun, so Mitra may have been an ancient sun goddess who was the twin or double of Mithras; or the goddess may have undergone reconstruction into a male god.

Mnasa Little is known of this Mycenaean goddess but her name, which means "memory" and is related to that of another Greek goddess, Mnemosyne. Mnasa was part of a trinity of goddesses worshiped in Pylos, far in the west of the Greek Peloponnese. Her companions were the young woman Potnia and Posidaeia ("wife of the husband"), the woman of childbearing years. This would make Mnasa, the third member of the common female trinity, an old woman wise in her years.

Mnemosyne The daughter of earth and sky, she was to the Greeks "memory" personified. She was mother of the nine Muses, goddesses of art, whom she conceived in nine days of continual intercourse with Zeus. In Boeotia, she was worshiped in the form of a spring; a fountain bearing her name was said to flow in the underworld of Hades.

Modgud The servant of Hel, the Scandinavian death queen, this maiden guarded the path to the underworld. To reach her realm, the newly dead had to cross Hell-Ways, the yawning caverns surrounding the World Tree Yggdrasil, at whose roots Hel lived. Spanning the abysses where the roaring River Gjoll flowed was a gold-paved bridge where Modgud stood her watch.

Moirae In Homeric times, there was just one "fate," and her name was Moira ("strong one"). Then, as often happened in antiquity, the Greek goddess began to multiply herself. Soon there were two Fates, one of birth and one of death, or for good and evil fortunes; in the Olympian gods' war with the Titans they appeared, brandishing brass pestles. Later there were four Fates. But most commonly, the original goddess triplicated into the three Fates, the spinners of destiny.

Sometimes the goddesses were said to be the daughters of Nyx the night queen; in other tales, they sprang from the womb of Themis the lawgiver. They were named Clotho ("spinner"), she who bore the distaff and spun the thread of life; Lachesis ("measurer"), to whom the thread was passed as it came off the spindle; and Atropos ("inevitable"), who snipped it with her shears. Among the most ancient pre-Hellenic goddesses of the region, they never lost their authority; even powerful Zeus could not countermand them. Only once were they gainsaid: Apollo got them drunk in an attempt to save a friend's life, and they agreed to cut another person's thread instead.

Mokosh The ancient Slavic culture worshiped the earth goddess under this name, and her religion survived into Christian times. As late as the sixteenth century, Christian chronicles complained that Slavic women still "went to Mokosh" ceremonially. A spinner goddess, her image was embroidered on ceremonial clothes, where she was depicted as a woman with a large head, bearing a spindle.

Outdoors, Mokosh was represented by stones, particularly those breastlike in shape. Rain was perceived as Mother Mokosh's milk, so she was invoked in time of drought. In the nineteenth century in the Ukraine, archaeologists moved some of Mokosh's stones during a survey; a drought ensued; the people of the area blamed the scholars, and the stones were restored. At such Mokosh-stones, people came on pilgrimages to pray for health and prosperity. The crippled and handicapped particularly brought offerings of grain and animals, begging for the restoration of wholeness.

Monje   The powerful larva-shaped witch of Yorubaland was so huge she filled the entire Niger river until it overflowed. In its water, she laid innumerable little water-witches, who spread across the land like a flood, killing everyone in their path. Human life would have been destroyed had it not been for magical birds that threw lightning bolts into the water. The electricity dried up the water, and Monje and her witches as well.

Mora   When you go to bed at night, Serbian lore said, you should beware of stray pieces of straw lying around the bedroom, for they could be Mora in disguise. The Polish version of her name, Mara, lives on in our language as *nightmare*, for she was the night-riding witch who entered bedrooms as a white shadow to strangle her victims and suck their blood. Alternatively, she tormented them with bad dreams, appearing in these visions as a leather band, a mouse, a cat, a snake, or a white horse. She did not confine her activities to the torture of humans, however; she was just as happy persecuting animals and plants. Behind this folkloric witch figure is the ancient fate goddess, seen in her deadliest aspect; the thread she uses to strangle her victims is the thread of their own life, which she earlier spun and cut.

Morgan Le Fay   *Mor* meant "sea" in several Celtic languages, and Morgan was a sea goddess whose name still survives in Brittany where sea sprites are called morgans. The most famous sea goddess was surnamed Le Fay, "the fairy"; in Welsh mythology, she was said to be a queen of Avalon, the underworld fairyland where King Arthur was carried—some said by Morgan herself—when he disappeared from this world. In some legends, Morgan was Arthur's sister, whereas in other tales she was an immortal artist and healer who lived with her eight sisters in Avalon.

Some scholars claim she was the same goddess as the one called, in Ireland, Morrigan. That crowheaded goddess was a battle divinity, which suggests that Morgan might also have been a goddess of death. Indeed, there is dispute over whether her surname means "the fairy" or "the fate." If Morgan were not a mere sea sprite but the goddess of death, that would explain her unfriendly character in Malory's *Morte d'Arthur*, where Morgan appears as the king's dreaded foe, constantly plotting his death, and in *Sir Gawain and the Green Knight*, where she seems similarly bent on the destruction of the king and his Round Table. If Morgan were once the queen of death, ruler of the underworld and of rebirth to the early Britons, a cultural shift could easily have seen her reinterpreted as a powerful demonic force bent on destruction.

Moriath   Her name means "sea-land," and she was an Irish princess who, finding a man named Labraid irresistibly attractive, set herself to win him with music and flattery—and succeeded.

Morrigan   There was a trinity of goddesses of war and death in ancient Ireland, and scholars argue about which one was the preeminent figure. Was Morrigan a form of Badb, or the other way around? Was Nemain the same as, or different from, Macha? Was the overall name Morrigan, with the component parts being Macha, Badb, and Nemain; or was there no overall name, with Macha being a completely different goddess?

The disputes are probably unresolvable. And the goddesses involved are difficult to distinguish; here one appears as the Bean Nighe or Washer-at-the-Ford, there the same figure bears a different name. All the goddesses could take the shape of a crow. All were giants when they took human form.

The only thing that distinguished Morrigan from the others was her association with magic; she sang runes and cast charms before battles to strengthen her favorites. Otherwise she was, like Badb, seen before battle washing the armor of the doomed; she was seen flying over the battlefield as a crow hoping for carrion; she could turn into a snake to observe the slaughter from that angle. From our point of view, this "great queen" is hardly a cheerful female image, but Anahita, the Valkyries, Bellona, and many other warrior goddesses show that other cultures and eras have not been so squeamish.

Moruadh   The brandy-drinking sea maiden of Ireland was said to have a red nose, green teeth and hair, and a pig's eyes. Like other sea spirits, she made a very good wife for a human man—if he could keep her, which entailed stealing her magic *cohuleen druith*, the cap that allowed her to breathe beneath the sea. Of course—like swan maidens and other enchanted lovers—should she ever find her cap, Moruadh would leave home, husband, and human children to return to freedom.

Mother Friday   The Russian and Slavonic harvest-goddess was very particular about her people keeping her feast days sacred. If, on the goddess' favored days, any woman worked on her spinning wheel or loom, or even mended cloth, the offending woman would be blinded by dust that rose from the earth.

Motsesa   In Mozambique, a legend is told which resembles that of the Greek heroine Psyche. The princess Motsesa, it is said, was married off to the water god Bulane. He lived far away in the mountains, so the girl sent by caravan to the designated place, where she was abandoned, alone in the wilderness. Fearful but exhausted, she fell asleep on the ground—and woke to find herself in a magnificent home. She was alone there, except for the invisble hands that served her and the invisi-

ble lover who slept with her. Strange as it was, she grew comfortable and, finally, happy. Soon she had a little son to keep her company, and her life seemed full. But when her sister Senkepenyana came to visit, the girl sang a mocking little song to the baby. "Where is your father?" it said. And the father—lest the family think he had abandoned his child—immediately appeared. The sight of the god terrified the girl, who fled, leaving the baby behind. Motsesa too was terrified when she returned and found a strange man holding her son, but when Bulane introduced himself, her happiness returned.

Mou-Njami   Among the Uralic speakers of Siberia, this was the name of mother earth, a goddess who carried eyes within her as other creatures carried eggs. When females became pregnant, Mou-Njami provided the eyes for the offspring, thus allowing them to see her. Because of their sacredness, hunters were forbidden to injure their prey's eyes, which had to be carefully cut out and buried as an offering to mother earth.

Mou-Njami looked like a huge green animal, for the grass was her fur. Every year, she shed her coat and grew another one. Because the soil was the mother's skin, her people never cut into it with metal knives or spears. Even needless digging or driving of fence posts was forbidden out of concern for the earth's skin.

Moye   Chinese mythology records the story of this famous woman blacksmith. Her husband had gathered iron and gold from five mountains and ten directions, but he was unable to use the metals until Moye—remembering that any transformation entails a sacrifice—offered her hair and nails to the fire. Then she ordered 300 young people to operate the bellows while she leaped into the molten metal. From her sacrifice, a famous sword bearing her name was cast.

Muhongo   The African Eurydice, this queen died young; her husband mourned her incessantly. He sent a magician to find her in the afterlife. But when the magician reached Muhongo she instructed him in the facts of life and death, telling him that the dead have joined another kingdom and cannot return to earth's surface.

Mujaji The Rain Queens of the Lovedu people of South Africa bore as a title the name of their primary goddess, whose incarnations they were believed to be. These women were highly regarded for their political prowess as well as their military might; they kept their people safe first from the Zulu and later from the European Boers. The goddess herself rarely left her home in the dragon mountains and was thus rarely seen among humans. A weather goddess, she had control over storms and floods, which she hurled at her enemies; those who worshiped her, however, were rewarded with gentle rain in sufficient quantities to make gardens flourish.

Muireartach Her name means "eastern sea," and this Irish goddess was the embodiment of the storm-torn ocean; she was so turbulent that the only way to kill her was to drown her in a calm sea or bury her up to her shoulders in soil. The one-eyed crone lived beneath the waves with the seasmith, loving only him and the sea merchants who massaged her surface. "Ill-streaming, bald-red, white-maned," Muireartach was eventually killed by the Irish warrior Fionn MacCumhail.

Mulhalmoni The Korean goddess of water is invoked when women shamans wish to cure eye disease or blindness. Coins are dropped in sacred springs, and rice steamed in a *nok* (sacred cauldron) is offered to the goddess. The dedicated rice is eaten by the patient, whose eyes are bathed in spring water. Sometimes this ritual is performed not to cure but to protect the eyes; then it takes the form of a family outing or picnic in the mountains.

Munanna In Irish legend, this woman was married to a man whom she found tedious. So she took a lover, a Scandinavian sea pirate with whom she plotted her husband's death. After the killing, the pair left for Norway. But the pirate, terrified of the power the woman had over him, pushed her into a lake, where she drowned. Even then, Munanna remained a powerful spirit, flying around the cliffs of Inishkea, crying "Revenge, revenge" at anyone who saw her cranelike figure.

Mu Olokukurtilisop Among the Cuna of the Isthmus of Panama, this was the name of the great preexistent goddess who parthenogenetically produced the sun, took him as her lover, birthed the moon and mated with him, and thus produced the entire skyful of stars. Still full of energy, Mu Olokukurtilisop took all the stars as lovers, thus producing the plants and animals of our world.

Muses The Greek goddesses of art and inspiration are probably the most familiar ancient divinities today. Daughters of Mnemosyne, they were born near Mt. Olympus in a place they later made their dancing ground. There they were raised by the hunter Crotus, who was transported after death into the sky as Sagittarius.

Usually there were nine Muses: Clio or Kleio ("famegiver"), ruler of history, depicted with an open scroll or a chest of books; Euterpe ("joygiver"), the fluteplaying lyric Muse; "the festive" Thalia who wore the comic mask and wreaths of ivy; the singing Melpomene, Thalia's opposite, who wore the mask of tragedy and vine leaves; Terpsichore ("lover of dancing"), who carried a lyre and ruled choral song as well as dance; another lyre-bearer, Erato ("awakener of desire"), ruler of erotic poetry; Polyhymnia or Polymnia, the meditating one whose name means "many hymns" and who inspired them; Urania ("heavenly"), the globe-bearing Muse of astronomy; and Calliope ("beautiful voiced"), ruler of epic poetry, shown with a tablet and pencil.

Sometimes, however, there were fewer than nine Muses. Three named by Hesiod were obviously symbolic: Melete ("practicing"), Mneme ("remembering"), and Aoide ("singing"). When there was only one Muse, she was called by any of the names of the nine. The group as a whole had many alternative names, derived from places sacred to them: Carmentae, Pieriades, Aganippides, Castalides, Heliconiades, and Maeonides.

Muso Koroni   Among the Bambara people of Mali, the earth goddess bears this name, which means "pure woman with ancient soul." She is the color of the dark rich African earth, sometimes appearing as a black panther or leopard; thus she is goddess of night. An ancestral mother, she gave birth to all life, human, plant and animal, after the sun god Pemba took the form of a tree and penetrated her with his roots. She is the goddess of life's passages, the one who causes girls to menstruate and who oversees initiations. Muso Koroni is both tame and wild, goddess of agriculture and of wilderness simultaneously. Millet is her favorite cultivated crop, and it is good to honor her with dances by old women to the sound of gourd rattles whenever harvest nears. But she rules the wild places as well, even those wildernesses within the human soul which are called *wanzo*.

Mut   Originally from Nubia, this bisexual world mother was sometimes a vulture, sometimes a crowned woman, to the Egyptians. Her name means "mother," but her character is now vague, for her ancient worship was slowly supplanted by that of such goddesses as Isis and Hathor.

Muzita   In Zaire, among the Bakongo people, Mahangu was the first human being. Created both male and female in one body, Mahangu attempted to embrace the creator—the force of which broke the being into two. Muzita was the female half, a hard-working farmer-woman.

Muzzu-Kummik-Quae   To the Ojibwa people of the north central American forests, the second smoke of tobacco is offered to this earth woman, with the following words: "To you, Mother, we give thanks. When I am hungry, you feed me; when I am cold and wet, you shelter me; when I am downcast, you comfort me. For this am I grateful, I am endebted to you." The earth mother was the great teacher of her people, showing the way to spiritual insight and the right way to live on this earth.

Mylitta   Actually the name of this goddess was Mulitta or Mu'Allidtu, but it was Hellenized by the Greek historian Herodotus when he described her worship in ancient Phoenicia. The ancient writer tells us how Babylonian priestesses of Mylitta, burning incense and wearing wreaths around their heads, awaited strangers with whom to perform the sacred rites of love. Mylitta's worshipers bobbed their hair at puberty and offered her these youthful locks; afterward they could offer themselves more totally. At her shrine beside the sacred spring of Afka—a name sometimes used of the goddess herself—these women set up booths or camped in the green groves, enjoying intercourse with those who came to them.

At the great spring of Afka, fire was said regularly to fall into the water, renewing the youth of its goddess. Thus Mylitta combined the force of flowing water and the force of heavenly fire into a highly sexual energy personified as a nude, bearded woman riding a tortoise or a billygoat. Ancient travelers from Greece and Italy, coming upon this image, called Mylitta after their goddesses of desire, Aphrodite or Venus.

Myrine   In addition to the huge Amazon queendom north of Greece, there was another one, possibly earlier, in Libya, where Myrine ruled. The "swift-bounding one," she invaded Atlantis and subdued it with 30,000 mounted women warriors supported by 3,000 infantrywomen, all armed with bows and protected by heavy snakeskin armor. Defeating the Atlantians, Myrine executed all the men and enslaved the women and children. Then she established a city in her name and signed a truce with the remaining Atlantians to protect them against the fierce neighboring tribe of Gorgons— not, presumably, the immortal ones the Greeks mentioned in other tales. When the Amazons relaxed, confident in their victory, the Atlantians concluded a secret alliance with the Gorgons and overthrew the women warriors.

Myrine escaped and pursued her military career eastward, conquering Lesbos, Samothrace, and Lemnos. Caught in a storm in the Aegean, she sacrificed to "the Mother" and was spared, thereafter setting up shrines in the goddess' honor. She died in battle in Thrace, when an alliance of kings invaded Amazon-held Asia Minor; her grave was covered by a huge hill built by women and called Baticia ("thorn hill").

Myrmex The warrior goddess Athena fell in love with this woman of Attica because of her skill with the loom, her hard-working nature, and her gracious piety. But the course of love does not always run smoothly: Myrmex began to boast that she had invented the plow, when her lover Athena had been the real inventor. Athena, furious, turned the girl into an ant in revenge.

Myrrha Across the ancient Near East the same story was told in various ways: how the earth fell in love with a beautiful youth in his springtime years, how he betrayed her and was punished by death, and how the kindly goddess brought him back to life again—the story of the springtime that flowers and fades on the face of the ageless earth. Sometimes the legend told, too, of the magical conception of the beloved vegetation god, and this was the case with Adonis, the young lover of Asia Minor's mother goddess, Aphrodite. At an autumn festival, white-robed women who had endured nine days of fasting and chastity offered the first fruits of the fields to the goddess who provided them. After this offertory, a communion: a public orgy during which the princess Myrrha mated with her own father and conceived the child whom the goddess would love. The tale, it seems clear, was allegorical, for Adonis was a tree spirit and thus his mother was a personified tree, the myrrh tree whose blossoms are fertilized by nearby, probably kindred, trees.

Naamah In ancient times this word, which means "pleasant," was used of the Canaanite goddess of sexuality, Astarte. But one people's deities are often their enemies' demons, and so the name Naamah was given by the Hebrews to one of their demon queens, a creature so beautiful that mortal men—even angels—could not resist her. She seduced them with her sweet cymbal music, but once they became aroused she stole their semen to form demon children. Like Lilith, Naamah also entertained herself by strangling sleeping babies, but she much preferred to endanger the human race by luring men from their appropriate mates. She is said to be still alive, living in the sea, where even the monsters of the deep, infatuated with her beauty, pursue her constantly through the waves.

Nahkeeta The goddess of Lake Sutherland in the Olympic Mountains of the Pacific Northwest was originally a delicate maiden, gentle as a water bird, with hair like a stream and a voice like a waterfall. She was beloved of her people, and she herself loved the dense forests where they lived.

One day while Nahkeeta was gathering wild plants, she lost her way in the thick rain forest. As the light dimmed beneath the great trees, she wandered until exhausted, then fell asleep beside a fallen tree. There, the next day, her family found her bloodied body, marked with the claws of a wild beast. They had loved her so much that their sorrow was unceasing—until the day that she reincarnated herself in a soft blue lake, a lake filled with water birds and the slow sound of wind, like a voice, on her surface.

Naiads To the Greeks, everything on earth had a resident spirit, often perceived in female forms called Nymphs. The Naiads, nymphs of water, were not so long-lived as oceanic Nereids or rocky Oreads, but did live longer than the tree women or Dryads. As long as the streams and rivers embodying them did not go dry, the freshwater Naiad lived.

Naina Devi The Bilaspur goddess of eyes was brought to earth by a supernatural cow, who gave great floods of milk at her sacred spot.

Nambi The first woman of Uganda lived in the sky as princess of heaven, but she desired an earthly man and descended to have intercourse with him. Then Nambi returned to the sky. Her family was appalled that she would lower herself to make love with an earthling. Nambi's father stole her lover's only cow, taking it to the sky and forcing it to feed on wild plants. Nambi returned to earth and told her lover Kintu where his cow was hidden, suggesting that he reclaim it—and her. Kintu traveled to heaven, where the sky father presented him with vast herds of identical cattle, demanding that he find his own cow. With Nambi's help he identified the beast, but the sky father subjected Kintu to other tests before allowing his daughter to live on earth with the man.

The sky father also warned Nambi that her brother, Death, might follow them to earth. The couple left in haste, taking the first animals with them. Halfway down, Nambi realized they had no seeds for edible plants; she stole back to heaven to get some. Death spied her and followed her to earth. Now, although humans have food to eat, they also have the unwelcome presence of Brother Death.

Nambubi Mother of gods among the Buganda people of Uganda, she was descended from the fish of Lake Victoria.

Nammu An early Sumerian goddess of the formless waters of creation, she was the great abyss which brought forth the entire universe. Later, Nammu assisted Mami in forming the human race. She also—when the goddesses Lahar and Ashnan failed to provide food and drink for the deities because they were drunk—tattled to the high god Enki; the result was the creation of humankind, formed to serve the immortals.

Nana The nymph who conceived Attis, beloved of Cybele, by carrying a ripe almond or pomegranate next to her skin, Nana may have been—like Myrrha, mother of Adonis—a tree spirit, for she gave birth to a tree god. Before being incorporated into the major seasonal myth of Anatolia, however, Nana starred in a similar one of her own. For Nana ("queen") was one of the old Babylonian names for Ishtar as patron of Lagash and Ninevah, used at the same time as the similar name Inanna. Ishtar's worship as Nana was long-lived, for the Assyrian conqueror Assurbanipal, while sacking the Elamite capital of Susa in 636

B.C.E., discovered an image of the goddess that the Elamites had carried off from Erech 1,635 years earlier.

Another Nana was the wife of the sacrificed Scandinavian god Balder; she had no other mythic role than accompanying Balder to the underworld. Her name, obviously, is identical to that of the mother-lover of the young vegetation god of the eastern Mediterranean. Some scholars believe that the story of Nana migrated northward to become part of Scandinavian tradition; there the mother was distinguished from the vegetation-god's lover, the former being named Frigg, while the latter retained the name Nana.

Nana Buluku The world creator was, to the Fon people of Benin in west Africa, the mother of the great goddess Mawu and her twin brother lover Lisa. The source of divinity, Nana Buluku retired from active participation in this world after Mawu's birth. Her worship was very ancient and so widely known that it is difficult to pinpoint its source; in some places she was the preeminent deity. In the African diaspora, she became St. Anne in Brazilian Macumba. Oldest of the water-orishas, she is celebrated with them on Saturdays, when she dances carrying a curved broom and wearing red, white and blue beads.

Nanshe This Babylonian water goddess was honored each year with a flotilla of boats sailing on her canals. At the city of Lagash, the flotilla joined a sacred barge bearing the goddess' image, and the procession floated about as Nanshe's worshipers reveled. A wise goddess, she was an interpreter of dreams and omens; she served each New Year's Day as the judge of each person's activities during the preceding year.

Nar Any Irish king who slept with this goddess died, says a legend that many scholars believe records a period of so-called ritual kingship, when a king "married" the earth goddess and was ultimately sacrificed to assure her fertility. Save for a suspicious repetition of kingly names at regular intervals and a coincidentally similar length of residence on the throne, there is scant evidence for the practice of sovereign murder in Ireland, but such ancient myths as this suggest it.

Naru-Kami The Japanese thunder goddess was the protector of trees and the ruler of artisans. Wherever she threw a bolt, that place was afterward considered sacred.

Natosuelta "Winding river" was this Celtic goddess' name; she was a raven goddess worshiped in Gaul as creator and destroyer of this world. Her images show her holding a house on a long pole, suggesting that one of her roles was as domestic goddess.

Nausicaa The princess who welcomed Odysseus back to human society may have been, in fact, the author of the famous Greek epic. So argued Samuel Butler (1835–1902) in *The Authoress of the Odyssey*, calling Nausicaa a Sicilian noblewoman who created the work from shreds of legend. He supported his argument by asserting that the writer was clearly more familiar with homelife than the sea and contending that Nausicaa used the story to frame portraits of the great Greek heroines: Calypso, Circe, and Penelope, for instance.

Navky In Slavic lands, children who drowned or babies who died in infancy haunted their survivors for seven years, half-naked and crying. Then they were transformed into lovely water-dwelling women who called out to passing travelers. When the passerby approached, the Navky (Mavky in Russian) leaped on him and tickled him to death.

Nawangwulan This Javanese swan maiden came to earth to marry a mortal. But as other mortals have done to other swan maidens, he betrayed her. The one rule she made in the household was that he should not watch her while she made rice; this was because she had the power to feed her entire family on one grain. But, unable to control himself, he observed her one day. A swan-maiden

divorce followed, wherein she reclaimed her winged garments and flew away.

Nchienge This water woman, in Zaire, was a primal goddess who gave birth to the first people; her eldest daugher was named Labama.

Nehalennia The Celtic dog goddess of sea traders, she was the primary divinity of the area now called the Netherlands, where over 120 altars and sculptures dedicated to her were found. She was depicted with baskets or cornucopia of fruit, with solar amulets around her neck, and with her companion/familiar dog by her side. She was invoked especially by those about to embark on sea journeys, for safe and successful completion of voyages.

Neith One of Egypt's most ancient goddesses, Neith was originally the essence of the tribal community perceived in its totems, two crossed arrows and a mottled animal skin. Later, as her worshipers politically dominated those of other Egyptian goddesses, Neith assumed the attributes of the conquered deities, becoming a complex figure who could boast (as Plutarch recorded her temple inscriptions), "I am all that has been, that is, that will be, and no mortal has yet been able to lift the veil that covers me." Despite accretions, however, Neith remained basically the mistress of handicrafts and industry—a warlike mistress who could protect her worshipers' property against invasion. (In this, the Greeks saw an image of their own Athena.) Wearing the double crown of unified Egypt, Neith eventually commanded the reverence of all Egyptians from her temple city of Sais.

In the beginning of time, it was said, Neith took up the shuttle, strung the sky on her loom, and wove the world. Then she wove nets and from the primordial waters pulled up living creatures, including men and women. Finally, in the shape of a cow, Neith invented childbirth by bringing forth Ra, who grew to be the mightiest of gods. During their lives, she was responsible for her worshipers' health—for her priests were doctors and healers—and after death, she guarded their remains while welcoming their souls into the afterworld.

Nekhebet The vulture-headed goddess of the Nile's source, she was called the twin of Uadgit after Egypt's political unification; together they formed the Neb-Ti, the "two mistresses." Nekhebet, the patron of laboring women and called by the Greeks Eileithyia, combined political and motherly roles in her mystic task of suckling the pharaoh-to-be.

Nemain Her name means the "venomous one" and is a cognate of the British goddess Nemetona; she was one of the powerful battle goddesses of ancient Ireland and was related to the crow goddess Morrigan.

Nemesis In late Greek mythology, she was monstrous, a fierce figure of revenge and anger, the bad-luck version of the fortune goddess Tyche. But in earlier days she was worshiped with Themis in Attic Rhamnus. The white-garbed, winged Nemesis tormented those who broke the social rules that Themis represented. Although sometimes said to be one of the Erinyes, her power was less narrow; hers was more the force of justice than retaliation.

When Zeus arrived in Greece with his worshipers, he conquered Nemesis, "night's dark daughter," in the same way that legends show him overcoming other goddesses. Intent on rape, Zeus chased Nemesis across the land. The powerful goddess changed shape once, twice, a third time, but the god transformed himself as well. Finally he overpowered her in bird form, and she laid an egg that hatched into the goddess Helen.

Nemetona The British "goddess of the sacred grove" was one of the divinities worshiped at Bath, where Sul was honored as patron of the thermal springs. Nemetona was depicted as a seated queen holding a scepter, surrounded by three hooded figures and a ram.

Nenakatu A long-haired midget woman, this little nature spirit of the Miwok of California was mishievious, even dangerous. As an antidote to her power, one wore leaf-necklaces or drank wormwood tea.

Nephele Originally a Semitic goddess whose name means "cloud," she came into Greek mythology as wife of a Theban king and mother of Helle. A cloud spirit, she became identified with the sky queen Hera.

Nephthys This Greek version of her name is more commonly used than her original Egyptian name, Nebthet. She was Isis' sister and opposite: Isis was the force of life and rebirth; Nephthys, the tomb-dwelling goddess of death and sunset. They had similarly opposite mates. Isis' consort was the fertility god Osiris, while her sister's mate was the evil god Set.

Set was not only wicked but sterile. So Nephthys, who wanted children, plied Osiris with liquor until, forgetting his loyalty to Isis, the god tumbled into bed with Nephthys. That night she conceived the god Anubis. Set, possibly out of jealousy, then killed and dismembered Osiris. This proved too much for Nephthys, who left Set to join in her sister's lamentations and helped to restore Osiris to life.

Nereids The daughters of Doris, the sea goddess, the fifty Nereids were famous for their rosebud faces and their oracular powers; not only could they predict shipwrecks but they could avert them. In their honor, the Greeks danced, imitating the ocean journeys of the demon-riding maidens, sometimes clad and sometimes naked. Some famous Nereids were Amphitrite, Clymene, Galatea, Glauce, Panope, and Thetis.

Nerthus One of the most famous passages from the Roman writer Tacitus described the common form of worship among the Germanic tribes dwelling north of the empire. Their primary deity, he said, was the earth goddess Nerthus. Her major sanctuary was on an island in the ocean, where a statue of her sat on a cloth-covered cart until the moment her priest divined the presence of Nerthus herself in the statue.

She then began a solemn procession among her people, drawn by oxen from tribe to tribe. All fighting ceased; all weapons and, indeed, all iron tools were locked away until the goddess' journey was completed. Festivities accompanied her, all doors were open in hospitality, and prosperity came to the countryside.

Finally, the accompanying priest realized that the goddess was tired of human company, and the procession started back to Nerthus' island sanctuary. In a hidden lake, the goddess and her chariot were bathed by slaves who, apparently unable to live a normal life after contact with the goddess' effigy, were offered to her in death.

Nessa Originally she was Assa ("gentle one"), a princess of Ulster in northern Ireland. But the evil Druid Cathbad murdered the tutors who made life pleasant for this studious girl, and she changed her nature entirely, becoming Nessa ("ungentle"). A warrior rather than the scholar she would have been, she defeated king after king and kept a strong hand on the reins of government.

But Cathbad still had designs on her. One day, while Nessa was bathing in a quiet spring and her armor was just out of reach, Cathbad surprised her. Weaponless, she could not resist him. He raped her and then demanded her friendship. "Better," she said diplomatically, "to consent than to be killed, and with my weapons gone."

Although kept hostage as a concubine, Nessa refused to bear Cathbad children. Knowing, however, that she would eventually give birth to a hero, she watched for omens. One day when she was sent to draw water for the Druid from a magical well, Nessa spied in the pail two tiny worms. She drank some water, swallowing the worms; they fertilized her; soon she gave birth to the famous king Conchobar. Lest anyone think that

he was the spawn of the Druid, the hero came from the womb clutching a worm in either hand, evidence of his miraculous conception.

Ngolimento The African people of Togo, the Ewe, believe that before birth, children live with this goddess, the mother of spirits. Their lives on earth will be happy if they obey her during that prenatal period, but if they do not, bad luck will follow them through the womb and into life.

Ngwa Ndundu In the Kongo mystery religion called Kimpasi, this is the ritual name of the woman who leads the initiations. She must be a woman of advanced age, one who has been bereaved of a young child, and one who has been possessed of spirits.

Niamh Her very name means "beauty," this daughter of the sea, the fairy queen of Tir na n'Og, the Irish Land of the Blessed far away in the western ocean, almost beyond human reach. Like many fairy goddesses, Niamh "of the golden hair" had a fondness for mortal lovers. Once, legend says, she stole the poet Oisin from the Fianna, the band of heroes with whom he lived.

For a long time—human speech has no words for the length of time, but the Fianna aged and died while Oisin lived young and blissful with Niamh— Oisin was happy in Niamh's domain. Finally, homesickness for the mortal world stirred the poet. The longing grew until, finally, Niamh could no longer stand the man's complaints. She put him on a magic horse and set the horse's head east, toward humanity, but she warned her lover not to dismount. Poor Oisin—when he landed on earth, the buckle on his fairy saddle broke, and he fell to the ground. The moment his young body touched the earth, all its accumulated human years fell on it. Instantly Oisin grew old, died, and turned to dust, never again to enjoy Niamh's embraces.

Nidra In Sanskrit, the word for the "sleep of time" is feminine in gender, and so assumes a feminine form as a black-skinned goddess clothed in yellow and dark blue silk, who practices ascetic rites in the Vindhya Mountains. When the demon Kamsha attempted to destroy the world, Nidra descended into the womb of the woman Yasoda while her brother, the god Vishnu, arranged to incarnate through the womb of a woman nearby. At the moment of birth, the two babies were exchanged, and Kamsha kidnapped the baby he thought was Vishnu and smashed its head against the rock. From the infant body, the magnificent goddess arose and flew back to heaven, while Vishnu was left alive to combat the demon. Nidra is sometimes called Yoganidra for her ascetic practices, or Vindhyavasini for the village in which her cult is practiced; sometimes she is viewed as a form of Maya, the goddess of illusion, although it is possible Nidra is a local goddess absorbed into the larger Hindu pantheon.

Nike   The most famous image of this Greek goddess stands atop a stairwell in the Louvre in Paris: "Winged Victory," Nike carved in marble with arching wings and flowing garments. The Greek goddess was the daughter of the fearsome river-goddess Styx and the sister of Zelos ("zeal"). She was honored throughout Greece, especially at Athens, as a companion—or form—of Athena.

Nimue   This is the Welsh name for the supernatural sorceress called the Lady of the Lake in Arthurian legend. She lived, surrounded by beautiful fairy-like immortal maidens, in an island realm where there was neither winter nor pain nor death. She was one of the mighty goddesses who took King Arthur to Avalon at the end of his earthly reign, a particularly appropriate action, for it had been Nimue who had invested Arthur as king.

Ningal   The "Great Lady" of the fruitful earth was courted by the moon god, the Sumerian and Ugaritic people said. He brought her necklaces of lapis lazuli and—for he was the rain provider—turned the deserts into orchards to win her heart.

Ningyo   This Japanese goddess looked just like a fish, but she had a woman's head, and when she cried her tears were pearls. Women tried to capture her, to take a bite out of her; this would guarantee them eternal youth and beauty.

Ninhursag   Long ago in a fine fair town, the Babylonian serpent goddess of birth and rebirth lived with the god of wisdom. In Dilmun, where Ninhursag and Enki made their home, there was no age or death, no sickness and no barrenness; not even the animals harmed one another.

One day Ninhursag's belly swelled up. Nine days later the goddess Ninsar (also called Ninmu) was born. The lascivious Enki seduced his daughter, who bore Ninhurra. Then Enki slept with his granddaughter, who bore Uffu, the goddess of plants. Of course Enki wished to sleep with his greatgranddaughter, but Ninhursag whispered to her that she must first demand a brideprice of cucumbers, apples, and grapes. The lustful Enki granted them, and Uttu agreed to occupy his bed.

From their affair sprang eight different kinds of plants, living things the world had never seen before. But Enki ate his offspring as quickly as they appeared, even before the mountain mother Ninhursag could name them. Furious with the greedy god, Ninhursag leveled so terrible a curse at him that he immediately fell down, stricken in eight parts of his body with eight different diseases.

The other gods grew concerned as Enki weakened and grew thin. But the goddess, still angry at the god, refused to heal him. Finally—when Enki was a breathing corpse—the congregation of heaven prevailed on Ninhursag to cure him. Still unwilling, for fear he would resume his upsetting behavior, the goddess agreed to a compromise: she would not heal him directly but would create eight tiny goddesses (among them Ninti) to control the health of Enki's afflicted parts; they could do the healing if they chose. Indeed, the little goddesses set to work, and soon Enki was well again. Some say, however, that Ninhursag did finally cure Enki herself and that she did so by placing him within her vagina, whence he could be reborn whole.

Niniganni In Guinea, the Baga people worshiped this python goddess of life and fortune. Huge wooden statues repesenting her have only recently been found by outsiders, so zealously did the Baga women guard their matron goddess. These statues are decorated with fourteen vertical lozenges, representing the fourteen days between dark and full moon—an apparent symbol of women's reproductive cycle.

Ninlil One day the young Sumerian goddess Ninlil was bathing in the stream Ninbirdu, a lonely spot far from all eyes. The god Enlil, happening by, took full advantage of the solitude: he raped the virgin goddess. The other deities, horrified at the deed, swiftly banished Enlil to the underworld. But Ninlil had conceived; she followed Enlil to the kingdom of the dead, her huge belly a reminder of his crime.

This development disturbed heaven even more, for in their omniscience the deities knew that the child in Ninlil's belly was the moon. If born in the underworld, he would have to remain there for eternity, for not even divinity grants freedom from the death queen Eriskegal's laws. When her time came, Ninlil performed magic: she bore three shadow children, one each for herself and Enlil, one for their child, each to remain a perpetual hostage to Eriskegal. Then, still pregnant, she climbed to earth with Enki. Thus was the moon god Sin born, on the horizon from which he can mount the sky.

"Mistress of winds," Ninlil was the ancient goddess of the city of Nippur, a mother figure whose emblems were the same as the other great earth-goddesses of the ancient Near East: the serpent, the heavenly mountain, and the stars. Because she was the earth, Ninlil had to approve any ruler of her surface. Thus each prince gained his throne by mating with the goddess, incarnate in one of her priestesses; then he ruled as Ninlil's consort. As the worship of Ishtar spread across Babylonia,

Ninlil was identified with her as "Ishtar of Nippur," eventually losing her identity entirely, while her name became a title of Ishtar.

Niobe Early Greek legend named her as the mother of humanity; her seven daughters, the Meliae or ash tree nymphs, produced human beings as fruit. Often called a goddess rather than a woman, Niobe was noted for her fruitfulness; some say her children were without number.

Later Greek legend called her a queen and said that she bragged of the number of her children and mocked the goddess Leto for having only two offspring. Those, however, were the powerful Artemis and Apollo, and they avenged their mother by slaughtering all but one of Niobe's children. (Her daughter Chloris survived to become one of Greece's great beauties.) Overcome by grief, Niobe was so transfixed by weeping that the gods took pity on her, transforming her into a stone from which a fountain eternally sprang.

Nirriti In Hindu India, humanity's misfortunes are embodied in this goddess: a weary old woman, starved and leprous, always holding out her hand for alms. All born into poverty and crime who, nonetheless, attempt to live righteously are protected by Nirriti; as the goddess who endures earth's misfortunes, she is naturally the one to whom those wishing for a change of luck would pray. Wearing black garments and ornaments, priests offer sacrifice to her, then put a stone into a pot of water and toss it to the southwest, transferring more disease and ill fortune to the already heavy shoulders of Nirriti.

Nisaba "She who teaches the decrees" of divinity to humans, this goddess brought literacy and astrology to a Sumerian king on a tablet inscribed with the names of the beneficent stars. An architect as well, she drew up temple plans for her people; she was also an oracle and dream interpreter. The most learned of deities, this snake goddess also controlled the fertility of her people's fields.

Nixies   The Germans—like many other peoples—considered the prophetic spirits of water to be feminine. Like the rivers they inhabited, the Nixies were changeable in nature: sometimes charming and peaceful, sitting in the sun to comb their long blonde hair; sometimes fierce and hungry, drowning people for food.

They could assume human form to go to market or to dance on the riverside; in this form, they were long-breasted young women about four feet tall, who might pass for completely human except for the wet hems of their skirts and aprons. Mortal men often fell in love with them, wasting away because of their beauty; sometimes a Nixie would agree to marry a human, always making him vow never to ask her origin. Excellent dancers, they would dance with human men, but should one steal her glove it meant the Nixie's death; the next day the river where she lived would be red with her blood.

Noika   In Oceanic mythology, she is the pearl goddess who lived with her sister Korina in a cave inventing magic and ritual which made their people wealthy and happy. They were inseparable as maidens, but once they were married, they began to disagree. As often happens, friends took one side or the other. After many years, the arguments were so severe that the entire village was forced to separate, half following Noika, half going with Korina.

No-Il Ja-Dae   The Korean goddess of the toilet was said to be perpetually angry, perhaps because her clitoris had been cut out and thrown into the ocean, where it became a seashell. She was especially hostile to women who tried to use the outhouse at night; she might make them sick or strike them blind. In some areas of Korea, she was called Nam-Sa Kui the ghostly maiden, and was said to be a lovely woman dressed in bright silks.

Nokomis   This word, meaning "grandmother," was the Algonquin name for the goddess called Eithinoha ("our mother") by the Iroquois. She ruled the earth and its produce; she created the food for the people and animals who dwelled on her land. But she did not only create it: she fed herself to her people, for the woodland Indians recognized that life continues only if it devours life.

They said that earth had a daughter, Onatah, the corn maiden. When the thirsty Onatah was wandering through the land, looking for dew, an evil spirit abducted her and held her under the earth; the sun eventually found her and led her back to the surface. The similarities between this North American myth and the Greek legend of Demeter and her daughter are obvious; both are expressions of a similar profound understanding of the vegetative cycle on which humanity depends.

Nomia   This shepherdess of Sicily loved Daphnis, son of the phallic god Hermes. Although the boy vowed fidelity to the woman, she did not entirely trust him and promised she would blind him if he were ever unfaithful. When she found him in the arms of a local princess, he claimed he had been kidnapped, made drunk, and forced into the compromising position. Nomia did not believe him and acted on her threat, then abandoned her faithless lover. Now blind, he pined after her, inventing bucolic poetry in hopes of winning her back—which never happened.

Norns   At the foot of the World Tree, Scandinavian religion said, lived three sisters, the most powerful of all deities; not even the gods, the Aesir, could undo what they had done, or do what they did not wish. Urd, Verdandi, and Skuld—the three Norns—drew water each day from Urd's well and, mixing it with gravel, carefully sprinkled the World Tree. They never overwatered, causing the tree to rot, neither did they allow the tree to parch, for on it not only human life but the universe itself depended.

Although these three were most familiar, there were actually innumerable Norns—one for each person born, for they were the Fates that ruled each life. Some legends said that each person had one Norn, who taught life's rules; your luck depended on the talent of your Norn, whom you were to honor at each meal by setting an extra place for her. Other legends said that each person had three Norns, two who promised good, one bringing evil.

The latter belief may represent the influence of Mediterranean culture, which also affected the Scandinavian conception of the three most powerful Norns. Urd, the eldest sister, may at first have stood alone, with Verdandi and Skuld joining her later. As finally perceived, each member of the trinity had distinct powers: Urd (whose name became our word *weird*) ruling the past, Verdandi the present, and Skuld the future.

Nortia   To the Etruscans, who occupied Italy before Rome conquered the peninsula, each entity had a preordained life span—each human being, and each nation or state as well. To them Nortia was a preeminent goddess, the force of time-linked destiny. In her temple in Volsinii, a nail was pounded into the wall at the close of each year; in this way people could know exactly how many years had passed, if not how many were to come, in their individual lives and in the collective life of Etruria.

Norwan   The "dancing porcupine woman" of the California Wintuns was a goddess of light who brought food to earth. Daughter of earth and sun, Norwan danced, light as warm air, above growing plants; she kept dancing each day until sunset. Once, it was told, she slept with a new man, angering her usual lover; this brought on the first war in human history.

Notambu   In Zimbabwe, this was the name of the priestess of the moon goddess Jezanna. At the time of her priesthood, the Mashona people practiced child sacrifice. Notambu was horrified by this practice, and when the time came for her to perform it, she called out instead for Jezanna to take pity on the selected child. The goddess heard her prayer, and such sacrifices were ended. It is said that you can still see the moon goddess playing with the child and with Notambu, on nights when the full moon strikes the waters of the Davisa River.

Nott   The Scandinavian primeval goddess Nott ("night") was the mother of the earth (the goddess Jord) and of the day as well. She rode forth each evening on her horse Frostymane, from whose foaming mouth the dew fell.

Nsomeka   The culture heroine of the Bantu of southern Africa brought riches to her people by boldly visiting the jungle home of the great mother goddess Songi, who taught a magical tooth-filing ritual that created prosperity. When Nsomeka returned to earthly life, Songi caused cattle and fowl and other domestic animals to crowd out through her tooth notches; entire villages of well-built houses and shade-producing trees appeared, too. Because of wealth produced by women, Bantu men lived peacefully with their mates, treating the women with utmost respect.

Nsongo   Ancestral goddess of the Bangala people of Zaire, she lived incestuously with her twin brother Lianja. When she died suddenly, her pregnant daughter-in-law suddenly heard singing from her womb. The voice told her that the baby would be Nsongo, reborn, and so it came to pass.

Nu Kua   The creator goddess of ancient China made the first human beings from yellow clay. At first, she carefully molded them. At length, finding this too tedious, Nu Kua just dipped a rope into slip-like clay and shook it so that drops splattered onto the ground. Thus were two types of beings born: from the molded figures, nobles; from the clay drops, peasants.

Later this serpent-bodied goddess quelled a rebellion against the heavenly order and, when the dying rebel chief shook heaven's pillars out of alignment, she restored order by melting multicolored stones to rebuild the blue sky. Finding other problems on earth, Nu Kua set about correcting them: she cut off the toes of a giant tortoise and used them to mark the compass' points; she burned reeds into ashes, using them to dam the flooding rivers. She also concerned herself with the chaos of human relations, and established rites of marriage so that children would be raised well. Order restored, Nu Kua retreated to the distant sky—her domain and her attribute.

Nuliayoq   On the western coast of Hudson Bay, the Inuit people consider the world's primary divinity to be this goddess who is similar to Sedna, the preeminent deity of other Eskimos. There are differences between the tales told of Nuliayoq and of Sedna, however. Nuliayoq was an orphan girl who, when her village moved to another place, had no one to watch out for her safety. She would have been abandoned, had she not jumped onto one of the departing boats. But she missed her footing and drowned in the sea, where, like Sedna, she became the controlling spirit of marine life. Nuliayoq was said to have a home in a warm heavenly land, where souls of good people and of suicides traveled to play ball with a talking walrus skull; these games flitted across the sky, visible as the aurora borealis. When not in her heavenly home, Nuliayoq guarded her animals and fish, waiting at the entrances to inlets and rivers to punish anyone who flouted her fishing and hunting regulations.

Numma Moiyuk   Ocean goddess of the Yulengor of Arnhem Land in Australia, she created herself in the form of a very fat woman—full of the unborn children who would someday populate the entire continent. Though she came from the sea, she knew the need for fresh water and created the first pools and wells. Then she gave birth to humankind and taught her descendants the necessary crafts to survive on earth, including the weaving of fishnets and the painting of sacred designs. Finally she died, offering her body as food to her children.

Nunnehi   Gourd-headed, hairless and tall, these Cherokee spirits like to attend funerals, for they know that dancing will follow. Men who become enamoured of them often follow them home after the dance—only to see the Nunnehi walk into a lake or directly through a rock, leaving behind one dazed suitor. Benevolent nature spirits, they worry about the difficulties that Cherokee people face. Once, they even tried to move all the Cherokee to their own world, so that the people would be free of suffering and pain. They visited each village in turn, telling its residents to fast for seven days and seven nights. That was too much for many, who sneaked some morsels of food during the preparatory week. Alas for the hungry ones, however, for when the Nunnehi returned and led the people through a mountain (said to be Pilot Knob in Tennessee), those who had kept faith disappeared while the rest remained. Since that time they have never reopened the offer of escape to Nunnehi heaven.

Nut   Once, long before our earth existed, the great sky goddess Nut lay across the body of her small brother the earth, holding him in constant intercourse. But—so said the ancient Egyptians—the high god Ra disapproved of their incessant incest, and he commanded the god Shu to separate the pair. Shu hoisted Nut into a great arch, but—such was the goddess' desire for her little brother Geb—he was forced to remain forever holding them apart, supporting the starspangled belly of the sky queen. And that is how we see Nut in Egyptian art: a woman standing on her toes and bending forward in a perfect arch, her fingers touching the earth opposite her feet, her hair falling down like rain. So she stood, on the inside of sarcophagi, where as mother of the dead she stretched her long body protectively over the mummy.

Ra cursed Nut for her love, forbidding her to bear children during any month of the year. But the god Thoth outwitted the curse, playing draughts with the moon and winning from him five intercalary days, days not attached to any month, which float between the years. And in these five days, from her brother's seed already within her, Nut produced five children: the sister goddesses Isis and Nephthys, their mates Osiris and Set, and the sun god Horus.

Sometimes Nut took the form of a huge cow; such was the shape she wore when the god Ra decided to abandon the earth. She kneeled so that he could climb on her. Then up, up she strained, bearing the god upon her back until she became dizzy from the weight. Four gods instantly rushed to hold up Nut's vast body, remaining thereafter as the world's four pillars.

Nuxiu   The ancestral mother of the Chin people, who gave their name to China, she became pregnant miraculously when she ate an egg dropped from the sky by a black bird. The child born from this pregnancy was the first ruler of the Chin dynasty.

Nyadeang   The Sudanese African people, the Nuer, name this moon goddess Daughter of the Sky-Spirit. A simple ritual honors her: rubbing ashes on the forehead as the new moon rises, while praying for long life and happiness.

Nyamitondo   Among the Nyanga people of Zaire, this heroine married the lightning, from whom she learned to grow bananas and who taught her how to forge iron tools. When a dragon attacked and ate Nyamitondo, she found herself in its belly together with all the people from earth. But she cut her way out, thus freeing the people to repopulate the world.

Nyamwanda   The Nyanga of Zaire say that this goddess lives in an iron house and owns a special whistle that brings the dead back to life.

Nyapilnu   Ancestral goddess of the Australian Yiritja people, she was the one who invented architecture when, stranded in a storm with her sister Wurdilapu, she discovered that tree bark could be used to build shelters.

Nyavirezi   This legendary Rwandan queen could transform herself into a lioness whenever she wanted to hunt. She was also a prophetess who could foretell the results of a hunt.

Nyi Pohaci   The rice goddess of the Sundanese, who live near Java, was the daughter of the serpent goddess Antaboga. Her mother, fearing to lose her in marriage to a god, gave her only fruit of the tree of paradise to eat. But this diet was not enough to sustain her, and she wasted away. Her death brought life, however, for as her body decomposed, rice sprang forth from her eyes, bamboo from her thighs, and the coconut palm from her head.

Nyina Mweru   A legendary princess of Uganda, she was the daughter of a celestial king who returned to heaven, abandoning her on earth. Mating with a handsome stranger, she produced a son who accidentally killed his grandfather. After that, kings of the country could not stay on the throne until death, but had to give up the crown once they had grown too old to rule.

Nyx   In mother-ruled cultures, some theorists contend, night was given precedence over day, the moon over the sun. The interpretation is arguable, but it is unarguable that the pre-Hellenic creation myth calls the goddess Nyx ("night") the first daughter of unruly Chaos, and these pre-Hellenic Greeks are believed to have been matriarchal or at least matrilineal.

Nyx gave birth to Erebus and mated with him to produce the first light ever seen, the Hesperides. Unfortunately, she did not stop there, spewing out many other often dreadful creatures like Age and Death and Fate. (Perhaps the light she birthed balanced the horrors.) She lived, like her daughter Hemera ("day"), beyond the horizon in Tartarus. Twice each day Hemera and Nyx passed at the brass gates of the other world, waving from their chariots as one went home and the other mounted the sky. There were few worshipers of this elderly goddess, but upon them Nyx bestowed one gift: that of prophecy, of seeing beyond the night of the present.

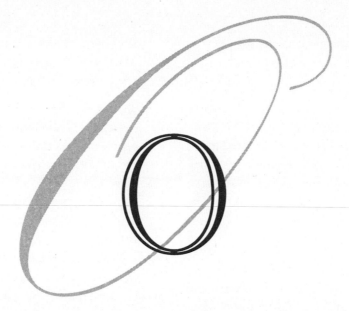

Oba Goddess of the African river that bears her name, she is a primary divinity of the Yoruba people. Her myth centers on Oba's rivalry with coquettish Oshun. Oshun desired Oba's mate Chango, and she would stoop to anything to get her way. One day, Oshun pulled a horrifying trick on Oba. Claiming that Chango preferred her cooking, she shared her secret: that she cut off parts of her ears and put them in the dishes—when it was really only mushrooms that Oba saw floating in the soup. The next time Oba cooked for Chango, she cut off a whole ear and mixed it with the food. This, alas, made the dish revoltingly foul-tasting, and Chango was even more revolted to see his mangled mate. When Oshun arrived to gloat, Oba attacked her. The two goddesses turned into rivers, and where their waters meet, there is always turbulence.

As did other Yoruba goddesses, Oba accompanied her people to the New World. When she possesses dancers, they wear a scarf that hides one ear—and they must be kept from other dancers who are embodying Oshun. Oba is sometimes syncretized with the Christian St. Catherine.

Obatallah This creator goddess is among the pantheon of four great female divinities of Brazilian Macumba, the others being Oshun, Oya and Yemanja.

Oceanids There were 3,000 of them, these elder sisters of the Nereids. Early Greek water goddesses, they were daughters of the sea queen Tethys and eventually were replaced in mythology by the latecomers.

Ochumare Yoruba and Santeria goddess of the rainbow, sometimes Catholicized into Our Lady of Hope.

Ocrisia One of the great Roman matriarchs was originally a servant of queen Tanaquil. One day, as Ocrisia was laying out the day's offerings by the hearth, a penis-shaped flame stretched out toward her. Tanaquil, skilled in reading omens, knew that the fire god lusted for the young woman and instructed Ocrisia to dress in bridal attire and lie near the fireplace. Apparently the fire's desire was satisfied, because nine months later Ocrisia gave birth to the child who grew to be Servius Tullius, sixth king of Rome.

Oddibjord In Scandinavia, prophets were women called Volvas or Voluspas. The one by the name of Oddibjord was very famous; she traveled about telling stories and fortunes, and the fortune you got depended on how well you fed her.

Oddudua   Primary mother goddess of the Yoruba of Nigeria, she is the great *orisha* (deity) of the earth as well as its creator. Her name means "she who exists for herself and to create others," and it was her energy that caused the primal matter which later formed itself into this universe. The spot where she descended from the sky onto the new earth is still pointed out in Yorubaland. Oddudua is called Saint Claire in Santeria.

Odras   In Irish legend, this human woman was strong enough—or foolish enough—to demand her rights from the queen of death, the Morrigan. Odras had a cow that the goddess wanted to mate with her bull, Slemuin the Smooth. The Morrigan simply stole the animal and carried it beneath the world.

Angry at her loss, Odras went to wild Connaught, to Hell's Gate in the Cave of Cruachen. But there enchantment overtook her, and she fell asleep under magical oak trees. The Morrigan came again to the earth's surface and, to punish the girl for her presumption, sang a spell over her that turned Odras into a pool of water.

Oeno   In Greek myth, Oeno ("wine") was a granddaughter of the wine god Dionysus, and sister of Spermo ("wheat") and Elias ("olive oil"). Their grandfather gave them a useful power: to change water to wine, grass into wheat, berries into olives. They lived peacefully on the island of Delos until the Greeks stopped by, looking for provisions for the trip to Troy. Oeno and her sisters helped them with their special powers, but the Greeks greedily fell upon the women, thinking to keep them prisoner until Troy fell. Dionysus came to their aid, turning them into doves so they could escape.

Ogdoad   In the primordial abyss, said the Egyptians, there were four female frogs—Naunet, Kauket, Hauket, and Amaunet, collectively called the Ogdoad—and four male snakes. Out of their ran-

dom movements a pattern began to emerge, which grew increasingly more regular until they had brought order out of chaos.

Ohoyo Osh Chishba   "Unknown Woman" was the name of the Cherokee vegetation goddess. The people of what is now southeastern America told the following story. Ohoyo Osh Chishba lived alone, an old woman full of wisdom but set in her ways. One day, as she walked along a familiar path, she saw blood on the ground. She covered it with a jar.

A few days later, she picked up the jar and found an infant boy, whom she raised to be a hunter, teaching him what animals to seek and how to kill them. But Ohoyo Osh Chishba taught him nothing of plants, for she provided all the maize and beans they could eat. And she gave him one caution: that he should never pass a certain blue mountain, visible from her home.

As he grew, the boy became curious. One day, peering in Grandmother's window, he saw her disrobe and scratch herself over a pot. As she did so, cornmeal and beans ran down her legs and into the pot, for she herself was food and she was creating meal for her child.

When he entered and refused his dinner, Grandmother knew instantly that he had spied on her. She sent him away with instructions that, as he left, he should set fire to her house. He did so sadly, and followed her dying instructions by seeking a wife from a distant tribe. When at last he brought his bride back to Grandmother's land, he found all the food plants of the world growing, enough to feed all their descendants.

Olwen   The Welsh sun goddess' name may mean "leaving white footprints" or "golden wheel." She was the opposite of the "silver-wheeled" moon goddess Arianrhod. Olwen was mentioned in early Arthurian legend as a princess who, attired in many rings and a collar of red gold, married a man named Culhwch, despite the knowledge that this marriage would kill her father.

The father, whose name translates as the "giant hawthorn tree," tried to prevent the consummation of her love for Culhwch by placing thirteen obstacles—possibly the thirteen lunar months of the solar year—in her path. But Olwen survived the tests by providing the thirteen necessary dowries.

That Olwen was specifically the summer sun seems clear from descriptions of her: she had streaming yellow hair, anemone fingers, and rosy cheeks; from every footstep a white trefoil sprang up. The "white lady of the day," she was called, the flower-bringing "golden wheel" of summer.

Omamama The ancestral goddess of the Crees of Ontario, Omamama was endlessly beautiful, although old as the earth herself; she was also endlessly loving to her children, the spirits and the divinities of the world. Her firstborn was the thunderbird; her second, the sorcerer frog; her third, the Cree hero Weesakayjac; and finally the wolf and beaver. After these powers, rocks and plants fell from her almighty womb until the earth was furnished and populated as we know it today.

Omecihuatl One day this Mexican goddess—the female half of divinity who, together with her consort, formed an androgyne called Ometeotl—squatted down to give birth. Her child was a stone knife, which she instantly threw down to the vacant earth, where it miraculously shattered into 1,600 heroes.

The heroes could have become gods and rejoined their mother in her heaven. But, both lazy and ambitious, they wished to remain on earth and be served by men. There were, however, no men then in existence. Turning to Omecihuatl ("star-skirted goddess"), they asked her to create some. She suggested instead that they improve their spiritual condition and seek eternal reunion with her.

The 1,600 heroes then sent the hero Xolotl to the underworld to gather ashes and bones. These they formed into the bodies of the first man and woman, destined ever after to serve the goddess' children.

Omphale This Amazon queen was said by the Greeks to rule the southern empire of Libya. As was customary, Omphale ("navel") purchased slavemen of attractive appearance and sensual manners; the Amazons knew no man could equal a queen, much less be superior, so their rulers enjoyed men as kings of other lands enjoyed female concubines. When the brawny Heracles came up for sale, in punishment for the murder of his wife and children, Omphale bought him and brought him home.

Omphale kept Heracles for three years. For amusement, she ordered him to wear transparent purple dresses. When not engaged in other duties, Heracles had to weave and spin and card wool. If he made mistakes at these unfamiliar chores, Omphale beat him with a golden sandal. Finally growing bored with him, Omphale sent Heracles back to his homeland.

Oniata Once the daughter of the sun came to live among the Iroquois people, legend says, being born with a beauty exceeding that of all other human women combined. Not only a beautiful girl, then woman, she was compassionate and noble in spirit. But the men around her, alas, were far from either. They left their wives and children to linger about the camp where Oniata lived; they fought each other at the least pretext, claiming they fought for Oniata's favor. When, finally, the Iroquois women complained bitterly and angrily about Oniata's presence among them, she explained sadly that she had never wished for the men's attentions. In order to ensure that the men would return to their families, she left the earth for good. She did, however, leave a trace of her beauty behind: the spring wildflowers.

Oona The most beautiful of Ireland's fairy queens, she was said to have golden hair so long it swept the ground; she flew through the earth robed in gossamer silver bejeweled with dew. Oona lived with the fairy king Finnvara, who was constantly unfaithful to her with mortal women; she retained, nonetheless, an even, benevolent temperament.

Ootonobeno-Kami   The goddess of the female element of primitive life forms, she emerged from primordial chaos shortly before the creator goddess of Japanese Shinto, Izanani.

Ops   Her name survives in our word *opulent*, and in Rome she represented the opulence of the earth's fruiting. Worshiped at harvest festivals on August 25 and December 19, she was associated with the god Consus, ruler of the "conservation" of the grain that Ops brought her people. Newborn children were put in her care, so that she would care for them as tenderly as she cared for the shoots of springtime plants. She was called by several titles: Consivia, the sower; Patella, stimulator of the wheat crop; and Rucina, promoter of the harvest. She was a very ancient Roman goddess, identified in later days with the Greek Rhea.

Orbona   In Rome, this goddess had an important, if poignant, function: she was the one to whom parents came to pray and offer sacrifice if they had lost a child to death. These sacrifices were not intended for the soul of the deceased, but for the safety of remaining children. Parents of ill children also prayed to this maternal force.

Oreads   The sweet-singing nymphs of mountains and rocks, they were slender, pale women who wore thin robes, woven in caves on fine looms visible only to the second-sighted. To honor these elemental spirits, the Greeks used to anoint rocks with fragrant oils, hang attractive belts on rocks, and leave offerings in caves.

Oreithyia   The daughter of Erechtheus and Praxithea, she was dancing by the River Ilissus one day when the north wind, Doreas, snatched her up, carried her to Sarpedon's rock in Thrace, and raped her. From this crime, two daughters,

Cleopatra and Chione, were conceived, as were the winged Argonauts, Calais and Zetes.

Orore   To the Chaldeans, there was nothing before creation except a goddess—an insect with a hugely pregnant abdomen and a giant eye—and her bullheaded fishtailed consort; they were the male and female principles of creation, the original egg and sperm.

Orthia   Artemis in Sparta was the "upright one" or "she who causes erections," a thirsty goddess particularly pleased with blood and semen released by the young male initiates whipped at her shrines.

Oshun   Originally the Yoruba goddess of the river named for her, Oshun's emblem is the brass bracelet worn by her worshipers, and a pottery dish filled with white stones from a river's bed. In her African homeland, Oshun mated with the god Chango, with whom she had human children. Their descendants, who still live along her waters, are forbidden to eat snails or beans, or to drink beer made from sorghum. Oshun is honored in Nigeria with an annual ceremony called *Ibo-Osun*. A feast of yams begins the evening, then women dance for the goddess, hoping to be chosen as one of her favorites. Those who are selected are granted new names, which include that of the goddess: Osun Leye ("gift of Oshun"), or Osun Tola ("treasure of Oshun"). Once selected in this way, the woman serves her community as advisor, particularly assisting with family problems and illnesses. Oshun is especially consulted by those who wish to have children, for she encourages this womanly activity.

Oshun is the primary divinity of Oshogbo, an African *orisha* religion, where she is honored with brass objects, as well as jewels and yellow copper. Her chief festival celebrates the arrival of the ancestral family on the banks of Oshun's river. While bathing, one of the princesses apparently drowned, but reappeared soon after attired in gorgeous garments which, she said, Oshun had given her. The alliance with the river goddess has continued to this day.

In the African diaspora, Oshun gained new names and titles: Oxum in Brazil; Ochun in Cuba; Ezili-Freda-Dahomey in Haiti. When she possesses dancers, their movements are those of a woman who loves to swim, who makes her arm bracelets jangle, and who admires herself in a mirror. Her appearance is greeted with welcoming shouts of "Ore Yeye o!" In Brazilian Macumba, Oshun is goddess of waters; she is depicted wearing jewels, holding a mirror, and wafting a fan. Altars to her hold copper bracelets and fans, as well as dishes of omuluku (onions, beans and salt). She rules love, beauty and flirtation. In Santeria, Oshun is revered as Our Lady of La Caridad, patron of the island of Cuba.

In Benin (formerly Dahomey) in Africa, art such as this wooden sculpture captures woman's power and sensuality. So does the mythic figure of Oshun, a goddess whose influence extended to the New World through the African diaspora.

Ostara The Germanic name for spring's goddess means "movement towards the rising sun." Ostara was celebrated in the fourth month of the year, April, according to the British scribe Bede the Venerable, writing in the seventh century C.E. Over a thousand years later, the Grimm brothers found that she was still honored in Germanic lands, where her name was used for the month she ruled. In Anglo-Saxon, her name became Estre or Eastre, which survives today in the festival of rebirth, Easter, and in the mood encouraged by springtime, estrus. She was honored among the Germanic people with painted eggs, a tradition that survives today.

Otiona An Athenian patriot, she offered herself as a sacrifice when her father, King Erechtheus, was waging war on the Eleusinians. Her death was apparently effective, because her side won.

Oto-Hime Of the sea goddess of Japan, almost the same story was told as of the Irish Niamh. Once a young fisherman met Oto-Hime. Impressed with his charm, she took him to her castle beneath the waves. There they lived for a little while, making love and enjoying court life. The young man, however, grew worried about his family and spoke of his homesickness to Oto-Hime. She agreed to let him go, but gave him two conditions: that he carry a tiny box, and that he never open it.

He left immediately, box in hand. But when he reached his home island, he found nothing he remembered: the faces and names were different, the clothes of a new style, the houses in a different shape. Puzzled, he finally found an ancient resident who had heard the name of his family.

He said they had been dead for hundreds of years. Baffled and sad, the young man sat down and, forgetting his promise, opened the little box. Out swept the years he had lived with Oto-Hime. Surrounding him like smoke, they withered his body, and he fell instantly into dust.

Otrere "Nimble" was the name given to the ancestral goddess of the Amazons; it also was a title of distinction bestowed on women leaders. This Amazon mother goddess was said to be a daughter of the war god Ares, although the name of her mother is not recorded. Alternatively, she was said to be the mother of the most famous Amazon queens, fathered by Ares.

Ovda A violent wanderer of the Finnish forests, the mightily powerful Ovda was almost always in ill humor. She had long breasts, which she threw over her shoulders, and long ragged hair; she wore no clothing as she wandered through her property, looking for trespassers to tickle to death. Those who encountered her tried to take advantage of a hole in her left armpit: if you could stick your finger in, Ovda would fall helplessly to the ground.

Oya Originally a goddess of the Yoruba in western Africa, she was goddess of storms on the Niger River. Her name means "she tore" in the Yoruba language, for her winds tear up the river's calm surface; she is also called "mother of nine," for the nine estuaries of the Niger. She is a warrior goddess as well as patron of female leadership.

Buffalo horns are placed on her altar, for Oya is a water-buffalo when not in human form. Once, it is said, a hunter saw a buffalo shed its skin; the beautiful woman who emerged hid the skin in a thicket of thorns and went to market. The hunter stole Oya's skin, forcing her to become his mate. But his other wives teased her about being a buffalo, and in anger, she killed them and reclaimed her buffalo hide. She stormed out to the fields to find the man who had betrayed her, but he bought his life for some bean fritters—Oya's favorite food.

The Yoruba people of Nigeria pictured woman's power this way. Yoruba goddesses like Oshun and Oya and Ymoja traveled with their enslaved worshipers to the New World, where they became part of such syncretic religions as Macumba and Voudou.

In addition to bean fritters, those who honor Oya offer her palm wine, goat meat and yams. Wednesday is her holy day, when her followers wear dark red beads to please her. When she enters a dancer, the dance becomes frenzied as Oya swings a sword (or a flyswatter). Sometimes she dances with arms outstretched to hold off ghosts, for she is the only goddess who can control them.

Oya emigrated with her children to the New World, changing form to suit her new surroundings. In Brazil, she was called Yansa; in Cuba, Olla, in Haiti, Aido-Wedo; in New Orleans, Brigette; she was also assimilated to the Catholic saints Theresa, Barbara and Catherine. A warrior storm goddess who also rules fire, she is one of the great divinities of Brazilian Macumba. In Santeria she is the nine-headed mate of the lightning god Chango. Patron of justice and memory, she is pictured holding a flame.

Pahto A mountain goddess of the Yakima and Klick-itat, she was embodied in a mountain in south-western Washington, today called Mount Adams. Once, it was said, she was a wife of the sun. But he had four other mountain wives, and two of them stood in the way of the sun's rays each morning. Plash-Plash (Goat Rocks) and Wahkshum (Sim-coe Mountain) received caresses of sunshine long before the god even noticed Pahto.

So Pahto killed the other wives; she exploded and dashed off their heads. Then she happily accepted the first rays of the sun on her wooded sides each morning.

But she grew restless and greedy. Having once felt her power, she decided to improve herself fur-ther. She went south, where she stole everything she could from other mountains, all the berries and ferns and trees and animals, the salmon and the trout, and she took them all back to her own hill.

The other mountains grew furious. Klah Klah-nee (Three Sisters) urged Wyeast, goddess of Mount Hood, to do something. First she offered Pahto a truce, if half of the stolen goods were returned; Pahto refused. So Wyeast blew her head off, leaving a pile of rocks on the north face, once Pahto's head. Then Wyeast took back what had been stolen, leaving only a few berry bushes and some elk and fish for the haughty mountain.

The sky spirit, seeing how Pahto had been humbled, offered her a new head: a great white eagle, a cap of snow that shone in the sunlight. This eagle was the law of generosity and freedom, the law that—in the shining of the sunlight on mountain snow—stood forever to remind Pahto's people to share the resources of her earth.

Paivatar In the Kalevala, the nineteenth-century compilation of Finnish mythological tradition, this was the name of the spinning sun virgin who wove daylight from a rainbow arch. "Competent maid," she was called, "resplendent on a shaft-bow of the sky." She held a weaver's batten, a heddle, and a golden shuttle. The cloth she wove was gold; her moon-sister's was silver.

One of the epic events of the Kalevala is the freeing of the captive sun from a dark cave where the witch Louhi had hidden her. As in the Japanese myth of Amaterasu, a mirror image of the sun was first forged from metal. But when hoisted into the sky, it proved unsatisfactory. So the poet Vain-omoinen demanded that Louhi say where the god-dess was hidden. "The sun got into the crag, the moon vanished into the rock, and they will never get free, never, never at all!" the witch taunted.

But Vainomoinen, undeterred, lopped off the heads of Louhi's henchmen as though they were turnip tops, and set out to free the sun. He went to Ilmarinen, the smith, and ordered a three-tined hoe, a dozen ice picks, and many keys. Louhi, seeing all the activity at the forge, disguised herself as a bird and flew over to spy on Ilmarinen. When she saw that it would be impossible to win over the determined heroes, she set the sun goddess free.

Pales For many years mythology texts called her a god, but recent scholarship confirms that the Roman divinity of cattle was a goddess. Although there was a god of this name among the Etruscans, all other tribes of Italy knew Pales as a feminine force. There is some evidence, indeed, that she was not only one goddess but two: the goddesses of small and of large cattle. At her festival, the Parilia on April 21, the stock-keeping farmers purified their animals by driving them between blazes of fragrant woods; then they offered a long prayer to Pales begging forgiveness for any unintended slight against nature committed in the previous year. Without such careful ceremony, the Romans were convinced, the animals would not bear healthy offspring and the farmers would suffer even for minor offenses like burning the wrong dead tree.

Pali Kongju This princess, according to Korean myth, was the ancestor of all shamans. Her story began when her father, King Upbi of Sam, decided to marry despite predictions of misfortune for his children. A large part of that misfortune came from their father's rejection of them, for he would have preferred a single son to all his first six daughters. When the queen birthed a daughter for the seventh time, the king ordered the child thrown into the ocean—hence her name, meaning "princess thrown away."

Unable to save her child, the weeping queen put her in a jewel box with a bottle of milk. Rough soldiers tore the box from her arms and threw it into the sea. But then, from beneath the waves, a horde of golden turtles slowly rose until they bore the little box above the water. Thus she was brought to shore where she was adopted by a peasant couple who, from the time they took her in, had great good fortune. She grew to be a happy, loving daughter.

Meanwhile, the king and queen had been stricken with a wasting illness from which diviners said they could only recover if Pali Kongju would aid them by fetching the medicinal water from the Western Sky. The desperate king repented his infanticide and begged his other daughters to get the water. They refused, claiming they were unable to bear the arduous journey.

But the god of the mountains found Pali Kongju and told her of her duty. Sad though she was to leave her foster parents, the princess returned home to the palace where the king and queen greeted her with disbelieving relief. She did not stay long; taking a pair of iron shoes and an iron stick, she set off.

She had to pass the North Pole Star and the South Pole Star, playing at their interminable games of chance; she had to pass the Old Farming Woman of Heaven, who made her plow and sow an immense field; she had to find the Laundress of Heaven and wash her clothes from black to white. Finally, she reached the Western Sky, where she was met with glittering golden turtles who formed a bridge to the beyond for her.

Nearly falling to hell from the cliffs above it, Pali Kongju struggled on until she found the ugly Guardian Armed Guard at the well of heaven. Of course he would give her the water, the god said, in return for money. Alas, though, the princess had not thought to bring money with her.

So she agreed to marry the god and bore him seven sons. Finally, he gave her a bottle of the water, and with her children she set off for home.

But she came too late, for the funeral was already underway for her mother and father. Desperate with grief, she sprinkled them nevertheless with the healing fluid. There was a stirring of life—then her parents sat up and embraced her. They wished to shower her with gifts and love, but she realized that her duty was to return to the world beyond so that she could help others in need. Taking her seven sons, she disappeared from this world.

Because of her sacrifice, she became the patron saint of the *mudang*, the women shamans who still practice in great number in Korea. During the *kut*, the danced ritual that is the heart of their religion, the mudang often don a stripe-sleeved multicolored robe and tell the tale of Pali Kongju as an incantation and an inspiration.

Pallas "Great maiden" was the name of this pre-Hellenic goddess whose independent identity became submerged in the great Athena. She survived in the myth that said she was an early friend of Athena and was accidentally killed by her, whereupon Athena took her friend's name as her own. (An almost identical story is told of Callisto and Artemis.)

Pamphile This great Greek sorceress could bring the moon into her garden with her spells, so powerful were they. Mistress of metamorphosis, Pamphile rubbed herself with ointment by a magic lamp's light to change her shape. Often she became an owl and flew through the night, bathing in spring water with anise and bay leaf when she returned to regain human form. But even her fabulous magic had its limitations. Once, it was said, she was infatuated with a young man and needed only a hair from his head or body to enchant him forever; never able to procure the hair, she never satisfied her love.

Pandia It is not known whether this goddess was a powerful one (her name means "all goddess" or perhaps "goddess of all") whose legend was lost or merely a local form of the moon goddess Selene. Some Greek tales called her Selene's daughter, the "entirely bright one," probably the full moon; she

was also said to be the mate of Zeus Pandion, the full-moon god.

Pandora Originally she was "rich in gifts," the "all-giver," the earth in female form, endlessly producing food for people and animals; the name may have been a title of the Greek Gaia. She was also called Anesidora ("sender-forth of gifts") and shown as a gigantic woman rising from the earth while little men opened her way with hammer-blows.

Later, as Greek society changed, she became the evil Eve of their legend, the one who brought all sorrow to earth. Gifted with all talents, the most beautiful creature imaginable, she was given a box and instructed never to open it. But, too curious to obey, she did so, and all the evils that afflict humanity escaped to run rampant through the world. Only one being, the hope goddess Spes, remained in the box to comfort us.

Yet even this late story has symbolic overtones that point to Pandora's earlier identity with the earth mother. Originally the "box" was a *pithos*, an earthenware jar used to store food and to bury the dead. This pithos symbolized the earth mother's womb, in which the dead were placed in fetal position to await rebirth. Thus when "Pandora's box"—the womb—is opened, we are born into our trials and even our death, though women continue to hold hope within us.

Pani A plant goddess of the Polynesian Maori, she was impregnated by a man who had sweet potato seeds in his testicles. Pani gave birth (naturally enough) to a plant and, realizing her duty, retreated to the underworld, where she tended the magical sweet potato patch in the divine garden.

Pantariste This heroic Amazon was on the scene when the Greeks attempted to steal the belt of queenship from the royal Hippolyta. She left the palace to track the Greek Tiamides, who was on his way to alert his shipbound countrymen of the women warriors' resistance; she killed the messenger with her bare hands.

Papa The word we use for father was used by the Polynesians to summon mother earth, who existed from the beginning in perpetual intercourse with her lover, the sky god Rangi. They left no room between them, creating darkness everywhere, which stifled the gods that resulted from the divine union. Finally, the young gods decided to separate their parents. Although apart, the pair remained lovers still; the earth's damp heat rose lustfully to the sky, and the rain fell from heaven to fertilize beloved Papa.

Papalluga In Serbian mythology, Papalluga is a spinning maiden who brought down an unfortunate fate upon herself when, dropping her spindle into a ravine, she caused her mother to turn into a cow. Happily, the cow could still speak and help her daughter—which was soon necessary, for the father quickly remarried a wicked jealous woman. The first thing this stepmother did was to order Papalluga to spin a ball of hemp overnight—or be killed. Papalluga's cow-mother came to the rescue, chewing the hemp and producing fine linen out of her ears. The stepmother caught on, however, had the magical cow killed, and commanded Papalluga to pick up a load of scattered millet. As she was doing so, the girl was visited by birds who brought her magical clothes and assisted her at her task. And so Papalluga was able to dress in fairy garments, go to church, and catch the eye of the prince. Three times this happened, until Papalluga found herself at church, dressed and shod in pure gold—and capturing the prince's attention, also caught his heart.

Paphos This name was given to the Greek love goddess Aphrodite at Paphos, where she was said to have risen from the waves; this name was applied to all women who devoted their bodies to the goddess' service, as well as being bestowed upon the daughter of Pygmalion and the statuesque Galatea.

Pare Some Polynesians used this name for their volcano goddess, but among the Maori, Pare was said to have been a flirtatious young woman who led on, and then rejected, a young man named Hutu. He exploded in fury at her; ashamed of toying with his desires, she hanged herself.

Hutu was so anguished at the news of Pare's death that he decided to convince her to return to life. He traveled to the underworld but could find no traces of her. Hoping to lure her from hiding, Hutu began to play island games, Pare's favorite sports. Secretly she began to draw near. Then Hutu pulled saplings down to his height, soaring with them as they snapped upward. Pare found this new sport irresistible. As soon as she joined Hutu, he swung a tree so high that he dragged Pare back into the light.

Parooa Among the Assam in northern India, this female spirit lurked where three roads met, hoping to lure wayfarers astray with her *taka*, a flutelike instrument made of bamboo with which she imitated the moan of a lost person. When the helpless traveler left the road, Parooa created a thick fog from which no way out was visible.

Parvati One of the greatest goddesses of India is the daughter of the Himalayas, known also as Uma, Gauri, and sometimes as Shakti ("energy"). She was the consort and enlivening force of Shiva, the lord of life's dance, and many myths surround her.

She gained Shiva's attention by practicing magical asceticism until she had such power that he could not resist her. Thereafter he spent this time sexually pleasing the goddess. Once, when interrupted before she was satisfied, Parvati cursed the gods so that their consorts were barren but they themselves were pregnant. They were most miserable with the affliction, until Shiva allowed them to vomit up the semen that had impregnated them.

Parvati had one son of her own. It was no thanks to her spouse, for Shiva did not want to be bothered with children. As they argued about it one day, Parvati cried out that she wanted a child to hold and caress. Shiva teased her, ripping a piece of her skirt and handing it to her, telling her to fondle that. Hurt and betrayed, Parvati grasped the red cloth to her breast, and—touching the nipples of the mother goddess—the cloth took form and began to nurse. Thus was Ganesha, the benevolent god, born. But Shiva, angry and jealous, found an excuse to behead the child, saying that he had slept in a ritually incorrect way. Parvati was desperate with grief, and Shiva, ashamed, told her he would find the boy another head. The only one he was able to locate—Parvati must have received this news suspiciously—was an elephant's. And so Ganesha was reborn half human, half elephant.

Shiva's Shakti is also called Kali and Durga, for she is at times a fierce form of femininity. One legend explains how the goddess divided herself. Originally, it seems, she had dark skin, about which Shiva teased her once too often. Furious at him—for she felt less than beautiful, wishing that her skin were golden like his—he set off for the mountains, intending again to practice asceticism until she gained her desire. Ganesha accompanied her; she left Viraka, Shiva's attendant, to guard his bedroom so that he didn't enjoy other women's company during her absence. But a demon disguised as Parvati attempted to kill Shiva. He lured the god to bed after loading his illusory vagina with real nails. Shiva, recognizing the deceit, put a sword on his penis and dispatched the demon.

Parvati's informants spread the word that a woman had been seen entering Shiva's bedroom, and Parvati exploded in anger. Her anger shot out of her mouth in the form of a lion; she cursed the false guardian Viraka to become a rock. Then she continued practicing yoga until Brahma took pity on her and asked her what she wished. When she said she wanted a pure golden skin, he blessed her. From her body sprang another goddess, one ugly and black, usually named Kali.

Now golden and beautiful, Parvati started home. Viraka, still on guard, refused to let her enter, not recognizing the goddess in her new skin. Realizing that she had made a mistake in cursing him—but unable, so powerful are a goddess' words, to recall her ill wish—Parvati mitigated it by allowing him to be reborn as a girl named Rock.

Pasiphae "She who shines for all" was a Cretan goddess, daughter of sun and moon; she mated with a magical bull who rose from the sea, as another Cretan goddess, Europa, mated with Zeus in bull disguise. Later, the Greeks made Pasiphae's story both more and less realistic, calling her a Cretan queen, who, conceiving an unnatural passion for a bull, satisfied her desire by having the artisan Daedalus build her a wooden cow in which she could have intercourse with her beloved. By this means, she conceived the bull-man, the Minotaur; her other children were Ariadne and Phaedra, who also figure in Cretan and Greek myths.

Pattini The one-breasted goddess of Sri Lanka is still served today by transvestite priests who enter shamanic trances. One of the major goddesses of the area, she is honored in long poems like the Shilipatikarum, the epic of the silver anklet, as well as in rituals and folkways. In myth, Pattini was born miraculously from a mango. Then she married a prince with whom, for some unexplained reason, she could not have intercourse. He left her for a prostitute, on whom he squandered his fortune, returning home penniless to Pattini, who was herself mired in poverty as an abandoned wife. But she, ever-loving, gave him her priceless silver anklet—her last possession—to sell in the marketplace. Unbeknownst to him, the queen had once had an identical bracelet, which had been stolen. When Pattini's luckless husband appeared with the apparently incriminating evidence, he was captured and executed for theft. Pattini herself went to the marketplace, then to the king himself. But too late—her husband lay there, already dead. Enraged, Pattini tore off her left breast and threatened the king with it. But he, scoffing, merely invited her to eat it. She threw it instead at the city. It burst into flame, destroying everything but the body of her husband, whom Pattini lovingly resurrected.

Pattini's solar identity is indicated directly in liturgies directed to her. She is born "of the pure dynasty of the sun," her ritual songs say, and "she banishes darkness," she "arrives like the sun in your midst in great beauty." Hers is the fire of the sun; summer's heat and drought are said to be caused by her fury at her husband's death. Pattini's fire can be dangerous, threatening to life. Thus cooling ceremonies are necessary; these include drinking sacred water in which an anklet has been dipped. Its circular shape connects this silver anklet both to the goddess' breast and to the sun itself; some versions of the epic, making the connection more plain, describe Pattini as throwing her anklet, not her breast, at the murderous king.

The most important divinity in Sri Lanka, she is also the only female figure in many village pantheons. Some legends, affected by Buddhist ideas, say that Pattini's claim to high position rests in her wishing to be reincarnated as a male—in order to attain to Buddhahood, the domain of men in that tradition. In these myths, she resisted intercourse with her husband by surrounding herself with a wall of flame.

Pawosee   As a girl, she was kidnapped from her people, the Kiowa of the American plains. She grew up knowing she did not belong, but did not know where else to go. When at last she escaped, she did not know which direction to run. But she stumbled upon a dead buffalo and took shelter under its fur-covered carcass. There she dreamed, a sacred dream, in which the buffalo showed her the way to use each of its parts, for food, for medicine, for clothing, for building. When she awoke, she set off with a sure sense of what her path was to be. Finding her people, she taught them how to use the buffalo, as the animal itself had taught her.

Pele   Even today, visitors to Hawaiian volcanoes report seeing a wizened old woman who asks for a cigarette, lights it with a snap of her fingers, then disappears. Others say that a red-robed woman dances on the rims of the fiery mountains, although it is not certain whether this figure is an incarnation of the goddess or one of her worshipers. Of all the world's goddesses, Pele is one of the few still living in the belief of her people, not as metaphor but as metaphysical reality, to whom offerings are still made when volcanic eruptions threaten Hawaiian towns.

A bright daughter of the earth goddess Haumea, Pele spent her girlhood watching fires and learning how to make them, thus revealing her temperament early. This did not please the sea goddess Namaka, who prophesied an unpleasant future for the fire-loving girl, but she, who lived in the ocean, may have been biased. But Namaka had a point: Pele did cause a conflagration in her mother's homeland once, toying with underworld fires.

The mother, knowing that Namaka would persecute Pele on her return, suggested that it was time for Pele to find a home of her own. So she set off in a canoe with several siblings including her sister Hiiaka ("cloudy one"). They were *malihini*, goddesses who migrated to Hawaii after human settlement there began. Hawaii was only an atoll when they arrived, so Pele used a divining rod to locate likely places to build islands, then caused them to be born in tempestuous eruptions from undersea volcanoes.

Namaka trailed her sister, furious at the destruction Pele had wrought in their original homeland. Ocean and fire met in a terrific brawl, and Pele got the worst of it, rising like a steamy spirit from the fray. No longer embodied, she disappeared into the Hawaiian volcanoes, especially in the fiery part of the crater of Kilauea called Halemaumau, said today to be one of her favorite haunts.

There she was honored by the Hawaiian people as the essence of earthly fire. Into her craters, offerings were cast: cut hair, sugar cane and flowers (especially hibiscus), white birds, money and strawberries. Some say that human beings were also tossed into the lava; others deny this, claiming there is no evidence for such rites.

There is one famous legend, however, that suggests that some were, if not sacrificed literally, at least consecrated to the goddess. This is the tale of the young Hawaiian man named Lohiau. Pele, it was said, sometimes dozed in her crater, sending her spirit wandering through the islands. One night, hearing the sweet melodies of flutes, she followed the sound until she came upon a group of sacred hula dancers.

Among them was Lohiau. Instantly attracted to him, Pele embodied herself in beautiful human flesh and seduced him. They spent three days making love before she decided that it was time to return to her mountain. Promising to send for him, Pele disappeared, awakening far away on Kilauea.

Not one to break a promise—and immediately desiring the young man again—Pele endowed her sister Hiiaka with magic and sent her off to fetch Lohiau. Hiiaka was a kindly goddess, given to singing with the poet goddess Hopoe and to picking blossoms from the tropical trees. But out of dedication to her sister, Hiiaka set off, first making Pele promise to tend her gardens.

Passing through many trials, often relying on her magic to defeat threatening monsters, Hiiaka reached Lohiau's home just as he died, pining away for his lover Pele. But Hiiaka caught his soul and pushed it back into his body, reviving him. Then they set off for Kilauea.

Although touched by the man's beauty, Hiiaka fully intended to fulfill her task and bring Lohiau untouched to her sister. But Pele was a jealous spirit, and she soon began to burn, imagining Hiiaka in Lohiau's arms. The crater began to spit out lava fretfully. Pele was growing angry.

Hiiaka understood the messages from the distant crater and hastened along. Even though challenged for possession of the man by a sorceress (probably Pele in disguise) and even though Lohinu told Hiiaka he loved her more than Pele, the goddess would not betray her sister's trust. All the way to the crater she conveyed the prize, only to find that Pele had not kept her part of the promise, that the volcano goddess had in jealous fury killed the poet Hopoe and scorched Hiiaka's lovely gardens.

Right then and there, on the rim of the crater, Hiiaka made love to Lohiau. Pele, erupting in fury, burned the man to death but could not destroy her immortal sister. Hiiaka, not about to lose to her angry sister, descended to the underworld to free Lohiou's soul. When she arrived at the deepest circle of the underworld, the point at which the rivers of chaos were held back by a gate, it occurred to her that flooding the entire world would thoroughly extinguish Pele and her wrath.

Her conscience kept her from such folly, however. Hiiaka, after freeing Lohiau's soul, determined to return to the surface and demand her lover from Pele. The lustful, angry goddess would not have been willing, except that Lohiau's comrade Paoa arrived in timely fashion to satisfy the goddess' heat. Hiiaka was reunited with Lohiau, and they retired to his country. Pele, meanwhile, found herself a lover of sturdier stuff in the combative hog god Kamapua'a, inventor of agriculture, whose idea of courting a goddess included all but dousing her flames with heavy rain and stampeding pigs across her craters. To this day, their turbulent affair continues on the islands called Hawaii.

Penelope   Behind the familiar figure of the faithful Greek wife Penelope, weaving by day and unwinding her work each night, looms a much more powerful queen: the spring goddess who, as owner of the land, chose its king; a goddess whose activity of weaving and unwinding showed her power over life itself. Even dwarfed into the queen of Ithaca, Penelope's original character was hinted at in the Odyssey's ending. After the happy reunion of Penelope and Odysseus, where our memories seem to end the tale, came the king's second banishment, which again left Penelope to rule alone. Then, the epic said, Odysseus returned again, to be killed, unrecognized, by his son by Circe; Penelope then married Circe's son while her own married Circe. Still other stories claimed that during Odysseus' absence his wife was far from faithful: it was Penelope who brought forth the wild woodland god, Pan, fathered on her by the ram-shaped Hermes—or by all her suitors in one long orgy.

Penthesilea   One of the greatest of the fighting Amazons, she led a troop to Troy to fight the Greeks; they nearly turned the tide of battle. Penthesilea herself engaged in single combat with the Greek hero Achilles. Some accounts of the war say that she killed him; the more common account is that the contest was close but Penthesilea was finally killed by the Greek warrior. Achilles, tearing off her helmet to see what worthy opponent he had bested, was overcome with her fierce beauty and regretted destroying her. But his destructiveness was untamable, for he then raped her corpse and killed a comrade who suggested that this lust was unnatural.

Perchta   An ancient mother goddess has survived throughout modern Germany, Switzerland, and Austria under the name of this "elf woman." Perchta is said to make the fields fertile and the cattle bear strong calves. Sometimes, it is said, you can see her float across the fields to nurture them, her white cape looking exactly like a soft mist.

She has her difficult side as well. She cannot tolerate laziness; she carefully inspects distaffs and spinning wheels, looking for wasted bits of wool. If she finds them, she scratches the guilty spinner or, worse yet, tears open her stomach and stuffs the remnants into the cavity. She herself, however, is rather sloppy in appearance, with long, white matted hair and tattered clothes. Her face is wrinkled like an apple doll, but her eyes are lively. Her favorite time of year is the "twelve days of Christmas," which culminate in Perchta's Day, when everyone eats pancakes of meal and milk in her honor. Leftover bits of the cakes are left for Perchta herself; she will come secretly to enjoy them, but if anyone tries to spy on her, he will be blinded for the year.

Perkuna Tete   The oldest goddess known in the Baltic was this "mother of thunder," who survives in only a single myth fragment as welcoming the sun goddess Saule, after her day's work, with a hot bath.

Pero   She was the granddaughter of Niobe and daughter of Chloris. A great beauty of Greek legend, she bore a title of the pre-Hellenic moon goddess, of whom Pero may be a vestigial form.

Perse   "Lightbearer" or "destroyer," she was the early Greek moon goddess, wife of the sun and daughter of the ocean. Her own daughters were the Cretan goddess Pasiphae and the famous witch Circe; possibly she later developed into Persephone.

Persephone   The Greek world was divided into three parts, in honor of the threefold goddess. Hecate, the moon, wandered through the sky; Demeter ruled the surface of the earth; and underneath the world, in the afterlife, the pale queen Persephone lived. Sometimes Hecate would join her there; sometimes Persephone would visit her mother, Demeter, on earth. But they were never completely separate, for these three goddesses were really a trinity, like the Christian god, three persons perceived as facets of the same divinity.

According to the Greeks, Persephone originally lived above-ground. One day, surrounded by companions, the maiden goddess was picking flowers. Suddenly the chariot of Hades appeared; the god of death snatched her up and carried her through a crack in the earth, which instantly closed after them. Hearing her daughter's cries, Demeter immediately sought her, but no trace remained.

Demeter went into mourning, broken only when the Olympian gods demanded the return of the raped maiden—on condition that she was not to have eaten anything in the afterworld. Hades, hearing the heavenly verdict, pressed a single pomegranate seed into Persephone's mouth. So the goddess was condemned to spend one-third of the year below ground, while the rest of the time she enjoyed the company of her mother on earth.

While Persephone was with her, Demeter caused the earth to spring forth with blossom and fruit. While Persephone was absent, however, the earth wilted and died, and the earth goddess mourned her annual separation from the daughter who was also Demeter's incarnate younger self. This annual cycle of joy and sorrow was celebrated at the town of Eleusis in solemn mysteries that the Greeks said made humans ready to face death, revealing the beautiful Persephone who waited to welcome them.

But what of those who died while Persephone was away from her domain? Did they wait for months to be initiated into the spirit realm? Persephone was known to be a gracious and gentle queen of the dead—indeed, she was called the reason for life itself, the goddess who lived with Eros, the goddess who had no children but allowed others to give birth. Some scholars, pointing out this confusion in the Greek conception of the afterlife, suggest that Persephone was originally the queen of death and that Demeter's daughter was Kore ("maiden"). As Greek theology grew, assimilating various figures into fewer but more complex ones, these maiden goddesses were joined.

That would explain variants of the Persephone story, like the one that tells how the goddess was sitting in a cave, guarded by snakes and weaving the entire world on a loom. Zeus came to her in the form of a snake and had intercourse with her; she gave birth to the wine god Dionysus, who was instantly ripped apart by Titans and died. This tale—which fits in poorly with the more familiar tale of the virgin goddess—shows Persephone more clearly associated with symbols of regeneration: the snake and the loom; she was perhaps a remnant of the earliest Persephone, the queen of death and rebirth. In another fragmentary story, Persephone is called Praxidice (or as multiple goddesses, Praxidicae) and given control over oaths, as well as the power to punish those who break them.

Phaedra   After the Athenian hero Theseus had abandoned the helpful Cretan heroine Ariadne, he returned to his city, ascended the throne, and married his deserted mistress' sister, Phaedra. She soon became infatuated with Theseus' son by another abandoned mistress, Hippolytus, son of Hippolyta. She offered her bed to her stepson, but he refused; she cursed him so that he was dragged to death by magical sea-dwelling horses. This Greek Phaedra seems to be a literary creation based on an original Cretan goddess of whom only the name, "bright one," survives intact.

Pherenice   This Greek woman bore a son who became a famous wrestler. She coached him to victory after victory, until he was ready to enter the Olympics. All women except Hera's priestesses were barred from the games, but Pherenice nonetheless put on male clothing to coach her son in the ring. He won, and her disguise was discovered; but in recognition of her coaching excellence, she was dismissed without punishment.

Philemon   Once, Greek legend says, there was an old man and woman who lived together so long and tenderly that they became inseparable, almost indistinguishable. Although age bent their backs, their eyes still shone with care and concern for each other; often they told themselves how empty life would be without such love.

Once, looking for adventure, the gods Zeus and Hermes went wandering the earth. Stopping at the poor hut where Baucis and Philemon lived, they begged a meal. The impoverished couple generously served what food they had, though they knew it meant a week of gruel for them. The gods revealed themselves; in recognition of the old couple's kindness, they granted a single wish. The pair wished quickly: to live together forever, never to be separated. Their hut instantly changed into a temple, where they served the gods for years. Then one day, as they stood outdoors, their feet took root and their arms stretched up to the sky, and they lived on forever as a pair of intertwined linden trees.

Philomena   In Thracian legend, this sister of Procne (or Progne) was raped by her brother-in-law, King Tereus, who, to keep her from reporting the crime, cut out her tongue. But Philomena still had hands to bear witness, and she wove a tapestry picturing the brutal act. When she sent this to her sister, the two women began to plot revenge. They cut up the five-year-old son of Procne and her husband and served the child to his father for dinner. During the meal, Philomena brought in the boy's head and flung it upon the table. At that point they were all transformed: Philomena into the first nightingale; Procne, into a swallow; King Tereus, into a hawk; and the boy Itylus, into a sandpiper.

Phyllis   There were two Greek heroines by this name. The first was a Thracian queen, courted by an Athenian king who sought to control her country. She agreed to wed him, thereby giving him title to Thrace. But he heartlessly left her to return to the pleasures of Athens. So Phyllis ended his rights to Thrace, and her life, by throwing herself into the sea. A more romantic legend, reminiscent of *Romeo and Juliet*, says that Phyllis went nine times to their meeting place but her lover was detailed; she hung herself and was turned into a leafless almond tree. When her lover arrived and saw what had happened, he embraced the tree and it burst into leaf.

Another famous Phyllis was a free-living woman who took as a lover the young Macedonian king, Alexander, who was wildly infatuated with her. His teacher, the philosopher Aristotle, warned him against giving such power to a woman. Phyllis found this attitude insulting; she avenged herself by so bewitching Aristotle that he served her as a mount, walking on his hands and knees while she rode astride, controlling his head with a bridle.

Pidari   This South Indian snake goddess was depicted with flaming hair and three eyes; she held a noose

and a drum, apparently to frighten away evil spirits from the villages she guarded. Her worship has been traced to the first millennium of the Christian Era.

Pietas   Roman goddess of duty and filial respect, she was sculpted offering her full breasts to wrinkled, aged parents. She protected children as well, and is represented by a sacred stork.

Pi-Hsia Yuan-Chin   The Princess of the Blue and Purple Clouds was, to Chinese Taoists, a major divinity and one of the most beloved. With her train of six divine helpers—one for each stage of labor—she attended every birth, bringing health and good fortune to the newborn, as well as protecting its mother. She was sometimes thought to be identical with the Buddhist Kuan-Yin and was called by the names Sheng-Mu ("holy mother"), Yu Nu ("jade maiden"), and T'ien Hsien ("heavenly immortal").

Pitho   This minor Greek goddess, said to rule seduction and persuasion, was the daughter (appropriately enough) of the lustful goddess Aphrodite and tricky Hermes. Other myths call her the daughter of Ate, goddess of disorder; with Eros, the god of love, she gave birth to the health goddess Hygiea. In another myth, the Greeks said that Penia, goddess of poverty, was the daughter of Porus (expediency), who was conceived on the birthday of Aphrodite (sex). Yet other records use this name as a title of Aphrodite herself.

Pitys   The Greek woodland god Pan desired this nymph, but she had no interest in him. Nonetheless he pursued her—literally, chasing her across the landscape. When she began to fall behind in the race, she changed herself to a pine, which thereafter was sacred to him and formed the headgear for his followers. Another version of the story says that Pan was in fact her lover, but that the wind god Boreas desired her. When she rejected him, he blew her off a cliff. As she was hanging there desperately, the earth mother Gaia took pity on her and transformed her into a weathered pine tree which weeps sap whenever the wind touches it.

Pleiades   The seven daughters of the nymph Pleione, they were born in wild Arcadia and followed the wild goddess Artemis until they were turned into the stars that bear their name, the "seven sisters." Individually, their names were Alcyone, Calaeno, Electra, Maia, Merope, Asterope and Taygete—almost all names also borne by early Greek goddesses, which suggests that the legend linking them has been lost.

Pohaha   This heroine of the Pueblo Cottonwood clan refused to marry or learn women's skills, preferring instead to hunt and raid with her male age-mates. Although she was mocked for this choice, the raillery ended when she became leader of the men's war-parties. Lest anyone question that this redoubtable warrior was female, she would raise her skirts as she approached an enemy—then soon claim victory. Named Chief Defender of the Clan, Pohaha held that title for the rest of her life.

Pohjan-Akka   In the European subarctic, among the Scandinavian Saami, this goddess was said to be mistress of the northern hell called Pohjan, where anyone who died a violent death would live forever, wearing blood-drenched garments. The "man-eating village" of Pohjan was sometimes thought to be the aurora borealis, floating with red fringes through the wintry sky. Witches were said to be able to visit Pohjan in their living bodies, but no other breathing humans could even find the place, located somewhere in the Arctic Ocean.

Po Ino Nogar   Among the Chams of Cambodia, the world's goddess-ruler, creator of rice, was called Po Ino Nogar ("Great One, mother of the kingdom"). Born either from seafoam or from clouds, she had ninety-seven husbands and thirty-eight daughters. One of her offspring was Po Bya Tikuh ("mouse queen"), a maleficent virgin goddess; another was the goddess of disease, Po Yan Dari, who lived in caves and grottoes to which worshipers would bring stones, asking for miraculous cures. Another Cham healing goddess was the divine priestess Pajau Tan, said to be a thirtyish woman who lived on earth as a healer but who was finally sent to live in the moon because she kept raising all the dead; there she still lives, providing flowers to the newly dead to ease their transition.

Poldunica   In eastern Europe, the goddess of midday was a white lady who floated about the fields on gusts of wind, killing people with a touch of her hand. That was her most familiar form, but there were variants. In Moravia, she was a white-gowned old woman with horse hooves, staring eyes, and wild hair. In Poland, Poldunica was very tall and carried a sickle; she asked difficult riddles of those she caught wandering the fields at midday, and if they could not answer she would reap them. In Russia, she was very beautiful—something her victims noticed just before she twisted their heads around, bringing death, or at least intense pain. In Serbia, she guarded the corn from thieves and careless children; in Finland, she kidnapped children caught abroad at noon. Finally, in Siberia, Poldunica appeared as a scantily clad woman of great age, who hid in nettle patches and pulled naughty children into her den.

Polycaste   The sister of the great Greek architect Daedalus, she bore a son who, as he grew up, was found to be even more brilliantly inventive than his uncle. Seeing the boy as a threat to his reputation, Daedalus murdered him; the grieving mother flew away, transformed by sorrow into a bird. When Daedalus' son died by his own carelessness and pride, Polycaste was there, chattering in derision as Daedalus dug the grave.

Polydamna   A famous queen of Egypt whom Helen of Troy visited as she traveled back to Greece, Polydamna was an herbalist who gave Helen a drug to banish melancholy and heartbreak.

Pomona   In the spring, the Romans honored Flora, the flower goddess; fall was the season of fruit, of Pomona. Although she had no actual festival, Pomona was nonetheless significant enough to be endowed with one of the twelve *flamines*, or high priests, of the city and with a shrine twelve miles from Rome called the Pomonal. Ovid tells us that she was courted by several of the male fertility gods, including Pan, Priapus, and Silenus. But she was won when Vertumnus came courting—disguised as an old woman, with whom Pomona fell in love.

Port-Kuva   Many cultures believe that a home has its own spirit, and the Cheremis of eastern Russia were no exception. They called her Port-Kuva ("house woman") and said she was invisible to human eyes unless a disaster or illness was about to befall the residents of her abode. She was a Norn or Fate, however, and controlled such events; people could, therefore, if they saw Port-Kuva, suspect that they had hurt her feelings and could repair the breach before ill befell them. Sacrifices of black animals, buried in the earth, were helpful in such events. Bread and pancakes, however, also sufficed; they were absolutely necessary to make Port-Kuva feel at home in a new house.

Poshjo-Akka   "She permits shooting" is the name of the Saami hunting goddess; to her, offerings were poured out on winter solstice in the hunting camps. The goddess' image stood within the storage hut of the hunters so that she could observe the condition of all slaughtered animals. Once butchered, their skulls were buried at the statue's feet in thanksgiving and in sorrow that we must kill to live. Without such care, the animals would be unable to reincarnate, and all life would cease.

Postvorta   The Romans, like many other peoples, considered prophecy related to childbirth; perhaps this represented a natural curiosity about the fate of newborns or a recognition of the wisdom of midwives. In any case, they provided two goddesses to assist the laboring mother and to provide oracles of the future: Postvorta and her companion, called Antevorta, Prorsa, or Porrina.

Poza-Mama   Among Siberian peoples, this most sacred goddess lived in the hearth fire; she was also mistress of the mountains. Like the Ainu Kamai Fuchi or the Roman Vesta, she was the bond that kept the family intact, as well as the heat that kept them alive. The Ulchi spit the first mouthful of every meal into the fire as a kind of grace and a prayer for food in the future; the Khakass had the same ritual to honor the braided-haired goddess.

The Negidals kept pictures of the fire goddess Kutuga next to the hearth and revered the spot as sacred to the goddess. Among the Shors, fire was called Otuz Pastu Ot Ana, "thirty-headed Mother Fire," and Altyn Tondu Ot Ana, "Mother Fire in her golden coat." The Altai called her Ot Ana, "Mother Fire," and Kyz Ana, "Virgin Mother," for it was believed that she perpetuated herself without need of a male principle; she was responsible for all family members, living and dead, for she lit the way to the afterlife with her bright flame.

Among the fire taboos of the Altai were the following restrictions: no garbage is to be thrown into the fire; the fire must never be unnecessarily put out; no iron may touch it; no one should jeer or mock the fire. Because mother fire was the mediator between humanity and the world beyond, no shaman functioned without first asking her help.

Prajnaparamita   This Buddhist figure represents "The Perfection of Wisdom," embodied in a young golden-skinned woman who emits rays of light. She was the "mother and begetter" of space and of the secrets hidden at the beginning of time, to be revealed when humankind is sufficiently advanced.

Prakriti   Two points of collision between patriarchal Indo-European culture and indigenous mother goddess religions saw the rise of splendidly complex mythologies: classical Greece and ancient India. In India, the melding of two disparate philosophies created Hinduism and its offspring, Buddhism, which both employ vocabularies compounded of insights from the two streams that converged to form them.

From the ancient religions of Devi ("The Goddess"), there remained a strong tendency toward the worship of female divinity. In Hindu philosophy, three concepts are given feminine form: Maya, the dancing goddess who keeps creation alive; Shakti, the force of life itself, and Prakriti, or nature. These three theological concepts are closely connected and—because no myths illustrate them—sometimes difficult to separate. In fact, each is identified with one or another of the triad, for the force of life cannot be segmented into neat categories.

As Prakriti, this energy is the creative principle, the unitary pattern behind all movement. Self-knowing, endless, and perfectly alone, Prakriti exists everywhere but is nowhere actually manifest, for although she herself, the material of the universe, is singular, that form takes immeasurably various individual forms. She is therefore paradoxical, divinely alone in her uncountable forms, which humans can perceive only because we, too, are parts of Prakriti.

Praxidike   A three-faced head symbolized this Greek goddess of vengeance and enterprise, who punished evil actions and rewarded the good.

Prithivi   Hinduism embodies the earth in female shape, calling her Prithivi ("broad one") and saying that she appears like a cosmic cow, full of milk for her children. She figures in few myths but appears in many prayers.

Procris   Princess of Athens, she married Cephalus. But the man soon drew the eye of the lustful dawn goddess Eos; she spirited him away, but Cephalus refused to sleep with her. Eos, disgusted, returned the man to earth, first changing his appearance completely. When Cephalus entered his home, he seemed a handsome stranger, and Procris, infatuated, welcomed him into her bed. When Cephalus resumed his own shape, Procris, horrified to be caught in infidelity, fled the palace.

In the forest, she joined a band of wild roaming women, servants of Artemis. Later reconciled to her mate, Procris grew jealous and possessive; she began to spy on Cephalus. Eos, to avenge Cephalus' rejection, had the man mistake Procris for an animal and kill her. Some interpreters see this as a nature allegory, in which the dew (Procris) is slain by the rays of the sun (Cephalus) while the dawn looks on.

Proserpina   There were many Roman agricultural goddesses, each ruling a moment in the life of the plants necessary for human survival. Before the Roman pantheon was joined with that of the Greeks, Proserpina was a maiden whose particular role was as nursemaid to the tender shoots of spring. She was called "The Savior" in Sicily, where images of the maiden with her mother Ceres were used for many centuries in place of those of Mary and the Christian god. Sheaves of grain and bouquets of wildflowers were placed before the divinities according to the season. But Proserpina's name became synonymous with that of Persephone, until her former identity was entirely lost.

Protagenia   The "firstborn" daughter of Pyrrha after the great flood, she was the legendary ancestor of many Greek tribes.

Psyche   The heroine of a Greek allegory, Psyche represented the human soul, married to the loving heart personified as the god Eros. Psyche, the story goes, spent her days alone, making love each night in darkness with a husband she never saw; only under these conditions would he remain faithful to her. For a while she lived happily enough. But finally a fearful curiosity about his identity and a deep spiritual loneliness drove Psyche to bring a lamp into the bedroom. Hardly had the woman seen the beautiful winged body of her lover than a bit of oil fell from her lamp, awakening him.

Instantly Eros flew away. Thus the soul, the Greeks knew, could remain happy in romantic union, until unmet needs demanded conscious knowledge of the lover's real identity.

Next, the tale goes, Psyche was charged with many near-impossible tasks to gain back her beloved: sorting overnight a roomful of seeds; catching the fleece of the sun's sheep; traveling to the underworld to ask for magical beauty ointment. Intent on regaining Eros, she overcame these obstacles one by one.

But as Psyche returned from Hades with Persephone's ointment box, vanity overcame her. She opened the jar to rub beauty cream on her weary face. Psyche fell into a swoon and might have died, but Eros persuaded the Olympian divinities that she had struggled enough. She ascended to heaven and was reunited with her lover, bearing two children named Love and Delight. In this allegory, the Greeks produced a magnificent tale of the relations of heart and mind, the journey through romance to real marriage, and the human joy born of the victorious struggle.

Pudicitia   The personification of modesty, she was called Aodos in Greece. In Rome, she went under two names: Pudicitia Patricia, the modesty of noble women; and Pudicitia Plebeia, that of women of the plebian class. At first, there was only one Pudicitia, but when lower-class women found they were frequently barred from participating in the shrine activities, they seceded and founded their own. Pudicitia is often considered a form of Fortuna, the fortune goddess, and as such is known as Fortuna Muliebris ("women's fortune").

Pyrrha   Many peoples have legends of a great flood sent in punishment for humankind's iniquity. The Greeks placed this flood far back in the mythic era, when Bronze Age people occupied the earth. Brazen indeed, they provoked the Olympian divinities to decide the whole race should be drowned.

There was, however, one honorable couple: Deucalion, son of Prometheus, and Pyrrha, daughter of the earth goddess Pandora. Only the perfect righteousness of their lives stayed the anger of the Olympians, who allowed the pair to escape death by floating nine days and nine nights in a wooden box. When the great flood receded, the couple found themselves on the sacred mountain of Parnassus. There they offered sacrifice for their salvation and, granted one boon, they asked that the earth be repopulated.

They received an answer: as they descended to the flood-wet valley, they should cast the bones of their mother behind them. Quickly Pyrrha penetrated the enigma. Picking up stones, the bones of the earth mother, she began to walk downhill. Deucalion joined her, throwing stones over his shoulder. Behind them sprang up the "stone age" people, men from stones cast by Deucalion, women from Pyrrha's.

Pythia   A woman had to have seen fifty years through mortal eyes before she could be called by this name, borne by the Oracle of Delphi; only women distinguished by age could endure the power that rose from the earth at that spot. Pythia also had to be married, in deference to the original owner of the shrine, the earth mother Gaia or Hera; in later Greek history, it was dedicated to the newly arrived god Apollo.

Pythia's duties were as follows: on the seventh of each moon, she underwent ritual purification. Then, seated on the three-legged stool, or tripod, she chewed bay leaves and breathed in fumes that rose from a chasm, inducing a state of ecstasy in the prophet. Eventually she spoke complicated, often enigmatic, prophecies, which were then interpreted to questioners by her male attendants. These seekers, who could ask questions of the oracle only once each year, had to be ritually purified beforehand.

Python This is one of the names—another being Delphyne ("womb")— given to the great snake of sacred Delphi, born of the mud left after the great deluge and a parthenogenetic daughter of earth. She nested near the flower-filled spring of the Greek shrine. Some legends said that she was killed by the invading god Apollo, when he took over the famous oracular spring; others, giving the name Python to her dead mate, said the she-snake lived forever at Delphi, where only women were allowed to prophesy even after the earth mother, the original owner of the oracle, was ousted by the Greek sun god.

Qadesh "Holy one," originally a title of Ishtar the wanton, was later applied to an Egyptian goddess who rode a lion, holding out snakes and lotus buds. Sometimes Qadesh wore the headdress of the local pleasure goddess Hathor, evidence that the holiness she embodied was a sacramental reverence toward sexuality as an expression of divine force.

Qamaits Among the Indians of the Pacific Coast, Qamaits was the highest heavenly goddess, a great warrior woman who lived in the east of the world. Although she created the earth, she brought death, famine, and disease to humanity when she visited; better for all the people, the Bellacoola and others said, when she stayed in her sea home with its salty bathing pool.

Her name means "sorrowmaker." She has another name, Dji Sisnaxitl ("slaveowner"), for to her all humans were merely slaves. Researchers in the early part of this century found evidence that she had once been the most important of the Bellacoola divinities, but in recent times, information about her has become scantier, and prayers were addressed to her less and less often. Thus, it seems this great death goddess, within very recent times, lost her grip on her worshipers, just as earlier underworld queens from Hel to Persephone became mere metaphors rather than divine aspects of femininity.

Qebhsnuf With Selkhet, she was an Egyptian guardian of the embalmed dead.

Ques We still know her name as our word for rest and serenity: *quiet*. The Roman goddess of tranquility, she was worshiped in shrines used as roadside rest-stops.

Queskapenek From the magnificently fertile Okanagan valley in southern British Columbia comes a lovely folktale which may have originally been a myth of the earth goddess. Queskanapenek, it was said there, was the first woman, and the first chief of the land. She lived near the blue lake waters and bore her children into the richness of its lands. When her time came to die, she worried about her descendants, and so she went on a long pilgrimage. Traveling throughout the region, she picked the most productive and tasty plants and, carrying them back to her valley, planted them so her children would be happy and comfortable.

Rabie Among the Indonesian islanders of Ceram, the moon was not originally in the sky but lived on earth with her parents. There her loveliness drew the eye of Tuwale the sun man, who demanded her in marriage. Her parents, however, loath to give up their daughter, waited till nightfall and put a dead pig into Tuwale's bed. Humiliated by the swap, he decided to get revenge. A few days later Rabie simply sank out of sight. After a three-day funeral feast, the people saw Rabie return, when the first full moon rose in the sky.

Rachel One of the four great matriarchs of Israel, she was the most loved of the husband they shared. Like her sister Leah and like their servant doubles Zilpah and Bilhah, she gave birth to sons from whom the tribes of Israel descended. As befitted her status as favored spouse, she gave birth to the favored sons, Joseph and Benjamin.

A prophet, she foresaw the birth of her second son, but was said to have been cursed for her pride, for she said at Joseph's birth, "I will bear another son," rather than praying that it might occur. She did bear one son more, but died in labor. Not herself Hebrew but Aramaic, Rachel continued the worship of the seraphim, or household gods, even after joining the Hebrew household of Jacob.

Radha "Beloved one," said to be an incarnation of the Indian goddess of abundance, Lakshmi, was the adulterous lover of Krishna, the incarnation of Lakshmi's consort, Vishnu. The love of Radha and Krishna is the source of some of the most famous love poetry in existence, and Radha is still honored today in the rituals of Shakti, female energy. Although other goddesses sometimes appear as priestesses of these rites, most often it is the voluptuous Radha who stands before her worshipers, putting on a mortal woman's body for the occasion. Naked except for jewelry and flowers, the woman is given reverence due the essence of femininity by groups of male and female worshipers, bound to utter secrecy about their participation in the ceremonies.

Radien-Akka On Saami shamans' drums, this goddess is pictured as part of a holy trinity of father, mother and child.

Radien-Kiedde Among the Saami, the creator goddess who handed over souls to mother goddess Madder-Akka just before they were to be incarnated.

Rafu-Sen The Japanese plum-blossom goddess, the hardy beauty of springtime, was said to be a lovely maiden, forever chaste, who wandered through moonlit groves of blossoming plums, drawing out their perfume, with her long veils floating in the springtime darkness.

Ra-mitovi-aman-dreniny   The "green princesses" or Andrianas of Madagascar were fairylike beings of dazzling beauty who bore this name, which means "the likeness or equal of her mother." They had long green hair, light green skin, and mirrorlike eyes. They are often the mothers of human heroes.

Ran   The great sea goddess was, to the Scandinavians, also the queen of the drowned. Ran was a mighty woman who held a seafaring ship steady with one hand while with the other, sweeping her magical net into the water, she snared the sailors. These captives she took under the waves to her realm, where they lived as if on earth; because it was believed they were allowed to return to earth to attend their funerals, anyone seen at his own wake was assumed to be safely in Ran's keeping. Because she loved gold, Scandinavian sailors kept gold coins in their pockets as tokens of admittance to her domain, in case of death by drowning, called "faring to Ran" in eddic poetry.

The sea, called "Ran's road," had a male form as well named Aegir. With Ran he had nine giant daughters, the waves, which poets also called "the claws of Ran." Like their mother, these wave women could appear to humans as mermaids. Ran was most likely to make herself visible during the cold, dark Scandinavian winter, when she splashed as close as she could to her worshipers' warm campfires.

Rana Neida   Among the southern Saami, this springtime goddess had a specialized task: she turned south-facing hills green with grass early in the season, giving winter-starved reindeer fresh growth on which to browse. To gain her favor—and an early spring—the Saami ritually rested a spinning wheel against her altar and covered it with blood, a sacrifice the goddess apparently liked.

Ranaghanti   This North Indian Assamese goddess of war was worshiped in the shape of a huge red stone; she granted not only victory but protection on the field of battle.

Rangada   In the Indian epic called the Mahabharata, this warrior maiden stumbled upon the sleeping hero Arjuna. Finding him extremely attractive, she sat on her heels watching him until he woke, then told him frankly that she wished to enjoy his body. Shocked at her frankness, Arjuna said that he had taken a vow of celibacy—and besides, he would never be tempted by such an aggressive woman. So Rangada departed and went to her home. There she dressed herself in womanly silks, perfumed herself, and went back to Arjuna's tent. It did not take him long to break his vow, and he did so frequently for the next thirteen months. But Rangada's people came looking for her, bemoaning the loss of their village protector. As they sang her praises—how well she rode, how strongly she fought—Arjuna began to wonder aloud what it would be like to love such a strong woman. Finally Rangada came from the tent to see her former comrades; they were overjoyed to see her, and Arjuna found himself thrilled to ride into battle beside his bedmate.

Rangda   In the dance-dramas of Bali, there is a moment when the curtain shakes, and a long-nailed hand slowly protrudes from it. Next comes a face, half-covered by a white cloth—an awesome face, with great fangs and bulging eyes. When Rangda the witch finally reveals all of herself, the audience sees long breasts and a long protruding tongue, a tangle of long hair, and flames rising from her eyes and mouth. She leaps forward in awkward strides, laughing hideously. Behind the mask of Rangda is always a man, because it is believed that if this part were danced by a woman, the power would be too great to contain, and all of Bali would be destroyed. Although often associated with the warrior goddess Durga, Rangda is probably a folk-memory of an ancient pre-Hindu goddess of the island.

Ranoro On the island of Madagascar off Africa, there is a race of demi-goddesses—not quite human, not quite divine—called Andrianas. One of them was Ranoro, who descended to earth to marry a human man, whom she pledged to never speak the word "salt." When he forgot himself, she leaped into the Mamba River and was never seen again.

Ranu Bai Barren women prayed to this ancient goddess of India's Nimadi people. On a silver cord she bore a golden pitcher with which she filled in all the rivers of India.

Rapunzel "Rapunzel, Rapunzel, let down your hair!" the prince would call from beneath the tower where this maiden was held prisoner by a wicked old witch named Mother Gothel, and then he would climb to her bed on the thick plaits of her long hair. Like other Germanic fairy tales, this familiar childhood story hides an ancient myth whose meaning we can only guess. The trapped sun maiden, who would bring spring if she were not held prisoner by the witch of winter, is a common mythic theme in northern Europe; Rapunzel is likely a folkloric memory of her.

Rati The goddess of passionate night in Indian Hinduism, Rati was an embodiment of Kali ("Mother Time"). But while Kali was the perpetual night that ends creation, the fruitful cosmic destruction from which all would be reborn, Rati was the "giver," the earthly night in which all beings rest, the time of greatest procreative activity. In esoteric tradition, Rati was one of the great symbols of enlightenment, for if Maya's dance of creation so confuses the senses that we cannot understand the universal essence, Rati's darkness permits somewhat less confusion and therefore—paradoxical as it seems—greater consciousness and clarity.

Ratu Kidul On the southern coast of Java, fisher folk are careful not to wear green garments near the ocean, so as not to offend this queen of the sea, who might dash their heads against her rocks or change her current to endanger them. Ratu Kidul is a pre-Indian figure of a sort found in many cultures: a seductive Lorelei who lures sailors to their deaths. She is worshiped not only by fishermen but also by those who gather swallows' nests from the sides of sheer seacliffs. In the 1500s, a king had intercourse with Ratu Kidul; only their descendants can see the goddess now.

Rauni The Finno-Ugric thunder goddess bore many names—Akko, Maan-Eno, Ravdna, Roonikka, in addition to Rauni—probably because she was one of the people's most powerful divinities. Wife of the oak god of thunder, Rauni was incarnated in the rowan tree or mountain ash, whose red berries were sacred to her. Some myths say that she first brought plant life to the earth's face by having intercourse with the thunder god.

Rebecca The counterpart in later Hebrew legend of the great heroine Sarah, she was the mother of Jacob and Esau—symbolically, of the Hebrews and their non-Hebrew neighbors in the ancient Near East. Like Sarah, with whom she shared many attributes, Rebecca came close to having the stature of the great earth goddesses of her territory: she was prescient, had an unearthly beauty, and lived under a magical cloud that never left her tent. Like Sarah, too, she lived with a man who, in times of danger, pretended she was his sister; divine sister-brother marriages were common to the mythology of the surrounding non-Hebrew tribes. A shrewd mother who, in classic matriarchal fashion, favored her younger son over her older one, Rebecca engineered the famous birthright-stealing episode whereby Jacob snatched Isaac's blessing from Esau.

Renenet When an Egyptian child was born, this goddess was on hand to pronounce its name, define its personality and bestow its fortune. Then she began to suckle the child, for Renenet was the

265

personification of the force of nurturing and its effect on a child's destiny. In a larger sense, she was the earth itself, which offered milk and grain to her people, who hoped to flatter her as the "goddess of the double granary."

Renpet   A newly sprouted palm was the emblem of this Egyptian goddess of youth and springtime, who also symbolized the extension of measurable time into immeasurable eternity. The goddess of "the year"—the meaning of her name—she was shown in ancient art wearing a calendar for a hat.

Rhea   In late Greek legend she was a vague motherly figure—the Titan who gave birth to the Olympian gods. But earlier, Rhea was the primary goddess, the great mountain mother (called Ida as goddess of Mount Ida), the earth who gave birth to the creatures of her wild and fruitful surface.

Rhea's name is Cretan. In the art of that island, Rhea was depicted as a huge stately woman surrounded by worshipful animals and small, subservient human males. Her religion was a fervent one, celebrated in great musical processions of pipes and cymbals, leading to mystical orgies among her reveling children. The blazing torch, the brass drum, and the double ax were her symbols, and she was invoked with these words: "Earth sends up fruits, and so praise earth the mother."

When the wide stream of Aegean mother worship touched the later freshet of patriarchal religion, the confusion of divinities was such that multiple pantheons were defined, forming what we now call Greek mythology. Rhea was incorporated into Greek legend as a Titan, one of the second generation of deities. It was said that she was the wife of Cronos ("time") and the mother of the most powerful gods and goddesses, among them Hera. But reminders of her majestic past crop up: she was said to have been transformed into Demeter, to have been a snake goddess raped by her own son Zeus, and to have borne as many fatherless children as she had fingers. Even in late legend, the earlier identity of Rhea as goddess of the living earth was subtly acknowledged.

Rhea Silvia   The mother of Rome was originally the daughter of a king, Numitor, who was unseated by his younger brother, Amulius. The usurper kidnapped Silvia and made her a Vestal to keep her from reproducing her father's royal line. But she secretly slept with the war god Mars and bore twin sons—the city fathers Romulus and Remus. Discovered with her infants, she was commanded by Amulius to drown the children. Instead, she took up with Tiberinus, god of the Tiber River, who gently carried the children in a box downstream to safety. (Upon landing, they were nursed by a she-wolf whom some say was Rhea Silvia herself.) Some modern interpreters consider this legend to be an expression of Italy's change from matrilineal to patrilineal succession.

Rheda   Bede, writing of the Anglo-Saxons, mentions her as one of their goddesses; no trace of her name is found among their Germanic cousins on the continent, however. Little is known of her except that the month of March—Rhedmonath—bore her name in that land; presumably she was a spring goddess.

Rhiannon   The beautiful Welsh underworld goddess traveled through earth on an impossibly speedy horse, accompanied always by magical birds that made the dead waken and the living fall into a blissful seven-year sleep. Originally named Rigatona ("Great Queen"), she shrank in later legend into Rhiannon, a fairylike figure who appeared to Prince Pwyll of Dyfed near the gate of the underworld. He pursued her on his fastest horses, but hers—cantering steadily and without tiring—exhausted any mount of Pwyll's. Finally, the queen decided to stay with Pwyll; she bore him a son soon afterward.

What can one expect of a goddess of death? Her son disappeared, and the queen was found with blood on her mouth and cheeks. Accused of murder, she was sentenced to serve as Pwyll's gatekeeper, bearing visitors to the door on her back; thus she was symbolically transformed into a horse. All ended happily when her son was found;

Rhiannon had been falsely accused by maids who, terrified at finding the babe absent, had smeared puppy blood on the queen's face.

Behind this legend is doubtless another, more primitive one in which the death queen actually was guilty of infanticide. This beautiful queen of the night would then, it seems, be identical to the Germanic Mora, the nightmare, the horse-shaped goddess of terror. But night brings good dreams as well as bad, so Rhiannon was said to be the beautiful goddess of joy and oblivion, a goddess of Elysium as well as the queen of hell.

Rhode A vague figure in late Greek mythology, she was the daughter of the sea queen Amphitrite and goddess of the island named for her, Rhodes—a place also sacred to her mate, the sun god Helios.

Rhpisunt The people of the Haida Wolf clan in southeastern Alaska possess a story of the Bear Mother, Rhpisunt, who long ago was a noblewoman, daughter of the Wolf clan's chief. Out walking one day, she stepped into the droppings of a bear and, a dainty and somewhat vain woman, became enraged that her feet should be soiled. Not only did she curse the bears then but she continued to exclaim against the animals for many days.

Later, while picking berries, Rhpisunt became separated from her party and, roaming farther and farther into the forest, finally filled her basket. But almost as soon as the basket was full, she felt the straps give way, and all her carefully harvested berries fell to the ground. It took some time to gather them together; by that time there was no sign of her friends' canoe.

Happily enough, she came upon a handsome young man who led her down a path until they came to his village. He introduced Rhpisunt to the chief, his father, a huge fat man who sat in a log house lined with bearskin cloaks. Suddenly, at Rhpisunt's side, a little fat lady named Tsects ("Mouse Woman") appeared; she whispered that Rhpisunt should give her some grease and wool and that she should never relieve herself without

breaking off a piece of copper and placing it on the ground above the buried excrement.

Rhpisunt did as she was told and soon saw why she'd been so instructed: the Bear People, finding copper left behind after the woman's trip to the bushes, judged her complaints about the bear's leavings justifiable, as she herself passed shiny metal. Thereupon, Rhpisunt was allowed to marry the Bear Prince, and Mouse Woman provided a huge feast, miraculously created from the bits of fat Rhpisunt had given her.

Found in a Tlingit shaman's grave, this mask represents the spirit of a woman of many years and was worn by the shaman to invoke such feminine power. For myths of the Tlingit and related people, see Dzalarhons, Gyhldeptis, Qamaits, Queskapenek, Rhpisunt, Sneneik, and Somagalags.

But the woman's family was seeking her; they'd found her prints, with those of bears, leading away from where she'd been lost. The Haida raged through the forest killing bears, and in the village of the Bear People there was mourning for the loss of life. Eventually, led by Rhpisunt's little lapdog,

Maesk, one of the woman's brothers found her, together with her Bear Prince and their twin sons, in a cave. The visionary Bear Prince knew he would die, so he shared magical formulas with his wife before he was speared by her brother. Rhpisunt was brought back to the Haida village, where she grew to a great and revered age. Her sons, taking off their bear jackets while in human company, returned at her death to their father's people, but afterward the people of the Wolf clan recognized bears as their blood relatives.

Ri The moon goddess of ancient Phoenicia, of whom little is known but her name, which seems to mean "light."

Rind In Scandinavian legend, Rind was originally a Russian princess who, it was prophesied, was the only one who could bear a child to avenge the death of the god Balder. The god Odin traveled to her court disguised as a soldier to conceive the avenger, but Rind rebuffed him. Odin came the next year disguised as a skilled smith able to make beautiful ornaments, but Rind still did not find her heart moved. A third time Odin came wearing a third disguise, that of a young courtier. Rind again refused his advances.

Finally Odin disguised himself as a young leech maiden, a healer, and became a servant of the princess. It was in this form that he finally drew Rind's eye and, when she fell sick of a strange malady (brought about, some legends say, by the curses of Odin himself), Odin cured her. At last Rind agreed to sleep with Odin, conceiving the hero Vali.

Worshiped throughout Scandinavia as a goddess, Rind was, some scholars believe, a symbol of the wintry earth, refusing the embraces of the fertilizing god. More convincing is the argument that Rind was a sun goddess, for she was described as "white as the sun" and as leaving her couch each morning and returning each evening. As the Scandinavian sun was considered to be female, this interpretation has the force of tradition behind it.

Rohini Once, Indian mythology tells us, Daksha had twenty-seven daughters, all married to the moon. But though the moon promised to spend his favors equally, he fell in love with Rohini ("Red One") and began to spend more and more time with her. Daksha cursed the moon with consumption, but his daughters prevailed on him to lighten his curse, so he allowed the disease to be chronic rather than fatal.

Rona To the people of New Zealand, the moon was a man, and a tease at that. One night when Rona was walking to the stream to draw water, the moon man covered himself with a cloud so that she could not see; Rona stubbed her toe on a big rock. Annoyed, she cursed the moon. She insulted him. She called him names. Irritated, he came down to argue with her. When the moon man reached earth, Rona was still so irritated that he grabbed her by the shoulder and took her and her basket with him back to the sky, where she still clings to the moon's face.

Rosmerta This continental Celtic goddess is depicted with a bulging basket of fruit, a full bag of food, or a plate held over a bucket. Her name means "Good Purveyor," which suggests that she was a goddess both of prosperity and of trading. Like many other Celtic goddesses, she is also associated with healing shrines and sacred springs.

Royot At the beginning of time, the universe was united and whole, and the greatest gods walked among us on earth. But, say the Southeast Asian mountain people called the Jarai, a young man once accidentally drank a love-potion intended for another man, which caused him to fall desperately in love with his sister Royot. She returned his love, but died giving birth to their first child. The gods were so stricken by this tragedy that they turned the doomed lovers into boulders. Then they abandoned the earth and retreated to the blue skies. Now humans no longer understand the language of animals or birds, all of whom sing a constant sad melody, for when Royot died, the universe was permanently torn apart. That tragedy sends ripples through time, and so any further actions that might exacerbate the rupture must be avoided or redressed.

Rozanicy   In the singular, Rozanica (Rodienitsa in Croatia) is the ancestral goddess mother of a Slavic clan, whose name means simultaneously "mother," "heritage" and "destiny." In the plural, she becomes Rozanicy, all the deified ancestral mothers. Two feasts celebrate her: the annual winter solstice feast, and the initiation of any child formally into the family, when a special Rozanicy porridge is served.

Rudabeh   In the Sha-Nameh, the gorgeous Persian poetry on mythological themes, Rudabeh was an exquisitely beautiful heroine—more beautiful than the sun, her body like rubies, her hair like amber. Falling in love with a man named Zal, she wandered to his camp, pretending to gather roses. Captivated by her, Zal agreed to visit her for a night of love. She prepared for him by decorating her palace with brocaded hangings, placing vats of fragrant flowers throughout it, and perfuming it with amber. When he arrived, Rudabeh made him pledge he would never raise a hand to her before she welcomed him to her bed.

Rugiu Boba   "The Old One of the Rye" was a Lithuanian harvest goddess honored, like the Carlin in Scotland, when the last sheaf to be reaped was formed into her likeness. Brought into the village at the time of the harvest festival, her effigy was kept in a place of honor in the home until replaced the next year.

Rukko   In the cosmology of the Native American Mandan people, Rukko was a goddess of materiality and darkness who created human bodies, while a male spirit provided animating souls.

Rumina   The Roman goddess of nursing mothers was worshiped at a fig tree. There the founders of Rome, the twins Romulus and Remus, were said to have been suckled by a wolf bitch. Fittingly, the offering made to Rumina was milk—to assure plentiful milk for healthy babies.

Rumor   The last-born daughter of the earth mother Gaia, Rumor was seen by the Greeks as feathered and fleetfooted. Rumor, they said, ran through the earth bearing messages that should be attended to, for some of them were disguised messages from the gods.

Rusalki   These Russian water spirits were originally human women who drowned or committed suicide. The company of naked, wild-haired Rusalki rose each spring from streams to beg bits of white linen from humans. The Rusalki hung them from trees after carefully laundering them. (One who accidentally stepped on the Rusalki's wash would be spastic thereafter.)

Their spring cleaning done, the Rusalki began their nightly magical dances that help plants grow and mature; sometimes for these occasions they wore long white unbelted tunics or robes of green leaves. Humans could lose their souls by witnessing the beautiful dances of the Rusalki, which usually brought rain to the growing plants. When summer was over, the Rusalki retreated to feather nests at the bottom of their streams, where they hibernated until the next spring.

Ryuhwa   This Korean goddess, daughter of the god of waters, was held captive in a room by her jealous father. But the sunlight was able to enter her room, and try as she might to shield her body from it, it managed to strike her and, finally, impregnate her. From this intercourse, she laid an egg, which her father threw to a dog. But the dog wouldn't eat it, so he gave it to a pig, which again refused to devour the egg. He tossed it onto a road, but horses carefully turned around it. He abandoned it in a field, but carrion birds sheltered it with their wings. Giving up, he gave it back to his daughter, who hatched it into the archer god Cumong.

Saba Although married to a warrior, this Irish heroine retained such a horror of bloodshed that she died of grief because of her husband's cruelty in war. The most famous legend concerning her tells how, bewitched by a jealous Druid, she was transformed into a deer and in that form bore her young son in the woods. He was born in human form, but Saba could not resist licking his brow—where he sprouted fawn's hair and hence he was named Oisin ("little fawn").

Sabulana The savior-heroine of the African people of Machakeni rescued her people from starvation when—although previously they had lived on the earth's bounty—they neglected proper sacrifice to the goddess and found themselves unable to gather food from their gardens. Even wild food escaped them. Women trying to gather wild honey found that their hands broke off at the wrist when they reached into honeybearing trees.

Only Sabulana apprehended the problem, and she instructed her people to seek divine help. Then she went alone—for no one was brave enough to accompany her—to the sacred ancestral grove. There she met ghosts and sang a melody for them so stirring that their hardened hearts melted. Telling Sabulana that her people

had been sacrilegious and to make offerings to the earth for her gifts, the ancestral spirits sent the young woman back to the village, where she and her mother were honored as chiefs.

Saga The all-knowing goddess came second, after Frigg, in the Scandinavian pantheon; to some scholars she was an aspect of the mighty Frigg herself. The eddas said that Saga lived at Sinking Beach, a waterfall of cool waves where she offered her guests drinks in golden cups. Her name, which means "omniscience," was applied to the epic heroic tales of her people.

Salacia We get our word *salacious* from her name, although there was nothing particularly lurid about the Roman figure of a sea goddess whose domain overlapped with that of Venilia, goddess of the shallow coastal waters, but more properly was the deeper saline waters. The sexual connotations for Salacia's name may be the connection of Aphrodite to the ocean, wherein she was born when the severed genitals of Uranus splashed down.

Salmachis In the Greek colony of Caria in Anatolia, this fountain nymph lived, a force so feminine that anything that drank her waters became female. Human males could not resist the power of Salmachis, nor could the gods. One day the son of Hermes and Aphrodite, who bore both parents' names, chanced by Salmachis' fountain. The nymph fell in love with him and reached to embrace him. Alas for her, he drowned in her waters. Salmachis pleaded with the Olympians to revive him and unite them forever; they approved her wish and the two became the first hermaphrodite in Greek myth. Earlier mythic hermaphrodite had been known, not coincidentally from the lands where this fanciful Greek story is derived.

Samdzimari In the Georgian Caucasus mountains, we find this demon-turned-goddess whose mythic power suggests that she was first a goddess-turned-demon. The sister of the heroic Giorgi, she was held captive by evil blacksmiths called Kadzhi. Giorgi, sewn into the skin of a dead horse, was smuggled into their hideout and killed them all. Then he captured Samdzimari, as well as a lot of Kadzhi loot: anvils, a cow with one horn, all their secret tools. The metal objects became sacred; the cow's horn became the official measure of a glass of beer; and Samdzimari was promoted to a goddess.

But the promotion didn't tame her, for she remained a force of wilderness even in her new sophisticated guise as "the lady with the necklace" (the meaning of her name). She sneaked around at night, taking the forms of other women in order to make love to their mates—but transforming herself into a demonic animal just as semen was released. Or she simply disappeared, leaving behind terrified sexual partners, about whom she sang little derisive ballads.

Samdzimari was especially likely to come to the beds of shamans or priests, serving as their link between this reality and another. She was, interestingly, also considered the matron goddess of marriage, which she invented in order to keep her hero-brother close to her. Like Artemis, a wilderness goddess from south of Samdzimari's land,

she cared for women in childbed and animals as they bore their young.

Samjuna "Knowledge" was the Indian wife of the sun, whose brilliance finally so tired her that Samjuna hid in the wilderness disguised as a mare, leaving behind a replica of herself. But he discovered her ruse and transformed himself into a stallion to seek her and, finding her, to have intercourse with her. From this union came the twin gods of agriculture, the horse-headed Aswins. Samjuna agreed to return to the sky with the sun god, but first she had her father trim away some of the sun's rays to diminish his brightness. From the extra pieces of the sun were fashioned the weapons of other gods.

Samsin Halmoni These three goddesses of birth in Korea are celebrated at birthday parties throughout life. Women shamans, or *mudang*, specializing in childbirth and birthday rituals, are called by the goddesses' name. These rituals include offerings of steamed rice, wine and soy sauce, laid out like a dinner for the divine women. When a child is born, the *mudang* uses a floating gourd like a drum to beat out prayers for a safe delivery.

Saosis The Egyptian goddess, identified with Hathor, who was emblemized in the acacia tree in which it was said that "death and life are enclosed."

Sao-Ts'ing Niang In Chinese legend, the reason the sky cleared after rain was that "broom lady" swept the clouds away. She also had the power to gather them, and she was called on in times of drought to save her people.

Sarah The greatest of the ancient Hebrew matriarchs, she also had the most in common with the ancestral goddesses of the non-Hebrew tribes of the ancient Near East. Her attributes and legend make it clear that she must be viewed as a vestigial goddess among the patriarchal Hebrews. Even as a mortal, Sarah was recognized as alien to the Hebrews. She was described as a Chaldean princess who bestowed wealth on Abraham by consenting to marry him.

Sarah was brilliantly beautiful and ageless; she was said to be so lovely that human women seemed like apes beside her. She did not bear a child until she had lived nearly a century; then, rather than exhausting her, the birth rejuvenated her. From her face an unearthly radiance shone; a miraculous cloud marked her tent as long as she was alive. Apparently her life had a particular health-giving power, for while Sarah was alive, her land was fertile and her husband did not age; when she died, the land ceased to bear and her husband, Abraham, suddenly aged and died.

She was so close to divine that she actually held conversations with Jehovah. She was prescient—called Iscah ("seer")—and acknowledged to be a more gifted prophet than her husband. Finally, she had a curious trait in common with the great goddesses of her region: she was called Abraham's sister as well as his spouse. Because the mythic intention was unclear to the Hebrews, they explained that Sarah was only called Abraham's sister when danger threatened, but in reality was only his wife. While so "disguised," Sarah married several kings, rather like goddesses who grant sovereignty to a man by "marrying" him, while remaining constantly in love with their "brothers," the fertile gods of growth and reproduction.

Sar-Akka Among the Swedish Saami, this daughter of Madder-Akka was considered the supreme deity and creator of the world. In one myth, she was said to have invented physical life when, given a soul by her mother, she formed a body to house it. This recalls her duty as a birth goddess; her specific charge was to create the fetal flesh within the womb. She is sometimes called Skile-Qvinde, ("dividing woman"), because of her rulership of the division of childflesh from motherflesh at birth. She appears, together with her mother and sister, on Saami drum paintings, recognizable by the forked stick in her hand, symbol of division.

Sarasvati As every Hindu god must have a Shakti, or enlivening female force, to function, so Brahma the creator needed Sarasvati for the world to come into being. She is not only the water goddess, one of a trinity that also includes Ganga and Yamuna, but she is also the goddess of eloquence, which pours forth like a flooding river.

Inventor of all the arts and sciences, patron of all intellectual endeavors, Sarasvati is the very prototype of the female artist. She invented writing so that the songs she inspired could be recorded; she created music so the elegance of her being could be praised. In her identity as Vach, goddess of speech, she caused all words to come into being, including all religious writings. Sometimes it is said that she is the rival of Lakshmi, goddess of material wealth; if anyone has the favor of one goddess, the other will turn away so that no one is ever blessed with both Sarasvati's genius and Lakshmi's riches.

Sarbanda The king of the Babylonian city of Erech worshiped this "queen of the bow" and declared himself her son, while the wealthy among Sarbanda's people enriched her temples with huge annual endowments. Like many other goddesses of the ancient Near East, however, Sarbanda was assimilated into the mighty figure of Ishtar.

Sati Anglicized, her name becomes Suttee, for Sati was the first woman to follow her husband into death. An incarnation of Devi, she was married to that aspect of the destroyer Shiva called Rudra; when he was killed, Sati committed suicide.

Another Sati ("she who runs like an arrow"), also known as Satis and Satet, was an Egyptian archer goddess who personified the waterfalls of the river Nile. Her sanctuary was at Aswan, in ancient upper Egypt, on the island of Seheil.

Satine The underworld queen, to the Indonesian people of the island of Ceram, was the daughter of the banana tree. At first she lived on earth, but after the death of the goddess Hainuwele (of whom some say Satine is an aspect)—who had been danced into the earth by human associates—Satine decided that she, too, would leave the earth and live on the death mountain. In that peaceful land, she ruled kindly, although to enter her domain humans had to pass through the black gate of death.

Saule The greatest goddess of the Baltic peoples—the Lithuanians and Latvians—was the shining sun, the sky weaver, the amber goddess Saule. She ruled all parts of life, from birth into her light to death when she welcomed souls into her apple tree in the west. Even the name of the ocean on which the Balts lived was hers, named for Balta Saulite ("darling little white sun") She was worshiped in songs and rituals that celebrated her nurturance of earth's life, for she was Our Mother, called various names like Saulite Mat ("little sun-mother") and Saulite Sudrabota ("little silver sun").

She was married in the springtime of creation to the moon man Meness. Their first child was the earth; after that, countless children became the stars of heaven. Saule was a hardworking mother, leaving the house at dawn each day and driving her chariot across the sky until dusk. Menesis, however, was fickle and carefree, staying home all day and only sometimes driving his moon-chariot.

The light of Saule's life was her daughter (variously named Austrine, Valkyrine, and Barbelina, but most generally called Saules Meita, the sun's daughter), the beloved lady of the morning star. Each evening, after she had bathed her weary horses in the Nemunas River, Saule looked for the child. But one evening she could not find her—for in her absence, Saule's beautiful long-haired daughter had been raped by Menesis.

Furious beyond words, Saule took a sword and slashed the moon's face, leaving the marks we see today. Then she banished him forever from her presence; thus, they are no longer seen together in the sky— the end of the happy paradise before the evil came into our world.

Saule was worshiped each day when her people would bow to the east to greet Mother Sun. But she was especially honored on summer solstice, Ligo, when she rose crowned with a braid of red fern blossoms to dance on the hilltops in her silver shoes. At that moment, people dived into east-flowing streams to bathe themselves in her light. All the women donned similar braided wreaths and walked through the fields, singing goddess songs, or daina. Finally, they gathered around bonfires and sang the night away.

Because Lithuanian is the oldest extant Indo-European language, it is thought that the Baltic mythologies hold clues to the original beliefs of that people. But scholarly convention has it that the Indo-Europeans worshiped a sky father embodied in the sun. Whence, then, this powerful sun mother? Marija Gimbutas, herself Lithuanian, believed Saule to be an Old European goddess of that woman-honoring culture that preceded the Indo-European invasions; Saule was too vital to her people, according to this theory, to give way to a male solar divinity. But sun goddesses in other Indo-European areas show there is room for study.

Saules Meita The daughter of the sun in the Baltic, sometimes called Austrine, Valkyrine or Barbelina, was called a "little sun," possibly a star. In Lithuanian and Latvian legends, there are many sun daughters who climb rose trees in the sky to follow their mother. When they stayed at home, they were charged with keeping the house clean; sometimes they played hooky and ran off to Germany to play with the sons of god.

Saules Meita was said to be courted by a pair of twin stars; in some songs they are her brothers. When she was in danger of drowning—as when she dropped her golden ring into a fountain—it was their duty to save her. These twin gods appear in other Indo-European myths as well as companions to the dawn maiden, as the Asvins to Hindu Ushas or the Dioscuri to Greek Helen.

Savitri The primary Hindu ancestor, Savitri was impregnated by Brahma early in creation. She gestated for a century, then began to give birth. From her womb poured music and poetry, the years, the months, and the days, the four ages of creation, and innumerable other offspring, including death. Called Sata-Rupa ("hundred-shaped"), she is also said to have been the first woman, daughter of Brahma and wife of the first man.

Sayo-Hime A legendary woman of Japan, she married a man who often traveled by sea. And so often she would stand by the seashore watching for his boat that she turned into the famous "Wife Rock" of Futami in the province of Shima.

Scathach The "shadowy one," who lived on an island near Scotland, Scathach was the greatest female warrior of her time. Heroes from all the Celtic nations would travel to study with her, for she alone knew the magical battle skills that made them unconquerable: great leaps and fierce yells, which seem in ancient legend like puzzled accounts of Oriental martial arts.

One of her most famous students was the Irish warrior Cuchulain. When the princess Emer sized him up as a possible husband, she thought him too unskilled in his profession; therefore, she suggested that he study with Scathach, the foremost warrior of her day. While Cuchulain was away, he learned more than martial arts, for through an affair with Scathach's enemy, Aiofe, the warrior produced a son whom he later unwittingly killed.

Scota A vague figure in Irish legend, she was called a "daughter of Pharaoh" in the post-Christian historical annals that amalgamated ancient lore with biblical legend. She was probably an Irish ancestor goddess, for the people of the island were called in ancient times *scoti* or *scots*, a name that later came to rest in another Celtic homeland.

Scylla Once this legendary Greek monster, Lamia's daughter, was a beautiful woman, so beautiful that she roused the jealousy of the sea queen Amphitrite, who poisoned her bath with magic herbs. When Scylla rose from the water, her twelve-footed body ended in six dogs' heads with six mouths each, each mouth with three sets of teeth. This horrible barking creature was no longer a threat to the sea goddess.

The embittered Scylla stationed herself on the seacoast, where she trapped sailors and ate them. But she hated her life so much that she flung herself into the sea between Italy and Sicily and was instantly transformed into rocks that continued to devour sailors. No one could safely pass the treacherous petrified woman, it was said, unless Hecate allowed it.

There was another figure in Greek legend with the same name, whom some scholars claim was actually the same woman. She was the princess Scylla, daughter of King Nisus who had a magical golden hair in the middle of his head that protected him from harm. But his daughter, infatuated with King Minos, during a Cretan siege of her city, betrayed her father by pulling out the golden hair and presenting it to Minos. The Cretan king spurned Scylla, however, and she committed suicide in shame; in death, she was transformed into a lark, and her father into a hawk.

Sedna Beside the Arctic Ocean, there once lived an old widower and his daughter, Sedna, a woman so beautiful that all the Inuit men sought to live with her. But she found none to her liking and refused all offers. One day, a seabird came to her and promised her a soft life in a warm hut full of bearskins and fish. Sedna flew away with him.

The bird lied. Sedna found her home a stinking nest. She sat, sadly regretting her rejection of the handsome human men. And that was what she told her father, when she listed her complaints when he visited her a year later.

Anguta ("man with something to cut") put his daughter in his kayak to bring her back to the human world. Perhaps he killed the bird husband first, perhaps he just stole the bird's wife, but in either case the vengeance of the bird people followed him. The rising sea threatened the escaping humans with death. On they struggled, until Anguta realized that flight was hopeless.

He shoved Sedna overboard to drown. Desperate for life, she grabbed the kayak with a fierce grip. Her father cut off her fingers. She flung her mutilated arms over the skin boat's sides. Anguta cut them off, shoving his oar into Sedna's eye before she sank into the icy water.

At the bottom of the sea, she lived thereafter as queen of the deep, mistress of death and life, "old food dish," who provided for the people. Her amputated fingers and arms became the fish and marine mammals, and she alone decided how many could be slaughtered for food. She was willing to provide for the people if they accepted her rules: for three days after their death, the souls of her animals would remain with their bodies, watching for violation of Sedna's demands. Then they returned to the goddess, bearing information about the conduct of her people. Should her laws be broken, Sedna's hand would begin to ache, and she would punish humans with sickness, starvation, and storms. Only if a shaman traveled to her country, Adlivun, and assuaged her pains would the sea mammals return to the hunters, which, if the people acted righteously, they did willingly.

In Adlivun, she lived in a huge house of stone and whale ribs. With one leg bent beneath her, Sedna dragged along the ground. A horrible dog guarded her, said by some to be her husband. Anguta himself lived there too; some versions of the myth say that, hoping the seabirds would think Sedna dead, he allowed her back into the kayak and returned home. But she hated him thereafter and cursed her dogs to eat his hands and feet; the earth opened and swallowed them. In any case, Anguta served Sedna by grabbing dead human souls with his maimed hand and bringing them home. These dead lived in a region near Sedna's home through which shamans had to pass to reach the goddess. There was also an abyss, in which an ice wheel turned slowly and perpetually; then a caldron full of boiling seals blocked the way; finally, the horrible dog stood before Sedna's door, guarding the knife-thin passageway to her home. Should the shaman pass all these dangers and ease Sedna's aching hands, the goddess permitted him to return, bearing the news that Old Woman had forgiven her people, that the seals would again seek the hunter, that the people would no longer starve.

Sekhmet Once, long ago, the lion-headed sun goddess of Egypt became so disgusted with humanity that she commenced a wholesale slaughter of the race. Her fury terrified even the gods, who deputized Ra to calm down the goddess. She refused to be restrained. "When I slay men," she snarled, "my heart rejoices."

Ra, attempting to save the remnant of humanity from the bloodthirsty goddess, mixed 7,000 vats of beer with pomegranate juice. He set the jugs in the path of the murdering lioness, hoping she would mistake them for the human blood she craved. Indeed she did, and she soon drank herself into a stupor. When she awoke, she had no rage left.

The intoxicating red drink was henceforth prepared and consumed on feast days of Hathor, so some say that Sekhmet was the negative side of that pleasure-ruling goddess. Others say that she was the opposite of Bast, the cat embodying the sun's nurturing rays; the lion, her destructive drought-bringing potential.

Sela In Kenya, the Luhya say the first woman bore this name and that she lived in a house on wooden stilts because the earth, in primordial times, was infested with crawling monsters. Her children—the human race—were bold enough to descend from her hut and live in houses built on the ground.

Sele Variations of this name appear all over Britain and Scotland, applied to fairy folk and sacred hills, to folkloric figures and festivals. The word is related to Old Norse *saell*, "happy," and old Teutonic *saeli*, "blessed," as well as to Sil and Silly, Sal and Sally, names used of female figures in folklore and tales. The original name may have denoted a harvest goddess, whom Michael Dames connects with the fabulous ancient monument Silbury Hill, whereupon a harvest ritual was enacted into historical times. Connections have also been suggested with the magical mermaid, the Silkie, and with the sun goddess Sul.

Selekana   In Lesotho, in Africa, this heroine was an obedient and clever girl who, alas, drew the envious attention of her peers. One day, as a cruel trick, the other girls pushed Selekana into the river as they were drawing water. Sinking to the bottom, Selekana met the River Woman, a one-armed and one-legged queen who immediately enslaved her. Forced to fetch and carry from the River Woman's palace, Selekana was so diligent that even River Woman was forced to admit her excellence. Freeing her from servitude, River Woman sent Selekana back to the village, decking her with jewels before she departed. When the girl returned, the haughty chief's daughter was outraged at her new wealth. Hearing the tale of what had occurred, the chief's daughter traveled to the river—but when River Woman tried to make her clean the underwater palace, she refused, and was eaten up by River Woman's crocodile husband.

Selene   Also called Phoebe and perhaps Helene, this early Greek full-moon goddess was the daughter of Thea (Titan of light) and spouse (or sister, or both) of the sun. Winged and crowned with a crescent, she drove the lunar chariot across the night sky, whose goddesses Leto and Hecate were her daughters; this radiant chariot was drawn by two white horses or oxen. When she was not visible, Selene was said to be in Asia Minor, visiting her human lover Endymion, for whom she had won the prize of eternal life and youth. Some legends say that he had to pay a price for this: he slept perpetually, even when his eyes were open, in his dark cave bed. In a fragment of poetry by Virgil, Selene was said to have been seduced by the wilderness god Pan, who used a beautiful white sheep's fleece to lure her into his woodland home.

Selkhet   In Egypt's pyramid tombs, mourners placed little golden figures of the guardian goddesses of the dead. One of these was Selkhet, a scorpion goddess of great antiquity who, with Qebhsnuf, protected the vessels that held the corpse's intestines. Selkhet was also one of the deities who led the deceased into the afterlife and offered instructions in the customs of that world. She was shown as a woman with a scorpion headdress, or as a scorpion with a woman's head, and symbolized the rebirth that follows death.

Semele   Daughter of Harmonia, she was called a mortal in late Greek legend, where she appears as the mother of the wine god Dionysus. But her name came from Asia Minor, where it meant the "subterranean," and Dionysus' mother was in some legends called the queen of death. Semele had been worshiped as a goddess for ages before the introduction of Dionysus to Greece; she probably represented the earth in its darkly fruitful form, the earth that devours life so that, fertilized, she may reproduce it.

The complex Greek story of Dionysus' birth has him first born of Persephone and killed in infancy. His father, Zeus, however, made a broth of the baby's heart and brought it to Semele, who became pregnant with the divinity to be reincarnated. But Semele recklessly asked Zeus to appear before her in Olympian glory. When he did so, she was consumed by his magnificence. Zeus picked up the fetus, sewed it into his thigh, and gave surgical birth to the child later.

But the young wine god, it was said, never really freed himself from the influence of his mother, whom he adored so much that he descended to death's realm to reclaim her, bringing her back to Olympus and installing her as the foremost of his Maenads under the title Thyone ("ecstatic madwoman"). Thus Semele, who started as a goddess and was demoted to mortality, was restored to divinity.

Semiramis   Some said the Syrian goddess Atargatis bore this daughter and placed her in the desert to be raised by doves. Others disagree: Semiramis was not originally divine but was a canonized queen, Sammuramat. In either case, when Semiramis was a nubile maiden, she attracted the attentions of Prince Omnes. They married, and he remained so infatuated with her that, when Semiramis decided to become queen of Babylon with a second husband, Ninus, as king, Omnes committed suicide in despair.

He was not the only man destroyed by love of Semiramis. "She of the exalted name" was one of the most lustful of queens. Unwilling to share her life with a man, she took handsome soldiers to bed and had them killed afterward (compare the Breton princess Dahut). Across western Asia, there are mounds of Semiramis, said to be graves of the one-night lovers she buried alive.

Once, they said in Armenia, Semiramis fell in love with the sun. When he did not return her affection, Semiramis attacked him with a huge army. The queen took the day, and Er, the sun, was killed in the battle. But then Semiramis repented her fury and begged the other gods to restore the sun to life—a tale that may have been derived from that of the Babylonian Ishtar.

Sequana   Among the Celts, the earth goddess was thought to be visible in the rivers that drained each land. Thus their earth-river goddesses could best be defined as watershed deities. Sequana ruled the Seine and its valleys; her special shrine was at the river's source. During festivals, an image of Sequana was drawn along the river in a ship that looked like a duck holding a berry in its bill. At the shrine, worshipers tossed votive offerings, often tiny statuettes, into the water as they prayed for health; many of these trinkets came to light in 1964 during excavations of the Seine's source.

The names of a number of other Celtic river-goddesses are known: Sabrina of the Severn; Clutoida of the Clyde; Belisama of the Mertey; Briant, whose river bears her name, and Devona of the Devon; Verbeia of the Wharfe; Matrona of the Marne. When depicted in art and statuary, these goddesses often reclined lazily, wearing long flowing dresses with folds as soft as river waves. Often they held cornucopias, fruit, or other symbols of the fertility their waters brought to the land.

In Ireland, where the goddesses' myths as well as their names were remembered, Boann and Sinann and Banna were all said to have been curious girls who, seeking immortal wisdom, traveled to the well at the mouths of their rivers, the Boyne, the Shannon, and the Bann. The wells, furious at being disturbed and unwilling to give forth secrets, rose from their holes and drowned the seekers. Thus, said Irish Celtic legend, were the great rivers of the earth formed. It is likely that similar stories of the river goddesses were told in Britain and Gaul.

Seyadatarahime   In the Kojiki, the ancient compilation of Japanese folklore, this woman was struck in the vagina by a red arrow while defecating outside her village. Taking the arrow home, she took it to bed with her. There it turned into a young man, a form of the snake god named Omononushi, to whom she bore a child. Carmen Blacker, scholar of women's shamanic traditions in Japan, finds in this tale a reflection of the tradition that shaman women took otherworldly or animal lovers.

Shait   This infinitely divisible Egyptian goddess was human destiny, born at the instant of birth. Invisible Shait rode through life with each person, observing all virtues and vices, crimes and secret prides. Thus it was Shait who spoke the final judgment on a soul after death, and that sentence, based on such intimate knowledge, was not only perfectly just but inescapable.

Shakti   Just as divinity is symbolized in Hindu India as a *lingam* (phallus) surrounded by a *yoni* (vulva), so goddess energy is thought to surround and animate the energy of a god. Maleness, in divine terms, is thought of as inert, a kind of passive being, while female divinity provides the activating energy that invigorates and empowers the god. Thus, in religious iconography, Hindu artists show the goddess having intercourse on top of the god, activating his previously languid body.

Worship of Devi ("The Goddess") appears to have been the rule in pre-Indo-European India. Generations of invasions by Indo-Europeans with their patriarchal mythology led to the apparent religious conquest of the area. But the goddess' worshipers did not give up her image; as the Indo-Europeans mingled with the indigenous races, the goddess began to reappear in Indian religious texts. Eventually, in the complexity of Hinduism that exists today, the goddess as the Shakti or energy of divinity was inseparable from the male god.

Each member of the Hindu trinity was provided with his Shakti: Maya enlivening creative Brahma; Lakshmi empowering nurturing Vishnu; and Parvati or Kali as the consort of destructive Shiva. But Shakti is sometimes used as a name for Shiva's energy alone, consistent with the philosophic understanding that all life, all energy, ultimately leads to destruction.

Shapash In the ancient Near East, the sun was more often female than male, and Shapash ("torch of the gods") was one of her names. In the Ugaritic Epic of Baal, this goddess retrieves the fertility-god's plaything from the underworld, an allegory of the return of moisture and growth to the earth's surface, of the annual defeat of drought.

Shauskha An Ishtarlike Hurrian divinity, whose winged beauty seduced even monsters. The kings of Anatolia served her; she commanded them through dreams, oracles, and the augury of her female soothsayers. Shauskha is probably a form of the Hittite sky queen Hannahanna.

Sheila na Gig Smiling lewdly out from rock carvings, this goddess of ancient Ireland can still be seen in surviving petroglyphs: a grinning, often skeletal face, huge buttocks, full breasts, and bent knees. What most observers remember best, however, is the self-exposure of the goddess, for she holds her vagina open with both hands.

She is the greatest symbol of the life-and-death goddess left in Ireland, where her stones have in some cases been incorporated as "gargoyles" in Christian churches. Her name means "hag"; her grinning face and genital display are complicated by the apparent ancientness of her flesh. Laughter and passion, birth and death, sex and age do not seem to have been so incompatible to the ancient Irish as they are to the modern world.

Sheilah Daughter of the careless Jephthah, this Hebrew maiden was sacrificed because her ambitious father promised to kill the first thing he met upon returning home from a battle. Furious at his lack of foresight, Sheilah uttered a famous lament when she realized that he could not be convinced to let her live. In particular, she wept that she would die a virgin. "Ye beasts of the forest," she wailed, "come and trample on my virginity." Her death did not go unavenged: Jephthah was cursed by Jehovah and died by dismemberment.

Shekinah The Talmud tells us that human senses cannot perceive Jehovah, but that we can see, hear, and touch his Shekinah. This word (meaning an emanation Jehovah allows us to sense) is feminine in gender. Eventually (like Sabbath and Hokkma) the word took on a feminine personality as well, until Shekinah became a rather disputative but compassionate demi-goddess who argued with the high god in support of his creatures. Like the Greek Dike, Shekinah was said to have abandoned the earth when humankind became too evil.

Sheshat Like Nisaba, a similar goddess to the east, this Egyptian goddess was "mistress of the house of books," inventor of writing, and secretary of heaven. She was also "mistress of the house of architects," the goddess charged with studying the stars to determine the axes of new buildings.

Finally, Sheshat invented mathematics, for which she was appointed goddess of fate, measuring the length of our lives with palm branches.

Shiwanokia   This primal divinity was, to the Zuni, a powerful being who, by spitting in her hand, caused the great earth mother, Awitelin Tsita, to be born. Her worshipers called their priestess Shiwanokia in honor of this creator.

Shulamite   The goddess whom the Assyrian city of Shulman was named after, she was the "heavenly female who designed heaven and earth." Her name survives, in part, in "Jerusalem," and in the mysterious Shulamite, the beloved of the biblical king Solomon. It was to this Jewish maiden that Solomon composed his famous "Song of Songs," those gorgeously erotic lyrics that are one of the treasures of Hebrew literature. According to her legend, Shulamite was a rural maiden who fell in love with a shepherd who was unfortunately judged as an inappropriate mate by her family. To destroy the relationship, Shulamite's brothers forced her to labor in the vineyards, hoping that as the sun blackened her skin, her suitor would reject her. Far to the contrary, her darkened visage drew the eye of Solomon's courtiers, who captured her and brought her to court. Solomon wrote his magnificent lyrics to win her heart, but Shulamite remained true to her shepherd-love and finally was returned to him.

Sibilaneuman   The goddess of songs to the Cagaba Indians of Colombia, she was hailed as the "mother of songs and dances, the mother of the grains and the mother of all things...She is the mother of dance paraphernalia and of all people, and the only mother we have."

Sibilja   A cow who was worshiped as embodying divinity, she accompanied Eysteinn Beli, a legendary Swedish king, into battle. Her presence was a sure token of victory, for her roaring and bellowing so frightened Beli's enemies that they lost their nerve and ran from the battlefield. Great sacrifices were offered to Sibilja, who was buried next to her chief worshiper, the king, when she died.

Si Boru Deak Parujar   Among the Batak of Indonesia, this creator goddess was born in the heavens together with her sister, Sorbayati. Their parents arranged for Sorbayati, the older sister, to marry the lizard god, but at a dance-party it was revealed that he really preferred Si Boru Deak Parujar. Humiliated, Sorbayati threw herself off heaven's balcony and fell to earth, which at the time was still a chaos of mud and slime. There her body disintegrated into those vital plants, bamboo and rattan, which readily grow in such primeval conditions. The bereaved sister then descended herself to earth, where—since she could not bring back Sorbayati—she set about creating land masses on the back of a snake. Only after doing so would she agree to marry the lizard god, who was transformed into a human at the wedding. From this union were born the first real humans, including the first woman Si Boro Ihat Manisia.

Sibyl   There were ten famous female prophets of the ancient world, one each in Persia, Libya, Delphi, Samos, Cimmeria, Erythraea, Tibur, Marpessus, and Phrygia, and one—most renowned of all—in Cumae near Naples, where Sibyl's cave was discovered in 1932 to have a sixty-foot-high ceiling and a 375-foot-long passageway entrance.

The Cumaean Sibyl wrote her prophecies on leaves, which she then placed at the mouth of her cave. If no one came to collect them, they were scattered by winds and never read. Written in complex, often enigmatic verses, these "Sibylline Leaves" were sometimes bound into books. It was said that the Sibyl herself brought nine volumes of these prophecies to Tarquin of Rome, offering them to him at an outrageous price. He scoffed, and she immediately burned three volumes, offering the remaining six at the same high price. Again—rather less casually—he refused. Again she burned three volumes, asking the original price. This time the king's curiosity was high, his resistance low, and he purchased the Sibylline prophecies.

The volumes were carefully kept in the Capitol and consulted only on momentous occasions by the Senate. Some were destroyed by fire in 83 B.C.E. while the rest survived until 405 C.E., when they perished in another fire. The people of Rome searched the world looking for prophecies to replace the Sibylline Leaves but were unable to find any. The Sibyl herself, it was discovered, had vanished. So the way was left clear for the production of pseudo-Sibylline prophecies, a profitable business until the end of the Roman Empire.

The Sibyl of Cumae gained her powers by attracting the attention of the sun god Apollo, who offered her anything if she would spend a single night with him. She asked for as many years of life as grains of sand she could squeeze into her hand. Granted, the sun god said; and Sibyl, glad to win her boon, refused his advances. Thereafter she was cursed with the fulfillment of her wish—eternal life without eternal youth. She slowly shriveled into a frail undying body, so tiny that she fit into a jar. Her container was hung from a tree; Sibyl needed, of course, no food or drink, for she could neither starve nor die of thirst. And there she hung, croaking occasional oracles, while children would stand beneath her urn and tease, "Sibyl, Sibyl, what do you wish?" To which she would faintly reply, "I wish to die."

Sicasica A mountain goddess of the Aymara of Bolivia, she was said to reside in the peak named for her and to try to seduce young men by taking the shape of a woman and luring them into her fatally cold glaciers.

Siduri When the hero of the Sumerian epic, Gilgamesh, sought treasure at the world's end, he found this bawdy innkeeper living on the border of the ocean abyss. The merry Siduri sang of the fleetness of time and the pleasures of life, telling Gilgamesh, "Dance and play, night and day...make each day a festival of joy." He refused, demanding instead directions to the ferryman of death. Siduri—who was the goddess Ishtar in her guise as a winemaker—told him, although the wise goddess knew Gilgamesh could not hold his prize once he found it.

Sif The beautiful Scandinavian grain goddess was most renowned, legend says, for her long golden hair—the autumn grass. Sif lived with the thunder-wielding Thor; the lightning was seen to mate with the fields on summer nights. The wicked Loki, however, cut off Sif's hair one night, and Thor made him travel to the lands of the dwarves to bring back master artisans. The dwarves were set to work making hair of spun gold that, when attached to Sif's head, grew like the original.

Sigurdrifta The wisest of the Valkyries, the Scandinavian battle maidens, Sigurdrifta once stole from battle a hero to whom Odin had promised victory; in punishment Odin stung her with sleep thorns. Sigurdrifta sank into a trance, saying she would never awaken until a man utterly without fear came to claim her as his wife.

When the hero Sigurd was riding in search of adventure, he found a mountain lit by fire; in the center of the light was Sigurdrifta, fully armored. Cutting her armor from her, he awakened the warrior and asked her to teach him wisdom. Sigurdrifta made reverent gestures toward night and day, toasting the deities of each, before answering. She spoke at length with the hero, telling him magic runes and the ways of sorcery. Finally, she sank back into sleep. Some legends, however, say she was the same woman whom Sigurd later encountered under the name of Brynhild.

Silewe Nazarata Both kindly and terrifying, this double-faced bisexual goddess of Indonesia lives in the upper world, from which she both creates and controls our world below.

Silkie She took her name from the silk clothing she wore, this Scottish house goddess who sneaked into homes to clean whatever was left in disorder;

of course, too careful housekeeping was as bad as slovenliness, for if she found nothing to clean, Silkie messed up the rooms instead. Some have connected her with the harvest goddess Sele and with the fairy folk called Silly Witches.

Silly Witches   In Celtic lands, it is considered bad form, if not actually dangerous, to discuss the fairy folk openly. A number of euphemistic phrases have sprung up over the centuries to refer to these semi-divine beings, who are probably ancient divinities banished upon the arrival of new religions. In Ireland, they are often the Good Folk; in Scotland, they are the Silly Witches or Silly Ones, a term whose origin may connect them to the harvest goddess Sele.

Sin   This Irish fairy woman was probably a remnant of an early goddess, for she was said to have created wine from water and swine from leaves to feed the battalions of warriors she had created with her spells.

Sinann   The goddess of Ireland's famous Shannon River was—like most other Celtic river goddesses—originally a curious and heedless woman. Seeking knowledge from the sacred well at the world's end, Sinann enraged the waters of wisdom with her audacity. Connla's Well, as it was called, rose up in fury and drowned her, but could not return to its cage and henceforth streamed through Ireland as a river. Virtually the same legend is told of the Boyne River goddess, Boann.

Sirens   Today we picture these sweet singers in only female bodies, but in early Greece the Sirens were both male and female bird-bodied prophets of the future and omniscient readers of the past. Above their strange egg-shaped bodies rose beautiful human heads; the breasts and faces of women were borne only in later days on the Sirens' feathered bodies.

There were variously two or three Sirens, given different names by different ancient authors. Homer mentions two Sirens but names only one:

Himeropa ("arousing face"). Three others are elsewhere named as Thelchtereia ("enchantress"), Aglaope ("glorious face"), and Peisinoe ("seductress"). Finally, in Italy, the Sirens were named Parthenope ("virgin"), Leucosia ("white goddess"), and Ligeia ("bright-voiced").

They were servants of Persephone the death queen, charged with bringing souls to her. This they did by singing sweetly to passing ships so that the enchanted sailors would be smashed on the rocks beneath the Sirens' coastal meadow. In form and function they are easy to confuse with Harpies, but the Sirens seem to represent death's sweet call, while their vulturelike sisters signify unsought, terrifying death.

Sita   The Hindu goddess Lakshmi incarnated herself as this girl so that she could marry her consort, Vishnu, in his incarnation as the hero Rama. Her name means "furrow," for Sita sprang forth from the earth when it was cut with a plow (appropriately, Lakshmi is the goddess of abundance and productiveness).

Sita came to earth to assure the destruction of the demonic King Ravena. While traveling with Rama, Sita was kidnapped by Ravena; Rama fought and destroyed Ravena. But even divine incarnations are imperfect, and Rama doubted Sita's chastity during her imprisonment. Though Sita successfully underwent a test of fire, Rama continued to doubt. Sita, pregnant, retreated to the wilderness to bear her twin sons who, recognized as adolescents by Rama, brought about the couple's reunion. But still Rama doubted and, wounded by his rejections, Sita called for a final test: earth, which gave her birth, should take her back if she were innocent. The earth opened and Sita disappeared, leaving Rama convinced of her purity and heartbroken at her loss.

Sitala   When one is stricken with smallpox in India, he is said to be possessed by the "cool goddess" Sitala, who owns all people and therefore can visit them in her feverish form. (The name "cool one" is clearly a flattering one, intended to keep the goddess at bay.) Sometimes said to be the death-goddess Kali, Sitala is still worshiped annually in India, particularly in Bengal. There it is said that Sitala, born after other goddesses, had difficulty getting humans to pay enough attention to her; she invented smallpox to force humanity to invent rituals for her. The tactic clearly worked, as Sitala is one of the most worshiped goddesses of India, called the Mata ("mother") of each village.

Sjofn One of the servants of the great Scandinavian goddess Frigg, this maiden had the special task of stirring infatuation in human hearts, a kindling that might lead to love.

Skadi The goddess for whom Scandinavia was named dwelled high in the snow-covered mountains; her favorite occupations were skiing and snowshoeing through her domain. But when the gods caused the death of her father Thjassi, Skadi armed herself and traveled to their home at Asgard, intent on vengeance. Even alone, she was more than a match for the gods, and they were forced to make peace with her.

Skadi demanded two things: that they make her laugh and that she be allowed to choose a mate from among them. The first condition was accomplished by the trickster Loki, who tied his testicles to the beard of a billy goat. It was a contest of screeching, until the rope snapped and Loki landed, screaming with pain, on Skadi's knee. She laughed.

Next, all the gods lined up, and Skadi's eyes were masked. She intended to select her mate simply by examining his legs from the knees down. When she'd found the strongest—thinking them the beautiful Balder's legs—she flung off her mask and found she'd picked the sea god Njord. So she went off to live in the god's ocean home.

She was miserable there. "I couldn't sleep a wink," Skadi said in a famous eddic poem, "on the bed of the sea, for the calling of gulls and mews." The couple moved to Thrymheim, Skadi's mountain palace, but the water god was as unhappy there as Skadi had been in the water. Thereupon they agreed on an equitable dissolution, and Skadi took a new mate, more suitable to her lifestyle: Ullr, the god of skis.

Skogsnuivar The woodwives of Scandinavia were said to be sweet-voiced, fur-garbed creatures whose duty was to herd wild woodland animals. Before any animal was hunted, the Skogsnufvar had to be contacted for assurance that the prey was not their pet. If well courted by the hunter, the Skogsnufvar would direct him to animals they were willing to do without; coins and food left at fallen trees signified the intent to honor the woodwives' will.

Skuld In Scandinavia, the goddess or Norn of the future was also a powerful sorceress and queen of the elves. Skuld was said always to be veiled and to carry the scrolls of fortune with her. There was also, in Norse legend, a half-elf mortal woman of this name, said to have the power to raise the dead, even if the bodies had been chopped in pieces; she was invincible because of this talent.

Smilax This Greek shepherd loved a man named Crocus; both were changed into the flowers that bear their names.

Snegurochka The heroine of a Russian fairy tale often known as the Snow Maiden, she was a little girl found by a childless couple one winter, a child who made their lives full of happiness and warmth. But human warmth was the only kind the girl could tolerate, for when spring came she melted away—she had been made of snow. Behind this folkloric figure hides an ancient winter goddess who changes form with the passing of her season.

Sneneik Along the Pacific Coast, the Bellacoola and others acknowledged the power of this cannibal woman, who sneaked through the world stealing children and robbing graves, throwing bodies into the woven basket she carried. She owned a home far away from our world, where she offered visitors food that, should they eat it, paralyzed them; she had many children, but they all were wolves.

When she visited this world, she appeared as a wild woman of the woods, a black-faced hag with sleepy eyes who emits low whistles that sound like *u, hu, u, u*. During winter ceremonies, a dancer disguised as Sneneik leaps forth and attempts to steal children and carry them away. Yet despite her fearsome appearance and threatening demeanor, Sneneik is also the bestower of gifts of coppers and food for feasts.

Solntse The Slavic sun goddess lives with the moon, her mate, in a little three-bedroom house in the sky. One room is hers, one is his, and the children—all the stars in the sky—bunk together in the last.

Somagalags The Bella Coola mountain mother, she arrived on earth at the Skeena River and began traversing what was then a flat, featureless terrain. Every time she met a man, she had intercourse with him and gave birth to another mountain. As the area is now very mountainous, it is clear that Somagalags had an active sexual appetite. Her children were hillocks when they were born, but she reared them up to be the enormous mountains that line the Pacific Coast of the North American continent today.

When her children looked substantial enough to take care of themselves, she settled down at the oceanside, where she built a cedar house and gave birth to four more children, all of them wolves. They were very hungry puppies, who wore her out gathering food for them. Every time she left the house to gather food, she heard human voices within, but when she entered, the sounds changed to wolf noises. But finally she crept upon the cabin and peeked through a window. There within were four strapping lads lounging about. She leapt through the window, a stick in her hand, and beat them each soundly. The boys admitted the error of their ways and, thereafter, took care of themselves. In return, Somagalags taught them all the secrets they needed to know to survive on this earth, including the proper ways to conduct rituals. Her sons went on to find wives and establish flourishing families, and Somagalags is therefore honored as the ancestral mother of the Bella Coola people.

Sophia The personification of Wisdom in the Judaeic scriptures, Sophia moved beyond metaphor to becoming truly personalized in later Hebraic, Gnostic, Kaabalistic and European philosophic text. In her original manifestations—in the biblical Proverbs, Wisdom songs and Sirach—she appears as Jehovah's companion, sometimes seen as opposed to a Lilith-like figure called the Foolish Woman. Created first after Jehovah (or sometimes at the same time as him, thus his equal), Sophia built her own house, one with seven pillars; she invites the faithful to dine at her heavy-laden table. Many images are used of her: she is a fruit-bearing tree, she is a garment that shrouds and protects us, she is a working craftswoman of great skill, she is veiled, she is open. Full of contradiction and mystery, Sophia remained a potent mythic symbol through many centuries and many countries, and continues to inspire the faithful of patriarchal regions today with a sense of feminine divinity.

Spako This name was given to the stepmother of King Cyrus, founder of the Persian Empire, but was originally that of a wolf goddess who nursed the king, thereby guaranteeing his power.

Spear-Finger One of the most powerful mythic figures of the Cherokee was Spear-Finger, a giantess who ate human livers. Though she could change her shape at will, her natural form was an old rock-skinned woman with a bony forefinger that she used for stabbing the unwary. She had special powers over stone: she could lift huge boulders, cement rocks together just by touching them, and build mountains of pebbles. Like the Cailleach and other winter hags, she had to die for life on earth to go on.

Always hungry, she often lured children from their play and stole their livers. She caused no pain, left no wound, but the afflicted eventually died. Thus, she was greatly feared. Anyone who ran into an old woman singing *"Uwela natsiku. Susasai,"* which means, "Liver, I eat it," quickly ran away.

When a council was held to rid the earth of Spear-Finger, it was decided that a trap would be the best way. So a pitfall was dug in a trail and a big bonfire lit to lure the old woman. It worked: very shortly she came down the path, looking for all the world like a member of the tribe. She was not shot immediately because the men felt kinship with her.

But when she fell into the hole they'd dug and immediately turned into a stone-skinned woman with a bone finger, they lost all sympathy for her. The hunters emptied their quivers to no avail. Nothing could penetrate her skin. She was immensely strong, and it seemed as though she would climb out and kill them. Then a titmouse nearby sang *"un, un, un,"* which the hunters thought meant *"unahu,"* or heart. So they shot at Spear-Finger's heart, but the arrows glanced off her stony chest. So they caught the bird and cut out its tongue for lying.

Then they heard another sound. It was the chickadee, who bravely flew into the pit and landed on Spear-Finger's right hand. The hunters began to shoot there, and the old woman fell down dead, for her heart was hidden in her wrist. The earth was freed from Spear-Finger, who lived on only in myth.

Spes An early Cretan goddess called Elphis in Greece, she was the one force left in the box of Pandora after evil had escaped into the world. Spes was ruler of the underworld and of death's cousin, sleep; her plant was the poppy, but otherwise nothing is known of her legends and meaning. In Greece and Rome, Spes became the personification of hope, worshiped in temples dedicated to her as early as the fourth century B.C.E

Sphinx The "strangler" started her life in Egypt, where the lion-bodied monster had a bearded male head and represented royalty. But in Greece—in a city with the Egyptian name Thebes—the Sphinx became female. She was said to have been a Maenad who grew so wild in her intoxicated worship that she became monstrous: snake, lion, and woman combined.

The guardian of Thebes, she prevented travelers from passing by strangling them if they could not answer a mysterious riddle. (Possibly she descended from the underworld guardian goddess who, in many cultures, prevented the passage of

Carved from limestone, this Egyptian figure is dated to the twenty-sixth Dynasty, more than 2,500 years ago. It represents the Sphinx, a human-lion hybrid who appears in Greek as well as Egyptian mythology.

the living into death's territory.) What, the Sphinx would ask, walked on four legs in the morning, two at noon, and three in the evening? Finally one traveler, who would become King Oedipus of Thebes, answered her: Human beings, who crawl as children, walk upright as adults, and rely on canes in age. Her reason for existence having been destroyed, the Sphinx destroyed herself.

Spider Woman Among the people of America's southwestern desert, the earth goddess was most familiar as a spider, big-bodied like the desert spiders who lived near the Zuni and Hopi. Another name for this earth goddess was Awitelin Tsita.

Sreca In Serbia, this was the name of the fate goddess when she appeared as a lovely maiden spinning golden thread; this vision meant good fortune. Bad luck, however, was brought by the same goddess, in the guise of Nesreca, a sleepy old woman with bloodshot eyes who could not be roused from bed when needed.

Srid-Icam 'phrul-mo-che The ancestral goddess, mother of all humanity, was to the early Tibetans this "Great Magical One, Lady of the Visible World." She lived in heaven with her parents, the primordial divinities, and her only brother. When a human man came to ask for her in marriage, she accepted. But before she departed the heavens, she asked for her half of the world as her inheritance—but was told that, as a girl, she only got one-third, as well as a spindle from her mother and an arrow from her father. These dowry gifts were sufficient, however, for Srid-Icam to create a comfortable world for her descendents.

Stepova-Baba Ukrainian great goddess, the "grandmother of the steppes," she is depicted in granite statues of a rotund featureless woman, which guard the rivers of her homeland. A single such statue is to be found outside the Ukraine, located on the Canadian side of Niagara Falls, where she is presumably doing the same duty.

Styx Under the earth, the Greeks said, lay the land of the dead, and between the two worlds wound the seven tributaries of the River Styx. The goddess of this sacred river was Styx herself, the "hated one" who prevented the living from crossing into the realm of Persephone without first undergoing death's torments.

The eldest, strongest daughter of the ancient sea, Styx was the mother of three daughters, the most famous of whom was Nike ("Victory"); the others were Strength and Valor. The mother of this triad was as much revered as feared. Because she sided with the Olympian gods in their battle with the land's earlier divinities, the Greeks said, Styx was honored as the source of all oaths. Even among the Olympians, an oath taken on the name of Styx was held inviolable; if broken, it meant the sinner was deprived of Hebe's ambrosia and nectar, the food and drink that kept the gods young and immortal.

Sudice The goddesses of fate in Eastern Europe had names that varied from land to land: Rojenice in Croatia; Sudicky in Bohemia; Sudzenici or Narucnici in Bulgaria; Sojenice in Slovenia; Sudice in Poland. All were said to be beautiful old women with white skin and white clothes, wearing white handkerchiefs on their heads and many necklaces of gold and silver. They glistened as they walked; sometimes they decked themselves with garlands of flowers or carried lit candles.

Generally these goddesses were invisible to human eyes, but they did appear at birth, when three of them arrived to cast the newborn's fate. Two spoke wishes for the child's fortune, but the words of the last could not be undone. To make sure she spoke good wishes, parents offered her gifts of wine, candles, and bread.

Suhijinino-Kami The goddess of settled sediments, a Japanese Shinto divinity who was among the first to emerge as the earth formed.

Sukulung In ancient Mali, this princess was the mother of the heroic Sundiata Keita. Although the hero is historic, his legend has mythic embellishments, including the statement that his mother's pregnancy lasted seven years.

Sul The ancient British goddess of healing waters had her special shrine at the spa we call Bath, where her power was strongest. Some scholars say that she was a solar divinity, deriving her name from the word that means "sun" and "eye." This interpretation may account for the perpetual fires at her shrines; the fact that her springs were hot, rather than cold, is additional evidence in favor of considering her a sun goddess.

She was honored into historic times; the Roman occupiers called her Minerva Medica ("healing Minerva"); occasionally she is called Sulivia. In statuary and bas-reliefs, she was shown as a matronly woman in heavy garments with a hat made of a bear's head and her foot resting on a fat little owl. In Bath and on the continent, she also appears in multiple form, as the tripartate Suliviae. The latter name is also used of the pan-Celtic divinity Brigid, suggesting a connection between these figures.

Sundi-Mumi The sun mother of the Finno-Ugric Wotjakians was invoked as follows: "We remember you with good broth and with bread. Give us warm days, and fair summer, and warm rain."

Sungmo In ancient Korea, this goddess lured a monk into her mountain sanctuary as he passed by, causing a stream to suddenly become a torrent. She then appeared to him as a giant, bewitched him with a spell, and made him her lover. From their union she bore eight daughters whom she trained as healers.

Sunna "Mistress Sun," the ancient Scandinavians used to sing, "sits on a bare stone and spins on her golden distaff for the hour before the sun rises." To the people of the north, as to many others, the bright day-bringing star was feminine, the goddess Sunna—still honored whenever we point to the sun.

Her people said that Sunna lived at first on earth; she was such a beautiful child that her father, Mundifiore, named her after the most brilliant star. But such presumption annoyed the gods of Asgard. They took Sunna from earth to her namesake, where she forever after rode the chariot of day. Pulling her were divine horses, Arvak ("early-waker") and Alsvid ("all-strong"); under their harnesses were bags of wind that cooled them and the earth as they traveled with their mistress through the sky. Likewise Sunna carried the shield Svalin ("cool"), which protected the earth from too intense contact with her rays.

Sunna was not really immortal, for like other Scandinavian gods, she was doomed to die at the Ragnarok, the end of this universe. She was said to be constantly chased through the sky by the Fenris-wolf, offspring of a female giant; on the last day he would catch her and devour her. But, say the eddas, "one beaming daughter the bright Sunna bears before she is swallowed," and this new sun daughter would take her mother's place in the new sky following the destruction of Sunna's realm.

The "bright bride of heaven" had, in addition to the familiar powers we grant the sun, a special function in Norse mythology. She was the "elf beam" or "deceiver of dwarves," for those creatures were petrified by her glance. Stone was important to her in another way, for her worshipers carved deep stone circles across the Scandinavian landscape as part of her sacred rites.

Surabhi One of the beings who emerged from the ocean as it was churned, says one of the most famous and evocative Hindu myths, was the cow Surabhi, goddess of plenty called the "fragrant one." She forthwith produced all luxury—and a daughter, Nirriti ("misery") as well.

Swan Maidens In Germanic and Scandinavian mythology, these women were Valkyrielike figures who flew through the air in bird disguises. They would, however, shed their feather cloaks to dance by the shores of quiet lakes. There, human men could capture the Swan Maidens as brides by stealing the victim's feather cloak and keeping it hidden from her. Should she find it, no matter how long and happily she had lived with the man or how many children she had borne, the Swan Maiden would don her cloak and fly instantly away. Sometimes, legend says, these women wore their souls on golden chains around their necks which, if removed, meant the girl's death.

Sweigsdunka This Lithuanian star goddess was bride of the sky and ruler of both the morning and evening stars. A weaver, she created the star cloth that covered the sky each night.

287

Syn The goddess gatekeeper of heaven was, among the Scandinavians, named Syn ("denial") because she denied entry to anyone she judged unworthy. Because she was all-seeing and perfectly just, Syn was the goddess on whom oaths were sworn; she was also invoked in lawsuits so that justice would prevail.

Syrinx This Greek nymph escaped from an attempted rape by changing herself into a reedy marsh. Her repentant assailant, the wilderness god Pan, cut down the reeds and made himself a pipe, which afterward was called by the nymph's name.

Syrith A golden-haired woman so beautiful that no one could look her in the face, this Scandiavian goddess may be an aspect of the love goddess Freya, one of whose alternative names is Syr ("Sow"). Imprisoned in a mountain wilderness by a giant who forced her to tend his goats—hence her name Syr Fen Tanna ("Syr of the Crags"), she was found and freed by the hero Othar (significantly, one of Freya's lovers). But she declined to return his love despite taking up residence in his parents' home. In exasperation, he finally announced that he would marry another maiden, at which time she changed her mind and agreed to wed.

Tabiti The Scythian great goddess ruled fire and animals. To her these early eastern Europeans swore oaths, suggesting a connection with the earth who witnesses all things. She was worshiped in southern Russia even before the Scythians arrived; little pottery statues of her were found there, showing an upright goddess bearing a child. The later Scythians showed her as half-serpent, often seated between a raven and a dog. Strabo says Tabiti was the protective goddess of the Black Sea sailors, who sacrificed to her anyone who strayed into their territory.

Tacoma The great earth goddess of the Cascade Mountains was embodied in the snowy peak of Mt. Rainier. Among the Salish, Nisqualli, Puyallup, Yakima, and other peoples of that area, Tacoma was the protector of the country's fresh waters, which brought nourishment upriver in the form of spawning salmon. Many legends were told of her, usually connecting her with the other mountains of the Cascades and Olympics.

One legend says that she was originally a hugely fat woman who shared a man with two other wives. The man, angered at their constant quarreling, set them far apart—two on one side of Puget Sound, and Tacoma on the opposite shore, where

there was plenty of room for her bulk. This did not deter her, however, from shooting insults at her co-wives.

Another version says that the woman was kept constantly on the move by her husband and co-wife until, exhausted, she just sat down and stayed put. But she continued to hate the other wife, at whose head she threw hot coals, so that Mount Constance today is bald.

Yet another story says that Tacoma was always a mountain, but that, when she was a womanly young mountain, she married a mountain prince. But not yet full-grown, she soon outstripped her husband in size. So, to make room for her husband and his people, she moved across Puget Sound, taking berries and salmon with her.

Tacoma grew so huge that she became a mountain that ate anything that set foot on her slopes. Voraciously, she ate people as well as animals. Finally the great god Changer turned himself into a fox and dared Tacoma to swallow him, after he'd magically pinned himself to another mountain. When Tacoma tried to swallow the god, she engorged vast quantities of rock and water, but Changer could not be moved. One more try—and she burst open, hot blood flowing down her sides. Her corpse still sits there, covered with snow, a petrified woman's body.

Tahc-I The sun goddess of the Louisianan Tunica was originally courted by the kingfisher, who took a man's shape for the occasion. Successful in his pursuit, he took Tahc-I home in the dark, telling her he lived in an upstairs room. When the girl woke up, however, she was out on the limb of a hackberry tree in a nest. She was perplexed and ashamed. She was also hungry and was not delighted when the kingfisher—now in bird form again—brought her a tasty lapful of minnows for breakfast. She began to sing mournfully, and as she did she rose into the sky, radiating light. In her honor the Tunica annually danced the sun dance and placed her statue, together with that of a frog, on altars in their homes.

Taillte The goddess of August in ancient Ireland was said to be foster mother of the light, embodied in the god Lugh. One of the great Irish earth goddesses, Taillte lived on the magical Hill of Tara, from which she directed the clearing of an immense forest, the wood of Cuan. It took a month to create the Plain of Oenach Taillten, where Taillte then built her palace; it remains on Irish maps today as Teltown, near Kells.

A festival was celebrated annually in her honor, lasting the whole of August. For generations it was celebrated, complete with mercantile fairs and sporting events; even into medieval times Taillte's festivities were held. Eventually they died out, but in the early part of this century the Tailltean Games—the Irish Olympics—were revived in an attempt to restore Irish culture.

Tai Yuan The Chinese saint of this name lived on clouds high in the mountains and remained celibate until the age of eighty, by which time she had become totally androgynous as well as ethereal. A beam of light, wandering by, saw the shining "Great Original" and penetrated her uterus; a year later Tai Yuan gave birth to a heroic child who became the ruler of the underworld.

Tamar There were two important figures by this name. One was a Hebrew heroine who outlived husband after husband. Her first was killed by a curse; she married his brother, who quickly died as well. So Tamar took matters into her own hands. A prophet, Tamar could see that her children would have glorious descendants. So, disguised as a holy woman, offering herself sexually as an embodiment of the goddess, she caught the eye of her husbands' father Judah. He failed to recognize her because Hebrews kept their women veiled, while promiscuous pagan women left their faces self-confidently uncovered.

Tamar took Judah to bed and conceived by him, later reveiling herself and returning to his household, where she lived as a widow. Although there was a period of tension when her pregnancy was discovered, Tamar showed Judah love tokens he had given the holy woman and forced him to acknowledge the fatherhood of the twin sons she bore.

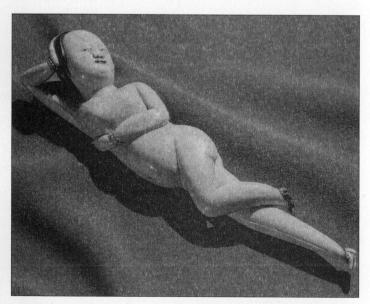

Made of ivory, this doll was used by eighteenth-century Chinese women to protect their modesty when they discussed physical ailments with male doctors; the woman could point out the site of pain without the doctor needing to touch her. Such modesty appears as a quality of many Chinese heroines; see Tai Yuan and Gum Lin.

The second Tamar was an ancient goddess of Georgia, an eternal virgin who rode through the air on a serpent saddled and bridled with gold. She lived high in the mountains in a palace built by storks and nightingales who flew in the necessary rock and wood. Tamar enslaved the morning star, who was master of winter; whenever he escaped, snow began to fall, but annually she captured him back and brought summer back to the land.

Although she was a virgin, Tamar was impregnated by a tiny beam of light that struck her through the thick walls of her castle. After a year, she bore a son, but she abandoned him in the woods, where he was raised by deer and grew up to become an angel. A sky goddess with control over the weather and the seasons, Tamar also has solar connections.

Tamayorihime Like her sister Japanese heroines Ikutamayorihime and Seyadatarahime, she was a young woman who became mother ancestor to an important family after mating with an otherworldly creature. This being used to come under cover of darkness, which apparently did not disturb the girl until she became pregnant. Then, to discover his identity, she sewed a long hemp thread to his hem, and, next morning, followed it to a dark cave. At its mouth she called out for her lover to show his face. "You would burst with fright," a deep voice answered from the earth's center. Unafraid, she continued to make her demand until he appeared, a scaly monster with a needle stuck in its throat. Tamayorihime fainted, but lived to bear the hero Daida, greatest warrior of Kyushu. The heroine's name, meaning a woman (*hime*) possessed (*yor*) by a god (*tama*), may have been a title borne by the Japanese shamans called *miko*. Similar stories are told of Psyche and Semele.

Tanaquil Behind King Tarquin of Rome stood the wise queen Tanaquil, interpreter of omens, political genius, domestic manager. She came with Tarquin from Etruria to Rome and, when an eagle swooped

Although considered a fierce goddess, the Green Tara depicted in this mask from Tibet seems calm and gentle. Her skin is green, with reddish cheeks and brows; her crown is composed of spiral designs.

down and stole his hat, she knew instantly that he was destined for success in the Italian town. When that success came, in the form of kingship, Tanaquil served as Tarquin's chief advisor. And she also provided the successor to the throne—not by giving birth, but by noticing an omen that Ocrisia would bear the next king and by generously ensuring that conception took place. In the late nineteenth century, J. J. Bachofen analyzed the myths of Tanaquil and contended that she was a legendary disguise for a goddess who, like Cybele or Ishtar to the east, granted kingship to her favorite but retained the land's sovereignty for herself.

Tangalimbibo In Zaire, this legendary chief's daughter was held prisoner by the river god despite the fact that she was nursing a new baby. Desperate to be together with her child, she agreed to the sacrifice of her favorite cow, after which she was released by the imprisoning divinity.

Tanit   When the conquering Romans saw the image of this goddess—just before they destroyed the Carthaginians who worshiped her—they named her Dea Caelestis or simply Caelestis ("heavenly goddess") for she seemed to rule the sky. Indeed, the winged goddess with a zodiac around her head and the sun and moon in either hand was the sky goddess of the Punic people. (Some oversimplify her status, calling her a moon goddess, but she ruled the sun and stars as well.) Her children called her "mother," seeing the sky as their source, just as other peoples have called themselves earth's children. Although the Carthaginians of history are a Phoenician people, Tanit may well have been an indigenous goddess of the Berbers whose identity meshed with the arriving Astarte to form the sky-queen of historic times.

Tara   In Indian Hinduism, the star goddess Tara is a manifestation of the queen of time, Kali. Her symbol, the star, is seen as a beautiful but perpetually self-combusting thing; so Tara is the absolute, unquenchable hunger that propels all life. As a Bodhisattva, a Buddha-to-be, she is considered second only to the great Avalokitesvara, of whom she is sometimes said to be a female aspect.

Among Buddhists and Jains, and particularly in Tibetan Lamaism, Tara became a symbol of other hungers as well, in particular the spiritual hunger for release from the purely physical world. As such, Tara is the goddess of self-mastery and mysticism, invoked under her 108 names on a rosary of 108 beads. The compassionate goddess, she appears as a playful adolescent, for Tara sees life for the game it is; she also appears as a celestial boat woman, ferrying her people across from the world of delusion to that of knowledge. As the Green Tara she is terrifying, but the White Tara of meditation stares at us from her three eyes to remind us that if we look through the terror of death she waits to enlighten us.

Across the many islands and atolls of the Pacific, innumerable forms of the goddess were honored, each under a name unique to the region. From Massim in New Guinea comes this ancestral figure in wood. For some Pacific goddesses, see Atanea, Biliku, Ciau, Papa, Satine and Taranga.

Taranga The mother of the Polynesian hero Maui did not carry him to term; she gave birth too prematurely for the fetus to live, and so wrapped him in her magical hair and tossed him into the sea. Then she offered prayers and sighs for the fetus, which protected it from turning into a demon, the usual fate of such children. In the sea's great womb, the child was carried to term and then raised by the gods until he was old enough to see Taranga's home. Happy to see her miscarried babe, Taranga welcomed Maui and made him her favorite son.

Taranga spent each day far from home, and her children did not know where she went. One day Maui decided to follow her; he saw her disappear beneath the earth. Continuing his pursuit, he found her tending the miraculous underworld gardens from which all food on this earth derives. Because of his obvious daring, Taranga allowed Maui to go through the manhood rituals earlier than other boys.

Tari Pennu In Bengal, this earth goddess was propositioned by the sun god. She refused him, and so he created human women to service him. But they took up the worship of the earth goddess, and the struggle between Tari Pennu and the sun continues to this day.

Tatsuta-Hime Each autumn this Japanese goddess wove a beautiful multicolored tapestry. She then incarnated herself as wind and blew her own work to shreds.

Tauret This was the animal form of the great Egyptian mother goddess Mut. As a nurturing force, she was a pregnant hippopotamus with long teats, standing on her hind legs and carrying the scrolls of protection. But as the fierce animal force, as the mother who defends her brood, she was a lion-headed hippo with a dagger.

Tefnut Taking her name from the dew that appears each dawn, she was an Egyptian goddess of daybreak like Eos, Aja, and Aurora. Like them, Tefnut

was associated with the mountains from which the sun rises. Sometimes, as the "heavenly cow of creation," she seemed to be a form of Neith; sometimes she was a lioness or a lion-headed woman, suggesting a similarity to Bast or Sekhmet.

The Green Tara was said, in Tibetan Buddhism, to be the fierce form of the kindly star goddess who also appears as the White Tara. This painting dates from the turn of the twentieth century.

Telesilla A poet of the Greek town of Argos, she was the heroine of a war with neighboring Sparta. When the Spartans besieged Argos, this poet fought her way out of the siege—at the head of an army of Argive women, worshipers of the ancient Hera.

Tellus Mater The Roman "Mother Earth" was honored each April 15, when a pregnant cow was sacrificed and its unborn calf burned. The Romans tried to offer appropriate tribute to each divinity and they felt that the earth—pregnant in spring with sprouting plants—would especially appreciate such a sacrifice.

Tellus' constant companion was Ceres, the grain goddess, and the two of them interested themselves not only in vegetative reproduction but in humanity's increase as well. Therefore, they were invoked at every marriage that they might bless it with offspring. Tellus too was considered the most worthy goddess on whom to swear oaths, for the earth, witnessing all doings on her surface, would see that an oath taker kept his promise. Finally, Tellus, to whom the bodies of the dead were returned as to a womb, was the motherly death goddess, for unlike her apparent Greek counterpart Gaia, Tellus was associated with the underworld as well as the earth's surface.

Telphassa "Wideshiner," she was an early Greek goddess of light who was probably imported from Phoenicia; she remains in legend only as the mother of the cow goddess Europa.

Telphusa This water nymph had prophetic powers, said the Greeks, but the water of her fountain was so bitterly cold that it killed anyone who tried to gain prophetic speech by drinking there. Some legends say that the famous seer Tiresias died when he tried to increase his foreknowledge by sipping Telphusa's water. When Apollo, the invading god who took prophecy from the ancient earth goddesses, was seeking a place for his oracle, he first selected Telphusa's renowned spring. But she persuaded him to look elsewhere, directing him to Gaia's Delphi—where the nymph knew Apollo would have a fierce fight with the guardian serpent Python before he could control the oracular spring.

Tethys The most ancient pre-Hellenic sea goddess, she was part of a trinity of world creators with Nyx, the primeval darkness, and Gaia, the fertile earth; all together they mothered the world we inhabit. Gradually, the ages eroded Tethys' power, until classical Greek mythology contained little information about her. Homer tells us she has ceased giving birth, being content with 6,000 children: half of them sons, half the daughters called Oceanids, most famous of whom is her mother's double with a similar name, Thetis. By Hesiod's time, Tethys was even less important; that poet scrambled her history by calling her a Titan, a created goddess rather than a creator. But she still remained important enough to have been named as the nurse of the infant Hera, the great women's goddess of Greece.

Thalassa In one Greek account of creation, she was the mother of all, possibly the same goddess as Tethys. Later she was said to be the fish mother, creator of all sea life. Her name, which means "sea," survives in the word for a mercantile sea kingdom, *thalassocracy*. Some find in her a personification of the Mediterranean Sea, others an image of all the world's oceans.

Thalestris This Amazon queen practiced an early form of eugenics. Rather than mating with anonymous males in the yearly fertility ritual, she kept her eyes open for likely kings and princes to press into sexual duty. She had apparently borne several children this way when she first cast eyes on Alexander of Macedon. Recognizing a superior specimen of manhood, she invited him to fertilize her, an offer that, apparently, he took as a high compliment.

Thea The pre-Hellenic goddess of light, mother of the dawn and the luminaries, bore a name that means simply "goddess." Although this hints at earlier eminence, nothing is left of Thea but her name and the list of her children; like many elder Greek goddesses, she was replaced by divinities of the invading Indo-Europeans.

Themis The "steadfast one," the daughter of Gaia, was the earth goddess personified as an unshakable power. By Homer's time, she had come to signify a second powerful steadfastness: the social contract among people living on the earth (similarly Fides). One of the most ancient and most hallowed of goddesses, Themis later became a vague and abstract personality. Yet evidence of her original precedence is suggested: no Olympian gathering could take place unless she called it, and neither could any divinity lift the cup of nectar before she had drunk.

In the language of her people, *themis* was a common as well as a proper noun, the former indicating the power of convention, of whatever is fixed in society as steadfastly as the earth beneath us. The personification of such social cohesion, Themis was shown bearing a pair of scales; as the fruitful earth, she was shown holding the cornucopia. She was mother of the seasons, or Horae, goddesses who determined the proper moment for the fruitful earth's budding and exhaustion, and the proper times as well for human events. One of Themis' daughters, the fierce Dike, was her own maiden self, a stern, uncompromising virgin. Her other children were the Horai (Order, Justice and Peace) and the Moirai (the spinning, allotting and cutting fate goddesses).

Themis ruled prophecy, for she knew human nature and the nature of human society and so could predict the outcome of any struggle; thus she shared with Mother Gaia the famous Delphic Oracle. For her worship, she demanded group dancing, the symbol of a group's bonding through graceful action. Eldest of Greek goddesses, she was the first to whom temples were built, for before her there was no human community to offer worship.

Thetis Reading late Greek mythology, you would believe this goddess was merely the mother of the hero Achilles. But clues in her legend suggest that she was originally one of the great goddesses, daughter and double of the sea queen Tethys, much as Hebe was to Hera. She was apparently a goddess of womanhood, for she was raised by the threefold deity of femininity, Hera. Thetis also nursed the two gods associated with women's

rites: the appealingly dissolute Dionysus and the crippled artisan Hephaestus.

Sometimes legend called Thetis not Tethys' daughter but an offspring of another sea goddess, Doris. In either case, she was gifted with the oceanic power of shapechanging. Thus, when the Olympians—fearing the prophecy that she would bear a son greater than his father—condemned Thetis to marry a mortal, she resisted in the time-honored fashion of sea queens. She changed herself into monsters and microorganisms, but her husband-to-be, alerted to her powers, held fast until she resumed human form.

This highly polished basalt figure shows Tauret, the hippopotamus goddess who was the animal form of the Egyptian mother goddess Mut.

She agreed to marry Peleus. At the wedding the prankster goddess Eris tossed her famous apple, marked "to the fairest," into the crowd, which resulted in the Trojan War and the death of Thetis' mortal son, Achilles. After Achilles' death, Thetis abandoned Peleus, who until that time had remained youthful by her immortal powers; he immediately aged and died.

Thorgerd Her full name was Thorgerd Holgabrud. Originally a human woman, she was deified because of her unprecedented skill in divinity and sorcery. She and her sister Irpa were the special goddesses of the Icelandic nobleman Jarl Haakon, who built them a special temple in the south of that volcanic island.

Thorgerd was a mighty warrior goddess, charged with protecting her people from enemies; if they were attacked, she sprang to life, arrows flying from each finger, each arrow killing a man. In addition, she had power over natural forces necessary for her people's happiness; thus she was invoked for luck in fishing and farming. Her worship was among the last vestiges of the ancient religion, remaining vital into Christian times. The Christians, denouncing her, called her Thorgerd HolgaTroll, although she had no troll blood in her.

Tiamat Before our world was created, said the Babylonians, there was only Tiamat, the dragon woman of bitter waters, and her mate Apsu, god of fresh water. In those timeless days in a frenzy of creativity, Tiamat began to bring forth offspring: monsters, storms, and quadrupeds, the like of which exist today only in our dreams. Finally, the gods came forth from the almighty womb of Tiamat and, growing swiftly, set up housekeeping in another part of the universe. But they were a rowdy bunch, who disturbed Apsu with their noise. He approached Tiamat with the suggestion that, because she had created them, she could readily do away with the gods. Mummu Tiamat ("Tiamat the mother") was taken aback by the suggestion and refused.

But the gods got wind of the conversation and, in retaliation, killed Apsu, the goddess' lover. At that her fury exploded and, with Kingu, her firstborn son, she attacked the gods. They waged a battle that, some say, goes on annually to this day, with the hero Marduk each year swallowed by the enormous dragon. Tiamat, according to this version of the story, became a civilizing fish mother (like Atargatis) to the people of earth. But others contend that Marduk, hero of the new gods, killed his mother in the battle. Her body fell into the lower universe; one half became the dome of heaven, the other half the wall to contain the waters.

Tien-Hou She was born Mei Chou, a natural psychic and the sister of four seafarers. One day she fell into a deep trance, which worried her parents deeply. They tried everything to break the spell and at last succeeded, much to Mei Chou's anger. Soon afterward, three brothers returned home with the news that the fourth had been lost at sea; they, too would have drowned, they said, had not their sister walked across the water in her astral body to save them. Mei Chou lived on earth only a few years longer before being elevated to the heavens as Tien-Hou, the Chinese Empress of Heaven. Not to be confused with Hsi Wang Mu, queen of the West and empress over all divinities, Tien-Hou was the ocean goddess who rode across the sky on clouds, consulting her wind servants to find sailors in danger. She then hastened to their rescue, just as she had when she lived on earth.

Tien-Mu To make lightning, this Chinese goddess had only to flash two mirrors at each other; from their intersecting rays, lightning bolts shot out.

Tisnawati In Java, this creator goddess was born after a serpent brought a sparkling jewel up from the underworld. That gem gave birth to Tisnawati, who attracted the unwanted attentions of a god. Resisting him, Tisnawati died—but in doing so, she gave life, for the first banana trees rose from the palms of her hands, rice sprang from her vulva, a coconut palm from her head, and corn from her teeth.

Titichane   A folkloric form of an African ancestral mother who took cat form, Titichane was said to have been a woman who married a man from another village. Traveling there to live with him, she took the family cat along with her, but failed to tell him of the animal's peculiar powers. It got free and killed some chickens, so the husband killed the cat. And with it, he killed his wife and her whole clan, for the cat was their external soul.

Tlazoltéotl   "Dirty lady" or "earth's heart" was the Aztec goddess of the fourfold moon, the witch-goddess of sexuality and license. Gambling, temptation, and black magic also fell to her rulership; however, she was also the purifier of her people, for only her priests could hear confessions of guilt. This confession was only effective once in a lifetime, so Aztecs put it off as long as they could, rather than die in an impure condition.

The four aspects of Tlazoltéotl had individual names: Tiacapan, Teicu, Tlaco, and Xocutxin. All were witches who rode broomsticks through the sky, clad only in the night and a tall peaked hat. Like other witch goddesses of other lands, they were particularly fond of crossroads: the literal ones, which they were said to haunt, and the crossroads of life, the points at which decisions lead to good or evil.

Tlitcaplitana   The Bellacoola of the Pacific Northwest were always eager to meet this heavenly woman, who descended from her home in the sky to heal the sick; often she would grant them secret knowledge and chants as well as health. Sometimes, alas, her power was too much for the human vessel, and they died from the contact. But that was not because of any ill will on the goddess' part, for she was the most generous of heavenly spirits, though ugly in the extreme, with a big snout and ropelike breasts. Her singing, however, which carried across the calm waters and through the dense rain forests, was as beautiful as she was not.

Toci   "Our grandmother" was one of the great Aztec goddesses, the embodiment of nature's healing powers, and therefore invoked in sweat baths where the body was purified. She was said to wear a skirt of shells and carry the sun disk on her shield. Toci's festival was particularly celebrated by doctors, midwives, surgeons, and fortunetellers, who danced for eight days as though entranced, moving only their blossom-filled arms. Without speaking, they danced before a woman chosen to represent the goddess. Some researchers contend that in early times, the people of Mexico did not sacrifice humans to their divinities; Toci may have originally been worshiped without human slaughter, but by the time of the Spanish invasion her festival ended with the midnight sacrifice of the woman who had received the prayers of the Aztec healers.

Tomyris   Most history books mention that Cyrus the Great died on a military campaign. But it is seldom acknowledged that he was bested in battle and executed by an Amazonian queen, ruler of the Massagetae, a Scythian people. When Cyrus' imperialism led him to invade Tomyris' country, she attempted to negotiate a truce. He refused; she sent her son against the invader, who took him prisoner; then the young prince killed himself in shame.

Just prior to the suicide, however, Tomyris gave Cyrus a last warning: "Restore my son to me…Refuse and I swear that, bloodthirsty as you are, I will give you your fill of blood." Cyrus was not disposed to listen to the queen's threats, and Tomyris forthwith destroyed his entire army and captured the king. Flaying his corpse and beheading it, she held his severed head above a skinful of blood and tossed it in, instructing him to drink his fill.

Tonan   One of the Aztec mother goddesses, she once challenged her son, a god who believed himself omnipotent, to produce mother's milk—to prove he could be as generous as he was fierce. He could not, and she became known as a protective divinity, one who answered the prayers of the poorest and who especially watched over birthing mothers.

Tonan was honored in a winter solstice festival at which a woman dressed entirely in white and covered with shells and eagle feathers danced, weeping and singing, through the crowds. A priest accompanied her and, taking the goddess' mask from the woman, killed the year's incarnate deity. The next day, Aztec men struck the women of the community with little bags full of green paper, apparently a magical act to renew the life force.

It was at Tonan's sacred shrine that the virgin now called Guadalupe manifested herself. But Tonan herself is still honored by the Nahua people, who celebrate a feast between December 20–24 for Tlakatelilis (Tonan's name in their language) which includes music and the placement of marigold garlands on statues of the goddess (or of her substitute, Guadalupe).

Torah   The "Law" was a female force in Jewish legend, as stern and demanding as any goddess. She appeared as an advisor to Jehovah, and a skeptical one at that. Torah opposed the creation of humanity on the grounds that "The man thou art creating will be few of days and full of trouble and sin." Only after Jehovah had convinced Torah that repentance was possible did she cease her protest.

Toririhnan   In the Oceanic mythology of New Caledonia, this goddess controlled storms, which occurred whenever she blew her nose on her finger. Once, it is told, she tried to pretend she was the chief's pregnant wife by stuffing her uterus with bits of pottery; the real wife, having survived Toririhnan's attempted drowning, gave birth to twin sons who set fire to the goddess' cabin, forcing her to reside forever in the mountains where thunderclouds gather.

Tou-Mou   The Chinese goddess of the polestar was the judge of all peoples, keeping records of their lives and deaths. In addition, she was the scribe of heaven, keeping a tally of all the divinities, their duties, and their various estates in the nine heavens.

Toyota-Mahime   This sea goddess, "Lady Abundance-of-Jewels," appears in the Kojiki, the Japanese scriptures. Like Melusine and other mermaids, she married a mortal but set a single condition on their happiness; in this case, the mermaid warned her husband not to look upon her while she was birthing their child. Then she hid in a hut thatched with cormorant feathers. Of course her mortal mate, unable to contain his curiosity, peered inside to see Toyota slithering around in her true serpent form. Discovering his perfidy, she retreated to the ocean and forever closed the door joining her realm to his.

Toyo-Uke   A food goddess whose gold-filigreed shrine stands at the great Shinto shrine of Ise, she is sometimes considered an early sun goddess whose worship was made secondary to that of the powerful Amaterasu, ancestor of the dominant Yamato clan and of their descendents who still occupy the throne of Japan.

Triduana   A Scottish name for Brigid from the Edinburgh area. Of Triduana was told the famous Brigid tale that she tore out her eyes to destroy her beauty, rather than be preyed upon by a lecherous king—in this case Nechtan, king of the Picts. Triduana's sacred place was a well beneath a Druidic oak.

Trung-Trac   The rain goddesses of the Tonkin were originally warrior women who led a revolt of their people against a tyrannical Chinese governor. The uprising was successful, and Trung-Trac, the elder sister, became queen while her sister Trung-Nhi was honored as a war hero. Later, however, they were again invaded and conquered by the Chinese. The women were deified after death.

Tsagigla'lal   On the Columbia River, which runs between the states of Washington and Oregon, this woman was a culture heroine of the Wishram people. She was originally a chieftain, but when Coyote decreed that women could no longer be chiefs, she refused to give up responsibility for her people. Instead, she turned herself into stone so that she could forever protect them. A petroglyph upstream from the Dalles depicts her watchful eyes.

Tse che nako Among the Pueblo people called the Keres, Tse che nako created this earth simply by thinking of it. Whatever she visualized, it came to be, including the sacred beings who help her manage the ongoing creation of this world.

Tsi-Ku When a Chinese woman wanted to know what the future held, she went to the toilet and asked Tsi-Ku ("purple lady"), the goddess of the outhouse.

Tsuru When Japan was under the rule of shaman queens, this woman offered herself as a human sacrifice in the building of a dyke against a raging flood in Oita prefecture. Buried alive in the river, she successfully diverted the waters so that the village was safe. Probably she was a *miko*, or shaman, for there is a tradition—the *hitobashira* or "human pillar" tales—that only such women could hold back ravaging floodwaters, provided they were willing to lay down their lives; in some interpretations, this death was metaphoric and meant retirement to an ascetic life in the shrine. Tsuru was worshiped at Aibara shrine near the site of her sacrifice.

Tuchulcha The Etruscans pictured death as a woman with horrifying eyes staring over a beak, ass' ears, serpent hair, and a snake twisted around one arm.

Tuli As the great father god of Samoa watched the watery chaos of primeval time, the bird goddess Tuli flew across it. As she tired, he threw stones from heaven, giving her temporary perches; these became the islands of Polynesia. As she rested on a rock, Tuli grew weary of the sun blazing on her head, so she flew back to heaven and brought herself a fresh vine as an umbrella. She left the vine behind her, and from it swarmed maggots who became the first human beings.

Tundr Ilona The Ugrians, including the Hungarians, said that this goddess created the world. The sun was an egg which she, taking the shape of a swan, laid in the sky.

Tu-Njami The Siberian "mother fire" looked like a small naked girl, but she was strong enough to protect the whole family that worshiped her at their hearth—especially the women, since she was their ancestor. She was a goddess of purification and healing whose special concern was the removal of disease and filth. Tu-Njami also ruled birth, for she was an incredibly productive mother herself, birthing small versions of herself—daughters—on every twig in the fire.

Tuonetar The queen of death, according to the Finnish Kalevala, lived in a jungle of darkness somewhere on the earth, divided from the land of the living by a black-watered river. It was thought to be possible to reach Tuonela, Tuonetar's country, by hiking seven days through underbrush, seven through woodlands, and a final seven days through dense forest. Finally, the traveler reached the banks of the River Manala, where Tuonetar's swans floated and where her daughters laundered their dark robes. Only these daughters could—if they would—convey the traveler into the country of Tuonetar. But few would survive their assistance, for they were goddesses of disease. Once Loviatar, Kipu-Tytoo, or another of Tuonetar's daughters had brought the visitor to the death queen, Tuonetar herself would offer a magical brew of frogs and worms; if one drank that, return to the land of life was impossible.

Turan Before Rome conquered the Italian peninsula, the area now called Tuscany was the home of a rich and complex culture. The Etruscans who lived there evolved a theology and a philosophy of life quite different from the Romans—a culture that perished with the Roman victory, leaving only vestiges in the most biased source possible, the records of their conquerors.

The Etruscans left their own words as well, but their inscriptions are written in a language not yet deciphered and apparently unrelated to any language known today. The mysterious Etruscan culture was said by Herodotus to be a migrant from Lydia, a woman-honoring culture where children bore their mothers' name and assumed their mothers' social status.

This Lydian heritage seems to have survived in Etruria, for Etruscan women enjoyed more social equality with men than did their peers in other Mediterranean countries of the ancient world. All the more unfortunate, then, that only the names of their goddesses survive. Although there is no proof that strong goddesses either lead to, or reflect, similar social prominence among their human counterparts, this connection seems probable; therefore, the Etruscan goddesses may have been the most feminist in the ancient world.

One Etruscan goddess about whom the modern world does know something is Turan—who survived as Turanna, the "good fairy" of peace and love in modern Italy. She took her name from the same word as the Greek *tyrannos*, or ruler. Thus Turan is assumed to be the queen of life, sometimes called Aphrodite. She was the mistress, in both modern senses of the word, a divinity of sex and dominance. And apparently her worship included the former, for her temples were placed outside the city walls so as to be less obvious to young people and mothers of small children.

Turesh   The Ainus of northern Japan remembered a golden age when humans did not have to work for a living, a happy time when the god Okikurumi caught fish in the celestial sea and sent down the catch in baskets with the goddess Turesh. But there was, as in many paradises, a single law in this land: no Ainu should ask their benefactress' name or seek to discover her appearance. One Ainu was villainously curious, however, and grabbed the ministering hand as it set food upon his table, pulling into the house a squirming sea monster. The wrath of heaven fell upon the Ainus that day, and since that time they have had to struggle for the meager food their harsh land provides them.

Turrean   The Irish wolfhound goddess was, legend said, originally human, but was changed by the spiteful fairy queen Uchtdealbh into the most beautiful bitch that ever lived. Turrean was kept prisoner for many years on Galway Bay until her nephew Fionn MacCumhaill freed her and restored her to human form. In the meantime, she bore two sons, who retained their canine shape; they lived with their uncle and traveled with him as his half-human dogs, Bran and Sgeolan.

Uadgit The sovereign cobra goddess of lower Egypt and the Nile delta, she joined with Nekhebet to form the two mistresses of the land, the Neb-Ti, a political symbol of the unification of Egypt.

Uinigumasuittuq Her names means "The one who did not wish to marry" or "refuser of husbands," and her story is found among most Inuit people, often attatched to the undersea goddess Sedna. Uinigumasuittuq, who lived with her parents and their dog Siarnaq, was known throughout the area as the girl who refused all suitors. But one day an especially handsome youth appeared in her village, and she began to entertain him every night in her bed. But it was not a human man; it was Siarnaq, metamorphosed—something that the father discovered. In fury, he evicted both girl and dog, banishing them to a little island. There the dog began to swim daily back to the village to get food for his family—for the girl was soon pregnant with puppies. But one day, tired of finding food for the growing family, the father filled the dog's baskets with rocks, and he drowned.

Uinigumasuittuq, furious, instructed her half-dog children to tear apart their grandfather's kayak. Then she sent them away so that they would not be killed for their crime. The first puppies she packed into the upper leather of a booth and sent off to the south; they became the white people. The others, whom she set off in other directions, became the ancestors of the native peoples. Then she stayed on in the area, continuing to refuse human suitors and finally finding a second husband among the sea-birds.

Uke-Mochi Japan's food goddess had her own way of providing for the world's needs: she vomited. When she faced the land, rice—boiled and ready to be devoured—poured from her mouth. Facing the sea, she regurgitated fish and seaweed. Looking to the mountains, she vomited game creatures ready for capture.

Unfortunately, she set her table this way when one of the male gods was visiting her. It disgusted him, so he killed her. Her fertile body, falling to earth, dissolved into food: cattle stampeding from her head, silkworms crawling from her eyebrows, rice plants popping up from her belly. The god's behavior, however, so angered heaven's queen, Amaterasu the sun goddess, that she withdrew her light, causing the world's first winter.

Uks-Akka The "door woman" of the Saami of Lapland, she was said to live under the doorway and to change girl children into boys in the womb, the doorway to life.

Umaj   Russian Siberia was home to many different ethnic traditions, but almost all worshiped a birth goddess of this name. The Khakass believed she lived in the placenta; among the Shors, she protected newborns. The nearby Altais believed the sacred mountains of their land were occupied by big-breasted women who appeared naked, even in winter; anyone who made love with one always had good luck in hunting. Under the name Umay, she was honored by the Turks, and Mongols worshiped this earth goddess who controlled human fertility and who lived in the placenta. Called Qatum (Empress), Umay was embodied in human queens. Her worship still lives on among the Yakuts, where she is called Avisit; she protects newborn children and horses. Among the Turks, rituals involving the placenta recall her early power in their area.

Unelanuhi   The sun was the primary object of worship to the Cherokee, the only deity to whom prayers were addressed. Each morning the people prayed to her by bowing towards the dawn—if possible over water—and saying *A ke yu ku gusqua ne lo ne hi*, "hail, sun, my creator." Her name was Unelanuhi (The Apportioner), for she divided the year into seasons. She was also called Aag:hu Gu:gu (Beautiful Woman), a word also used of the glow of the dawn, and Sutalidihi (Six-Killer), a name whose meaning is lost.

Early in creation, the sun lived on the other side of the world. Over here, everyone was always bumping into things and stubbing their toes, so a council was called to determine a remedy. When fox said there was plenty of light around the world, possum volunteered to bring it to this side. He tried, but when he'd stolen part of the sun's fire, it burned off his tail and fell away. Buzzard tried, but the fire burned off the feathers on his claws. Then Grandmother Spider, Kanene ski Amai yehi, wove herself a little basket and spun a web on which she traveled across the sky. She

wove and wove until she reached the sun. Then she reached out, grabbed the sun, roped it into her basket, and fled back across her waiting web to light our sky.

But the new sun sat too low in the sky for comfort. People were dying from its extreme heat. So, handbreadth by handbreadth, the animal elders moved the sun upwards. Up and up she went, until she stood seven hands high in the air. There the sun was just right, and there she has stayed to this day.

This too-hot sun appears in the Cherokee story that the north went traveling and fell in love with the daughter of the south. He carried her to his country, where all the people lived in ice houses. The next day, when she got up, the houses started to leak. As she climbed higher and higher, the walls began to collapse. People begged the young man to divorce his wife so that their houses would not be ruined. Because he loved her, he held out against them for a time, but finally he had to let her go. She went back south, far enough away not to burn down the villages.

Unelanuhi had a daughter, whom she visited every day in her house on the high point of noon. Every day, as the sun looked down, she saw people squinting up at her, faces contorted in an attempt to gaze upon her brilliance. This made her think them ugly, so she decided to kill them all. Every day she scorched the earth, until everyone on earth was perishing. The spirit people, the Little Men, told their human kin that, in order to survive, they would have to kill the sun. The Little Men transformed two people into snakes—a copperhead and a spreading adder. They traveled to heaven and hid near the sun daughter's house to wait Unelanuhi's arrival.

As she stopped there, the adder got ready to strike. But the sun's brilliance blinded him, and he just spit some yellow slime. Angered, the sun-mother called the snakes foul names, and they slunk off in disgrace. So the Little Men turned two more people into snakes—this time, into a rattlesnake and into the monster called Uktena. They traveled to the sky to kill the sun. But the overeager rattlesnake rushed at the sun's daughter rather than wait for the sun herself. He struck, he bit her, he killed her—and then, terrified, ran away with Uktena back to earth.

The sun mother, finding her daughter dead, shut herself up in the house and refused to come out. Darkness descended on the earth; people began to freeze. The Little Men told the humans that now it was necessary to bring back the sun's daughter from the ghost country Tsusgina'i, in the Darkening Western Land of Usunhiyi. Seven men were outfitted for the journey, with sourwood rods and a box for carrying the sun daughter's soul. When they arrived in the land of ghosts, the travelers found all the spirits dancing in a circle. Every time the sun's daughter passed in this circle dance, they stuck her with a sourwood rod until she fell to the ground helpless. Her soul was then placed in the box for return to the land of the living. Under no circumstance, the people were warned, should they even peek into the box.

Was ever such a warning heeded? The girl awoke and pleaded to be let out. She was hungry, she said, she was suffocating. Please, she cried— and finally they listened. They didn't open the box, really; they just pulled the lid back a hair's breadth to allow the girl to breathe. Something flew past. Then they heard, from a nearby tree, the call of a cardinal. When they returned to the land of life, the box was empty, for that red bird had been the daughter of the sun. Since that time, because of that failure, no one who dies can be brought back from the land of ghosts.

The sun, all her hope vanished, dissolved into tears that threatened to flood the world. A council was held. It was decided that young people should be sent to entertain the weeping sun. They danced, they sang, they waved their articulate arms telling fascinating stories, but the sun never even glanced at them. Then the drummer suddenly changed the beat. Surprised, the sun mother looked up. A dazzling array of human beauty surrounded her. She smiled—and so it was that the sun returned to us. But now we must die, because only the bringing back of the redbird would have banished death forever.

After she had been reconciled to humanity, Unelanuhi became a helpful, watchful goddess. Myths tell of how she offered assistance to those on earth who needed it, as she did when the world's first couple had the world's first argument. The woman became furious at her husband. Leaving him, she began to wander over the empty earth. The man, not willing to part with her, followed at a distance, but she took no notice of him. The sun goddess took pity on the lonely beings. "Do you still desire her?" she asked the man. When he nodded, she decided to help.

First, she created huckleberries, bright purple bits that sparkled before the woman's eyes. The woman squashed them with her feet as she walked over them. Then the sun goddess created the service tree, dangling its red fruit into the woman's face. Again she passed by. Finally, the sun created tender red strawberries. The woman, tempted at last by this new food, stopped. She filled her hands, then her mouth, with the berries. The moment she tasted them she thought about sex. She kept eating and eating, thinking about having sex—with her husband, the only man on earth. She ate and ate, not moving from the patch. Then she stood up and waited. Soon her mate came up behind her. She did not move. He moved closer to her; she did not run. He embraced her, and she embraced him back. And the sun goddess left the strawberries behind to remind women of sensual pleasure.

Unelanuhi herself used to sleep with a young man who visited her once a month, a lover who refused to tell her his name. Determined to discover who was pleasuring her, she dipped her hands in ashes and rubbed his face in the dark. When daylight came, her brother met her at breakfast with ash on his face—the same one visible today in the moon, for the young man ran in shame from his sister and stayed as far away in the sky as he could. Once a month, however, he could not resist visiting her in the new moon's darkness.

Uni One of the few Etruscan goddesses whom the modern world knows, Uni—her name may later have evolved into Roman Juno—was benefactor of Tuscan cities and of the women who lived there. Queen of the sky, she hurled thunderbolts when angered and, when pleased, granted safe passage to infants at birth. Her major sanctuary was at Pyrgi, a port of the city of Caere, where she was endowed with silver and gold by her worshipers.

Ursula The Slavic moon goddess of this name was honored on her feast day, October 21. Later, Christians in the same area adopted her as a saint, calling the old moon feast St. Ursula's day.

Urvasi When the Hindu gods churned the ocean, among the beings that emerged were the Apsaras ("daughters of pleasure"), multiple spirits of all possibility, incarnations of parallel worlds that exist beyond our perception. The dancers and singers of the heavens, they are renowned for wantonness, taking as lovers whomever they please, never counting the number of men and gods who have shared their beds.

They are described as large-hipped and languid, with soft, inviting eyes. Most famous was Urvasi (a name sometimes used of the dawn goddess Ushas), born when a sage surrounded by tempting Apsaras slapped his thigh. One, like other such heavenly nymphs on occasion, Urvasi consented to live with a human king, but she told him that human nakedness disgusted her. He promised she would never have to see him unclothed, but he forgot one day, and she fled. When he promised to leave his throne and become an erotic singer-dancer, she agreed to return.

Ushas The Hindu dawn goddess—sometimes called Urvasi—was said to stay eternally young but to make men grow constantly older. She appeared each morning, throwing off her blouse to reveal shining breasts that filled the heavens with splendor. Like other dawn goddesses, she was wanton, and said to be either the mother or the lover of the sun.

Uti Hiata This is the Pawnee name for "mother corn," one of the most important divinities of the Plains Indian culture. Their neighbors, the Arikara, told the corn mother's story in detail. From the great blue lake of creation, diving ducks brought up bits of silt to build prairies and foothills. Sky father Nesaru, seeing giants populating the earth, sent a great flood to destroy them; he replanted the earth with maize seeds, which sprouted into human beings. Then he sent Uti Hiata to assist at their birth.

Finding no one on earth, Uti Hiata walked and walked. Suddenly the thunder kidnapped her and hid her beneath the earth. There, she gathered the underworld animals—the mole, the mouse, the badger—and with their help dug through the ground and burst out into the sun. As she emerged, so did the people of the plains, to whom she taught secrets of life and magic and the methods of agriculture and of religious ritual. Satisfied that humanity would live in abundance, she disappeared from the earth, leaving the cedar as an emblem of her existence.

Utset and Nowutset The first mothers of humanity were, to the Sia and Navaho of the southwestern American desert, two sisters who were the first humans in this world. They lived for a time in peace, until a rivalry began between them. Some stories said they started a riddle contest, and that Nowutset, being the duller sister, lost to Utset, who then killed her. Another version says that the sisters argued and decided that the one whom the sun touched first in the morning would be judged the winner. Nowutset was taller, but Utset cheated and won. The contest was restaged; Nowutset pushed her sister suddenly and a fierce fight began. The sisters, unable to live with each other, separated. Utset became the mother of pueblo-dwelling people, and Nowutset, of all the others.

Uyu-sum Among the Indian mountain people called the Koraput, this mythic woman cut her own daughter's throat in order to have something to eat. But the child's soul blazed out through the wound and threatened the world with a holocaust. To avoid the world's destruction, Uyu-sum swallowed her daughter. She then rose up from the earth into the sky where, lit from within by her daughter, she is now the sun.

Uzume Ancient Japan's shaman goddess was the one who lured the sun goddess Amaterasu from the cave where she'd hidden. She did so by a merry mockery of shamanic ritual. Tying her sleeves above her elbows with moss cords and fastening bells around her wrists, she danced on an overturned tub before the heavenly Sky-Rock-Cave. Tapping out a rhythm with her feet, she exposed her breasts and then her genitals in the direction of the sun. So comic did she make this striptease that the myriad gods and goddesses began to clap and laugh—an uproar that finally brought the curious sun back to warm the earth.

Shaman women who followed Uzume were called *miko* in ancient Japan. First queens like Himiko, later they were princesses and even later, common-born women. Some Japanese women today, especially those called *noro* and *yuta* in Okinawa and the surrounding islands, still practice shamanic divination.

This Japanese woodcut by Hokkei shows the shaman goddess Uzume dancing before the heavenly sky-rock-cave in which the sun goddess Amaterasu had confined herself. It was Uzume's quick and inventive actions that saved the earth from perishing, according to the Japanese scriptures.

Vacuna This early agricultural goddess evolved into a Sabine divinity of license and fun, for her festivals were held when the labor of the farming year had ended; her name is related to our word *vacation*. The later-coming Romans decided she was a goddess of war (perhaps their idea of a good time) and identified her with Bellona.

Vajravaraki The goddess "wanderer of the air" was said in Tibet to incarnate herself regularly as a Buddhist abbess who never slept; she had magical powers to protect the nuns under her care. Once, when a Mongol chieftain tried to take over the abbey, he could not find it. In its place, there was a herd of pigs with a very large wild sow at its head. After the danger passed, the spell of metamorphosis was unnecessary, and the nuns were restored to human form.

Valkyries The helmeted battle maid, the chooser-of-the-slain who flew on her supernatural horse over war's carnage, is probably the only still-familiar female image from Scandinavian mythology. But there was another picture of the Valkyries—one more violent and powerful—that has been virtually forgotten. For before the battle started, the Valkyries wove the web of war, raising the warp of spears and weighting it with human heads, running a dripping red weft through the spears, using arrows as shuttles. When they had determined the battle's outcome, they flew from their blood-drenched house like carrion-seeking ravens to devour the bodies of the slain.

These goddesses thus had much in common with the Moirae, the Norns, and other fate rulers who spun or wove human life in a supernatural home. The Anglo-Saxons identified the Valkyries with the Greek Erinyes, goddesses of vengeance who hunted down anyone spilling the blood of kin. Current interpretation sees these divine women simply as the servants of Odin, flying to earth to retrieve his select heroes; this ignores stories that show the Valkyries opposing Odin's will, selecting their own favorites, and teaching magic to the heroes they intended to save.

They did not always ride horses to battle; sometimes they appeared on wolves or disguised themselves as ravens. Some writers claimed there were two kinds of Valkyries: divine ones, of whom there were nine, or nine times nine; and the half-mortal Vaetter-maidens, visible as humans to the second-sighted, while the average eye saw only the aurora borealis leaping excitedly over the field of battle.

Vanths   The most famous of the winged beauties called the Vanths was Culsa, the serpent goddess of the underworld. The Etruscans thought death spirits were numberless and pictured the Vanths as hunters in short skirts and high boots, carrying torches or snakes, waiting to accompany each of us past the grave.

Var   Although this Scandinavian love goddess would have nothing to do with marriage, she did concern herself with promises lovers made to each other outside wedlock. She took fierce vengeance on anyone who broke such vows. An aspect of the all-knowing earth, Var saw and heard everything that happened; nothing could be hidden from her, so when a lover complained of wrongdoing by a love partner, Var knew instantly if the accusation were correct.

Varia   This legendary Irish woman had such a temper that one day Donagha, her lazy husband, drove her into an extremity of anger. She leveled so furious a curse at him that it flung him to the farthest point distant from her in Ireland—to Donaghadee in Ulster, opposite her home in Kerry, Teach na Vauria.

Vashti   A minor Elamite goddess, she appears in the Hebrew Book of Esther as a queen of the Persians who served also as the state's high priestess. A diplomat and daughter of a king, Vashti was unfortunately married to a fool, who drunkenly demanded that she appear before his friends naked. She refused. "Have you lost your reason from drinking? I am Vashti, daughter of Belshazzar, a son of Nebuchadnezzar who scoffed at kings. Shall you, a fool, be the master of so much beauty as mine?" But a Hebrew adviser, intent on replacing Vashti with a woman of his tribe, urged the king to sentence her to death as a fearful example to other women who insisted on control of their own bodies. The king, proving himself more foolish by the moment, followed the Hebrew's advice. Queen Vashti's people rose against him, and the uprising was only put down when Esther ascended the throne.

Vasilisa   This Russian heroine's name means "queen," and it is likely that she was an ancient goddess of the area, for she appears as the maiden in a folktale in which the other two stages—mother and crone—of the classic feminine trinity appear as well. Vasilisa, it is said, was born to a loving mother who, alas, died when the girl was but eight. As she lay on her deathbed, the mother conveyed a magical doll to Vasilisa, warning her to keep it secret and safe. If she were in trouble, the mother told Vasilisa, she should ask the doll for advice.

After her mother's death, Vasilisa's father married a widow with two children, but the new marriage was an unpleasant one for the girl, who was tormented by the new wife. She turned often to the doll for comfort. Finally, things became unbearable, for the stepmother sent Vasilisa to the dark forest where lived Baba Yaga—the frightening ogressmother who ate disobedient children like chickenmeat—to get a candle. When Vasilisa consulted her doll-oracle, she was told to obey her stepmother, but to take the doll with her into the forest.

And so she did. The girl walked all night, passing a rider dressed in white and riding a white horse, just at the moment dawn broke; then a rider dressed in red and riding a red-saddled horse, just as the sun rose; and finally a rider on a black horse who brought night. Even more unusual was the Baba Yaga's home, which was bolted with skeleton arms and locked with a skull, and surrounded by a fence on which more skulls stood guard. As night fell, the eye sockets of the skulls began to gleam with an unearthly glow, and suddenly Baba Yaga appeared, riding through the air in a mortar and rowing with a pestle. "Ugh, it smells of Russians here," she said, and Vasilisa came forward and, shaking from head to toe, introduced herself to the hag.

Baba Yaga took pity on the girl and said she would help her. But first she had to become Baba Yaga's servant for a few days. She gave an impossible series of orders—things that had to be accomplished before dawn—and went to bed. That night Vasilisa secretly consulted her doll, which told her to just go to sleep, that all would be well. And, to the girl's surprise and delight, when she awoke the next morning all the assigned work had, indeed, been accomplished. The same thing happened for several nights, until Baba Yaga grew suspicious of her power and, giving her one of the flaming skulls, sent Vasilisa on her way.

When she got home, Vasilisa gave the stepmother the candle she had requested—but the skull flamed up and killed her, and the step-children as well. Then Vasilia found a new home with a woman who sewed shirts for the king, who fell in love with Vasilisa, and she ended her life living happily in the palace, her doll always with her.

Vatiaz Among the Mongolian Buryat, this heroine was said to have traveled to heaven after her brother's murder in order to compete for the hands of three daughters of the chief god. There were many games of physical skill, all of which she won. Even though shamans warned the gods that she was a woman, they could not deny her strength and skill. So she was allowed to take the sisters back to earth, where she had them revive her brother.

Ved-Ava One of the most important goddesses of the Finno-Ugric Mordvins was Ved-Ava, the water mother or water hostess. The spirit of the earth's fertility and of all who live on her face, she was also the one who sent fish into the nets of fisherfolk.

Veden Emo The Finnish "mother of the water" was responsible for guiding fish into the nets of the hungry. She is a very ancient goddess; her worship was recorded almost 2,000 years ago by Agricola.

Vegoia When the Etruscans were first settling Tuscany, this goddess appeared to help them form a civilization pleasing to the gods of the land. Vegoia showed the Etruscans how to worship properly in rituals, how to divine the wishes of the deities through augury, and finally how to measure the land and set boundaries for human territory.

Veleda One of the most famous of the legendary warrior queens of the ancient Continental Celts, Veleda ruled the Bructeri people. They once captured a Roman ship and towed it up the River Lippe as a present for their queen, outraging the Romans. But the legions, afraid of war with the fierce Bructeri, used diplomatic means to regain their vessel. Although she seems to have been a historical queen, the Roman writer Tacitus said that she was worshiped as a goddess, so it is possible that Veleda was a goddess name borne by human queens as a title of honor.

Vellamo The Finnish sea goddess lived underwater with her daughters, the waves, who tended cattle and raised mysterious crops on the ocean's floor.

Venus We use her name, or words related to it, often: in *vain, winsome, fain,* and *win*—and in that particular form of adoration, *veneration.* (She was the goddess of *venereal* as well.) But when we speak of "Venus on the half-shell," we confuse her with the Greek Aphrodite rising from the sea.

The confusion is ancient, for the Romans themselves identified their kitchen-garden goddess with the great goddess of sexuality from the East, so that it is now impossible to completely distinguish Venus from Aphrodite. The Roman goddess was originally a spirit of charm and beauty, goddess of wild strawberries and herbs, of pine cones and cypress trees, served by virgin priests and priestesses. Wherever a large stone rested near a tall tree, there was Venus' sanctuary; there her altar could be erected for bloodless sacrifices. In this early Italian form, Venus was far less complex than the goddess with whom she was merged: a delicate, delightful, and, yes, winsome goddess of a youthful kind of love, the kind that took place on berry-picking excursions and in flirtations in Venus' own kitchen-gardens.

The name Venus is also given to statues of goddesses so ancient that we have no knowledge of the languages her worshipers spoke, much less the names they gave to her. Found across Europe, the often-tiny statues of these robust Venuses, carved as much as 30,000 years ago, are identified with the places where they were found. Thus there is the Venus of Laussel, carved into stone, lifting her cornucopia on which lines representing the menstrual cycle are drawn; Venus of Lespugne, an abstraction of womanly power with androgynous references; Venus of Willendorf, round and faceless, her small arms barely stretching across her milk-filled breasts; Venus of Brassambouy, her little head crowned with the earliest-known evidence of hair styling (perhaps, in fact, the oldest profession).

These Venuses were somewhat sarcastically named, a sarcasm made plain when scholars deride the fleshiness of these figures, as though only goddesses whose beauty is acceptable under today's conventions could be goddesses of love. Yet among people living at a near-subsistence level, such fleshiness would have been an indication of child-bearing potential, for very gaunt women could have ceased to menstruate so that their bodies could sustain their own life. How the figures of these goddesses were used—even whether we should call them goddesses at all—is disputed, although they seem clearly religious objects that may well have had a part in ritual or prayer.

Veshtitze In Slavic tradition, this was an old woman who left her body at night and flew through the air in a hen's body. She sought human children to kill, for she existed on the hearts of infants.

Vesta Vergil said that Vesta is more easily felt than explained. Ovid, another great Roman poet, said Vesta and fire required no effigy—because Vesta was fire, and fire was Vestal. Like the Greek Hestia, Vesta was never originally shown in human form;

when, in later days, she was pictured on coins, it was as a veiled figure.

Behind that veil was the central divinity of the Roman family, the goddess to whom a daily offering was made in each home at her sacred place, the hearth. In her public worship, Vesta was honored in the only round Roman temple, where a sacred fire burned, tended by the famous sisterhood of Vestal virgins. One day a year, on March 1, the Vestals doused and then relit the fire. Vesta's other sacred day was June 9, the Vestalia, when barefoot Roman matrons offered food baked on their own hearths and the Vestals sacrificed salt cakes baked on Vesta's fire; after eight days of such offerings, the Vestals closed the temple, cleaned it

Among the splendors of European art are the prehistoric figures called "Venuses." This one, found in Laussel, France, shows a robust goddess figure with a horn marked with thirteen stripes, apparently indicating a lunar calendar.

thoroughly, threw the refuse into the Tiber River, and reopened for the year.

Unlike her virgin priestesses, however, Vesta was honored as a mother, and there is evidence that a phallus-shaped effigy was reverenced in her temple down to imperial Roman times. That and the tradition of rekindling the Vestal fires by rubbing wood together—always a sexual symbol—indicate that Vesta was a goddess of generation, a symbol of the continual renewal of the family and of the Roman state. The light of the Vestal hearth, and of the hearth in each Roman home, showed the intention of the people to reproduce and continue their state; it was considered an ill omen for the public fire to go out, an omen of the end of the civilization. But if war threatened the city, the Vestal abbess was considered the appropriate person to mediate a peace.

Vila One of the most powerful eastern European goddesses was called Samovila, Vila, or Judy according to the language of the people, who pictured this woodland force as a fair-skinned winged woman with glistening garments and golden hair falling to her feet. She lived deep in the woods, where she guarded animals and plants as well as cleaning rubble out of streams and assuring sufficient rainfall.

Hunters were wary of beautiful, well-dressed women speaking the languages of animals, for Vila was fiercely possessive of her wild herds. Should one be injured or—worse yet—killed, Vila mutilated the offender or lured him into a magic circle and danced him to death. Alternatively, Vila might bury him in rocks by starting an avalanche, or simply cause him to keel over with a heart attack.

Vila was able to masquerade as a snake, swan, falcon, horse, or whirlwind. Cloud Vilas could transform themselves into clouds or fog. Born on a day of soft misty rain, when the sun formed miniature rainbows on the trees, she knew all the secrets of healing and herb craft. Should a human wish to learn her skills, blood-sisterhood was forged with Vila. The applicant appeared in the

This charming pottery vase from South Italy is typical of the "red-figured" ware of early Roman times. It may represent Venus, goddess of flirtation, or Juno, goddess of each woman's individual gifts.

woods before sunrise on a Sunday of the full moon. Drawing a circle with a birch twig or a broom, she placed several horsehairs, a hoof, and some manure inside the circle, then stood with her right foot on the hoof calling to the Vila. Should the spirit appear and be greeted as a sister, Vila would grant any wish.

Vitsa-Kuva "Cattleyard lady" lived among the Cheremis people of eastern Russia, appearing every night among the flocks in the folds, a white-

311

dressed lady who caused animals to mate if she liked their owner, thus increasing the family wealth. Woe to the person, however, to whom Vitsa-Kuva took a dislike; she would drive the cattle through the fields all day until, unable to stop long enough to eat, they fell down dead.

Viviane   The father of this Welsh sorceress was Dyonas, the fosterling of the forest goddess, who promised him that his first daughter would be mated with the world's wisest man. And in fact, Viviane drew the eye of the mighty magician Merlin, whom she refused until he revealed his secrets to her. Once she had mastered them, she was stronger than her lover. When Viviane decided to assure herself that Merlin would never wander, she lured him to the magical forest of Broceliande, in the center of Brittany. There, as he slept in a flowery meadow, she bewitched him into believing himself trapped in a high tower. Yet, it is said, Merlin was happy in his imprisonment, for he was close to his beloved Viviane.

Vodni Panny   These Slavic water goddesses appeared to human eyes as beautiful sad women dressed in green translucent robes; they lived under the rivers in crystal castles surrounded by silver paths.

Voluptia   This Roman goddess represented sensual pleasure, especially that of the sexual sort; we invoke her every time we call something *voluptuous*. Interestingly, she shared her temple with the goddess of anguish, Angerona.

Voluspa   This name, or the similar word *volva*, was used of wise women in Scandinavia. The most famous seer in Norse legend was the one for whom the poem *Voluspa* is named. Born before this world began, Voluspa was asked to tell the history of the world. Once started, she did not stop, even though the gods did not wish to hear of their own death at Ragnarok, the doom of gods.

Vut-Imi   From the Siberian village of Kazym comes this creator goddess' myth. She first lived on the Arctic Ocean from whence she traveled around the world, occasionally leaving mittens that became rivers, sleds that became hills, and reindeer that became pine trees. After thus creating the Arctic world, she retreated to an island in Lake Numto, her principal sacred site.

The highest divinity of the Khanty tribespeople of Kasym and neighboring areas, Vut-Imi was honored with songs at bear festivals, sacrificial fires at other times. Her image was made of sheets of silver or gold; it was kept in a small building near which cauldrons were hung on human-shaped hooks.

Wa According to Chinese writings from the first century C.E., this was the name of a divine woman who, in ancient times, "produced the ten thousand beings through metamorphosis." It is difficult to tell exactly how this creator goddess populated the world—whether she was transforming parts of herself into other beings, or transforming rocks, clay or other substances as mother goddesses in other cultures prove wont to do.

Wahini-Hai The demonic mother figure of Polynesia looked like a seductive woman, except for her protruding eyes and her tongue, hanging to her toes. She sneaked through the world stealing and eating small children.

Wah-Kah-Nee The "drifting maiden" was born among the Chinook people of the Pacific Coast, a people once struck with a terrible endless winter. The ice never moved on the rivers, neither did the warming winds blow across the forests, and people began to fear for their survival, for they would soon have no food.

A council was called, and the elders recalled that endless winter always resulted from murdering birds. Each person was asked if he or she had been guilty of such a crime. Everyone denied it.

But the children pointed to a little girl who, crying, confessed that she had struck a bird with a stone, and it had died.

The Chinook dressed the girl in the finest garments and exposed her on a block of ice as an offering to the winter spirits. Almost immediately the ice crashed from the river, and summer came like a flood into the country. Nearly a year later, when the ice again was moving, they saw a block of ice containing the girl's body and fetched it to shore. Miraculously, the girl revived and afterward lived among them as a sacred being, able to walk unprotected, even barefoot, through the winter and to communicate with its spirits.

Wakahirume Favorite weaving maiden of the Japanese sun goddess Amaterasu, she died when the evil Susanoo threw a flayed piebald colt through the roof of the Heavenly Weaving Hall. Terrified, Wakahirume fell onto her shuttle, which fatally punctured her vagina. This so enraged Amaterasu that she closed herself into the Sky-Rock-Cave, and only the creation of the world's first mirror could lure her hence. In some interpretations, Wakahirume is the sun goddess' younger sister or a younger dawn form of the divinity.

Waldmichen "The wood nymph" was a form of the Germanic goddess Freya found in Lower Saxony. Her servants were rabbits; two of them held the train of her cloak while two others lit her way with candles. She lived in a grotto, where a visitor could see the souls of unborn babies cavorting; she owned a mill where she ground old men and women young again.

Walo The Australian aboriginals of Arnhem Land called the sun goddess by this name and said that she lived with her daughter Bara and her sister-in-law, the world mother Madalait, far to the east. Each day Walo journeyed across the sky accompanied by Bara, until one day the sun goddess realized that the reason the earth was so parched was their combined heat. She sent her daughter back to the east so that the earth could become fertile and bloom.

Walutahanga The eightfold snake goddess of Melanesia was born to a human mother who was afraid of her husband and hid the serpent girl. But he discovered the deception and, shocked at his daughter's form, cut Walutahanga into eight pieces. After eight days of rain, the girl's body rejoined into a whole. Walutahanga traveled through the islands, tormenting humans in retaliation for her murder. Captured, she was again chopped into eight pieces and her bones thrown into the sea; everyone except a woman and her daughter ate the goddess' body.

It rained for another eight days. Then the bones under the sea again formed themselves into the goddess. To punish humanity, Walutahanga covered the islands with eight huge flooding waves, which killed everyone but the woman and her child, the only one who had not eaten the goddess' flesh. The goddess gave them many gifts, including coconut and clearwater streams, before again retreating to the ocean.

Wanne Thekla In the Netherlands, this elf queen ruled witches' gatherings; she may have been a form of Habondia, ruler of abundance. She is believed to be of Celtic origin.

Waramurungundji The all-creating mother of Australia, a figure similar to the important goddess Kunapipi, she gave birth to the earth and then fashioned all its living creatures. She then taught her creations to talk and divided each language group from the next.

Wari-Ma-Te-Takere In the Cook Islands of Polynesia, this goddess was "the beginning and the bottom," a coconut-shell divinity who parthenogenetically produced the other gods from her right and left sides. The first part of her name means "mud," and Wari symbolizes the fertile slime of primordial times.

Wave Maidens Also called Billow Maidens, these nine Scandinavian giantesses—Atla, Augeia, Aurgiafa, Egia, Gialp, Greip, Iarnsaxa, Sindur, Ulfrun—were daughters of the sea goddess Ran. When they favored a sailor, they played in the waves around his ship, pushing him forward to his destination.

Wawalag Sisters The civilizers of Australia, these two mythic women wandered the continent domesticating plants into edible foodstuff, evolving language for each territory, and naming all the land's creatures. At the end of their journey, they camped with their children next to the pond where the great mother serpent Julunggul lived, a taboo place where menstrual blood was prohibited. Unaware of the taboo, however, the older Wawalag bathed. Julunggul reared out of the water in fury, calling on the skies to drench the women with rain. The women danced and sang, hypnotizing the snake, but every time they stopped she moved toward them. Worn out at last, the Wawalag Sisters fell asleep, and Julunggul swallowed them whole.

But the snake goddess, when visiting the other supernatural snakes of the universe, was made to feel ashamed for eating the women and their children. She vomited them up; the women were revived by ant bites, but Julunggul could not restrain herself and ate them again. Again she vomited them up. Again she ate them—as she probably does to this day.

Weisse Frauen The "white women" of Germany and other northern European locations were said to be goddess-worshiping witches who disappeared ages ago into the woods. They lived deep in the forests where they helped lost travelers, foretold the future, and helped the earth produce its fruit by their ritual dances. Some say they were the ghosts of old goddesses, enchanted by Christianity, seeking magic to release them into fuller life again.

Whaitiri One of the common figures of Polynesian mythology was "blind grandmother," a powerful figure who owned the thunder and ate human flesh. Once she descended to earth to marry a warrior chief, misunderstanding his title, "mankiller." When Whaitiri had taken up residence with her husband, she found that he did not, after all, share her affection for eating humans. Not only that, but he complained about the smell of their children's excrement. She invented the latrine, showed humans how to use it, and returned to the sky, where she still lives.

White Buffalo Woman Ages ago, this sacred woman brought secret knowledge to the Oglala of the Midwestern forests and plains. It was said that she first appeared to two young men, a white-clad lady whose clothing was lavishly embroidered with porcupine quills in exquisite patterns. One of the young men was overtaken by lust, but the second recognized that she was no earthly woman. The first, although warned, could not contain himself; he rushed open-armed toward the woman. She smiled, and a soft white cloud descended to cover their embrace.

When it passed, the woman stood alone with the young man's skeleton at her feet. Smiling, she told the second man that the dead had been awarded just what he sought. She instructed the man to return to his village and set his people to building a huge sacred tent. Then she entered the village, and the people were enraptured by her presence. Walking seven times around the central fire, she spoke to them, giving them a bag containing a sacred pipe and teaching them the ceremonies that went with these objects. Then, recalling that this was the third of seven revelations to the Oglala, she reminded them of the mysteries of their mother, the earth. Urging them always to honor her, she disappeared in the shape of a white buffalo.

Wigan The first woman among the Ifugao of the Philippines wanted to populate the world beneath her sky, but her daughter Wigan and her son Bigan were resistant to leaving home. So she sent them into the forest to pick tubers, and then unleashed a huge flood on the world. Floating upon the raging waters, Wigan and her brother found houses, pigs, cats, chickens, dogs and jars full of food. They soon had a nice homestead on earth, but populating the land was difficult because, as brother and sister, the couple was forbidden from having sexual relations. But one night Bigan came to his sister while she was asleep and impregnated her. The taboo against brother-sister incest was reimposed as soon as the earth was populated.

Wilden Wip The forest women of Germany were usually seen alone, seeking a human as a playmate. But they disappeared after lovemaking, never staying long enough to share their vast knowledge of healing and magic.

Winonah In the mythology of the Ojibwa of the north-central American forests, this was the name of the daughter of the great goddess Nokomis. Winonah ("nourisher") was a virgin mother who was raped four times, over many generations, by the same manitou or spirit. It happened that she was in the forest picking berries one day, and overtaken with a need to urinate, she forgot the warning that women should never face west while making water. When the manitou saw her vagina, he took form and had intercourse with her immediately. Through this spirit-union, she not only acquired magical powers of fertility and longevity, but also gave birth to four heroic sons.

Wlasca After more than a generation of rule by princesses, the women of Bohemia refused to be led by the magician Przemislaw. Instead, under the leadership of the warrior Wlasca, they drank a magical potion to make them heartless, then killed all the men in their region—lovers and sons included. They ruled themselves for seven years (c. 690 C.E.) before Przemislaw took over their fortress by magical means.

Wuriupranili In northern Australia, this sun goddess was said to make bark into a torch, carrying the flame through the sky from east to west. At the western sea, she dipped it in the water, then used the embers to guide her under the earth to reach her eastern starting point again. The brilliant skies of dawn and dusk, it was said, came from Wuriupranili's red ochre body paints misting up into the sky as she powdered and beautified her body.

Wurusemu The Hittite sun goddess, also called Arinna. Her consort was the weather god; her rituals were performed by a high priestess, who also ruled the country as queen.

Xatel-Ekwa The Hungarian goddess of the sun, who rode through the sky mounted simultaneously on three horses.

Xochiquetzal The goddess of flowers, this Aztec divinity was, like the Roman Flora, a deity of sexual license as well. Marigolds were her favorite blooms, but she loved every plant and every creature to such excess that she was sometimes called "bitch mother." Her other names were "flower of the rich plume," "flower-feather," and "blue-skirted lady." Much loved by Aztec women, she was honored with little pottery figurines that showed her with feathers in her hair; these are still frequently unearthed in Mexico.

In some legends, this goddess was the only female survivor of the great flood that destroyed the world preceding this one. With a man, she escaped the torrent in a small boat. Faced with the prospect of repopulating the world, they set to work as soon as the flood receded. But all of their children were born without speech. Finally a pigeon magically endowed them with language, but every child received a different tongue so that each was unable to communicate with the others.

Xoli-Kaltes The Hungarian goddess of the dawn, a hot-blooded young woman who baked men who came to court her.

Yabme-Akka Death appeared to the Scandinavian Saami as Yabme-Akka ("old woman of the dead"), a goddess who demanded black cats buried alive to appease her ill temper. Her servant was a blue-clad little man who tortured souls in the afterlife.

Yama-no-Kami In Japan, this goddess was a spirit of sacred mountains, one who brought good luck to hunters and woodsmen who attended to her rites but who could be quite stern with those who did not. One-legged and one-eyed, she was invoked as a protector for women in childbed under the name of Juni-sama, for she has a secret box of souls from which she endows each new being. As a seasonal goddess, she annually gives birth to twelve children, the year's twelve months. In singular form, she is Yama-no-Shinbo, the mountain mother.

Yamato-Himeno-Mikoi This early Japanese princess of the imperial family became possessed by the goddess Amaterasu, ancestral mother of her clan, and under the goddess' influence founded the Great Shrine at Ise as Amaterasu's sanctuary.

Yaoji This Chinese goddess was said to have been worshiped in the form of a sacred rock at the summit of a hill called the Mount of the Sorceress. According to legend, an ancient king encountered her on that hill in a dream, revealing not only her name but the location of a plant to be used in love magic. She was also called Yunhua Furen, "Blossoming Lady of the Clouds."

Yaya-Zakurai This Japanese cherry-tree goddess was a beautiful young woman each spring. She remained celibate while her beauty lasted, only taking lovers when her petals had fallen.

Yhi The goddess of light and creator goddess of the Karraur, an Australian aboriginal group, she lay asleep in the Dreamtime before this creation, in a world of bone-bare, windless mountains. Suddenly, a whistle startled the goddess. She took a deep breath and opened her eyes, flooding the world with light. The earth stirred under her warm rays. Yhi drifted down to this new land, walking north, south, east, west. As she did, plants sprang up from her footprints. She walked the world's surface until she had stepped everywhere, until every inch was covered with green. Then the goddess sat to rest on the treeless Nullarbor Plain.

As she glanced around, she realized that the new plants could not move, and she desired to see something dance. Seeking that dancing life, she descended beneath the earth, where she found evil spirits who tried to sing her to death. But they were not as powerful as Yhi. Her warmth melted the darkness, and tiny forms began to move there. The forms turned into butterflies and bees and insects that warmed around her in a dancing mass. She led them forth into the sunny world.

But there were still caves of ice, high in the mountains, in which other beings rested. Yhi spread her light into them, one at a time. She stared into the cave's black interiors until water formed. Then she saw something move—something, and another thing, and another. Fishes and lizards swam forth. Cave after cave she freed from its darkness, and birds and animals poured forth onto the face of the earth. Soon the entire world was dancing with life.

Then, in her golden voice, Yhi spoke. She told her creatures she would return to her own world. She blessed them with changing seasons and with the knowledge that when they died they would join her in the sky. Then, turning herself into a ball of light, she sank below the horizon. As she disappeared, darkness fell upon on the earth's surface. The new creatures were afraid. There was sorrow and mourning, and finally there was sleep. And, soon, there was the first dawn, for Yhi had never intended to abandon her creation. One by one the sleepy creatures woke to see light breaking in the east. A bird chorus greeted their mistress, and the lake and ocean waters that had been rising in mists, trying to reach her, sank down calmly.

For eons of Dreamtime the animals lived in peace on Yhi's earth, but then a vague sadness began to fill them. They ceased to delight in what they were. She had planned never to return to earth, but she felt so sorry for her creatures that she said, "Just once. Just this once." So she slid down to the earth's surface and asked the creatures what was wrong.

Wombat wanted to wiggle along the ground. Kangaroo wanted to fly. Bat wanted wings. Lizard wanted legs. Seal wanted to swim. And the confused Platypus wanted something of every other animal. And so Yhi gave them what they wanted. From the beautiful regular forms of the early creation came the strange creatures that now walk the earth. Yhi then swept herself up to the sky again.

She had one other task yet to complete: the creation of woman. She had already embodied thought in male form and set him wandering the earth. But nothing—not the plants, not the insects, not the birds or beasts or fish—seemed like him. He was lonely. Yhi went to him one morning as he slept near a grass tree. He slept fitfully, full of strange dreams. As he emerged from his dreaming he saw the flower stalk on the grass tree shining with sunlight. He was drawn to the tree, as were all the earth's other creatures. Reverent and astonished, they watched as the power of Yhi concentrated itself on the flower stalk. The flower stalk began to move rhythmically—to breathe. Then it changed form, softened, became a woman. Slowly emerging into the light from which she was formed, the first woman gave her hand to the first man.

Ymoja   She is one of the great goddesses of Africa and of the African diaspora. In her original homeland, she was the Yoruba goddess of the Ogun river, where she was said to be the daughter of the sea into whose waters she empties. Her breasts are very large, because she was mother of so many of the Yoruba gods. She is also the mother of waters—Mama Watta—who gave birth to all the world's waters. Even as she slept, she would create new springs, which gushed forth each time she turned over. At her main temple, at Abeokuta in the Ibara district, she is offered rams, yams and corn.

In the African diaspora, Ymoja has remained a popular divinity. She is Imanje or Yemanja in Brazilian Macumba, where she is ocean goddess of the crescent moon. In Cuba she is Yemaya, appearing in many variants: Yemaya Ataramagwa, the wealthy queen of the sea; stern Yemaya Achabba; violent Yemaya Oqqutte; and the overpowering Yemaya Olokun, who can be seen only in dreams. She is Agwe in Haiti, La Balianne in New

Orleans. She is syncretized with Our Lady of Regla and Mary, Star of the Sea; in Brazil, she is Our Lady of the Immaculate Conception, whose followers wear crystal beads and greet her appearance with shouts of "Odoya." On her feastday on February 2, crowds gather on the ocean beaches of Bahia to offer her soap, perfume, jewelry and fabric which, together with letters bearing requests to the goddess, are thrown out to sea.

Yolkai Estsan The sister of the turquoise-sky goddess Estsanatlehi, she was a Navaho moon goddess. Called "white shell woman" because she was made from abalone, Yolkai Estsan ruled the dawn and the ocean; she was also creator of fire and maize. Some legends said she was an aspect of the great Estsanatlehi rather than her sister.

Yondung Halmoni An ancient Korean wind goddess, she is celebrated in shamanic rituals when she is fed rice cakes. Like many goddesses, she is sometimes transformed into a male god, though her female form takes historical precedence.

Yuki-Onne The "snow maiden" of Japan was the spirit of death by freezing, a calm, pale woman who appeared to the dying, making their passage quiet and painless. To those lost in blizzards, struggling futilely against the cold, she came, soothing them, singing to lull them to sleep, then breathing a deathly cold breath on them.

Once, it was said, a young man and an old man were lost on a snowy mountain. Yuki-Onne appeared, easing the older into death but merely touching the younger, telling him never to speak of their meeting. Terrified, he kept silent when searchers found him and the body of the old man.

Years later he met and married a thin, pale woman named Yuki, with whom he was very happy. One evening, as a storm roared by their home, he casually told her the story of his meeting with the snow maiden—told it as an amusing tale, as though she had been a fantasy. Instantly his wife stood up, her face draining of blood, her body growing thinner until she seemed to be just a bit of snowy mist. In cold fury, she reminded him of his promise that night on the mountain, said that only their children kept her from murdering him, and disappeared.

Masks such as this one, from the Bundu women's society in Sierra Leone, were used in celebrating rites specific to women. For African goddesses of women's power, see Ymoja, Nyina Mweru Oeno and Muso Koroni.

Zaramama   The "grain mother" of ancient Peru was occasionally incarnated in her own fields in the form of strangely shaped ears of corn or ears that joined in multiple growths. Sometimes these goddess images were made even more like Zaramama by being dressed as human women in a robe and shawl with a silver clasp; or they were created from precious metals or stone. Sometimes, Zaramama came to earth in cornstalks, which were hung by her worshipers on willow trees; festive dances were held around the willows, then the cornstalks were burned, assuring a plentiful supply of corn, while Zaramama's Andean people drank fermented corn beer and ate the meat of sacrificed llamas, whose blood anointed their faces.

Zarpandit   "Silver-shining" or "seed-creator" was an early Assyro-Babylonian pregnant goddess who was worshiped each night as the moon rose.

Zemyna   Because all life came from her, the Lithuanian earth goddess was honored at the birth of every child, when the soil was tenderly kissed both morning and evening; food offerings were laid in front of stones, tied to tree boughs, or cast into flowing water to thank Zemyna for the new life.

Her name means simply "earth," and Baltic poems exalt her productiveness by calling her "blossomer," "bud raiser," and "flower-giver." Her special area of concern was plant life—not only foodstuffs but weeds, trees, the algae scum of ponds, the arctic lichen. Trees with three leaves or nine branches were especially connected with Zemyna; the oak, the linden and the spruce were her favorites. And of those trees, the most revered part was the top, where the secret of life was believed to hide.

Plant and human life were believed to flow together, with souls taking up residence after death in trees. Women lived on in lindens and spruce; men, in oaks, maples and birches. Virginal young girls survived as lilies; village ancestors resided in fruit trees. The passionate love of the Baltic people for the earth's plant life resounds through the dainas, the spiritual and mythological folksongs of the culture. "Green linden, my mother," a poem addresses a tree, or "green oak tree, my father." Even the most familiar tree in the yard easily became the cosmic tree leading to the sun mother Saule's heaven; the birds that rested there became emblems of the force of life itself.

Zipaltonal   In Nicaragua, Zipaltonal was the creator goddess who made everything on earth. She lived in the east, whence souls of the elect went after death; souls of evildoers were confined to beneath her surface.

Zipporah   The magical wife of the Hebrew hero Moses, she could only wed a man who could touch a man-eating tree. Moses, by a miracle, was able to survive the tree's attack, but Zipporah's father then threw him into a deep pit. The girl, however, liked Moses' looks, secretly fed him for seven years, and then suggested to her father that if Moses had survived then he was indeed a man of miracles. Moses, emerging from the pit hale and well fed, became Zipporah's husband. Later in his life, she had to save him from death again— this time by outwitting the evil angel Lucifer.

Zirna   The Etruscan moon goddess was the companion of the love goddess Turan; she was represented with a half-moon hanging from her neck.

Zisa   The Germans devoutly honored this goddess in a festival on September 28, suggesting that she was connected with the harvest.

Zonget   The ancient goddess of hunting among the Mansi and Khanty of Siberia, she ruled all bird and animal life, as well as those who hunted it. At her command, birds and animals would either come to the snare or leave it empty. To human eyes she looked like a greyhen, a kind of arctic bird.

Zorya   There were three Slavic dawn goddesses, "three little Zorya," as the folksongs say. There was Zorya Utrennyaya, the morning star; Zorya Vechernyaya, the evening star; and the midnight Zorya. All have the same job: to guard a chained dog who tries to eat the constellation Ursa Minor, the little bear. If the chain should ever break, if the dog should ever get loose, the universe will surely end. Thus the Zoryas are guardian goddesses; they appear that way, too, as virgin warriors who keep their favorites safe under a long veil that shields them in battle.

Zuleika   The most passionate woman of Jewish legend, she is often referred to merely as "Potiphar's wife," as though her own given name were unrecorded. She fervently desired the Hebrew prince Joseph, so much so that she tied him down while she fondled herself in front of him; he, however, utterly rejected her advances at first, though later she nearly had her desire satisfied.

Once, to show her friends how unnerving Joseph's beauty was, she threw a banquet. At each place, she set knives and put oranges on each plate. When Joseph entered, the guests lost awareness of anything but him, cutting their hands unconsciously as they tried to peel their oranges; the table ran with blood and orange juice while the guests felt no pain, entranced by Joseph's presence. Afterward they sympathized with the woman's passion for the man.

Like Phaedra and other spurned mythic women, Zuleika got her revenge on Joseph by accusing him of the opposite of his crime. Sick with longing, she contended that he had assaulted her in bed. Joseph was thrown into prison and whipped.

Zvezda Dennitsa   The Slavic morning star goddess was the wife of the man in the moon. In Serbia, when she has not been seen for a while, the moon sings to her, "Where hast thou been, star Dennitsa, where has thou been? Where hast thou wasted thy days, three bright days?" She may be a localized form of the warrior maiden Zorya.

Symbols of the Goddess

In art and in ritual, in dreams and in poetry, the goddess takes on symbolic as well as human form. What follows is an index that points to some of the ways in which the goddess is symbolized. There are many ways, and reasons, to use this index. There might, for instance, be an image that is important to you in dreams and in creative work; following its traces through many myths can deepen your self-understanding. Or you may appreciate a specific goddess' energy and wish to locate similar others for ritual or meditation. You may wish to discover a new goddess of gardening, for example, or one for health. This index offers a way to get started. The major goddesses appear in the "Myths of the Goddess" section; minor goddesses are defined in the "Names of the Goddess" section.

Celestial Bodies and Events

Sun Aclla, Aega, Aine, Akewa, Akycha, Amaterasu, Ban Noamha, Bara, Bast, Beiwe, Bila, Bisal-Mari-amna, Bomong, Brigid, Chup-Kamui, Cinderella, Dia Griene, Djanggawul Sisters, Etain, Gnowee, Grian, Hae-Sun, Hathor, Hekoolas, Hsi-Ho, Kanene Ski Amai Yehi, Ilankaka, Jumala, Keca Aba, Klu-mo, Kn Sgni, Kou-Njami, Marici, Medusa, Mitra, Olwen, Paivatar, Paive, Pattini, Rapunzel, Rind, Rosmerta, Saule, Sekhmet, Shamshu, Shapash, Solntse, Sul, Sundi-Mumi, Sunna, TahcI, Toyo-Uke, Unelanuhi, Walo, Wuri-upranili, Wurusemu, Xatel-Ekwa.

Moon Aponibolinayen, Andromeda, Anunit, Arian-rhod, Artemis, Auchimalgen, Bil, Biman Chan, Britomartis, Candi, Chango, Coatlicue, Coyolx-auhqui, Dae-Soon, Dewi Shri, Diana, Europa, Gleti, Gnatoo, Gorgons, Hanwi, Hecate, Helen, Helle, Hina, Huitaca, Io, Ishtar, Isis, Ix Chel, Jata, Juno, Klu-mo, Leucothea, Mama Quilla, Mawu, Metzli, Notambu, Nyadeang, Pandia, Pero, Perse, Rabie, Ri, Sadarnuna, Selene, Tapa, Teczistecatl, Tlazolteotl, Ursula, Ymoja, Yohuatlicetl, Yolkai Estsan, Zarpandit, Zirna.

Stars Al-Uzza, Andromeda, Astarte, Austrine, Belit-Ilani, Cassiopeia, Cynosura, Esther, Gendenwitha, Hesperides, Hulluk Miyumko, Ishtar, Istehar, Kachina, Klu-mo, Lemkechen, Maya Owichapaha, Maia, Matariki, Mayi-Mayi, Meropc, Omeahuatl, Pleiades, Saules Meita, Sweigsdunka, Tara, Tou-Mou, Vakyrine, Zorya, Zvezda Dennitsa.

Sky Aditi, Agasaya, Amayicoyondi, Andriam-Vabi-Rano, Anatu, Aponibolinayen, Atargatis, Azer-Ava, Bau, Biman Chan, Chih Nu, Diana, Dione,

Dunne Enin, Estsanatlehi, Ganga, Geezhigo-Quae, Hannahanna, Hathor, Hebat, Hera, Jata, Inanna, Irdlirvirisissong, Klu-mo, Kuan-Yin, Lemkechen, Luonnotar, Maia, Mawu, Mayahuel, Mitra, Mylitta, Naila, Nambi, Nu Kua, Nut, Qamaits, Saule, Shauskha, Samjuna, Tamar, Tanit, Tien-Hou, Tlitcaplitana, Uni, Yeshe Tsoquel.

Weather Abhramu (clouds), Anahita, Ardat Lili (storms), Aryong-Jong (rain), Azer-Ava (rain), Bardaichila (storms), Cailleach, Cally Berry, Coatrischie, Dames Vertes (wind), Doda (rain), Feng Pho-Pho (wind), Frau Holle, Fulgora (lightning), Gentle Annie, Gna (wind), Guabancex (wind), Horae, Idothea, Ino (rain), io (rain), Iphigenia, Irdlirvirisissong (aurora borealis), Iris (rainbow), Julunggul (rainbow), Junkgowa, Kadlu (thunder), Kanuga (winds), Kunapipi (rainbow), Louhi (storm), Mardeq Avalon (wind), Mokosh (rain), Muireartach (storm), Mujaji (rain), Naru-Kami (thunder), Nephele (cloud), Ninlil (wind), Nut, Ochumare (rainbow), Oya (storm), Pa (drought), Panope (storm), Perkuna Tete (thunder, lightning), Rauni (thunder), Rudrani (storm), Sao-Ts'ing Niang, Shina-To-Be (wind), Siris (rain), Tamar, Tatsuta-Hime (wind), Tempestates (storm), Tien-Mu (lightning), Trung-Trac (rain), Toririhnan (storms), Uni (thunder), Whaitiri (thunder), Yondung Halmoni (wind), Yuki-Onne.

Time and Times of Day

Time At-Em, Juno, Kali, Laima, Menat, Mens, Nidra, Nortia, Prajnaparamita, Renpet, Savitri, Unelanuhi.

Light/Day Akewa, Aja, Alectrona, Anunit, Bau, Bila, Bisal-Mariamna, Bomong, Brigid, Circe, Diana, Gerd, Helen, Inaras, Jocebed, Kanene Ski Amai Yehi, Lampetia, Lucina, Norwan, Poldunica, Prajnaparamita, Ri, Sala, Sipna, Telphassa, Thea, Yhi.

Dark/Night Achlys, Black Madonna, Breksta, Brunissen, Eriskegal, Eumenides, Evaki, Hecate,

Guadalupe, Khon-Ma, Korrigan, Klu-mo, Laima, Laume, Leto, Maia, Marinette, Mayahuel, Muso Koroni, Nidra, Nott, Nyx, Rafu-Sen, Rati, Rhiannon, Rukko, Shulamite, Tuonetar, Zarpandit, Zorya.

Dawn Aja, Al-Uzza, Amba, Astarte, Atanea, Aurora, Austrine, Bau, Eos, Gendenwitha, Hanwi, Hekt, Hina, Hine-titama, Ishtar, Mater Matuta, Tefnut, Thea, Ushas, Wakahirume, Xoli-Kaltes, Yolkai Estsan, Zorya.

Evening/sunset/twilight Akusaa, Astarte, Bast, Belit-Ilani, Hanwi, Hesperides, Ishtar, Nephthys, Norwan, Zorya.

Elements, Directions and Seasons

Earth Aeracura, Agischanak, Aje, Ala, Al-Lat, Altan-Telgey, Ama, Amymone, Anieros, Asintmah, Asase Yaa, Atira, Augralids, Awitelin Tsita, Banba, Becuma, Berecyntia, Beruth, Chaabou, Chthonia, Coatlicue, Da, Damkina, Demeter, Dharti Mata, Diti, Dewi Shri, Dzivaguru, Ebhlinne, Egime, Erce, Eriu, Etugen, Frigg, Fulla, Gaea, Gefjon, Hegemone, Hertha, Hippia, Hlin, Hu-Tu, Hybla, Ibu Pertiwi, Ila, Ja-Neba, Jata, Jord, Kamadhenu, Klu-mo, Ki, Lilwani, Luminu-Ut, Madder-Akka, Ma-Emma, Maeve, Mami, Mastor-Ava, Mati, Mawu, Mayahuel, Medusa, Meter, Mindhal, Mokosh, Mou-Njami, Muk Jauk, Muso Koroni, Nar, Nerthus, Ninlil, Nokomis, Nott, Nsomeka, Oanuava, Omamama, Omeahuatl, Onatah, Ops, Oreads, Pandora, Papa, Prithivi, Rhea, Rind, Semele, Shiwanokia, Si Boru Deak Parujar, Sita, Tacoma, Taillte, Tamar, Tari Pennu, Tellus Mater, Themis, Umaj, Waramurungundji, Yak, Zemyna.

Air Gna, Guabancex, Iphigenia, Litae, Mardeq Avalon, Ninlil, Norwan, Nut, Poldunica, Shina-To-Be, Tatsuta-Hime, Vajravaraki, Yondung Halmoni.

Fire Aetna, Aibheaog, Agischanak, Biliku, Brigid, Brynhild, Camilla, Chuginadak, Cinderella, Darago, Davata, Dayang Raca, Dunne Enin, Durga, Dzalarhons, Elena, Eos, Feronia, Fuji, Goga, Gula, Hestia, Het, Holika, Izanami, Kupalo, Kahindo, Latiaran, Loo-Wit, MahuiIki, Maia, Masaya, Matergabiae, Mylitta, Ocrisia, Oya, Pele, Perasia, Pheraia, Poza-Mama, Radha, Tabiti, Tu-Njami, Vesta, Yolkai Estsan.

Water Aige, Ailsie, 'Aisha Qandisha, Amberella, Amphitrite, Annalia Tu-Bari, Aryong-Jong, Aveta, Anahita, Angeyja, Anuket, Aphrodite, Asherah, Atanea, Atargatis, Atla, Avfruvva, Bentakumari, Boann, Britomartis, Camenae, Chalchiuhtlicue, Cipactli, Cleone, Dabaiba, Danae, Doris, Egeria, Fand, Fatima, Fideal, Galatea, Ganga, Giriputri, Gum Lin, Guabancex, Hypermnestra, Ix Chel, Julunggul, Juras Mate, Jurate, Ka Ahu Pahau, Korobona, Korrigan, Lakshmi, Liban, Limnades, Louhi, Luonnotar, Ma Tsu-Po, Mem Loimis, Mere-Ama, Miriam, Motsesa, Mulhalmoni, Monje, Nakkeeta, Naiads, Nakineitsi, Nammu, Nanshe, Navky, Nemetona, Nereids, Niamh, Nimue, Ningyo, Niobe, Nixies, Nuliayoq, Oshun, Oto-Hime, Pattini, Ran, Ranu Bai, Rosmerta, Rusalki, Ryuhwa, Salacia, Sarasvati, Sarvari, Sayo-Hime, Selekana, Sinann, Tiamat, Toyota-Mahime, Ved-Ava, Veden Emo, Vellamo, Vodni Panny, Yamuna, Ymoja, Wigan.

North Branwen, Helle, Lemkechen, Louhi, Pohjan-Akka, Uadgit.

South Hekoolas, Kou-Njami, Nekhebet, Nirriti, Omphale, Rana-Neida.

East Aja, Al-Uzza, Atse Estsan, Aurora, Bau, Bila, Britomartis, Changing Woman, Eos, Hekt, Keca Aba, Mater Matuta, Muireartach, Ninlil, Qamaits, Ushas, Walo, Wuriupranili, Zipaltonal.

West Akusaa, Ament, Bast, Bo Find, Echtghe, Estanatlehi, Hesperides, Hsi Wang Mu, Kadlu, Niamh, Pali Kongju, Saule.

Spring Anna Perenna, Antheia, Flora, Freya, Frigg, Gillian, Gauri, Hebe, Hlin, Hu-Tu, Juturna, Kachina, Kono-Hana-Sakuya-Hime, Kore, Kostrubonko, Libera, Maia, Ma-Ku, Nana, Oniata, Ostara, Pais, Penelope, Persephone, Proserpina, Rafu-Sen, Rana Neida, Renpet, Rapunzel, Rheda, Rusalki, Vesna, Yaya, Zakura.

Summer Aine, Beiwe, Ceres, Diana, Ebhlinne, Freya, Frigg, Furrina, Inghean Bhuidhe, Kupalo, Luot-Hozjit, Ma-Emma, Pattini, Olwen, Onatah, Sele, Taillte, Tamar.

Autumn Ahrenkonigin, Anieros, Anapurna, Athana Lindia, Baba Yaga, Demeter, Feronia, Fides, Idem-Huva, Inari, Latiaran, Mama Allpa, Mamapacha, Morgay, Mother Friday, Pomona, Rugiu Boba, Sif, Tatsuta-Hime, Zisa.

Winter Acca Larentia, Angerona, Befana, Black Annis, Bona Dea, Bronach, Cailleach, Cally Berry, Carlin, Carravogue, Colleda, Frau Holle, Louhi, Marzana, Poshjo-Akka, Rind, Rozanicy, Snegurochka, Tonan, Tonantzin, Wah-Kah-Nee, Zima.

Parts of the Earth

Mountains Agdos, Aine, Almha, Anu, Ararat, Agischanak, Banba, Becuma, Berecynthia, Cailleach, Cally Berry, Clidna, Cybele, Dali, Ebhlinne, Echo, Echtghe, Giriputri, Hagar, Hsi Wang Mu, Huldra, Ida, Irnini, Jord, Kupapa, Kusumamodini, Mamapacha, Min Mahagiri, Momu, Ninhursag, Oreads, Pahto, Poza-Mama, Rhea, Saule, Sicasica, Skadi, Sungmo, Somagalags, Tacoma, Tefnut, Umaj, Yama-Uba.

Volcanoes Aetna, Chimera, Chuginadak, Darago, Dzalarhons, Feronia, Fuji, Iztaccihuatl, Loo-Wit, Masaya, Pare, Pele.

Rivers, Streams, Fountains Amymone, Anuket, Arnamentia, Avfruvva, Biblys, Boann, Brigantia, Camenae, Castalia, Coventina, Danae, Dryope, Egeria, Epona, Ganga, Korobona, Korrigan, Limnades, Io Shen, Logia, Mere-Ama, Miriam, Mnemosyne, Mylitta, Nekhebet, Nixies, Oba, Ranu Bai, Rusalki, Sabrina, Saga, Salmacis, Samundra, Sati, Sequana, Sinann, Styx, Sulis, Tacoma, Telphusa, Yamuna, Ymoja.

Oceans, Lakes, Pools Aige, Ailsie, Amberella, Amphitrite, Anuanaitu, Andriam-Vabi-Rano, Aphrodite, Asherah, Atanea, Atargatis, Bentakumari, Benvarry, Britomartis, Calypso, Ceasg, Cethlion, Ceto, Charybdis, Clidna, Creiddylad, Dea Syria, Dione, Domnu, Doris, Dubh Lacha, Eurynome, Galatea, Gamsu, Huixtochuatl, Idothea, Isis, Julunggul, Junkgowa, Juras Mate, Jurate, Lakshmi, Liban, Lorop, Luaths Lurgann, Luonnotar, Mama Cocha, Mere-Ama, Meri, Morgan Le Fay, Moruadh, Muireartach, Mutyalamma, Naamah, Nahkeeta, Nereids, Niamh, Nuliayoq, Numma Moiyuk, Oceanids, Odras, Oto-Hime, Panope, Pohjan-Akka, Qamaits, Ran, Scylla, Sedna, Sjojungru, Sjora, Tethys, Thetis, Tien-Hou, Toyota-Mahime, Turesh, Vellamo, Walutahanga, Wave Maidens, Yemanja, Yolkai Estsan.

Forests Ardwinna, Aricia, Artemis, Budhi Pallien, Buschfrauen, Callisto, Cuvto-Ava, Dames Vertes, Dea Dia, Dhat-Badan, Dziwozony, Fangge, Flidais, Giane, Gidne, Gwyllion, Gyhldeptis, Huldra, Irnini, Ivithja, Juno, Keca Aba, Kono-Hana-Sakuya-Hime, Kunapipi, Kupalo, Lignaco-Dex, Mardeq Avalon, Metsannetsyt, Naru-Kami, Nemetona, Ovda, Parooa, Risem-Edne, Skogsnufvar, Vila, Waldmichen, Weisse Frauen, Wilden Wip.

Deserts Al-Lat, Al-Uzza, Dhat Badan, Hagar, Menat, Ningal, Pa, Semiramis.

Vegetation

Trees Ailinn (apple), Asherah, Askefruer (ash), Akoya (pine), Aze (pine), Ba'Alat, Buan (hazel), Carya (walnut), Cuvto-Ava, Dia, Daphne (laurel), Druantia (fir), Dryads, Dunne Enin, Dryope (poplar), Egle (fir), Embla (elder), Esther (myrtle), Eve (apple), Fangge, Helen, Heliades (poplar), Hsi Wang Mu (peach), Idunn (apple), Kono-Hana Sakuya-Hime (cherry), Kualchink, Kupalo (birch), Leelinau (pine), Lotis (lotus), Mayahuel (cactus), Meliae (ash), Myrrha (myrrh), O-Ryu (willow), Philemon (linden), Pitys (pine), Puta, Rafu-Sen (plum), Rauni (rowan), Renpet (palm), Rumina (fig), Saosis (acacia), Sarna Burhi, Saule (apple), Uti Hiata (cedar), Venus (cypress), Yaya-Zakura (cherry), Zemyna (oak, linden, spruce).

Flowers Acantha, Blathnat, Blodewedd, Clytie, Flora, Hebe, Lakshmi, Limoniades, Mary, Mehurt, Olwen, Oniata, Proserpina (wildflowers), Smilax, Spes (poppy), Xochiquetzel (marigold).

Plants Alakhani, Ariadne, Athana Lindia, Cocomama, Damia, Demeter, Dewi Shri, Haumea, Itzpapalotl, Kachina, Limnades, Mentha, Muso Koroni, Nokomis, Norwan, Ohoyo Osh Chishba, Pandora, Si Boru Deak Parujar, Rana Neida, Rauni, Tulsi, Uttu, Venus, Wawalag Sisters, Yhi, Zemyna.

Animals

Reptiles, Dragons Abuk, Aida-Wedo, Angitia, Aspelenie, Antaboga, Bachue, Benten, Britomartis, Campe, Carravogue, Cipactli, Coatlicue, Corchen, Echidna, Eingana, Eurydice, Eurynome, Eve, Ezili-Freda-Dahomey, Fatouma, Gorgons, Hecate, Hekt, Hit, Hydra, Ix Chel, Janguli, Julunggul, Kadi, Kadru, Kunapipi, Lamia, Leviathan, Mafdet, Mamapacha, Manasa, Medea, Medusa, Melusine, Mertseger, Morrigan, Nasa, Ninhursag, Nisaba, Nu Kua, Olosa, Pidari, Python, Qadesh, Rhea, Selci Syt

Emysyt, Sphinx, Tabiti, Tiamat, Toh Sri Lam, Toyota-Mahime, Turesh, Uadgit, Vanths, Walutahanga.

Mammals Acca Larentia (wolf), Aige (deer), Aine (horse, cattle), Aakuluujjusi (caribou, walrus), Ajysyt (cattle), Amalthea (goat), Amashilamma (cow), Anat (cow), Anu (cat), Artemis (bear), Artio (bear), Audhumbla (cow), Bast (cat, lion), Bo Find (cow), Budhi Pallien (tiger), Callisto (bear), Cybele (lion), Dali (mountain sheep), Durga (lion), Epona (horse), Eriskegal (lion), Etain (horse), Freya (cat, boar), Godasiyo (puppies), Godiva (horse), Grand-Aunt Tiger (tiger), Hathor (lion, cow), Hecate (dog, horse), Hedrun (goat), Henwen (pig), Hera (cow), Hippia (horse), Hsi Wang Mu (tiger, cat), Inari (fox), Kara-Kura (goat), KuzunoHa (fox), Laume (cat), Le-Hev-Hev (rat), Lupa (wolf), Lyssa (dog), Macha (horse), Mafdet (cat, mongoose), Mahakh (dog), Mala Liath (pig), Mbombe (elephant), Mehit (lion), Mehurt (cow), Menalippe (horse), Muso Koroni (leopard), Nehalennia (dog), Neith (cow), Ninkharak (dog), Norwan (porcupine), Nut (cow), Pales (cattle), Prithivi (cow), Pawosee (buffalo), Nyavirezi (lion), Rhea Silvia (she-wolf), Rhiannon (horse), Rhpisunt (bear), Samjuna (horse), Scylla (dog), Sekhmet (lion), Sibilja (cow), Spako (wolf), Suki (cow), Surabhi (cow), Tauret (hippopotamus), Tefnut (cow, lion), Titichane (cat), Turrean (dog), White Buffalo Woman (buffalo).

Birds Aedon, Aife, Aithuia, Aje, Asteria, Athena, Badb, Barbmo-Akka, Blodewedd, Branwen, Brunissen, Caer, Clidna, Corra, Dechtere, Devorgilla, Elena, Fand, Fionnuala, Frigg, Graeae, Halcyone, Holzweibel, Huitaca, Kasum-Naj-Ekva, Kilili, Kling, Liban, Loddis-Edne, Macha, Marinette, Mertseger, Minerva Medica, Morrigan, Munanna, Mut, Natosuelta, Nawangwulan, Nekhebet, Nemain, Nemesis, Pamphile, Panes, Philomena, Polycaste, Rhiannon, Scylla, Shiju-Gara, Silige Fraulein, Sirens, Siris, Swan Maidens, Tuli, Tundr Ilona, Uso-Dori, Valkyries, Vasilia, Veshtitze, Vinata, Zonget.

Fish, Aquatic Mammals Amphitrite, Atargatis, Avfruvva, Ban Naomha, Bentakumari, Boann, Britomartis, Ceasg, Ceto, Chelone, Derceto, Hit, Ka Ahu Pahau, Liban, Lorop, Mama Cocha, Mere-Ama, Moruadh, Ningyo, Noogumee, Nuliayoq, Olosa, Sedna, Thalassa.

Insects Arachne, Biliku, Hatai Wugti, Ituana, Itzpapalotl, Kanene Ski Amai Yehi, Le-Hev-Hev, Lucina, Melissa, Mellonia, Nasa, Orore, Selkhet, Tsan Nu.

Sustenance and Abundance

Hunting Ardwinna, Arganthone, Artemis, Artio, Banka-Mundi, Dali, Diana, Dziewona, Flidais, Hastseoltoi, Ja-Neba, Karpophoros, Kasum-Naj-Ekva, Ko, Luot-Hozjit, Mielikki, Nyavirezi, Pohaha, Poshjo-Akka, Pukimna, Sedna, Skogsnufar, Thorgerd, Tuulikki, Uke-Mochi, Umaj, Vanths, Vila, Viran-Akka, Umaj, Zonget.

Farming and Gardening Abuk, Abundita, Ahrenkonigin, Ala, Anesidora, Anna Puma, Ashnan, Athana Lindia, Carna, Ceres, Charila, Chicomecoatl, Cihuacoatl, Cocomama, Damia, Demeter, Emboq Sri, Eshara, Eumenides, Hainuwele, Haumea, Hegemone, Idem Huva, Inari Ino, Junkgowa, Kait, Kornjunfer, Libera, Ma-Emma, Mama Allpa, Mamapacha, Marcia, Metanira, Morgay, Mother Friday, Onatah, Pandora, Pani Perchta, Po Ino Nogar, Pok Klai, Pomona, Puta, Qocha Mana, Rugiu Boba, Saning Sri, Seia, Selu, Sibilaneuman, Sien-Tsang, Sif, Taranga, Thorgerd, Toyo Uke, Uke-Mochi, Uti-Hiata, Wanne Thekla, Vacuna, Venus, Zaramama, Zisa, Zytniamatka.

Animal Raising Ajysyt, Amalthea, Amashilamma, Beiwe, Challalamma, Damona, Dil, Falvara, Lahar, Lampetia, Luot-Hozjit, Mala Liath, Pales, Pandora, Pukimna, Vitsa-Kuva.

Feasting and Drinking   Ashnan, Bast, Bona Dea, Dis, Dugnai, Flora, Ganymeda, Gauri, Hathor, Hebe, Hedrun, Huitaca, Inaras, Lyssa, Maenads, Maeve, Mami, Mayfihuel, Ninkasi, Potina, Sakkala-Khatun, Sekhmet, Siduri, Siris, Sura, Thyone.

Hearth and Home   Anna Purna, Aspelenie, Athena, Caca, Cardea, Chinnintamma, Chuang-Mu, Dugnai, Fornax, Ghar-Jenti, Gorgons, Groa, Haltia, Hestia, Hlin, Hlodyn, Kamui Fuchi, Kikimora, Laugo-Edne, Matergabiae, Port-Kuva, Poza-Mama, Silkie, Tu Njami, Uks-Akka, Vesta, Vesuna Erinia.

Desired Qualities

Wisdom   Ceibhfhionn, Danu, Egeria, Gatamdug, Genetaska, Hokkma, Kathirat, Metis, Providentia, Samjuna, Sigurdrifta, Snotra, Tanaquil, Tara, Thordis, Vashti, Vegoia, Veritas, Voluspa, Vor.

Beauty   Aega, Antiope, Aphrodite, Bebhionn, Becuma, Blodewedd, Clidna, Deirdre, Echo, Emer, Fand, Freya, Gerd, Guinevere, Helen, Leanan Sidhe, Lilith, Lieu Hahn, Lorelei, Malika Habashiya, Macha, Morgan Le Fay, Naamah, Niamh, Ningyo, Nixies, Omamama, Oniata, Oona, Oshun, Parvati, Pero, Poldunica, Radha, Rafu-Sen, Ra-mitovi-aman-dreniny, Rebecca, Rhiannon, Rudabeh, Sarah, Scylla, Sedna, Shauskha, Sipna, Sudice, Sunna, Venus.

Wealth   Aje, Aida-Wedo, Amberella, Anu, Ashiakle, Benten, Bona Dea, Chichinguane, Copia, Fulla, Dzivaguru, Gonzuole, Ganga, Gollveig, Habondia, Hada Bai, Jocebed, Kamadhenu, Kuan-Yin, Kuma, Lakshmi, Lan Ts'ai-Ho, Liberalitas, Louhi, Maruwa, Mbombe, Mokosh, Mutyalamma, Nsomeka, Ops, Sarah, Selekana, Surabhi, Wanne Thekla, Yaparamma.

Scholarship, Learning   Aife, Alaghom Naom Tzentel, Brigid, Ceibhfhionn, Danu, Durga, Edda, Fu-Pao,

Hiedono-Ame, Minerva, Mnasa, Mnemosyne, Muses, Nisaba, Saga, Samjuna, Sarasvati, Sheshat, Tou-Mou.

Fairness and Justice   Aeval, Ain, Ala, Arete, Augralids, Basilea, Belit-Seri, Beruryah, Concordia, Daughters of Zelophehad, Deborah, Djigonasee, Egeria, Erinyes, Genetaska, Harmonia, Ishtar, Kadi, Litae, Maat, Marcia Proba, Megaera, Metis, Nanshe, Nemesis, Oya, Praxidike, Shait, Syn, Tanaquil, Themis, Torah, Tou-Mou.

Peace   Athana Lindia, Concordia, Djigonasee, Ececheira, Eleos, Fengi, Genetaska, Horae, Irene, Kuan-Yin, Mengi, Saga, Turan.

Magic and Prophecy

Fate and Destiny   Ananke, Auchimalgen, Ban Naomba, Bean Nighe, Bona Dea, Buan, Camenae, Brizo, Carmenta, Cassandra, Cethlion, Cihuacoatl, Corra, Coventina, Deborah, Dekla, Dione, Dis, Dolya, Egeria, Eve, Feithline, Felicitas, Fortuna, Gestinanna, Gollveig, Hathor, Hecate, Istustaya, Laima, Lavercam, Mamitu, Manto, Masaya, Mati, Menalippe, Menat, Meskhoni, Minu Anni, Miriam, Moirae, Morgan Le Fay, Nanshe, Necessitas, Nereids, Nessa, Nisaba, Nixies, Norns, Nortia, Nyx, Oddibjord, Papaya, Parca, Phoebad, Port-Kuva, Postvorta, Pythia, Python, Rachel, Rebecca, Renenet, Sar-Akka, Sarah, Shait, Shauskha, Sheshat, Sibyl, Sirens, Skuld, Sreca, Sudice, Tamar, Tanaquil, Telphusa, Themis, Tien-Hou, Tlazolteotl, Valkyries, Vegoia, Voluspa, Weisse Frauen.

Sorcery and Shamanism   Adsagsona, Amaterasu, Angitia, Anuanaitu, Banba, Boann, Carman, Cerridwen, Chichinguane, Chuginadak, Circe, Dayang Sumbi, Devera, Devorgilla, Dzivaguru, Eriu, Freya, Groa, Hecate, Hekt, Hild, Himiko, Huitaca, Isis, Istehar, I-toeram-bola-totsy, Jingo, Jocasta, Junkgowa, Kamrusepas, Kasum-Naj-Ekva, Kongsim, Kuma, Lara, Louhi, Marinette, Mbombe,

Medea, Mella, Monje, Meroe, Moncha, Morrigan, Muses, Nimue, Ninlil, Noika, Papalluga, Pali Kongju, Pamphile, Sigurdrifta, Sin, Skuld, Sungmo, Thorgerd, Tlazolteotl, Uti Hiata, Uzume, Vajravaraki, Vila, Viviane, White Buffalo Woman, Wilden Wip, Wlasca, Vasilisa, Winonah, Yaoji, Zipporah.

Shapeshifting Aife, Aige, Blodewedd, Carravogue, Cerberus, Cherubim, Dectere, Epona, Hippia, Inari, Iphis, Julunggul, Junkgowa, Kla, Lan Ts'ai-Ho, Lilith, Meta, Nemesis, Pamphile, Spear-Finger, Thetis, Vajravaraki, Valkyries, Vila.

Luck and Fortune Acca Larentia, Akonadi, Benten, Dolya, Fama, Felicitas, Ghar-Jenti, Haltia, Nirriti, Norns, Pi-Hsia Yuan-Chin, Praxidike.

Boogey-women and witches Agrat Bat Mahalat, Adsagsona, Baba Yaga, Bila, Black Annis, Broxa, Cailleach, Carman, Ceiuci, Cer, Churalin, Cihuateteo, Dakini, Gollveig, Heith, Jezenky, Kalwadi, Khon-Ma, Kishimogin, Kunapipi, Lamasthu, Lamia, Lilith, Mabb, Mahalat, Mara, Medea, Meroe, Mormo, Munanna, Naamah, Nasa, Navky, Orthia, Ovda, Pahto, Parooa, Poldunica, Ptrotka, Rakshasi, Rusalki, Siren, Sneneik, Spear-Finger, Surasa, Tlazolteotl, Veshtitze, Vila, Vitsa-Kuva, Wahini-Hai, Whaitiri.

Arts, Crafts and Other Skills

Handicrafts Arachne (weaving), Athena, Aclla (weaving), Brigid (goldsmithing), Chih Nu (weaving), Dactyls (smithcraft), Eileithyia (spinning), Elen (building), Frau Holle (spinning), Giane (weaving), Gnatoo (tapa), Habetrot (spinning), Hsi-Ling Shih (weaving), India Rosa (pottery, weaving), Ishikore-Dome (smithcraft), Isis (weaving, spinning), Istustaya (spinning), Ix Chebel Yax (weaving, dyeing, spinning), Ix Chel (weaving), Kanene Ski Amai Yehi (weaving, pottery), La Reine Pedaque (spinning), Lohasur Devi (ironworking),

Mami (pottery), Matergabiae (cooking), Myrmex (weaving), Minerva, Moirae (spinning), Moye (blacksmithing), Nyamitondo (blacksmithing), Nyapilnu (architecture) Naru-Kami, Neith (weaving), Paivatar (spinning), Papaya (spinning), Penelope (weaving), Philomena (weaving), Potina (weaving), Papalluga (spinning), Rana Neida (spinning), Saule (weaving), Sreca (spinning), Sunna (spinning), Sweigsdunka (weaving), Tatsuta-Hime (weaving), Valkyries (weaving), Wakahirume (weaving).

Music Akoya, Asintmah, Bast, Canola, Cred, Graces, Hathor, Hesperides, Huldra, Jugumishanta, Lan Ts'ai-Ho, Leanan Sidhe, Limnades, Lieu Hahn, Minerva, Moriath, Morrigan, Muses, Naamah, Oreads, Parooa, Sarasvati, Savitri, Sibilaneuman, Sirens, Syrinx, Tahc-I, Tlitcaplitana, Urvasi, Uso-Dori, Wawalag Sisters, Yuki-Onne.

Art Castalia, Crocale, Graces, Hathor, Morgan Le Fay, Muses, Numma Moiyuk, Sarasvati.

Dance Bast, Caryatids, Eurynome, Graces, Hathor, Hit, Huldra, Kachina, Kinnari, Ko, Kali, Laka, Leanan Sidhe, Limoniades, Mahalat, Maya, Mera, Muso Koroni, Muses, Nereids, Nixies, Norwan, Nunnehi, Rangda, Rusalki, Saule, Sibilaneuman, Swan Maidens, Themis, Urvasi, Uzume, Vila, Wawalag Sisters, Weisse Frauen, Yhi.

Poetry Brigid, Cred, Deborah, Eadon, Edda, Fachea, Gonlod, Ila, Karaikkal-Asmmaiyar, ' Koevasi, Lavercam, Leanan Sidhe, Miriam, Muses, Nausicaa, Saga, Sarasvati, Saule, Savitri, Telesilla.

Healing

General Healing Airmed, Ajysyt, Angitia, Argante, Aveta, Black Madonna, Bebhionn, Brigid, Caolainn, Carna, Coventina, Cura, Eir, Ganga, Glispa, Groa, Gula, Habetrot, Juturna, Isis, Kamrusepas, Kongsim, Mella, Mama, Meditrina, Minerva,

Mokosh, Morgan Le Fay, Neith, Ninhursag, Nirriti, Pali Kongju, Panacea, Pi-Hsia Yuan-Chin, Rosmerta, Salus, Sarah, Shatagat, Sitala, Sulis, Thordis, Tlicaplitana, Toci, Tu-Njami, Vila, Wilden Wip.

Specialized Healing   Aibheaog (toothache), Airmed (herbs), Angitia (herbs), Brigid (eyes), Buschfrauen (herbs), Caolainn (eyes), Circe (herbs), Dziwozony (herbs), Kaya-Nu-Hima (herbs), Kiri Amma (childhood diseases), Mahalbiya (fevers and ulcers), Orbona (childhood diseases), Mulhalmoni (eyes), Polydamna (herbs).

Love and Sexuality

General   Branwen, Graces, Hnossa, Ingebord, Lofn, Milda, Oshun, Radha, Rangada, Sjofn, Var, Venus.

Sexuality   Achtland, Agrat Bat Mahalat, 'Aisha Qandisha, Anat, Aphrodite, Astarte, Blathnat, Cotys, Eostre, Flora, Freya, Harmonia, Hathor, Ino, Ishara, Ishtar, Jezebel, Lilith, Mal, Mylitta, Myrrha, Naamah, Qadesh, Samdzimari, Sheila na Gig, Tlazolteotl, Turan, Vacuna, Voluptia.

Fertility   Al-Lat, Anahita, Anna Perenna, Artemis, Asase Yaa, Bo Find, Boann, Brag-srin-mo, Deae Matres, Djanggawul Sisters, Epona, Eumenides, Fortuna, Freya, Helen, Hertha, Isong, Madder-Akka, Megaera, Niobe, Numma Moiyuk, Omamama, Po Ino Nogar, Ranu Bai, Ymoja, Zarpandit.

Partnership and Affection   Ailinn, Cherubim, Deirdre, Edain, Eri, Eurydice, Galatea, Halcyone, Hero, I-toeram-bola-totsy, Lopamudra, Niamh, Oto-Hime, Penelope, Philemon, Psyche, Pyrrha, Rebecca, Saibya, Sayo-Hime, Zipporah.

Baudy Women and Lewd Jokers   Baubo, Hit, Iambe, Sheila na Gig, Siduri, Tlazolteotl, Uzume.

Wild Women and Wantons   Achtland, Agave, 'Aisha Qandisha, Anat, Anna Perenna, Antianara, Arianrhod, Asherah, Astarte, Belit-Ilani, Bona Dea, Buschfrauen, Cocomama, Dakini, Dziwozony, Eos, Ezili-Freda-Dahomey, Grainne, Ino, Ishtar, Jeh, Kilili, Kunti, Leucippe, Lyssa, Maenads, Maeve, Mylitta, Myrrha, Ostara, Paphos, Pele, Phyllis, Qadesh, Semele, Semiramis, Sphinx, Thyone, Urvasi, Ushas, Uzume, Vacuna, Wlasca, Xochiquetzal, Zuleika.

Defense and Protection

Amazons and Athletes   Aella, Aiofe, Aigiarm, Alfhild, Al-Uzza, Amazons, Anahita, Atalanta, Bia, Brynhild, Caenis, Callisto, Camilla, Candace, Cartimandua, Cloelia, Cyrene, Dejanira, Ess Euchen, Galiana, Gondul, Hera, Hervor, Hiera, Hina, Hippo, Hippolyta, Hyrrokin, Jingo, Judith, Luaths Lurgann, Lysippe, Macha, Maeve, Mami, Marpesia, Melanippe, Myrine, Nessa, Omphale, Otrere, Oya, Pantariste, Penthesilea, Pherenice, Pohaha, Qamaits, Sati, Scathach, Semiramis, Sigurdrifta, Taillte, Telesilla, Thalestris, Thorgerd, Tiamat, Tomyris, Trung-Trac, Valkyries, Vatiaz, Veleda, Wlasca.

Mother Protector   Abeona, Adeona, Agave, Alemona, Anahita, Aphrodite, Akonadi, Auchimalgen, Caireen, Cerberus, Cuba, Cydippe, Dakini, Dea Nutrix, Djigonasee, Edusa, Ess Euchen, Europa, Fides, Fionnuala, Fylgja, Gnowee, Gula, Hlin, Hlodyn, Juks-Akka, Kasum-Naj-Ekva, Kishimogin, Korobona, Kuan-Yin, Lasa, Macris, Matuta, Nut, Pi-Hsia Yuan-Chin, Rumina, Sarah, Sasura, Saule, Tabiti, Taranga, Tauret, Tien-Hou, Uks-Akka, Umaj.

Stages of Life

Maiden   Alfbild, Antheia, Artemis, Athena, Britomartis, Caer, Callisto, Cavillaca, Colleda, Despoina, Eir, Eos, Fionnuala, Gefjon, Hebe, Kore, Lolita, Ma-Ku, Ninlil, Odras, Oniata, Ostara, Pais, Pallas, Pare,

Persephone, Proserpina, Rafu-Sen, Renpet, Sar-Akka, Saules Meita, Scota, Sheilah, Sreca, Uma, Wah-Kah-Nee, Wakahirume, Yamato-Himeno-Miko, Yaya Zakura, Yuki-Onne.

Mother Aka, Ama, Amba, Ba'Alat, Bau, Bontene, Ceres, Cybele, Cydippe, Damkina, Deae Matres, Demeter, Epona, Eve, Frigg, Genea, Hera, Mami, Mut, Nowutset, Ocrisia, Oddudua, Ops, Pandora, Papa, Parvati, Renenet, Selci Syt Emysyt, Sundi-Mumi, Tava-Ajk, Tellus Mater, Utset, Vesta, Yemaya, Zaramama.

Mother Creator Aakuluujjusi, Aditi, Ararat, Asherah, Ataensic, Atse Estsan, Bhavani, Biliku, Bonto, Cally Berry, Cerridwen, Cipactli, Cleone, Coatlicue, Dabaiba, Danu, Deae Matres, Demeter, Devi, Diti, Eingana, Ekhe-Urani, Epona, Eriu, Eurynome, Eve, Frigg, Gaea, Ganga, Hera, Hina, Ila, Inanna, Indara, India Rosa, Ishtar, Isis, Isong, Ituana, Izanami, Kadru, Kali, Katau, Kumei, Khon-Ma, Koevasi, Korobona, Kottavi, Kuma, Kunapipi, Kurukulla, Liomarar, Lla-Mo, Lorop, Luonnotar, Madalait, Madder-Akka, Mahakala, Mami, Mawu, Mayahuel, Mehurt, Mokosh, Muk Jauk, Neith, Nemesis, Ninhursag, Nu Kua, Obatallah, Omamama, Omecihuatl, Parvati, Pattini, Pheraia, Po Ino Nogar, Qamaits, Radien-Kiedde, Rhea, Sarah, Sar-Akka, Sarasvati, Sedna, Sela, Shiwanokia, Stepova-Baba, Tabiti, Tanit, Tethys, Thalassa, Thetis, Tiamat, Tundr Ilona, Wa, VutImi, Waramurungundji, Wari-Ma-Te-Takere, White Buffalo Woman, Yebaad, Yhi, Zywie.

Parthenogenetic Mother Aditi, Arianrhod, Asase Yaa, Atabei, Ataensic, Bugan, Ceto, Dechtere, Diti, Djanggawul Sisters, Djigonasee, Eurynome, Finchoem, Fu-Pao, Gaia, Henwen, Hera, Kongsim, Ligoapup, Luminu-Ut, Mary, Mu Olokukurtilisop, Nana, Neith, Nessa, Nyx, Parvati, Poza-Mama, Shiwanokia, Tai Yuan, Thalassa, Tiamat, Wari-Ma-Te-Takere, Wawalag Sisters.

Crone Baba Yaga, Befana, Bronach, Bugady Musun, Cailleach, Cally Berry, Edda, Eileithyia, Ess

Euchen, Elle, Goga, Graeae, Hathay, Haumea, Hecate, Hel,Hsi Wang Mu, Menat, Mnasa, Muireartach, Nirriti, Nokomis, Ngwa Ndundu, Ohoyo Osh Chishba, Pele, Poldunica, Sarah, Sedna, Sheila na Gig, Sibyl, Spear-Finger, Sreca, Sudice, Stepova-Baba, Ukepenopfu, Voluspa, Weisse Frauen, Whaitiri.

Ancestral Mother and Grandmother Abigail, Abuk, Acca Larentia, Adah, Amaterasu, Ammavaru, Angerboda, Alan Qo'a, Anu, Apasinasee, Asase Yaa, Atabei, Atse Estsan, Awitelina Tsita, Bachue, Bestla, Bhavani, Bilhah, Brigantia, Bugan, Cessair, Claudia Quinta, Dido, Dinah, Dis, Don, Doris, Edda, Embla, Eve, Hagar, Hathor, Helle, Hina, Hybla, Itiba Tahuvava, Ja-Neba, Junkgowa, Kasum-Naj-Ekva, Kuma, Leah, Ligoapup, Luminu-Ut, Mama Ocllo, Mami, Mehurt, Meliae, Mokosh, Mu Olokukurtilisop, Muk Jauk, Mut, Nambi, Nammu, Nana Buluku, Natosuelta, Neith, Niobe, Nu Kua, Numma Moiyuk, Omamama, Otrere, Pali Kongju, Protagenia, Pyrrha, Rachel, Rebecca, Rhpisunt, Sarah, Savitri, Scota, Sela, Tamayorihime, Toci, Ukepenopfu, Vegoia.

Birth and Death

Birth and Rebirth Ajysyt, Artemis, Cihuateteo, Decima, Devayani, Eileithyia, Ermutu, Erua, Eve, Ituana, Ix Chel, Latona, Leto, Lucina, Madder-Akka, Mawu, Meng-Po Niang-Niang, Meskhoni, Nagar-Saga, Neith, Ninhursag, Nintur, Nona, Partula, Persephone, Saibya, Samsin Halmoni, Sar-Akka, Sasti, Saule, Savitri, Selkhet, Sheila na Gig, Sinjang Halmoni, Skuld, Tu-Njami, Uks-Akka, Umaj, Ved-Ava, Vesta, Waldmichen, Wari-Ma-Te-Takere, Ymoja, Zarpandit, Zemyna.

The Underworld Ahemait, Ala, Alecto, Ambika, Angerona, Ariadne, Adsagsona, Asase Yaa, Atalanta, Belit Seri, Blathnat, Ceres, Clidna, Coatlicue, Erinyes, Eriskegal, Eve, Freya, Hathor, Hecate, Hel, Hikuleo, Hina, Husbishag, Ishtar, Izanami, Kali,

Kalma, Kurukulla, Lara, Lyssa, Mahakala, MahuiI-ki, Malophoros, Mania, Mari-Ama, Meilichia, Mem Loimis, Mertseger, Mictecaa'huatl, Miru, Modgud, Natosuelta, Nephthys, Ninazu, Ninkigal, Persephone, Pohjan-Akka, Proserpine, Qamaits, Rhiannon, Saosis, Sati, Satine, Sedna, Semele, Sheila na Gig, Snutqutxals, Spes, Styx, Tellus Mater, Tsun Kyankse, Tuchulcha, Tuonetar, Vanths, Yabme Akka, Yuki-Onne.

Helpers and Midwives

Spirit Guides Ament, Cihuateteo, Fylgja, Harpies, Hindi, Iro Duget, Le-Hev-Hev, Libitina, Maat, Maman Brigitte, Mania, Marzana, Matronit, Miru, Modgud, Naenia, Neith, Poza-Mama, Qebhsnuf, Ran, Selkhet, Shait, Sirens, Sphinx, Srinmo, Styx, Vanths, Yabme-Akka, Yuki-Onne.

Midwives Adamanthea, Artemis, Asintmah, Bhavani, Biddy Mannion, Candelifera, Carmenta, Cynosura, Dekla, Egeria, Eileithyia, Ermutu, Haumea, Hekt, Intercidona, Jocebed, Kapo, Luaths Lurgann, Mabb, Maia, Mami, Meskhoni, Miriam, Pi-Hsia Yuan-Chin, Postvorta, Sar-Akka, Uks-Akka, Umaj, Uni.

Aescetics and Meditators Kalisha, Karaikkal-Asmmaiyar, Parvati, Tai Yuan, Tara, Vajravaraki, Volumna, Yaya-Zakura.

Challenges and Tragedies

Punishment Aura, Cer, Clytemnestra, Cyone, Erinyes.

Revenge Althaea, Antigone, Anuanaitu, Caenis, Clytemnestra, Echenais, Electra, Erinyes, Furrina,

Hecate, Itzpapalotl, Lemna, Medea, Melusine, Minachiaman, Munanna, Nemesis, No-Il Ja-Dae, Pele, Philomena, Poine, Praxidike, Sita, Skadi, Valkyries, Var, Zuleika.

Rape Akycha, Alcippe, Asteria, Austrine, Caenis, Cybele, Cyone, Danae, Daphne, Dryope, Hera, Hina, Leda, Lotis, Marpessa, Menalippe, Merope, Nemesis, Nessa, Ninlil, Oreithyia, Penthesilea, Persephone, Philomena, Proserpine, Rhea, Saules Meita, Syrinx, Winonah.

Victimization Athaliah, Bebhionn, Iphigenia, Meta, Sedna, Sheilah, Vashti, Wakahirume, Walutahanga.

Death of Loved One Achall, Aedon, Airmed, Althaea, Antigone, Banshee, Buan, Carman, Clytemnestra, Demeter, Etain, Isis, Korobona, Lysippe, Nana, Niobe, Polycaste.

Suicide Andraste, Arachne, Arria, Brynhild, Charila, Dido, Erigone, Hathay, Ia, Ixtab, Jocasta, Macaria, Metzli, Nuliayoq, Otiona, Pare, Phyllis, Rusalki, Sati, Scylla, Sphinx, Tsuru.

War Aeron, Agasaya, Alecto, Amazons, Anat, Andraste, Ankt, Artemis, Ate, Badb, Baduhenna, Bellona, Dilbah, Eshara, Hariasa, Harimela, Kara, Minerva, Morrigan, Nemain, Ranaghanti, Sinjang Halmoni, Sroya, Vacuna, Valkyries, Zorya.

Incest Akycha, Anat, Austrine, Biblys, Echidna, Giri Devi, Larissa, Matronit, Nut, Quetzapetlatl, Rebecca, Royot, Sarah, Saules Meita, Tamar, Unelanuhi.

Names of the Goddess

On the following pages is a listing of all goddess names, well known and obscure, that I have discovered and researched. This listing provides all of the variant spellings and alternative names mentioned in the original references, as well as titles or "surnames" (such as corn maiden), which sometimes substitute for names.

Where there are many variations of a name, the most common will appear in boldfaced type. This is the name that is used in the "Myths of the Goddess" section; for example, As-Ava is a less common spelling for Azer-Ava; therefore it is listed as follows:

As-Ava. **Azer-Ava**.

Please note that only goddesses whose myths are told in the "Myths of the Goddess" section are listed in boldfaced type.

When little is known or recorded about a goddess, her name appears only in the "Names of the Goddess" listing along with a brief description of her myth.

When one goddess myth has strong associations to another goddess myth this is indicated by italics; for example, under the goddess Varma-Ava you find:

See Azer-Ava.

Variant spellings emerge because of different ways of transliterating non-English into English words. Sometimes such spelling variations can be minor, as with the Irish "Finnola" and "Fionnuala," both of which will be found in approximately the same area of a dictionary. However, others are sufficiently different that they would present difficulties to someone unaware of the alternative possibilities. The German "Habondia" and "Abundia" are the same goddess, but the first transcriber heard the breath that begins the word as more emphatic than the second—thus creating alternatives that would be many pages away from each other in an alphabetical listing. Finally, changes in approved transliteration occur occasionally; thus all Chinese words are now spelled differently than thirty years ago, and readers are likely to happen upon old spellings as often as newer ones.

A

A. **Aja.**

Aa. **A.**

Aag:hu Gu:gu. **Unelanuhi.**

Aakuluujjusi

Abeona. Roman goddess ruling child's first departure from home.

Aberewa. **Asase Yaa.**

Abhramu

Abigail

Ablabaiae. **Eumenides.**

Abrya

Absusu. **Ishtar;** originally independent Sumerian deity.

Abtagigi. "She who sends messages (of desire)"; **Ishtar.**

Abuk

Abunciada. **Habondia.**

Abundita. "Agricultural abundance," Roman farm goddess.

Abyzu. **Lilith.**

Acantha

Acca Larentia

Achall

Achamantis. One of **Danaids.**

Acheloides. Patronymic of Sirens.

Achlys

Achtan

Achtland

Achununa. Obscure Etruscan goddess.

Acidalia. **Aphrodite** as fountain goddess.

Aclla

Acme. One of **Horae.**

Adah

Adamanthea

Adamma. **Kubaba.**

Adamu

Adath

Adeona. Roman goddess ruling child's return home from school.

Adi Maya. **Lakshmi.**

Adicia. Greek goddess of injustice; opposite of Dike.

Adis(h)akti. **Shakti.**

Aditi

Adrastea. Nurse goddess; *see Adamanthea.*

Adrasteia. "Unyielding" **Nemesis.**

Adsagsona

Ae(l)lo. **Harpy.**

Aeaea. **Circe,** named for her island.

Aebh. **Fionnuala.**

Aedg. Mother of Fand and Etain.

Aedon

Aedos. **Pudicitia.**

Aega

Aegeria. **Egeria.**

Aegilae. One of **Heliades.**

Aegle. One of **Heliades.**

Aegophagos. "Goat-eater," **Hera** at Sparta, where Heracles sacrificed goats to her.

Aella

Aellopos. "Swift-footed as storm winds," **Iris.**

Aeracura. Celtic earth mother of Rhine Valley.

Aeron. Welsh goddess of slaughter and war.

Aertha. **Hertha.**

Aetheria. One of **Heliades.**

Aethra. One of **Oceanids.**

Aetna

Aetole. Javelin-throwing **Artemis** at Naupatcus.

Aeval

Afka. **Mylitta.**

Agasaya

Agave

Agdos

Aghyu Gugu. "Beautiful woman" or "excellent woman," **Unelanahi.**

Agirope. **Eurydice.**

Agischanak

Aglaia. One of **Graces.**

Aglaope. One of **Sirens.**

Aglauros. One of **Augralids.**

Agoraea. "Protector of assemblies in the Agora," **Athena** or **Artemis.**

Agrat Bat Mahalat

Agrotera. **Artemis** as "Huntress."

Agusan Devi

Agwe

Agwe. **Ymoja.**

Ahemait

Ahrenkonigin. Austrian "queen of corn ears," harvest goddess.

Ahsonnutli. **Estsanatlehi.**

Ai-Willi-Ay-O. **Sedna** on west coast of Hudson Bay.

Aibheaeg

Aido-(H)wedo. **Oya.**

Aife. **Aoife.**

Aige

Aigiarm

Ailbe. Mother of Deirdre's lover.

Ailbhe. **Ailbe.**

Ailinn

Ailsie

Ain

Aine

Aine An Cnuic. **Aine** "of the Hill."

Ainippe. Greek warrior; *see Amazons.*

Airmed

'Aisha Qandisha

Aisyt. **Ajysyt.**

Aithuia

Aja

Ajysyt

Aka

Akewa

Akka/o. **Aka.**

Akna. Mayan birth goddess worshiped in Yucatan.

Akonadi

Akoya

Akusaa. Egyptian goddess of sunset.

Akycha

Ala

Alagabiae. *See Deae Matres.*

Alaghom Naom Tzentel

Alakhani

Alan Qo'a

Ala Nur

Albina

Alcippe

Alcyone. **Halcyone; Pleiades.**

Ale. **Ala.**

Alecto

Alectrona

Alektro. **Alecto.**

Alemona. Roman goddess who guards fetus.

Alera. **Turan.**

Aletheia. Greek for **Veritas.**

Alexandra. **Cassandra.**

Alfhild

Alfhild Solglands. **Sunnu.**

Alfsol. **Sunnu** as "elf-sun."

Algea. **Ate.**

Alicibie. **Amazon** in Penthesilea's troupe.

Alilat. **Al-Lat.**

Al-Karisi

Al-Lat

Al-Uzza

Allatu(m). Akkadian **Eriskegal.**

Allita. **Al-Lat; Dido.**

Alm(h)a/u. Irish goddess of Tuatha de Danann.

Alpan(u). **Turan.**

Altan-Telgey

Althaea

Altyn Tondu Ot Ana. *See Poza-Mama.*

Alukah. Canaanite **Eriskegel.**

Am. **Ama.**

Ama

Amadubad. **Mami.**

Amalthea

Amara. **Mamapacha.**

Amarapati. "Immortal lady," **Kiri Amma** in Sri Lanka.

Amashilamma. Sumerian cow goddess.

Amata. Name of Vestal virgins after election; *see Vesta.*

Amaterasu

Amaterasu-Omi-Kami. **Amaterasu.**

Amatudda. **Mami.**

Amaunet. **Ogdoad.**

Amayicoyondi

Amazons

Amba

Amber. **Amba.**

Amberella

Ambika

Ambologera. "Delaying old age," **Aphrodite** of Sparata.

Ambrosia. One of **Heliades.**

Ament

Ameretet. *See Armaiti.*

Amma. *See Edda.*

Ammavaru

Amphitrite

Amudubad. **Mami.**

Amymone. **Danaid**; also fountain goddess.

An.Zu.

Ana. **Anu.**

Anadyomene. "She who rises from the waves," **Aphrodite.**

Anaea. **Anaitis.**

Anagke. **Ananke.**

Anahita

Anaitis. Greek for **Anahita.**

Anakis. Greek for **Anuket.**

Ananke

Anapurna

Anat

Anath/a. **Anat.**

Anatole. One of **Horae.**

Anatu

Anaxarete

Anchiale. Mother of Dactyls.

Andarta. **Artio.**

Andraste

Andriam-Vabi-Rano

Andromeda

Andromena. **Andromeda.**

Ane. **Ala.**

Aneitis. **Anaitis.**

Anelanuhi. **Unelanuhi.**

Anemotis. "Subduer of Winds," **Athena.**

Anesidora. "She who sends up gifts," **Demeter** and **Pandora.**

Angerboda

Angerbotha. **Angerboda.**

Angerona

Angeyja. Scandinavian water goddess, daughter of Ran.

Angitia

Anguitia. **Angitia.**

Angwushahai'i. *See Kachina.*

Ani. **Mami.**

Anieros

Anima Mundi

Anit. **Anat.**

Ankamma. **Ammavaru.**

Ankt

Anna. **Hannah.**

Anna Perenna

Anna Purna. **Anapurna.**

Annalia Tu-Bari

Anouke. **Ankt.**

Anta. **Anat.**

Antaboga

Antandre. **Amazon** in Penthesilea's troupe.

Antevorta

Antheia. "Blooming One" or "Friend of the Flowers," **Hera** at Argo.

Antianara

Antibrote. **Amazon** in Penthesilea's troupe.

Antigone

Antiope

Antu(m). **Anatu.**

Anu

Anuanaitu

Anuket

Anukis. Greek for **Anuket.**

Anunit. **Anunitu.**

Anunitu

Aobh. **Fionnuala.**

Aoide. One of **Muses.**

Aoife

Apaea. **Britomaris** on Aegina.

Apasinasee

Apet. **Tauret.**

Aphek. **Mylitta.**

Aphrodita. Italian for **Aphrodite.**

Aphrodite

Apia-Fellus. Scythian earth goddess.

Apito. **Atabei.**

Aponibolinayen

Apsaras. *See Urvasi.*

Arachne

Aranrot. Early Welsh for **Arianrhod.**

Ararat

Ardat Lili

Ardat Lilitu. **Ardat Lili, Lilith.**

Arduinna. **Ardwinna.**

Ardvi Sura Anahita. **Anahita.**

Ardwinna

Areia. "Warlike." In Sparta, **Aphrodite.** In Athena, **Athena.**

Arete

Argante. Healer queen of British Avalon.

Arganthone. Thracian mistress of animals, hunting goddess.

Ariadne

Arianhod. **Arianrhod.**

Arianrhod

Aricia

Aridella. Deified **Ariadne.**

Arinna. **Wurusemu.**

Ariope. **Telphassa.**

Ariu. Sister of Liban.

Arktos. **Callisto.**

Armaiti

Arnarkuag(s)sak. "Old Sea-Woman," **Sedna.**

Arnementia. Celtic goddess of healing springs.

Arrand. **Aine.**

Arrang Dibatu

Arria

Artemis

Artemisia

Artimpaasa. Scythian love and moon goddess.

Artini. Etruscan **Artemis.**

Artio

Artumes. Etruscan **Artemis.**

Aruru. **Mami.**

Aryong-Jong

As-Ava. **Azer-Ava.**

Asakhira. **Ishara.**

Asase Efua. **Asase Yaa**, in Fante dialect.

Asase Yaa

Ashdar. **Ishtar.**

Asherah

Ashiakle

Ashnan

Ashtoreth. **Astarte.**

Asia. **Athena** in Colchis.

Asintmah

Askefruer. "Ash women," Danish woodland spirits.

Aspclcnie

Asrapas. **Dakini.**

Assa. **Nessa,** as a young girl.

Assesia. **Athena** as city goddess of Assesus.

Astarte

Astateia. **Artemis.**

Asteria

Asterope. One of **Pleiades.**

Astraea

Astraia. **Astraea.**

Astronoe. Phoenician mother goddess; story resembles that of Cybele.

Asynjr.

At-Em. Egyptian mother goddess of all-devouring time.

Atabei

Ataensic

Atalanta

Atanea

Atargatis

Ate

Atea. *See Atanea.*

Atete

Athaliah

Athana Lindia

Athena

Athene. **Athena.**

Athirat. **Asherah.**

Athtarath. **Astarte.**

Atira

Atla. A **Wave Maiden.**

Atlantides. Greek star goddesses.

Atropos. Oldest of **Moirae.**

Atse Estsan

Attabeira. **Atabei.**

Au Set. "Exceeding queen," Greek for **Isis.**

Au-Co

Auchimalgen

Audbumbla

Audhumla. **Audbumbla.**

Aufruvva

Augeia. A **Wave Maiden.**

Aughty. **Echtghe.**

Augralids

Aura

Aurgiafa. A **Wave Maiden.**

Aurora

Ausrine. **Austrine.**

Austrine

Autonoe. "Wise unto herself," sister of Agave.

Auxo. One of **Graces.**

Auzit. **Isis.**

Avaris. Egyptian form of **Anat.**

Aventina. Many-breasted **Diana** worshiped on Rome's Aventine Hill.

Averna

Aveta

Avilacoq. **Sedna.**

Avisit. **Umay.**

Awehai. **Atansic.**

Awitelin Tsita

Axiocersa. **Auiocersa.**

Axiopoenois. **Athena** as "Avenger."

Aya. **Aja.**

Ayaba. Hearth goddess of Fon of Benin.

Aze. Japanese pine-tree spirit.

Azer-Ava

Azesia. **Demeter** or **Persephone** as goddess of harvest.

B

Ba'Alat

Baaltis. **Ba'Alat.**

Baau. **Bau.**

Baba Yaga

Baba. **Baba Yaga.**

Bacchantes. **Maenads.**

Bachue

Badb

Badb Catha. "Raven of Battle," **Morrigan.**

Baduhenna. "War-maddened," Scandinavian war goddess.

Bahu. **Bau.**

Bakkah. Arab love goddess.

Balta Saulite. **Saule.**

Ban-Ava. *See Azer-Ava.*

Ban-Chuideachaidh Moire. "Midwife to Mary," **Brigid.**

Banba

Banbh. **Banba.**

Bandae. **Banna.**

Bandia. Irish generic for "goddesses."

Banka-Mundi

Banna Naomha. **Ban Naomha.**

Banna. Goddess of River Bann; *see Sequana.*

Ban Naomha

Banshee

Bara. *See Walo.*

Barbata

Barbelina. **Saules Meita.**

Barbmo-Akka

Bardaichila

Base. Cappadocian name for **Athena.**

Basho. Japanese goddess of basho plant.

Basilea. Ancient Celtic queen who civilized her people.

Bassarae. **Maenads.**

Bast

Bastet. **Bast.**

Bau

Baubo

Bawin Jata Balawang Bulan. **Jata.**

Be Bind. **Bebhionn.**

Bean Nighe

Bebhionn

Bechoil. Early Irish ancestor goddess like Danu.

Becuma

Befana

Begoe. **Vegoia.**

Beiwe

Beiwe-Neida. Daughter of sun among Saami. *See Beiwe.*

Beli-Sheri. **Belit-Seri.**

Belili. **Ba'Alat.**

Belisama. Celtic goddess of Mersey River; *see Sequana.*

Belit-Ilani

Belit-Ile. **Belit-Ilani.**

Belit-Matate. "Lady of Lands," Babylonian title of **Ninlil.**

Belit-Seri

Bellona

Belqis. Islamic name for Queen of Sheba. *See Candace.*

Beltis. **Ba'Alat, Zarpandit.**

Bendis

Bentakomari

Benten

Benvarry. Friendly Manx mermaid.

Benzaiten. **Benten.**

Bera. **Scota.**

Berchta. **Perchta.**

Berecynthia

Beregyni

Berit. **Beruth.**

Berlusianhena. **Deae Matres.**

Berooch. Irish mermaid.

Beroth. **Beruth**.

Bertha. "Swan," **Freya**.

Beruryah

Beruth

Bestla

Bhagvati. **Mindhal**.

Bharat Mata. Mother India, goddess of nation.

Bhavani

Bhdrakali. "Gracious" **Kali**.

Bhrkuti. Tibetan heavenly goddess.

Bia

Bibli(o)(u)s. **Biblys**.

Biblys

Bibracte. Continental Celtic earth goddess.

Biddy

Biddy Mannion

Bil

Bila

Bildjiwuraroju. *See Djanggawul Sisters*.

Bilhah

Biliku

Billow Maidens. **Wave Maidens**.

Biman Chan

Bina. The **Matronit**.

Biobhonn. **Bebhionn**.

Birrin. Daughter of Cessair.

Bisal-Mariamna

Bjort. Serving maid to Menglod.

Black Annis

Black Goddess. **Black Madonna**.

Black Madonna

Blaithine. **Blathnat**.

Blama. Daughter-in-law of Cessair.

Blanaid. Maid to Ethne.

Blathnat

Blodewedd

Bo Dhu. *See Bo Find*.

Bo Find

Bo Ruadh. *See Bo Find*.

Boabhan Sith. Highland Scots **Banshee**.

Boadicca. *See Andraste*.

Boann

Boba. Lithuanian **Baba**.

Bodua. Continental Celtic war goddess; *see Badb*.

Bohu. **Bau**.

Bokoj. **Tu-Njami**.

Bomong

Bomu Rambi. *See Mella*.

Bona Dea

Bontene. "The Mother" at Thyiateria, a Greek colony.

Bonto. Mordvin creator goddess.

Boudicca. *See Andraste*.

Boulaia. "Counselor," or "upholder of law," title of **Athena**.

Bouvinda. *See Bo Find*.

Brag-srin-mo

Branwen

Brauronia. "Bear," **Artemis** or **Callisto**.

Breksta

Bremusa. **Amazon** in Penthesilea's troupe.

Bri. Beautiful Irish fairy queen.

Briant. Welsh river goddess; *see Sequana*.

Bricta. Celtic fertility goddess.

Bridgit. **Brigid**.

Brig(h)it/d. **Brigid**.

Briganda/o. Southern French **Brigid** as goddess of hot springs.

Brigantia

Brigette. **Oya**.

Brigid

Brimo. "Angry one," **Demeter** in Eleusinian mysteries; also **Rhea, Hecate, Persephone**.

Britomartis

Brizo

Bronach

Bronwen. **Branwen**.

Broxa

Brunissen

Brynhild

Brynhilda. **Brynhild**.

Buan

Bubona. Roman goddess, protected oxen and cows.

Buddhi. "Intelligence," Hindu goddess.

Buddhi Nagin. "Old Female Snake," rainbow-snake goddess of north Indian Kulu.

Budhi Pallien

Buffalo Calf Maiden. **White Buffalo Woman**.

Bugady Enintyn

Bugady Musun

Bugan. Philippines; mother of humanity after great flood.

Bunzi. Serpent-rainbow goddess of Zaire.

Buschfrauen

Buschgrossmutter. **Buschfrauen**.

Buto. **Uadgit**.

Butterfly Maiden. Hopi springtime spirit; *see Kachina*.

Byul-Soon. Korean star goddess; *see Hae-Soon*.

C

Caca. Ancient Roman goddess later replaced by **Vesta**.

Cacce-Jienne. "Water mother" of Russian Saami.

Caelestis. **Tanit**.

Caenis

Caer

Caileach Cinn Boirne. **Bronach**.

Cailleach

Cailleach Beara. **Cailleach**.

Caireen. Heroic mother of Irish legend.

Caitileen Og. **Clidna**.

Calaeno. One of **Pleiades**.

Caligo

Calligo. **Caligo**.

Calliope. One of **Muses**.

Callipateira. **Pherenice**.

Callipygos. "Beautiful buttocks," title of **Aphrodite**.

Callirrhoe

Calliste. **Callisto**.

Callisto

Callithyia. **Callihrroe**.

Cally Berry

Calva

Calypso

Camenae

Camilla

Campe

Campestres. Latin name for Celtic field goddesses.

Camunda. **Durga** as warrior goddess.

Candace

Candelifera. Roman goddess who assists at births.

Candi

Candika. "Fearful," name for **Kali, Durga**.

Canola

Caolainn

Cap(i)ta. **Minerva**.

Caprotina. **Juno**.

Cardea

Carley. **Carlin**.

Carlin

Carline. **Carlin**.

Carman

Carme. **Charmel**, mother of Britomartis.

Carmenta

Carmenti/es. **Carmenta.**

Carna

Carpo. **Horae** of Atumn.

Carravogue

Cartinandua

Carya

Caryatids

Caryatis. **Carya.**

Casmenae. **Camenae.**

Cassandra

Cassiop(i)e. **Cassiopeia.**

Cassiopeia

Castalia

Cat Ana. **Anu.**

Cathubodia. Continental Celtic **Banba.**

Cavillaca

Ceasg

Ceibhfhionn

Ceiuci

Celaeno. "Screamer," a **Harpy.**

Cer. **Ker.**

Cerberus

Ceres

Cerridwen

Cessair

Cethlion

Cetnenn. Great woman warrior of Irish legend.

Ceto

Ch'll Kongju. "Seventh Princess," **Pali Kongju.**

Chaabou. Semitic earth mother.

Chalaiope. Sister of Medea.

Chalchiuhtlicue

Chalinitis. "Restrainer," **Athena** who helped bridle Pegasus.

Challalamma. Buttermilk goddess of eastern India.

Chamaine. **Demeter.**

Chandi. **Candi.**

Changing Woman

Chang-O

Chantico. Ancient Mexican fire goddess.

Charila

Charis. One of **Graces.**

Charites. **Graces.**

Charmel. Mother of Britomartis.

Charshamba Karisi. **Al-Karisi.**

Charybdis

Chelone

Chera. **Hera** as old wise woman.

Cherubim

Chia. **Huitaca.**

Chichinguane

Chicomecoatl

Chien-Ti

Chih Nu

Chimera

Chinnintamma. Household goddess of eastern India.

Chitone. "With her garment tucked up for freedom," **Artemis.**

Chlaus Haistic. Powerful Irish witch.

Chloe. "Green," **Demeter.**

Chloris. **Flora, Niobe.**

Chochmingure (pl). Hopi Corn Mothers.

Chochmingwu. Hopi Corn Mother.

Chokmah. **Hokkma.**

Chthonia

Chu-mana. Hopi snake maidens.

Chuan Hou. **Tien-Hou.**

Chuang-Mu. Chinese goddess of bedroom.

Chuginadak

Chunwang. **Sungmo.**

Chup-Kamui

Churalin

Chwimbian. **Viviane.**

Chysothenius. Homer's name for **Iphigenia;** possibly historical Greek woman poet.

Ciau

Cihuacoatl

Cihuapipiltin. **Cihuateteo.**

Cihuateteo

Cinderella

Cinxia. "Loosener of girdles," **Juno.**

Cipactli

Circe

Cisa. **Zisa.**

Citlalinicue. **Omecihuatl.**

Ciza. **Zisa.**

Claudia Quinta

Cledoxa. One of Niobe's murdered daughters.

Cleodora. One of **Danaids.**

Cleone

Cleta. One of **Graces.**

Clidna

Clio. One of **Muses.**

Cliodna. **Clidna.**

Cloelia

Clonie. Amazon in Penthesilea's troupe.

Clotho. One of **Moirae.**

Clothru. *See Maeve.*

Clutoida. Celtic goddess of Clyde River; *see Sequana.*

Clymene

Clytemnestra

Clytia. **Clytie.**

Clytie

Coatlicue

Coatrischie. Tempest-raising goddess of Antilles.

Cocomama

Colleda

Comedovae. Continental Celtic healing goddesses.

Conciliatrix. "Peacemaker," **Juno.**

Concordia

Consivia. **Ops.**

Copia

Cora. **Kore.**

Corchen. Early Irish snake goddess.

Cordelia. **Creiddylad.**

Cori Ocllo. *See Mama Ocllo.*

Coronis. One of **Heliades.**

Corra. Scottish crane goddess of prophecy.

Cotys

Cotytto. **Cotys.**

Coventina

Coyolxauhqui

Cred

Creiddylad

Creide. **Cred.**

Creidwy. **Cerridwen.**

Creta. Mother of Pasiphae.

Crete. **Creta.**

Crobh Dearg

Crocale. Hairdresser of Artemis.

Cuba. Roman goddess who guarded toddlers.

Cuda. British Celtic goddess of prosperity.

Culsa. *See Vanths.*

Cunina

Cupra. **Turan.**

Cura

Curiatia. **Juno** as guardian of fiances.

Cuvto-Ava

Cybele

Cydippe

Cynosura

Cynthia. **Artemis.**

Cyone

Cypris. **Aphrodite.**

Cyrene

Cyther(ei)a(s). **Aphrodite.**

D

Da
Dabaiba
Dactyls
Dae-Soon. Korean moon goddess. *See Hae-Soon.*
Dagini. **Dakini.**
Dah-Ko-Bed. **Tacoma.**
Dahud. **Dahut.**
Dahut
Dakini
Dakshinakali. "Black Kali," worshiped in Bengal.
Dali
Damatre. Early Italian mother goddess.
Damatres. "The Mothers," **Demeter** and **Persephone** in Sicily.
Damballah. **Oya.**
Dame Habondia. **Habondia.**
Dames Vertes
Damgalnunna. Sumerian **Damkina.**
Damia
Damkina
Damona. Continental Celtic serpent healing goddess, also ruler of cattle.
Dana. **Danu.**
Danae
Danaids
Danu
Daoine Sidhe. *See Danu.*
Daphne
Darago
Darine. **Fithir.**
Darzamat. Latvian mother of gardens.
Daughters of Zelophehad

Daukina. Damkina, in Greek.
Davata. Indian fire goddess.
Dayang Raca
Dayang Sumbi
Dea Artio. **Artio.**
Dea Caelestis. Roman name for **Tanit.**
Dea Dia. **Dia.**
Deae Matres
Dea Nutrix
Dea Syria
Deborah
Decca. *See Fionnuala.*
Dechtere
Decima. Roman goddess of last month of fetal gestation.
Deianira. **Dejanira.**
Deichtire. **Dechtere.**
Deino. One of **Graeae.**
Deirdre
Dejanira
Dekla
Delia. **Artemis.**
Deliphobe. One of **Sibyls.**
Delphine. **Python.**
Delphinia. **Artemis** at Athens.
Delphyne. **Python.**
Demeter
Dendritus. **Helen.**
Dennitsa. **Zvezda Dennitsa.**
Dercetis. **Derceto.**
Derceto
Derk/ceto. **Atargatis.**
Despoina
Devana. Czechoslovakian **Dziewona.**
Devayani. Indian goddess who knew secret of raising dead.
Devera. Roman goddess ruling brooms used to purify ritual sites.
Devi

Devo Dukryte. "God's Daughter," **Saule.**
Devona. Goddess of Devon River; *see Sequana.*
Devorgilla
Dewa Anta. **Anta.**
Dewi Danuh. Balinese water goddess.
Dewi Nawang Sasih
Dewi Shri
Dharti Mata. "Mother Earth" in Bombay.
Dhat-Badan
Dhat-Hami. **Dhat-Badan.**
Dia
Dia Griene
Diana
Diana Nemorensis. **Diana** "of the wood."
Dice. **Dike.**
Dictynna. **Britomartis.**
Dido
Digi No Duineach. **Cailleach.**
Digne. **Cailleach.**
Dii Involuti. Roman **Moirae.**
Diiwica. Serbian **Dziewona.**
Dike
Dil. Irish cattle goddess.
Dilbah. **Ishtar** as war-provoking morning star.
Dinah
Dindymene. **Cybele,** from shrine on Mount Dindymon in Phrygia.
Dione
Dirae. "Curses," **Erinyes.**
Dirphya. **Hera.**
Dis
Disciplina. Roman goddess of discipline.
Discordia. Roman **Eris.**
Disir
Diti

Diuturna. **Juturna.**
Divi-Te Zeni. Bulgarian **Dziwozony.**
Divozenky. Bohemian **Dziwozony.**
Djanggawul Sisters
Dji Sisnaxitl. **Qamaits.**
Djigonasee
Dod(ol)a. Serbian goddess of rain.
Doh Tenagan. Malaysian patroness of women.
Dolya
Domduca. **Juno** as goddess of marriage.
Domnu ."The Deep," Irish sea goddess.
Don
Donna Beatrice. **Kimpa Vita.**
Doris
Draupadi
Druantia. Continental Celtic goddess of fir trees.
Dryads
Dryope
Dubh Lacha. Irish sea goddess.
Dugnai
Dunne Enin
Durga
Dwyn(acm). **Branwen.**
Dzalarhons
Dziewona
Dziwozony
Dzonokwa. *See Tsonoqua.*

E

Eadon. Irish goddess of poetry.
Ebhlenn. **Ebhlinne.**
Ebhlinne
Ececheira
Echenais
Echidna
Echighe

Echo

Edain

Edda

Edji. **Eve.**

Edulica. Roman protectress of children.

Edusa. Roman goddess, ruled weaning of infants.

Eergatis. *See Ergane.*

Egee. Amazon general of Libya; *see Myrine.*

Egeria

Egia. A **Wave Maiden.**

Egime. Sumerian earth mother.

Egle

Eidothea. **Idothea.**

Eile. Sister of Maeve.

Eileithyia

Eingana

Eir

Eire. **Eriu.**

Eireisone

Eirene. **Irene.**

Eithinoha. **Nokomis.**

Eithna/e. **Ethne.**

Eka Obasi. **Isong.**

Ekash-Taka. Indian mother of moon.

Ekhe-Urani. "Colorless one," southeast Asian goddess.

Ekki. **Aka.**

Elat

Ele. Sister of Maeve.

Electra

Elen

Elena

Eleos

Elias. Greek "Olive Oil," *see Oeno.*

Elionia. Birth goddess of Argo, possibly Eileithyia.

Elissa. **Dido.**

Elle

Elpis. Greek **Spes.**

Embla

Emboq Sri. "Bride Rice," food goddess of Java.

Emer

Empanda

Eni Mahanahi

Enyo. One of Graeae; also minor Greek war goddess.

Eodain. *See Leanan Sidhe.*

Eos

Eostre. **Ostara.**

Epaine. "Awesome," title of **Persephone.**

Ephesia

Epicaste. **Jocasta.**

Epona

Erathipa

Erato. One of **Muses.**

Erce

Erda. **Hertha.**

Ereskigal. **Eriskegal.**

Eri

Erigone

Erinyes

Erioboa. **Amazon.**

Eris

Eriskegal

Eriu

Ermutu. Egyptian birth goddess, similar to Meskhoni.

Ertemi. *See Eni Mahanahi.*

Erua. "Conception" or "pregnant," **Mami.**

Erycina. **Aphrodite,** for famous temple on Mount Eryx in Sicily.

Erysiptolis. "Protector of the city," **Athena** in times of war.

Erytheis. One of **Hesperides.**

Erzulie-Freda-Dahomey. **Ezili-Freda-Dahomey.**

Eset. **Isis.**

Eshara

Ess Euchen

Ester. **Esther.**

Esther

Estine. **Estiu.**

Estiu. Irish Warrior and bird goddess.

Estsanatlehi

Etain

Ethausva. Obscure Etruscan goddess.

Ethlenn. **Ethne.**

Ethna. **Ethne.**

Ethne

Etna. **Aetna.**

Etugen

Eudora. One of **Heliades.**

Eumenides

Eunomia. One of **Horae.**

Euphrosyne. One of **Graces.**

Europa

Euryale. One of **Gorgons.**

Eurycleia. Greek daughter of Ops.

Eurydice

Eurynome

Euterpe. One of **Muses.**

Eutychia. Greek goddess of happiness; in Rome, **Felicitas.**

Evadne. **Amazon** in Penthesilea's troupe.

Evaki

Evan. Obscure Etruscan goddess.

Eve

Eye Goddess

Ezili Danto. Rum-drinking, chain-smoking **Black Madonna** of Haiti.

Ezili-Freda-Dahomey

F

Fachea. Irish goddess of poetry.

Fadzja. **Tu-Njami.**

Fainen. *See Weisse Frauen.*

Fakahoutu. **Papa.**

Falvara

Fama

Fand

Fangge

Fata Morgana. **Morgan Le Fay.**

Fates. **Moirae.**

Fatima

Fat Lady

Fatouma

Fatua. *See Bona Dea.*

Fauna. *See Bona Dea.*

Fea. "Hateful" name for **Morrigan.**

Feithline

Felicitas

Feng Pho-Pho

Fengi

Fenya. **Fengi.**

Feronia

Ffraid. Welsh "Saint" **Brigid.**

Fideal

Fides

Finchoem

Findabar

Finncaev. "Fair love," powerful fairy queen of Ireland.

Finola. **Fionnuala.**

Fiongalla

Fionnuala

Fiorgyn(n). **Fjorgyn.**

Firanak

Firebird. *See Elena.*

Firgunia. **Hertha.**

Fithir

Fjorgyn

Fjorgynn. **Fjorgyn.**

Fland. *See Flidais.*

Flidais

Flora

Fluonia. **Juno** of menstrual flow.

Fluusa. Early Italian name for **Flora.**

Fluvonia. **Juno** of menstrual flow.

Fodhla. *See Eriu, Eire.*

Folta. *See Banba, Eriu.*

Fons. Roman goddess of fountains.

Fornax. Roman goddess of bread-baking, identified with Vesta.

Fors. "Force," *see Fortuna.*

Fortuna

Frau He/arke. **Hertha**.

Frau Holda. **Frau Holle**.

Frau Holle

Fraud. Roman goddess of treachery.

Freda. *See Ezili-Freda-Dahomey.*

Frejya. **Freya**.

Freya

Frigg

Frigga. **Frigg**.

Friis Avfruvva. *See Avfruvva.*

Frith. Maid-servant to Menglod.

Fru Gode. **Frau Holle**.

Fubau. **Fu-Pao**.

Fuji

Fulgora. Roman goddess of lightning.

Fulla

Fu-Pao

Furiae/Furies. **Erinyes**.

Furrina

Fylgja

Fylgakona. **Fylgja**.

Fyorgynn. **Fjorgyn**.

G

Gabiae. "Givers" or "Controllers," continental Celtic mother goddesses.

Gaca. **Gaia**.

Gaia

Galatea

Galiana

Gamlat. Babylonian goddess merged with Ishtar.

Gamsu. Chaldean sea goddess merged with Zarpandit.

Ganga

Ganna. Continental Celtic oracle-woman.

Ganymeda

Ganzir. **Eriskegal**.

Gaomei

Garbhog. Carravogue.

Garmangabis. "Weaver of faith," continental Celtic mother goddess.

Gasan-ia. "My Lady," *see Wurusemu.*

Gatamdug

Gauri

Gauri-Sankar

Gawaunduk

Ge. **Gaia**.

Geezhigo-Quae

Gefjon

Gefjun. **Gefjon**.

Gefn. **Freya** as "generous one."

Geirronul. "Spear-Bearer," a **Valkyrie**.

Gello. *See Lilith.*

Gemmyo. *See Hiedono-Ame.*

Gendenwitha

Genea. Phoenician mother of humanity.

Genetaska

Gentle Annie

Gentle Hannie. **Gentle Annie**.

Gerd

Gersimi. *See Freya.*

Geshtinnanna. **Gestinanna**.

Gestinanna

Ggigantia

Ghar-Jenti

Gheareagain. **Carravogue**.

Gialp. A **Wave Maiden**.

Giane

Gidne. Saami long-tailed forest goddess.

Gillagriene. Irish daughter of sun.

Gillian

Gilou. **Lilith**.

Giri Devi

Giriputri

Girya. "Mistress of House," **Parvati**.

Glas. "Blue one," magical Irish milch-cow.

Glauce. A **Nereid**.

Glaukopis. "Owl-eyed" **Athena**.

Gleti

Glispa

Gna

Gnatoo. Tapa-making moon goddess in Friendly Isles.

Gnowee

Godasiyo

Godiva

Goga

Gogyeng Sowuhti. Hopi **Spider Woman**.

Goleuddydd

Gollveig

Gondul

Gonlod

Gonzuole

Gorgons

Graces

Graeae

Graine. **Grainne**.

Grainne

Grainne ni Malley

Grand-Aunt Tiger

Grandmother Toad. *See Ataensic.*

Grania. **Grainne**.

Gratia. *See Graciae.*

Green Ladies. **Dames Vertes**.

Greip. A **Wave Maiden**.

Grian

Grimbild. *See Brynhild.*

Grimes Grave Goddess. *See Albina.*

Griselicae. Continental Celtic healing goddesses of thermal springs.

Groa

Guabancex

Guacarapita. **Atabei**.

Guadalupe

Guanyin. **Kuan-Yin**.

Guatauva. Messenger goddess of Antilles.

Gudiri-mumy. Mother-Thunder of Finno-Ugric Votyaks.

Gudrun. *See Brynhild.*

Guenloie. **Guinevere**.

Guimazoa. **Atabei**.

Guinevere

Guizi mu. "Mother of demon children," Chinese **Hariti**.

Gula

Gula-Bau. **Gula**.

Gum Lin

Gumshea. Babylonian vegetation goddess, merged with Ishtar.

Gunabibi. *See Kunapipi.*

Gunlad. **Gonlod**.

Gusts-of-Wind. *See Ataensic.*

Guth. A **Valkyrie**.

Guurmu. Daughter of Gula.

Gwendolyn. **Gwendydd**.

Gwendydd

Gwenh(w)yfar. **Guinevere**.

Gwragedd Annwn. Welsh lake maiden; *see Nimue.*

Gwyar

Gwyllion

Gyhldeptis

H

Habetrot

Habonde. **Habondia.**

Habondia

Hada Bai

Hadassah. **Esther.**

Hae-Soon

Hag of Beare. **Cailleach.**

Hagar

Hainuwele

Hakahotu. **Papa.**

Halcyone

Hallat. **Al-Lat.**

Halmasuit

Haltia

Hamadryads. **Dryads.**

Haminga. **Fylgja.**

Hanata. **Ishtar** as warrior.

Hannah

Hannahanna

Hanwi

Hard Substances Woman. Hopi name for **Estanatlehi.**

Hariasa. Germanic war goddess.

Harimela. Germanic war goddess.

Hariti

Harmonia

Harmonthoe. **Amazon** in Penthesilea's troupe.

Harpies

Hastseoltoi. Navaho goddess of hunting.

Hatai Wug(h)ti. **Spider Woman.**

Hathay

Hathor

Hauket. *See Ogdoad.*

Haumea

Haurvatat. *See Armaiti.*

Hawwah. "Life" or "life-giver," Hebrew name for **Eve.**

Hebat

Hebe

Hecaerge. "Hitting at a distance," name of **Artemis** for marksmanship; **Aphrodite,** when she throws darts of love.

Hecate

Hedrun

Hegemone

Heh. **Het.**

Hehewuti. "Warrior Mother," *see Kachina.*

Heian. **Pele.**

Heid. **Gollveig.**

Heimarmene. Greek personification of fate.

Heith

Heithrun. **Hedrun.**

Hekate. **Hecate.**

Heket. **Hekt.**

Hekoolas

Hekt

Hel

Helde. "Brilliant," **Valkyries.**

Helen

Helene/a. **Helen.**

Heliades

Helle

Hemera. *See Eos, Nyx.*

Heng-O. **Chang-O.**

Henge. **Chang-O.**

Henwen

Hepatu. **Hebat.**

Hera

Herentas. Early Italian form of **Venus.**

Herfjoter. "Panic-Terror," a **Valkyrie.**

Hero

Herophile. A **Sibyl,** daughter of Lamia.

Herse. "Dew," one of **Augralids.**

Hertha

Hervor

Hervor. "Warder of the Host," a **Valkyrie.**

Hespera. Sunset, last phase of **Eos.**

Hesperide. *See Eos.*

Hesperides

Hestia

Het. Egyptian serpent-fire goddess.

Het-Her. **Hathor.**

Hetaira. **Aphrodite** as protector of courtesans.

Hgoptchae Poridok. "Seventh Princess," **Pali Kongju.**

Hi. **Hekoolas.**

Hiaka. *See Pele.*

Hiedono-Ame

Hiera

Hiiaka. *See Pele.*

Hikuleo

Hild

Himaji. "The Pearly," **Parvati.**

Himbuto. **Uadgit.**

Himeropa. One of **Sirens.**

Himeros. "Desire," attendant on Aphrodite.

Himiko

Hina

Hindi(ra). **Durga** as pomegranate-carrying death queen.

Hine-ahu-one

Hine-titama

Hintaku. **Hekoolas.**

Hippia

Hippo

Hippodamia

Hippolyta

Hippolyte. **Hippolyta.**

Hippothoe. "Impetuous Mare," **Amazon** in Penthesilea's troupe.

Hiquit. **Hekt.**

Hit

Hiyedano-Are. **Hiedono-Ame.**

Hlathguth. "Necklace-adorned Warrior maiden," a **Valkyrie.**

Hlif. Maidservant to Menglod.

Hlifthrasa. Maidservant to Menglod.

Hlin

Hlodyn

Hlok. "Shrieker," a **Valkyrie.**

Hluodana. **Hertha.**

Hlyn. **Hlin.**

Hnos. **Hnossa.**

Hnossa

Ho Hsien-Ku

Hokkma

Hokmah. **Hokkma.**

Holdja. Estonian **Haltia.**

Holika. Goddess of Indian fire festival.

Holle. **Frau Holle.**

Holzfraulein. **Holzweibel.**

Holzweibel. **Buschfrauen** in form of owls.

Homadhenu. **Kamadhenu.**

Hopoe. *See Pele.*

Hora. Roman name for **Graces.**

Horae

Horephoros. **Demeter** as bringer of favorable weather.

Horn. **Freya.**

Horsel. **Ursula.**

Horta. **Angerona.**

Hou-T'u. **Hu-Tu.**

Hozbrauen. **Holzweibel.**

Hrede. **Rheda.**

Hrist. "Shaker," a **Valkyrie.**

Hsian Fu-Jen. Chinese double water goddess.

Hsi-Ho

Hsi-Ling Shih

Hsi Wang Mu

Hua-Henga. **Taranga.**

Huaxu

Huitaca

Huixtocihuatl

Huldra

Huligamma. Obscure Indian goddess with transvestite priests.

Hulla. Daughter of Wurusemu.

Hulluk Miyumko

Hun-Ahpu-Mtye

H'Uraru. **Atira.**

Husbishag

Hu-Tu

Hybla

Hydra

Hypermnestra

Hypsipyle. Queen of Lemnos; *see Lemna.*

Hyrrokin

I

Ia

Iahu Anat

Iaine. **Ain.**

Iambe

Ianthe. *See Iphis.*

Iarnsaxa. A **Wave Maiden.**

Iarnvithja. Scandinavian troll wives.

Iaso. Greek goddess of healing, sister of Hygia.

Ibu Pertiwi

Icovellauna. Continental Celtic water goddess.

Ida

Idaean Mother. **Ida.**

Idem-Huva

Idisi. German **Valkyries.**

Idothea

Idunn

Idya. **Oceanid**, mother of Medea.

Iella. **Atabei.**

Igirit. **Agrat Bat Mahalat.**

Iha-Naga. *See Kono-Hana-Sakuya-Hime.*

Ikutamayorihime

Ila

Ilamatecuhtli. **Tonan.**

Ilankaka

Ilia. **Rhea Silvia.**

Ilithyia. **Eileithyia.**

Ilma(ter). Finno-Ugric sky goddess.

Imberombera. **Waramu-rungundji.**

Imbrasia. **Hera**, of Imbrastus River, beside which she was born.

Imd. Scandinavian water goddess, daughter of Ran.

Impae. Daughter of Gula.

Ina. **Hina.**

Inaba. Japanese heroine, story similar to Andromena.

Inada Dao. Indonesian primal mother.

Inanna

Inara. **Inaras.**

Inaras

Inari

Inaruchaba

Indara

India Rosa

Inferna. **Proserpina** as goddess of underworld; also **Juno.**

Inga Woman

Ingebjord. **Ingebord.**

Ingebord

Inghean Bhuidhe

Inkanyamba. Zulu goddess of waters, hail and storm.

Innini. **Inanna.**

Ino

Intercidona

Interduca. **Juno**, invoked by newly married couples.

Invidia

Io

Iord. *See Hertha, Jord.*

Ipa Huaco. *See Mama Ocllo.*

Iphianassa. **Iphigeneia.**

Iphigenia

Iphis

Irdlirvirisissong

Irene

Iris

Irkalla. **Eriskegal.**

Irnini

Iro Duget. Melanesian death queen.

Irpa. *See Thorgerd.*

Iscah. **Sarah.**

Iseult

Ishah. **Eve.**

Ishara

Ishikore-Dome

Ishtar

Isis

Ismene

Isolde. **Iseult.**

Isong

Istar(u). **Ishtar.**

Istehar

Istustaya. Hittite spinning fate goddess.

Ite. *See Hanwi.*

Itiba Tahuvava

I-toeram-bola-totsy

Ituana

Itugen. **Etugen.**

Itzpapalotl

Iunones. "Protectors of women," continental Celtic **Matronae.**

Ivithja. Scandinavian female forest monster.

Iwa-Naga-Hime. Japanese rock goddess, sister of Kono-Hana-Sakuya-Hime.

Ix Chebel Yax. **Ix Chel.**

Ix Chel

Ixtab. Mayan goddess, cared for souls of suicides.

Iyalode. "She who leads all the town's women," **Oshun.**

Iynx. *See Echo.*

Izanami

Iztaccihuatl. Central Mexican volcano goddess.

Izushio-Tome. "Grace maiden," Japanese folklore heroine.

J

Ja-Neba

Jadi. **Jaki.**

Jaki

Jana. **Diana.**

Janguli

Jangulitara. **Janguli.**

Jata

Jeh

Jezanna. *See Notambu.*

Jezebel

Jezenky

Jiandi

Jiangyuan

Jil(l)ian. **Gillian.**

Jingo

Jiuzi mu. Chinese **Hariti.**

Jocasta

Jocebed

Jord

Judith

Judy. **Vila.**

Juga(lis). **Juno** as goddess of marriage.

Jugumishanta

Juks-Akka

Julian. **Gillian.**

Julunggul

Jumala

Juni-Sama

Juni-sama. **Yama no Kami.**

Junkgowa

Juno

Juras Mate

Jurate

Jurt-Azer-Ava. *See Azer-Ava.*

Jusas. **Saosis.**

Juturna

Juventas

Jyestha. "The elder," **Devi** or **Kali.**

K

Ka Ahu Pahau

Kachina

Kadesh. **Qadesh.**

Kadi

Kadlu

Kadru

Kaguya-Hima. "Brilliant lady," Japanese mirror goddess.

Kaikara

Kait. Hittite grain goddess.

Kakia

Kala-Pidari. **Pidari.**

Kalas-Ava. *See Azer-Ava.*

Kali

Kalika. **Kali.**

Kalisha

Kalliste. **Callisto.**

Kalma. "Corpse odor," Finnish death goddess.

Kalwadi

Kamadhenu

Kamaduh. **Kamadhenu.**

Kamala. **Lakshmi.**

Kami Naru. **Naru-Kami.**

Kamilla. **Camilla.**

Kamrusepas

Kamui Fuchi

Kamui Katkimat. **Nish-Kan-Ru Mat.**

Ka Nam

Kandi. **Durga.**

Kandiu. Great mother of Sri Lanka.

Kandra. **Durga.**

Kanene Ski Amai Yehi

Kannagi

Kantarupi

Kanuga

Kapila. "Red one," **Kamadhenu.**

Kapo. Hawaiian midwife goddess of childbirth and abortions.

Kapruk-arasi. **Kannagi.**

Kara

Karaikkal-Asmmaiyar

Kara-Kura

Kara. **Valkyrie.**

Kardas-Jurt-Ava. *See Azer-Ava.*

Karpophoros. **Lady of the Beasts.**

Kasum-Naj-Ekva

Katau Kumei. "Queen of women," Cambodian earth goddess.

Kathirat

Kauket. *See Ogdoad.*

Kaumaii. **Shakti.**

Kausiki. "Sheathed one," shadow-side of **Parvati.**

Kausiki. **Durga.**

Kaya-Nu-Hima. Japanese goddess of herbs.

Keca Aba

Ker

Keres. *See Ker.*

Kerres. Early Italian **Ceres.**

Kesara. **Cessair.**

Ketche Avalon. **Keca Aba.**

Kethlenda. **Cethlion.**

Ketq Skwayne. *See Ataensic.*

Khala Kumari. Water goddess of Bengal.

Khebe. **Kubaba.**

Khegirnunna. Daughter of Gula.

Kheshagga. Daughter of Gula.

Khipa. **Kubaba.**

Khon-Ma

Ki

Kichijoten. *See Vasudhara.*

Kidaria. **Demeter.**

Kijoten. Japanese for **Lakshmi.**

Kikimora

Kilili

Kimpa Vita

Kinnari

Kipu-Tytoo. *See Tuonetar.*

Kiri Amma

Kirisha. **Ki.**

Kirke. **Circe.**

Kishar. **Ki.**

Kishimogin

Kiwakweskwa

Kla

Klah Klahnee. *See Pahto.*

Kleio. One of **Muses.**

Klete. One of **Graces.**

Kling

Klotho. One of **Moirae.**

Klu-mo

Klu-rgyal-mo srid-pa gtan-la phab-pa. **Klu-mo.**

Kn Sgni

Ko

Koevasi

Kokyangwu(h)ti. Hopi **Spider Woman.**

Koliada. Colleda.

Kongsim

Kono-Hana-Sakuya-Hime

Kore

Korina. *See Noika.*

Kornjunfer. Germanic corn goddess.

Korobona

Korobonako. **Korobona.**

Korrigan

Korythalia. **Artemis** at Sparta.

Kostrubonko

Kotta-Kiriya. **Kottavi.**

Kottavi

Kottutto. **Cotys.**

Kotus. **Cotys.**

Kotyto. **Cotys.**

Kou-Njami

Krimba. Slavic house goddess.

Kualchink. Tree goddess of Tierra del Fuego.

Kuan-Yin

Kubaba

Kubabat/s. **Kubaba.**

Kubele. **Cybele.**

Kud-Azer-Ava. *See Azer-Ava.*

Kuma

Kumari. **Shakti.**

Kunapipi

Kunti

Kupala. **Kupalo.**

Kupalo

Kupapa. **Kubaba.**

Kurukulla. Tibetan **Kali.**

Kururumany. **Korobona.**

Kusumamodini. Mountain goddess of Himalayas.

Kutuga. *See Poza-Mama.*

Kuwanlelenta

KuzunoHa. Japanese fox goddess.

Kveldrida. "Nightrider," Scandinavian witch name.

Kwannon. **Kuan-Yin.**

Kweetoo. *See Kadlu.*

Kyn-Fylgja. **Fylgja.**

Kyz Ana. *See Poza-Mama.*

L

La Balianne. **Ymoja.**

Labama. *See Nchienge.*

Lachesis. *See Moirae.*

Lacinia. **Juno.**

Lada

Lady Godiva. **Godiva.**

Lady of the Beasts

Lady of the Lake. **Nimue.**

Laetitia. Roman goddess of unfounded joy; *see Fama.*

Lahar. Babylonian goddess of sheep and flocks.

La'ila'i

Laima

Laima-Dalia. **Laima.**

Laime. **Laima.**

Lair Derg. **Aine.**

Laka

Lakhamu. **Lamamu.**

Lakshmi

Laksmi. **Lakshmi.**

Lalal. Etruscan moon goddess.

Lalita. **Lolita.**

Lamamu

Lamasthu

Lamethusa. One of **Heliades.**

Lamia

Lampetia

Lan Tstai-Ho

Laosoos. "Rouser of Nations," usually **Athena,** sometimes **Eris.**

Lara

La Reine Pedaque

Larentia. **Lara.**

Larissa

Lasa

Lat. **Al-Lat.**

Latiaran

Latis. Ancient water goddess of Celtic Britain.

Lativrena. **Laverna.**

Latona

Laugo-Edne. Saami laundry goddess.

Laukamat. Latvian mother of fields.

Lauma. **Laume.**

Laume

Lavercam

Laverna. Roman goddess of thieves and impostors.

Leah

Leanan Sidhe

Leda

Leelinau

Le-Hev-Hev

Lemkechen

Lemna

Lenae. **Maenads.**

Lernaea. **Demeter** at Lerna.

Lethe

Leto

Leucippe

Leucosia. One of **Sirens.**

Leucothea. **Ino.**

Levana

Leviathan

Lha-mo. **Lla-mo.**

Lhianna Shee. **Leanan Sidhe.**

Li Chi

Lia

Liban

Libentina. **Venus** as goddess of sex.

Libera

Liberalitas. Roman goddess of generosity.

Libertas

Libitina

Licho. Slavic **Dolya.**

Lieu Hahn

Liganakdikei. **Lignaco-Dex.**

Ligeia. "Shrill-sounding," one of **Sirens.**

Lignaco-Dex

Ligoapup

Ligoband. Carolina Island goddess similar to Lorop.

Ligoububfanu. *See Ligoapup.*

Likko. Slavic **Dolya.**

Lilith

Lilwani

Lilwanis. **Lilwani.**

Lim(enti)a. Roman goddess who protects threshold.

Limnades

Limoniades. **Limnades.**

Liomarar. Creator goddess of Yap Island; *see Lorop.*

Litae

Litai. **Litae.**

Ljod. A **Valkyrie.**

Lla-Mo

Lo Shen. Chinese goddess of rivers.

Locha. *See Maeve.*

Locia Amai. **Tu-Njami.**

Loddis-Edne

Lofn

Logia. Goddess of Lagan River in Ireland.

Lohasur Devi. Goddess of iron forgers in India.

Lolita

Lona. *See Mele.*

Loo-Wit

Lopamudra

Lopemat. Latvian mother of cattle.

Lorelei

Lorop

Losna. **Lalal.**

Lotis

Louhi

Louisa. "Kindly" **Demeter.**

Loviatar. *See Tuonetar.*

Lua

Lua Mater. **Lua.**

Luaths Lurgann

Luatia. **Juno.**

Lubenti(n)a. **Venus** as goddess of sex.

Luchuch. Obscure Etruscan goddess.

Lucina

Lucitia. **Juno.**

Lucna. Etruscan moon goddess.

Lueji

Luideag. **Cailleach.**

Luisa. "Kindly" **Demeter.**

Luminu-Ut

Luna. Minor Roman moon goddess.

Lung Nu. *See Kuan-Yin.*

Luonnotar

Luot Chozjik. *See Luot-Hozjit.*

Luot-Hozjit

Lupa

Luperca. **Lupa.**

Lyceia. "Wolfish" **Artemis.**

Lygodesma. **Artemis** in Sparta.

Lysippe

Lyssa

M

Ma. **Mami.**

Maa-Ema. **Ma-Emma.**

Maan-Eno. **Rauni.**

Maat

Mabb

Macaria

Macha

Macris

Madalait. *See Walo.*

Madam Pele. **Pele.**

Madame St. Urzulie. Voudoun *loa* of nocturnal emissions.

Madder-Akka

Mae d'agua. **Ymoja.**

Ma-Emma

Maenads

Maeve

Mafdet

Maga. Mother of Dechtere.

Magna Mater. "Great Mother," Roman name for **Cybele.**

Mah. **Mami.**

Mahakala. **Kali** in Tibet

Mahakh. Aleut dog goddess.

Mahalat

Mahalbiya

Mahaliah. **Mahalat.**

Mahamaya. **Maya.**

Mahr. **Mora.**

Mahuea. **MahuiIki.**

Mahui(ka). **Mahui-Iki.**

MahuiIki

Maia

Maitreya

Majesta. **Maia.**

Makhut. **Matronit.**

Makore-Wawahiwa. "Fiery-eyed canoe breaker," one of Pele's sisters.

Ma-Ku. Chinese maiden goddess of springtime.

Mal

Mala Liath

Mala Lucina. "Evil **Lucina,**" **Juno** as "evil midwife."

Malavis. Obscure Etruscan goddess.

Malha. **Rangada.**

Mali'O. Hawaiian goddess of music.

Malihini. *See Pele.*

Malika Habashiya

Malina. **Akycha.**

Maliya. Anatolian goddess like Athena.

Malophoros. Greek underworld goddess.

Mama

Mama Allpa. Peruvian mother goddess of harvest.

Mama Cocha

Mama Coya. *See Mama Ocllo.*

Mama Cuna. Chief vestal of Accla.

Mama Huaco. *See Mama Ocllo.*

Mama Ocllo

Mama Quilla

Mama Rahua. *See Mama Ocllo.*

Mama. **Mami.**

Maman Brigitte

Mamapacha

Mamazara. **Zaramama.**

Mami

Mamitu

Mami Wata. **Ymoja** as "Mother Water."

Mamlambo. Zulu river mother.

Mana Geneta. **Mana.**

Mana. Roman birth goddess.

Manasa. Snake goddess of Bengal who inspires women.

Manat. **Menat.**

Maneca

Mania

Maniae. "Madnesses," **Erinyes.**

Manto

Mar. **Mari-Ama.**

Mara. **Mora.**

Marahi Devi. *See Sitala.*

Marai Mata. **Sitala.**

Marcassa

Marcia. Ancient Italian agricultural goddess.

Marcia Proba

Mardeq Avalon

Mardol. "Light on the sea," **Freya.**

Marena. **Marzana.**

Marga/o. Mother of Etain.

Maria

Mari-Ama

Marici

Mari Llweyd. Welsh midwinter goddess, depicted as horse.

Marinette

Marpe. Amazon warrior.

Marpesia

Marpessa

Martialis. "Warlike" Juno.

Maruwa

Marwe. **Maruwa.**

Mary

Mary Lucifer. "Mary Light-Giver," **Mary Magdalene.**

Mary Magdalene

Marzana

Masaya

Mastor-Ava. *See Azer-Ava.*

Mat' Xyra Zemlia. **Mokosh.**

Matariki. **Maori Pleiades.**

Mater Larum. **Lara.**

Mater Matuta

Mater Turritia. Roman name for **Cybele.**

Matergabiae

Mati

Matka Boska. **Black Madonna.**

Matres Coccaae. British "red-mothers," Celtic cosmic goddesses.

Matres Domesticae. Britain Celtic earth goddesses.

Matres Glanicae. Continental Celtic mother goddessess from Provence.

Matronae Aufaniae. Celtic earth goddesses of Bonn, Germany.

Matronae Gabiae. Continental Celtic mother goddesses.

Matronae. **Deae Matres.**

Matronis Assingenehis. Celtic earth goddesses of Rhine valley.

Matronis Mahlinehis. Celtic earth goddesses of Rhine valley.

Matronit

Matronita. **Matronit.**

Ma Tsu-Po. Chinese water goddess.

Matushka Krasnogo Solntsna. **Solntsna.**

Matuta. Mater Matuta.

Mauitikitiki-a-Taranga. **Taranga.**

Maut. **Mut.**

Mawu

Maya

Mayahuel

Maya Owichapaha

Mayi-Mayi. Australian star goddesses.

Mbaba Mwana Waresa

Mbombe

Mean. Obscure Etruscan goddess.

Meave. **Maeve.**

Mebhdh. **Maeve.**

Mechanatis/Mechanites. "Inventor," **Athena** as mechanic; **Aphrodite** as deviser of love messages.

Medb. **Maeve.**

Medea

Meditrina. Roman goddess of medicine.

Medusa

Megaera

Megaira. **Megaera.**

Mehit. Lion-headed Egyptian goddess.

Mehitabel. Cabbalistic goddess, mother of Lilith the younger.

Mehurt

Mei Chou. *See Tien-Hou.*

Meilichia. Obscure Greek underworld goddess.

Melanie

Melanippe

Mele

Melete. One of **Muses.**

Meliae

Meliot. *See Melusine.*

Melissa

Mella

Mellon(i)a/s. Roman goddess of bees.

Melpomene. One of **Muses**.

Melusine

Mem Loimis

Menalippe

Menat

Mene. **Selene**.

Menerva. **Minerva**.

Meng-Jiang Jyu

Menglod

Mengloth. **Menglod**.

Meng-Po Niang-Niang

Mengi/a. *See Fengi*.

Menrva. Etruscan **Minerva**.

Mens

Mentha

Menya. *See Fengi*.

Mera

Mere-Ama

Meri. **Isis** as sea goddess; also **Hathor**.

Meroe

Merope

Merseger. **Mertseger**.

Mertseger

Meskhent. **Meskhoni**.

Meskhoni

Messia. Roman goddess of agriculture.

Mestra. **Meta**.

Meta

Metanira. *See Demeter*.

Meter

Methe. Greek goddess of drunkenness, a **Maenad**.

Metis

Metlitodes. "Sweet as honey," **Persephone** in hell.

Metsannetsyt

Metsarhatija. Finnish forest goddess.

Metz. Celtic water goddess found at Trier, Germany.

Metzli. Aztec moon goddess.

Mezamat. Latvian forest-mother.

Miao Shan. **Kuan-Yin**.

Mictecacihuatl

Mielikki

Mife. Goddess of Luo River in China.

Milda

Minachiamman

Mindhal

Mindhal Devi. **Mindhal**.

Minerva

Minerva Medica

Minithya. **Thalestris**.

Min Mahagiri

Minthe. **Mentha**.

Minu Anni. Assyrian fate goddess.

Minu Ulla. Assyrian fate goddess.

Miralaidji. *See Djang-gawul Sisters*.

Miriam

Miru

Misere

Mist. "Mist," **Valkyrie**.

Mitra

Mitylena/e. **Myrine**.

Mnasa

Mneme. One of **Muses**.

Mnemosyne

Modgud

Modjadji. **Mujaji**.

Modron. British name for **Matrona**.

Moira. **Moirae**.

Moirae

Mokosh

Mokuskha. Multiple **Mokosh**.

Momona. **Atabei**.

Momu. Scottish goddess of wells and hills.

Moncha. Irish Druid priestess.

Moneta. **Juno**.

Monje

Mor-Ava. *See Azer-Ava*.

Mora

Morana. **Marzana**.

Morgain. **Morgan Le Fay**.

Morgan La Fay. **Morgan Le Fay**.

Morgan Le Fay

Morgay. North English harvest goddess.

Moriath

Moriath Morca. **Moriath**.

Mormo. Greek female boogie like Lamia.

Morrigan

Morrigu. **Morrigan**.

Mortlock. *See Lorop*.

Moruach. **Moruadh**.

Moruadh

Mother Friday

Mother Ndundu. **Ngwa Ndundu**.

Mother Trudy. Germanic **Baba Yaga**.

Mothir. *See Edda*.

Motsesa

Mou-Njami

Mousae. **Muses**.

Mousso Coronie. **Muso Koroni**.

Moye

Mu'Allidtu. **Mylitta**.

Muhongo

Muilearthach. **Muireartach**.

Muime Chriosda. "Foster mother of Christ," Christianized **Brigid**.

Muireartach

Muiriath. **Moriath**.

Mujaji

Mujingga. **Kalwadi**.

Muk Jauk. "Black lady," Cambodian earth goddess.

Mulhalmoni

Mulindwa. Ugandan warrior goddess.

Mulitta. **Mylitta**.

Mulua Dapie Bulane. Indonesian moon goddess.

Mulua Hainuwele. **Hainuwele**.

Mulua Satene. **Satene**.

Mummu Tiamat. **Tiamat**.

Mumuna. *See Kunapipi*.

Munanna

Munthuch. Obscure Etruscan goddess.

Mu Olokukurtilisop

Muriranga-whenau. Maori goddess of wisdom.

Muses

Muso Koroni

Mut

Muta. **Lara**.

Mutyalamma. Pearl goddess of eastern India.

Muzita

Muzulla. *See Wurusemu*.

Muzzu-Kummik-Quae

Mwatikitiki. **Taranga**.

Myesyats. Slavic moon goddess.

Mylitta

Myrine

Myrkrida. "Darkrider," Scandinavian witch.

Myrmex

Myrmix. **Myrmex**.

Myrrha

N

Naamah

Na Bo Nok'o. Sky goddess of Chinese Ch'uan Miao.

Naenia. Roman goddess of funerals.

Nagar-Saga "Framer of fetus," **Mami**.

Nahab. Snake-headed Egyptian goddess.

Nahkeeta

Naiads

Naila. "The Blue," Arabian goddess, perhaps the sky.

Naina Devi

Nair. **Nar.**

Nakineitsi. Finnish and Estonian water goddess.

Namaka. *See Pele.*

Nambi

Nambubi

Nammu

Nam-Sa Kui. **No-Il Ja-Dae.**

Nana

Nana Buluku

Nana e votres. Albanian hearth goddess.

Nana. **Inanna.**

Naneae. **Anaitis.**

Nanshe

Naotsiti. *See Utset.*

Nar

Nar-Azer-Ava. *See Azer-Ava.*

Narucnici. Bulgarian **Sudice.**

Naru-Kami

Nasa. Persian fly-dragon goddess.

Nascio. Roman birth goddess.

Nata. **Nana.**

Natal. *See Nana.*

Natalis. **Juno.**

Natosuelta

Naunet. *See Ogdoad.*

Nausicaa

Navky

Nawangwulan

Nchienge

Ndundu. **Ngwa Ndundu.**

Neal. *See Niamh.*

Neb-Ti. "Two-mistresses," **Uadgit and Nekhebet.**

Nebaunaubaequae. Ojibway mermaid.

Nebthet. **Nephthys.**

Necessitas. Roman goddess of destiny; mother of Fates.

Nedolya. *See Dolya.*

Neeve. *Niamh.*

Nehalennia

Neith

Nekhebet

Nemain

Neman. **Nemain.**

Nemausicae. Continental Celtic spring goddess.

Nemesis

Nemetona

Nemon. **Nemain.**

Nenakatu

Nephele

Nephthys

Neptunis. **Artemis.**

Nereids

Nerio. "Valor," Roman war goddess.

Nerrivik. **Sedna.**

Nerthus

Nesreca. *See Sreca.*

Nessa

Net. **Neith.**

Nevinbimbsau. Melanesian goddess of initiation.

Ngolimento

Ngwa Ndundu

Niamh

Niang-Niang Sung-Tzu. **Pi-Hsia Yuan-Chin.**

Nicnevin. "Bone mother," Scottish **Cailleach.**

Nicostrata. *See Carmenta.*

Nidra

Nike

Nikkal. **Ningal.**

Nimue

Nina. **Nana.**

Ninazu. **Eriskegal.**

Nindum. "Lady of procreation," **Mami.**

Nin-Edin. **Belit-Seri.**

Ningal

Ningul. **Ningal.**

Ningyo

Ninhurra. *See Ninhursag.*

Ninhursag

Nin-Si-Anna. "Lady eye of heaven," **Ishtar.**

Nini. **Inanna.**

Niniganni

Ninkasi. "Lady horn face," Sumerian beer/wine goddess, merged with Ishtar.

Ninkharak. "Lady of the mountain," healing dog goddess merged with Ishtar.

Ninkhursag. **Ninhursag.**

Ninkigal. "Lady of dead land," **Eriskegal.**

Ninkkarsagga. **Ninhursag.**

Ninkurra. **Ninhurra.**

Ninlil

Ninmah. "Lady Mother," Sumerian **Mami.**

Ninmu. *See Ninhursag.*

Ninsar. *See Ninhursag.*

Ninsikilla. "Pure queen," **Mami.**

Ninti. *See Ninhursag.*

Nintu. **Nintur.**

Nintur. "Lady of the womb," or "Lady life-giver," birth goddess merged with Ishtar.

Niobe

Nirdu. **Hertha.**

Nirriti

Nisaba

Nish-Kan-Ru Mat. Ainu sky goddess worshiped at Festival of Falling Tears.

Niski-Ava. *See Azer-Ava.*

Nitya. "Eternal woman," **Manasa.**

Nixies

No-Il Ja-Dae

Noika

Nokomis

N'okomiss. **Nokomis.**

Nomia

Nomoi. *See Lorop.*

Nona. Roman goddesses of second-to-last month of fetal gestation.

Noogumee. Whale mother of Canadian Micmac.

Norns

Norov-Ava. *See Azer-Ava.*

Nortia

Norwan

Notambu

Nott

Nowutset. *See Utset.*

Nox. **Nyx.**

Nsomeka

Nsongo

Nuala. **Fionnuala.**

Nu Gua. **Nu Kua.**

Nu Kua

Nuliajuk. **Nuliayoq.**

Nuliayoq

Numma Moiyuk

Nunnehi

Nun of Beare. **Cailleach.**

Nut

Nuwa. **Nu Kua.**

Nuxiu

Nyadeang

Nyamitondo

Nyamwanda

Nyapilnu

Nyavirezi

Nyi Pohaci

Nyina Mweru

Nymphenomene. "Seeking a mate," Hera's second stage.

Nyx

Oanuava. Celtic earth goddess worshiped in France.

Oba

Oba Do. Mother of Oshun.

Obasi Nsi. **Isong.**

Obatallah

Oceanids

Ochumare

Ocrisia

Ocypete. "Swift," a **harpy.**

Ocyrrhoe. **Menalippe.**

Oddibjord

Oddudua

Odras

Oeno

Oettar-Fylgja. **Fylgja.**

Ogdoad

Ohoyo Osh Chishba

Oiorpata. "Men-Killers," Scythian word for **Amazons.**

Olla. **Oya.**

Olosa. Santeria crocodile goddess who assists fisherfolk.

Olrun. "Rune-reader," a **Valkyrie.**

Olwen

Oma. **Bona Dea.**

Omamama

Omecihuatl

Omphale

Onatah. Daughter of Nokomis.

Onaugh. **Oona.**

Onc/ga. **Athena** as oracular goddess.

Oniata

Oona

Ootonobeno-Kami

Opet. **Tauret.**

Ophthalmitis. **Athena** as goddess of good eyesight.

Ops

Orbona

Oreads

Oreithyia

Orore

Orsel. **Ursula.**

Orthia

Orthosia. **Artemis.**

O-Ryu. Japanese willow-tree goddess.

Oshun

Os Keca Aba. **Keca Aba.**

Ossa. Greek **Fama.**

Ossipago. **Juno,** as strengthener of infants' bones.

Ostara

Osun. **Oshun.**

Ot Ana. *See Poza-Mama.*

Otiona

Oto-Hime

Otrera. **Otrere.**

Otrere

Otsuved-Azer-Ava. *See Azer-Ava.*

Otuz Pastu Ot Ana. *See Poza-Mama.*

Ovda

Oya

P

Pa. Chinese goddess of droughts.

Pachamama. **Mama-pacha.**

Padma. **Lakshmi.**

Padrita. Lycian **Aphrodite.**

Paeonia. "Healer," **Athena** as serpent goddess.

Pahto

Pais. "Girl," **Persephone,** also **Hera.**

Paivatar

Paive. Norwegian **Saami Beiwe.**

Pajau Tan. *See Po Ino Nogar.*

Paks-Ava. *See Azer-Ava.*

Palagia. "Sea," **Aphrodite.**

Palden Lhamo. **Lla-mo.**

Pales

Pali Kongju

Pallas

Pallor. Roman goddess of fear.

Pamphile

Panace(i)a. "All-healing," Greek and Roman goddess of healing.

Pandemos. **Aphrodite** of the commoners.

Pandia

Pandora

Pandrosos. *See Augralids.*

Panes. Bird goddess of Acagchemen of California.

Pani

Panope. **Panopea.**

Panopea. Nereid invoked by storm-tossed sailors.

Pantariste

Papa

Papalluga

Papatuanuku. **Maori Papa.**

Papaya. *See Istustaya.*

Paphia. **Paphos.**

Paphos

Parca. Roman **Fate** or **Moira.**

Pare

Parewhenua-Mea. Maori multiple rain goddesses.

Parooa

Parthenia. "Virgin," **Athena** or **Hera.**

Parthenope. One of **Sirens.**

Partula. Roman goddess of parturition.

Parvati

Pasht. **Bast.**

Pasikrateia. **Persephone** or **Artemis.**

Pasiphae

Pasithea. A **Nereid**; also one of **Graces.**

Patell(an)a. Roman agricultural divinity.

Pattini

Pavor. Roman goddess of fear.

Pawosee

Pax. **Concordia.**

Pedrite. Lycian **Aphrodite.**

Peisinoe. One of **Sirens.**

Pele

Pemphredo. One of **Graeae.**

Penelope

Penia. *See Pitho.*

Penthesilea

Pepromene. Greek goddess of individual destiny.

Perasia. Cappadocian goddess served by priestesses who walked through fire.

Percht. **Perchta.**

Perchta

Perkuna Tete

Pero

Perone. **Pero.**

Perrephatta. **Persephone.**

Perse

Persea/Perseis. **Perse.**

Persephone

Persipnei. Etruscan **Persephone.**

Per Uadjit. **Uadgit.**

Pessinuntica. Ancient Phyrgian mother goddess.

Phaea. Greek monster-sow goddess.

Phaedra

Phaenna. One of **Graces.**

Pharmacides. Theban sorcerer goddess with great skill in drugs.

Phatusa. One of **Heliades.**

Pheme. **Fama.**

Pheraia. Thessalian ancestral moon goddess.

Pherenice

Philemon

Philia. Greek goddess of friendship; also **Aphrodite**.

Phillippis. An **Amazon**.

Philomela. **Philomena**.

Philomena

Phlea. "Fruitful," **Demeter**.

Phoebad. Delphic priestess; used of any Greek prophetic woman.

Phoebas. **Phoebad**.

Phoebe. **Selene**.

Phosphoros. "Lightbringer," **Artemis** as birth goddess, **Eos** as dawn, **Hecate** as torch bearer.

Phratria. "Lawgiver," **Athena**.

Phyllis

Phyrne. "Toad," **Hecate**.

Phytia. "Creator," **Leto** in Crete, who protects threatened children.

Pidari

Pietas

Pi-Hsia Yuan-Chin

Pinga. **Sedna**.

Pitali. **Pidari**.

Pitho

Pitys

Plash-Plash. *See Pahto*.

Plataia. **Hera** as woman seeking a mate.

Pleiades

Plutos. "Richness," **Persephone**.

Po Bya Tikuh. *See Po Ino Nogar*.

Podarge. One of **Harpies**.

Pohaha

Pohjan-Akka

Poine. Greek attendant of Nemesis; Roman goddess of righteous punishment.

Po Ino Nogar

Pok Klai. Agricultural goddess of upper Burma.

Poldare. One of **Harpies**.

Poldunica

Poli-ahu. Hawaiian goddess of storm and of Manua-Kea.

Polias. "Guardian of the City," **Athena** at Athens.

Polycaste

Polydama. **Polydamna**.

Polydamna

Poly(hy)mnia. One of **Muses**.

Pomona

Pontia. **Aphrodite**.

Populonia. **Juno**.

Porne. "Titillator," **Aphrodite**.

Porrima. *See Antevorta*.

Port-Kuva

Poshjo-Akka

Posidaeia. *See Mnasa*.

Postverta. **Postvorta**.

Postvorta

Potina. Roman goddess of weaving and drinking.

Potnia. "Lady," goddess title in Crete. *See Mnasa*.

Potniae. "Awful ones," **Erinyes**.

Po Yan Dari. *See Po Ino Nogar*.

Poza-Mama

Prajna. "Wisdom," **Sarasvati**.

Prajnaparamita

Prakriti

Prakrti. **Prakriti**.

Prascovia. **Mother Friday**.

Praxidic(a)e. *See Persephone*.

Praxidikae. "Vengeful ones," **Erinyes**.

Praxidike

Primigenia. "Firstborn," **Fortuna**.

Pritha. **Prithivi**.

Prithivi

Procne. *See Philomena*.

Procris

Progne. *See Philomena*.

Promachos. "Champion," **Athena**.

Promoakkos. "Forefighter," **Athena**.

Pronoea. "Forethought," **Athena**.

Pronuba. **Juno**.

Prorsa. **Antevorta**.

Proserpina

Proserpina/e. Roman **Persephone**.

Protagenia

Prothoe. Famous Amazon warrior.

Prothyraea. **Giane**.

Providentia. "Forethought," Roman goddess.

Prthivi. **Prithivi**.

Psi-Hsia-Yuan Chun. **Pi-Hsia Yuan-Chin**.

Psyche

Psylla. "Springer," Greek divine mare.

Ptesan-Wi. Brule **White Buffalo Woman**.

Ptrotka. Name for **Lilith** as "winged creature."

Pudicitia

Pukimna. Igulik (Eskimo) protector of land animals.

Purich. Obscure Etruscan goddess.

Puta. Roman goddess of tree-pruning.

Pyatnitsa. **Mother Friday**.

Pyrrha

Pythia

Python

Q

Qadesh

Qamaits

Qatun. **Umaj**.

Qebhsnuf

Qocha Mana. Hopi "white corn maiden."

Querquetulanae Virae. Roman green-oak nymphs with prophetic powers.

Ques

Queskapenek

Quetzapetlatl. Incestuous twin sister of Mexican god Quetzacoatl.

R

Rabie

Rachel

Radha

Radien-Akka

Radien-Kiedde

Rafu-Sen

Rakshasi. Indian female demon.

Rambha. Seductive Indian female demi-goddess.

Ramitovi-aman-dreniny

Ran

Rana Neida

Ranaghanti

Rangada

Rangada Malha. **Rangada**.

Rangda

Rangild. "Shield-Bearer," a **Valkyrie**.

Ranoro

Ranu Bai

Rapunzel

Rat. "Female sun," **Bast**.

Rata. *See Laka*.

Rathgild. "Plan-Destroyer," a **Valkyrie**.

Rati

Ratis. British Celtic fortress goddess.

Ratu Kidul

Rauni

Raura. "Fierce" **Durga.**

Rav-Ava. *See Azer-Ava.*

Ravdna. **Rauni.**

Raz-Akka. *See Madder-Akka.*

Re. **Ri.**

Rebecca

Rebekah. **Rebecca.**

Regina. "Queen" **Juno.**

Reginleif. "Companion of Gods," a **Valkyrie.**

Renenet

Renpet

Renph. **Renpet.**

Rescial. Obscure Etruscan goddess.

Rhamnub(s)ia. **Nemesis** in Africa.

Rhea

Rhea Silvia

Rheda

Rhiannon

Rhode

Rhodos. **Rhode.**

Rhpisunt

Ri

Rigatona. **Rhiannon.**

Rind

Rinda. **Rind.**

Risem-Edne. "Twig Mother" of Norwegian Saami.

Ritona. Continental Celtic goddess from Trier, Germany.

rNam-rgyal. Tibetan serpent goddess.

Rodienitsa. Croatian singular **Rozenicy.**

Rohini

Rona

Roonikka. **Rauni.**

Roro Kidul. **Ratu Kidul.**

Rosamond. British figure associated with bowers and mazes; *see Gillian.*

Rosmerta

Rota. A **Valkyrie.**

Royot

Rozanica. *See Rozanicy.*

Rozanicy

Rucina. **Ops** as promoter of harvest.

Rudabeh

Rudrani. Indian goddess of storms who spreads disease and death.

Rugiu Boba

Rukko

Rumina

Rumor

Rusa. **Al-Lat.**

Rusalki

Rusalky. **Rusalki.**

Ryuhwa

S

Saar. **Saba.**

Saba

Sabala. **Kamadhenu.**

Sabia. **Saba.**

Sabitu. **Siduri.**

Sabrina. Goddess of Severn River; *see Sequana.*

Sabulana

Sadarnuna. Sumerian goddess of new moon.

Sadsta-Akka. **Sar-Akka.**

Sael. **Sele.**

Saga

Saibya

Sakambhari. **Devi**, or **Durga**, as mother goddess.

Sakhmis. Greek for **Sekhmet.**

Sakkala-Khatum. Drunken Mongolian fire goddess.

Sal(ly). **Sele.**

Sala. Babylonian light goddess.

Salacia

Salmaris

Salpinx. "Trumpet," **Athena.**

Salus. Roman goddess of health.

Samdzimari

Samjna. **Samjuna.**

Samjuna

Sammuramat. **Semiramis.**

Samovila. **Vila.**

Samsin Halmoni

Samundra. Indian goddess of rivers.

Sangarius. **Nata.**

Sanghyang Sri. *See Nyi Pohaci.*

Sangiang Serri. Rice goddess of Celebes, Indonesia.

Saning Sri. Javanese rice goddess.

Saosis

Sao-Ts'ing Niang

Sapta Matrika. "Seven Divine Mothers." **Matrika.**

Sarah

Sarai. **Sarah.**

Sar-Akka

Saramama. **Zaramama.**

Saranya. **Samjuna.**

Sarasvati

Sarbanda

Sar-Edne. **Sar-Akka.**

Saris. Ancient goddess of Armenia, merged with Semiramis.

Sarna Burhi. Tree goddess in Bengal.

Sarvari. Indian water goddess.

Sasti. "Goddess of the sixth," birth goddess form of **Durga.**

Sasura. **Mami** as protector of fetus.

Sata-Rupa. **Savitri.**

Satet. **Sati.**

Sati

Satine

Satis. **Sati.**

Saturnia. **Juno.**

Saule

Saules Meita

Saulite Mat. **Saule.**

Saulite Sudrabota. **Saule.**

Savitri

Sayo-Hime

Scathach

Schwarzen Mutter-Gottes. **Black Madonna.**

Scota

Scylla

Seal(e). **Sele.**

Sedna

Seena. **Sinann.**

Seewa. **Mother Friday.**

Segetia. Roman goddess of sprouting seeds.

Sehmet. **Sekhmet.**

Seia. Roman goddess of seeds beneath the earth.

Seille. **Sele.**

Seimia. "Star of Babylon," city goddess of Babylon.

Sekhmet

Sekmet. **Sekhmet.**

Sel. **Sele.**

Sela

Selchie. **Silkie.**

Selci Syt Emysyt. Siberian "mother of all snakes."

Sele

Selekana

Selena. **Selene.**

Selene

Selie. **Sele.**

Selk. **Selkhet.**

Selkhet

Selkie. **Silkie.**

Selquet. **Selkhet.**

Selu. "Old corn mother" of Cherokee.

Semele

Semiramis

Semmes Mate. **Zemyna.**

Semnae. "Kindly ones," **Erinyes.**

Sengen Sama. **Kono-Hana-Sakuya-Hime.**

Sengen-Sama. Japanese volcano goddess of Mount Fujiyama.

Senkepenyana. *See Moseka.*

Sentia. Roman goddess who heightened feelings.

Sentu. **Nintur.**

Senuna. **Sinann.**

Seqinek. **Akycha.**

Sequana

Serk. **Selkhet.**

Seshatu. **Sheshat.**

Sessrymner. "Large-wombed," **Freya.**

Seyadatarahime

Shait

Shakti

Shala. **Shulamite.**

Shamash. **Shapash.**

Shams(hu). Arabian sun goddess.

Shapash

Sharrat Shame. "Queen of heaven," title of **Ishtar.**

Shatagat. Ugaritic healing goddess who could conquer death.

Shauskha

Sheila na Gig

Sheilah

Shekinah

Sheng-Mu. "Holy mother," **Pi-Hsia Yuan-Chin.**

Shenmei. "Divine Matchmaker," **Nu Kua.**

Sheol. Hebrew underworld goddess, a "clamorous woman."

Sherua. Ancient goddess merged with Ishtar.

Sheshat

Shiduri. **Siduri.**

Shiju-Gara. Bird goddess of Manchuria.

Shina-To-Be. Japanese wind goddess.

Shita-Teru-Hime. Japanese heroine of family loyalty.

Shitla. **Sitala.**

Shiwanokia

Shri. **Lakshmi.**

Shulamatu. **Shulamite.**

Shulamite

Si Boro Ihat Manisia. *See Si Boru Deak Parujar.*

Sibilaneuman

Sibilja

Sibille. **Weisse Frauen.**

Si Boru Deak Parujar

Sibyl

Sibylla. **Sibyl.**

Sicasica

Siddhi. "Success," Hindu goddess.

Siduri

Sien-Tsang. Chinese goddess of silk cultivation.

Sieroji Zemele. **Zemyna.**

Sif

Sige. "Silence," Phoenician goddess worshiped in Egypt.

Sigurdrifta

Sil. **Sele.**

Sila. "Good behavior," Indian goddess.

Silewe Nazarata

Silie. **Sele.**

Silige Fraulein. **Buschfrauen** that appear as vultures.

Silkie

Silly Witches

Silly Wychtis. **Silly Witches.**

Silvia. **Rhea Silvia.**

Sin

Sinann

Sindur. A **Wave Maiden.**

Sinend. **Sinann.**

Sinjang Halmoni. Korean military goddess, also assists birthing mothers.

Sinmara. Scandinavian cave-dwelling fire giantess.

Sipendarmith. **Armaiti.**

Sipna. Etruscan mirror goddess.

Sipylene. "The Mother," goddess of city of Smyrna.

Siqiniq. **Seqineq.**

Sir(ri)du/a. **A.**

Sirah. **Siris.**

Sirens

Siris. Babylonian bird goddess of banquets and rainbearing clouds.

Sirona. Continental Celtic sky goddess.

Sita

Sitala

Sitala-Devi. **Sitala.**

Sito. **Demeter** as giver of food or grain.

Siva. Polish and Russian goddess of life.

Sjofn

Sjojungru. Scandinavian sea goddess.

Sjora. Swedish sea goddess.

Skabas-Ava. *See Azer-Ava.*

Skadi

Skegjold. A **Valkyrie.**

Skeyh. "Axetime," a **Valkyrie.**

Skile-Qvinde. **Sar-Akka.**

Skogol. "Raging one," a **Valkyrie.**

Skogsnuivar

Skuld

Smashanakali. **Kali** of charnel ground.

Smert. Russian goddess of death, also Bohemian winter goddess like Marzana.

Smilax

Sml. West Semitic Mother of Eagles, possibly related to Semele.

Smyrna. **Myrrha.**

Snegurochka

Sneneik

Snotra. Scandinavian goddess of wisdom.

Snow Maiden. **Snegurochka.**

Snutqutxals. Bellacolla death goddess.

Sojenice. Slovenian **Sudice.**

Sol. **Sunna.**

Solntse

Somagalags

Songi. *See Nsomeka.*

Sophia

Sorbayati. *See Si Boru Deak Parujar.*

Sororia. "Sister," **Juno.**

Sospita. "Savior," Juno.

Soteria. Roman goddess of safety and recovery.

Spako

Spakona/ur. **Voluspa.**

Sparta. Mother of Eurydice and Danae; ancestral goddess of Sparta.

Spear-Finger

Spendarmat. **Armaiti.**

Spendta Armaiti. **Armaiti.**

Spermo. *See Oeno.*

Spes

Sphinx

Sphinx. *See Anuket.*

Spider Woman

Sreca

Sri. **Lakshmi.**

Srid-Icam 'phrul-mo-che

Srin-mo (wSrin-mo). *See Brag-srin-mo.*

Sroya. Slavic virgin war goddess.

Stata Mater. **Vesta.**

Stepova-Baba

Sterope. One of **Pleiades.**

Sthenno. One of **Gorgons.**

Stone-Dress. **Spear-Finger.**

Strenua. Roman goddess of strength.

Styx

Suad(el)a. **Pitho.**

Subharda. **Lakshmi.**

Sudice

Sudicky. Bohemian **Sudice.**

Sudzenici. Slovenian **Sudice.**

Suhijinino-Kami

Suki. Indian cow goddess, wife of sun.

Sukulung

Sul

Sulevia(e). *See Sul.*

Sulis (Minerva). **Sul.**

Sumi-Zome-Zakura. **Yaya-Zakura.**

Sunbikib Nabuj. Creator goddess of Toraja of south Celebes, Indonesia.

Sundi-Mumi

Sungmo. **Chunwang**

Sunkalamma. Goddess of south Indian pariahs.

Sunna

Sunnu. **Sunna.**

Suonetar. Finnish lifegiving goddess.

Sura. Indian goddess of wine.

Surabhi

Surasa. Demon queen of India.

Sutalidihi. **Unelenuhi.**

Svatantrya. **Shakti** as "independence."

Swan Maidens

Sweigsdunka

Syama. "Darkness," Durga.

Syn

Syr. "Sow," **Freya;** *see Syrith.*

Syr Fen Tanna. **Syrith.**

Syrinx

Syrith

T

Tabiti

Tabiti-Vesta. **Tabiti.**

Tacita. **Lara.**

Tacobud. **Tacoma.**

Tacoma

Ta-Dehnet. The "peak," **Mertseger.**

Tahc-I

Taillte

Tailtiu. **Taillte.**

Tai Yi. **Tao.**

Tai Yuan

Takkobad. **Tacoma.**

Takobid. **Tacoma.**

Talar-Disir. **Disir.**

Talitha. Obsure Etruscan goddess.

Talliju. In Katmandu, **Tulsi.**

Tamamono-Maye. *See Inari.*

Tamar

Tamayorihime

Tambon. **Jata.**

Tamfana. Obscure Germanic goddess.

Tamtu. **Tiamat.**

Tana Ekan. Earth goddess among Lamaholot of eastern Flores, Indonesia.

Tanais. **Anaitis.**

Tanaquil

Tanetu. **Hathor** as goddess of light.

Tanfana. **Tamfana.**

Tangalimbibo

Tanit

Tanith. **Tanit.**

Tapa. **Hina** as moon goddess.

Tapele. Earth goddess in Ceram, Indoneesia.

Tara

Taranga

Tari Pennu

Tarkhu. Hittite goddess, possibly original of **Atargatis.**

Tasimmet. Hittite weather goddess.

Tatsuta-Hime

Taur. **Tauret.**

Tauret

Taurice. **Artemis.**

Tauthe. Babylonian female first principle.

Tava-Ajk. Saami mother goddess.

Taygete. One of **Pleiades.**

Tea. *See Taillte.*

Teczistecatl. Mexican moon goddess.

Tefnut

Tehom. Hebrew Tiamat.

Tehoma. **Tacoma.**

Teicu. **Tlazoltéotl.**

Te Kore. Maori goddess of the void.

Teleglen Edzen. Mongol earth goddess.

Teleia "Full-grown," **Hera**'s second phase.

Telesilla

Telete. Roman spirit of mystery religions.

Tellus Mater

Telphassa

Telphusa

Tempestates. Roman goddesses of wind and storm.

Tenso-Daijun. **Amaterasu.**

Te Po. Maori goddess of darkness.

Terpsichore. One of **Muses.**

Teteoin(n)an. **Toci.**

Tetetka. *See Kasum-Naj-Ekva.*

Teteu Innan. **Toci.**

Tethys

Tha(i)na. Obsure Etruscan goddess.

Thalassa

Thalath. **Thalassa.**

Thal(e)ia. One of **Muses, Graces.**

Thalestris

Thallo. One of **Horae.**

Tha(l)na/r. Etruscan dawn goddess.

Tharatha. Armenian name for **Atargatis.**

Thea

Thei(r)a. **Thea.**

Thelchtereia. One of **Sirens.**

Themis

Theotokos. **Mary,** holding or nursing divine child.

Thermodosa. **Amazon** who fought with Penthesilea.

Thesmia. "Law-giver," **Demeter** or **Persephone.**

Thesmophoros. "Law-giver," **Demeter** or **Persephone.**

Thetis

Thia. **Thea.**

Thjothvara. Maidservant to Menglod.

Thora. Scandinavian ancestral mother.

Thordis. Scandinavian wise woman and healer.

Thorgerd

Thung. **Freya.**

Thurd. "Might," daughter of Sif.

Thurgai. *See Minachi-amman.*

Thyiades. *See Maenads.*

Thyone. "Ecstatically raging," deified **Semele.**

Tiacapan. **Tlazoltéotl.**

Tiamat

Tien Fei. **Tien-Hou.**

Tien-Hou

Tien Hsien. "Heavenly Immortal," **Pi-Hsia Yuan-Chin.**

Tien-Mu

Tifantina. **Diana.**

Tikuiwuti. Hopi mother of animals' spirits.

Tisiphone. One of **Erinyes.**

Tisnawati

Titania. Roman moon goddess.

Titichane

Tkuriz. **Tu-Njami.**

Tlaco. **Tlazoltéotl.**

Tlakatelilis. **Tonan.**

Tlaltecuhtli. *See Cipactli.*

Tlazoltéotl

Tlitcaplitana

Toci

Toeris. **Tauret.**

Togo Musun. **Tu-Njami.**

Toh Sri Lam. Crocodile goddess of Indochina.

Tol-Ava. *See Azer-Ava.*

Tomyris

Tonan

Tonantzin. **Tonan.**

Torah

Toririhnan

Tou-Mou

Toyo-Uke

Toyo-Uke-Bime. *See Uke-Mochi.*

Toyota-Mahime

Triduana

Trivia. "Three," **Diana,** sometimes **Hecate.**

Trung-Nhi. *See Trung-Trac.*

Trung-Trac

Tsagigla'lal

Tsan Nu. Chinese silkworm goddess, Lady Horsehead.

Tse che nako

Tsects. *See Rhipsunt.*

Tsi-Ku

Tsi Ku Niang. **Tsi-Ku.**

Tsiporah. **Zipporah.**

Tsonoqua. **Sneneik.**

Tsun Kyanske. Khymer goddess of afterlife.

Tsuru

Tuchulcha

Tuli

Tulsi. Indian goddess of basil plant.

Tundr Ilona

Tu-Njami

Tuonetar

Turachoque. **Bachue.**

Turan

Turanna. **Turan.**

Turesh

Turrean

Tursa. Early Italian goddess of terror.

Tutilina. Roman goddess who protects harvest; possibly same as **Ops.**

Tuulikki. Finnish goddess of forest animals.

Tuurm. **Tu-Njami.**

Tuwabontums. Ancestral mother of Hopi.

Tuwapongtumsi. Hopi mother of animals' bodies.

Tyche. Roman city goddess. *See Fortuna.*

Tzitzimitl. *See Mayahuel.*

U

Ua-'Apuakea. Hawaiian rain goddess.

Uadgit

Uairebhuidhe. Irish bird goddess.

Uathach. Daughter of Scathach.

Uaziit. **Uadgit.**

Uinigumasuittuq

Uinigumissuintung. **Uinigumasuittuq.**

Uke-Mochi

Ukepenopfu. Ancestor mother of Argami Nagas of India.

Uks-Akka

Ulsiga. "**Ishtar** of heaven and earth," title of reverence.

Uma. Hindu virgin goddess, *see Amba, Ganga, Parvati.*

Umaj

Umay. **Umaj.**

Umm. **Ama.**

Umm Attar. "Mother Attar," Arabian goddess of sexuality and reproduction.

Unelanuhi

Uni

Unxia. Roman goddess of wedding anointment.

Upis. **Artemis** of Ephesis.

Upsu Nusa. Earth mother of central Moluccas, eastern Indonesia.

Urania. Muse of astronomy; also title of **Aphrodite** in Sparta.

Urd. One of **Norns.**

Ureantaea. Daughter of Bau.

Uretsiti. **Utset.**

Ursa Major. **Callisto.**

Ursula

Urvasi

Ushas

Uso-Dori. Japanese goddess of singing who appears as bullfinch.

Uti Hiata

Uto. **Uadgit.**

Utset and Nowutset

Uttu. Sumerian goddess of spinning.

Uyu-sum

Uzume

Uzza. **Al-Uzza.**

V

Vacallinehae. Continental Celtic **Deas Matres.**

Vach. **Sarasvati.**

Vacuna

Vagitanus. Roman goddess who induced babies' first cries.

Vajravaraki

Vakarina/e. **Saules Meita.**

Vala. **Norns** as prophetesses.

Valetudo. Early Italian goddess of health.

Valkyries

Valkyrjr. **Valkyries.**

Valnad. Swedish name for **Fylgja.**

Vama. "Left-handed," **Devi,** or **Kali** as battle goddess.

Vamesvari. **Kali** as power of consciousness.

Vanabruder. **Freya.**

Vanadis. **Freya.**

Vanths

Var

Vardogr. Norwegian name for **Fylgja.**

Varia

Vari-Ma-Te-Takere. **Wari-Ma-Te-Takere.**

Varma-Ava. *See Azer-Ava.*

Varuni. **Gauri.**

Vashti

Vasilisa

Vatiaz

Vechernyaya Zvezda. Slavic star goddess who tends sun's horses.

Ved-Ava

Ved-Azer-Ava. **Ved-Ava.**

Veden Emo

Vegoia

Ve/irplace. Roman goddess of family harmony.

Vejamat. Latvian mother of wind.

Veleda

Vellamo

Venilia. Roman goddess of coastal waters and winds; *see Salacia.*

Venus

Verbeia. Goddess of River Wharfe in northeastern England.

Verdandi. One of **Norns.**

Vergilia. Roman **Pleiades.**

Veritas. Roman goddess of truth.

Verticordia. Roman goddess of chastity.

Veshtitze

Vesna. Slavic goddess of spring; *see Ostara.*

Vesta

Vesuna Erinia. Early Italian hearth goddess; like Vesta, but married.

Vete-Ema. **Mere-Ama.**

Victrix. **Venus** as "Victor."

Vila

Vimarsa. "Being many things at the same time," **Shakti.**

Vinata. *See Kadru.*

Vindhyavasini. **Nidra.**

Viran-Akka. Saami hunting goddess.

Vir(Azer-)Ava. *See Azer-Ava.*

Virginia. Roman goddess of politics.

Virilis. **Fortuna** who makes women attractive to mates.

Viriplaca. "Placator," **Juno.**

Virtus. Roman goddess of courage.

Visha-hara. "She who takes away venom," **Manasa** as protector against poisonous snakes.

Vitsa-Kuva

Viviane

Vodni Panny

Volla. **Fulla.**

Volumna. Roman goddess of will power.

Voluptas. **Voluptia.**

Voluptia

Voluspa

Volva. *See Voluspa, Gollveig.*

Vor. Scandinavian goddess of prudence.

Vrou-Elde. Dutch goddess of spring.

Vut-Imi

Wang-Mu Niang-Niang. **Hsi Wang Mu.**

Wanne Thekla

Wannon-Sama. Japanese **Kuan-Yin.**

Waramurungundji

Wari-Ma-Te-Takere

Wauwalak Sisters. **Wawalag Sisters.**

Wave Maidens

Wawalag Sisters

Wazit. Original name of **Uadgit.**

Weisse Frauen

Weiwobo. **Hsi Wang Mu.**

Werzelya. Abyssinian name for **Lilith.**

Whaitiri

White Buffalo Woman

Wigan

Wilden Wip

Winona. **Winonah.**

Winonah

Wisin Wif. **Nixies.**

Wlasca

Wuriupranili

Wurusemu

Wyeast. *See Pahto.*

X

Xatel-Ekwa

Xenia. **Athena** who protects strangers.

Xiwang Mu. **Hsi Wang Mu.**

Xochiquetzal

Xocutxin. **Tlazoltéotl.**

Xoli-Kaltes

Xulsigiae. Continental Celtic water goddess worshiped at Trier.

Y

Yabme-Akka

Yak. Mother earth in Malaysia.

Yama no Kami

Yama no Shinbo. **Yama no Kami.**

Yama-Uba. Japanese mountain goddess.

Yamato-Himeno-Miko

Yamuna. Hindu river goddesses, ruler of Jumna.

Yanan. **Oya.**

Yansa. **Oya.**

Yaoji

Yaparamma. Business goddess of eastern India.

Yasoda. *See Nidra.*

Yauni. *See Ganga.*

Yaya-Zakura

Yebaad. Female chief deity of Navaho.

Yemanja. **Ymoja.**

Yemaya. **Ymoja.**

Yeshe Tsoquel. Tibetan Tantic female Buddha, "Sky Dancer."

Yhi

Ymoja

Yoganidra. **Nidra.**

Yohuatlicetl. Mexican moon goddess.

Yolaikaiason. **Yolkai Estsan.**

Yolkai Estsan

Yondung Halmoni

Yrsa. "She-Wolf," ancestral mother of Scandinavia.

Yuki-Onne

Yunhua Furen. **Yaoji.**

Yu Nu. "Jade maiden," **Pi-Hsia Yuan-Chin.**

Z

Zaarmu. Daughter of Bau.

Zanaru. "Lady of lands," **Ishtar.**

Zaramama

W

Wa

Wahini-Hai

Wah-Kah-Nee

Wahkshum. *See Pahto.*

Wakahirume

Waldmichen

Walo

Walutahanga

Zarpandit

Zarya. **Zorya.**

Zazuru. Daughter of Bau.

Zemes Mate. **Zemyna.**

Zemina. **Zemyna.**

Zemyna

Zemynele. **Zemyna.**

Zerbanit. **Zarpandit.**

Zerbanitu(m). **Zarpandit.**

Zib. **Ishtar** as evening star who provokes desire.

Zilpah. *See Rachel.*

Zima. Slavonic Mother Winter, like **Marzana.**

Zinthrepus. Obscure Etruscan goddess.

Zintuki. Granddaughter of Wurusemu.

Zipaltonal

Zipna. Obscure Etruscan goddess.

Zipporah

Zirna

Zisa

Ziva. *See Siva.*

Zleja. *See Bresksta.*

Zlota-Baba. **Jumala.**

Zonget

Zorya

Zosteria. "Girded for Battle," **Athena.**

Zuleika

Zvezda Dennitsa

Zvoruna. Lithuanian forest goddess.

Zygia. "Joiner," **Hera** presiding over marriage.

Zytniamatka. Prussian Corn Mother.

Zywie. Polish great goddess, "The Living."

Feasts of the Goddess

The following are dates on which goddess feasts are or were traditionally celebrated. For details of the rituals involved, refer to the "Myths of the Goddess" section.

January 1: Nanshe
January 5: Befana
January 11–15: Carmenta
January 12: Mania
February 2: Brigid
March 1: Juno, Vesta
March 15: Anna Perenna
March 17: Libera
March 19–23: Minerva
March 25: Mati Syra Zemlja
April 15: Tellus Mater
April 19: Ceres
April 21: Pales
April 28–May 3: Flora
May 1: Maia
May 6: Inghean Bhuidhe
June 9: Vesta
June 11: Matuta
June 21: Aine, Beiwe, Hu-Tu

July 7: Juno
July 25: Furrina
August 15: Diana
August 25: Ops
September 28: Zisa
October 1: Fides
October 13: Camenae
October 21: Ursula
October 31: Carlin
November 15: Feronia
December 1: Bona Dea
December 12: Guadalupe
December 14: Halcyone
December 19: Ops
December 21: Angerona, Beiwe, Colleda, Tonan
December 23: Acca Larentia
December 25–January 6: Frau Holle, Perchta

Bibliography

Adams, Charles, editor. *Reader's Guide to the Great Religions.* 2nd ed. New York: The Macmillan Company, 1977.

Adams, David. *The World of Myth: An Anthology.* Leeming, NY: Oxford University Press, 1990.

Aeschylus. *Plays.* Translated by John Herington. New Haven: Yale University Press, 1986.

Akurgal, Ekrem. *The Art of the Hittites.* New York: Harry N. Abrams, Inc., n.d.

Albright, William Foxwell. *Yahweh and the Gods of Canann.* New York: Doubleday & Co., 1968.

Allen, Paula Gunn. *The Sacred Hoop: Recovering the Feminine in American Indian Traditions.* Beacon Press, Boston. 1986.

Anati, E. *Palestine Before the Hebrews.* New York: Alfred A. Knopf, 1963.

Anderson, Jorgen. *The Witch on the Wall.* London: George Allen & Unwin, Ltd., 1977.

Andrups, Janis, and Vitatus Kalve. *Latvian Literature: Essays.* Stockholm: M. Goppers, 1954.

Apuleius, Lucius. *The Transformations of Lucius, or The Golden Ass.* Translated by Robert Graves. London: Penguin, 1951.

Arriaga, Pablo Joseph De. *The Extirpation of Idolatry in Peru.* Translated and edited by L. Clark Keating. Lexington, KY: University of Kentucky Press, 1968.

Ashe, Geoffrey. *The Virgin.* London: Routledge and Kegan Paul, 1976.

Avalon, Arthur, and Ellen Avalon *Hymns to the Goddess, Translated from the Sanskrit.* London: Luzac and Company, 1913.

Bachofen, J. J. *Myth, Religion, and Mother Right.* Translated by Ralph Mannheim. Bollingen Series. Princeton: Princeton University Press, 1967.

Baily, Cyril. *Religion of Ancient Rome.* London: Archibald Constable & Co., 1970.

Banks, M. MacLeod. *British Calendar Customs, Vol. 2: Scotland.* London: William Glaisher, Ltd., 1939.

Bare, Lawrence A. *The Divine Hierarchy: Popular Hinduism in Central India.* New York: Columbia University Press, 1975.

Barton, George A. *The Royal Inscriptions of Sumer and Akkad.* New Haven: American Oriental Society, 1929.

Batchelor, John. *The Ainu of Japan.* London: The Religious Tract Society, 1892.

Beier, Ulli, ed. *Yoruba Poetry: An Anthology of Traditional Poems*. Cambridge: Cambridge University Press, 1970.

Belianjus, Vytautas F. *The Evening Song: Vakarine Daina. Lithuanian Legends and Fables*. Los Angeles, CA: Bonnie Press, 1954.

Benjamins, esq. *Dearest Goddess*. Virginia: Current Nine Publications, 1985.

Bennet, Florence Mary. *Religious Cults Associated with the Amazons*. New York: AMS Press, 1967.

Bernal, Martin. *Black Athena: The Afroasiatic Roots of Classical Civilization*. 2 Volumes. New Brunswick, NJ: Rutgers University Press, 1987, 1991.

Bhrolchain, Murrean Ni. "Images of Woman in Early Irish Myths and Sagas." *The Crane Bag*, 4, No. 1: The Irish Woman. Dublin: Blackwater Press (1977–1981).

Bierhorst, John. *The Mythology of North America*. New York: William M. Morrow & Co., Inc., 1985.

Billson, Charles J., ed., collector. *Folk-Lore of Leichestershire and Rutland*. County Folk-Lore, Vol I. London: David Nutt, 1895.

Blacker, Carmen. *The Catalpa Bow: A Study of Shamanistic Practices in Japan*. London: George Allen & Unwin, Ltd., 1982.

Bleeker, C. J. *Hathor and Thoth: Two Key Figures in the Ancient Egyptian Religion*. Leiden: E. J. Brill, 1973.

Bloc, Raymond. *The Ancient Civilization of the Etruscans*. Translated by James Hogarth. New York: Cowles Books Co., 1969.

———. *The Etruscans*. New York: Praeger Publishers, 1956.

Blofeld, John. *Bodhisattva of Compassion: The Mystical Tradition of Kuan Yin*. Boulder, CO: Shambhala, 1978.

Boas, Franz. *The Central Eskimo*. 1888 Reprint. Lincoln, NE: University of Nebraska Press, 1964.

———. *The Eskimo of Baffin Land and Hudson Bay*. Bulletin of the American Museum of Natural History, 15, 1901.

Boer, Charles, tr. *The Homeric Hymns*. Chicago: Swallow Press, 1970.

Bonnefoy, Yves, ed. *Mythologies*. A Restructured Translation of *Dicionnaire des mythologies and des religions des socieites traditionnelles and du monde antique*. Prepared under the Direction of Wendy Doniger. Volumes 1 and 2. Chicago: University of Chicago Press, 1991.

Bord, Janet, and Colin Bord. *The Secret Country*. New York: Walker & Co., 1977.

Brandon, S. G. F., ed. *Dictionary of Comparative Religion*. New York: Charles Scribner's, 1970.

Branson, Brian. *Gods of the North*. New York: Vanguard Press, 1955.

Bratton, Fred Gladstone. *Myths and Legends of the Ancient Near East*. New York: Thomas Crowell, 1970.

Bray, Frank Chapin. *Bray's University Dictionary of Mythology*. New York: Thomas Crowell, 1935.

Briggs, Katherine. *An Encyclopedia of Fairies*. New York: Pantheon Books, 1967.

Brown, Cheever MacKenzie. *God As Mother*. Hartford, VT: Claude Stark & Co., 1974.

Brown, Emily Ivanoff. *Tales of Ticasuk: Eskimo Legends and Stories*. Fairbanks, AK: University of Alaska Press, 1987.

Brown, Vinson. *Voices of Earth and Sky*. Harrisburg, PA: Stackpole Books, 1975.

Bruchac, Joseph. *Return of the Sun: Native American Tales from the Northeast Woodlands*. Freedom, CA: The Crossing Press, 1989.

Budge, E. A. Wallis. *The Gods of the Egyptians: Studies in Egyptian Mythology*. Vol. 1. New York: Dover Publications, Inc., 1969.

Bullfinch, Thomas. *Bulfinch's Mythology*. Middlesex: Hamlyn Publishing Group, 1964.

Buttrich, et al. *Interpreter's Dictionary of the Bible*. New York: Abingdon Press, 1962.

Campbell, John G. *Popular Tales of the West Highlands.* Edinburgh: Edmonston and Douglas, 1862.

———. *Superstitions of the Scottish Highlands.* Glasgow: James MacLehose and Sons, 1900.

Campbell, Joseph R. *The Fians.* London: David Nutt, 1891.

Campbell, Joseph. *The Masks of God.* 4 vols.: *Oriental Mythology, Primitive Mythology, Occidental Mythology, Creative Mythology.* New York: The Viking Press, 1959–1965.

Carmichael, Alexander. *Carmina Gadelica: Hymns and Incantations Collected in the Highlands and Islands of Scotland in the Last Century.* Hudson, NY: Lindisfarne Press, 1992.

Chamberlain, Basil Hall. *Ainu Folktales.* London: Folklore Society xxn, 1888.

Chapman, John W. *Ten'a Texts and Tales from Anuik, Alaska.* vol. 6. Publications of the American Ethnological Society. Leiden: E. J. Brill, 1914.

Chin, Yin-Lien C., Yetta S. Center and Mildred Ross. *Traditional Chinese Folktales.* Armonk, NY: M. E. Sharp, 1989.

Clark, Ella. *Indian Legends of the Pacific Northwest.* Berkeley: University of California Press, 1953.

Colegrave, Sukie. *The Spirit of the Valley: The Masculine and Feminine in Human Consciousness.* Los Angeles: J. P. Tarcher Inc. 1979.

Converse, Harriet Maxwell. *Myths and Legends of the New York Iroquois.* Port Washington, NY: Ira J. Friedman, 1962.

Covell, Alan Carter. *Ecstasy: Shamanism in Korea.* Elizabeth, NJ: Hollym International Corp., 1983.

Coxwell, C. Fillingham. *Siberian and Other Folk-Tales.* London: The C. W. Daniel Company, ND.

Crawford, O. G. S. *The Eye Goddess.* London: Phoenix House, 1957.

Cross, S. H. *Slavic Civilization through the Ages.* Edited by L. I. Strakhovsky. Cambridge: Harvard University Press, 1948.

Crossley-Holland, Kevin. *The Norse Myths.* New York: Pantheon Books, 1980.

Curtin, Jeremiah. *Creation Myths of Primitive America.* 1898 Reprint. New York: Benjamin Blom, Inc., 1969.

———. *Myths and Folklore of Ireland.* Boston: Little, Brown, & Company, 1890.

Dames, Michael. *The Silbury Treasure: The Great Goddess Rediscovered.* London: Thames and Hudson, 1976.

Danaher, Kevin. *The Year in Ireland: A Calendar.* Cork: The Mercier Press, 1977.

Danielou, Alain. *Hindu Polytheism.* Bollingen Series. New York: Pantheon Books, 1964.

Davidson, H. E., and Peter Geller. *The Chariot of the Sun and Other Rites and Symbols of the Northern Bronze Age.* New York: Praeger Publishers, 1969.

Davidson, Hilda Ellis. *Scandinavian Mythology.* London: Hamlyn Publishing, 1969.

Davis, Elizabeth Gould. *The First Sex.* New York: Penguin Books, 1971.

Dejubainville, H. D'Arbois. *The Irish Mythological Cycle and Celtic Mythology.* Dublin: Hodges, Figgis & Co., 1903.

Deighton, Hilary J. *The Weather-God in Hittite Anatolia: An Examination of the Archaeological and Textual Sources.* BAR International Series, 143 (1982).

Deutsch, Helene. *A Psychoanalytic Study of the Myth of Dionysius and Apollo.* New York: International University Press, 1969.

Dexter, Miriam Robbins. *Whence the Goddesses: A Sourcebook.* New York: Pergamon Press, 1990.

Dillon, Myles, ed. *Irish Sagas.* Cork: Mercier Press, 1968.

Dioszegi, V., and M. Hoppal, eds. *Shamanism in Siberia.* Budapest: Akademiai Kaido, 1978.

Dioszegi, V., ed. *Popular Beliefs and Folklore Traditions in Siberia.* Bloomington, IN: Indiana University Press, 1968.

Domitor, Teckla. *Hungarian Folk Beliefs*. Bloomington, IN: Indiana University Press, 1982.

Dorsey, George. *Traditions of the Arikara*. Washington, D.C.: Carnegie Institute, 1904.

Dowson, John. *A Classical Dictionary of Hindu Mythology*. London: Trubner & Co., 1874.

Dragamanov, M. P. *Notes on the Slavic Religio-Ethical Legends*. Russian and Eastern European Series, vol. 23:2. Bloomington, IN: Indiana University Press, 1961.

Dumezil, Georges. *Archaic Roman Religions*. Volumes. 1 & 2. Translated by Philip Krapp. Chicago: University of Chicago Press, 1966.

———. *Gods of the Ancient Northmen*. Edited by Enar Haugen. Los Angeles: University of California Press, 1973.

Durdin-Robertson, Lawrence. *Goddesses of India, Tibet, China and Japan*. Ireland: Caesara Publications, 1976.

———. *The Goddesses of Chaldea, Syria, and Egypt*. Ireland: Caesara Publications; 1975.

Eastman, Elaine Goodale. *Indian Legends Retold*. Boston: Little, Brown & Company, 1929.

Eliade, Mircea. *Shamanism: Archaic Techniques of Ecstacy*. Willard Trask, translator. New York: Pantheon Books, Bollingen Series, Vol. 76, 1964.

Ellis, Hilda Roderick. *The Road to Hell*. New York: Greenwood Press, 1968.

Ellis, Normandi. *Awakening Osiris*. MI: Phanes Press, 1988.

———. *Dreams of Isis*. Wheaton, IL: Quest Books, 1995.

Elwin, Verrier. *Myths of the North-East Frontier of India*. Shillong: North-East Frontier Agency, 1958.

———. *Tribal Myths of Orissa*. Edited by Richard M. Dorson. Oxford: Geoffrey Cumberledge, 1954.

Emerson, Nathaniel B. *Pele and Hiiaka: A Myth from Hawaii*. Tokyo: Charles Tuttle Co., 1978.

Erdoes, Richard, and Alfonso Ortiz, eds. *American Indian Myths and Legends*. New York: Pantheon Books, 1984.

Euripides. *Helen*. Translated by Robert Emmet Meagher. Amherst: University of Massachusetts Press, 1986.

Evans, Arthur. *The Earlier Religion of Greece in Light of Cretan Discoveries*. London: The Macmillan Company, 1937.

Evans, E. Estyn. *Of Irish Ways*. New York: Devin-Adair, 1957.

Ferguson, John. *Encyclopedia of Mysticism*. New York: Seabury Press, 1977.

———. *The Religions of the Roman Empire*. Ithaca, NY: Cornell University Press, 1970.

Ferm, Vergilius, ed. *Forgotten Religions*. New York: The Philosophical Library, Inc., 1950.

Flood, J. M. *Ireland: Its Myths and Legends*. London: Kennikat Press, 1916.

Foreman, Carolyn Thomas. *Indian Women Chiefs*. Washington, D.C.: Zenger Publishing Co., Inc., 1954.

Forlong, J. G. R. *Encyclopedia of Religions*. New York: University Books, 1964.

Fowler, W. W. *Roman Ideas of Deity*. Freeport, New York: Books for Libraries Press, 1914.

Frazer, Sir James George. *The Golden Bough,* 3rd ed. New York: The Macmillan Company, 1935.

Friedrich, Paul. *The Meaning of Aphrodite*. Chicago: University of Chicago Press, 1978.

Gantz, Jeffrey, tr. and introduction. *The Mabinogian*. New York: Barnes & Noble Books, 1976.

Garber, Clark. *Stories and Legends of the Bering Strait Eskimo*. Boston: Christopher Publishing House, 1940.

Gaster, Theodor. *Thespis: Ritual, Myth and Drama in the Ancient Near East*. Garden City, NY: Doubleday Anchor Books, 1961.

Getty, Adele. *Goddess: Mother of Living Nature*. London: Thames & Hudson. 1990.

Giddings, J. L. *Kobuk River People*. College, Alaska: University of Alaska, Department of Anthropology and Geography, Studies of Northern People, No.1, 1961.

Gimbutas, Marija. *Goddesses and Gods of Old Europe.* Berkeley: University of Califomia Press, 1974.

———.*The Balts.* New York: Praeger Publishers, 1963.

———.*The Slavs.* New York: Praeger Publishers, 1971.

Ginzburg, Louis. *Legends of the Jews.* Translated by Henrietta Szold. Philadelphia: Jewish Publishing Society of America, 1909.

Gitlin-Emmer, Susan. *Lady of the Northern Light: A Feminist Guide to the Runes.* Freedom, CA: The Crossing Press, 1989.

Gleason, Judith. *Orisha: The Gods of Yorubaland.* NY: Atheneum, 1971.

Godolphin, F. R. B., ed. *Great Classical Myths.* NY: The Modern Library, Random House, 1964.

Goldenberg, Naomi. *Changing of the Gods.* Boston: Beacon Press, 1979.

Gombos, Imbre, and George F. Gushing, translators. *Zyrian Folkore Texts.* Akademiai Kiado, Budapest, 1978.

Goodison, Lucy. *Women, Death and the Sun.* London: London Archaeological Institute, 1989.

Grace, Patricia. *Wahine Toa: Women of Maori Myth.* Paintings and Drawings by Robyn Kahukiwa. Sydney: Collins. 1984.

Graves, Robert. *The Greek Myths.* 2 Volumes. Baltimore, MD: Penguin Books, 1955.

———. *The White Goddess.* New York: Farrar, Strauss, Girou, 1948.

Gray, L. H., ed. *Myths of All Races.* 13 Volumes. New York: Cooper Square Publishers, 1946.

Green, Miranda. *The Gods of Roman Britain.* Aylesbury, Bucks: Shire Archaeology, 1983.

———. *The Gods of the Celts.* Totowa, NJ: Barnes and Noble Books, 1986.

———. *The Sun-Gods of Ancient Europe.* Hippocrene Books, London, 1991.

Greenway, John, ed. *The Primitive Reader.* Hatboro, Pa.: Folklore Associates, 1965.

Grigson, Geoffrey. *The Goddess of Love: The Birth, Triumph, Death and Return of Aphrodite.* New York: Stein and Day, 1977.

Grimm, Jacob. *Teutonic Mythology.* Translated by James Steven Stallybrass. London: G. Bell Sons, 1883.

———. *The Complete Fairy Tales of the Brothers Grimm.* Translation and introduction by Jack Zipes. New York: Bantam Books, 1987.

———. *The Complete Grimm's Fairy Tales.* Introduction by Padraic Colum. Commentary by Joseph Campbell. NY: Pantheon Books, Random House, 1972.

Guerber, H. A. *Myths of Northern Lands.* Detroit, MI: Singing Tree Press, 1970.

Gupta, Sanjukta, translator. *Laksmi Tantra, A Pancaratra Text.* Leiden: E. J. Brill, 1972.

Gurney, O. R. *Some Aspects of Hittite Religion.* Oxford: Oxford University Press, 1977.

Guyot, Charles. *The Legend of the City of Ys.* Translated by Deirdre Cavanaugh. Amherst, MA: University of Massachusetts Press, 1979.

Hackin, J., et al. *Asiatic Mythology.* New York: Thomas Crowell, 1963.

Harrison, Jane Ellen. *Prolegomena to the Study of Greek Religion.* 1903 Reprint. New York: Meridian Books, 1955.

Hastings, James, ed. *Encyclopedia of Religion and Ethics.* New York: Charles Scribner's, 1924.

Hawkes, Jacquetta. *Dawn of the Gods.* New York: Random House, 1968.

Hawley, John Stratton, and Donna Marie Wulff. *Devi: Goddesses of India.* Berkeley: University of California Press, 1996.

Henderson Joseph, and Maud Oakes. *The Wisdom of the Serpent.* New York: George Braziller, 1963.

Herodotus. *The Histories of Herodotus of Helicarnassus.* Translated by Henry Carter. Baltimore, MD: The Heritage Press, 1959.

Highwater, Jamake. *Myth and Sexuality.* New York: New American Library, 1990.

Hinnells, John R. *Persian Mythology.* London: Hamlyn Publishing, 1973.

Hoch-Smith, Judith, and Anita Spring. *Women in Ritual and Symbolic Roles.* New York: Plenum Press, 1978.

Hoddinott, R. F. *The Thracians.* London: Thames & Hudson, 1981.

Hollander, Lee M., tr. *The Poetic Edda.* Second edition, revised. Austin: University of Texas Press, 1988.

Hooke, S. H. *Middle Eastern Mythology:* Baltimore, MD: Penguin Books, 1963.

Hookham, Hilda. *A Short History of China.* New York: New American Library, 1969.

Horace. *The Odes and Epodes of Horace.* A Modern English Verse. Translation by Joseph P. Clancy. Chicago: University of Chicago Press, 1960.

Hubbs, Joanna. *Mother Russia: The Feminine Myth in Russian Culture.* Bloomington: Indiana University Press, 1988.

Hubert, Henri. *The Greatness and Decline of the Celts.* London: Kegan Paul, Trench Brubner and Co., 1934.

Hull, Eleanor. *The Cuchulain Saga in Irish Literature.* London: David Nutt, 1898.

Hurtado, Larry W., editor. *Goddesses in Religions and Modern Debate.* Atlanta, GA: Scholars Press, 1990.

Hutter, Catherine. *The Norsemen.* Greenwich, CT: New York Graphic Society Publications, Ltd., 1965.

Hyde, Douglas, tr. *Beside the Fire: A Collection of Irish Gaelic Folk Stories.* New York: Lemma Publishing, 1973.

————. *A Literary History of Ireland.* London: T. Fisher Unwin Ltd., 1899.

Idowu, E. Bolaji. *African Traditional Religion.* Maryknoll, NY: Orbis Books, 1973.

Jackson, Kenneth Hurlstone. *A Celtic Miscellany: Translations from the Celtic Literatures.* London: Penguin Books, 1971.

James, E. O. *Prehistoric Religion.* New York: Praeger Publishers, 1957.

Jaynes, Julian. *The Origin of Consciousness in the Breakdown of the Bicameral Mind.* Boston: Houghton Mifflin Company, 1990.

Jenness, Diamond. *The Corn Goddess and Other Tales from Indian Canada.* Bulletin no. 141, Anthropological Series no. 319. Ottawa: National Museums of Canada, n.d.

Jochelson, W. with Suvorov and Yachmeneff. *Aleut Traditions.* Fairbanks, Alaska: Native Language Center, 1977.

Johnson, Buffie. *Lady of the Beasts: Ancient Images of the Goddess and her Sacred Animals.* San Francisco: Harper and Row Publishers, 1988.

Johnston, Basil. *The Manitous: The Spiritual World of the Ojibway.* New York: Harper Collins, 1995.

Jonval, Michel. *Les Chansons Mythologiques Lettones.* Paris: Librarie Picart, n.d.

Joyce, P. W. *Old Celtic Romances.* New York: Devin-Adair, 1962.

Jung, C. G., and K. Kerenyi. *Essays on a Science of Mythology.* Bollingen Series. Princeton: Princeton University Press, 1949.

Karas, Sheryl Ann. *The Solstice Evergreen: The History, Folklore and Origins of the Christmas Tree.* Boulder Creek, CA: Aslan Publishing, 1991.

Karsten, Rafael. *The Religion of the Sameks.* Leiden: E. J. Brill, 1955.

Katzenelenbogen, Uriah. *The Daina: An Anthology of Lithuanian and Latvian Folksongs.* Chicago: Latvian News Publishing Company, 1935.

Kennedy, Patrick. *Legendary Fictions of the Irish Celts.* London: The Macmillan Company, 1866.

Kerenyi, Karl. *Athene: Virgin and Mother.* Translated by Murray Stein. Houston, TX: Spring Publications, 1978.

———. *Goddesses of Sun and Moon.* Dallas, TX: Spring Publications,1979.

———. *Zeus and Hera.* Bollingen Series. Princeton: Princeton University Press, 1975.

Kinsella, Thomas, tr. *Tain bo Cuailnge.* Dublin: Dolmen Press, 1969.

Kinsley, David. *Hindu Goddesses: Visions of the Divine Feminine in the Hindu Religious Tradition.* Berkeley: University of California Press, 1986.

———. *The Sword and the Flute.* Berkeley: University of California Press, 1975.

Kirk, G. S. *The Nature of Greek Myths.* Woodstock, N.Y.: The Overlook Press, 1975.

Knappert, Jan. *Kings, Gods and Spirits from African Mythology.* New York: Peter Bedrick Books, 1986.

———. *The Aquarian Guide to African Mythology.* Wellingborough: The Aquarian Press, 1990.

Kramer, S. N. *The Sacred Marriage Rite.* Bloomington, IN: Indiana University Press, 1969.

———., ed. *From the Poetry of Sumer.* Berkeley: University of California Press, 1979.

Krause, Aurel. *The Tlingit Indians: Results of a Trip to the Northwest Coast of America and the Bering Straits.* Translated by Erna Gunther. Seattle: U of Washington Press, 1970.

Kuhn, A. B. *The Lost Light.* Elizabeth, NJ: Academy Press, 1940.

Kupelrud, Arvid. *The Violent Goddess: Anat in the Ras Shamra Texts.* Oslo: Universitets-forlaget, 1969.

Laing, Gordon J. *Survivals of Roman Religion.* New York: Cooper Square Publishers, 1963.

Leland, Charles. *Algonquin Legends of New England.* Boston: Houghton Mifflin Company, 1884. Reprint. Detroit Singing Tree Press, 1968.

Lind, L. R., ed. *Ten Greek Plays in Contemporary Translations.* Boston: Houghton Mifflin, 1957.

Logan, Patrick. *The Holy Wells of Ireland.* Gerrards Cross: Colin Smythe, 1980.

———. *The Old Gods: The Facts about Irish Fairies.* Berkeley, California: Appletree Press, 1981.

Lonnrot, Elias. *The Old Kalevala and Certain Antecedents.* Prose translations with foreword and appendices by Francis Peabody Magou, Jr. Cambridge: Harvard University Press, 1969.

Lonsdale, Steven. *Animals and the Origins of Dance.* London: Thames and Hudson, 1981.

Macalister, R. A. S. *The Archaeology of Ireland.* London: Methuen Co., 1928.

MacGregor, A. A. *The Peat-Fire.* Scotland: The Moray Press, n.d.

MacKenzie, Donald A. *Scottish Folk-Lore and Folk Life.* London and Glasgow: Blackie & Son Ltd, 1935.

———. *Egyptian Myth and Legend.* London: The Gresham Publishing Co., 1907.

———. *The Myth of China and Japan.* London: The Gresham Publishing Company, 1923.

MacNeill, Maire. *The Festival of Lughnasa.* 2 Volumes. Dublin: Comhairle Bhealoideas Eireann, 1982.

Mails, Thomas E. *The People Called Apache.* Englewood Cliffs, NJ: Prentice Hall, 1974.

Markale, Jean. *Women of the Celts.* Translated by A. Mygind, C. Hauch and P. Henry. Rochester, VT, Inner Traditions, Inc, 1986.

Marriott, Alice and Rachlin, Carol. *American Indian Mythology.* New York: Thomas Crowell, 1968.

Matthews, W. H. *Mazes & Labyrinths: Their History and Development.* New York: Dover Publications, 1970.

McCrickard, Janet. *Eclipse of the Sun.* Glastonbury: Gothic Image, 1989.

McIlwraith, T. F. *The Bella Coola Indians.* Toronto: University of Toronto Press, 1948.

McKay, John G. *More West Highland Tales,* Vol. 2. Edinburgh: Oliver and Byrd, 1960.

McNeill, F. Marian. *The Silver Bough.* Glasgow: William Maclellan, 1959.

Meagher, Robert Emmett. *Helen: Myth, Legend, and the Culture of Misogyny.* New York: Continuum, 1995.

Merriam, C. Hart. *The Dawn of the World: Myths and Weird Tales Told by the Mewuk Indians of California.* Cleveland: The Arthur H. Clark Company, 1910.

Metraux, Alfred. *Voodoo in Haiti.* Translated by Hugo Charteris. New York: Oxford University Press, 1959.

Mills, Clark, and Albirgis Landsbirg. *The Green Linden: Selected Lithuanian Folksongs.* New York: Voyages Press, 1962.

Mookerjie, Ajit. *Kali: The Feminine Force.* New York: Destiny Books, 1988.

Moor, Edward. *The Hindu Pantheon.* Delhi: Indological Bookstore, 1968.

Mueller, F. Max, and Richard M. Dorsson, eds. *Peasant Customs and Savage Myths: Selections from the British Folklorists, vol. 1.* Chicago: University of Chicago Press, 1968.

Mundkur, Balaji. *The Cult of the Serpent: An Interdisciplinary Survey of Its Manifestations and Origins.* Albany, NY: State University of New York Press, 1983.

Munro, Neil G. *Ainu: Creed and Cult.* New York: Columbia University Press, 1965.

Neumann, Erich. *The Great Mother.* Translated by Ralph Manheim. New York: Pantheon Books, 1963.

Newman, Paul. *Gods and Graven Images: The Chalk Hill-Figures of Britain.* London: Robert Hale: 1987.

Nicholson, Irene. *Mexican and Central American Mythology.* London: Hamlyn Publishing, 1967.

Nicholson, Shirley, ed. *The Goddess Reawakening. The Feminine Principle Today.* Wheaton, IL: Quest Books, 1989.

Nilsson, Martin. *Greek Folk Religion.* New York: Harper Torchbooks, 1965.

Obeyesekere, Gananath. *The Cult of the Goddess Pattini.* Chicago: University of Chicago Press, 1984.

Ochs, Carol. *The Myth Behind the Sex of God.* Boston: Beacon Press, 1977.

O'Connor, Norrey Jephson. *Baffles and Enchantments.* Freeport, NY: Books for Libraries Press, 1922.

O'Faolain, Sean. *The Silver Branch.* Freeport, NY: Books for Libraries Press, 1968.

O'Flaherty, Wendy Doniger. *Hindu Myths.* Baltimore, MD: Penguin Books, 1975.

O'Heochaidh, Sean. *Fairy Legends of Donegal.* Translated by Maire MacNeill. Dublin: Comhairle Bhealoideas Eireann, 1977.

Oinas, Felix J., and Stephen Soudakoff, trs. *The Study of Russian Folklore.* Hawthome, NY: Mouton Publishers, 1975.

Okenstierna, Eric. Catherine Hutter, translator. *The Norsemen.* Greenwich, CT: New York Graphic Society Publications Ltd, 1965.

Olson, Carl, editor. *The Book of the Goddess, Past and Present.* Crossroad, New York, 1985.

Onassis, Jaqueline, ed. and introduction. *The Firebird and other Russian Fairy Tales.* Illustrated by Boris Zvoyrkin. New York: The Viking Press, 1978.

O'Rahilly, T. F. *Early Irish History and Myth.* Dublin: Institute of Advanced Studies, 1957.

Osborne, Harold. *South American Mythology.* London: Hamlyn Publishing, 1968.

Ovid. *The Metamorphoses. Complete New Version.* Horace Gregory, translator. New York: New American Library, The Viking Press, NY 1958.

Pakrasi, Mira. *Folk Tales of Assam, vol. 3.* Mystic, CT: Lawrence Verry Inc., 1970.

Pallotino, M. *The Etruscans.* London: Penguin Books, 1955.

Park, Yong Jum. *Traditional Tales of Old Korea.* Seoul: Hanguk Munkwa Publishing Company, 1974.

Parker, Derek and Julia Parker. *The Immortals.* New York: McGraw-Hill Book Co., 1976.

Parringer, Geoffrey. *A Dictionary of Non-Christian Religion.* Philadelphia: Westminster Press, 1971.

———. *West African Religion.* London: The Epworth Press, 1949.

Patai, Raphael, and ROBERT GRAVES. *Hebrew Myths: The Book of Genesis.* New York: Greenwich House, 1983.

———. *The Hebrew Goddess.* New York: KTAV Publishers, 1967.

Paton, C. I. *Manx Calendar Customs.* London: London Folklore Society, William Glaisher, Ltd., 1934.

Patterson, Adrian, translator. *Old Lithuanian Songs.* Lithuania: Pribacis Kaunas, n.d.

Paulson, Ivar. *The Old Estonian Folk Religion.* Translated by J. K. Kitching and H. Kovamees. Bloomington, IN: Indiana University Press, 1971.

Persson, Axel W. *The Religion of Greece in Prehistoric Times.* Berkeley: University of California Press, 1942:

Phillipi, Donald. *Norito: A New Translation of the Ancient Japanese Ritual Prayers.* Tokyo: Institute of Japanese Culture and Classics, 1959.

Pollard, John. *Seers, Shrines and Sirens.* London: George Allen & Unwin, Ltd., 1965.

Porras, Tomas Herrera. *Cuna Cosmology, Legends from Panama.* Translated by Anita G. McAndrews. Three Continents Press/Shantih, 1978.

Powell, T. G. E. *The Celts.* London: Thames and Hudson, 1980.

Powers, William K. *Oglala Religion.* Lincoln, Neb.: University of Nebraska Press, 1975.

Preston, James J., editor. *Mother Worship: Theme and Variations.* Chapel Hill, NC: University of North Carolina Press, 1982.

Rafy, K. U. *Folktales of the Khasis.* New York: The Macmillan Company, 1920.

Ralston, W. R. S. *The Songs of the Russian People.* New York: Haskell House Publishers, 1970.

Ranke, Kurt. *Folktales of Germany.* Translated by Lotte Baumann. Chicago: University of Chicago Press, 1966.

Redgrove, Peter. *The Black Goddess and the Unseen Real.* New York: Grove Press, 1987.

Reichard, Gladys. *Navaho Religion: A Study of Symbolism.* Bollingen Series. New York: Pantheon Books, 1959.

Rhys, John. *Celtic Folklore.* Oxford: Clarendon Press, 1901.

Rice, Patty. *Amber, the Golden Gem of the Ages.* New York: Van Nostrand Reinhold Co., Inc., 1974.

Richardson, N. J., translator. *The Homeric Hymns.* Oxford: The Clarendon Press, Oxford, 1974.

Rink, Johannes. *Tales and Traditions of the Eskimo.* London: W. Blackwood & Sons, 1875.

Robert, J. J. M. *The Earliest Semitic Pantheon: A Study of the Semitic Deities Attested in Mesopotamia Before Ur III.* Baltimore, MD: The Johns Hopkins University Press, 1972.

Roheim, Geza. *Hungarian and Vogul Mythology.* Seattle, WA: University of Washington Press, 1954.

Ruskin, John. *Queen of the Air.* New York: Hurst & Company, n.d.

Rydberg, Victor. *Teutontc Mythology.* New York: Norroema Society, 1907.

Sandars, N. K., tr. and introduction. *Poems of Heaven and Hell from Ancient Mesopotamia.* . London: Penguin Books, 1971.

Sargent, Thelma, translator. *The Homeric Hymns.* New York: Norton, 1975.

Scott, Lionel. *Tales of Ancestors and Orisha.* New York: Athelia-Henrietta Press, 1994.

Sebeok, Thomas A., and Frances J. Ingemann. *Studies in Cheremis: The Supernatural.* New York: Viking Fund Publications in Anthropology, No. 22, 1956.

Seros, Kathleen, adaptor. *Sun and Moon: Fairy Tales from Korea.* Elizabeth, NJ: Hollym International Corporation, 1982.

Sobol, Donald. *The Amazons of Greek Myth.* New York: A. S. Barnes & Co., 1972.

Sokolov, Y. M. *Russian Folklore.* Translated by Catherine Ruth Smith. Hatboro, PA: Folklore Associates, 1966.

Soupaul, R. E. *Breton Folktales.* London: G. Bell & Sons, 1971.

Spence, Lewis. *The Minor Traditions of British Mythology.* New York: Benjamin Blom, Inc., 1972.

Spiden, Herbert Joseph. *Songs of the Tewa.* New York: The Exposition of Indian Tribal Arts, Inc., 1933.

Stapleton, Michael. *A Dictionary of Greek and Roman Mythology.* New York: Bell Publishing Co, 1978.

Starhawk. *The Spiral Dance: A Rebirth of the Ancient Religion of the Great Goddess.* San Francisco: Harper & Row, 1979.

Sterne, Carus. "The Northern Origin of the Story of Troy." Open Court, Chicago. August 1918, p. 449-ff.

Stone, Merlin. *Ancient Mirrors of Womanhood: Our Goddess and Heroine Heritage.* 2 Volumes. New York: New Sybilline Books, 1979.

Sturluson, Snorri. *The Prose Edda.* Translated by Arthur Gilchrist Brodeur. New York: The American-Scandinavian Foundation, 1929.

Tacheva-Hitova, Margarita. *Eastern Cults in Moesia Inferior and Thracia.* Leiden: E. J. Brill, 1983.

Tacitus. *The Agricola and the Germania.* Translated with an Introduction by H. Mattingly. Translation revised by S. A. Handford. London: Penguin Books, 1981.

Taylor, Colin F. *Native American Myths and Legends.* New York: Salamander Books, 1994.

Teish, Luisah. *Jambalaya: The Natural Woman's Books of Personal Charms and Practical Rituals.* Harper and Row, San Francisco, 1985.

Terry, Patricia, ed. *Poems of the Vikings: The Elder Edda.* New York: Bobbs-Merrill Co., Inc., 1969.

Thompson, Stith. *Tales of the North American Indians.* Bloomington, IN: Indiana University Press, 1972.

Thorpe, Benjamin. *North German Traditions.* London: Edward Lemley, 1852.

Toulson, Shirley. *The Winter Solstice.* London: Jill Newman and Hobhouse, 1981.

Trevelyan, Marie. *Folklore and Folk Stories of Wales.* London: Eliot Stock, n.d.

Twille-Petre, O. G. *Myth and Religion of the North: Religion of Ancient Scandinavia.* New York: Holt, Rinehart & Winston, 1964.

Uchtheim, M. *Ancient Egyptian Literature: A Book of Readings.* Vol. 2: The New Kingdom. Berkeley: University of California Press, 1976.

Uguwiyuak. *Journey to Sunrise: Myths and Legends of the Cherokee.* Claremore, OK: Egi Press, 1977.

Vermaseren, Maarten S. *Cybele and Attis.* London: Thames & Hudson, 1977.

Vernalekan, Theodor. *In the Land of Marvels: Folk-Tales from Austria and Bohemia.* London: Swan Sonnenschein & Co., 1889.

Vieyra, Maurice. *Hittite-Art.* London: Alex Tiranti, Ltd., 1955.

Voegelin, C. F. . "The Shawnee Female Deity." Yale University Publications in Anthropology No. 10. Reprinted by Human Relations Area Files, New Haven, 1970.

Von Franz, Marie-Louise. *Problems of the Feminine in Fairy Tales.* Switzerland: Spring Publications, 1972.

———. *Shadow and Evil in Fairy Tales.* Boston: Shambhala, 1995.

Warner, Marina. *Alone of All Her Sex.* New York: Alfred A. Knopf, 1976.

Waters, Frank. *The Book of the Hopi.* Drawings and source material recorded by Oswald White Bear Fredericks. London: Penguin Books, 1977.

Weber, Max. *The Religion of China.* Translated by Hans Gerth. New York: The Macmillan Company, 1951.

Weigle, Marta. *Spiders and Spinsters.* Albuquerque: University of New Mexico Press, 1985.

Wellard, James. *The Search for the Etruscans.* New York: Saturday Review Press, 1973.

Werblowsky, R. J., and Geoffrey Wigoden, eds. *Encyclopedia of the Jewish Religion.* New York: Holt, Rinehart & Winston, 1966.

Wheeler, Post, translator and editor. *The Sacred Scriptures of the Japanese.* New York: H. Schuman, 1952.

Wherry, Joseph H. *Indian Masks and Myths of the West.* New York: Funk & Wagnalls, 1969.

Whitehead, Henry. *The Village Gods of South India.* Calcutta: The Association Press, 1916.

Whitlock, Ralph. *The Folklore of Wiltshire.* Totowa, NJ: Rowman & Littlefield, Inc., 1976.

Wilde, Lady Jane Francesca Elgee. *Ancient Legends, Mystic Charms and Superstitions.* London: Chatto & Windus, 1925.

Wilde, William. *Irish Popular Superstitions.* New York: Rowland & Co., 1973.

Witt, R. E. *Isis in the Graeco-Roman World.* Ithaca, NY: Cornell University Press, 1971.

Wolkstein, Diane, and Samuel Noah Kramer. *Inanna: Queen of Heaven and Earth, Her Stories and Hymns from Sumer.* New York: Harper and Row, 1983.

Yoongsook, Kim Harvey. *Six Korean Women: The Socialization of Shamans.* St. Paul: West Publishing Co., 1979.

Yu, Anthony C., translator and editor. *The Journey to the West.* Chicago: University of Chicago Press, 1977–1983.

Zielinski, Thaddeus. *The Religion of Ancient Greece.* Translated by G. R. Noyes. Freeport, NY: Books for Libraries Press, 1926.

Zimmer, Heinrich. *Myths, and Symbols in Indian Art and Civilization.* Edited by Joseph Campbell. Bollingen Series. New York: Pantheon Books, 1946.

Zimmerman, J. E. *Dictionary of Classical Mythology.* New York: Bantam, 1964.

Zobarskas, Stepas. *Lithuanian Folk Tales.* Brooklyn, NY: Gerald Rickard, 1958.

Zong, In-Sob, editor. *Folk Tales from Korea.* New York: The Grove Press, 1953.

Zuntz, Gunther. *Persephone.* Oxford: Clarendon Press, 1971.

Stay in Touch...
Llewellyn publishes hundreds of books
on your favorite subjects.

On the following pages you will find listed some books now available on related subjects. Your local bookstore stocks most of these and will stock new Llewellyn titles as they become available. We urge your patronage.

Order by Phone

Call toll-free within the U.S. and Canada, **1–800–THE MOON.**

In Minnesota call **(612) 291–1970.**

We accept Visa, MasterCard, and American Express.

Order by Mail

Send the full price of your order (MN residents add 7% sales tax) in U.S. funds to:

Llewellyn Worldwide
P.O. Box 64383, Dept. K465-0
St. Paul, MN 55164–0383, U.S.A.

Postage and Handling
   • $4.00 for orders $15.00 and under
   • $5.00 for orders over $15.00
   • No charge for orders over $100.00

We ship UPS in the continental United States. We ship standard mail to P.O. boxes. Orders shipped to Alaska, Hawaii, the Virgin Islands, and Puerto Rico will be sent first-class mail. Orders sent to Canada and Mexico are sent first-class mail.

International orders: Airmail—add freight equal to price of each book to the total price of order, plus $5.00 for each non-book item (audiotapes, etc.).

Surface mail: Add $1.00 per item

Allow 4–6 weeks delivery on all orders. Postage and handling rates subject to change.

Group Discounts

We offer a 20% quantity discount to group leaders or agents. You must order a minimum of 5 copies of the same book to get our special quantity price.

Free Catalog

Get a Free copy of our color catalog, *New Worlds of Mind and Spirit*. Subscribe for just $10.00 in the United States and Canada ($30.00 overseas, first-class mail). Many bookstores carry *New Worlds*—ask for it!

The Mysteries of Isis
Her Worship and Magick
de Traci Regula

For 6,000 years, Isis has been worshiped as a powerful yet benevolent goddess who loves and cares for those who call on Her. Here, for the first time, Her secrets and mysteries are revealed in an easy-to-understand form so you can bring the power of this great and glorious goddess into your life.

Mysteries of Isis is filled with practical information on the modern practice of Isis' worship. Other books about Isis treat Her as an entirely Egyptian goddess, but this book reveals that she is a universal goddess with many faces, who has been present in all places and in all times. Simple yet effective rituals and exercises will show you how to forge your unique personal alliance with Isis: prepare for initiation into Her four key mysteries, divine the future using the Sacred Scarabs, perform purification and healing rites, celebrate Her holy days, travel to your own inner temple, cast love spells, create your own tools and amulets, and much more. Take Isis as your personal goddess and your worship and connection with the divine will be immeasurably enriched.

1-56178-560-6, 320 pp., 7 x 10, illus., softcover   **$19.95**

Maiden, Mother, Crone
The Myth and Reality of the Triple Goddess
D. J. Conway

The Triple Goddess is with every one of us each day of our lives. In our inner journeys toward spiritual evolution, each woman and man goes through the stages of Maiden (infant to puberty), Mother (adult and parent) and Crone (aging elder). *Maiden, Mother, Crone* is a guide to the myths and interpretations of the Great Goddess archetype and her three faces, so that we may better understand and more peacefully accept the cycle of birth and death.

Learning to interpret the symbolic language of the myths is important to spiritual growth, for the symbols are part of the map that guides each of us to the Divine Center. Through learning the true meaning of the ancient symbols, through facing the cycles of life, and by following the meditations and simple rituals provided in this book, women and men alike can translate these ancient teachings into personal revelations.

Not all goddesses can be conveniently divided into the clear aspects of Maiden, Mother and Crone. This book covers these as well, including the Fates, the Muses, Valkyries and others.

0-87542-171-7, 240 pp., 6 x 9, softcover   **$12.95**

To order, call 1-800-THE MOON
Prices subject to change without notice

Celtic Myth & Magic
Harness the Power of the Gods & Goddesses
Edain McCoy

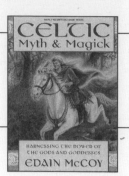

Tap into the mythic power of the Celtic goddesses, gods, heroes and heroines to aid your spiritual quests and magickal goals. *Celtic Myth & Magic* explains how to use creative ritual and pathworking to align yourself with the energy of these archetypes, whose potent images live deep within your psyche.

Celtic Myth & Magic begins with an overview of 49 different types of Celtic Paganism followed today, then gives specific instructions for evoking and invoking the energy of the Celtic pantheon to channel it toward magickal and spiritual goals and into esbat, sabbat and life transition rituals. Three detailed pathworking texts will take you on an inner journey where you'll join forces with the archetypal images of Cuchulain, Queen Maeve and Merlin the Magician to bring their energies directly into your life. The last half of the book clearly details the energies of over 300 Celtic deities and mythic figures so you can evoke or invoke the appropriate deity to attain a specific goal.

This inspiring, well-researched book will help solitary Pagans who seek to expand the boundaries of their practice to form working partnerships with the divine.

1–56718–661–0, 7 x 10, 464 pp., softcover $19.95

Magick of the Gods and Goddesses
How to Invoke Their Powers
(formerly titled *Ancient & Shining Ones*)
D. J. Conway

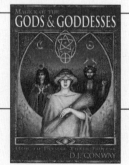

Magick of the Gods and Goddesses is a handy, comprehensive reference guide to the myths and deities from ancient religions around the world. Now you can easily find the information you need to develop your own rituals and worship using the Gods/Goddesses with which you resonate most strongly. More than just a mythological dictionary, *Magick of the Gods and Goddesses* explains the magickal aspects of each deity and explores such practices as Witchcraft, Ceremonial Magick, Shamanism and the Qabala. It also discusses the importance of ritual and magick, and what makes magick work.

Most people are too vague in appealing for help from the Cosmic Beings—they either end up contacting the wrong energy source, or they are unable to make any contact at all, and their petitions go unanswered. In order to touch the power of the universe, we must re-educate ourselves about the Ancient Ones. The ancient pools of energy created and fed by centuries of belief and worship in the deities still exist. Today these energies can bring peace of mind, spiritual illumination and contentment. On a very earthy level, they can produce love, good health, money, protection, and success.

1-56718-179-1, 448 pp., 7 x 10, 300 illus., softcover $17.95

To order, call 1-800-THE MOON
Prices subject to change without notice